The Youth
of
André Gide

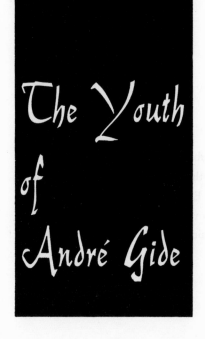

The Youth of André Gide

by Jean Delay

Member of the Académie Française

Abridged and translated by June Guicharnaud

CHICAGO AND LONDON
The University of Chicago Press

This book was originally published in 1956–57
by Librairie Gallimard, Paris,
under the title, *La Jeunesse d'André Gide*

The translations of the original works, published and unpublished, of André
Gide used in this book were prepared by the translator, June Guicharnaud. It
should be pointed out that the authorized English translations of the works of
André Gide published in the United States vest exclusively in Alfred A. Knopf,
Inc. Their permission to publish Miss Guicharnaud's translation is gratefully
acknowledged.

The University of Chicago Press, Chicago & London
Published simultaneously in Canada by
The University of Toronto Press

English translation © 1963 by The University of Chicago.
All rights reserved. Published 1963.
Composed and printed by The University of Chicago Press,
Chicago, Illinois, U.S.A.

Library of Congress Catalog Card Number: 63-13063

Designed by Theo Jung

to Roger Martin du Gard

this essay, which will have failed
in its objective if it does not—
through its thoughtful attention—
convey a deep concern for friendship

Foreword

This study of André Gide in his formative years could not have been made without the documents that his family and friends were kind enough to provide. I should like to express my sincere gratitude to M. and Mme. Jean Lambert-Gide, M. Dominique Drouin, Mme. Théo van Rysselberghe, and the members of the publication committee of Gide's complete works: MM. Roger Martin du Gard, Jean Schlumberger, Pierre Herbart, Jacques Naville, and Mme. Marie Dormoy. Thanks to them, I was able to consult all the unpublished material pertaining to his youth: his notes, letters, and *cahier de lectures* or reading notebook.

The notes for *Si le grain ne meurt* are classified year by year, dated from 1874 to 1900, and entitled: *De me ipso et de aliis.* They contain chronological references, an enumeration of reminiscences, scribbled down in their raw state before literary art gave them form, rough drafts which are often rather different from the final versions, and texts which are not included either in Gide's works or in his *Journal,* such as the notebook written at a café in Alençon in 1897.

The most important of Gide's letters are those written to his mother. They constitute the principal document on his youth. As soon as he began to travel without her—that is, in May, 1890—to her death in May, 1895, he kept up an enormous correspondence with her. Needless to say, he could not tell her everything, but it is surprising to see how much he did. Although it would appear that he did not keep the daily letters from his mother, she kept all of his, sometimes annotating them and always dating them when he forgot to do so. We know that André Gide's correspondence, probably just as important, with his first cousin Madeleine Rondeaux, who in 1895 became Mme. André Gide, was largely destroyed in 1917, for reasons explained in *Et nunc manet in te.* Certain letters to Jeanne Rondeaux, who became Mme. Marcel Drouin, and to his cousin Albert Démarest give useful and precise details concerning his childhood and adolescence. His "literary" correspondence which has been, is being, or will be published, began during his last year at the Ecole Alsacienne, when he met Pierre Louis, the future Pierre Louÿs. The most important of such letters are addressed to Pierre Louÿs, Paul Valéry, and Marcel Drouin.

André Gide began to keep his *cahier de lectures* in October, 1889, directly after he had passed his second *baccalauréat* and found himself free from all academic duties. He scrupulously kept the "subjectif," as he called it, day by day, noting down his impressions as they came, until October, 1893, the date of his first trip to Algeria. Certain aspects of it make one regret that his creative genius prevailed over his taste for "incidents" and "pretexts." From my point of view, his *cahier de lectures* makes it possible to determine exactly what literature influenced the young writer during those four years and the role such influences played in his development.

Bibliographical references or sources for the various works and commentaries quoted in the text are given in footnotes. Occasionally I allude to personal conversations with André Gide during his last years (June, 1946 —February, 1951), to the extent that they contribute to clarifying the origins of some trait of character. But my recollections of the great writer, whom I knew only in his old age, would be irrelevant in a study whose objective is his youth.

Contents

Illustrations

BOOK ONE

André Gide before André Walter
(1869–90)

Introduction to a Psychobiography

The works of André Gide are one of the most successful attempts made by man to explain and understand himself. Whether tale, journal, or fiction, each work is a portrait of the author. Many other writers have tried to portray themselves, but few have gone about it as persistently and with such diversity of means. At the end of his life, Gide liked to comment: "Now I have said what I had to say." He had expressed himself and felt that he had thus accomplished his main task.

Much has been said about the vanity of a literature of confession. However, it has contributed considerably to what Sainte-Beuve called the natural history of minds, a branch of study which is not restricted to describing and classifying their forms but is meant to discover the laws of their structure, how they became what they are, how they could have not become what they are. Gide said of La Bruyère: "He portrays men as they are but does not say how they became that way. And that's what is important. His portraits, so honest in themselves, lack the third dimension." The portrait Gide drew of himself has a third dimension. Every one of its features has its history and so becomes less enigmatic.

The genesis of an artist must be traced back to its main source, his youth. Even though later on he tries to forget or repudiate his past, he is indelibly marked by his family milieu, including both heredity and upbringing, and his first conflicts and moments of solitude. Gide was twenty-three when he wrote: "This terrifies me: to think that the present, which we are living today, will be the mirror in which we shall recognize ourselves later on; and that by what we have been, we shall know what we are." For him, at the end of his twenty-fifth year, the chips were down. Such as he was, so he would remain. Of course his changeable personality continued to develop indefinitely and was even re-created, in relation to his works, but his basic character had by then acquired its permanent traits. And it was Gide's character that gave their particular style to the evolutions and revolutions of his mind, as it evolved and resolved around itself.

Just as Pascal reproached Montaigne for portraying himself, so Paul Valéry reproached Gide. The author of *Eupalinos* generally considered autobiography as very mediocre indeed. "Je m'appele: Personne," he wrote in his *Mauvaises Pensées.* "Those who have something great within themselves do not attach it to their persons. On the contrary. What is a person? A name, needs, idiosyncrasies, absurdities, absences; someone who blows his nose, who cough, eats, snores, etc.; a plaything of women, a victim of the heat and the cold; an object of aversion, hate, or mockery . . . ." Monsieur Teste, who probed the faculties of "The Hon. Myself" on every level, said very little about himself in that sense. Eupalinos did admit that his architectural masterpiece had been inspired by a woman he had happily loved in his youth, but he said no more than that, and anyone curious about him as a person is reduced to meditating on the harmonious proportions of a temple, seeking something in perfection other than itself. Works like André Gide's are more likely to satisfy such curiosity.

The desire to be known as one quite naturally antagonizes anyone who does not share it. If the reader finds confessions beside the point or scandalous, *Si le grain ne meurt* will put him in a state of hostility from the very first page, and its author will quickly become "an object of aversion or mockery" in his eyes. If he is puritanical, he will find enough to become indignant at, for Gide's confessions are no less brazen than Jean-Jacques Rousseau's. If he is a particularly elevated soul, who judges everything from a vantage point of the stars, he will find an opportunity on every page to cry out: "What matters all that is not eternal!" The innumerable details about parents, uncles, aunts, cousins, maids, and friends, about games, outings, children's diseases, and the writer's own idiosyncrasies will constantly exasperate him. But if he is more interested in a study of the ways of man than in ethics, and if he is convinced that nothing of man is insignificant, then he will consider *Si le grain ne meurt* not only a literary success but a considerable piece of research. "Anyone who would eliminate all the passages in which Montaigne talks about himself would reduce the volume by a third. . . . For my part, it is precisely that third that I should particularly want to keep." What Gide says of Montaigne could doubtless (except for the proportion) be said about his own works. And because he dared to talk about himself, they have a great chance of survival, for any confession that touches on human truth is guaranteed to last.

An autobiographer has many obvious advantages over a biographer. First of all, he knows his subject better than anyone else. If he deigns to talk about his troubles, his weaknesses, his manias, he will not be reproached with being an iconoclast, a reproach often made to biographers of great men. "The biographer watches out for their common pettiness and all their inevitable and universal troubles," wrote Paul Valéry, whose only interest was to bring out the greatness that had attracted him. "He counts their socks, their mistresses, their foolishness. . . . His illusion consists in believing that what he seeks can generate or 'explain' what the other has found or produced."

In *Si le grain* Gide did not actually count his "socks," but he did give similar details. For example, he takes an entire page to tell how his mother made him wear a starched shirt every day when he was a child. The incident might be called foolishness and the biographer looked down upon for having related it. And yet that small detail did have quite some importance for the child who was thus armored by a good Victorian upbringing. In *Si le grain* Gide was able to count up his "mistresses" in short order, but he talks as freely as Henri Beyle about certain "fiascos" and even about many scabrous "contacts." If a biographer told similar stories about the pure author of *La Porte étroite,* had they remained unknown, he would have created a scandal. But here the great man got a head start. It was he himself who drew attention to his share of "common pettiness" and "inevitable troubles," and he himself was the biographer whose "illusion consists in believing that what he seeks can generate or 'explain' what the other has found or produced." But is it an illusion?

A literary genius is rarely created by spontaneous generation. In other words, he has a history, and his history is not often pleasant. Anyone whose works are original has generally experienced difficulties since childhood. "At the origins of every great moral reform, if we look well, we will always find a little physiological mystery, some dissatisfaction of the flesh, an anxiety, an anomaly." It is not surprising to see an immoralist who felt that way give such attention to the problem of his own origins in order to find an explanation for the drama of his life and the genesis of his works. "I must frankly dare to admit it: it was my solitary and sullen childhood that made me what I am."

In that perspective the reader of *Si le grain ne meurt* stops being irritated by so many details of Gide's childhood. A man who has reached maturity, in full possession of his intelligence, with an artist's vocation and an "anomaly" in his flesh, avidly examines the past and looks for the secret of his vocation and his anomaly in the child that he was. Behind the charms of a style that cannot help but be exquisite, there is deep seriousness in his inquiry. Why did he waste time on so many anecdotes? Probably for the pleasure of recounting them, but mostly because he did not know a priori what was important in his formation, and who does know? "Others form man," said Montaigne, "I describe him. . . . I speak the truth, not my fill of it, but as much as I dare speak it." Actually, Gide dared a great deal: "I see it as more than impudence; rather as a certain protest against propriety; what usually is passed over in silence and hidden is what he had most pleasure in telling, in flaunting." But when it came to his "imperfections," Gide was no more certain than Montaigne that "what was considered one thing in his time does not have some value, unknown to himself and hidden, for other countries and other times." And there lies his greatest originality. He felt that what seemed useless, laughable, or hateful yesterday could seem important tomorrow. He explored like a psychologist who learns that everything has been said about man but who knows that everything has yet to be understood.

Gide was convinced that what was most peculiar to him was the most important thing in him. He plunged into the "darkness" of his child-hood, just as the legendary hero goes back to the time of his "nocturnal crossing." He felt that there was a mysterious link between the nervous disorders of his childhood and adolescence and the demands of his voca-tion, a link more or less similar to that which he tirelessly emphasized in many other artists. He felt that the relation between the first anguish in their lives and the final greatness of their works was not fortuitous. Far from believing, like those who tend to deify the man of letters, that one must not reveal his weaknesses, he considered that his human value is really due to their transmutation. When he dwells on the ailments from which so many creators have suffered, it is certainly not to disparage those he gives as examples.

He wrote in his *Dostoevsky:* "Doubtless there will always be delicate and easily offended learned people who prefer to see only the busts of great men—who revolt against the publication of private papers, private letters; they seem to notice nothing more than the flattering pleasure such writings would bring to the mediocre minds that see heroes subject to the same infirmities as they. They then speak of indiscretion and, when they write in a romantic way, of 'the violation of tombs,' or at least of unhealthy curiosity; they say: 'Let us forget the man; only his works are important!'—Obviously! but what is admirable, what for me continues to be an inexhaustible lesson is that he wrote them *in spite of that."* In Do-stoevsky's private journals and letters, one does indeed find a moving testi-mony of his desperate struggle against sickness, and the spectacle of the struggle is in itself a rare lesson in energy. But Gide goes much further and, in relation to the great Russian novelist, raises a psychological prob-lem of "extraordinary importance": that of the relation between a lack of balance and creation.

Of course he did not go back to the theories of Lombroso and Nordau, who likened genius to "degeneration." His point of view was quite dif-ferent. He saw illness as "a source of anxiety" which could become a factor of inner progress, and showed how what begins as inferiority can be the starting point of superiority. Gide, who did not feel "the same as others," was forced by his very lack of balance to revise the norms and values in order to adapt them to his own use. In so doing, he created an individual protest and his works are the expression of it in more or less symbolic form.

In his early *Journal* Gide spoke of a "system of compensations" in regard to literary creation. His Pascalian meditation on the good use of illness ("The use of illness. Illness as a source of anxiety. Nothing to expect from those who are 'satisfied.'") contains the following notes, characteristic of his personal conception:

Illness offers a man a new anxiety which has got to be justified. Whence Rousseau's value, as well as Nietzsche's. Without his illness, Rousseau would merely have been an unbearable orator in the manner of Cicero. . . .[1]

Concerning the illusions we have as to the health of great men: see Molière, Racine, etc. The man who has the best things to say about the question is precisely the one generally cited as the model of a healthy man of letters: Goethe. See *Faust* (admirable dialogue with Chiron). He was unquestionably conscious of the advantage in, etc. See *Torquato Tasso,* etc.

Which brings us to the famous question as to why Sparta had no great men. . . . By suppressing the sickly, you suppress the rare variety—a well-known fact in botany or at least in *floriculture,* for the most beautiful flowers often come from puny looking plants.

Gide later amplified the theme of his study of Nietzsche and the psychology of reformers:

It is *natural* that any great moral reform, what Nietzsche would call any transmutation of values, be due to a physiological *lack of balance.* In well-being, thought is at rest, and as long as the state of things satisfies it, thought cannot propose to change it. (I mean the *inner* state, because for outer or social states, the reformer's motive is quite different; the former are chemists, the latter mechanics.) At the origins of a reform there is always discomfort; the discomfort from which a reformer suffers is that of an inner lack of balance. Densities, positions, and moral values seem different to him, and the reformer works at reconciling them; he seeks a new equilibrium, his works are but an attempt at the reorganization, according to his reason and his logic, of the disorder he feels within himself; for any state of disorder is intolerable to him. And naturally I am not saying that one has only to be unbalanced to become a reformer—but rather that every reformer is, to begin with, unbalanced.

In his *Dostoevsky,* which he admitted was "often only a pretext for my own thoughts," Gide ventured to follow his own thinking through and formulate it with extraordinary intransigency:

[1] He was to come back to the subject in his *Dostoevsky:* "Rousseau without his madness would probably have been no more than an indigestible Cicero. Let no one tell us: 'What a pity he was sick!' Had he not been sick, he would not have tried to resolve the problem created by his anomaly" [pp. 267–68].

I do not know that a single one can be found, among those who have offered humanity new evaluations, in whom those Messrs. Binet-Sanglès cannot discover, and quite rightly, what they will perhaps call a taint.

The innovator, then, is impelled by his anomaly to search for new norms and driven to originality by his illness. Gide contrasted "geniuses who were in perfectly good health," such as Victor Hugo, whose "inner balance posed no new problem," and reformers like Socrates and Pascal, Luther and Rousseau, Nietzsche and Dostoevsky, who in varying forms, had to suffer from "thorns in the flesh," as, much before Kierkegaard, Saint Paul had phrased it. According to Gide, a well-balanced creator is doomed to be no more than a resounding echo, whatever its sonority, and only a creator without balance can speak with a new voice, because he is forced to find "a harmony that does not exclude his dissonance."

There are of course many objections that might be raised to such a plea, and the examples cited are not equally convincing. Not only do Hugo's heredity and personal problems make it impossible to consider him "a genius who was in perfectly good health," but the ailments of the reformers he mentions seem so dissimilar that there is no common measure among them. Gide wrote: "Mohammed was epileptic, as were the prophets of Israel, and Luther, and Dostoevsky. Socrates had his daemon, Saint Paul his mysterious 'thorn in the flesh,' Pascal his abyss, Nietzsche and Rousseau their madness." His list calls for many reservations. Just because a man of genius has nervous breakdowns, visions, or goes into trances, many have believed themselves authorized to diagnose one or another of such disorders as epilepsy. Whereas in the majority of cases, what was diagnosed as epilepsy was in fact a neurosis, that is, not a brain disease but a psychological disorder. Dostoevsky really did suffer from epilepsy, but it would be impossible to come to Gide's conclusion: "Dostoevsky's insistence on bringing epilepsy into his novels adequately enlightens us as to the part he felt his illness played in the formation of his ethics and the evolution of his thinking." Now that we are better acquainted with the Russian novelist's life, it would seem that for a long time, epilepsy masked the real problem which was a guilt neurosis. His works, which are a long confession, reveal that the brain disease was but one factor of a fundamental anguish. Gide made the same mistake in using Nietzsche's "madness" to explain his genius. For Nietzsche's mental disorder also masked the real problem which was a compensation neurosis representing a psychological overcompensation for an inferiority complex. The creation of his works was interrupted by the general paralysis that led to his insanity, and the syphilis which attacked his nervous system did no more than destroy a personality that had been largely built up by a neurosis.

Although morbid factors have contributed to making such creators into men who represent a certain way of understanding relations between the ego and the world, they are certainly not anomalies as foreign to mankind in general as a mental disorder, but rather neuroses which are merely the exaggeration of the psychological traits of a personality. The problems of such men are the same as those of many others, only more acute. There is nothing exceptional in the conflicts they experienced, but they experienced them so intensely that they carried them to an extreme. They used their art to find a solution to inner difficulties that would have led others to defeat. Indeed, the same neurotic structures that habitually lead to failure can lead to creation in men gifted enough to transform a basic necessity into an original finality and convert weakness into strength. "Our art," wrote Renan, "is knowing how to make our illness into a charm." What concerns a psychologist is not the "charm" or aesthetic value of an artist's experience, any more than he is concerned with the religious value of a mystic's experience, but the transformation of a personality which, unbalanced to begin with, manages to find a new equilibrium in and through creation. "A work of art," wrote young Gide in his *Journal,* "is an equilibrium outside of time, an artificial health."

The value Gide attributed to anxiety recalls the mystical conception of it. "If anyone claims to know nothing of anguish," said Kierkegaard, "I would gladly give him my explanation: namely, a great spiritual insensitivity." Or again: "If man were an angel or a beast, he would not experience anguish; being a synthesis, he becomes capable of it." When Gide was twenty, he used the same conflict between two natures to explain André Walter's malady: a struggle between the angel and the demon, between the soul and the flesh. His transcendant interpretation leaves André Walter's "little physiological mystery" and Kierkegaard's "thorn in the flesh" in the dark. Here one realizes the frightening disproportion between the physical and metaphysical explanations of anguish. But is not the "little physiological mystery" itself a psychological problem? According to psychoanalysts, a neurosis is much less the result of a constitutional anomaly than a lack of balance in the formation of a personality. And it is closely linked in origin to each individual's background and, in particular, his childhood. Stekel, interpreting anguish as the result of an insoluble conflict between individual demands and moral or social imperatives, sees creation as an effort, more or less successful, to work out the conflict in an original way: "Neurosis is an attempt and a man of genius is its successful outcome."

There is no doubt that the general problems posed by Gide with regard to the psychology of creators and reformers correspond to his own particular problem. To the names of the great writers, "Rousseau, Nietzsche, Dostoevsky, Flaubert," mentioned in his early *Journal* to illustrate "the good use of illness," he added a new illustration. But what "continues to be an inexhaustible lesson" in himself as in the others is not anguish but the very personal way he reacted to it. The art with which he built up his protective and defensive mechanisms and succeeded in achieving catharsis through literary creation is surprisingly ingenious. That is the reason his psychobiography, a consideration of the events of his life in relation to his psychological evolution and the genesis of his creations, is of exceptional interest, on condition that he told the truth.

Gide had passed middle age when he wrote *Si le grain ne meurt.* And we all know the usual reservations as to the veracity of youthful reminiscences evoked in maturity. In what Nietzsche spoke of as "the erosion of contours," a distinction must be made between what eroded of itself and what the writer eroded intentionally.

The historical value of reminiscences depends first of all on the reliability of memory. Gide complained that his was "hardly trustworthy" and talked about its "anti-historicity." He generally remembered people and places perfectly well but found it difficult to situate his memories in time. "I get tangled up in chronology." However, the unpublished notes he used to construct his book are classified and dated year by year; and it is probable that the synopsis Mme. Paul Gide drew up in 1894 of her son's *curriculum vitae,* dating at his request the most important events of his childhood, was useful to him as a reference. As unreliable as his memory may have been in certain respects, he did have enough documents to reinforce it. He had begun to keep a diary at sixteen and found the story of his life in it almost day by day. At thirteen he was already a prolific letter writer and was able to reread those letters that had remained within the family circle, especially the many addressed to his mother and cousins. In addition, he had always remained attached to the people who had surrounded him in his youth, and Madeleine Rondeaux, who became Mme. André Gide, had shared much of his childhood. Thus his reminiscences were seconded by a diary, letters, and testimony which helped him to re-establish his past, even to reconstruct it. And there lies the main problem.

"I did that, says my memory; I did not do that, says my pride; and my memory invariably yields." Much before psychoanalysis, Nietzsche's aphorism pointed out the affective origins of forgetfulness. Chamfort, even more briefly, said that memory is at the heart's disposal. But any omission of that kind is more readily attributed to hypocrisy. In practice, it is not always easy to distinguish between an unintentional but advantageous disregard of the past and intentional reticence, or to figure out what is due to which. We know that Gide's sincerity, which has given rise to so many commentaries, has recently been questioned once again by the "rectification" of "Victor."[2] To proceed to doubt the veracity of a writer, found wanting on one particular point, is a big step; but the anecdote would be enough, were there any need to show that Gide was capable of dissembling, intentionally or unintentionally, when his passions were involved. Honest as his demand for sincerity was, no one would claim that he was always faithful to it. Yet although he did not tell the truth in places, he almost always ended by telling it. One has only to refer to the whole of his writings to find certain gaps filled in and certain distortions rectified.

One of the greatest enigmas of *Si le grain ne meurt* is the contrast between the first and second parts: we leave a shy young Huguenot; we then discover a bold immoralist. Whatever happened? The text gives one to understand that the change was absolutely spontaneous. Yet it was partly provoked, as usually happens to studious adolescents, by books. In another of his texts Gide was eloquent about the "first carving" cut in his mystical soul by his reading of the second part of *Faust* at eighteen; he was more reticent about the writer who, somewhat later but not much, deepened the "carving" made by Goethe. He even claimed not to have discovered Nietzsche until he was writing *L'Immoraliste,* but finally, in a letter to Mme. Renée Lang, he most explicitly admitted that his assertions were "inaccurate." Just as dissimilation was part of his nature, so was his frank admission. No doubt such "oversights" can be attributed to a lack of gratitude toward the "Mothers," a rather commonplace trait in creators who prefer to be the sons of no one and ascribe everything to themselves.

A novelist who tells the story of his life is in danger of fictionalizing it. He is subject to the distortions of memory common to all, but also to distortions that in a way are professional. An artist's memory itself tends to become a work of art, as do all his faculties, which are geared to aesthetic creation. The novelist, a man of imagination who spends his life on the borders of the imaginary and the real, is more especially apt to overstep the boundaries. Flaubert was not the only one who could say: "Madame Bovary, c'est moi"; most of his emulators are inclined to bovarysm, the word by which Jules de Gaultier designated a tendency to see reality and oneself as other than they are. Gide's most tragic mistake, disclosed in his painful *Et nunc manet in te,* was due to that propensity, which led him to put "an ideal figure invented by me" in the place of a real figure. He did much the same thing with himself. He composed himself artfully; he made himself artificially.

On January 3, 1892, Gide noted in his *Journal:*

---

[2] *Translator's note:* A young man who protested against inaccuracies or distortions in Gide's account of their relationship.

A man's life is his image. At the hour of death, we shall be reflected in the past and, leaning over the mirror of our acts, our souls will recognize *what we are*. Our whole life is spent in drawing an ineradicable portrait of ourselves. The terrible thing is that we don't know it; we don't think of making ourselves beautiful. We think about it in speaking of ourselves; we flatter ourselves but later on our terrible portrait will not flatter us. We recount our lives and we lie to ourselves; but our lives will not lie. They will recount our souls, which will stand before God in the usual posture. One can therefore say the following, which I see as a kind of inverted sincerity (on the part of the artist): Rather than recount his life as he lived it, he must live it as he will recount it. In other words: his portrait, which his life will be, must be identical with the ideal portrait he desires; and, in simpler terms, he must be as he wants to be.

This early text, in which Gide considers his existence in terms of portraiture, shows the desire to conform to an imaginary objective and the romantic notion that life should form a picture. However, the painter who creates an "ideal portrait" must submit to aesthetic exigencies. If in *Si le grain ne meurt* Gide had wanted to tell everything about his youth and reconstruct it in its inextricable complexity, his book would not have been the masterpiece it is. He had to choose. Whether he wanted to or not, he had to simplify the lines, erode the contours, bring together into one single scene happenings that took place at different periods of his life, arrange the play of shadow and light, thicken the "darkness" in one place, purify the transparency in another, touch up the real; in short: intervene. What is lost by science is gained by art. That ability to stylize which so pleases the creator is of great interest to bis biographer. Moreover, Gide was a stylist who was sensitive to the slightest attraction of words. "May the word never precede the idea," he noted in his *Journal* of 1891, trying even then to go against his inclination. But when he found the exact word, the perfect expression, how could he resist, even at the price of suffering or of some slight deviation from the truth? It is difficult for a born writer not to allow himself to be led by his pen, not to prefer sometimes virtuosity to virtue, and not to prefer *himself*, as it were. Yet the descendant of Huguenots from Uzès had a need for rectitude, therefore of rectification, and was innately severe when it came to mistakes due to complacency. There is a great deal of honesty in his "afterthoughts," and his retractions themselves make his approach less approximate. However carried away he was by his talent, he intended to bind himself to the truth, and he doubtless came nearer to it than many other artists when he wrote his autobiography and posed for posterity, giving obvious attention to making himself life-size, without a pedestal and without trimmings.

Although a novelist's temperament may cause him to deviate from historical truth, it may by the same token bring him closer to psychological truth. Consequently the liberties he may happen to take with accuracy enchant the psychologist as much as they antagonize the historian. There is all the seriousness of humor in the following sally from *Paludes:* "I arrange the facts in such a way as to make them more consistent with truth than they are in reality." But what then is that truth if not his own, if not the personal equation, the cipher, the symbol in which his personality is projected? He does not reflect the real; he refracts it, but according to his personal requirements, which are of course more completely fulfilled the freer he is to arrange, in his own way, an imaginary world, reconstructed according to the laws of his fancy.

An introverted novelist, "who draws his characters from himself," creates and creates only in his own image. His heroes are more or less his doubles; his doubles are more or less his possibilities. None of them is exactly himself, but each one is an emanation of himself. None of them resembles his creator as he is, but as he might have been, as he was, as he will perhaps be, as he would have been or would be if. . . . Each of Gide's characters represents a part of himself. He entrusts them with the care of expressing his virtualities and his tendencies, for the "Hell and Heaven of his characters are within him." He well knows that they are not real but feels that they are true because they share in his truth. Whether or not he gives them a civil status is a question of technique, but he would not waste time doing it if he did not mean to set up an adventure that corresponded to his inner needs. He entrusts them with his virtues and vices, his wealth or his poverty, and in a suitably chosen milieu, he watches them prosper or fall, like an experimenter who is avid to learn and whose curiosity is anything but gratuitous. Their adventures educate him, their failures warn him, their follies predispose him to prudence, their poisons give him immunity. He tests himself in them. His personality is constantly developing, disintegrating, and reforming in his characters, a progeny whom he alone recognizes as his own.

"What each of my characters, which I hewed from my very flesh, lacks is that bit of good sense that keeps me from pushing their follies as far as they did." Each one of them is an exaggeration, but an exaggeration of his own tendencies. And to begin with André Walter, his first fictional double, the double of his adolescence:

I soon could not say which of us was leading the other; for although there was nothing in him which I had not first felt myself, nothing, so to speak, I had not tried out on myself. I often pushed my double ahead of me, ventured out after him, and it was in *his* madness that I was preparing to founder.

One can learn more about André Gide's state of mind at twenty from *Les Cahiers d'André Walter* than from the corresponding pages of *Si le grain ne meurt*. Still, André Walter was both similar to Gide and different from him. Their situations and characters were analogous but not identical, and they correspond only relatively. It would be quite as absurd to rely on Walter for an understanding of Gide's character as not to take him into account at all. And what is true of one is true of the other doubles, so that several of Gide's imaginary psychobiographies could be used as an introduction to his own problems at various stages of his development.

It is difficult for a man who projects himself onto the three mirrors of tale, journal, and fiction to keep the same close watch on all three images and make them coincide according to clock time. But it is precisely a comparison between the delays of some and the headway of others that makes cross-checking possible, and one then discovers that the events of André Gide's imaginary life almost always preceded the events of his real life. The novel preceded history, the adventure of a fictional double preceded the novelist's future. "Things BECOME true," André Walter prophetically said, "we have only to think them . . . our mind creates its own Truths." Would that mean that at the time Gide portrayed André Walter, he knew everything that he was portraying? A writer of genius says more about himself than he knows, and it is doubtless that unknown—"that part of the subconscious I should like to call the part of God"—in which lies the principal mystery of literary creation. That part, which psychoanalysis has tried to make somewhat too clear, had already been pointed out by Montaigne: "The same can be said for painting; a painter sometimes applies a stroke not only without inventing it, but without being conscious of it."

Before he was twenty-five, Gide had written five fictional works, given here in the order of completion, not necessarily of publication: *Les Cahiers d'André Walter* (1890), *Le Traité du Narcisse* (1891), *Le Voyage d'Urien* (1892), *Le Tentative amoureuse* (1893), *Paludes* (1894). None of these books, with the exception of the enigmatic *Paludes,* is generally thought of as a major work. All the same, their psychological interest is considerable, for each is closely linked to one of Gide's personal problems, whether it be André Walter's malady, the inclinations of Narcissus and the aesthetics of his mistake, the travels of Urien, "sad brother," through the fears and desires of the subconscious, Luc's vain attempt, or the stagnation of *Paludes,* "a sick man's work," as Gide called it, but a sick man who ridicules his sickness and stagnation with salutary irony and prepares himself to be cured or to leave. In addition to those of his first books, many other fictional characters lead back to Gide's youth. Alissa, in *La Porte étroite,* the feminine replica of André Walter, goes back to his adolescence; little Boris, in *Les Faux-Monnayeurs,* to his childhood. For that matter his autobiography, *Si le grain ne meurt,* must not only be completed by all his intimate writings, but considered in relation to all his fictional works, in order to sort out the historical truth from the psychological truth.

André Gide was twenty-four when in 1893 he wrote to his friend Marcel Drouin:

How do I understand my whole life? For a long time now, my works appear to me, before me, ready, awaiting nothing except to be written. There is nothing irrational in my undertakings. While making *the greatest allowance possible for change,* I seem to see each new work take place, not following but in the midst of the others, so real do the works yet to be done appear to me, as real even now as those in the past. I know the importance that each must have, which will only be explained afterward, so that one can be a good judge of one part only after having known the whole—that is, after me—for each act of our lives is in a sense a preface or an indication of those that will follow.

Did Gide have an idea even then, a kind of intuitive premonition not unknown in literature, of what he would have to say, of the whole of his themes and even their sequence? I think so, "while making the greatest allowance possible for change" caused by the experiences of life, and for the "implex," as Paul Valéry put it, in contrast to the complex. At that point he already possessed, but only potentially, the basic scheme that existence and art would later convert into realities and images, the rough sketch of psychological traits that he would use to compose his destiny and his design. "No works were more intimately motivated than mine—and anyone who does not see that will not have much insight into them." Whatever the incidence of eventuality or the role of fabrication in the genesis of his works, they first issued from a personal motivation that goes back to the beginnings of a life. It was in Gide's youth that the secret web that was to orient his life and works, their complicated knots and their foreseeable disentangling, was woven. No epigraph would be better suited to a study of Gide's youth than Montaigne's words, as valid here as they are debatable elsewhere: "For my part, I believe that our minds are as developed at twenty as they are ever likely to be, and that they then promise all of which they will ever be capable."[3]

Although André Gide was already "almost whole" in *Les Cahiers d'André Walter,* he was not completely so. The publication of *Les Cahiers* is the dividing line between two different periods of his youth, one closely confined to the family milieu, the other increasingly open to outside in-

---

[3] Montaigne had first written "of which they are capable."

fluences.[4] "After having created André Walter," he wrote to his mother on May 27, 1892, "I felt that I *had* to move completely out of that atmosphere of tears, religious gloom, and the same solitary brooding in which I had lived for twenty years. I intentionally plunged into an altogether different life with the aim of forgetting my old personality."

Gide's protest was partly due to his rejection of the state of mind disclosed in his first book, and resulted in the decisive crisis he passed through during the years 1893–95. That battle between "the old man" and "the new man" continued to recur in his successive books for a quarter of a century. André Gide's youth contains all the situations and all the characters of the drama that was resolved in and by his works.

[4] That is why this study of André Gide's youth is divided into two books: *André Gide before André Walter (1869–90)* and *From André Walter to André Gide (1890–95)*.

PART I

Origins and Childhood

1: The Rondeaux and the Gides

> "... the fruit of two races, two provinces, and two faiths."
>
> Si le grain ne meurt

J ULIETTE RONDEAUX, wife of Paul Gide and mother of André Gide, came from a Norman family, established in Rouen for five generations.[1]

The earliest known ancestor, Nicolas Rondeaux (1620–1695), an illiterate farmer, went into business and became a bourgeois in Rouen. His second son, Marin (1642–1721), learned the techniques of business from him so well that he became rich and gout-ridden. Marin Rondeaux's only son, Jean-Claude (1720–1805), was brought up by the Jesuits, became councilor at the Cour des Comptes of Normandy, and was made a noble by Louis XV. His interest in natural science led him to accompany Bernard de Jussieu on several botanizing trips. He had six children, one of whom was the great-grandfather of André Gide.

Charles Rondeaux (1753–1820), called Rondeaux de Montbray, then—during the Revolution—Rondeaux-Montbray, and finally Rondeaux as before, inherited his father's fortune, a position in the Cour des Comptes of Normandy, and a taste for natural science and liberal ideas. He was twice married, and his second wife was a Protestant, Anne-Marie Dufou (not

---

[1] The main sources of information concerning Gide's mother's family are the following: P. Le Verdier, *Histoire de la famille Rondeaux;* R.-G. Nobécourt, *Les Nourritures normandes d'André Gide;* Anna Shackleton's Notebooks and Correspondence, unpublished; *Lettres de Guizot à Laure de Gasparin;* André Gide, *Si le grain ne meurt* and unpublished notes.

Dufour as Gide wrote in *Si le grain ne meurt*). From that time on (October, 1781), the Catholic tradition of this branch of the family was broken. As a heading to his unpublished notes on his ancestors, André Gide wrote: "All Catholics until Mlle. Dufour."[2]

Edouard Rondeaux (1789–1860), son of Charles and Anne-Marie, was a Voltarian bourgeois. He had been baptized but remained outside of Catholicism all his life. Like his father, he married a young Protestant, Julie-Judith Pouchet. He agreed to be married by a Protestant minister and to have his five children brought up in the Reformed Church. Guizot, his neighbor in Calvados, described him as a capable man, "a real businessman, intelligent, sensible, active, valuing above all success and the profits of success."[3] Success in business and in local politics seems to have been the main occupation of his life. He added several branches to his father-in-law's printed cotton manufacturing busines and his ventures were prosperous. In 1860 his estate was estimated at a million and a half francs. It was he who acquired most of the Normandy residences at which André Gide spent much of his time: the house in the rue de Crosne in Rouen, the châteaux and land of La Roque–Baignard in Calvados and of Cuverville in the Caux. Although not a doctrinaire like his half-brother Jean, as vice-president of the Rouen Chamber of Commerce, he had a strong voice in the General Council of the Seine-Inférieure. Very sociable, fond of jokes, and good-natured except during his attacks of gout, he generally kept open house, although in business he had the reputation of keeping a close watch on his interests and of being "stingy."[4]

It would be difficult to imagine anyone more different in character than his wife, Julie Pouchet, as pious, reserved, and shy as he was skeptical, enterprising, and prone to good living. Julie-Judith Pouchet (1798–1873) was born in the vicinity of Bolbec on an estate called "Le Montpellier," where the Protestants of the region assembled to worship. She came from an old Huguenot family, part of which had left the Caux and emigrated to England at the time of the revocation of the Edict of Nantes. In a province as Catholic as Normandy, the Protestants constituted an all the more united minority, and every Sunday, "Le Montpellier" was one of the places at which they met. Although married to the skeptical Edouard Rondeaux, Julie Pouchet remained passionately faithful to her religion, and as much through piety as her charitable works, became one of the best known figures in the Reformed Church of Rouen.

In the same atmosphere of ardent Protestantism, Julie Rondeaux-Pouchet

[2] Unpublished notes for *Si le grain ne meurt.*

[3] Letter from François Guizot to Laure de Gasparin, June 21, 1859.

[4] "I am by nature miserly," Gide noted in *Ainsi soit-il.* "In that, I must take after my Norman ancestors."

brought up her five children: Charles (1820–1890), Claire (1822–1901), Henri (1825–1882), Emile (1831–1890), and Juliette (1835–1895). The tragedy of her life was her son Henri's conversion to Catholicism. André Gide recalled it in *Si le grain ne meurt* in the laconic phrase: "My grandmother, on opening a wardrobe in her son's room, fell back in a dead faint: it was an altar to the Virgin." At about twenty-four, Henri Rondeaux had decided to become a Catholic. After a long series of discussions with Father Hanin, the parish priest of Bolbec, and Pastor Vermeil of Paris, and despite reproaches from the people around him, he carried out his plan and was baptized and took communion on March 30, 1849, in the convent of the Sisters of Compassion. The stages of his conversion and its painful repercussion in the family circle can be reconstructed from the correspondence between Henri Rondeaux, his mother, and Father Hanlin.[5] Mme. Edouard Rondeaux wrote a vehement letter to the parish priest of Bolbec, whom she held chiefly responsible for her son's renunciation, in which she attacked the Catholic faith, denied the virginity of the mother of Christ, called her worshipers superstitious, and rejected the belief in purgatory. Edouard Rondeaux, who was relatively indifferent to religious matters, told his son: "I believe it would be unfortunate if one could be saved only by religion and I am convinced that behaving like a gentleman is quite enough."

Juliette Rondeaux, born on April 11, 1835, in Rouen, was twelve when the family dissension began and there is no doubt she was deeply marked by it. Separated by a great difference in age from the eldest children, Charles and Claire, who in 1842 married a Parisian lawyer, Guillaume Démarest, she lived largely in the company of her two brothers, Henri and Emile. In 1850, following Henri's conversion, as Juliette was going to be fifteen, her mother provided her with a Protestant and Scottish governess, Miss Anna Shackleton.

Anna Shackleton (1826–1884) was only nine years older than her charge and seemed hardly that, so pretty and blooming was she. She was the daughter of a foreman who had come to Rouen with a small English colony, brought over by an industrialist, M. Rowcliffe, whose foundry on the Elbeuf route was helping in the construction of the railway from Paris to Le Havre.

Pious, intelligent, learned, and cultured, with a fluent reading knowledge of German, a fair reading knowledge of Italian, and a gift for music and painting, Anna Shackleton had considerable influence on her pupil and brought a taste for literature and the arts into an extremely bourgeois milieu. Her letters, written in a lively and charming style, have been kept, as well as a reading notebook which testifies to great curiosity, translations,

---

[5] The correspondence has been assembled by M. Pierre le Verdier.

particularly that of Goethe's *Reinecke Fuchs,* and drawings and water-colors of La Roque, which are in fact rather cold and do not seem to express the true quality of her sensitivity. When Juliette's nephew Maurice Démarest asked her why she was so timid in her paintings and put so little of herself into them, she answered that the circumstances of her life had killed her personality and had not allowed her to develop. It would seem that a kind of modesty, which was extraordinary according to those close to her, had kept her from expressing herself freely. The same was true when she played the piano with that discretion and controlled sensitivity recalled by Gide in *La Porte étroite.*

Juliette Rondeaux became passionately fond of her governess, and "ces demoiselles," as they were called, became inseparable. Having until then been subjected to the rigors of a puritanical and Victorian upbringing, Juliette discovered another world. With Anna she read poetry and took lessons in music and painting, and her lack of aptitude was offset by her good will. Her governess wrote to Maurice Démarest:

Your aunt fervently works at her piano and is making progress. We paint from nature with quite some success and much perseverance, in spite of the heat; up until now we have found pretty subjects. Your aunt has acquired facility, and she once had very little for this type of drawing.[6]

Anna Shackleton's relationship with Juliette passed rapidly from governess to companion to friend, even too rapidly for Mme. Edouard Rondeaux and Claire Démarest. André Gide was most explicit about it in *Si le grain ne meurt:*

My grandmother was certainly not hard-hearted; but without setting too much store by it, she had a keen sense of hierarchies. Her daughter Claire had the same sense, but not her kindness; in fact that was the only sense Claire had and was irritated at not finding it in her sister. Instead she found her instinctively, if not exactly rebellious, at least insubordinate. Juliette had probably not always been that way, but the instinct was awakened in her through her friendship for Anna. Claire found it difficult to forgive Anna her sister's friendship; she thought that friendship must have degrees and nuances, and that it was not proper for Miss Shackleton to forget that she was a governess.[7]

But Juliette did not see it that way. She refused to dress more elegantly than her governess and everything that showed an outer dfference in their social positions shocked her. Gide's commentary shows what pleasure he felt in recalling his mother's slight irreverence in regard to precedence. "Through her friendship for Anna," Juliette had become impatient with social prejudice and even somewhat independent, but she continued to conform strictly to moral and religious laws. In her observance of puritan-

---

[6] Letter from Anna Shackleton to Maurice Démarest, June 25, 1858.

[7] *Si le grain ne meurt,* I, 30, 31.

ical rules and in worship, she brought to bear a precise and methodical mind. Anna was just as virtuous and Christian, but in her own way, which was not as limited. One saw Christianity mostly as interdiction and prohibition, the other as love and grace.

As different as their two natures may appear, the two young girls were so attached to each other that they were unable to live apart for any length of time. But Mme. Edouard Rondeaux and her daughter Claire were worried about Juliette not getting married and feared that the comparison between governess and charge was not to her advantage.

More than one thought that Anna Shackleton, still young herself, and in addition extremely pretty, might overshadow her pupil. Besides, young Juliette Rondeaux, it must be confessed, was a somewhat difficult person to manage. Not only did she constantly withdraw into the background and efface herself when she should have stood out, but she never lost an opportunity of pushing Miss Anna forward.[8]

When at a social gathering Juliette effaced herself, as if wanting to point up Anna's natural ease, she doubtless did it out of tactfulness, but perhaps also because near her young friend, who was prettier, more gifted, more cultured, and, in short, much more attractive than she, she was deeply affected by the feeling of inferiority that played so great a part in the formation of her character. Although she gave the impression of being determined, she was in fact hiding her timidity and lack of self-confidence. When Gide tried to give a picture of his mother as a young girl, according to her stories and those of Anna Shackleton or Claire Démarest, the trait he emphasized was a lack of assurance, which moreover he said he inherited from her. Just as she dreaded making an appearance at a social gathering and had to force herself literally to take part in the social life of Rouen, so her son, at over twenty, felt "dead with embarrassment" when he had to visit fashionable Parisian salons: "An unconquerable shyness held me back."

Although Juliette Rondeaux was hardly encouraging, she did receive marriage proposals from "the most brilliant matches of Rouen society." But she refused them all. Her mother and sister began to worry about it seriously and, as usually happens in bourgeois families who have marriageable daughters, Juliette's future became the central problem of the rue de Crosne household. Anna Shackleton let herself be won over by the family's concern and her pride was wounded. On November 22, 1859, she wrote:

Still another Rowcliffe girl is getting married! The tall one, she's marrying the young minister who was just ordained here and is settling in Elbeuf! And my poor Juliette! Ah! I'm peeved, I'm furious, I should like to create a paragon of virtue and offer him to her.[9]

[8] *Si le grain ne meurt,* I, 30.

[9] Letter from Anna Shackleton to Maurice Démarest, Nov. 22, 1859, unpublished.

A husband was easy to find, but "perfection" is rare. Perhaps, in the Rondeaux-Pouchet's milieu of rich bourgeois industrialists and business-men, Juliette had not met the personification of the moral and intellectual ideal she had conceived under the influence of her mother and Anna Shackleton. Perhaps, being shy by nature, she was somewhat apprehensive of marriage. In any case, she refused all offers.

In 1859 the minister of the Reformed Church of Rouen, M. Paumier, having reached the age of retirement, was replaced by M. Roberty. Roberty was young and full of fervor and energy. He and his wife, who was of Scottish extraction, were immediately welcomed in the rue de Crosne. Juliette confided in the new minister and he thus became aware of her ardent Protestantism and great moral ideal. He got the idea of having her meet a young jurist, Paul Gide, who had just brilliantly passed his *agré-gation* in law. Paul Gide was the son of a Huguenot judge, president of the Uzès Tribunal and known for his high integrity and exemplary piety.

According to a note written by a M. Gide from Mulhouse in the nineteenth century,[10] the Gides are descended from a noble Italian family, the Guidos, who came from Florence to France at the end of the fifteenth century and whose name figures in Hozier's armorial. They gallicized their name, adopted the Reformation, and after the revocation of the Edict of Nantes, separated. The main branch stayed in Nîmes; one emigrated to Geneva, another to Berlin, and a third to Alsace. The only portrait Gide kept of his father's ancestors was that of a Théophile Gide, born in Lussan in 1682, who lived in Berlin.

The cradle of the Uzès Gides,[11] connected with the Nîmes branch, is the little town of Lussan, about eleven miles from Uzès, where another branch of the family owns the château of Fan. Professionally, Gide's pa-ternal ancestors were flour-mill owners, glassmakers, and lawyers. His great-grandfather Théophile, born in Lussan, was the notary public of Uzès.

He was one of those tall, angular Huguenots, as solid as Cévenol granite, of sober appearance and rather gloomy disposition—they had endured long persecutions

10 The note was found in Paul Gide's files. But his son would seem to have known nothing about it.

11 The main sources of information concerning Gide's father's family are the fol-lowing: A. Lavondès, *Charles Gide;* A. Esmein, *Paul Gide,* a biography published as a preface to the second edition of Paul Gide's book *Etude sur la condition privée de la femme dans le droit ancien et moderne;* speeches and articles published after Paul Gide's death, 1880; Paul Gide's files and personal papers, unpublished; Charles Gide's correspondence with André Gide, unpublished; André Gide, *Si le grain ne meurt* and unpublished notes; André Gide's correspondence with his mother, unpublished.

and their piety had kept an austere fervor. During the first days of toleration, he had negotiated the buying of a church for his coreligionists.[12]

Théophile Gide was known for his great integrity. A very strict Protestant, his moral dogmatism went along with intellectual liberalism, as is frequent in true sons of the Reformation.

Théophile's son Tancrède (1800–1867), also born in Lussan, studied law and in 1830 became justice of the peace in Uzès, then judge; and from 1839 until he died, he remained president of the Tribunal. On May 7, 1831, at Nîmes, he married Clémence Aglaé Granier (1802–1894), also descended from an old Cévenol Protestant family, several of whom were ministers. They had five sons, but the three born between Paul and Charles died shortly after birth, "badly nursed," according to Gide, who attributed the lack of care to his grandfather's contempt for the art of medicine.

André Gide never knew his grandfather, who died two years before he was born, but he learned about him from his mother's enthusiastic stories of his high-mindedness and piety:

She described him to me as an austere Huguenot, whole-hearted, very tall, very strong and angular, scrupulous to excess, unyielding, and pushing his confidence in God to a sublime extreme. . . . Those of my grandfather's generation continued to keep alive the memory of the persecutions that had hammered away at their ancestors, or at all events a certain tradition of resistance; a great inner stubbornness had resulted from the attempt to break them. Each one of them distinctly heard Christ say to him and to all the little tortured flock: "Ye are the salt of the earth: but if the salt have lost his savor, wherewith shall it be salted?"[13]

Tancrède Gide belonged to the last generation of men who addressed God as "thou" and who worshiped with their great felt hats on their heads, in memory of "services held out-of-doors, under a burning sky, in the secret recesses of the dry Languedocian hills."

Persecuted until the second half of the eighteenth century, marked by the experience of the *culte du désert* and Camisard resistance, southern Protestantism has kept a tradition of nonconformity, a taste for the little flock and the virtues of an elite, a pride in its poor and unassuming churches, intended to be so in contrast to Roman pomp, and an austere notion of worship which has definite similarities to Jansenism.

According to certain documents,[14] it would seem that Tancrède Gide, a true Cévenol, was actually less granitic than his grandson had imagined him. Among the appraisals of his superiors at court, we find:

A learned judge, capable, conscientious, but absolutely lacking in the basic qualities necessary to a leader of men: firmness and dispatch. M. G. is an obstacle

[12] A. Lavondès, *Charles Gide,* p. 21.

[13] *Si le grain ne meurt,* I, 41, 45.

[14] Paul Gide's files, unpublished.

to the repression of numerous violations that have been introduced into this district by the greed of businessmen and the nonchalance of certain magistrates.

Another, after having paid tribute to his modesty, a quality he possessed to the highest degree, added:

M. G., in an unsuitable position at the head of the Uzès Court where he is criticized for his slowness, a weakness due to the extreme gentleness of his character, would be more in his place as councilor to the Court, to which he would bring the example of a sober and austere life and the respect attached to upright intentions and the love of good.

Rectitude, irreprochable morality, seriousness, and austerity are words that constantly recur in descriptions of the judge; but we also find the words: extreme gentleness, weakness, lack of firmness and dispatch, slowness, an absence of the qualities necessary for leadership. It would also seem that a certain tendency to live in the realm of ideas rather than in that of practical realities, and a very distinct kind of indecision, perhaps encouraged by "Protestant doubt," were more or less passed on to his two sons, Paul and Charles, and in considerably accentuated form, to his grandson André.[15]

At first cold and difficult to approach, Tancrède Gide did like certain staunch friends to visit his house in the rue Saint-Etienne and, later, his fine apartment in the Trinquelague house. His wife, friendly, gay, and with southern vivacity, liked to entertain. But his main preoccupation was to bring up his sons according to the religious and moral principles he himself put into practice. "From an intellectual and even moral point of view," Charles Gide wrote to his nephew André, "your grandfather alone made us what we are."[16]

Paul Gide was born in Uzès on May 15, 1832. Until the age of fifteen, when his brother Charles was born, he remained an only child. He went to secondary school in Uzès, where the teaching of the humanities was far more advanced than that of the sciences. He quickly showed a keen interest in literature, was always first in his class in Greek, Latin, and French, and acquired considerable knowledge in the classics which was to be of great value to him in his future career as professor of Roman law. At the University of Aix, Paul Gide, at twenty-one, received the prize for Roman law and, two years later, the gold medal for his doctorate thesis. In November, 1856, accompanied by his father, he went to Paris to take the competitive examinations for the *agrégation* in law, but he failed the

[15] "Disposed, as my father had been, to attaching less importance to realities than to ideas," wrote André Gide.

[16] Letter from the economist Charles Gide, Paul Gide's younger brother, to André Gide, Jan. 14, 1894, unpublished.

orals. When it was given again three years later, Paul Gide took first place. The following year he gave a course in administrative law in Grenoble, and less than three years after the *agrégation,* at barely thirty, he was given a full professorship in law at the University of Paris.

A talented professor, Paul Gide was also a highly esteemed scholar. His colleagues nicknamed him *vir probus,* as much for his intellectual honesty as for his knowledge of Roman law. His book *Etude sur la condition privée de la femme dans le droit ancien et moderne* ranked him, according to Ernest Lehr, among the "wisest, most profound, and most elegant of law historians." André Gide knew that it was his father's masterpiece. Yet his other works show the same intellectual qualities and the same concern with form. Paul Gide was a humanist in the broadest sense of the term. But he was more especially an orginal thinker, rich in personal ideas and open to all forms of progress. It was he who, shortly after the war of 1870, interested his brother in the field of political economy, a science that was just developing and to which Charles Gide contributed greatly for more than half a century. Remarkable as Paul Gide's own works are, he did not have the time to show all he was capable of: he died at the age of forty-seven.

From the time of his success in the competitive examinations for the *agrégation,* Paul Gide was the focus of attention of Protestant intellectuals, for the name Gide was well known in the Reformed Church. Pastor Roberty's suggestion of a possible marriage between Paul Gide and Juliette Rondeaux seemed worthy of Mme. Rondeaux-Pouchet's consideration. "Le Montpellier" itself, where she had been brought up and which was the Norman counterpart of the Gard stronghold, seemed to predestine a bond with the descendent of Languedocian Huguenots.

In June, 1859, Laure de Gasparin of Nîmes, a friend of the Gides, wrote to her faithful correspondent, the former Prime Minister François Guizot, whose country estate Val-Richer was close to the Edouard Rondeaux estate La Roque–Baignard, to ask for information about Juliette Rondeaux. Guizot's answer, dated June 21, 1859, is valuable for the picture it gives of Juliette at twenty-four and of her family:

I shall give you the information you desire without delay. The Rondeaux-Pouchets are indeed my neighbors. A few years ago, the father, a big manufacturer in Rouen, bought the estate of La Roque, about two miles from Val-Richer. He comes for a few weeks every summer with his family. We see each other at those times. He is capable, a real businessman, intelligent, sensible, active, valuing above all success and the profits of success. His wife is an excellent person, pious, charitable, and high-minded, with shy and awkward ways. Everyone who knows her values her. She herself is rich, and manages her household quite well. They have four children, two sons and two daughters.[17] I don't think you know much about their means. They are certainly very rich and their finances are well handled.

The daughter is not pretty. Not ugly either, but a bit awkward. She was very well brought up by a person of great merit, who has instilled in her good sentiments and good habits in every respect. My daughters say she is well-educated and has a taste for good literature. Their impressions of both mother and daughter are good. The family is well-established in Rouen; the father has long been and still is, I think, a member and secretary of the General Council. He has an elder brother, now very old, for a long time a member of the Chamber of Deputies in our days and one of the most faithful and intelligent allies of our party. A true liberal conservative. A cultured man as well, even learned.

I have told you all I know. On the whole, I can pass on only good impressions of the family and the person in question. I believe her health is very good. At any rate she seems healthy, neither tall nor fat.

Adieu my dear friend.

FRANÇOIS GUIZOT

Guizot's information must have greatly impressed the Gides. But his answer is dated June, 1859, and the "introduction" did not take place until 1862. The delay can doubtless be explained by Edouard Rondeaux's illness and then his death on October 17, 1860. The deep mourning, and the sorrow and anxiety that followed, are enough to account for the fact that any plans for marriage were temporarily set aside. Besides, 1861 was a year of great change in the rue de Crosne. Juliette gradually took over the running of the house, for her mother was sick and grief-stricken. With Anna Shackleton, she took the initiative of sending away most of her father's servants, who were not very particular about their morals. The valet, Louis, a great ladies' man, and his wife Henriette, who blithely encouraged his adventures, were dismissed along with the housemaid, Adèle. "Ces demoiselles," wanting to live only among people of irreproachable morals, cleaned house. On that subject, Juliette Rondeaux stood for no weakness and no joking. She had been irritated by the tolerance of her father, who was as little puritanical as it is possible to be.

It was not until 1862 that Claire Démarest and her eldest son Maurice, who lived in Paris, were invited to the Pastor Rognon's in the rue de Seine to meet Paul Gide, then a lecturer at the Faculty of Law. Pastor Rognon, who had prepared Maurice Démarest for his first communion, was one of Pastor Roberty's friends. Like him, he was a champion of orthodox Protestantism and an avowed adversary of M. Athanase Coquerel.[18] The

---

[17] Actually five children, three sons and two daughters.

[18] In 1864 Athanase Coquerel was dismissed from his duties as probationer by the so-called orthodox ecclesiastical party because of his "liberal" ideas. The measure was a signal for strife among the Reformed Churches of France.

Démarests, who "came in the capacity of scouts for a first look at the candidate,"[19] were most impressed. They were as pleased by his distinction as by his culture, and agreed that he was the personification of Juliette Rondeaux's moral and intellectual ideal. Their only reservation was that Paul Gide seemed "in rather weak health." A short time after, Juliette and Paul were finally brought face to face.

Juliette Rondeaux had long disdained the most brilliant matches of Rouen society, when at last everyone was completely surprised to hear that she had accepted a penniless young professor of law, from the depths of the *Midi,* who would never have dared ask her for hand had he not been urged to and introduced by the excellent Pastor Roberty, who well knew my mother's views.[20]

Juliette Rondeaux's views were formed by a fervent Protestantism. She was so enthusiastic about the Gard Huguenots that some time after, on returning from Uzès, it took her a few days, her sister Claire noted, to "settle down again in Normandy."

The marriage contract was signed in Rouen on February 23, 1863. Paul Gide contributed his talent, Juliette Rondeaux her fortune. The marriage certificate was countersigned according to the old custom by many relatives and friends. Among the signatures is that of a Flaubert, not Gustave but his brother Achille, the Rondeaux's family doctor. The religious ceremony took place on Friday, February 27, at the Saint-Eloi church.

The couple settled in Paris at 19 rue de Médicis. The young professor was near the Faculty of Law where he taught; his wife was the neighbor of her sister Claire Démarest, then living at 24 rue Soufflot, whom she saw every day. Anna Shackleton had stayed in Rouen as companion to Mme. Edouard Rondeaux. She remained there until Mme. Rondeaux's death in 1873 and then came to live in Paris, in the rue de Vaugirard, not far from her friend.

For six years the Paul Gides had no children. Then on Monday, November 22, 1869, their son André was born. The announcement, one copy of which has been kept, was engraved with the initials G. R. P. (Gide-Rondeaux-Pouchet). Four or five years later, Paul Gide appeared on the balcony of their rue de Médicis apartment with his son, throwing "paper dragons" into the wind, which carried them toward the chestnut trees of the Luxembourg Gardens. And with that scene in mind, Gide opened *Si le grain ne meurt.*

[19] Maurice Démarest's notebooks, unpublished.
[20] *Si le grain ne meurt,* I, 31.

2: Father Image

"Ah! my taste for literature I owe to him, not to my mother."

ANDRÉ GIDE, in Conversation

ℱ OR eleven years (1869–80), from his birth to Paul Gide's death, André Gide, an only child, lived between his mother and father. It matters little whether or not the image he formed of his parents and their marriage corresponds to objective reality. A child's mind is not formed by his parents such as they are but as he sees them, as he first saw them at an age when impressions are ineradicable. Whether an image is authentic or deceptive, it has the same suggestive force and determines the reactions of identification or rejection so fundamental in the formation of character. In other words, Paul and Juliette Gide's actual personalities are of less consequence in our study than their son's image of them.

"I recall my father, with his square-cut beard and rather long and curly black hair, from a photograph; without it, I should have remembered only his extreme gentleness."[1] André Gide may not have kept a precise image of his father's physiognomy, but he well remembered his

[1] *Si le grain ne meurt*, I, 15. One characteristic of Gide's memory was his difficulty in recalling faces: "I cannot describe a face; the features vanish, even the color of the eyes." There is a contrast in all his works between the subtle precision of psychological analyses and the vagueness of physical descriptions. We know his characters from the inside, but we hardly see them, except perhaps for those of a secondary or anecdotal interest. It has been said that Gide could only describe souls.

character. When he talked about him, he never failed to contrast his father's good qualities with his mother's virtues, as if he had loved him both for himself and against her. One had charm, gaiety, tolerance, and intellectual culture, the other a rather heavy seriousness, austerity, authority, and a devotion to ethics.

There is a kind of magical charm in André Gide's first recollections of his father:

On certain fine summer evenings, when we had not dined too late and my father was not too busy, he used to ask: "Would my little friend like to come for a walk with me?" He never called me anything but his "little friend." "You'll both be sensible, won't you?" said my mother. "Don't come back too late." I liked to go out with my father; and as he rarely showed me much attention, the few things we did together had a strange, solemn, and somewhat mysterious air about them that enchanted me.[2]

Turning off the rue de Tournon,[3] they would cross the Luxembourg Gardens and walk along the avenue de l'Observatoire. The School of Pharmacy had not yet been built and instead there were street stalls where one could buy second-hand things or rent velocipedes. The "strange" lighting on the chestnut trees, the "wonder" of a *café-concert* glimpsed through planks that were badly joined, the roll of drums announcing the closing time of the gardens, the broad paths filled with shadow and "mystery" were all visions of a fairyland. "On those evenings I fell into bed intoxicated with shadow, sleep, and strangeness."

The sense of mystery is one of the fundamental aspects of Gide's childhood. Before sinking into sleep, he often thought:

There is reality and there are dreams; and there is a *second reality* as well. The vague, indefinable belief in something else besides the acknowledged reality of everyday life inhabited me for many years. . . . During the day my suspicions remained uncertain, but at night, just before falling asleep, I felt them grow more sharply defined and positive. I did not try to fathom the mystery; I felt that I might put an abrupt stop to something I was trying to catch unawares.[4]

His gentle and rather distant father belonged to that mysterious world and somehow took part in it, as if he also shared in its aura. His presence did not interfere with the dream but accompanied it, while the stiff and methodical mother was excluded from it: "She repeated far too often and about too many things: 'You will understand when you are older.'"

Professor Gide knew how to become a gay and simple man when he played with his little boy. We get that impression from the very first

[2] *Si le grain ne meurt,* I, 17, 18.

[3] In 1874 Gide's parents left their apartment at 19 rue de Médicis for one at 2 rue de Tournon.

[4] *Si le grain ne meurt,* I, 27, 28.

page of *Si le grain ne meurt*. When Gide had outgrown the usual child-hood games, he and his father would play guessing and word games and charades. The child felt that his father was trying to amuse him and every gesture he made filled his son with gratitude, due perhaps less to the game itself than to the intention behind it:

My father would go and look for some big book on the common law of Bur-gundy or Normandy, a heavy folio which he opened on the arm of an easy chair so that together we might follow, from page to page, the trail left by a perse-vering bookworm. While looking through an old text, the jurist had admired the little secret tunnels and said to himself, "Ah! this will amuse my little boy." And it did amuse me very much, with the added pleasure of the amusement he himself seemed to take in it.

He was more especially grateful to his father for playing with him, for, being an only child, he had almost no companions:

When I was not at school or in my room . . . mother, tired of having me at her skirts, would suggest that I go and play with my little friend Pierre, in other words, all by myself.

The fact that his father liked to participate in his diversions, without condescending, was one more bond between them, for André Gide had always been and remained fond of playing.

Vacations, for the university professor, were times of great relaxation. Paul Gide's laugh, the happy, pure laughter that showed "the extreme amusement it is natural for the soul to take in life," had left an even more ringing echo in the memory of a boy whose mother never laughed. "Miss Shackleton and he would go off into fits of childish mirth, in which, as far as I remember, my mother never joined." At Easter the family and Anna Shackleton would walk about in the country around Uzès, discover-ing wild plants and avoiding the generally harmless snakes they found in their path. The different attitudes and feelings of all four can be seen clearly from the following anecdote:

My father dawdled about and was amused by everything. My mother, aware of the hour, vainly spurred us on. Night was already falling when we finally came out from between the steep banks of the river. The village was still a long way off and we could just about make out the angelic sound of its bells. . . . I can still hear the angelus and see the charming path, the rosy sunset, and the encroaching darkness climbing up behind us from the Gardon river bed. I was amused at first by the long shadows we cast; then everything melted into the grey of twilight and I let myself be won over by my mother's anxiety. My father and Anna, gripped by the beauty of the hour, idled along without worrying about the time. I remember that they were reciting poetry; my mother thought that "it was not the moment" and cried out, "Paul, you can recite that when we get home."[5]

[5] *Ibid.,* pp. 39, 40.

And so even on those sunny days, his mother cast a shadow and cut a stern figure, caring more about respecting a schedule than enjoying the moment.

From time to time, in the rue de Tournon, Paul Gide asked his son to join him in his study. The little boy entered on tiptoe "as if in a temple." The bookcase rose out of the semidarkness like a "tabernacle." The enormous table covered with books and papers, the lectern, the thick carpet, dark and richly colored, increased his "rather fearful veneration." But as soon as the lord of the kingdom of books began to pay him some attention, the solemn study turned into a place of enchantment. Once he foresook the Pandects, the jurist became the wondrous storyteller his son wrote about with such nostalgia. He would read aloud and comment upon passages from the *Odyssey,* the adventures of Sindbad or Ali Baba, scenes from Molière, *Pathelin's Farce, Télémaque,*[6] the illustrations of Italian comedy in Maurice Sand's *Les Masques.* "I also admired the pictures of Harlequin, Colombine, Punchinello, and Pierrot after I had heard them converse with my father's voice." One day Paul Gide even undertook to read him the first part of the Book of Job. It

made the deepest impression on me both because of the solemnity of the story and because of the gravity of my father's voice and the expression on my mother's face as she alternately kept her eyes closed in order to indicate or shield her pious absorption and opened them, only to throw me a questioning look, full of love and hope.

On that occasion Mme. Paul Gide was present. Her husband's reading of a biblical text took place not in the study but in the small parlor "where we felt more especially in her domain." In giving that precise detail, Gide perhaps meant to emphasize the fact that secular reading was more in his father's line, religious reading in his mother's.

The adventures of the heroes of the *Odyssey* and the *Arabian Nights,* which Gide was to later read in the unexpurgated translations of Leconte de Lisle and Dr. Mardrus, were always linked in his imagination to the magical charms of the rue de Tournon library. When he lectured at the Libre Esthétique of Brussels on the evolution of theater, he quoted one entire passage that had filled him with terror and enthusiasm as a little boy.

I am thinking of what voyages were before we had maps and an exact but limited catalogue of the known. I reread these words of Sindbad: ". . . the captain suddenly cast his turban on the deck. Then he buffeted his face like a woman and plucked out his beard and fell down in the waist of the ship well-nigh fainting for stress of grief and rage. . . . So all the merchants and sailors came around about him and asked him: 'O master! What is the matter?' for the light had

[6] Unpublished notes for *Si le grain ne meurt.*

become night before their sight. And he answered, saying: 'Know, O folk, that we have wandered from our course and left the sea whose ways we wot, and come into a sea whose ways I know not.' " I am thinking of Sindbad's vessel.

Gide was often to think of Sindbad's vessel. . . .[7]

The first books read to him made an all the more vivid impression because they were read aloud by someone he loved. As a deeply emotional child, he constantly associated his tastes with the people who brought them out. His father's influence on the awakening of his poetic emotions was comparable to his mother's on the awakening of his moral conscience —which perhaps partly explains the strange division he made for so long between the world of art, which he saw as masculine, and the world of ethics, which he saw as feminine.

The books in his father's study seemed to him like the custodians of magic secrets, treasures that would solve all riddles. He felt they belonged to the world of the "second reality," extending it in a way by making it real. When his father died, André Gide was already eleven but he was unable to believe that the magician who held the key to dreams was "really dead" and imagined "that he was only dead to our visible daily life, but that at night, while I was asleep, he would secretly come back to my mother." But from then on she locked up the "tabernacle."

After my father died, my mother no longer allowed me to go in. The room was kept locked; and although it was at one end of the apartment, it seemed the center of it to me. My thoughts, my ambitions, and my desires all gravitated around it.

Mme. Paul Gide forbade her son access to his father's library until he was almost sixteen. In his last years he still talked about his excitement at finally being able to go back to the magic moments of his childhood. One day when I went to see him in the rue Vaneau, he showed me his father's notorious library, especially his collection of Greek lyric poets in "the exquisite little Lefèvre edition" mentioned in *Si le grain ne meurt.* Then, with the sudden emotion so characteristic of him, he said: "Ah! my taste for literature I owe to him, not to my mother." Since that day I have often thought about his words and the tone in which they were said. And one can so well measure the gratitude of a man for whom literature was a constant occupation and indeed a passion. The same day he told me, with what seemed like a touch of bitterness: "I think that if my father

[7] *Nouveaux Prétextes,* pp. 26, 27. Jean Paulhan, comparing Gide to Sindbad, brought out one of the main themes in the personal mythology that haunted Gide from the time of his childhood and naturally took increasingly symbolic forms. "Whoever reads him quite naïvely . . . thinks of Sindbad the sailor. . . . All the same, he has no compass and is always on the verge of shouting (like Sindbad): 'Here we are beyond the confines of the world!' " (Jean Paulhan, *Gide le marin, hommage à André Gide,* N.R.F., 1951.)

had seen to my upbringing himself, my life would have been very different."

Paul Gide's ideas on how to bring up a son differed greatly from his wife's. They were not in agreement either about permissible reading matter or about the problem of obedience. One was as broad-minded and tolerant as the other was narrow-minded and dogmatic:

... my mother holding that a child must give in without trying to understand, my father always inclining to explain everything to me. I remember very well that in those days my mother would compare the child I was to the people of Israel and assure me that before living in grace it was good to have lived under the law.

The idea of the categorical imperative, the unquestionable and unquestioning moral obligation, was not propagated by the Cévenol Huguenot but by the Norman, who on that subject as well as many others was more a Cévenol than her husband. Disputes over their son were frequent. It is not difficult to imagine whose side Gide was on during their discussions about "the suitable nourishment for a small child's mind." In fact, he was preparing to fight his mother tooth and nail. "My attitude toward her was frequently marked by insubordination and constantly by disputes, while my father with one word would have obtained from me anything he pleased." "He" had merely to ask, but he never did, and "she" finally did what she pleased. In the debates between he who "was inclined to . . ." and she who "held that . . . ," the most stubborn always won and the jurist returned to his study, leaving the future immoralist, after a few fruitless attempts, to close his mouth and pull in his claws. Like many meditative intellectuals, little given to polemics, Paul Gide was not bent on triumphing over a less intelligent but stubborn adversary and, hating scenes, he retired into his library of Roman law as if it were the Aventine. When André Gide emphasized his father's "gentleness," it was certainly well meant, but the adjective "extreme" was perhaps less so. The little boy would probably have preferred that his father, whatever his innate civility, defend his point of view more vigorously, at least in the disputes with his wife concerning their only son's destiny.

Recalling his mother's authoritarianism and narrow-mindedness, Gide added: "Conflicts arose which helped to convince me that I resembled my father . . ." That simple sentence reveals his initial desire for identification with his father's image. Nevertheless, the emotional identification, which might have been ardent and decisive in the formation of his character, remained incomplete and hardly effective. His father—tender but distant, charming but absent, gentle but inattentive, who "gave in to the needs of his heart more than he applied principles"—always seemed to him a somewhat enigmatic character, playing a part in his "second reality" and dreams, rather than in direct reality, where the omnipotent Mme. Gide obviously held sway. "Taken up by the preparation of his course at the Faculty of Law, my father gave me very little of his time. He spent most of the day shut up in his vast and somewhat dark study, into which I was only admitted when he invited me to come." Here we almost feel a touch of resentment, or at any rate regret, the feeling of receiving too little from a person by whom one would have wished to be loved more.

It would be an exaggeration to claim that André Gide felt deprived of paternal affection, but he was surely disappointed that it was shown rarely and unobtrusively. The incoercible emotional outburst, the sob that seized him one day late in life, on seeing Poil de Carotte, on the screen of a theater in Paris, walk hand in hand with his father, the taciturn M. Lepic, who could have been his friend, perhaps had its origin in his most distant past. What Gide called his "insatiable need to love and be loved" had no way of being satisfied by literature during his childhood. "I have often convinced myself that the worst scoundrels are those who lacked affection in their youth. It is no doubt strange that my parents' affection was not enough. . . ."[8] Moreover, as part of the family unit, the father had no authority in the household; he played only a secondary role. And the child more or less realized that his gay holiday companion and the magician of his evenings in the kingdom of books did not claim to exercise supreme rule in the family's daily life.

[8] *Si le grain ne meurt,* I, 80.

3: Mother Image

"She would have liked people to be not as they were but as they should have been so as to conform to her puritanical exigencies."

Si le grain ne meurt

THERE were times when André Gide reproached himself with the severity of the portrait he drew of his mother in *Si le grain ne meurt*: "I'm glad that I somewhat revised it in my *Feuillets d'automne*." He was referring to the pages he had written rather late in life and which he called *Ma Mère*. All the same, the specific revisions in *Feuillets d'automne* are simply an accentuation of his initial regrets that came through in the first portrait, which was not nearly as hard and sharply defined as one might think at first sight. Indeed, the writer's hesitations were perceptible even then. Although a first reading of *Si le grain ne meurt* might give the impression that Mme. Paul Gide's character was all of a piece, further study discloses psychological nuances that constitute a second portrait and seem to correspond to another nature. One impression constantly superimposed on another leads to confusion, due perhaps to the subject's actual duality, perhaps to the ambivalence of the author's filial sentiments.

As soon as Juliette Gide became head of the rue de Crosne household, she took command. She was precise and thorough in the exercise of her duties, for "with her, the idea of duty would often crumble into a pile of little obligations." The first to get up, the last to go to bed, alert from the minute she opened her eyes, helped by her faithful Swiss maid Anna Leuenberger (called Marie to avoid any confusion of names with Anna

Shackleton), she established a rule of impeccable order in her house. The numerous ledgers, still in existence, in which she kept her accounts and noted even the slightest expenses, up to and including "André's expenditures" as a very small boy, testify to bourgeois virtues carried to a high degree of perfection and an extraordinary rigor in household management. Meals in her house were at an appointed time, and she never stood for anyone arriving even slightly late.[1] The linens were put away in vast Norman cupboards according to immutable rites, on a prescribed day, and exact and niggling inventories were taken. The servants were always strictly surveyed, with an eye to costs. When her young son was allowed out for a walk, she gave him two sous to have a treat at old Clément's shop in the Luxembourg Gardens, where one could buy aniseed and sticks of sugar candy, but also at a higher price, tops and cockchafers. The child tried to get more money, but in vain; his mother assured him that two sous were more than enough. Mme. Gide was parsimonious.

Her successive apartments in the rue de Médicis, rue de Tournon, and rue de Commaille were always managed with the same horror of carelessness and the same love of cleanliness, reaching all the way to the nooks and corners. The floors were waxed to such a degree that, to Marie's indignation, André persisted in wanting to skate on them. Each piece of furniture was in its place, arranged as symmetrically as possible, absolutely gleaming when not protected by its perfectly fitted white percale slipcover, finely striped with bright red. Many of the tables and chairs were upholstered in "silk and wool" tapestry, a product of Mme. Gide's patient and persevering handiwork. The fine armchairs covered in Genoese velvet were forbidden to the tempestuous little boy. Furthermore, he himself was full of consideration for the furniture his mother treated with such care, and it was only later, at about nineteen, when Gide began visiting the Laurens, that he realized how "ugly" the furniture was. He also then understood why his father sometimes became impatient. One day, on his birthday, Paul Gide went into his rue de Tournon study and was appalled by the sight of a screen of silk tapestry-work in very bad taste:

In front of the fireplace stood a screen of silk tapestry-work representing a kind of Chinese bridge under a bower of wild roses. I can still see the blues in it. Its bamboo frame was decorated with pendants, from which swung silk tassels of the same blue as the tapestry, hanging in pairs from the heads and tails of mother-of-pearl fish and fastened by gold threads.[2]

The tapestry, alas, was the work of Mme. Gide, who had secretly embroidered it as a surprise for her husband.

[1] "I can't urge you strongly enough to try and be on time for meals. . . ." Letter from Mme. Paul Gide to her husband, 1873, unpublished.

[2] The screen has been kept.

Gentle as he was and adoring my mother, he almost lost his temper: "No Juliette!" he burst out, "no, I beg of you. The study is mine. Let me arrange at least this room myself, in my own way." Then, recovering his good disposition, he persuaded my mother that although the screen gave him great pleasure, he preferred it in the living-room.

It would seem that Mme. Gide had as little taste in her own dress as in her furnishings. She herself was rather wanting in charm. Most people who knew her are agreed that she could hardly have been called feminine. One describes her as "somewhat masculine," another still remembers that, as a child, he disliked kissing her "because it scratched." Very dark, big-boned, and awkward, she did have "naturally solemn and sweet" features but either never knew how or did not deign to make the most of them and, adept at detracting from herself, wore her hair in "most unbecoming" ways. She dressed rather clumsily, without undue expense, without affectation, yet without simplicity, so that in the eyes of a reputedly elegant witness, she seemed "astonishingly dowdy."

Under Anna Shackleton's influence, Juliette Rondeaux had acquired a great respect for "music, painting, poetry, and generally everything that was over her head." She had devoted herself with method to becoming accomplished. As soon as she married, she gave up painting and her watercolors, but not the piano. When she played, she would count aloud with the exact precision of a metronome and her interpretation of fiery passages was particularly mechanical; yet when she reached the end of the piece, she would play more quickly and then vigorously strike the final chord. Not partial to sentimental music, she divided composers into those who were healthy, such as Haydn, and those who were unhealthy, like Chopin. And the fact that for a long time she forbade her son either to play or listen to Chopin partly accounts for André Gide's early preference for his music.

Mme. Paul Gide's opinions on literature were based on the judgments of righteous critics, those who wrote for the *Temps*, the *Journal des Débats politiques et littéraires*, and the *Revue des Deux-Mondes*, particularly Ferdinand Brunetière, whose dogmatism she appreciated. She distrusted "anything new" and in order to judge correctly, she referred to the opinions of well-known critics for fear of admiring "in the wrong way," not enough, or not at all. She considered poetry and novels as frivolous genres and preferred reading historical or critical works, especially those that were dense and arduous. She was excited more by the effort of reading than by reading itself and felt that the more difficult the book, the more praiseworthy the effort. She tried less to broaden her mind than to strengthen it.

Instead of reading plays themselves, where the best and the worst are so dangerously mingled, she read Saint-Marc-Girardin's *Cours de littérature dramatique,* which prudently separated the wheat from the chaff. She divided writers into those who were good and those who were bad, not according to how well they wrote but according to whether or not their morality corresponded to her own puritanical and Victorian ethics. For example, Maupassant and the so-called realistic images he gave of Norman society disgusted her. She made a distinction between books to read and books to banish, in accordance with categorical imperatives that had little to do with literature. One might assume that she would have severely judged her son's books and would have condemned them as a whole. Yet she did approve of *Les Cahiers d'André Walter* because of its many biblical quotations. She died before *Les Nourritures terrestres* was published but the overappetizing title displeased her and she fought to make him change it.

Ethics was Juliette Gide's prime concern and everything else was subordinated to it. She had been taught the Calvinist or Jansenist doctrine that egotism is hateful and had fervently adopted it in her own very limited way. Duty to her meant making a "constant effort" to thwart nature, and she brought up her son in that spirit. As in any Huguenot upbringing, emphasis was put on sexual purity. We shall come back to this important aspect of André Gide's education and the difficulties it caused between mother and son from childhood on. But Puritanism is not limited to an attitude toward sexuality; it extends to all forms of sensual pleasure, even to the religious. Mme. Gide was austere in her practice of religion. She would go to the church of Pentremont every Sunday, help in the works of Protestant missions as her mother had done, and, like her, was fond of surrounding herself with ministers, whose relatives were often entrusted with the care and entertainment of her son during the holidays. Another of her characteristics was her hate of any self-complacency. Always ill at ease herself and "never lapsing into a state of self-satisfaction," she could not bear self-satisfaction in others. She not only scolded André for every show of vanity but for every show of pride as well. "She did her best to sweep out everything that in my own eyes could inflate my self-importance," and thus created the perpetual disputes between them, ending only when he held his tongue and obeyed. Everyone who knew André Gide as a child was struck by the family scenes. His Uncle Charles wrote to him:

I didn't love you when you were a child because I held you responsible, perhaps rather unjustly, for the irritation I felt at those perpetual disputes at table and elsewhere.[3]

Young André held his own: "In those days my attitude toward her was frequently marked by insubordination and constantly by disputes." When

[3] Letter from Charles Gide to André Gide, 1894, unpublished.

she realized that the use of authority had little effect on the small boy, she tried to reason with him according to Paul Gide's principles. But as soon as she became involved in controversial discussions, she had a powerful opponent. After having reasonably explained her point of view, prudently beginning with "I should like to point out . . ." or "I should like to draw your attention to the fact that . . . ," she would await a definite answer. But instead of the hoped-for yes or no, she got a yes *and* a no, followed by a lengthy commentary on the ambiguity of the problem at hand. The discussion would then grow worse than ever, without either yielding. "Ah," she would shout, "you'll drive me crazy!"[4] Finally, she would go back to discipline, pure and simple, as the only means to power for the head of anything, even a family. And so began, in childish form, the struggle of André Gide's youth: an attempt, at first timid, then increasingly impatient, to throw off the yoke of maternal authority.

I think it might have been said of my mother that the qualities she liked were not those of the people she tyrannized over, but rather those she hoped to see them acquire. In any case, that is how I try to explain her unceasing attempts to work on other people, and on me in particular; and I was irritated to such a point that I now wonder whether my exasperation had not ended by destroying all my love for her. She had a way of loving me that sometimes made me hate her and put my nerves on edge. You whom I arouse to indignation, imagine the effect of being constantly worried about and watched, incessantly and harassingly advised as to what to do, what to think, what to spend, what to wear, what to read, what title to give a book. . . .[5]

Mme. Gide may have loved her only son badly, but there is no doubt she loved him very much. She "tyrannized" over him for his own good, or what she believed it to be. "You owe it to your son." Those words took priority over any personal preference she may have had, even over her horror of spending money. When Paul Gide died, the rue de Tournon apartment had become too large and she wanted to move to more modest accommodations, for her tastes were simple and further simplified by her inclination to live economically. But she came up against her elder sister Claire Démarest's intransigence. Claire gave her to understand that she had to "keep up her position" for her son. Then the anachronistic discussions began about the degree of bourgeois respectability of the neighborhood, the rent, the floor, and about the eminent dignity of having a *porte-cochère* or carriage gateway. "Yes, the floor might do," said Aunt Claire, pouting slightly. "You could, I suppose, live high up. But as for the other point, no Juliette, I would go so far as to say: absolutely not." The "other point" was the *porte-cochère*. Then, seeing that her sister remained silent,

---

[4] I learned of this from Mme. Théo van Rysselberghe who heard about it from André Gide.

[5] *Si le grain ne meurt,* II, 363.

Claire Démarest slowly let drop the magic words: "You owe it to your son." And out of duty to her son, Juliette Gide chose an even larger and more expensive apartment than the old one. And just as she "owed" it to her son to live in an apartment house with a carriage gateway, so she "owed it to him," as Aunt Claire would say, to travel first class, take the best seats at theater, and so forth.

The words "you owe it to your son" had a sovereign effect on Juliette Gide except when there was question of a higher duty. One day she learned that a severe epidemic of typhoid fever had broken out at La Roque:

Mamma no sooner heard of it than she went off to look after the patients, considering it her duty since they were her tenant-farmers. My Aunt Claire had tried to keep her from going, saying that her first duty was to her son, not to her tenant-farmers, and that she was running a great risk in order to be of small assistance. . . . Advice, reproaches, nothing availed. What mamma recognized as her duty, she carried out against wind and tide.

That Juliette Gide had a certain nobility of character cannot be denied. And she was just as ardently patriotic as she was Protestant. Had she ever found herself in a situation that called for a show of her religious or patriotic convictions, it is likely she would have done her duty to the very end.

Gide's rather biased opinions of Corneille may often seem surprising, but his prejudice was not of a literary nature. When Ramon Fernandez claims that Gide "never met Corneillian heroes, nor would he have been much interested in them," I think he is quite wrong. As a matter of fact Gide spent his entire childhood in the lap of an almost Corneillian heroine. No doubt, circumstances kept Rouen's Juliette Rondeaux from rising to the ancient heights of tragedy, but she did bring a somewhat bourgeois form of tragic nobility into the scenes of her domestic life. The tendency that warped Gide's opinion of Corneille was of a personal nature. He could never read his plays without associating, rightly or wrongly, Corneille's ethics with his own mother's conception of duty and moral heroism.

Such, in general and in detail, is the first portrait of André Gide's mother and one that leaves a striking impression on those who read *Si le grain ne meurt*. Exactitude pushed to an extreme, domestic order carried to punctiliousness, an inflexible regularity of habits, a great sense of economy if not actual stinginess, a moral rigor applied to even the slightest action, an obsession with behaving properly and doing-what-one-should, an excessive love of duty, a disdain for facility in all its forms, a distrust of elegance and adornment, a horror not only of any familiarity and lack of constraint but even of an easy manner, a prudish and extreme restraint in any show of feeling, except in sublime circumstances, an austere and formal religion, more Calvinistic or Jansenistic than truly Christian, the most severe bourgeois conformity, putting respectability above everything else, and a tyrannical watchfulness over all her entourage, such are her most obvious characteristics. She seems like the embodiment of virtue without grace, of ethics without complacency, of religion without love. She is the Roman mother of the Ancients, the Corneillian mother of the classics, the virile mother of psychoanalysts, thus creating a horror of the Roman virtues, Corneille, and authority in her son. In short, she was *the* Puritan.

Yet the mask hid another face and the *persona* another person. Behind the strong authoritarian mother, Gide gives us a glimpse of a shy woman, worried to the point of anxiety and deeply lacking in self-confidence. As a young boy he noticed how very much her attitude changed when she was outside the house or the family circle. She became embarrassed, "extremely reserved," and seemed to be "afraid of her own opinion." An even slightly fashionable personage would impress her so much that she would "withdraw"; and when she needed to consult a doctor about her son, even one she had known well but who had since become eminent, she was "prevented from doing so by some shame or other, which I certainly inherited from her and which also paralyzes me in front of successful people." She never liked to go out "in society," for she felt as awkward and self-conscious as she had when, as a young girl, she was forced to attend social gatherings in Rouen. When visiting, "she would lose her self-assurance." Consequently, she reduced her acquaintances to a strict minimum, "not too distant cousins or the wives of a few of my father's colleagues at the Faculty of Law." Her social life was limited to the few obligations she judged indispensable, for "every one of mamma's actions was always well thought out." She forced herself to see the people one has to see, but always seemed to come away with the depressing and specious impression that she was "not as good as the others."

\André Gide remembers having seen his mother at ease in society only once, and it made such an indelible impression on him that he felt the need of recalling it in one of the later pages of his *Feuillets d'automne*. It took place at their Saussine cousins', where Gide, then an adolescent, went rather halfheartedly to take dancing lessons. The Saussines were receiving that day:

There were many introductions and the conversation, much the same as all social conversation, consisted in small talk and affectation. I paid more attention to my mother than to the others. I hardly recognized her. Ordinarily so modest, reserved, and afraid of her own opinion, she seemed full of confidence in the fashionable salon, and without pushing herself forward at all, she was perfectly at ease. . . . I was really amazed, and as soon as we escaped from that Vanity Fair and found ourselves alone, just the two of us, I told her so.

He had a dinner engagement with Pierre Louis that evening but was so anxious to get back to her that he returned to the rue de Commaille with unusual haste. The scene that took place seems to me of such great importance and so pathetic in its restraint that I shall transcribe it here in its entirety:

She had taken off her fine clothes and I found her dressed in the simple and dull costume she wore every day. The acacia was then in bloom and filled the air with its fragrance. My mother seemed worried; she never willingly talked about herself, and no doubt the springtime helped loosen her tongue.

—Is it true what you told me as we left our cousins? she began with great effort. Do you really think I was . . . well, as good as the others?

And as I began to protest, she continued sadly:

—If your father had only once been able to tell me that . . . I never dared to ask him, and I should have so much needed to know if, when we went out together, he was. . . .

She was silent for a moment. I watched her try to keep back the tears. She finished in a lower voice, hardly audible:

—. . . if he was pleased with me. . . .

Hidden, as so often happens, under an authoritarian mask was a lack of self-confidence and a great need for reassurance. The shy young girl who "disdained" Rouen society and its "brilliant matches" no doubt used the pretext of disdain to conceal a kind of fear of living. When she married Paul Gide it seems that she was disconcerted by his spirit of tolerance, his eclectic tastes, and his humanism. With the result that the feeling of inferiority she had already experienced in regard to Anna Shackleton was accentuated. Knowing the poor estimation she had of herself, one can image her reaction when she saw Anna Shackleton and Paul Gide laugh with the same laugh, be charmed by the same poets, enjoy the same natural beauties, while she, for whom only duty counted, was excluded from their pleasure. She felt no petty jealousy, for her heart "never gave in to anything base," but she grew to have even less confidence in herself than before. The Gides's only son was hardly left with an impression of marital harmony, and he probably sensed the fact that there was little communication between his parents. Otherwise he would not have tried to explain the contradictions in his own nature by the "contradictory influences" in his heredity.

I am afraid I have not really shown what a *person of good will* she was (I use the word in its most evangelical sense). She was always striving toward something good, something better, and never lapsed into a state of self-satisfaction. It was not enough for her to be modest; she was constantly trying to diminish

Paul Gide

Catherine Gide

André Gide with his mother

Students and members of the faculty at the Ecole Alsacienne.
André Gide is on the far left in the third row

André Gide

her imperfections or those she came upon in others, to correct herself or others, to educate herself.

Because of the unremitting effort she made, André Gide's mother seemed not natural but constrained, not serene but anxious. Her anxiety itself pushed her toward an ever-growing submissiveness to moral laws, and she became all the more rigorous and conforming in that she freed herself from a lack of inner confidence only by gaining another and systematic confidence in prescribed obligations. She transferred her need for greatness and for security to a belief in absolute obedience to the law, and found the constraint so salutary that she wanted to make her son fully profit by it.

Despite the relentlessness and heroism Mme. Paul Gide put into trying to appear only as she thought she should be in order to conform to her puritanical exigencies, her child got the impression of an inner duality. When as a man he thought about the great enigma of the beginning of life, he understood that what he both detested and admired in his mother was not what she was but what she had made herself become. By continually correcting, scolding, and deflating her son, she tried to instil in him a feeling of self-contempt, which according to certain Jansenist doctrines is the means to salvation. Convinced that one's most bounden duty is to conquer oneself, she felt she was doing what was right.

Yet one of Gide's remarks would seem to contradict the impression he gave of her self-restraint. He said that she gave herself up to duty "not through devotion so much as through natural inclination." Once the nature of the inclination becomes clear, the paradox is merely on the surface. A deep lack of self-confidence, by what seems a natural reaction, can lead to a search for laws that are all the more strict and all the more rigid. A state of inner anxiety, aggravated by a particularly tender conscience, is often counterbalanced by a great exactitude in observing laws and fulfilling duties, punctuality, punctiliousness, rigorism, formalism, and, as a matter of fact, pettiness. Indeed the two somewhat complementary aspects of a scrupulous person are closely linked. Anyone who is always uncertain, undecided, and rather uncomfortable, as if a small pebble (*scrupulus*) were painfully irritating him, is compelled by the difficulty itself to make a disproportionate effort to rid himself of it. This secondary compensation sometimes completely conceals the secret weakness, even from the eyes of his family, and then everything happens as if the mask of severity were hiding a tormented face.

It would no doubt be easy but unfair to attribute Mme. Gide's severity to Calvinism alone. Her character would seem less related to the fact that she was Protestant than to her way of being Protestant, dependent on her general way of being. Protestant or Catholic, there are so many ways of being Christian—in the spirit of unquietism or quietism, anguish or love, fear or grace—that every kind of mind, from the broadest to the narrowest, can adapt Christianity to its own needs. Gide was fond of subscribing to the interpretation of the anxiety-ridden Lucretius who, in connecting the word religion with *religare,* interpreted it in the sense of "tying up" and not of "joining." And it was precisely the narrow ties, denying all latitude, that Mme. Gide seemed to have sought in her religion. In a letter to Pastor Ferrari, Gide recalled "the admirable Christian figures" that hung over his childhood: his mother and Anna Shackleton. But the figures had no resemblance to one another:

Anna Shackleton! I still see your calm face, your pure brow, your slightly severe mouth, your smiling eyes that shed such kindness on my childhood. I should like to invent more vibrant, more respectful, and tenderer words in which to speak of you. Shall I one day tell the story of your life? I should like your humility to shine in my story as it will shine before God on the day the mighty are cast down and the lowly magnified.

Anna Shackleton's Protestant faith, identical to Juliette Gide's, had not taken away her charm, nor her smile, nor her radiance, nor "the extreme amusement the soul naturally takes in life"; no doubt it did the opposite and intensified them. Religion gives to each according to his tendencies, and what is often taken for a deformity brought about by a type of religion is in fact an innate form of personality. So that in this case the same "religion" had two faces: the stern face of Juliette Gide and the amiable face of Anna Shackleton.

4: Between Uzès and Rouen

"Holidays . . . in Rouen with my mother's family . . . holidays in Uzès with my paternal grandmother."

Si le grain ne meurt, *I, 21, 22*

URING the holidays André Gide, born in Paris of two transplanted stocks, came back into contact with his provincial ties. In accordance with unchanging customs, every New Year's Day would be spent in Rouen, every Easter in Uzès, and the summer months at La Roque–Baignard and at Cuverville in Normandy. In Uzès he went back to his paternal and Languedocian family, in Rouen to his maternal and Norman family.

From the edge of the Norman woods I evoke a burning rock-perfumed air, whirling with sun and rolling the scents of thyme, lavender, and the shrill crackle of the cicadas all intermingled. At my feet, for the rock is steep in the narrow valley which falls away, I evoke a mill, washerwomen, water all the cooler for being the more desired. A bit further on I evoke the rock once again, but not as steep now and milder, enclosures, gardens, then roofs, a gay little town: Uzès. It is there that my father was born and there that I came as a very young child.[1]

Paul Gide, his wife, and child would leave the train at Nîmes and take a carriage to Uzès. After the region of the dwarfed and prickly holm oak came the wheat fields, the vineyards, the olive trees. They would cross the Gardon at the Saint-Nicolas bridge. And soon appeared the little town with its three towers and its Romanesque belfry:

[1] "La Normandie et le Bas-Languedoc," *Prétextes,* p. 72.

O little town of Uzès! Were you in Umbria, tourists would flock from Paris to see you! Perched on the edge of a rock, whose steep slopes are partly covered by the shady gardens of the duchy, with tall trees at the bottom, sheltering the river crayfish in the tangle of their roots. From the terraces of the Promenade or the Park, through the nettle-trees of the duchy, one can see, on the other side of the narrow valley, an even steeper rock, jagged and riddled with caves, arches, needles, and escarpments like those of seacoast cliffs; then above it all, the harsh *garrigue,* completely laid waste by the sun.[2]

It was not the rich historical associations of the dukedom that struck young André Gide's imagination[3] but rather the beauty of the Uzès landscape, the valley of the Fontaine d'Eure, and more especially the *garrigue,* those hard dry hills of Languedoc, covered with holm oak and aromatic herbs.

Since the death of Tancrède Gide in 1867, André Gide's Uzès family was reduced to his grandmother and his Uncle Charles.[4] They lived on the second floor of the Trinquelague house on the Boulevard de l'Esplanade, in a spacious and uncomfortable apartment in which all the rooms were connecting—the dining room to the living room to the Paul Gides' room to their son's room to the grandmother's room to the back room that once was Uncle Charles'—so that going from one room to another meant meeting the family at every hour of the day.

Although Gide never knew his grandfather, he knew his grandmother well, for she lived to the age of ninety-two. According to A. Lavondès, she was a pious, kind, and amiable woman. When Gide came to spend his holidays in Uzès, she was already very old and lived with one servant, Rose, almost as old and wrinkled as she but not quite as deaf. On Sundays he would accompany her to church where she shocked him by chatting with other old ladies in such loud tones that their voices drowned the minister's. "Some people who might otherwise have been indignant excused the widows in memory of their husbands."

The Uzès grandmama would "put herself out" to receive her children from Paris and would see to it that the spiritual austerity of her family was compensated for by excellent food, in accordance with the local traditions. In Uzès, a town where, as Racine put it, "twenty caterers could have thrived," there was such abundance that the *pâtés en croûte,* the cream puffs, the round and golden loaves of bread, and the *mille-feuilles* made by the baker and pastry cook Fabrégat brought about the lay union of Catholics and Protestants who, in their choice of tradesmen, were gen-

[2] *Si le grain ne meurt,* I, 53, 54.

[3] He was, in fact, never interested in history.

[4] For valuable information not only about Charles Gide but about the entire Uzès family, see A. Lavondès, *Charles Gide.*

erally divided by their respective faiths. But as Mlle. Lavondès happily points out, "the sight of such wonders had most certainly not weakened the wills of our fathers, who were very sober people and temperate in everything they did." Be that as it may, when Gide remembered his grandmother, he remembered also the patty shells filled with quenelles, the flaky *brandades,* the *croûtillons au lard,* and the delectable *sultanes* that came from Fabrégat's. "Oh! Fabregas . . . Fabregas!" she would say with the local accent, "he's getting careless!" for nothing was good enough for the "little man." Mme. Paul Gide vainly fought against such a profusion of the fruits of the earth, so contrary to hygienic if not moral principles. As to the "little man" with the capricious appetite, the meals seemed interminable, in such a hurry was he to run out to the *garrigue.*

"Grandmother knitted stockings; it is the only occupation I ever saw her engaged in." She walked about with a bunch of knitting needles behind her ear, between her beribboned tulle cap and the strands of her grey hair. She knitted perpetually but never finished the stockings she began because she would mislay them here and there during the day, on some piece of furniture or in some drawer where Rose would find them again. Her conversation was limited to an inquiry into the news of the family and a discourse on how worried she was that the Paul Gides, accustomed to modern apartments and luxurious Norman houses, would be uncomfortable in Uzès. Moreover, her deafness made any conversation difficult. Exactly as André Gide knew her when he was a small boy, so she remained for him to the end of her life. In January, 1894, his Uncle Charles wrote to him in Biskra,[5] warning him of the serious condition she was in. And he spoke with gratitude of the woman whose "only thought in this life was for us—for me perhaps even more than for your father, probably because I was the child of her old age."[6]

Uncle Charles was usually in Uzès with his mother when André Gide visited. A rather impertinent portrait of the famous economist, as seen by his little nephew during the Easter holidays, appears in *Si le grain ne meurt:*

My uncle, at that time, was not yet interested in political economy; I discovered later that he was then particularly drawn to astronomy, a subject that suited his taste for figures, his way of being taciturn and contemplative, and that denial of individuality and of all psychology which soon turned him into a being with less knowledge of himself and others than anyone I know. He was then (I mean: at the time I was just a child) a tall young man with long black hair plastered behind his ears in strands, rather nearsighted, rather strange, silent, and most intimidating. My mother greatly irritated him by her

[5] Letter from Charles Gide to André Gide, Jan. 14, 1894, unpublished.

[6] When Charles Gide was born (1847), his mother was forty-five, his father forty-seven.

constant attempts to thaw him out; although she meant well, she had very little tact, and my uncle, unable or unwilling to take the will for the deed, was even then preparing to be indifferent to the charms of anyone but a bluffer. It seemed as if my father had monopolized all the graciousness in the family, leaving none behind to temper the callous and sullen manner of its other members.[7]

The portraits André Gide drew of his father and uncle are in direct opposition to one another. But the portrait of his Uncle Charles, as it appears in *Si le grain ne meurt,* should be considered in the light of circumstances, literature, humor, and mood. So towering a figure as Charles Gide, "the great and lofty figure of my Uncle Charles," as André Gide was to put it in his old age, cannot be comprehended from a few sarcastic details. And there can be no question of describing here, in all his complexity, the man who was considered "the most representative French Protestant at the beginning of the twentieth century."

Although for several years he was a professor in Bordeaux, Charles Gide continued to spend his vacations in Uzès. And because of his nostalgia for the south, for he liked "the dry exhilarating air" and sunny skies of Languedoc as much as his nephew did, he asked for an appointment at the Faculty of Law in Montpellier, thus drawing nearer to his mother in Uzès and his wife's parents in the neighborhood of Nîmes. He obtained his transfer and settled in Montpellier, where André Gide spent a memorable seven months in 1882 and revisited often in his youth, perhaps not so much attracted by the Charles Gide family as by the young brother of one of Charles Gide's colleagues at the Faculty of Law, Paul Valéry.

From the edge of the flaming *garrigue* I evoke thick grass that is always damp, sinuous boughs, deep shaded paths; I evoke a wood into which they plunge. . . . There, no crackle of cicadas; all is softness and luxury; under the plant growth, no naked rock ever appears. . . . On reaching the region of Caux, everything changes; great fields replace the meadows. . . . On this fifteenth of July, as I write, near Etretat,[8] now sitting down, now walking under the full noonday sun, never has this country seemed more beautiful to me. Some flax is still in bloom. The colza is being cut; the rye has been mown. In just a few days the wheat has turned golden. The harvest looks wonderfully promising. Here and there, in spots, everywhere, large poppies give a redness to the land.[9]

From the time of his childhood, André Gide was in contact with the land of Normandy and there he spent the greater part of his life.

The family house in Rouen, situated at the corner of the rue de Crosne

---

[7] *Si le grain ne meurt,* I, 41.   [8] At Cuverville-en-Caux.

[9] "La Normandie et le Bas-Languedoc," *Prétextes,* p. 73.

and the rue de Fontenelle, was bought by André Gide's maternal grand-father, Edouard Rondeaux, in 1832. After his death, his wife Julie Rondeaux-Pouchet remained in the house with her children, and, when they married, lived on there alone with Anna Shackleton as her companion. Every New Year's Day she had all her family assemble there, and the tradition was continued by Henri Rondeaux when in 1874, after his mother's death, he moved to the rue de Crosne.

Henri Rondeaux was an industrialist. He was director of an important printed cotton factory in Houlmes, a few miles from Rouen. Gide's description of his uncle is one of those concise and perfidious portraits at which he excelled: "My Uncle Henri was the best of men: gentle, benevolent, even a bit saintlike; his face had no character either; I did mention that he turned Catholic, did I not?" Nothing we know about Henri Rondeaux's life confirms the blandness Gide describes, and the story of his conversion testifies, on the contrary, to strength of character in the young man of twenty-five who carried out his convictions despite the solemn entreaties of his mother and the entire family. Also, under his direction and up until his death in 1882, the factory was highly prosperous and regularly expanding. In 1852 he had married Lucile Keittinger, herself the granddaughter and daughter of Rouen industrialists in the same field:

An orderly person, of great good sense and great feeling, my aunt was the exact counterpart of her husband; and yet she was judged his superior; for a man on the same moral level as a woman must be of great intelligence not to remain considerably inferior to her.

And there we have one of André Gide's favorite themes.

The Rondeaux-Keittingers were very Catholic and very little republican, to the extent that republicanism was identified with secularization. They read the *Croix,* a pious and regular paper, as well as the *Triboulet,* a satirical and short-lived paper, opposed to Jules Ferry. If it was true that, as Gide said, "my family's house had reverted to Catholicism and become more Catholic and *bien pensant* than it had ever been," it was true only for the masters of the house and their children, certainly not for the family guests who were invited on New Year's Day. When they saw numbers of the *Croix* and the *Triboulet* "defiantly" lying about on living room tables and even the billiard table, the Gides and the Démarests closed their eyes and refused to be corrupted. "The elder Démarests and my mother pretended not to see anything; Albert grumbled indignantly under his breath."

Guillaume Démarest (1808–1879), whose family was Catholic, had married Claire Rondeaux (1822–1901) and their children were brought up in the Protestant faith of their mother. They were much older than their first cousin André and seemed to him like grownups living in another world, with the exception of Albert, who, despite the difference in age—almost twenty years—had considerable influence on him and played a major role in his youth. Like the Gides, the Démarests lived in Paris and spent their holidays in Normandy.

In spite of certain differences in their religious and political beliefs, Juliette Gide, Lucile Rondeaux-Keittinger, and Claire Démarest got along "like three fingers on one hand." All three were "models of decency and honesty," as André Gide was to describe them in *Et nunc manet in te*, paying homage to his "Aunt Claire and Aunt Lucile" as well as to his mother and Anna Shackleton. They had a highly developed family or caste spirit and Aunt Claire's "we owe it to ourselves" could have been the motto of each one. They were consequently all agreed that the behavior of their sister-in-law Mathilde, wife of Emile Rondeaux, also living in Rouen, had to be treated with strict disapproval.

On the dreary rue de Lecat, at number 18, lived Emile Rondeaux, his wife, and their six children. Emile Rondeaux (1831–1890) had married Mathilde Pochet in April, 1866. It was soon apparent to the Rouen family that they were ill-matched. Although every year they had a child—Madeleine (1867), Jeanne (1868), Valentine (1870), Edouard (1871), Georges (1872), Lucienne[10]—their future seemed shaky. And actually a few years later they did divorce, an unprecedented occurrence in the family history.

Those who knew Emile Rondeaux have described him as a kind and distinguished man, cultured, dignified, scrupulously honest, but erratic and somewhat listless. While his father was alive he worked with him at the plant, but after his death, having inherited a large fortune, he worked solely to administer the estate of Cuverville-en-Caux which was part of his inheritance. At thirty-five, very nearly a confirmed bachelor, he met Mathilde Pochet, then twenty-one and exceedingly attractive. She was often taken for a Creole because of her dark beauty and nonchalant manner, and was in fact born on the island of Mauritius but descended from an old family of Havre merchants. Accustomed to a luxurious and easy life, she seemed "exotic and cosmopolitan" to Emile's family. Her sensual beauty, rather flashy elegance, and indolent, frivolous habits were hardly in tune with the austere Rondeaux. They were as suspicious and reticent with her as they were warmly approving of Paul Gide. In *La Porte étroite* she is Aunt Lucile, whose attitude shocked little Jérôme's mother and gave Jérôme himself "a feeling of uneasiness mixed with a kind of

[10] Neither the biographers of the Rondeaux family (P. Le Verdier, R.-G. Nobécourt) nor André Gide ever spoke of the sixth child, Lucienne. When the Emile Rondeaux were divorced, her mother took her away with her. Lucienne herself had two daughters.

admiration and terror."[11] André Gide found out about Mathilde Rondeaux's infidelity when he was thirteen, from his desperate cousin Madeleine. And it was one of the most important events in his youth.

Cuverville-en-Caux, the Fongueusemare[12] of *La Porte étroite*, was the place André Gide spent part of the summer holidays in the company of his Uncle Emile's children. He had little in common with his cousins Edouard and Georges but had great brotherly affection for Madeleine, Jeanne, and Valentine, and called them his "three sisters."[13] They were all three very different in character: Madeleine, the eldest, was gentle, sensible, serious, and weighed down by "a secret sadness"; Jeanne was gay, playful, and bold; Valentine was romantic, with "an extraordinary sense of mystery." For Gide the Cuverville house, "a white, two-storied building, much like many country houses of the century before last," was "the house of cousins." It was there that he situated Jérôme's love for Alissa in *La Porte étroite*, a transposition of André Gide's love for Madeleine Rondeaux who later was to become Mme. André Gide.

Cuverville was Emile Rondeaux's country house, La Roque–Baignard, the Paul Gides'—an old château that had belonged to the Labbey de La Roque family before becoming the property of Edouard Rondeaux, very picturesque and romantic, and as André Gide wrote in a letter to Francis Jammes, the "paradise lost" of his childhood. On a small island, surrounded by a pond and a moat, stood three buildings: a postern "of small but exquisite proportions," a building of brick and stone dating back to Henri IV, and another built at the beginning of the nineteenth century. At opposite ends of the island were little turrets; beyond the pond, a pigeon house. At La Roque, André Gide was isolated, even insular, separated from the world by a brick bridge which replaced the former drawbridge. "Words cannot describe the delight of a child living on an island, a tiny little island, from which moreover he can escape whenever he pleases."

The La Roque estate was so vast[14] and so varied, with its meadows, moors, rivers, and forests, that Gide hardly ever left it as a child and endlessly explored its land. With Anna Shackleton, his summer companion, he went out botanizing: "the herbarium reigned supreme at La Roque." There were trout in the moat and the pond, and Théodomir, a nephew of

[11] In *La Porte étroite* Lucile Bucolin is a fictional transposition of Mathilde Rondeaux, just as Jérôme's feelings for his Aunt Lucile are a transposition of André Gide's feelings for his Aunt Mathilde.

[12] The name was taken from a village in the vicinity of Cuverville.

[13] In *Si le grain ne meurt* Gide changed their names to Emmanuèle, Louise, and Suzanne, respectively.

[14] Almost a hundred acres of farmland and over sixty acres of woods.

Bocage,[15] the gamekeeper ever since Juliette Rondeaux was a young girl, taught him to fish. But the main attraction of La Roque was the wood. Late in life, from Sidi-ben-Saïd,[16] Gide nostalgically recalled the time of his discoveries in the Norman forest:

I dream of the mysterious inner woods at La Roque into which, being but a child, I never ventured without trembling; of the banks of the pond thick with flowering plants; of the evening mists over the stream.

La Roque–Baignard is La Morinière in *L'Immoraliste,* and the region of Auge gave the novel more than its "décor," for throughout the book, Gide wrote, "I have intently sought its likeness."

When Mme. Paul Gide was at La Roque–Baignard, she did not much like to leave it. She would occasionally take her son to Lisieux, Cambremer, or Boissière, and she kept up friendly relations with her neighbors, the owners of Val-Richer and Formentin.

Val-Richer, the Blancmesnil in *Si le grain ne meurt,* was the estate of the Guizot de Witt-Schlumberger family. André Gide's childhood friend at La Roque, François de Witt, the "Lionel" in *Si le grain ne meurt,* was the eldest son of Pauline Guizot and Cornelis de Witt. And the daughter of Henriette and Conrad de Witt, Mme. Paul Schlumberger, had a son, Jean Schlumberger, who later became one of André Gide's most intimate and faithful friends.

The other neighboring château was Formentin, the Quartfourche in *Isabelle,* about two miles from La Roque–Baignard. It belonged to a former clerk at the court of Rouen, Pierre-Amable Floquet, who had devoted his leisure time to a biography of Bossuet. He lived there with his wife and sister-in-law, Mme. de Saint-Alban, calm and pious women who, according to M. Floquet, "preferred quiet happiness to great tempests." But Mme. Saint-Alban had a daughter, Louise, who preferred great tempests to quiet happiness, and she became the heroine of André Gide's *Isabelle.*[17]

Just as André Gide would spend part of each summer at Cuverville in "the house of cousins," so the girls would come for about two weeks to La Roque–Baignard. The arrival of his "three sisters," Madeleine, Jeanne, and Valentine, was a special and long-awaited event. In the 1891 agenda that Gide kept day by day, we find under September 19: "They are arriving!" and under October 6: "Their departure." Between these small notations lies all the joy of Gide's holidays for a period of many years.

[15] Gide used his name in *L'Immoraliste.*

[16] *Journal,* September, 1942.

[17] M. Floquet was called "M. Floche," Louise de Saint-Alban became "Louise de Saint-Auréol," and her son was named "Casimir." See R.-G. Nobécourt, *Les Nourritures normandes d'André Gide,* IV.

5: Reflections on Two Families

> *"Nothing could be more different than these two families, nothing more different than these two provinces of France . . ."*
>
> Si le grain ne meurt, *I, 22*

*I*N HIS preface to *Les Nourritures normandes d'André Gide,* Thierry Maulnier seeks to explain Gide's interest in the "inheritance" of the writer and what he makes of his unique materials: Every work is unique in itself and any explanation of it must be unique. But that does not necessarily mean that the elements, the aliments which served in its construction, were of no consequence and should be considered as of no particular importance. They were merely materials and circumstances put at the disposal of the organizing laboratory of an *incomparable* personality, but the product of that laboratory would have been different had the materials and circumstances been different. A work, such as it is, does not exist because of them, but it would not have been as it is were they themselves not what they were.[1]

The fact that André Gide was so concerned about his heredity shows that he was conscious of how important was the contribution of those elements and aliments. But he seems to have greatly exaggerated the specific differences in his two families when he used the "contradictory influences" of two provinces of France and two faiths to explain not only his fundamental ambivalence but his vocation as arbiter and artist.

In February, 1920, Gide published a highly interesting article called "Hérédité" in the *Nouvelle Revue Française* and later reprinted it in his

[1] Thierry Maulnier, preface to R.-G. Nobécourt's *Les Nourritures normandes d'André Gide.*

Morceaux choisis and in *Si le grain ne meurt*. After having recalled the fact that as a child, he spent his holidays in Normandy with his mother's family and in Uzès with his father's family, he added:

Nothing could be more different than these two families, nothing more different than these two provinces of France, whose contradictory influences are combined in me. I have often convinced myself that I was forced to create because only through art could I reconcile those discordant elements which would otherwise have remained in a state of warfare or at any rate in a state of dialogue. No doubt the only ones capable of powerfully asserting themselves are those pushed in one direction by the impetus of their heredity. I believe that arbiters and artists are, on the contrary, products of cross-breeding in whom opposing forces coexist and neutralize one another as they grow.

The fact that Gide was a "product of cross-breeding" would then account not only for his being a congenitally determined "creature of dialogue," living in a dialectical state, but for his neutralizing vocation as arbiter, forced to reconcile contrary elements through inner strife, and his vocation as artist, forced to harmonize the dissonant voices of his two races.

In a letter to Francis Jammes, Gide wrote somewhat the same thing:

You know I am complicated, born a cross-breed, seated at a crossroads of religions, feeling within me all the pull of a Norman toward the south, all the pull of a southerner toward the north, bearing within me so many reasons for being that one alone perhaps remains impossible: that of *simply being*.[2]

Later on, in his *Journal,* in connection with his sixtieth birthday, he adds still more to his constellation of inner difficultes:

I have discovered, quite by chance and without much believing in astrology, that on precisely November 21, my birthday, our earth leaves the influence of Scorpio to enter that of Sagittarius. Is it my fault if your God took such great care to have me born between two stars, the fruit of two races, two provinces, and two faiths?[3]

Our God, portrayed here as a mischievous experimenter coupling the influences of which he disposes, stars and lands, churches and races, to create an ambivalent seed intended for the "garden of hesitations," is a bit too much like the game-loving millionaire in *Le Prométhée mal enchaîné:* "I play as a Dutchman sows; as he plants a secret onion." The two stars are Scorpio and Sagittarius. Should we then believe that had André Gide been born a few days earlier or later, at the very height of Scorpio or at the very height of Sagittarius, he would have had an assertive and not a hesitant nature? That would mean explaining the mysteries of innateness

[2] Letter from André Gide to Francis Jammes, Aug. 6, 1902, *Correspondance Jammes-Gide,* p. 199.

[3] *Journal,* 1929, p. 959.

by those of astrology. In point of fact, that kind of reference to the stars, common to many famous writers, is to my knowledge the only one in Gide's works, but the same can certainly not be said for the theme of two faiths, two provinces, and two races. Indeed, it comes back again and again like a leitmotif.

André Gide portrayed himself as "sitting at a crossroads of religions," but actually his religious foundation was exclusively Protestant. The contrast between the Rondeaux's Catholicism and the Gides' Protestantism is not really justified. At André Gide's birth, the Rondeaux, or at any rate those lineally descended, were almost completely removed from the old Catholic influence. Ever since Charles Rondeaux de Montbray's marriage to Anne-Marie Dufou in 1781, the family had been freethinkers on the men's side, Protestant on the women's. André Gide's great-grandmother, grandmother, and mother all belonged to the Reformed Church, and Julie Rondeaux-Pouchet, known to have been a fervent Protestant, brought up her daughter Juliette herself.

True, a Roman Catholic enclave was once again set up after Henri Rondeaux's conversion (1849) and marriage to "the very Catholic Mlle. Lucile K." (1852), and on Mme. Edouard Rondeaux's death (1873) it became established in the family house on the rue de Crosne. But it did no more than reinforce the Protestants' resistance. Moreover, with the exception of the Henri Rondeaux and their children Fernand and Marguerite, with whom Gide was never really intimate, his great-grandparents, uncles, aunts, and cousins were all Protestants, as much on the Rondeaux side as on the Gide.

In both his families André Gide found a general mentality that was more or less characteristic of the French Protestant: devotion to the Bible, considered the supreme religious authority, and its free interpretation; self-examination without the intermediary of a priest; moral dogmatism and puritanism; a refusal of the ecclesiastical hierarchy, of the cult of the Virgin and saints, and certain sacraments; the feeling of belonging to a minority or, more precisely, to an elite that had long been unjustly persecuted and which, although a minority in the region of Caux, had become a majority in the Cevenol country. Every one of those characteristics was to be found in André Gide, occasionally in surprising forms.

The history of both families well shows that, as the Catholic faction had been nearly decimated since the end of the eighteenth century, Gide's inner conflict between his "Catholic blood" and "Protestant blood" could not have taken place, for lack of anything conflicting. Notwithstanding, while his ambivalence cannot be explained by a conflict between two religions, it could in part be explained by the influence of one. I shall return to this point in connection with the effect of a Protestant upbringing on his personality.

In the absence of a war of religions, might André Gide's inner dissensions have originated in a war of races? While the Rondeaux and the Gides were of the same faith, there is no doubt that they were not of the same provenance or in any case of the same province. His mother's ancestors were Norman, probably much before the seventeenth century; his father's ancestors were Cevenol, at least since the sixteenth century. To proceed from this and see the well-known opposition between northerners and southerners (in as much as the Gides were of Italian origin) is a big step, and Gide took it.

I understand both the *langue d'oc* and the *langue d'oïl,* the thick Norman jargon and the singsong speech of the south. . . . I have a taste both for wine and cider, a love both for deep woods and the *garrigue,* for the white flowering apple tree and the white flowering almond.[4]

Such eclecticism in regard to dialects, regional products, and regional sites is not compromising, but his ideas about the mentality of the people are clearly more so, for they always risk being tendentious and influenced by emotional factors:

I think sadly that if some chance were to bring together the Norman peasant whom I know and the southerner whom I know, not only would they not love each other, but they could not even understand each other.

Chance, in the form of Pastor Roberty, did bring together—on a certain day in 1863—a pure Languedocian, Paul Gide, and a pure Norman, Juliette Rondeaux. Were they able to love one another or even understand one another? At all events they had a son laden with contradictory gifts. "Is it my fault? . . ." Or could it have been the fault of Normandy and Bas-Languedoc? It is hard not to believe that Gide conceived of the Languedocian mentality in terms of his father's and the Norman mentality in terms of his mother's. And we know that, since childhood, he felt the deep opposition between their two natures.

André Gide contrasted "southern subtlety" with "Norman heaviness." He praised the natives of Bas-Languedoc, "an almost Latin land of deep laughter, lucid poetry, and beautiful severity," for their vivacity, joyfulness, civility, "vivid and precise" language, indifference to any personal advantage, nobility, and taste for the arts and letters. Next to them the Norman race seemed to him dense, dull, boring, grasping despite their well-being, and economical to the point of avarice. The psychological par-

[4] "La Normandie et le Bas-Languedoc," *Prétextes,* p. 72.

allel is hardly to the Norman's advantage until the end, when Gide qualifies it:

But perhaps the qualities of the Norman race, less evident than those of the southerners, take on added strength from the heavier and restraining flesh, and gain in gravity and depth what they lose in brilliance and surface effects.[5]

The laughter and joyfulness of the Uzès hiker who "dawdled about and was amused by everything," the lucid poetry of the humanist, a friend of Greek and Latin poets, the beautiful severity of the *vir probus,* the vivid and precise language of the professor and writer, indifference to any personal advantage, and, above all, subtlety were indeed the characteristics of Paul Gide as described by his son. But Gide's Uncle Charles was also from Uzès and yet, if his nephew is to be believed, he was devoid of subtlety, laughter, and poetry, if not severity. Gravity, in the heavy and serious sense of the word, dull qualities and boring virtues, an absence of any aptitude for the delights of singing in particular and delights in general, a very strict sense of economy despite real affluence, obstinacy, and constant restraint were all characteristic of Juliette Gide. But are they specifically Norman?

André Gide likened the marriage between the Languedocian Paul Gide and the Norman Juliette Rondeaux to "cross-breeding" and saw himself as a "product" of it. Had he been a half-breed, he would not have expressed it in any other way. Psychological differences between Normans and Languedocians, or more generally between northerners and southerners, surely exist, but they do not necessarily have ethnological origins. On the other hand, had his mother and father both been from Uzès or from Rouen, is there any reason to believe that Gide would not have been divided and that the unity of provincial stock would have brought about a union within him just as its duality had brought about a division? That would mean according very determinant properties to the earth and the dead.

All the same, the racial interpretation of Gide's ambivalence was enthusiastically accepted by a German geopsychologist, L. Schreiber, who sees Gide's conflict between a French and Latin being and a "Norman or Teuton being" as a conflict which must indeed create many difficulties within an individual, judging by those it has generally created in history. But if we consult Thibaudet, we find that he attributes Gide's "bilateralism" or ambivalence to the properties of his Norman blood alone. Indeed, he considers Gide's tendency to "endow contrary forms with the same existence and the same rights" as a product of "litigious Normandy."[6] It would seem that here the systematic regionalization of minds leads to very strange conclusions. It is true that in classical French a Norman answer is

[5] *Prétextes,* p. 74.   [6] Albert Thibaudet, *Gide et Flaubert.*

an ambiguous one that says neither yes nor no or says both yes and no, bringing about an always possible conciliation between contraries and, in a way, a resumption of the question. But that sly kind of peasant ruse or cunning is far from the profound "quartering" that exists within innumerable divided people, whatever their earthly origins. Gide himself found remarkable examples of the "coexistence of contradictory feelings" in Flaubert, a Norman, but also in Montaigne, a native of Périgord, Baudelaire, a Parisian, Dostoevsky, a Russian, and so forth. Ambivalence is not a regional product, nor is it the product of the "contradictory influences" of two regions.

When in his inner dialogues Gide thought he heard an echo of the Gides' Languedocian voices and the Rondeaux's Norman voices, he seems to have been misled by a too prejudiced and, at that time, too Barrésian ear. And his explanation of an arbiter's and artist's vocation being brought about by the contrary regional influences of heredity is equally specious. Moreover, by beginning his well-known passage from *Si le grain ne meurt* with "I have often convinced myself that," Gide himself appears to have limited the importance of his theory to self-persuasion. Such reasons are merely on the surface and, as Pascal said, conceal the difficulty without removing it; they are no more than pretexts.

Taine, whose influence on Gide's development was considerable, admitted that race is "the character transmitted with the blood," a group of "innate and hereditary psychological tendencies," but in connection with his theory on "the transmission of national characteristics through blood," his nephew, André Chevrillon, commented:

Their continuance is more probably due to an accumulation of moral causes: the reciprocal suggestions of individuals in a group, the esteem sons have for their fathers, the influence of an established educational system, submissiveness to a prevailing ideal which varies, like reality.

In other words, the so-called ethnopsychological influences are more likely to be the result of a social heritage than of biological heredity.

The emphasis geopsychology puts on the idea of race, sociopsychology tends to put on the idea of class and, more generally, social influences. Although André Gide dwelled on the racial or provincial differences between the Rondeaux and the Gides, he never stressed the fact that they belonged to the same class and the same eminent *bourgeoisie.* The Rondeaux, of peasant origin, progressively became a "family of the upper middle class in Rouen." The Gides, of aristocratic origin, were typically representative in Bas-Languedoc of a family of Notables, in the full sense of that obsolete word. And although these *bourgeoisies* differed somewhat in regard to wealth, profession, and culture, they were all bourgeois.

Moreover, they were all French. Whatever the interest in regional characteristics, there is unquestionable unity in a country as integrated as France, despite its apparent diversity. Whether Norman or Languedocian, André Gide's maternal and paternal ancestors were part of the same country, the same civilization, and spoke the same language. They were all deeply patriotic and their attitudes during the wars and, for the Normans, during the invasions, is ample proof of it. No one could be more French, even more "old" French, than the ancestors of André Gide.

With the exception of inbreds, our common lot is to have been born of two different bloods; but what Gide claimed to be his particularity was the fact that he was born of two conflicting, even incompatible, bloods. The word "blood" as applied without reservation to religious and provincial influences is unacceptable except as a literary metaphor. In the matter of psychological heredity, it is not traditions, the reflections of social institutions, which are transmitted by chromosomes, but rather a person's psychobiological traits. No one disputes the existence of psychological differences produced by religions and regions, but such characteristics are basically of an institutional nature, in other words, acquired. Gide was not divided because he was born of a mixture of "Protestant Languedocian blood" and "Catholic and Norman blood," but the differences between his paternal and maternal families did play a part in his division, for he resembled them both.

Nothing is more conjectural than a retrospective interpretation of so-called hereditary psychological resemblances, and any attempt at it meets with insurmountable difficulties. For example, according to *Si le grain ne meurt*, Gide's "callous" Uncle Charles had little in common with his nephew; yet others found that he strangely resembled him. "Charles Gide's mystery is not the least attractive aspect of that lofty figure," wrote M. Poujol, and he concludes that the key to the enigma was: "indecision." Teissier du Cros, both a jurist and a psychologist, even tried to draw a parallel between the personalities of uncle and nephew whom he considered "twins in temperament."[7] He points out Charles Gide's "innate taste for contradiction" and relevantly comments: "One is often given to contradicting because of an inner state of contradiction"; and he sees the spirit of contradiction as the "entire" explanation of Charles Gide's mystery, "assuming of course that all its very numerous and diverse sources could be successfully determined." According to him, Charle Gide, also, had an ambivalent mind, and indeed it would seem so from certain of his letters:

I have not tried to influence you because I feel incapable of directing anyone—even my children—and the fact that people take me for a leader makes

---

[7] Teissier du Cros, postface to A. Lavondès' book, *Charles Gide*.

me laugh. The point[8] of this letter is perhaps the only point on which I have a decided conviction.

But his intellectual ambivalence was in contrast to an intransigent moral dogmatism, as often happens in true Huguenots. "To doubt intellectually is to seek for God; to doubt morally is to flee from Him" could only have been formulated by a Protestant philosopher.

On the Rondeaux side, much the same can be said for André Gide's mother. So seemingly strong, sure of herself, and authoritarian, she was in fact shy, anxiety-ridden, and self-doubting, except in the case of moral duty. Her rigid façade hid a secret weakness which can also be found in her son and was due no doubt as much to the constitution he inherited from her and the dominance of her genes as to the way she brought him up and the domination of her authority. It is probable that in reaction to her own anxiety and her own ambivalence, André Gide's mother constantly and compulsively restrained herself.

It then becomes clear that Gide's psychological ambivalence, which he interpreted as being a result of the fusion of two conflicting bloods, was in fact characteristic of both sides of the family, although it is impossible here to say how much was due to nature and how much to upbringing. It is also true that, although the personalities of Paul Gide and Juliette Rondeaux were actually very dissimilar, André Gide did seem inclined to exaggerate their differences. He was somehow led into it by his beginning position, having decided to explain his own personality in terms of such antagonisms, thus putting the responsibility for his fundamental division on his heredity. Yet had the differences between his parents been even more profound, they would not have been enough to explain their son's ambivalence. Any man who analyzes himself with a grain of sincerity will more or less recognize the coexistence within him of contraries, and to a certan degree his ambivalence is natural, for as Montaigne said, it carries within itself "the entire form of the human condition." Everyone is born more or less divided and only ceases being so through an effort of the will which alone makes decision and action possible. But if he remains divided and wants to remain divided, if he cannot or will not leave the marshlands of ambivalence, he then has a personality problem. And his problem is less related to the "coexistence of contradictory feelings" than to an ambiguous attitude in regard to his contradictions and a suspicious complacency, implying more concern with maintaining them than with resolving them. The more he becomes aware of his differences, the more he becomes attached to them; the more he listens to his inner dialogues, the more time he spends analyzing them and the more difficult it is to choose.

[8] He is referring to the sexual question. Letter from Charles Gide to André Gide, Aug. 20, 1894, unpublished.

Here we have what Montaigne called a "difformity" of character and one about which he spoke as insistently as Gide.[9] Important in the development of the habit, at least in part, are the first emotional attitudes with regard to the parents and the reactions of identification or rejection so essential in the formation of the ego. It would seem to me that they played a great part in the way Gide interpreted his heredity, portraying himself as the fruit of the contradictory influences of two faiths and two provinces, whereas in reality he was descended from families of one and the same Protestant, bourgeois, and French tradition. The similarities between his two families are far greater than the differences.

Such was the family background of André Gide's childhood and adolescence. The man who wrote "Families, I hate you" knew perfectly well that he had nothing to complain about in regard to his own. On his father's side he found high intellectual and moral qualities and three remarkable men on various scores—Tancrède Gide, a judge with rare nobility of soul, Paul and Charles Gide, two eminent jurists both of whom made original contributions; on his mother's side, he found a rich, industrious, and esteemed family, bourgeois privileges and virtues, an obviously domineering mother but also three "sisters," one of whom was to give him what was perhaps the best of herself. Bas-Languedoc contributed its burning *garrigue,* its landscapes of grapevines and olive trees, its special light, and the crackle of its cicadas as a setting for his holidays; Normandy, its large and beautiful houses, deep forests, fertile countryside, and rich granaries. "Suppressing either of the two regions would show ingratitude." The happy, often sunlit memories of Languedocian springtimes and Norman summers are in contrast to what Gide called his "gloomy childhood," as if he had wanted to deepen, perhaps excessively, its shadowy side.

[9] "The more I haunt myself and know myself, the more my difformity astounds me, the less I understand about myself."

6: First Years

*"The games of my early childhood . . .
were all solitary games. I had no playmates. . . ."*

Si le grain ne meurt, *I, 14*

A N ONLY child, born in Paris of a well-to-do and cultured family, brought up by parents who loved him, each in his own way, André Gide would seem to have grown up under privileged conditions. Yet his childhood was not happy; inwardly he lived in a state of agitation and nervous tension. During his last years, when he recalled his most distant past, one might have thought that he intentionally made it gloomy, he so emphasized its darker side. Even in *Si le grain ne meurt* he had written: "One would like to believe that in that age of innocence the soul is all light, tenderness, and purity, but I still see mine as nothing but shadow, ugliness, and deceitfulness."

When at middle age he wrote his confessions, Gide seemed to want to keep away from virtuous protestations like Rousseau's,[1] which were often contradicted by the text. Instead, he took a deliberately contrary point of view, fortunately also contradicted by many pages of his text. "I still see mine as . . ." does not signify "mine was," and when he gives in to the charm of certain memories, he is forced to go back on some exaggeratedly distressing assertions: "It seems to me that I made the darkness of my long-suffering childhood too obscure."

[1] According to his unpublished *cahier de lectures,* Gide read Rousseau's *Confessions* for the first time during his first stay in Biskra (November, 1892–March, 1893).

André Gide took great care to make himself out a perverse child, but he was mostly an anxious child. Fears played a considerable part in his first years. He never spoke about them in *Si le grain ne meurt*,[2] but rather in his *Journal* and in *Ainsi soit-il*:

When I was a child I was easily frightened; I had frightful nightmares from which I would awaken in a deep sweat. . . . And suddenly the gland stopped functioning.[3] At present I can have frightful dreams, see myself pursued by monsters, knifed, cut up in pieces . . . but it never becomes a nightmare.[4]

Or again:

When I was very young I often launched out at night into the most appalling nightmares from which I would awaken trembling and bathed in tears. Then, I don't know what happened in my system, nor what endocrine glands had suddenly began to function differently, but the feeling of fear left me. I would still dream about the same bogy-men but without taking them seriously; I could still be gobbled up by the *Crique* but I thought it was too funny.[5]

His childhood nightmares must have deeply impressed him, judging from the fact that he remembered them even in his old age, and their theme was obviously the aggression of imaginary and threatening beings who made darkness a thing to be feared. His fear of the dark was a fear in the dark, where he saw himself "pursued by monsters, knifed, cut up in pieces" or "gobbled up" by the *Crique*. Etymologically, the English word nightmare and the French *cauchemar* evoke the intervention of a demon (*mar*), while *cauchemar* also implies anguished oppression.[6] Actually, both the demon's personality and the kind of torture he inflicts are of great interest. There is nothing unusual about a child who has bad dreams, but when they insistently repeat the same terrifying theme and the child awakens "with a start and in a deep sweat," we are dealing with the nocturnal terror, the *pavor nocturnus* which the Ancients had pointed out as frequent in the childhood of anxious people. Ambroise Paré even carefully studied the varieties of demons appearing in children's nightmares. In Gide's we find the *Crique*, a classic devourer of children similar to

[2] With the exception of his actual attacks of anguish, his *Schaudern*.

[3] Gide's theory that a gland secretes fear as others secrete tears is very curious indeed, and I would not have pointed it out were it not connected with a strong tendency on the part of Gide to overestimate the psychological importance of the endocrine glands. Other examples of it can be found in his *Journal*. Thus he attributed his lack of a "sense of reality" to an endocrine gland that was supposedly "atrophied."

[4] *Journal*, 1924, pp. 799, 800.   [5] *Ainsi soit-il*, p. 98.

[6] *Caucher* comes from *calcare* (to press, to squeeze) and indicates anguish.

Plato's Mormo or the Languedoc's *Chaouche-vielio*.[7] The punishment he inflicted was that of cutting a body up in pieces. It might seem "too funny" to an adult, but the process was in all probability less amusing to a child imagining it *hic et nunc*. And the phantasm of the "body cut up in pieces," now being seriously looked into with regard to children's dreams and primitive myths, does not seem without significance in relation to the psychological structure of a subconscious that begets such demons of the night.

Gide scandalized people by confessing the precociousness of his solitary habits in the very first pages of *Si le grain ne meurt*: "Personally, I cannot say whether I learned about sexual pleasure from someone or in what way I discovered it; but as far back as I can remember, I knew about it." He described himself as a very young boy under the dining room table, playing with or alongside the *concierge*'s son in a way that an adult would hardly consider innocent. More surprising than the episode itself is the place he gave to it in his memoirs. Some claim that it shows a deliberate defiance of convention. But it is more likely that he found it necessary to emphasize the precociousness of an inveterate vice which, like Jean-Jacques Rousseau, he believed had a lasting effect on his habits. Also, at the time he was writing his confessions, he was well aware of psychoanalytical theories on the importance of infantile sexuality.

Just as significant as the precociousness of his sexual instincts is what Gide had to say about the precociousness of his instincts of aggression. He described himself in a photograph dating from his early childhood as hiding in his mother's skirts, "rigged out in a ridiculous little checked dress, looking sickly and bad tempered, with shifty eyes."[8] When his nurse, Marie Leuenberger, took him to play in the Luxembourg Gardens, near the rue de Médicis apartment, he never played with the other children. "I had no playmates." But he did have one, a "delicate, gentle, quiet," and frail little boy called Mouton "because of his little white fleece coat." When he learned that Mouton was going blind, he fell into violent despair:

I ran away and cried in my room, and for several days I practiced keeping my eyes shut a long time, going about without opening them, trying to experience what Mouton must have been feeling.

[7] Literally "the old woman who squeezes," *chaouche-vielio* is the Languedocian word for nightmare.

[8] Judging from the photograph, he did not exaggerate. "As a child he was ugly," declared Marie Leuenberger in a letter to Madeleine Rondeaux, July 10, 1895, unpublished.

But his sympathy for the little blind boy was equaled by his antipathy for the boisterousness of the other children. "Their games were as noisy as mine were quiet and I felt as peaceable as they proved quarrelsome." Yet his alleged gentleness was merely on the surface. In the gardens the future immoralist stayed close to his nurse, apart from the children, and sullenly looked at their "pretty" mud pies. "Suddenly, when my nurse was looking the other way, I rushed over and trampled down all the pies."

In trying to interpret the impulse, which seemed to denote a mean nature, Gide added: "I no doubt went up to the other children asking expectantly 'May I play with you?' And I so much resented their refusal that I wanted to destroy their games." His cruelty then was merely friendly spite or, as Stendhal would have put it, "suffering sympathy." But how exact is this adult interpretation of childish aggression? Other examples would seem to contradict it.

One day in Uzès his mother took him to meet his cousin Marguerite de Flaux, the future baroness of Charnizay and a great friend of Charles Gide. Marguerite de Flaux lived in an old mansion in a romantic park situated at the very foot of the Uzès towers. She was known as much for beauty as for her wit, and her house was a center for theater, particularly the repertory of Labiche, and for Uzès social life. Young André, then five, had not yet met his "beautiful" cousin:

"Go quickly and give your cousin a kiss," said my mother as I came into the drawing room. . . . I went up and my cousin drew me close to her. But at the sight of her bare and dazzling shoulder, I don't know what madness possessed me: instead of putting my lips to the cheek she offered me, fascinated by the dazzling shoulder, I dug my teeth into it and bit. My cousin screamed with pain and I with horror. She was bleeding. I spit out with disgust. I was quickly taken away and I think everyone was so dumbfounded that they forgot to punish me.

Mme. Gide's stupefaction at her son's outburst of nonconformity in the venerable drawing room of the De Flaux mansion was quite understandable. Yet his young voraciousness has highly distinguished literary precedents, such as the incident of little Henri Beyle who, sitting on the ramparts of Grenoble next to his big cousin Pison de Galland, cruelly bit her on the cheek and was called a "monster" by his Aunt Séraphie.

It is interesting to note that the mud pies were "pretty" and the cousin "beautiful." Later on, at an age when little boys are passionately fond of tin soldiers, Gide made use of them in a special way, which shocked collectors of the proud regiments:

I too had tin soldiers, and I too played with them; but my way of playing was to melt them down. You stand them upright on a shovel which you heat;

then you watch them totter on their bases, pitch forward, and soon out of every tarnished uniform comes a little soul—brilliant, glowing, stripped bare. . . .

At about the age of ten, "the idea of plunder took the shape of my spoiling a favorite toy" and became a subject of "sexual excitement."

For the most part, however, André Gide's childhood games were not of the same Neronian nature. Thy were quite simply games of patience, decalcomanias, erector sets, marbles, tops, kites, propellers, the many toys that can be played with in apartments or out-of-doors, and the famous kaleidoscope that Charles Du Bos found a bit lengthily described in *Si le grain ne meurt.* "The shifting of the rose patterns" plunged young André into a state of "unspeakable rapture." Yet the aesthetic pleasure was not enough and, wanting to force "the worker of marvels" into betraying its secret, he took it apart and replaced the "little bits of glass with the strangest objects." The result of his experimentation was not sensational but did have a "certain geometrical interest." Among the "strange" objects, between a pen point, a match end, a blade of grass, etc., was "the wing of a fly." That tiny fragment of an insect brings to mind the way it was removed by the young experimenter, the budding naturalist, who even then was fascinated by "the play of living matter."

Chasing insects was one of his favorite games in Uzès, at La Roque, and in Paris, where he attended lectures at the Museum of Natural History with the assiduous botanist Anna Shackleton and went along on her Sunday botanizing excursions with "old maids and friendly monomaniacs." Because of his precocious taste for the things of nature, his "uncle" Georges Pouchet gave him the magnificent entomological collection of his father, great-uncle Brutus-Archimède, once director of the Rouen Museum of Natural History. André Gide, also, was fond of collecting and, when he reached the so-called age of reason, of experimenting with cultures, although the results were generally unfortunate. Anna Shackleton had taught him to work carefully and zealously in the herbarium, and he did the same with his swarms of insects which he himself "pinned" in cork-lined boxes. Later on he used the wash basins to raise larvae of various species, even larvae of the beautiful rhinoceros beetle which, alas, died before reaching pupation.

As a projection of personality, nothing is less insignificant than a child's choice of games. Charles Du Bos reproached Gide with the complacent description of his first pastimes, but Gide was himself astounded at the fact that Charles Du Bos never played, and was particularly indignant to learn that he had never seen "snails in freedom" before having seen them prepared as a gourmet dish at the restaurant Lapérouse. Never having played, he said, leads to "an enormous deficiency," for "he who has never played does not see." His own taste for games remained constant. The way he continued to amuse himself with children's toys, quite alone and for long periods, and the pleasure he took in them show the importance he gave to play and diversion as a means of relaxation. He was inclined "to consider art itself as a game, a game of the gods," and he thought that children's games, to the extent that they require some imagination, are an early form of escape, an evasion of reality through play, which prepares for evasion through art.[9]

André Gide's early pastimes were less imaginative than those of other poets. As they were directed toward "living matter," they seem to point more to a future naturalist; but at the same time as he observed outer reality, much of his interest was turned toward what he called "the second reality." He had a precocious taste for daydreaming, the pastime that plays such a great part in the beginnings of poetic life:

The vague, indefinable belief in something else besides the acknowledged reality of everyday life inhabited me for many years; and I am not sure that even today I have not still some remnants of it left. It had nothing in common with tales of fairies, ghouls, or witches, nor even with those of Hoffmann or Andersen. No, I really think it was more a clumsy need to give life more density—a need that later on religion was able to satisfy, and also a certain propensity for imagining life's hidden side.[10]

A short episode in *Si le grain ne meurt* might strike the reader as pleasant but insignificant were it not for Gide's commentary, describing it as one of the many moments of poetic grace in his youth. On the occasion of their daughter Marguerite's "coming of age," the Henri Rondeaux gave a ball at the house in the rue de Crosne. As his cousin Marguerite came of age in 1878, André Gide must have been eight at the time:[11] "How could I know what a ball was? I had attached no importance to it and had gone to bed as usual. But suddenly the distant murmur . . ." He got up, groped his way out of his room, crossed the dark corridors, noiselessly arrived at the staircase, and from one of the steps discovered that the distant murmur consisted of the sounds of voices, the rustling of dresses, whispering, and laughter:

[9] The work being done today in child psychology and psychoanalysis (Karl, Groos, Moeder, Anna Freud, Mélanie Klein), comparing the analysis of play to that of dreams, has confirmed Schiller's idea of play as a preparation for art (*On the Aesthetic Education of Man, in a Series of Letters*).

[10] *Si le grain ne meurt*, I, 28.

[11] Gide situated the ball three years after his grandmother's death (1873), therefore in 1876. He would then have been six. But the date does not coincide with that of his cousin's coming of age (1878). In any case it makes little difference whether he was six or eight.

Everything seemed different than usual; I felt as if I were going to be suddenly initiated into another life, a mysterious, differently real, more brilliant, and more moving life which began only after little children were in bed.

At the sound of dance music, splendidly dressed ladies whirled about, "far more beautiful than in the daytime." Everything was stranger and more beautiful. He looked on with wonder and thought he recognized, among the "lovely ladies," one of his mother's friends whom he had seen just that morning, but he was not sure that it was "really she." Whereupon Marie promptly put the young spectator back to bed:

And when I was back in my bed, my mind was in a turmoil, and before sinking into sleep I thought in a confused way: "There is reality and there are dreams; and there is a *second reality* as well."

Most of the time Gide experienced the feeling of a second reality—which is neither the reality of a waking state nor the dream of a sleeping state—in the intermediary state between waking and sleeping. "During the day my suspicions remained uncertain, but at night, just before falling asleep, I felt them grow more sharply defined and positive." The *praedormitio,* the moment of somnolence before sleeping when the mental syntheses that assure an adjustment to reality and attention to life are relaxed, is indeed an eminently favorable time for that obscure perception. We have all experienced it more or less but—and this is what counts—more or less.

The real interest of the little anecdote, banal in itself (what child has not watched a party and found it like a fairy tale?), is that Gide considered the inner experience it brought about as one of the links in an invisible chain that gave him the feeling or the illusion of a second reality. He felt that one of the basic traits of his character was a certain difficulty in believing in the authenticity of reality, and all through his life he often got the impression of being a spectator at a theatrical production, as if he were waiting, after the comedy or tragedy, for the actors to come back and bow. In early childhood, as a delighted and hidden spectator of the rue de Crosne ball, he had the same feeling of seeing reality "like a spectacle *outside reality*."

7: At the Ecole Alsacienne

"I was sent away from school for reasons . . . which I shall venture to tell."

Si le grain ne meurt, I, 66

Εxcept for the children's classes held by Mlle. Fleur and Mme. Lackerbauer, school was not easy for André Gide. His real troubles began with the Ecole Alsacienne. At the age of eight, André Gide's father introduced him to M. Brünig, director of the "lower classes" at the Ecole Alsacienne. The very same day he took his place among "the others." The ninth form was under the direction of M. Vedel, an excellent, straightforward and good-natured man, with a kindliness typical of the South of France. That morning he was explaining what a synonym was and gave as an example the words *coudrier* and *noisetier,* both meaning hazel tree. He asked the new boy to repeat what he had just said, but Gide remained silent, incapable of uttering a single word. M. Vedel slowly repeated the definition and the example, then patiently awaited an answer. But the answer never came and his patience gone, he sent the new boy out into the playground and told him to repeat twenty times running that *coudrier* and *noisetier* are synonyms. When Gide came back to class his teacher questioned him a third time. Gide continued to remain silent. The boys then burst into uncontrollable laughter. "My stupidity had overjoyed the whole class."

The stupidity Gide somewhat complacently described in *Si le grain ne meurt* was no doubt an inhibition. Outside the family circle André Gide was then extremely shy and "paralyzed" in public. Although a kind of stage fright on the first day of school is not surprising for an emotional child brought up at home and an only son into the bargain, total inhibition is rare. For days and weeks the situation remained critical. Gide collected zeros for "conduct" and for "order and cleanliness," and he was among the lowest in his class. He used to be sent to the back of the room next to Paul Laurens, who would cover his notebooks with whimsical and fantastic drawings, using the chewed end of a penholder dipped in ink. Laurens would look very studious as he drew, but as soon as M. Vedel questioned him, "Paul, lost in the clouds and wild-eyed, looked so startled that the whole class would burst out laughing."[1] Neither Laurens nor Gide tried to be clowns despite their mirth-provoking talents. "I was simply stupid." The future Nobel Prize winner began school as a dunce. But a boy can be a dunce for many reasons.

When Gide was asked to leave the Ecole Alsacienne, it was not because of his low grades. He had "bad habits," and M. Vedel became aware of them one morning, having caught him in the act. The evening before, Mme. Paul Gide had given one of her banquets for her husband's colleagues and their wives. On his way to school, her son had filled his pockets with the pralines left over from dessert. During class, while eating one of them, he kept a hand in his pocket, and as M. Vedel talked about the lesson, Gide increased his sensual pleasures. "Suddenly I heard my name being called: 'Gide! You seem very red to me? Come here. I'd like to have a word with you.'" Gide became redder still, the effects of embarrassment adding to those of congestion, and walked up the steps of the platform. His classmates "snickered." M. Vedel questioned him, he confessed, and went back to his bench "more dead than alive." That very evening his father received a letter from the vice-principal asking him not to send André back to school for three months.

The same evening his parents seriously discussed the matter in the rue de Tournon study. Their decision was to take the guilty boy to a doctor, and a consultation was arranged with Dr. Brouardel, professor of medical jurisprudence at the Faculty of Medicine in Paris. Dr. Brouardel's solution was to threaten the delinquent with the radical suppression of the instrument of his act:

"I know all about it," he said, putting a threatening tone into his voice, "and there's no need to examine or question you today, my boy. But if your mother finds it necessary to bring you here again, that is, if you haven't mended your ways, well (and at that point his voice became terrifying), here are the instruments we should have to use, the instruments with which we operate on little boys like you!" And without taking his eyes off me, rolling them and scowling, he pointed behind his chair at a display of Touareg spearheads. He was too obviously inventing for me to take his threat seriously!

[1] *Si le grain ne meurt,* I, 235.

It is highly doubtful that the nine-year-old schoolboy took the threat with that much composure. But according to what Gide wrote, he was less afraid of corporal punishment than of the moral punishment implicit in "my father's silent grief" and his mother's "anxiety," tears, entreaties, and admonishments. In any case, this time the guilty boy finally realized the seriousness of his misconduct, which seemed to have eluded him until then.

In Gide's unpublished papers, there is a rough draft of his account of the episode:

As it offended no one, I was far from . . . I could not really bring myself to believe in the importance of my misdeed. Moreover, I could not really bring myself to believe in the seriousness of a misdeed which hurt no one. A month before I had been terrified by something else. Caught absolutely short, I pissed in my pants. It was one of those exam days when the recreation period is dispensed with and no doubt I had not taken the necessary "precautions" beforehand. At first I had hoped that it would not go further than my wet clothing and pass unnoticed; but deplorably profuse, it had formed what seemed like an enormous pool at my feet, which out of the corner of my eye I viewed with indescribable horror. Ah! I really had something to blush about that time! M. Brünig, the vice-principal, who certainly was everything, was present at the examination, as were all the parents, including my own. I was intensely embarrassed. After the examination was over, walking home between my father and mother, a prey to dejection, I was as silent as a condemned man. For surely this time I deserved being sent away from school. But not at all; to my indescribable astonishment I got off with a heavy cold. When I finally sobbed out my shame to mamma, she even smiled; she smiled as she kissed me and promised to write a note to M. Brünig apologizing for me. But this time, alas, it was quite different; on the very evening of the day M. Vedel had caught me, my father received a . . . [2]

It would seem then that the schoolboy had been surprised by the difference in his mother's attitude with regard to the first and second incidents. She smiled at one, she cried over the other. But the first was no more than a violation of civility, the second a transgression of morality.

While desolation reigned in the rue de Tournon, the great World's Fair of 1878 was about to open and a visit to the newly constructed Palais du Trocadéro with its succession of wonders was a salutary distraction for the guilty and repentant child. Anna Shackleton showed him round the fair and managed to amuse him so well that three months later he reappeared in the classroom of the Ecole Alsacienne cured, "at any rate about as much as one ever is." But, shortly after, he got the measles, and his parents decided to send him off to La Roque with Anna to recuperate. When he arrived he found the swallows already there.

[2] Unpublished notes for *Si le grain ne meurt*.

When classes began again in October, 1878, André Gide started over in the ninth form. M. Vedel, who was perhaps sorry for his hasty intervention, paid special attention to him. A feeling of relative security took the place of the strangeness he had felt as a new pupil and, with unaccustomed self-confidence, Gide received good grades. Moreover, directly after the holidays that preceded the school year, a family event of some importance took place: Albert Démarest began to take notice of his young cousin:

What could he have seen in me to attract his sympathy? I don't know; but I was probably all the more grateful for his attention in that I felt how little I deserved it. And I immediately did my best to be a bit more worthy of it.[3]

He became more sensitive to Albert's approval or disapproval than to his parents', for there was nothing of the "censor" about Albert and even his reprobation seemed prompted only by sympathy:

I distinctly remember the autumn evening he drew me aside, after dinner, in a corner of my father's study, while my parents were playing bezique with my Aunt Démarest and Anna. He began by saying in a low voice that he could not quite see what interest I had in life outside myself, that it was the mark of an egoist, and that I certainly gave the impression of being one. . . . Never before had I been spoken to in that way; Albert's words touched me more deeply than he ever supposed or than I myself realized until later.[4]

Albert Démarest, although twenty years older than his young cousin, was André Gide's first friend.

Despite an exceptionally hard winter that year and his rather delicate constitution, Gide went to school without a break, learned to ice skate, and went in for gymnastics. In fact he was champion of his class after Adrien Monod and "even better than he" on the ropes. In the spring he would play ball with his schoolmates in the Luxembourg Gardens. On Tuesdays, from two to five, he and the pupils of the Ecole Alsacienne would visit the Paris monuments and the Jardin des Plantes, where M. Brünig would point out a great variety of animals and plants. In his free time, he and Julien Jardinier, the son of one of his father's colleagues at the Faculty of Law, would spend their sous at old Clément's shop in the Luxembourg Gardens. He was not overly fond of young Jardinier. And when he wanted to raise silkworms, Julien showed such insurmountable aversion to caterpillars that they simply stopped seeing one another.

André Gide looked for another playmate and found one. He was a Russian. Gide had forgotten the boy's name but not the "real passion" he had felt for him:

[3] *Si le grain ne meurt,* I, 80.

[4] *Ibid.,* p. 81.

He was frail and extraordinarily pale; he had very fair, rather long hair and very blue eyes; his voice was musical and his slight accent gave it a singsong quality. His whole being exuded a kind of poetry, which I think came from the fact that he felt he was weak and wanted to be loved. He was somewhat looked down on by the other boys and rarely took part in their games; as for me, he had only to look at me and I felt ashamed of playing with the others, and I remember certain recreation periods when, suddenly catching his eye, I left the game then and there to go and join him. The boys made fun of me because of it. I so much wanted someone to attack him so that I could come to his defense.

Then the Russian stopped coming to school. "I kept secret about one of the first and deepest sorrows of my life."[5]

Every year during Lent, on Carnival Day, the Pascaud Gymnasium would give a costume party for the children in its clientele. The idea of dressing up threw Gide into a kind of "delirium." "What! Could the mere prospect of depersonalization cause such bliss? Already at that age? No: the pleasure consisted rather . . . in pretending to be someone else."[6] His taste for mimicry, which was one day to reach a point of intoxication, was obvious even in his childhood. The idea that putting on a new costume meant putting on a new personality enraptured him even then. But the future Proteus, who was to make "depersonalization" his personal luxury, was disappointed on the first occasion. Mme. Paul Gide's sense of economy limited his new personality to that of a little pastry cook, and the white calico costume made her son look like a "pocket handkerchief."

The boy who later on was to disguise himself as gloomy André Walter, the explorer Urien, Prometheus, Philoctetes, a "miglionaire," a traveler, a clergyman, a mandarin, an Oxford doctor, an old man of the mountains, Oedipus, and Theseus, found his first disguise very prosaic indeed, even though the pockets of his white apron were filled with cookies. And as he awkwardly stood around, brandishing one of Marie's enormous saucepans, he fell "positively in love" with a "little devil," dressed in black tights covered with steel spangles, who fascinated everyone by his capers, nonchalance, and glibness:

As people crowded round to see him, he jumped and tumbled and pirouetted, as if drunk with joy and success; he looked like a sylph; I could not take my eyes off him. I so much wanted to attract his attention and at the same time I was afraid to because of my ridiculous getup; I felt ugly and miserable.[7]

The little pastry cook went home "sick at heart," in the state of dereliction anthropomorphically attributed to the moth in love with a star. He had such a "fit of despair" that his mother promised him a more attractive disguise for the next year. And she kept her word. A year later he

[5] *Ibid.*, pp. 86, 87.   [6] *Ibid.*, p. 88.   [7] *Ibid.*, p. 90.

went to the Pascaud Gymnasium party as a picturesque "Neopolitan lazza-rone." But he searched in vain for the sparkling imp who had left him so dazzled and frustrated. Perhaps he never came, perhaps he had only changed his costume, if not his personality.

When school reopened in October, 1879, André went into the eighth form and had a new teacher. Because his mother probably felt that M. Vedel had been a good influence on her son, she decided to have André board with him. M. Vedel did take in an occasional day student of the Ecole Alsacienne, and André soon became one of his boarders. After he had been there a short time, he received the one letter from his father that is still in existence. His parents were then still on holiday in Uzès:

Uzès, Sunday,
October 28, 1879

My dear little André,

It's now almost a week since you left us and I hope that all has gone well and that you've been a good boy; I'm happy to see that your marks are high. I also hope that now that you've got into the habit of behaving well at M. Vedel's, you will continue to do so and when you're back with papa and mamma, you will not revert to your demanding and capricious behaviour of the past.[8] I'm sure that although your mamma isn't there, you continue to say your prayers morning and evening, and that you haven't forgotten that although we may be far away, God is always with you.

Your little cousin Jeanne (as you call her) is very nice; but tiny as she is, she has her whims. When they had to send her wet nurse away and get her a new one, would you believe it, she got angry. She pushed the new wet nurse away with all the strength in her little hands and for more than four hours she screamed, preferring hunger to taking milk from a wet nurse she didn't know. But now she's very good.

Mamma and I haven't yet made any big excursions. We haven't gone up on the Sarbonnet rock.[9] Summer is already over: there are no more little lizards on the walls or gnats in the alcove or pretty morning-glory on the rocks. However your mamma has pulled up one or two plants for you. She has sent them to Anna, who will dry them and bring them to you when she comes back to Paris.

Adieu my dear little André. We all send you our love, your grandmamma, mamma, and myself.

Your papa, who loves you very much.

Paul Gide

[8] That is probably the very simple reason for his having been sent away from home.

[9] "Mount Sarbonnet," where André hunted for caterpillars.

M. Vedel's house had once belonged to Sainte-Beuve, whose bust remained there in his honor, and under his undaunted eye, fist fights often
took place. André Gide's exceptionally protected childhood had hardly
prepared him for living with others. Frail and even puny, "thin as a rail,"
he was terrified by the brutality of some of the boys, yet it was mostly
their jeers that increased his painful feeling of physical inferiority. But on
one occasion Gide rebelled against "a great big redhead with a low brow."
That day, instead of repressing his aggression, he brilliantly exteriorized it:

Twice, three times, I put up with his sarcasm; but suddenly I was seized with
a holy rage; I jumped on him and got him in a grip, while the other boys
stood around us in a circle. He was considerably bigger and stronger than I;
but his surprise was in my favor; and then, I hardly recognized myself; my
fury unleashed all my strength; I punched him, I shoved him, and down he
went. Then when he was on the ground, drunk with my triumph, I dragged
him off in the ancient way, or what I thought was such; I dragged him by his
mop of hair and he lost a good handful of it. I was even a bit disgusted with
my victory because of all the greasy hair he left between my fingers; but I was
dumbfounded at having been able to win; beforehand it had seemed so impossible to me that I must have lost my head to have risked it. My success won
me the respect of the others. . . .[10]

André Gide seems to have gradually adapted to the life at Vedel's and to
have finally got along with "the others," once having earned their respect.

When school reopened in October, 1880, André Gide began his second
year as a boarder at the Vedel's.

Shortly after the beginning of classes, André Gide's parents came back
to Paris. He was at the Vedel's when Anna Shackleton rushed over to get
him and take him back to the rue de Tournon: his father was dead.

[10] *Si le grain ne meurt,* I, 93.

8: Death and Anguish

> *"I have done my best to describe the kind of overwhelming suffocation, accompanied by tears and sobs, to which I was subject. . . . Yet I fear it will remain absolutely incomprehensible to those who have never experienced anything like it."*
>
> Si le grain ne meurt, *I, 195*

P AUL GIDE was never particularly robust. Very slim, of narrow build, a bit stooped, he had what doctors call the *habitus* generally considered as favorable to tuberculosis. In 1880, at the end of summer, he had some digestive disorder that was at first diagnosed as "indigestion from figs" or "dysentery." Then it was discovered that what in fact he had was intestinal tuberculosis:

Actually he was suffering from intestinal tuberculosis, and I think my mother knew it; but in those days tuberculosis was an illness which people hoped to cure by ignoring. Besides, my father was already too far gone for any hopes of his getting over it.[1]

Paul Gide returned to Paris knowing that his case was hopeless, took to his bed, and became deeply engrossed in a book which never left him:

A heavy book lay on the sheet before him, open but face down so that all I could see was its leather binding; my father must have turned it over just as I came in. My mother told me afterward that it was a Plato.

The last book read by Tancrède Gide's son was not the Bible but Plato. And probably an idealist such as he could not have found any more suitable company.

The scene took place just a few days before Paul Gide died. André Gide

[1] *Si le grain ne meurt,* I, 93.

knew that his father returned sick, but he never for a moment thought that he would die. When Anna Shackleton came to get him at the Vedel's and told him the news, he was dumbfounded. In his unpublished notes for *Si le grain ne meurt* he wrote: "Papa—Anna's grief—my astonishment." When he saw his mother in deep mourning, his own grief burst out:

My grief did not burst out until I saw my mother in deep mourning. She was afraid the shock to my nerves would be too great and tried to get me to drink a little tea. I was on her lap; she held the cup, offered me a spoonful, and I remember she said, as she forced herself to smile: "Let's see now! Will this one get there safely?" And I suddenly felt completely enveloped in her love which from then on was to close in on me alone.

The motherly gesture, although perfectly natural, would seem to have provoked ambiguous feelings in her son, for at the same moment he felt she was gently protecting him and taking possession.[2]

An event as dramatic as a father's death, especially in the case of a beloved father, would be expected to cause a deep emotional upset. Therefore Gide's psychological reactions, as described in *Si le grain ne meurt* and which doubtless do honor to his sincerity,[3] cannot fail to be disconcerting. Once the first shock was over, Gide added: "As for my loss, how could I have realized it?" The question is curious for as intelligent and sensitive a child of eleven, more especially as he had already learned what death was the year before when his uncle Guillaume Démarest died. But the context is even more surprising:

I would speak of my regret, but alas! I was mostly sensitive to the kind of prestige my bereavement gave me in the eyes of my schoolmates. Imagine! Every one of them wrote to me, just as every one of my father's colleagues had done when he was decorated!

Such apparent insensitivity in really moving circumstances, in contrast to the ease with which Gide was affected "by the slightest thing," was not a trait confined to Gide's childhood. It would be oversimplifying to see it as a sign of coldness; for it was rather the result of a temperament which must be discussed in more detail. The fact remains that he was certainly very impressed by the letters he received from M. Brünig and the pupils of the seventh form, for he kept them all his life in a large envelope, where they still remain.

Although he seemed not to understand the extent of his loss, André

2 The same ambiguity was evident fifteen years later on Mme. Gide's death (May 31, 1895), when André Gide felt drunk "with love, grief, and liberty," like a "prisoner suddenly set free" (*Si le grain ne meurt,* II, 369).

3 Unless he was influenced by the more or less subconscious tendency to disparage himself which was one of the fundamental characteristics of his personality.

Gide was not long in discovering it. He often yearned for his father in the years to come. Paul Gide's advice and tolerance had toned down the severity of a puritanical upbringing that was laying the groundwork for future rebellion. A widow at forty-five, Mme. Gide never considered re-marrying. She decided to devote herself entirely to educating her only son and bringing him up according to strict principles. She became "the lady in black," whose son refused to see her in anything but mourning. As Gide wrote in his unpublished notes:

The first time after papa's death that mamma wore violet ribbons, I was shocked but said nothing. It seemed to me indecent that she should wear color; it made her look younger.

He was then preparing for the *baccalauréat* and nine years had passed since his father's death.

Gide situated two strange events in his life with relation to his father's death, one before and one after, and they were often to repeat themselves in his youth:

The first takes me far back into the past; I should like to give the exact year, but all I can say is that my father was still alive. We were at table; Anna was lunching with us. My parents were sad because they had learned that morning of the death of a little four-year-old child, the son of our Widmer cousins; I had not yet heard the news, but I made it out from the few words my father said to Nana.[4] I had only seen little Emile Widmer two or three times and had no particular feeling for him; but I no sooner understood he was dead than an ocean of grief broke over my heart.

His mother tried to quiet his sobs but

to no avail, for it was not exactly my little cousin's death that made me cry but something I did not understand, an indefinable anguish, which it was not surprising I could not explain to my mother, for I am incapable of explaining it any better even today. Ridiculous though it may seem to some people, I must say that later in life, on reading certain pages of Schopenhauer, I suddenly seemed to recognize it.[5]

Gide himself noted that his first attack of anguish had but little relation to the death of Emile Widmer, whom he hardly knew and was relatively indifferent to:

Mamma told me that we must all die and that Little Emile was in Heaven where there were no more tears or suffering, in short, all the most consoling things a loving mother can think of.

[4] Anna Shackleton was usually called Nana until Emile Zola's novel gave the name a significance considered incompatible with Miss Shackleton's character.

[5] *Si le grain ne meurt*, I, 135.

She probably thought that pity had provoked his inexplicable grief and so it had, in part, but there was something else, "something I did not understand." Neither the death of Albert's father, his uncle Guillaume Démarest, in 1879, nor his own father in 1880 had caused such explosions. This time it was more a question of fright and panic than of grief. Some reason can always be found for anguish, even a reason that seems to justify it, but the anxious person feels, and he is the only one to feel it, that there is "something else" and precisely "something I did not understand," as if the motive he knew hid another which remained unknown.

The second of these tremors is stranger still: It was a few years later, shortly after my father's death; in other words I must have been eleven. The scene again took place at table, during a morning meal, but this time my mother and I were alone. I had been to school that morning. What had happened? Nothing, perhaps. . . . Then why did I suddenly fall apart and why, sobbing convulsively in mamma's arms, did I again feel that inexpressible anguish, the very same that I felt at my little cousin's death? It was as though the special floodgate of some universal, inner, unknown sea had suddenly opened and an overwhelming wave rushed over my heart; I was more terrified than sad; but how was I to explain it to my mother, when all she could make out through my sobs were the jumbled words, repeated over and again in despair: "I'm not like the others! I'm not like the others!"[6]

In order to convey the abruptness, the violence, the unexpected and upsetting nature of such *erlebnis,* Gide twice used the same metaphor, which might seem emphatic were it not for its perfect suitability: the breaking of an "inner unknown sea" and "an ocean of grief." During the experience of anguish, consciousness sometimes appears to be submerged by the gushing forth of an emotional flux which seems to break through the controlling floodgate. A flood, a tempest, a breaking up of ice, an inner quake, are the metaphoric approximations that anguished people borrow from the seisms of nature in order to communicate to others the accidents of their own natures, incomprehensible to anyone who has not experienced them.

Later on, Gide wrote about a third and similar attack:

I have done my best to describe the kind of overwhelming suffocation, accompanied by tears and sobs, to which I was subject, and which, in its first three manifestations . . . surprised me so much. Yet I fear it will remain absolutely incomprehensible to those who have never experienced anything like it. Since then, I have become acclimatized to the attacks of this strange aura; they are far from being less frequent but are now tempered, controlled, and tamed, as it were, so that I have learned not to be any more frightened of them than Socrates was of his familiar daemon. I soon understood that drunkenness without wine was nothing other than lyrical ecstasy. . . .[7]

[6] *Ibid.,* pp. 135–36.
[7] *Ibid.,* p. 195.

Thus André Gide himself linked his first attacks of anguish in child-hood to the lyrical raptures of the future André Walter's adolescence. One and the other were states of emotional drunkenness, states of fear or joy very nearly without an apparent object, similar in some ways, different in others. In order to designate those strange states, Gide found it neces-sary to resort to a foreign word: *Schaudern,* meaning tremor or quiver. His choice of a German word probably corresponds to the feeling of strangeness he later thought he could ascribe to his own country, having at nineteen discovered German Romanticism and Schopenhauer. "When I read Schopenhauer's *The World as Will and Idea,* I immediately thought: then it's that!"[8] The fact that a writer as sure as Gide showed hesitation in expressing the ineffable is not without psychological interest, but the French word *angoisse,* taken in its etymological sense,[9] translates the un-translatable as well as *Schaudern,* and does convey the "overwhelming suffocation" Gide truly experienced since childhood.

It is always difficult, in a child who cannot yet clearly make out the difference between the real and the unreal and cannot gauge danger, to distinguish between fear and anxiety. Anxiety is at once more indefinite and more dramatic than fear. It is not an apprehension of this or that, of this person or that one; it is fear with no object, unexplained if not inex-plicable. Whereas fear is provoked by the perception of an outer and known[10] danger, anxiety is the apperception of an inner and unknown danger, whence its mysterious nature. More precisely, it is less an apper-ception than an expectation, the foreboding of a vague but immanent and imminent peril; it is both painful insecurity and uncertainty.

Anxiety is relatively frequent in nervous children, but a real attack of anguish is much less so. It differs not only in its intensity as a physical disorder,[11] the feeling of suffocation that can be "overwhelming," but also in its paroxysmal evolution. It has the nature of a living experience and, in my opinion, that is its greatest difference. Anxiety is the expectation of a

---

[8] *Journal,* p. 800.   [9] From *angere,* meaning to constrict.

[10] Or imagined, as when Gide as a child was terrified by the "monsters" in his nightmares. But to the extent that monsters are merely symbolic and disguised pro-jections of the subconscious, the fear in this case would be anguish.

[11] For many years psychologists have tried to use the physical component of anguish, namely suffocation, to distinguish it from anxiety. "Anguish," Brissaud once wrote, "is a physical disorder expressed by a feeling of constriction, suffocation. Anxiety is a psychic disorder expressed by a feeling of indefinable insecurity." The very neat opposition is hardly convincing, for in anxiety there is also a feeling of oppression and a difficulty in breathing deeply. Moreover, there can be attacks of anguish without constriction and attacks of constriction (*angor*) without anguish.

future danger, whereas anguish is the actual experience, *hic et nunc,* of an inner seism. It is consciously felt as the brutal appearance of a new phenomenon. Comparing it to an absence, a vacuum, a nothingness,[12] as has often been done, is wrong, for it is not a negative phenomenon but a positive phenomenon, a presence, even if its appearance has been provoked by a disappearance. It is an emotional eruption, a lyrical ejaculation, a purely affective drunkenness. In that perspective it might be said that anxiety is the expectation of anguish.

As for Gide's two early attacks of anguish, the first would seem to have been provoked or occasioned by the news of his little cousin Emile Widmer's death, the second by the sudden impression of feeling "cut off, excluded." And with regard to the third *Schaudern:* "Suddenly I felt overwhelmed and panic-stricken by something enormous, religious, like at the time of little Emile's death or like the day I felt cut off, excluded."[13] There are many possible interpretations of eleven-year-old André Gide's anguished cry "I'm not like the others," and they will be considered subsequently. But given his comment: "What had happened? Nothing, perhaps . . . ," it would be preferable not to attribute too precise a meaning to that moment of intuition which was both acute and vague and in fact inexpressible in its strangeness. With the help of his emotional paroxysm and while he desperately repeated: "I'm not like the others! I'm not like the others!" he became keenly aware, in a more dramatic way than ever before, of the permanent feeling of discomfort, insecurity, and inferiority that weighed on his anxious childhood.

[12] The feeling of emptiness is quite a different state: depression; although when depression reaches a certain point, it can provoke a real attack of anguish, and must not be confused with it. Most literary descriptions of "anguish" concern depression, which is itself the experience of nothingness.

[13] *Si le grain ne meurt,* I, 194. Gide wrote "little Raoul," for he changed the names of most of the characters in *Si le grain ne meurt.* But here he would seem to have forgotten that, the first time, he had given his cousin his real name.

9: A New Regime

*"And so I began that erratic and un-
regulated way of life and that desultory
education which I came to find only
too much to my taste."*

Si le grain ne meurt, *I, 98*

A NDRÉ GIDE's mother, now a widow living alone with her son,
wished to bring him up according to strict rules; but she was
thwarted by André's character and health. He was a difficult and
disconcerting boy. Ambivalent, undecided, hesitant, full of contradictions,
he was fundamentally unstable. In class he was considered an erratic student. He was subject to sudden "fits" of nervous tension, accompanied by
"headaches" which made any effort at attention momentarily impossible.
Such sudden changes of mood or "tension" gave him the reputation of
being lazy or capricious, and he often spoke about it later in life as one
characteristic of his nervous temperament; but during his childhood his
uncle Emile Rondeaux, himself a sensitive man who was considered weak,
was the only one who understood the nature of his trouble: "André," he
said, "is not lazy and will always love work, but he's erratic." The adjective stuck with him for some time after.

The word "erratic" did refer to the inconstancy of his work at school
but also, and much more generally, to a restless changeability that astonished everyone around him. He went with surprising speed from joy to
sadness, from enthusiasm to despair, from excessive and almost feverish
activity to apathy; he was as easily exalted as depressed, as easily fatigued
as restored. In his relations with his mother, he perpetually oscillated between obedience and rebellion, sometimes submissive, sometimes insubordinate. His resolutions could hardly be counted on, for as soon as he made

a decision, he would change his mind and do the contrary. He seemed to be doubting and impulsive, going from affirmation to negation, easily changing his mind, quick to retract, and yet in other circumstances he proved to be stubborn and opinionated. His reactions were unpredictable and the stories he told were not necessarily trustworthy. It was said that "with him, one could never know what was true."

He was considered a liar, "as much a liar," specified his Rondeaux cousins, "as Charles Pochet,"[1] which it seems was saying a great deal. However, everyone admitted that Charles lied for his own interest and André for pleasure, a habit not nearly so bad, according to André's "three sisters." For example, when he was at the top of the cedar tree in Cuverville and would shout: "I see the sea," it was more a graceful mistake than a lie, and so it was much of the time, for he had a poetic imagination. He lied less than he made up stories, and tended to take his imaginings for reality, fooling himself as much as he fooled others. But Mme. Gide would not agree to such deformation of the truth. She held that what is true is true and that what is false is false, to such a degree that the often aesthetic nature of young André's stories did not appear to her as an attenuating circumstance. With great and sometimes brutal simplicity, she refused to make the distinction between a dream and a lie. Nor did she appreciate the casuists' distinction between reticence or mental reservation and the sin of insincerity. She also had her hands full with her son's yes—no habit, trying to lead his evasive spirit back to the simple straight and narrow path. Moreover, having learned about her son's "bad instincts" from the episode at the Ecole Alsacienne, she remained suspicious and very much on the alert, convinced—as a good Puritan—that someone capable of sexual impurity will sooner or later be capable of anything.

She was therefore of the opinion that her son was in great need of living "under the law," but on the other hand he was so nervous that the law could not be applied in all its rigor. An extremely emotional child, he was sometimes stricken with paralyzing shyness in front of others. He had had terrifying nightmares, and his nights continued to be sleepless and agitated. He often had headaches and unexplained fatigue. Very thin and frail, with an especially narrow chest, he had the same constitution as his father, and since Paul Gide's illness, she could not help but fear that the same would happen to him.

André did not fail to notice how much his health worried his mother. She resorted to precautions that were more likely to weaken than to strengthen him. He referred to it in *La Porte étroite* in connection with Jérôme's childhood, which in certain ways was similar to his own:

[1] A first cousin to Emile Rondeaux's children.

My health was delicate. The solicitude of my mother and Miss Ashburton, their constant attempt to keep me from tiring myself, could easily have made me an idler. The fact that it did not shows that I have a real taste for work. At the first sign of good weather, both of them would become convinced that it was time I left the city, that I was growing pale; toward mid-June we would leave for Fongueusemare in the vicinity of Le Havre, where we were invited every summer by my Uncle Bucolin.[2]

We know that Miss Ashburton is Miss Shackleton, Fongueusemare the country house in Cuverville, and Uncle Bucolin, Uncle Emile Rondeaux. André Gide's mother, however, did not take him directly to Cuverville after his father's death but to Rouen, to the large family house in the rue de Crosne. No doubt leaving Paris with M. Vedel's ex-boarder was not an easy decision to make. "And so I began that erratic and unregulated way of life and that desultory education which I came to find only too much to my taste."

Until then Mme. Gide had been very worried about André's regularity at school. During that winter in Rouen at the Emile Rondeaux's, she took particular care that he did not overtax himself. A professor, "M. Hubert,"[3] came to make him work "a little" at the house, with his cousin Jeanne Rondeaux who was about the same age.

The great event of the winter was the founding of a newspaper by André Gide. He set it himself on a copying machine and published the poetry and prose of his three cousins Madeleine, Jeanne, and Valentine for all the family to read. His own contribution was limited to choosing texts of Boileau and Buffon in order to give the rue de Crosne gazette a classical tone and lofty style. Even so, this may very well have been the beginning of his literary career, for in his unpublished notes of 1881, he wrote: "my first poems."[4] But his occupations were cut short by Mme. Gide's decision, at the end of winter, to leave for La Roque.

At La Roque a tutor, "M. Gallin,"[5] was put in charge of André's instruction. But André hated him and, as a result of his violent antipathy, did almost nothing during his six-month stay, for he always refused to work with a professor unless he liked or admired him. He did find some consolation in the study of nature, and fortunately, in the course of the summer, his cousins arrived.

[2] *La Porte étroite*, p. 8.

[3] His real name was M. Huard, "M. Huard with his square fingers" (unpublished notes for *Si le grain ne meurt*).

[4] Unpublished notes for *Si le grain ne meurt*.

[5] Romard, *ibid.*

André Gide was then very superstitious and considered a whole group of numbers, gestures, magic formulas, and omens as lucky or unlucky. He emphasized that aspect of his personality as a child in his *Journal* and in *Ainsi soit-il.*[6] There is one game he never spoke of in *Si le grain ne meurt* but to which he attached particular importance, for he remembered the state of "trance" it put him in.[7] As a child, Valentine Rondeaux had "an extraordinary sense of mystery." She had, somewhat unwillingly, let her cousin in on the secret of some magic formulas made up of a long string of meaningless syllables, which for him took on the importance of a real talisman: " 'Please, Valentine, say it once very slowly so that I can remember it!' 'It has no value when it's not said very quickly.' And out of a kind of jabbering, I barely made out: 'Hossalaps allalip derfous.' " Certain consecrations of magic phrases, banal only to the non-initiated, required a solemn and complicated ceremony, and the slightest deviation from it would immediately take away all its value, or more precisely, its charm, for indeed it had to do with a charm in the magical sense.

That ritual ceremony, described in *Si le grain ne meurt,*[8] and its formal perfection were particularly disturbing to Gide as a child because they corresponded to his own tendency toward obsessive rites to exorcise anxiety. It was during his adolescence, at André Walter's age, and later on, episodically, in his *Journal,* that he spoke of his obsessive tendencies; but even in childhood he suffered from doubt, was obsessed by scruples, and had discovered the exorcising properties of rites. For example, when his mother left the rue de Tournon apartment for one on the rue de Commaille, André Gide, then age twelve, became apprehensive at the idea of changing his residence. He could not enter the new apartment without anguish. To neutralize his feeling of insecurity, he told me he had discovered "a trick." Before going in he "rapped on the door three times" or repeated some meaningless formulas "three times," but always the same ones. He felt reassured immediately, but for several weeks afterward he was "forced" to repeat systematically the rite or, had he fogotten to perform it, to go back, having been warned about his lack of observance by a new feeling of insecurity. And that was one among many traits characteristic of his anxiety as a child.

---

[6] The trait is common in anxious children (see Charles Odier, *L'Angoisse et la pensée magique*). Later on, when Gide had become "a rebel," he forced himself "somewhat as a challenge" (at least in the beginning) to seek out everything considered ill-omened "for the fun of thinking that everything that brings bad luck to the submissive must be favorable to rebels. . . . And so I never missed the opportunity of going under a ladder, travelling on Friday, or putting my trust in a thirteen."

[7] Gide did not use the word "trance" in *Ainsi soit-il* in that respect, but he used it during a conversation.

[8] *Ainsi soit-il ou Les jeux sont faits,* pp. 95–96.

Meanwhile, Mme. Gide could not stop worrying about André's almost complete idleness during the school year that had just passed. In October, 1881, she made the big decision to settle in Montpellier near the Charles Gides. She thought the southern climate would be good for ·her son's health and counted greatly on her brother-in-law's moral influence as a guide in his upbringing. Having tried the Rouen side of the family, she would try the Uzès side.

Charles Gide, fifteen years younger than Paul, had loved and admired his elder brother. He was deeply grieved by the death of the one person he had considered somewhat as his guide. He came to Paris to be the chief mourner and, after the funeral, Mme. Paul Gide asked him to act as a father to André, now that his own had prematurely disappeared.[9] Uncle Charles took his new duties seriously and resolved to keep up a regular correspondence with his nephew. As soon as he left Paris to rejoin his aged mother in Uzès, he wrote to André, and the first letter was the beginning of a highly interesting correspondence.

In October, 1881, Mme. Gide, her son, and her faithful servant Marie settled in Montpellier very near to the Charles Gides. The funished apartment she chose for the year was "small, ugly, and squalid; the furniture was sordid." André soo missed the rue de Tournon and even the Ecole Alsacienne. He could not get accustomed to his Montpellier lodgings, and his description of them was sinister. A feeling of material insecurity ("the hideousness of our lodgings made me think that my father's death had brought about our ruin") increased his feeling of general insecurity. The *lycée,* where Rabelais had been a student, seemed to him even more dismal than the apartment, and he immediately felt unhappy there. He was shyer than ever, "became depressed and sullen, and only associated with my schoolmates because I could not do otherwise."

His class was divided into two factions: the Catholic party and the Protestant party. "As the Catholic aristocracy sent their children to religious schools, all that was left for the *lycée,* apart from the Protestant boys who were almost all cousins, was a group of plebeians who were often fairly disagreeable and clearly full of hatred toward us." The persecutions to which he, a descendant of the Camisards, was subjected, however, were inflicted not because of religious or class hatred but because of a hatred for poetry. Or at least such was Gide's explanation, ideally suited to a future man of letters, for the hostility manifested by "Gomez and his pack."

At the Ecole Alsacienne, André Gide had learned to say poetry instead

[9] "She who, after your father's death, had told me: 'You will teach him to remain pure.' " Letter from Charles Gide to André Gide, Aug. 20, 1894, unpublished.

of monotonously reciting it. His natural inclination was to put a great deal of feeling into his speech and probably also some of the vocal mannerisms he had such difficulty in ridding himself of later on.[10] Whatever the reason, when Gide's turn came to recite a poem at the *lycée* of Montpellier, he did it in his own mannered way. But the artistic experience did not provoke the desired reaction among the listeners. The whole class was briefly stupefied and then immediately burst out laughing. The teacher himself, M. Nadaud, could not suppress a fleeting smile, but he quickly pulled himself together and, as a good professor of literature, entrusted with the care of the muses, he imposed silence: "Gide, ten.[11] So that makes you laugh, gentlemen. Well! Let me tell you, that is how you should all recite." And it was said in a calm voice which, at the memorable moment, Gide found "august." But alas! *Ad augusta per angusta!* The poetic diction was shocking to ears that were indifferent to the muses and particularly to those of the students in the sixth form at the *lycée* of Montpellier. Gide's way of pitching his voice seemed to them unbearably affected. A few tough guys took it upon themselves to beat the lyricism out of him. But the mishaps that followed were not peculiar to André Gide: many of the future budding Romantics experienced the same thing and learned on the playground the way a childish collectivity treats anyone it judges different from itself. Of course, the fact that Gide was frail and shy, an only child brought up by two highly moral women, and convinced into the bargain that he was not like the others, which they probably sensed, marked him out as a perfect victim for the persecution of pugnacious boys. He who was later to be exempt from most social experiences—competitive sports, military service, and the fight for material survival generally known to members of a profession—had a rather nasty experience of collective life at the *lycée* of Montpellier.

One of his schoolmates called Gomez, an "athletic brute" whose "vicious expression, hair plastered down low on his forehead, shining with pomade," and, *horresco referens,* "flowing bow tie the color of blood" were recalled by Gide forty years later, chose the puny Parisian for a scapegoat because he made the exasperating mistake of speaking too well. "I was jeered at, thrashed, hunted." Gomez ("he led the gang and he really wanted blood") was in command of the pack and as soon as class was over, they chased Gide down the streets of Montpellier:

For fear of ambush, I devised enormous detours; but when the others became aware of this, instead of stalking me, as they had been doing, they hunted

[10] It came back again in his last years when he was intimidated or embarrassed in public. "I did a lot of work on my voice," he told me. And only then was it apparent.

[11] *Translator's note:* The highest possible mark.

me down; it could really have been amusing; but I felt that their love of the game itself was less than their hatred for me, poor miserable game that I was.[12]

On certain days he returned home in a lamentable state, "my clothes torn and muddy, my nose bleeding and teeth chattering, absolutely haggard. My poor mother was in a state." André Gide must have remembered the savage hostility of his schoolmates and his own great fear when in *Les Faux-Monnayeurs* he described the despair of little Boris Lapérouse, faced with the "brotherhood of Strong Men." Just as Gomez hated Gide, so Ghéridansol hated Boris. And the cries of "the pack," hunting down the terrorized little Gide in the streets of Montpellier, correspond to the mort of the "gang" as they bought Boris to bay. Just as Gide took refuge in a nervous illness, so Boris took refuge in suicide.

Gide got "smallpox" just in time to protect him from his persecutors and put an end to that "hell." But at night his fever revived the terrifying images: "In my dreams I saw the ferocious Gomez; I fled panting from his pack; I again wiped from my cheek the loathesome sensation of the dead cat he one day picked up out of the gutter and rubbed against my face, while the others held my arms; I would wake up in a deep sweat." And he was immediately overcome by "unspeakable anguish" at the idea of going back.

Instead of the imaginary monsters in the nightmares of Gide's early childhood, the bogy-men and the *Criques*, the threatening characters now had human faces and were no more reassuring.

[12] *Si le grain ne meurt*, I, 114.

10: Nervous Attacks

*"I leave it to neurologists to disentangle
what was due to self-indulgence in the
nervous illness that followed my smallpox."*

Si le grain ne meurt, *I, 115*

Cᴇʀᴛᴀɪɴ illnesses can be cured, and so it was with André Gide's
"smallpox," which was more probably chicken pox. When Doctor
Leenhardt declared with satisfaction that his young patient
would soon be able to return to school, Mme. Gide greeted the happy news
with gratitude but her son was dismayed. The idea of going back into
harness and particularly of being once again faced with his persecutor,
Gomez, filled him with "frightful anguish." He trembled at the thought
of again serving as "game" for the cynegetic exploits of the pack. And yet
he was almost well, and every step he took toward recovery brought him
closer to the school door. It did not take Gide long to understand that it
was in his interest to make the step unsteady:

This is how I think it began. On the first day I was allowed to get up, a kind
of dizziness made me unsteady on my legs, as was only natural after three
weeks in bed. If this dizziness got a bit worse, I thought, could I imagine what
would happen? Yes, indeed: I would feel my head fall backward; my knees
would give way (I was in the little corridor that led from my room to my
mother's), and suddenly I would collapse. "Oh!" I said to myself, "if only I
could imitate what I imagine!" and even as I was busy imagining, I could tell
what a release, what a respite it would be to give in to the suggestion of my
nerves. One look behind to make sure of a spot where the fall would not hurt
too much. . . .[1]

[1] *Si le grain ne meurt,* I, 115.

Gide then described the different varieties of nervous movements he broke into, first in front of Marie who came running, then in front of all sorts of witnesses and for several weeks, on the floor or on his bed, standing, sitting, or lying down: muscular jerks, abrupt convulsive movements, diverse twitches and spasms, forward leaps or jumping in one spot, protracted rhythmical and sinuous dances, high kicks "in cadence, like those of Japanese jugglers," which were performed "in bed with the covers thrown back." In his unpublished notes Gide particularly recalled "the day I was jumping on all sides—mamma's terror—I wanted to throw myself out of the window."[2] After having reproached himself, in *Si le grain ne meurt,* for the part he was playing in front of his startled mother, he added:

Although the movements I was making were conscious, they were only partly voluntary. In other words I could, at the most, have controlled them a little. But I felt the greatest relief when I made them. Ah! How often, long afterward, when suffering from my nerves, have I deeply regretted that I was no longer at an age when an *entrechat* or two. . . .

The chaotic movements of the capricious child, who was acting a part in order not to be sent back to school, would obviously seem voluntary and feigned to an unbiased mind. And that was no doubt Uncle Charles's diagnosis. When Charles Gide saw his nephew's contortions, he treated them scornfully, and they immediately, although temporarily, disappeared. In his notes Gide recalled the scene in these terms: "Fury because my uncle does not take me seriously, I feign the most dreadful suffering, under a piece of furniture, he passes by without seeing me; I start groaning; he says: 'Well, well! What are you doing there?' And I, believing in the sublime, answer: 'I'm suffering!' "[3] In *Si le grain ne meurt* he added:

But I was immediately aware of my fiasco: My uncle put his glasses back on his nose and his nose back in his newspaper and closed himself in his study, shutting the door behind him with the greatest calm. O shame! What else could I do but get up, shake the dust off my clothes, and detest my uncle— which I did with all my heart.[4]

Was this proof of Uncle Charles's "denial of individuality and of all psychology"? Or, on the contrary, were his nearsighted eyes seeing far and clearly? The twitches, the twisting, and the spasmodic contractions of a throat choked with sobs all disappeared as if by magic under the cold shower of his icy indifference. But after a brief abatement, and to Mme. Gide's despair, the "entrechats" came back worse than ever.

[2] Unpublished notes for *Si le grain ne meurt.*

[3] *Ibid.*

[4] *Si le grain ne meurt,* I, 118.

Three doctors, Doctor Leenhardt and two consultants, gathered at the little patient's bedside, while he went on "jigging," and they decided he had to be sent to Lamalou-les-Bains, a spa for nervous cases. Gide described the memorable consultation in his notes as follows:

In that room in the Hotel Nevet (Montpellier), three doctors examined me. Leenhardt, who had looked after me during my smallpox, explained my case to Theulon and Boissier. My nervous state greatly worried my mother and I did my best so that it would. Recovery meant going back to the *lycée;* I preferred anything to that. My illness was like the adventurous unknown. The doctors decided on a season at Lamalou. Boissier, a doctor at the spa, looked at me. Theulon wanted to help me rebutton my jacket. Boissier tapped him on the shoulder saying: "Let him do it himself. I want to see . . ." I realized that he was examining me, trying to find out about my nervous state from my smallest gestures. So as I rebuttoned my jacket, I improvised a few jerks—not too many. "With you, sir, I shall have to play it close," I was thinking; and thereupon I despised the other doctor.[5]

And so persuaded he had outwitted everyone, if not himself, young Gide took off for a long period of truancy. He left with his mother and Marie for "ten months of laying fallow" at Lamalou and then at Gérardmer, ten months of idleness and outings, scarcely interrupted by baths in the Lamalou-le-Haut pool, which gave him "cooked skin and frozen bones," and from there to a soft bed that had been carefully warmed in his absence. Gomez and his boisterous pack, Uncle Charles and his severity were far in the distance. André Gide, in his own way, had written the first page of a rather long supplement to the existing treatises on the good use of illness.

"I leave it to neurologists to disentangle what was due to self-indulgence in the nervous illness that followed my smallpox." But in the complicated knot it is difficult to disentangle the threads knotted by Gide himself from those knotted in spite of him. One of the fundamental problems of Gide's personality was posed during that childhood illness: that of his sincerity toward others as well as toward himself. "While thinking that I am fooling them, I am no doubt fooling myself." Were his nervous attacks simulated? They were, of course, but only in part; that is, a definite simulation was added to a certain disposition. The fact that the intimidating Charles Gide made them temporarily disappear by his chilling attitude is less important than it would seem. Moral or physical intimidation can inhibit involuntary as well as voluntary movements. Although it may be true that people's anxious solicitude increases any outward manifestations and their indifference makes them lessen, it would be very unwise to consider such

[5] Unpublished notes for *Si le grain ne meurt.*

emotional criteria as proof of pure and simple simulation. For one to simulate something well, one must have it to begin with. For a thwarted child to give such a masterly exhibition of nervous disorders, an intention is not sufficient; he must be naturally predisposed to them.

Falling "where it would not hurt too much," the measured and rhythmical muscular discharges, the release of "relief" that followed, expressions like "if only I could imitate what I imagine," "although the movements I was making were conscious, they were only partly voluntary," and particularly "self-indulgence" correspond quite exactly to formulas used by doctors to characterize a nervous reaction that falls into the category of hysteria, or more precisely, a hysteroid reaction. The reaction, frequent in nervous children, does not deserve its bad reputation, based on a pure and simple assimilation to intentional simulation,[6] but it does indicate on the part of those who are victims of it, a "self-indulgence" made up of both a more or less unconscious duplicity of the mind and a more or less involuntary complicity of the body.

Such duplicity, the *homo duplex* denounced since antiquity, is less that of a liar than of a hypocrite, meaning actor in the Greek sense of the word. It is that of an actor who needs an audience in order to express himself and has already understood "the importance of an audience," but is so good in his part that he is caught in his own game. He makes an exhibition of himself for others but also for himself and, having become his own spectator, he no longer quite knows whether he is playing or being played.[7] "An actor perhaps," André Walter was to say later on, as he practiced in front of a mirror, "but I am playing myself," a dangerous game which ends by becoming a simulation before oneself and puts the apprentice sorcerer into the power of forces over which he no longer has control. Even if he has the illusion of directing them when actually he is merely obeying them or, as Gide said, "giving into the suggestion" of his nerves, he ends by being carried along by motorial storms which he is incapable of channeling in his own way. It is impossible to play with a body, malleable and suggestible enough to adapt to such relatively unconscious complicity, with impunity. The indeterminate limit between consciousness and

[6] Doctors sometimes make the assimilation for reasons which Freud has rather humorously analyzed. "Confronted with an attack of hysteria," he wrote, "a doctor's anatomical and physiological science leaves him in the dark. Faced with it he is incompetent, which is hardly pleasing when you are in the habit of holding your own science in high esteem. Therefore, hysterical patients lose the doctor's sympathy. He considers them like people who break the law, just as the faithful consider heretics. He thinks they are capable of everything base, and accuses them of exaggeration and intentional simulation."

[7] "Artificial prolongation of illness—nervous illness—real and feigned," André Gide lucidly noted (unpublished notes for *Si le grain ne meurt*).

the unconscious is the ideal borderline separating simulation from hysteria, but the lies of the body usually participate in one and the other. And when a child, after a nervous attack of that kind, triumphantly declares: "I was feigning," he is no less insincere than had he said the opposite.

When Gide fervently wrote: "Oh! If only I could imitate what I imagine," he did not yet know that an image, once actualized and in the physical realm, can become part of the body through a mysterious complicity. But in what does that most unequally distributed somatic self-indulgence consist? Is it linked to an abnormally porous, malleable, plastic quality of the nervous temperament, suggestibility? Is it linked to an intentional finality, rooted so deeply in the biological unconscious that it stems from the origins of instinct, as psychoanalysis has tried to prove? I shall come back to the problem when I discuss the psychological interpretation of these nervous attacks and the rather diverse advantages Gide learned to derive from them and then anticipate.

In *Si le grain ne meurt* André Gide's descriptions of his treatment at Lamalou-le-Haut are indicative of a temperament highly sensitive to physical impressions, even voluptuous. In addition to his cure, he spent a great deal of time walking, fishing, and reading. And in his unpublished notes he underlined the words: "I am starting Pascal—discovery." Very little is known about the month he spent at Gérardmer, but one sentence, written late in life, from *Et nunc manet in te,* is worthy of comment.

In one page of *Et nunc manet in te* Gide decided to say what he had "neglected to say in *Si le grain ne meurt*" and "which nevertheless has a certain importance as a refutation of certain theories which claim that our sexual tastes depend on opportunities we happened to come upon at a tender age when instinct, still undecided, is hesitant and questioning." He believed he could point out certain particularities in his childhood "in which I think a shrewd psychologist might already have seen the very sign of my inclination." He undoubtedly means his homosexual inclination. But it would take great shrewdness to give importance to the signs he brings out, especially the following:

My modesty in front of men was excessive and, when my mother, on the advice of our doctor, had decided to have me take showers (I must then have been barely over twelve), the very idea of standing naked in front of the shower attendant made me sick with apprehension. Had the shower been administered by a woman, I believe I should have accepted with no fuss at all.[8]

André Gide was twelve when he took the hydrotherapeutic cure at Gérardmer, ordered by Dr. Boissier, but at that age a child, brought up ex-

[8] *Et nunc manet in te,* p. 32.

clusively by women and innately timorous, could perfectly well show
"apprehension" before a male shower attendant without having it lead to
absurd conclusions. Besides, as a pederast, mature virility never excited his
desire. Therefore, his "excessive modesty" in front of "shower attendants"
cannot be taken as a convincing sign and seems hardly related to the kind
of temptations that later beset young André Walter.

When André Gide was sufficiently impregnated with Gérardmer's
gentle and balsamic air, his mother, believing him cured, took him back
to Paris, and immediately sent him back to the Ecole Alsacienne after two
years' absence. Before two weeks were up, new difficulties arose which
posed the same problem as the nervous attacks but in other forms.

"I had not been there two weeks before I added headaches to my repertory of nervous disorders, as they were less conspicuous and therefore more
practical in class." Were his headaches then quite simply feigned, as the
word repertory would seem to indicate? After having acted out Saint Vi-
tus' dance or variations on it, was he now acting out cephalalgia? The
hasty and confident statement is immediately qualified by a much less
confident one:

As my headaches left me completely at twenty, and even earlier, I judged them
very severely for some time afterward, accusing them of being, if not altogether feigned, at any rate greatly exaggerated. But now that they have come
back I realize that those at forty-six are exactly like those at thirteen and admit
that they could well have discouraged my attempts to work. . . . There is no
doubt they came at the right moment; I cannot say to what extent I used them.[9]

In other words, he used his migraines for utilitarian ends, but they existed
all the same and were only partly simulated.

The headaches were accompanied by sudden waves of fatigue, making
the schoolboy incapable of any protracted effort. "I was overcome by sudden waves of fatigue, fatigue of the mind, a kind of break in the current,
which continued after the migraine had stopped or, to be more exact,
succeeded it and lasted for days, weeks, months." Gide must have experienced similar "lapses" all through his life. At the same time as the fatigue,
he had an overwhelming impression of ennui, the kind of depression he
would describe so well in *Paludes*. He writes in *Si le grain ne meurt:*

What I then felt was an unspeakable disgust for everything we were doing
in class, for the class itself, the whole idea of lectures and examinations, competitive examinations, even recreation periods, and the fact of sitting motionless on a bench, as well as the general slowness, vapidity, and stagnation.[10]

As always happened in his periods of depression, he slept badly and not

[9] *Si le grain ne meurt,* I, 121–22.
[10] *Ibid.*

more than three or four hours a night. All the disorders were real and yet could be immediately changed by diversion or persuasion: "You say that you can't sleep more than three or four hours a night. Then try and convince yourself that you don't need any more," he was told by the doctor in whom he had confidence,[11] and "comforted by those words," he slept better.[12] His insomnia was due in great part to anxiety; in other words, it was provoked by the fear of not sleeping. Here again is evidence of a characteristic suggestibility.

As the nervous diathesis continued, a new doctor was consulted and he prescribed a sedative that was then fashionable: a bromized syrup of bitter orange peel and chloral. Later in life Gide could not be sarcastic enough with regard to "M. Lizart," who had prescribed the relatively harmless potion:

Nothing is more dangerous than a fool. How can I forgive him his prescriptions and his treatment? As soon as I felt or claimed to feel nervous: bromide; as soon as I was unable to sleep: chloral. For an almost unformed brain! All my later lapses of memory or will I attribute to him. If one could take action against the dead, I would sue him.[13]

The upshot of the "Lizart affair" was that, ever after, Gide deeply distrusted medicines and generally anything toxic. Moreover, he was extremely sensitive to their effects, as are many nervous people, and normally innocuous doses were enough for him. At seventy-nine, Gide was still talking about it and told me: "The bromide I was given when I was a child left me with a dimness of the mind," a dimness he alone noticed.

In October, 1882, after the summer holidays at La Roque, André Gide entered the fifth form at the Ecole Alsacienne. His nervous disorders became so much worse that at the end of the month Mme. Gide, completely at a loss, decided to take her son to Rouen, to the family haven in the rue de Crosne, just as she had done two years before on Paul Gide's death. "My mother resigned herself to treating me like an invalid and accepted the fact that I would learn nothing except by a fluke. In other words, my education was again interrupted and for a long time."

When he recalled the time of his depression at the Ecole Alsacienne, Gide described it as "unspeakable disgust." He found his life tasteless and flat, and his general want of appetite, as a result, was not unrelated to his attack of anorexia, in the alimentary and medical sense of the term. The

11 Doctor Boissier. It would seem that the episode took place during his second stay at Lamalou, in the fall of 1882.

12 *Ainsi soit-il*, p. 130.

13 *Si le grain ne meurt*, p. 123.

episode is important because it shows, for the first time in Gide's life, the psychological origins of the inhibition of an instinct. The disgust for food that he experienced can be put into the category of nervous anorexia or, to use one of his own expressions, into the "repertory" of his nervous disorders.

His appetite did not improve in the rue de Crosne and the change of family air did not have the expected result. Mme. Gide became increasingly worried, watching her son grow thinner from day to day. She was more especially concerned as she thought she saw he threat of Paul Gide's fatal illness hovering over him. As for André, since he was officially considered to be physically ill, he seemed not to be the slightest bit concerned with anything, particularly his health. His anguish was replaced by a kind of indifference or apathy. He let himself float about in the comfortable and padded atmosphere of the large Rouen house, "waited on hand and foot" and in a state of "sluggishness" perhaps not unrelated to the famous bromized syrup of bitter orange peel. It was then, at the end of December, 1882, that a moving event occurred, an event that was to give his life a completely new direction.

André Gide was then thirteen and at the most critical point of what is generally considered to be the awkward age. His health seemed in such jeopardy that his mother had to spare him any effort, and morally, he was right in the midst of a depression:

Decidedly the devil was lying in wait for me; I was completely the prey of shadows and there was no sign of a break through which a ray of light might touch me. It was then that the following angelic intervention occurred to snatch me away from the devil. The event seemed most insignificant but was as important in my life as revolutions are for empires—the first scene of a drama which is not yet played out.[14]

It was in these solemn tones that Gide announced the event that was to follow and which caused him to discover both his love for his cousin Madeleine Rondeaux and the "mystic orient" of his life.

The very seriousness of his words authorizes us to consider that "revolution" as a psychological and moral crisis of very great importance. Before going on with the new stage in Gide's life, let us first try to understand his "gloomy" childhood from the inside.

[14] *Ibid.*

11: The Delicate Seed

> *"I did not yet know to what degree native qualities predominate over acquired ones."*
>
> Si le grain ne meurt, *I, 192*

*M*OST of Gide's nervous disorders would have little significance taken individually, but together they unequivocally indicate a constitutional nervous state or, more precisely, neurosis. When Stekel studied the childhood of numerous poets, he very frequently found symptoms of an anxiety neurosis, even in Goethe whose old age was the image of serenity. The fruitfulness of existential anguish is one of the themes Gide insistently developed. In his essay on Dostoevsky he referred to the feeling of an inner lack of balance "at the origins" of the personality of creators and reformers, "a little physiological mystery, an anxiety, an anomaly." Whatever the explanation, the existence of nervous or neurotic disorders in the childhoods of men who were later to become true creators is a fact, and one too frequent to be negligible.

Most psychologists are agreed that to discover "the secret of a human being in the making,"[1] one must go back to the time of his youth. André Gide thought that the end of a life was constructed during its beginnings, and no one was more persuaded than he that the child is father to the man. Having noticed the frequency of children or "hardly formed" creatures in Dostoevsky's works, he praised the great Russian novelist for his interest in "the genesis of feelings" and added: "He was particularly attached to disconcerting cases, to those who rose up in defiance against morality and accepted psychology."[2] And in fact the only way to under-

---

[1] François Mauriac, *Le Jeune Homme,* p. 87.   [2] *Dostoevsky,* p. 183.

stand those who rise up in defiance is through an analysis of their mal-adjusted childhoods.

If Gide was fond of going back to the beginnings of his life, it was in the hope of finding a deeper and more adequate explanation of himself, a hope he never gave up. "I must frankly dare to admit it: It was my solitary and sullen childhood that made me what I am."

Although Gide transposed certain aspects of his childhood into fictional characters—André Walter in *Les Cahiers* and Jérôme in *La Porte étroite,* whose most distant memories are centered on a love for their first cousins, Emanuèle in *Les Cahiers* or Alissa in *La Porte étroite*—most of their feelings belong to a somewhat later period of Gide's life. On the other hand, the childhood of one character in *Les Faux-Monnayeurs,* little Boris Lapérouse, offers several important analogies with that described in the autobiographical *Si le grain ne meurt.* Boris is a thirteen-year-old child whose health is delicate and who is treated by the psychoanalyst Sophroniska for nervous disorders. His malady is an exaggeration of the one Gide suffered from at the same age, just as André Walter's malady is an exaggeration of Gide's difficulties as an adolescent. In that respect it is true that "the work of art is an exaggeration,"[3] but the exaggeration itself is of great psychological interest in that an artificial magnification of traits makes it possible to more easily understand a personality by making its characteristics perceptible to the most unpracticed eye.

Gide had learned of the death of a boy called Nény at the *lycée* of Clermond-Ferrand from an article in the *Journal de Rouen* dated June 5, 1909. The child had been pushed into suicide by a gang of schoolboys who accused him of being different from them. Gide was more especially drawn to the dramatic anecdote in that it immediately reminded him of the great fear of his childhood at the *lycée* of Montpellier. The emotion he felt while reading the news item was in all probability the birth certificate for the future Boris Lapérouse, who was born in the novelist's imagination out of sympathy, as it were. But it was to take much time and many circumstances for that potential character—in the sense that he corresponded to one of André Gide's potentialities, to one of his possible lives—to come into fictional existence.

During the years of *Les Faux-Monnayeurs'* formulation, Gide was initiated into psychoanalysis not only through the reading of Freud but more directly through a Czechoslovakian psychoanalyst, Mme. Sokolnicka, a former student of Freud then living in Paris. Mme. Sokolnicka found her most sympathetic audience in literary circles, principally the group of the

[3] *Journal,* 1893, p. 33.

Nouvelle Revue Française, and Gide and his friends attended many of her lectures. Gide became so interested that he himself went into analysis with her, but he found the sessions tedious and after the fifth one he "cut," which his doctor doubtless interpreted according to the Freudian catechism as "resistance" on the part of her illustrious patient. However, Gide had an extraordinary talent for turning the slightest events in his life to literary account; he was rich in what Paul Valéry called the "implex"—that is, our disposition for being "contingent," but also the obstinacy that makes it possible for a writer to "redeem" any mishaps by relating them to his inner needs. He made Sokolnicka into a fictional character with the Hellenized name of Sophroniska, its Greek root signifying wisdom. He brought her into the yet unborn world of *Les Faux-Monnayeurs* and entrusted her with a case that was particularly difficult to resolve: that of little Boris Lapérouse.

In *Les Faux-Monnayeurs* the novelist Edouard follows Boris' treatment with an interest that does not appear to me as gratuitous. Gide, having attended the psychoanalytical lectures of the *Nouvelle Revue Française,* had been quite naturally led to wonder whether Freud's discoveries were not applicable to his own childhood; Freud's interpretation of personality problems in terms of early family conflicts and the clumsy repression of infantile sexuality awakened certain of Gide's memories. Could the method have cured him at the time he was struggling with his unacknowledged inner difficulties, tormented by a state of nerves which doctors treated by hydropathic cures and sedatives? That was no doubt the question Edouard, his alter ego, asked himself. At the height of his strength and lucidity, Gide was evaluating his former weakness and disorders, and with a curiosity all the more persistent in that it took him back to his early problems, he followed Sophroniska's attempts to cure Boris of his anxiety neurosis.[4] My theory is that the episode in *Les Faux-Monnayeurs* is a kind of confrontation of André Gide's adult ego with his childhood ego or, more precisely, of one of his adult egos with one of his childhood egos. Besides, that retrospective self-examination will help us to understand him at the same age as his fictional alter ego, who was as anxiety-ridden as he and, like him, suffered "abominably"[5] from being "not like the others."

[4] In his old age Gide had grown extremely skeptical with regard to the success of psychoanalysis. Moreover, I have heard him congratulate himself on the fact that at the time of his childhood, the treatment had not yet been discovered and he thus avoided any possibility of having to undergo it. He felt that any such intervention would perhaps have made him different from what he was, and he believed that an artist must alone rid himself of his "complexes" through his works which act as a catharsis, as it were. Of course a neurotic can cure himself through art, but obviously he must be an artist.

[5] "He suffers abominably from being excluded." *Les Faux-Monnayeurs,* III, 481.

When at eleven, André Gide cried out "I'm not like the others!" it was a cry of anguish: "I was more terrified than sad." It seems that nothing particular happened preceding the emotional explosion except the sharp and unexplained intuitive feeling of being "cut off, excluded." Diverse interpretations of the enigmatic phrase have been given. Some saw it as a precocious awareness of his future homosexuality; yet his homosexuality did not become evident until many years later and was, in my opinion, more a consequence than a cause of the evolution of his personality. The factor of sexual guilt was, of course, part of it, but it would be impossible to give that exclusive a meaning to a state of panic in which the entire being felt strange and foreign. Others blamed it on the influence of the very special milieu—the Huguenot *bourgeoisie*—in which Gide was brought up, and certain French Protestants have thus tried to explain their own feeling of solitude.

Regardless of the theories, Gide did feel the mysterious foreboding of a difference as an immeasurable danger, as a threatening inferiority at the beginning of his struggles for life. Whether the perils that terrified Gide as a child were real or imagined is of small importance. What is important is the fact that he believed he was in danger and that he was excessively or fallaciously aware of it. The feelings of insecurity and inferiority appear here to be closely related, and we must go back to the source of the anguish—that is, to find the origins of the weakness, imaginary or real.

A feeling of inferiority is always a complicated knot made up of many twisted threads which are easier to cut than to disentangle. Many are the factors, physical and psychological, moral and social, that could have played a part in causing the painful impression of being not only different but inferior to others. It is necessry to try and distinguish between what came from the seed and what from the milieu, between how much was innate and how much acquired, between how much was due to temperament and how much to conflicts, or more generally, between how much was constitutional and how much institutional, in the broad sense with which Montaigne, for example, speaks of the "institution of children." It is, in fact, the conjunction of all those elements that provoked the conjuncture of Gide's anxieties at the age of thirteen.

To start with, Gide's puny appearance and weak constitution were a cause for humiliation and fear in the vulnerable child. He felt, or convinced himself, that he was weaker and less well-armed than the others. He constantly compared himself to them, and they appeared to him "perceptibly more strapping." When at the age of belligerent games he carefully avoided them, it was less because he felt "peaceable" than out of the fear of "being defeated." The fear was so deeply rooted in him that his brief "triumph" at the Vedel's, which won him "the respect of the others," was not enough to do away with it. Even more than the blows and brutalities inflicted on him by certain of his schoolmates, he suffered from their disdain. The battles on the playground foreshadowed a universe of games in which he felt defeated in advance.

On the other hand, if we are to believe Gide's recollections—and they seem to be confirmed by photographs and Marie Leuenberger's testimony —he was an ugly child, a fact of small importance had he not been excessively aware of his ugliness. He found the others better looking than he and more especially in that he felt ashamed of the "ridiculous getup" his mother forced him to wear. "How badly your mother dresses you, my poor boy!" says beautiful Aunt Lucile to her dismayed nephew in *La Porte étroite*. The "poor boy" was grieved about his inferiority with regard to clothes (he was later to compensate brilliantly for it), and the episode at the Pascaud Gymnasium, where he felt so humiliated at wearing a mediocre costume, is significant. He felt "sick at heart" when he compared himself to a sparkling little devil. And his abjection was caused, no doubt, more by a burning feeling of inferiority than by a flaming attraction at that point for the devil.

A feeling of physical inferiority would appear to have played a part in André Gide's early sympathy for lame, sickly, destitute children, "Mouton," for example, and all those who are not up to the others. And the trait remained constant in the future author of *Acquasanta*.[6] In that respect, one of M. Pierre Herbart's remarks seems pertinent:

I don't believe it can be seen as a perversion; but on the contrary, how can I express it? a kind of humility. Gide suddenly became human. It seemed that between him and those scrofulous creatures, those village idiots, those cripples, there was some common measure. He then expressed what was perhaps the best of himself (and it was not pity). As though he felt bound up with their deformities; as though he *recognized* himself in them.[7]

Yet Gide had none of those organic infirmities so often said to be at the origins of an inferiority complex: no congenital anomaly, none of those diseases or humiliating malformations such as Jean-Jacques Rousseau's enuresis, Sainte-Beuve's hypospadias, or Byron's clubfoot, no endocrine or even sexual insufficiency. If André Gide, like his young double Boris Lapérouse, "seemed like a girl" to his schoolmates, it was because of his upbringing and his manner, his shyness, his emotivity, his blushing modesty, even his dislike for using slang expressions which were considered a definite sign of virility by the "brotherhood of Strong Men." A young boy

6 *Feuillets d'automne*, p. 48.

7 Pierre Herbart, *A la recherche d'André Gide*.

brought up according to Victorian standards is easily considered by a collectivity of schoolboys as a traitor to his sex. In *Le Journal des Faux-Monnayeurs* Gide points out that Boris' schoolmates made fun of his "chastity" and derisively implied that it was "impotence." Young Gide's chastity, like Boris', was merely on the surface, and in fact his sexual instinct was as precocious as it was long-lived. He was normally built, and during puberty all the secondary sexual characteristics of virility were apparent. Biologically he had no sexual inferiority, which does not mean that a feeling of sexual inferiority—quite a different matter—did not have considerable importance in creating his later inhibitions with the feminine sex and in developing his pedophilia.

Yet there was one anomaly in his constitution, but the anomaly was of a nervous not a sexual nature. Although generally unrecognized except by Gide himself, it did not elude the Swedish psychologist Göran Schildt. In his book *Gide and the Man* he devotes a preliminary study to what he calls "the morbid point in Gide": "If we examine his life closely enough, we notice in effect that he, more than anyone, can be numbered among those whose lives are attempts to re-establish a threatened equilibrium."[8] What then is the anomaly? Here the problem is not a sexual one but rather that of a psychological tendency which Schildt calls "a complex of self-awareness, a mania for introspection, a tendency toward a dual personality," and to which he attributes the feelings of ambiguity, of the unreality of the real, and of bad faith. He points out that the anomaly dates from childhood and he relates it to an "innate weakness," made worse by a Protestant upbringing. He even seems to interpret that innate weakness as a weakness in vital energy. His conception singularly recalls that of Pierre Janet, who was the first to interpret the difficulties in adjusting to reality as a constitutional disturbance in nervous energy or, more precisely, in the flow of psychological tension. In that perspective the delicate nature of the source is much more of a handicap to the vital impetus than the obstacles that impede its flow, for a more vigorous nature would not have been hindered.

A study of André Gide's constitution could only be made together with that of the whole of his personality, but from childhood the fundamental traits of his nervous temperament were evident. To say that a child has a nervous temperament does not indicate much, for there are many ways of being nervous. Gide's way was rather special and corresponds to what the Ancients called irritable weakness, a mixture of excitability and nervous depression, and what today is called constitutional anxiety. Anxiety is of course far too complex to be explained simply by a temperament, but it is true that one is predisposed to it by a certain type of nervous tempera-

[8] Göran Schildt, *Gide et l'homme*, p. 16.

ment and is therefore especially vulnerable to conflicts. The so-called anxious constitution combines an excessive emotivity (the irritability) and a basic ambivalence (the weakness), shown by a feeling of doubt and indecision. These would be natural traits, inscribed in the organism from birth, innate forms of sensitivity and intelligence, as it were, more or less passed on by heredity. From that point of view, one is born anxious and doubting and remains so definitively, whatever the fluctuations linked to the vicissitudes of situations, complexes, and conflicts. The "native" qualities, to use Gide's expression, predominate over the "acquired" ones, and the role of the constitution over that of the institution or the events of an individual's history.

Of course, the idea of constitution or innateness, which amounts to the same thing, should not be confused with that of heredity. Every birth is a creation, and nothing is in the individual which is not in his parents except the individual himself. Congenitally, he depends less on his donors than on their combined gift, and through the conjunction of their two strains, they might have endowed him with qualities and defects they themselves never had. Yet it is rare for a weak, nervous person not to have descended from very sensitive stock, for him not to have been prefabricated, so to speak, by long generations of emotional doubting and scrupulous ancestors who prepared the delicacy of his "natural fabric," its weave, and its texture. It is rare not to find in the ancestors of an anxious child some analogous tendencies, sometimes obvious, sometimes latent, either because of their moderation or because they have been hidden by a "constant effort" at self-domination and a rigidity of compensation, of which André Gide's mother seems to be a living example.

A general nervous irritability, not in the sense of irascibility but of excitability, is relatively frequent in the childhoods of those who make up the *genus irritabile vatum,* an emotional, imaginative, and often capricious tribe. From the nocturnal terrors of his early years to the inhibitions of the schoolboy paralyzed in class by shyness, everything testifies to the fact that Gide had been a hyperemotional child. Even at eighteen, when studying for the first part of the *baccalauréat* at the Ecole Alsacienne, he was to feel "nervous and much less stimulated than embarrassed by the presence of twenty-five other boys," and when Pierre Louis, a fellow student, spoke to him for the first time, he felt incapable of answering. He was also subject to true emotional drunkenness, as shown by his excessive joy as well as his excessive suffering. Indeed, he belonged to that race of anxious children described by a poet as discovering life "from shudder to shudder."

His exaggerated emotivity was accompanied by a nervous erethism which in a sense is the physical aspect of an emotional constitution: a particular sensitivity to impressions transmitted by the nerves, extreme reactions of the sympathetic nervous system and a predisposition to spasmodic states, and finally a light and disturbed sleep, that great regulator of excitability.

As a child, Gide's excessive sensitivity gave him both pleasure and pain. His tactile hyperesthesia was such that even contact with rough material was painful and made wearing a hard collar and starched shirt "real torture." On the other hand, he was particularly responsive to the subtle and varied sensations he discovered at Lamalou and in its pool, and at almost the same age, his senses were also awakened on the Cour Vesque farm at La Roque, where he played with his friend Lionel:

Perhaps our greatest pleasure came from our contact with the fruits of the earth, our plunging into the thick of the harvest, our bathing in varied odors. O the perfume of the dried alfalfa, the pungent scents of the pigsty, the stable, and the cowshed! the heady vapors of the cider press, and there, further on, between the casks, those icy draughts carrying a smell of stale cider mixed with a slight touch of mold. Yes, later on I came to know the intoxicating fumes of the wine harvest but, like the Shulamite who asked to be comforted with apples, I breathe in their exquisite ether in preference to the dull sweetness of new wine.[9]

Getting drunk on the exquisite ether of apples shows a temperament that is hardly astonishing in the future author of *Les Nourritures terrestres,* and that page, among many others, shows Gide's natural disposition for "sensory interests," as some psychologists delicately put it.[10]

An intense organic sensitivity to variations in temperature, air pressure, or the hygrometric degree of the atmosphere was another aspect of his hyperesthesia. His sensitivity to cold—"I really feel the cold"—was less extraordinary than Proust's but very unusual all the same. His mood was greatly influenced by climate, and there was certainly something physical in the "boredom" and the "heaviness" which he described as caused by the rainy climate of Normandy, or the "joyfulness" he derived from "the dry, exhilarating air" of the south of France. He also had a great nervous sensitivity to storms. At twenty he wrote to his mother from the mountains: "The moral effect of these storms is extraordinary—on me at any rate—I cringe with terror."[11] And as a child his nervous erethism was such that during the night he would wake up with a start at the slightest noise, as if his whole system were on the alert even while he slept.

His natural inclination to blush when under the strain of emotion did

[9] *Si le grain ne meurt,* I, 171–72.

[10] In his *Traité pratique d'analyse du caractère* Gaston Berger uses Gide's temperament for his examples of "sensory interests."

[11] Letter from André Gide to his mother, June 22, 1890, unpublished.

not elude his classmates, and the fear of blushing in public made him blush even more. Outside of such vasomotor difficulties, his general tendency to have spasms can be seen in the many physical disorders of his childhood: nervous attacks, respiratory problems including "deep suffocation," migraine headaches. But the most distressing of all was surely his insomnia, the price he paid for all the rest. Gide suffered from it all his life, from childhood on: "I have always had insomnia. . . . It is a question of temperament."[12]

On the other hand, he had a tendency to exteriorize his emotions, contrary to the repressed nervous type's tendency to inhibit any outward manifestation. Perhaps because of his temperament but also out of a concern for security and a taste for thwarting his own nature, a result of his upbringing but later on more a question of aesthetics, he learned to control the pantomime and gestures of emotion, except when it was irrepressible, and affected a feigned impassiveness that could have made him seem stiff or cold. "There was so much hidden nervousness in my case. . . ." Those words, which he used in regard to later disorders, could well describe certain of his childhood difficulties.

Repressed emotion can be dangerous for nervous equilibrium. The motor expressions of emotion—for example, the gestures of aggression in anger, the gestures of flight in fear—can be inhibited, but everything happens as if the obstacle to the outer derivation of the discharge had as a corollary an even more powerful inner derivation. In fact, the repressed emotion is not accompanied by the relief that follows motor reactions; it produces an afflux of inner irritations which are not resolved and the tension remains. For example, if a state of irascible excitement does not result in muscular or verbal aggression against the object that provoked the anger, it creates a lasting impression of malaise. At the Ecole Alsacienne, except for the one memorable episode, Gide put up with his schoolmates' hazing and even their blows with apparent patience, and controlled his aggression as well as his other emotions. When he had his nervous attacks in Montpellier at the age of eleven, his outward manifestations gave him great "relief."

Another aspect of his nervous temperament was apparent during the Montpellier "attacks": an emotional suggestibility, a certain plasticity which made possible a physical actualization of the image and in a sense its embodiment. The "I convinced myself," which Gide so often repeated it became almost a habit of style,[13] shows an innate tendency toward self-

---

[12] *Ainsi soit-il*, p. 128.

[13] He repeated it as frequently as the "Ah!", an emotional interjection in which Saint-Clair sees "the very respiration of his lyricism." (M. Saint-Clair, *Galerie privée*, p. 154). *Translator's note:* Saint-Clair is the pseudonym of Mme. Théo Van Rysselberge.

persuasion, obvious ever since childhood. An inclination to imitate what he imagined can be seen in other episodes of *Si le grain ne meurt,* such as the ones concerning Mouton or the costume party. His incentive for putting himself in Mouton's place was of course sympathy, but a sympathy that should not be mistaken for true charity although it could have been its point of departure. The episode implies what André Gide's sympathy was to become, a kind of surrender of the ego to another, which appears more as empathy or emotional parasitism than as *agape.* It was less altruism than a thirst for the presence of someone else or of a transformation by someone else in a common emotion, an ecstasy, a giddiness. Losing his heart was a way for him to lose himself, but only momentarily: he became infatuated, he forgot himself in a state of emotional intoxication, but once the raptures had passed, he was ashamed at having thus been at the mercy of his nerves.

In the episode of the Pascaud Gymnasium costume party, the prospect of a disguise not only pleased him, which is indeed natural at that age, but threw him into a real "delirium" as he imagined the joy of "pretending to be someone else." Pretending to be someone else is obviously one of the pleasures of acting, but becoming someone else is true acting. The idea of a disguise to such an emotional and suggestible ego meant the act of becoming someone else, which is one of the reasons Gide attached such great importance to costume, and not only during his childhood. But even as a child he in no way needed a disguise to convince him that his inner self depended on his outward appearance. He had only to look at himself in the little mirror he received from Anna Shackleton to notice that his feelings were more determined by his expressions than his expressions by his feelings.

Gide's intense and suggestible emotivity was also subject to astonishing changes. The child who became excited and even upset by the slightest thing could be surprisingly indifferent, or at any rate unpredictable, in other circumstances. He went from an abundance of "heart," as André Walter was to say romantically, to a distressing coldness, just as all his life Gide was to oscillate between fervor and depression, like the symbolic Urien between two perils, the emotion of the Pathetic Ocean and the boredom of the Saragasso Sea. Ever since childhood he had experienced that boredom or "ennui" he described in *Si le grain ne meurt* as his "lapses" explained in terms of "variations of inner temperature or pressure."[14] Gide's word "pressure" is equivalent to the word "tension" used by Pierre Janet to designate variations in psychological and nervous potential. Gide kept coming back to that particular characteristic as if to emphasize its importance. For example, in *Ainsi soit-il:*

[14] *Journal,* 1944, p. 204.

A lack of self-confidence can become paralyzing. Not to be able to count on oneself. Will the person who keeps an appointment be the same as the one who made it? Whence my withdrawals, my escapes, my flights, my apparent inconstancy. Not to recognize others is bad enough; but how annoying not to recognize oneself![15]

With regard to inconstancy, Gide wrote: "I think the real question is hidden behind that word. And it is there that I shall begin my search."[16] The word inconstancy does hide many inner drives, but one of them is certainly nervous lability, one of the constants of the psychophysiology of an inconstant disposition. An intense and capricious emotivity, a receptivity to suggestions of the imaginary, an instability of the great vital rhythms, a lability of mood give the feeling of inconstancy and contribute to creating anxiety and lack of self-confidence.

All such characteristics of nervous irritability are common to the emotional constitution and the anxious constitution, which is merely an exaggeration of it, adding a permanent feeling of insecurity with regard to everything and nothing, a basic uneasiness, vague and diffuse, which because of diverse influences becomes anxiety or anguish. Consequently, the childhood of a man who is constitutionally anxious usually leaves him with the impression of a painful beginning. Whatever its joys, he will, like Gide, tend to remember it as "gloomy" and to darken it even more. He harbors an indefinable bitterness about his early life, which itself will cast gloom over its most radiant moments because, more than anyone else, he has the feeling of their precariousness: "Medio de fonte leporum, quid amari surgit, quod ipsis in floribus angat nescio."

Although the idea of nervous irritability is easily understandable, the same is not true for the other aspect of the so-called anxious constitution: nervous weakness. It is not at all an intellectual weakness, for it is compatible with the highest intellectual qualities and even seems to favor them to a certain extent; it is not especially a physical weakness in the usual sense, and those who are victims of it can look as robust as Gide looked sickly and puny during his childhood; nor is it actually a weakness of the will, although indecision is a result of it and has often been thus interpreted. It consists in a very special psychological weakness in energy or in the nervous structure which makes adjustment to reality, a grasp of reality, acts of belief, and reasons for action abnormally difficult.

The nervously weak person is always a doubter who dreads making decisions and translating them into action. He tends to withdraw into

[15] *Ainsi soit-il*, pp. 104–5.
[16] *Essai sur Montaigne, O.C.*, XV, 15.

himself and incessantly examines his inner world, which is often troubled by doubts, hesitations, obsessing scruples, and sometimes even true obsessions. He suffers from a feeling of inadequacy and ambivalence, a feeling heightened by his conflicts but pre-existing them, for here we are dealing with the innate characteristics of a temperament. We have only to open André Gide's *Journal* at random to find a description of the feelings of inadequacy, strangeness, duality, the unreality of the real, the state of doubt and ambivalence, obsessing and compulsive constraints, the same that had been described and patiently analyzed by Pierre Janet. Such passages are a combination of literary self-observation and scientific objective observation, of which there are many other instances in Gide's works.[17] The combination is all the more extraordinary in that Gide—and of this I made certain —had no direct knowledge of Janet's works. But what is important to note here are the early signs of the nervous weakness Gide chose to call his "deficiency" and which he later analyzed with admirable lucidity.

"I believe it comes . . . from my lack of a certain *sense of reality*. I can be extremely sensitive to the outer world, but I never completely manage to believe in it." What Gide here attributes to some mystery of the endocrine glands is an extremely complex mental synthesis, the very one that Pierre Janet analyzed in his memorable studies concerning what he called the "function of reality."[18] He considered that a weakness in the function of reality is the cause for the entire range of the feelings of inadequacy or what Gide would call "lack," of strangeness or what Gide would call "estrangement," of duality or what Gide would call "second reality," of inconsistency or what Gide would call "deconsistency." Gide experienced those feelings all his life, but even as a small child he had feelings of unreality and the duality of reality: for example, his impression of a "second reality" at the rue de Crosne ball and his doubt that the woman he recognized was "really she," or his impression of "exoticism" with regard to his young friend Armand Bavretel's family, the "estrangement" which "went to my head and after a short time made me completely lose the notion of reality; everything began to float around me, to lose consistency, to turn into fantasy, not only the place, the people, the talk, but myself, even my own voice seemed to come from a distance and its sound astonished me."[19]

[17] For example, certain passages from his 1893 *Journal* in relation to *La Tentative amoureuse* are remarkable in that they anticipate certain of Freud's texts.

[18] It consists in "the apprehension of reality through perception or through action, and modifies all the other operations according to whether it adds to them or does not add to them" (Pierre Janet).

[19] *Si le grain ne meurt,* I, 183.

The impression of being split into actor and spectator, and of living in a world that is not quite real, creates a feeling of theater or, at any rate, of illusion. Later in life that psychological characteristic was heightened in Gide by various influences, particularly that of being a professional littérateur, but it was no less innate. It is always the same type of nervously weak person who experiences the feelings of inadequacy, strangeness, duality, and the inconsistency of reality, whether in regard to the outer or the inner world.

There is something enigmatic about the will of a nervously weak person. Anyone who knows he is at the mercy of his nerves, who knows he is at the mercy of the whims or breakdowns of his nervous mechanism, is more especially in need of a *quid inconcussum*. The more fluid, inconstant, and inconsistent he feels, the more he needs a constraint that will make it possible for him to hold his being together and keep it in control. He is lost and bewildered if he does not find a religion that will bind his separate states together like the pages of a book. As a kind of compensation, the mobility of his nature calls for the restraining rigor of an ideal. Of course, the weakness of his belief makes it difficult for him to concentrate on a single objective, but when he has found that objective he clings to it with an obstinacy that determines his whole life. He thus replaces his indecision by a spirit of obstinacy, with all the artificial strain that the word implies. Gide as a child had not yet found that support, that *idée fixe* he was to discover later on in the exigency of an artistic ideal to which he subordinated everything, just as Maine de Biran had discovered it in the exigency of a philosophical system based on a sense of effort, without overlooking the fact that such an ideal corresponded to the demands of his nervous temperament.[20] *Faiblesse oblige.*

The conjunction of an intense, labile, capricious emotivity and the ambivalence of a doubter makes reality and action abnormally difficult and creates an anxious feeling of inconstancy and inconsistency. Whatever the intellectual superiority associated with that type of temperament (in many cases even becoming an instrument of it, as evidenced by the long list of talented men who were endowed or afflicted with it), it does, from the elementary viewpoint of a struggle for existence, represent an inferiority,

[20] Maine de Biran, whose nervous temperament from childhood on offers so many analogies with André Gide's, understood the relation of nervous weakness to the necessity of effort. If he based his philosophy on a sense of effort, it was because his personality constantly brought him back to the problem of the will, the sore point of any nervous person.

at least at the start. The destiny of a nervous child appears to be something to worry about because the child's complicated constitution implies more possibilities of failure than chances of success; and sucess, when it comes, is all the more praiseworthy in that it is a triumph over an innate weakness; but the effort needed to compensate for the initial lack of balance will have its price and the man, however great, who grows from that delicate seed, will always be somehow incomplete.

12: A Guilty Child

> *"Decidedly the devil was lying in wait for me."*
>
> Si le grain ne meurt, *I, 123*

URING Gide's childhood, most doctors were little concerned with the moral origins of anxiety. It was attributed to constitutional nervousness, bound up with a nervous temperament. The innate factor is indeed very important, but the part played by psychological conflicts is equally so. Without conflicts there would be no neuroses, but without a constitutional predisposition, the conflicts would not lead to neuroses.

Today the influence of pyschoanalysis has made it apparent that certain childhood anxieties are closely linked to early sexual problems, or more precisely, to the conflict between instinctive demands and opposing moral constraints. We know that before the publication of *Si le grain ne meurt,* André Gide knew about Freud's conceptions of infantile sexuality. "Here's something that will bring grist to your mill," Jacques Rivière had said to him with regard to a number of the *Disque vert* devoted to Freud. Although he claimed not to have been influenced by the Viennese psychiatrist, Gide did admit that he had found in his works a kind of "authorization"[1] to say what was generally kept hidden:

It seems to me that what I should be most grateful to him for is to have accustomed readers to hearing certain subjects treated without having to protest or

---

[1] "It seems to me that had I not known Dostoevsky, or Nietzsche, or Freud, or X, or Z, I would have thought in exactly the same way, and that I found in them an authorization rather than an awakening. Above all, they taught me to stop doubting myself, not to be afraid of my own thought, and to let myself be led by it, since in any case *I found them in it*" (*Journal,* 1924, p. 781).

blush. What he brings us mostly is audacity; or more exactly, he rids us of a certain false and embarrassing modesty.[2]

On several points Gide's autobiographical anecdotes in *Si le grain ne meurt* seem to illustrate the Freudian theories of the infantile libido. "Personally I cannot say whether I learned about sexual pleasure from someone or in what way I discovered it; but as far back as I can remember, I knew about it." The solitary habits he seemed at first to take for relatively innocent games appeared to him as really sinful after he was sent away from the Ecole Alsacienne. When at nine years old he was sent to Doctor Brouardel, was he not terrified by the doctor's solemn threat of an operation? It is rare for that allusion to the most primitive of punishments (etymologically, the words castigation and castration have the same root) not to cause an emotional shock in nervous children, and consequently every subsequent reference to sexual pleasure revives an anguish that can even lead to impotence. Repression thus goes beyond its objective and connects sexuality with danger, making any manifestations of it threatening. In the fable the guilty child Osiris was cut up in pieces and although he managed to gather his broken bits together, he always lacked, according to certain legendary versions, a choice piece: the phallus. So that the myth of Osiris became the symbol of the castration complex.

However if we refer to what Gide wrote, it was not the corporal punishment he feared, for he never really believed it would take place, but the moral punishment implicit in his father's "silent grief" and his mother's much more loquacious despair. The shame of being responsible for their distress, the fear of losing their affection, the reprobation he felt around him overwhelmed the lonely little boy living between the two household gods. And we must realize how dishonorable, considering the milieu and the circumstance, being immediately sent away from school was and the proportions the incident took in a childish and apprehensive imagination. Besides, it is probable that the guilt feeling was only partly linked to the clumsy repression of masturbation, which was itself no doubt responsible for reviving older prohibitions connected with the very first training of the instincts.[3] From the very beginning, bringing up a child means teaching him to give up forbidden pleasures in order to obtain promised love.

Under the immediate influence of prohibitions, Gide seemed to have abruptly renounced his habits and three months later reappeared on a bench at the Ecole Alsacienne, "cured, at any rate about as much as one ever is." In all events it is certain that he did not again give in to the

[2] *Journal*, 1924, p. 785.

[3] We know almost nothing about Gide's very first years, and the gap will be regretted by those who believe in the importance of the initial stages in the formation of the personality.

temptation until after an obsessing struggle which continued well beyond childhood and filled André Walter's *Cahier noir*.

Yet the solitary sins were gradually replaced by most ambiguous reveries. Commenting in his 1924 *Journal* about the number of the *Disque vert* devoted to Freud, Gide noted:

Ah! how annoying Freud is! and it seems to me that we would have surely managed to discover his America without him! . . . But how many absurd things in that imbecile of genius![4] Were it as thwarted as sexual appetite, mere appetite (hunger) would be the great supplier of Freudianism (just as we see thirst prompt the dreams of those who lack water while crossing the desert). In other words: certain fears are violent because they have no outlet. It is true that sexual desire, when not directly satisfied, is prone to manifold hypocrisies—I mean: of taking the most diverse forms—which the other hunger can never do.[5]

Do those "manifold hypocrisies," created by sexual repression, refer to the strange and anguishing reveries Gide experienced from the age of ten and which followed the abrupt repression of masturbation in his ninth year?

The special nature of the phantasms that followed the repression of masturbation seems to me the link between the images of failure, punishment, destruction, and sensual pleasure. That undoubtedly dangerous link, brought back by the emotional shock due to the recent prohibitions, was probably of long standing and contemporary with the early stages of the development of infantile sexuality. We know the importance Freud attached to the initial stages in the development of sadistic and masochistic tendencies—that is, the pleasure of punishing and destroying, or of punishing and destroying oneself. And those are indeed the tendencies underlying the sensual reveries of Gide's childhood, but naturally reduced to a puerile scale which could mask their true nature: no desire for others, no need to caress, kiss, or embrace, but images that signify something quite different from the love impulse.

In *Si le grain ne meurt* Gide explains that at about the age of ten, when his maid Marie would take him to the Luxembourg Museum, it was not the paintings and statues of nudes that suggested sexual pleasure to him, nor did sexual pleasure evoke such images. "No connection between the two. The things that excited me sexually were quite different."[6] And among them he particularly mentioned:

The idea of the urgency of some important act which I should perform, which people count on, which they expect from me, which I do not perform,

[4] A phrase just as brilliant and unfair as his too-well-known "Hugo, alas!"

[5] *Journal*, 1924, pp. 785–86.

[6] *Si le grain ne meurt*, I, 61.

which instead of performing, I imagine; and also the related idea of plunder which took the shape of my spoiling a favorite toy.

It was again the idea of surrendering himself to obscure forces, losing himself in them, annihilating himself by them, the impression of dissolving in a watery element,[7] the Protean dreams (even then!) of depersonalization and transformation that went as far as magical metamorphosis.[8]

Gide then added the example of George Sand's character Gribouille who, as he floated in the river, was transformed into a delicate branch of oak, remarking that for him the vegetal metamorphosis became one of his "themes of sexual pleasure." And there were others, such as the disaster of a smashed pile of dishes in Madame de Ségur's play *Les Dîners de Mademoiselle Justine* which made him "swoon"[9] and where we see the indissoluble connection between anguish and sensual pleasure.

One component of those phantasms was aggression, whether it was turned against himself or against others. An indication of the instinct for destruction, a primitive tendency or a secondary reaction to an early frustration, can be found in André Gide's early childhood. It is apparent in the games he played at the time he described himself from a photograph as "looking sickly and bad tempered, with shifty eyes," when he took pleasure in destroying what he loved, his tin soldiers, for example, or what others loved, such as the "pretty" mud pies of the children in the Luxembourg Gardens, or bit his "beautiful" De Flaux cousin to the point of drawing blood. We have already seen that certain of his solitary and somewhat Neronian games showed a precocious aggression which his upbringing taught him to conceal and which reappeared later on in other forms. But the less his aggression was exteriorized, the more it was turned inward and thus against himself.

The phantasms resulting from the brutal attempt at sexual repression and, later on, the obsessive nature of his solitary habits are marked by the same self-aggression. Masturbation gradually ceased being the naïve hedonism of his early childhood and became involved with a far more dangerous pleasure, a certain taste for harming himself, destroying himself, "madly exhausting himself," a surrender to the "abyss" where he giddily foundered after an obsessing and vain struggle. It was precisely that dangerous side of masturbation, which in certain neurotics can reach the point of becoming the equivalent of a search for exhaustion, that Gide emphasized in *Les Faux-Monnayeurs* with regard to little Boris: "He felt that

[7] Water phantasms continued to play a part in his personal mythology, and I shall come back to them with regard to the symbolism of *Le Voyage d'Urien.*

[8] Gide emphasized the link between sexuality and magic with regard to little Boris Lapérouse's magic formulas in *Les Faux-Monnayeurs.*

[9] *Si le grain ne meurt,* I, 62.

he was going to his ruin, that he was sinking very far from heaven; but he enjoyed going to his ruin and made that very perdition a sensual pleasure."[10]

Many have tried to explain Gide's future homosexuality by the instinctive manifestations of those first years, as well as his pathetic comment "I'm not like the others!" which to my mind should be interpreted much more generally. None of Gide's friendships up to the age of thirteen was homosexual. In *Si le grain ne meurt* he tells about the "real passion" he felt for a Russian boy at the Ecole Alsacienne, and how at the Pascaud Gymnasium costume party he fell "positively in love" with a "little devil" dressed in "black tights covered with steel spangles." The words *passion* and *love* evoke extreme feelings which could possibly slip into sensuality, but the fact is that they did not. And even had Gide been involved in homosexual friendships as a child, it would be impossible from that to predict anything for the future. It is frequent for children, before their sexual instincts are mature, to be undecided as to their choice of one sex or the other. In fact, mutual masturbation between boys is so widespread in certain school collectivities that it would be more likely to give rise to the feeling of being "the same as others" than that of being not the same as others. At any rate, André Gide's childhood gives no evidence of alloeroticism, but it does show a very ambiguous autoeroticism that was to become André Walter's narcissism: self-love and self-hate. And that abnormally prolonged narcissism did play a large part in the development of Gide's pedophilia.

André Gide transposed his own early sexual conflict to the character little Boris. In *Les Faux-Monnayeurs* Boris' nervous disorders and anguish are attributed by the psychoanalyst Sophriniska to the same "big shameful secret" as Gide's. Since the age of nine Boris indulged in masturbation and called his solitary vice "making magic." He had been caught by his mother, who reprimanded him to such a degree that he became frightened, and then his nervous illness began. The novelist Edouard, to whom Sophroniska explained her theory, was not convinced that the reason for it lay in the big shameful secret. Yet he was extremely interested in the disastrous role she attributed to the mother's severe reproaches and Boris' resulting anxiety. "If I understand you correctly, you think it would have been less harmful for Boris to continue peacefully indulging in his practice of 'magic?'" And Sophroniska replied: "I think there was no need to frighten him in order to cure him. . . . Nothing good is ever accomplished through terror."[11]

[10] *Les Faux-Monnayeurs*, III, 483.　　　　　　　[11] *Ibid.*, II, 265.

Like Sophroniska, most analysts see an anxiety neurosis not as a result of sexual frustration, as Freud had first interpreted it, but as a completely psychological reaction to the moral repression of instincts, leading to a feeling of guilt. According to them, it is the sin as such which links the anguish to a pleasure that has become a fault; in other words, it is not the revenge of sexuality but the retribution of morality, not the result of frustration but of prohibition. The anguish of guilt is then in a sense self-punishment by the conscience.

In Gide the guilt feeling created by the pressure of his instincts was all the more intense in that his conscience was formed by a puritanical upbringing. In fact, his conscience was essentially formed under the influence of his mother. Juliette Gide was as severe as a Protestant minister when it came to sexual purity, which she considered the most categorical imperative:

In bourgeois society the greatest sin is stealing; for a Puritan society it is any sexual infringement. Encouraged by that limitation of the moral domain is the idea that anomalies such as pride, hypocrisy, hardheartedness, and avarice can be considered as outside the moral problem, which is so taken up by the supposedly formidable sexual problem.[12]

For a true Calvinist, an offence against purity is the deadly sin par excellence. In his *Journal* Gide was to compare humorously his condition to that of "a little boy who amuses himself combined with a Protestant minister who bores him." That coexistence of two characters of different ages, habits, and morals, became peaceable in the course of time, but at the beginning it was intolerable. The word "boredom" is hardly strong enough to evoke the distress the guilty boy was caused by his vigilant minister.

Gide himself told how, brought up by austere Christian women "to whom the attribution of any slight disturbance of the flesh would have been an insult," he precociously made sexuality into a real "monster," a "dragon." When his mother put him to shame because of his bad habits, he certainly felt crushed with guilt in front of such an irreproachable judge. In *Les Faux-Monnayeurs* he described Boris' confusion in a similar situation in the following terms:

His mother, I imagine, scolded him, implored him, lectured him. Then his father died. Boris was convinced that this was the punishment for the secret practices he had been told were so sinful; he held himself responsible for his father's death; he thought he was criminal, damned. He took fright. . . .[13]

It is fairly common for nervous and religious children, terrified by touching admonitions, to believe that their "deadly sin" made them responsible

[12] Paul Arbousse-Bastide, *Optimisme catholique et pessimisme protestant,* quoted by E.-G. Léonard, *Le Protestant français,* p. 199.

[13] *Les Faux-Monnayeurs,* II, 264.

for the death of someone, as if the death stood for their punishment. They interpret any catastrophe or unfortunate occurrence that touches them closely, especially the death of a loved one, as a kind of collective chastisement brought about by their own particular sin. That belief is common to all prelogical mentalities. Boris sees his father's death as a punishment brought about by his sin; was the same true for Gide? There is no conclusive evidence of it. I should only like to point out that he was full of guilt at the time of his first anguish attacks. When he analyzed them retrospectively, he felt the need to situate them in relation to his father's death. Was his choice of that chronological reference purely objective and fortuitous, or did it correspond to an inner need? *Unconscious* motivations of that type are too often given as a reason for the guilt anxiety in children who masturbate to ignore them, even though such theories would surely appear absurd to logical minds.

Ever since childhood, Gide lived in a state of guilt. He experienced a bad conscience, dissimulation, temptation, downfalls, resistance, relapses, remorse, a whole series of moral conflicts later described in *Les Cahiers d'André Walter,* a novel about a carnal obsession pushed to madness in the delicate soul of a Protestant adolescent, and in *Les Faux-Monnayeurs,* in the episode about little Boris Lapérouse, the story of a child who was just as sensitive and just as Protestant.

Many other novelists have testily treated the theme of the young Puritan who became a neurotic because of the severity of his religious upbringing, sometimes by oversimplifying the given elements of the problem. Although it is quite absurd to make Calvinism bear "all the neuropathic sins of the world," it is still true that the puritanical attitude, which severely condemns the sins of the flesh so as to more satisfactorily exalt the ideal aspirations of the soul, contains the potential division of two human natures, the animal and the angelic, which made up André Walter's noble torment and Armand Vedel's dogged malice: "You don't know what an early puritanical upbringing can do to you. It leaves you with an incurable resentment in your heart . . . if I am to judge by myself."[14]

For a Christian child, all the temptations of the flesh, normal or abnormal (although not yet known as such), come from the devil, and it is not astonishing for a mind trained in that belief to be anguished by sexuality; the extraordinary thing would be if it were not. What in the last analysis he finds deadliest in the deadly sin are not the temporal punishments but the loss of his soul, hence on a more or less long-term basis, the eternal tortures of hell. And if Gide as an adult no longer believed in the devil, he did as a child, and if he did not feel the same as the others, it was also because he believed that within himself was the deadly and criminal

[14] *Ibid.,* III, 474.

presence of the "Other."[15] Careful readers of *Si le grain ne meurt* thought they breathed in a smell of sulphur and could sense the *sugillae diaboli,* so well known to inquisitors and exorcisers. In the greenest years of the future immoralist, they could recognize a person "possessed," as Henri Massis said, or "inhabited," as Paul Claudel put it. Whatever such insights are worth, it is probable that in the "darkness" in which he was then struggling, he recognized with terror the presence of the bad Prince, whose kingdom for all eternity has been darkness. The fears of his childhood nightmares were no more anguishing than his fear of being "damned" at the hour of trial. As a solitary child, he had no one to confide in to help him out of such anguishing darkness, nor as a Protestant child did he have the help of confession.

In the Catholic religion confession brings relief with the verbal expression of sin. Psychoanalysis, that secular faith, has been said to be successful in Anglo-Saxon countries because of their Protestantism and relatively unsuccessful in Latin countries because of their Catholicism. But the sacrament of confession goes much further than psychoanalysis: it makes it possible to relegate a sin to the past, for it absolves it after an act of penitence followed by a firm resolution not to commit it again, and ends by an act of grace, which is perhaps its most "saving" psychological element. A Catholic child relies on the confessor to judge his acts and his thoughts. A Protestant child learns very early to judge them all by himself, and gets into the habit of examining his conscience without a priest as intermediary. Thus every night Gide examined his conscience, a practice he continued almost all through his life: "Actually I no longer keep accounts as I once did; I no longer, at night before trying to fall alseep, practice what the Protestant calls self-examination; I act as if I had passed the examination."[16] That happy Pharisaism was not shared by the child of *Si le grain ne meurt;* on the contrary, he had the depressing impression of failing and, with justifiable terror, drew the logical conclusions.

The terror of a deadly sin is just as intense in a Catholic child as in a Protestant child, if both are scrupulous and afflicted with *memento mori;* yet the differences are considerable. As a Protestant psychologist once said with regard to his coreligionists:

Their consciousness, both personal and metaphysical, of Evil is one of the differences that most separate them from Catholics. For them every sin is deadly. Not that they don't make a practical distinction between the various

[15] "On the days when I happen to believe in the devil . . . I seem to hear the *other* laughing and rubbing his hands together in the shadows" (*Si le grain ne meurt,* I, p. 198).

[16] *Ainsi soit-il,* p. 41.

kinds of sin, but they reproach themselves for it as an adjustment to the world which will perhaps lead them toward the sin against the Holy Ghost, the one that will never be forgiven.[17]

An anxious child's suffering is not very different in a Catholic and in a Protestant, but their forms of Christian happiness are unequal. They have neither the same feeling of grace, divine love, and redemption, nor the same joys in worship. The devotion to the Virgin, the intercession of the saints, the superhuman nature of the minister of worship who has the power of saying Mass, of summoning God into the Host, and of telling the sinner, in the half-light of the confessional, to "go in peace," the belief in purgatory and in the souls for whom one prays for they still belong to the community of Christians, the reversibility of merit, and the famous "indulgences" Gide made such fun of, all the devotions of the Church of Saint Peter are so many moral supports. And the solemnity of the liturgical feasts gives the Catholic child all kinds of religious enchantment.

There was nothing comparable for André Gide as a child. In fact, he seemed only to remember the constraints and threats of his religion. Like all Protestants, he was fed on the Bible, but only later, at thirteen, did he seem to read it with fervor, at almost the same time that he discovered the Gospel "with transports of love." The young Huguenot Walter was to congratulate himself with some nostalgia for not having known "the candles, the incense, and the organs," nor the "voluptuous surrender in the arms of the Crucified God," and he was to write proudly: "The austere worship, the inhospitable chapels kept me from false prayers. I did not adore images." The austerity of Protestantism certainly has its grandeur, but the puritanical intransigence can, in a child who feels guilty and weak, increase his feelings of guilt and weakness without bringing him the support of liturgical escape or, between God and himself, the intercession of a Church that gives absolution.

[17] E.-G. Léonard, *Le Protestant français,* p. 139.

13: A Divided Child

> " 'Yes, no . . . Yes, I will. No, I won't.'
> The two contradictory sentences were
> pronounced in the same breath."
>
> Les Faux-Monnayeurs, *II, 223*

W HEN the novelist Edouard furtively listened to little Boris speaking on the terrace at Saas-Fée, the first words he copied into his *Journal* were the following: "Yes, I will. No, I won't." And he commented: "The two contradictory sentences were pronounced in the same breath." That almost theatrical entrance introduces us directly *in medias res* and immediately gives Boris' fundamental trait: indecision and irresolution. He is a child divided between contrary feelngs. André Gide also precociously went through the anguishing struggle of not being able to choose. He was a divided child before becoming the living symbol of a divided man. In his essay on Dostoevsky, in which he talked so much about himself in connection with the great Russian novelist that it is more a portrait of the painter than the model, he noted: "There is no doubt much about him that is unexplained. I do not think there is much about him that is unexplainable, as soon as we accept, as Dostoevsky asks us to, the coexistence in man of contradictory feelings." And he was right to consider ambiguity[1] the key to his personality.

Was Gide's ambiguity innate or acquired? In studying the delicate seed,

---

[1] We know that the word comes from *ambigere,* which means to doubt and is etymologically translated: to push in two directions at the same time (from *amb:* around, and *igere* for *agire:* to push). Originally this Latin verb designated the act of placing weights on both scales of a balance, provoking either an unstable equilibrium or alternate movements. The verb is very representative of the Gidian being.

we saw how nervous weakness predisposes one to psychological ambiguity, which in certain constitutions would be an innate form of sensitivity and intelligence. Yet the explanation is far from adequate, and many other factors contribute to the development of an ambiguous personality. There is no need to go back to Gide's theory about how important the duality of his heredity and his heritage was with regard to his division, but the influence of upbringing and of early affective conflicts must be considered here to the extent that it could have contributed to his doubting personality as a child.

A Protestant upbringing has often been said to encourage psychological ambiguity because free inquiry, entailing introspection, develops the division of the ego into judge and party. According to Göran Schildt:

The Protestant doctrine on the voice of conscience encourages self-observation; it forces man to keep a watch on himself, thus dividing the ego into an observing part and an acting part. When severely applied, the doctrine makes any naïve faith impossible, and flings the door wide open to doubt and complexes. Gide's encounter with Protestantism was almost catastrophic. It increased his difficulties and accentuated his innate weakness to such a degree that he never succeeded in conquering it. In that sense he remained Protestant all his life.[2]

Catastrophic is perhaps an exaggeration, but the encounter of a temperament given to doubt and a religion that can encourage it is surely not negligible.

Encouraged by systematic self-examination, doubt as to the sincerity of feelings and beliefs can indeed creep in very precociously. "And so begins the experience of hypocrisy in the very course of the most truly moral effort."[3] The story of André Gide's youth proves that statement. His assiduous practice of free inquiry from childhood on gave him an early experience of hypocrisy in the course of trying to be sincere with himself. Many of his fictional heroes, from André Walter to Armand Vedel, remember it more or less painfully:

When one is divided in that way, how in the world can one be sincere? I've come to the point of no longer even understanding what the word means. . . . Whatever I say or do, part of myself always stays behind and watches the other part compromise itself, observes it, makes fun of it and hisses at it, or applauds it.[4]

Yet that rather Luciferian character would seem to be wanting in lucid-

[2] Göran Schildt, *Gide et l'homme*, II, 35.

[3] P. Arbousse-Bastide, *Optimisme catholique et pessimisme protestant.*

[4] *Les Faux-Monnayeurs*, III, 469.

ity when he attributes the demon of introspection that possesses him to the Protestant upbringing given him by his father, Pastor Vedel. Rather than hold him responsible for it, Armand Vedel, author of a *Treatise on Inadequacy,* would do better to blame it on his own inadequacy, which is of course not intellectual, for he is intelligent (even diabolically so), but nervous. Introspection makes no one sick unless he already is: it strengthens the strong and weakens the weak. But the bent for it, acquired during one's very first years, encourages withdrawal into oneself. The very fact of keeping watch on all his inner workings, and subjecting the most obscure impulses of his heart to the eye of that witness, his psychological conscience, and to the approbation of that judge, his moral conscience, increases the introversion of any introvert, the doubt of any doubter, the scruples of anyone scrupulous, and more generally, the division of an ego which is all the more easily divided in that it is congenitally weak.

What is true for all culture is true for a religious heritage: it leads to different results in different natures, and accordingly it can either restrain or liberate, divide or bind together. The influence of André Gide's Protestant heritage was early and considerable. Sometimes he was pleased about it, other times he deeply regretted it. His attitude toward his childhood religion remained ambiguous to the end. And it is not surprising, for it was but one aspect of a general and basic ambiguity which his religion helped to increase but did not create. The same trait is just as evident in others who, as small children, belonged to no church. Gide's early reactions of identification or rebellion with regard to his family milieu must be analyzed here, for they obviously played a fundamental role in the division of his ego.

The ego asserts itself by rebelling or identifying, but it first asserts itself by the choice of an object outside itself. Before becoming conscious and voluntary, the choice is unconscious and involuntary, prompted by reasons that reason does not yet know. When its affective forces are at cross-purposes, the ego experiences a difficulty in being and its existence remains problematical. Now the first object of love or hate put forward to a child is obviously represented by his parents. His attitudes toward them mark him to such a degree that certain men merely repeat them throughout their lives toward substitutes, real or symbolic, of the parental images.

André Gide tried first to identify with his father's image: "Conflicts . . . helped to convince me that I resembled my father." That identification, resulting in certain traits of character, might have been decisive, but it remained incomplete. Paul Gide had little time for his son, and, since domestic disputes were distasteful to him, he gradually let his wife do as she saw fit. Moreover, he died prematurely, before his son was eleven. The father's death marks the end of a first type of family unit and the beginning of another monad reduced to the mother-son couple, and their psychological relationship was profoundly transformed. Indeed, the mother was the main character of André Gide's childhood, the one on whom he really depended. Gide made fun of the Freudian habit of explaining conflicts between children and parents by systematically bringing in the too-well-known Oedipus complex: "Don't you find that since Freud, there has been a spreading oedipemic?" he once said to me. His own childood situation could not have been less Oedipian, in the sense implied by Freud's first schema: love and desire for the mother, hate and envy of the father, sexual suppression linked to the prohibition of incest, the beginning of a guilt feeling. Nothing of that could be applied to Gide; there was no problem with regard to the father, for whom he never felt the slightest resentment, but quite obviously there was a mother problem. To speak of "inversion" or "shifting" of the Oedipus complex does not get us very far, and I see no interest in systematically applying the phrase to all the tendencies of attraction and repulsion of a child toward his parents.

The important thing is that the role of authority in the family unit, usually played by the father, and its assimilation in the child's imagination with the God of severity, was, in the case of André Gide, played by the mother. Indeed, I think the unquestionable affective complex provoked in him by the maternal image must not be interpreted on the level of hypothetical sexual fixations but on the level of the authority-submission conflict.

André Gide's affective attitudes toward his mother were not characterized by love or hate but by a mixture of love and hate, by ambivalence. We know that the word ambivalence, introduced into psychological language fifty years ago, designates a simultaneity of diametrically opposed feelings, resulting in contradictory and disconcerting attitudes; more precisely, it implies a kind of equivalence between a positive tendency and a negative tendency, for example, propulsion and repulsion, love and hate, or within each tendency, between the play of a positive component and that of a negative component, maintaining a dual play. Gide said of his mother: "She had a way of loving me that sometimes made me hate her," but also: "I admired the way her life had been one continual effort to draw a little nearer to everything that . . . was worthy of being loved," and he spoke in memorable terms of his "admiration for that heart which never allowed anything vile to enter it, beat only for others, and incessantly gave itself up to duty."[5]

He was divided between love for her "solicitude" and hate for her "tyranny," desire for her vigilance and fear of her supervision, admiration for her virtue and resentment of her coldness. He revered her as an

[5] *Si le grain ne meurt,* II, 367.

austere saint and hated her as a severe master. Overwhelmed by moral attentions and deprived of physical tenderness, he was caught between sentiment and resentment. The current that drew him toward her and the countercurrent that pushed him from her tossed him about between the ebb and the flow of contrary impulses, in such a way that he always resisted her authority with a heavy heart and gave into it begrudgingly. His attempts to protest never lasted very long against the omnipotent despot who demanded obedience without discussion and intended to make all her son's choices for him, leaving him neither freedom nor latitude. She was not only fighting his taste for pleasure but any attempt at personal affirmation, or what is more or less accurately called the instinct of self-assertion. That puritanical woman, imbued with the doctrine of self-hate, could not bear any manifestation of vanity, complacency, or even pride in her son, and she "did her best to sweep out everything that in my own eyes could inflate my self-importance."

One example of Gide's lasting resentment of his mother was his attitude toward the "ridiculous" way she dressed him as a child. One day, in his old age, I complimented him on a suit he was wearing: "Ah," he answered in a somewhat joking manner, "I really think I shall never get over the pleasure I take in dressing my own way, wearing gay materials, soft, colored shirts, yes, soft shirts!" Then his tone suddenly changed and became waspish: "It is my way of protesting against what my mother made me wear as a child: the navy-blue uniform and the stiff collar almost choked me. Ah! those stiff collars and especially the starched shirts, what torture! But it did me no good to kick, she forced me to wear that iron collar!" Those words in the mouth of a man of his age were surprising; but what surprised me even more was his tone of voice. I could feel the explosion of irritation, the return of a flame of animosity which, after a lifetime, had not yet been extinguished.

But there was nothing more ambivalent than the son's attitude to the strict way in which he had been brought up by his mother. And after having recalled that before living in grace, she wanted him to live under the law, he added: "Today I think my mother was in the right," a most Gidian retraction: "It never occurred to me that every mother, conscious of her duty, did not necessarily force her son to obey; but I also found it quite natural for the son to refuse to be subjugated."[6]

André Gide's reactions as a child to the ethics he was taught were merely the projection of his affective reactions to the mother who prescribed them. He was divided, with regard to her, between religious reverence and fearful protest, and the ambiguous mixture made any frank acceptance as prob-

[6] *Ibid.*, p. 363.

lematical as any frank opposition. Had he loved his mother without reservation, he would perhaps have accepted total submission and identified with her Puritan conscience, as Emmanuel Kant had done. Had he wholeheartedly detested her, he would have rebelled, exactly like Henri Beyle as a child did against his father. As it was, his hostility was slow to take the lead and did not become a reaction of opposition taking the form of an open and declared protest until about the age of twenty-three, and then after painful crises.

For Gide, the mother image was identified with a religion, an ethics, a social class, and a province, and in his feelings toward Protestantism, puritanical customs, the traditional *bourgeoisie,* and Normandy there was always a secret attraction behind an obvious hostility. His decision to actualize his dissimilarities with relation to his mother became all the more voluntary and conscious as he became more aware of his similarities. After having recalled that he had first thought he resembled his father, Gide added: "The most profound ancestral resemblances are not discovered until late in life." By fighting her, he was fighting a part of himself, the part that was the introjection of an admired and hated image, so that behind the iconoclast's victories we can sense the regrets and remorse of the idolater. If he wrote of his mother: "She had a way of loving me that sometimes made me hate her," he might have written about the values she embodied: "I had a way of hating them that sometimes made me love them."

Here perhaps is one of the affective roots of Gide's fondness for his adversaries, a weakness that he realized he always had.[7] He believed that "the fear of being right"[8] was one of the constants of his nature. It possibly dated from the time any attempt at self-assertion came up against his mother's intransigency. Perhaps, at the beginning, one of the reasons for his fear of being right was the feeling that his mother was right and that he was right to be afraid. In a psychoanalytical perspective, the ambiguity of Gide's character would represent the repetition[9] of childhood relationships, branded with an ambivalence toward a both revered and dreaded mother, and its extension to all the domains of mental life.

That is far from being the "explanation" of Gidian ambiguity, but there is no doubt that as an only child, brought up in a family unit in which

---

[7] "Recognizing the enemy's good qualities and virtues has always been my weakness, and it may well make me pass for a traitor among the supporters of either side" (*Journal,* 1943, p. 106).

[8] "Clouard was very perspicacious to head his article: *Gide or the Fear of Being Right.* That was very long ago; but it has remained one of the few constants of my nature; which means that in politics I'm worthless: I understand the adversary too well" (*Journal,* 1946, p. 254).

[9] What Freud called the automatism of repetition.

the mother had the authority and, after the father's death, was the sole authority, André Gide lived in an abnormally intense and prolonged state of dependency with regard to her. He felt that his dependency was an indispensable protection and an unbearable frustration. He loved her because she defended him and he felt weak; he hated her because she forbade him all that he hungered for: pleasure and fredom. For him, she was the image of security at the price of renouncing the satisfaction of the instincts. To obey her meant a gain of security and a loss of independence; to rebel meant a loss of security and a gain of independence. The conflict, which extended to all the entreaties of his nature, had a predominant sexual aspect, owing to his precocious sexual awakening and the particularly strict prohibitions his puritanical mother prescribed in that domain. In that sense we might say that he had a potential castration complex, linked to the tyranny of a graspingly possessive and, with regard to her son's virility, castrating mother.

Given André Gide's upbringing as a child and an adolescent, to assert his sexuality or his independence meant losing maternal love and affection, losing his guarantee of security; and on the other hand, to give up his sexuality or his independence meant sacrificing pleasure and freedom to the moral demands his mother embodied. He had the choice of satisfying her or satisfying himself, of hating her or hating himself. He therefore sometimes tried to oppose her, sometimes tried to identify with her, and one proved as vain as the other. He failed in his attempts and doubted himself just as he doubted her, and feared himself just as he feared her. He thus lived in a state of compromise, with clandestine satisfactions spoiled by a feeling of guilt and hypocritical obedience irritated by the feeling of frustration. He lived in a state of ambivalence, equally unable to suppress his instincts or accept them, powerless to choose between pleasure and security, between nature and morality, divided between obedience and rebellion. Torn between the desires of a "little boy" and the orders of a "Protestant minister," the ego could not give one up without regret or disobey the other without remorse. Even then he did not want to sacrifice anything of himself and wanted to avoid a choice which he felt in advance would be a mutilation.

In *Les Faux-Monnayeurs* Sophroniska says with regard to Boris: "His mother loves him very much, but to tell the truth it would be preferable for him to stop living with her."[10] She admits that Boris' mother loves her son but, in her opinion, loves him badly and brings him up too strictly. In other words, she thinks Boris has, as psychoanalysts are apt to say somewhat too often, a "mother problem." Clearly Gide had the same problem. When Mme. Paul Gide, irritated by her son's disobedience, decided to

---

[10] *Les Faux-Monnayeurs,* II, 226.

have him board with the Vedels, an entire school year went by with almost no troubles. When she decided to have him return for a second year, he did not protest. In fact, he seemed to take to his life as a boarder, as if the main reason for his conflicts had disappeared. But a few days after school started, his father died and from then on he did not leave his mother again until the age of twenty-three, and I mean did not leave her for one day.

The constraints of his strict upbringing prevented Gide from going forth into the outer world with confidence and encouraged his innate tendency to withdraw into himself. The "sullen" child took refuge in an ambiguous narcissism. The affective ambivalence that characterized his relationship with his mother was just as characteristic of his relationship with himself. It can be clearly seen in the disorders and dangerous reveries he delighted in. When Albert Démarest reproached him at the age of ten with being interested in nothing but himself and made him ashamed of it, his words left a lasting and staggering impression:

Albert's words touched me more deeply than he ever supposed or than I myself realized until later. What I generally like least in a friend is indulgence; Albert was not indulgent. If necessary, with him one could find arms against oneself. And, without really being aware of it, that was what I was looking for.[11]

What then was that need for finding arms against himself to fight himself with? Was it a natural need or a product of his upbringing? The inclination to fight oneself, unequally distributed in human nature, was a constant tendency of Gide's. His nature was of course fundamentally narcissistic, but in the sense that narcissism is both self-love and self-hate. The rivalry between the two opposing forces—one leading to the concentration, organization, and integration of the ego, the other to its dispersion, disorganization, and dissolution—played a basic part in Gide's life. It existed from childhood on, masked by the moral ambivalence which was then its predominant aspect. The "centrifugal and disintegrating force,"[12] the force of self-destruction which would have pushed Gide's ego into surrendering itself and "losing itself" had it not been held in check by a rival force of self-preservation, is not rare, at least not in the great doubters, those self-executioners. What we are dealing with is psychological masochism.

At the end of his life, Freud developed the notion of a fundamental duality of human instincts, opposing a life instinct or *libido* to a death instinct or *destrudo*. Most psychologists refuse the idea that the second

[11] *Si le grain ne meurt*, I, 81.

[12] André Gide's preface to Baudelaire's *Les Fleurs du mal*.

tendency is innate and that certain people, before any experience whatever, have a taste for both building and demolishing, a taste for building themselves and demolishing themselves, the rival attraction of construction and destruction. When the tendency becomes apparent, and no one can deny that in certain nervous children it is apparent very early, it is generally interpreted as the secondary result of a conflict, linked to suppression and to the shifting of aggression against others toward oneself, as it were. It is a fact of observation that frustration in a child is accompanied by an outburst of aggression against the object that is held responsible for the lack of satisfaction. But the aggression is suppressed by the guilt feeling linked to a moral upbringing, a fear of retaliation, and also, on occasion, an ambivalent attachment to the object that caused the frustration. Aggression that cannot find an outlet is thus inhibited but turns against the subject himself and creates a desire for self-punishment whose manifestation is anguish.

Between guilt and anguish there is then a basic link, the suppression of aggression and its change into self-aggression. Such at any rate are the most recent psychoanalytical findings,[13] showing the connection between masochism and anguish in certain anxious children. All the links of the chain of reactions—frustration, aggression against others, guilt, aggression turned against oneself, anguish—can be found in André Gide's childhood. He felt frustrated by his mother, he hated her at the same time he admired her and tried to rebel against her, he experienced an anguishing guilt feeling, he turned his aggression against himself as it appears from certain of his phantasms, and he felt that very self-aggression as anguishing and voluptuous, as pain and pleasure, in a vertiginous state of insecurity. And so he discovered what it was to suffer and take pleasure in the throes of being torn apart, which he subsequently sustained for literary ends.

[13] See Sacha Nacht, *La Peur*.

14: From Anxiety to Escape

"For you must understand, my children, that each of us, when adolescent, encounters at the beginning of his journey a monster. . . ."

Oedipe, *p. 82*

T HE factors of anxiety in André Gide's childhood were both acquired (linked to moral conflicts) and innate (linked to a temperament). And they combined to create the insecurity and inferiority feelings of his formative years. Many children have similar conflicts and yet become neither anxious nor weak. But Gide's innate weakness made him a priori ill-fitted to surmount the difficulties and obstacles he was to encounter "at the beginning of his journey." His terrified comment "I'm not like the others" shows a state of alarm implying that the ego is in danger. Weak and divided, divided because he was weak, and weak because he was divided, he did not feel capable of facing the enemies that were besieging him from outside and in. Contrary forces were oppressing him, immobilizing him, antagonizing him to the point of agony. The intense feeling of insecurity was a premonition of failure. It is probable that from this period on, whether Gide was aware of it or not, the elements of his inner drama were established and at work.

The feeling of a weakness of the ego quite naturally calls for a reaction of compensation which, in various and sometimes disconcerting forms, always finally tends toward a protest—that is, toward self-assertion. A person whose character and personality are governed by an inferiority complex is defiant. He lives with the illusion that nature, or the gods, or the devil, or his heredity, or his upbringing, or the others have challenged him, and with the conviction that he will need all his strength to take up the challenge. His protest, at first unconscious, then conscious, ends by reversing the situation of inferiority, even if it is also necessary to reverse all the values. That kind of inferiority complex, it would seem to me, played an important part in André Gide's formative years and was at work from his childhood on. It clarifies the meaning of his behavior at times, for seen in this perspective it can be explained in terms of defense reactions, intended to eliminate more or less permanently the humiliation due to the inferiority feeling and its resulting anguish. The unconscious finality which tends to restore value to the ego and remove its guilt can be found in much of Gide's behavior during his formative years, behavior that gave those years their very special flavor of flight and escape.

André Gide had Oedipus make the following rash speech to his two young sons, Etocles and Polynices:

You must understand, my children, that each of us, when adolescent, encounters at the beginning of his journey a monster which confronts him with a riddle that can prevent him from moving ahead. And although that particular sphinx puts a different question to each of us, my boys, you must convince yourselves that the answer to each question is always the same; yes, there is but one and the same answer to such different and varied questions; and the one answer is: Man; and the one man for each of us is: Himself.

One can only hope that Oedipus' young sons will not take his words literally and will not solve the riddle in the same way their father did. But a myth is fortunately open to manifold interpretations. The monster that each of us encounters at the beginning of his journey, and which has a different face for all, is in the most general sense that which opposes self-realization; it symbolizes the obstacle to the development of one's personality. What then was the monster Gide encountered at the beginning of his life? It was not outside him but inside him. Whatever its changeable appearance, it has but one name: anguish; and what Gide wanted to attack throughout his life were the reasons for his anguish, in order to triumph over his weakness, in order to conquer fear and self-doubt.

A "virile protest," the expression of an inferiority complex, aims at self-assertion, even if paradoxically it means self-destruction. The denouement of Boris' drama—his theatrical suicide—represents on a childish scale, in both a tragic and a ridiculous perspective, an attempt to rebel: the birth, from the depths of despair, of what is called a "superman"; and in the background the spirit of the Nietzschean Strouvilhou, the *deus ex machina* of *Les Faux-Monnayeurs,* gives the childish drama its transcendent significance.

All the symbolic situations that were to a certain extent his own, but spread out over different periods of his development, Gide transferred to little Boris and presented on a small scale: his flight into illness, his possession of imaginary goods, his escape into a purely mystical love, and finally his revolt and his no longer disguised act of protest. But at the age of thirteen Gide had not yet discovered more than one way to run from anguish, and that was the flight into bodily illness. When Sophoroniska tries to interpret Boris' attacks and nervous disorders, she says: "I say they began as a protest. . . . He took fright; and it was then that his weakly organism, like a hunted animal, invented all those little subterfuges which rid him of his inner suffering and which are so many confessions."[1] The anxious child took refuge in a nervous illness and, by means of that bodily subterfuge, got rid of his guilt feeling and escaped from humiliating inferiority. In a paradoxical way, strange no doubt but discovered by many other anxious children, his illness became a means of gaining security, and his nervous collapse an instrument of his will to power.

The elementary reaction to danger is flight, but in psychology there are many roads along which one may flee, and certain roads are actually subterfuges whose ultimate aim is to get round the obstacle and overcome it. The subterfuges are not only circuitous and artificial means of getting out of a difficulty; they are also, as the etymology indicates (*subter-fugere:* to flee underneath), clandestine means. In the realm of psychology such clandestine or subliminal means are those which are decided below the threshold of consciousness: they are sub-conscious or infra-conscious.

The most archaic and childish of subterfuges is the flight into illness. And its mechanism is obvious in Gide's childhood. Starting with his nervous attacks, which mark his official entry, as it were, into illness, he managed to turn his new condition to account both unconsciously and consciously: "I cannot say to what extent I used them." The avowed objective of the nervous attacks at age eleven was to avoid going back to the *lycée* of Montpellier so that he need not face the schoolmates who had been terrorizing him. The intention was clear, and the strategy proved effective. But in addition to the voluntary and conscious intention, which was quite simply a simulation, there was an unconscious and involuntary intentionality—and that was the real subterfuge.

When Gide broke out into the most varied nervous movements in his little room in Montpellier, he noticed that the exercises led to a very agreeable feeling of release. For a long time it has been an established fact that when an anxious person has a nervous attack, his anguish is reduced or disappears; the state of painful tension is replaced by an impression of release which can become voluptuous. Indeed, part of the need for reproducing the attacks and prolonging them is an obscure avidity for he-

[1] *Les Faux-Monnayeurs,* II, 264–65.

donic sensations which are satisfied clandestinely, sheltered from the stern eye of conscience. The "greatest relief" brought to Gide by his nervous attacks and which he nostalgically remembered as an adult, was a nervous release, more or less equivalent to an orgasm. That erotic significance gave the illness its name, but the Platonic myth of hysteria was singularly rejuvenated by Freud. In a nervous attack of this type, everything happens as if the suppressed instinctive energy turned into somatic manifestations which according to Freud are substitute satisfactions and in a sense, derivations. It was that kind of satisfaction, essentially libidinal but disguised and thus relieved of the guilt feeling, that he called the primary profit of illness.

But the profit is not only physical, it is moral. On the one hand, it is a nervous release, more or less linked, as Freud thought, to a sexual equivalent, but it is also the relief of anguish, inasmuch as anguish is linked to a guilt feeling. Through a kind of balancing of forces, as soon as the physical symptoms of a "conversion" become apparent, the moral anguish disappears or is reduced. The subterfuge, which is the fact of improvising, for others and for oneself, "a naïve tableau of physical illness,"[2] cancels out the guilt, transforms the personal fault into an accidental situation independent of the will, and thanks to an alibi—the indictment of the body which is from then on made responsible and incriminated—the mind is exonerated. One excuses itself by accusing the other. The bad conscience that accompanies obvious pleasure is transformed into a good conscience, since from then on the pleasure is realized in a concealed way, eluding the judge's eye; for the judge does not see or does not want to see anything that happens in a *fornix* more entrenched than the conscience. However, when neurosis is added to the simulation, the child still feels partially responsible and the primary profit is reduced. And actually that was André Gide's situation at the time of his first oversimulated attacks: a conscious and voluntary simulation exaggerating the real disorders. Therefore he reproached himself for "acting" in front of his mother and felt guilty for torturing her with worry. When as a nervous child he struggled in his little room in Montpellier, Gide was already in a state of ambiguity created by the mixture of a good and bad conscience. And he was already caught in the dilemma: "to be moral or to be sincere."

More obvious than the primary profit are the secondary profits: the advantages gained from the family through illness. Thanks to illness, Gide avoided having to return to school and disarmed his stern mother; he took the sword away from Dame Justice and tampered with the scales of bal-

[2] A. Hesnard, *L'Univers morbide de la faute.*

ance by throwing in the weight of a defect. From then on he was no longer a depraved child who had to be reformed, he was a sick child who had to be cared for. With the help of his new condition, he more or less innocently discovered how to change the authority-submission conflict that characterized his relations with his mother. "My mother resigned herself to treating me like an invalid." Having gained new value through his neurosis, he undertook to reverse the roles and substitute the filial despotism of illness for the maternal despotism of ethics. His nervous weakness became the instrument of his will to power. Nothing is more significant from that point of view than the evolution of his disorders and the way in which he used them to lay the foundations for a new policy within the family unit.

Most of the nervous disorders of Gide's childhood—motor attacks, migraines, insomnia, anorexia, diverse spasms—seem to me in great part to fall into the category of psychosomatic medicine, a relatively new word for an old reality, the very one Plato had seen when he reproached the Greek doctors for wanting to separate the body from the soul in the treatment of illness. Many organic disorders are merely nervous disorders of emotional origin translated into organic language. Distraction, in other words a change of moral climate, is of course beneficial, but as soon as the anxious child is again faced with his conflicts, he again tries to find subterfuges. And the part played by secondary profits in the creation of subterfuges is far from being negligible. Gide more or less unconsciously used all his disorders to change the nature of his relationship with a mother whose severity he dreaded; he used them to change a strict upbringing with established rules into a broader, more flexible regime, made to measure. It is strange how his most spectacular nervous disorders did not begin until after his father's death—that is, the minute he felt the maternal grasp "close in" on him. His illness made it possible for him to get out of her grip somewhat and to gain a certain freedom of movement. With its help, he maneuvered his way toward independence as others do toward a closer dependency.

At almost the same age and in almost the same year, another nervous child had also discovered the secondary profits of illness. In a room in Paris on the boulevard Malesherbes, Marcel Proust was learning to "almost flaunt" his "state of suffocation," thus reinforcing and adding even more alarm to the worried tenderness of Mme. Adrien Proust. Proust magnified his illness in order to increase his love dependency; Gide did the same to gain an already hostile independence. The two delicate executioners reproached themselves for the torment they inflicted in their homes, yet their remorse was not enough to make them give up the torment or the benefits they obtained therefrom. Indeed, both of them shifted their guilt feelings to the body, which, as Proust said, "has no pretensions to philosophy"; they exonerated themselves by indicting the body; they excused themselves by accusing the body, as if it had furnished them with an alibi.

But for future artists there is yet another kind of profit in illness. Actually one might wonder if the "acting" of the body does not to a large degree prepare for the play of the soul, and if the lies of neurosis do not sketch out the dreams of art. The artisan of his illness is already creating an artful work and learning to tame the devil. Such gamelike and solitary subterfuges open the way to other forms of escape. A bodily sickness, to the extent that it is imaginary, shows its inventor how to play the triple role of spectator-author-actor; it shows him what Diderot called the "mobility of the entrails," which leads him to discover the paradoxical sincerity of an actor. "An actor perhaps . . . ," André Walter cried out in front of his mirror, "but I am playing myself. The most skilful are the best understood." Nervous attacks and the refuge in the fiction of a bodily sickness are too often found in the childhoods of great actors and great writers for the theory to be purely gratuitous. But the flight into the lies of the body is but an elementary subterfuge and, Protean as it may be, the pantomime remains limited in relation to forms of escape that open a way for a flight into the imaginary, for the innumerable possibilities of dream, and then of art.

PART II

Adolescence

15: Madeleine Rondeaux

> *"Until that day, I had been wandering about aimlessly; then suddenly I discovered the mystic orient of my life."*
>
> Si le grain ne meurt, *I, 129*

ᖴʀᴏᴍ childhood on, André Gide had had a marked preference for his cousin Madeleine. Two years older than he, she was very different from her gayer and more playful younger sisters, Jeanne and Valentine. Jeanne was radiant with joy and health, but "beside her sister's grace, her beauty seemed all on the surface and available to everyone at the first glance." Madeleine's charm, in certain respects very similar to Alissa's in *La Porte étroite,* was something different from that of beauty:

I am unable to describe faces; the features escape me, even the color of eyes. I can only recall the expression of her smile, almost sad even then, and the line of her eyebrows, so extraordinarily high over her eyes, raised above them in large circles. I have never seen any like them anywhere . . . but yes: on a Florentine statuette of Dante's time; and I like to imagine that Beatrice as a child had very highly arched eyebrows like those. They gave her eyes, her whole being, a questioning expression that was both anxious and trusting—yes, passionately questioning. She herself was all question and expectation.[1]

Alissa's features were indeed those of Madeleine as Gide described her in *Et nunc manet in te:*

On the little photograph, now half effaced, which shows her to me at the age she then was,[2] her face and the strangely evasive line of her eyebrows

---

[1] *La Porte étroite,* I, 22.

[2] At the end of December, 1882. Madeleine Rondeaux was then fifteen.

give the impression of a kind of questioning, of apprehension, of fearful astonishment on the threshold of life.[3]

Gide knew very little about his cousin's childhood. "As she never talked about herself, I know nothing about her earliest personal recollections," but the few traits he points out do give us a glimpse of Madeleine's character. She took almost no part in games, especially if they were boisterous. She had little taste for exercise, particularly gymnastics, and proved to be as "fearful" as Jeanne was "fearless." When the others climbed up into the tall cedar in the Cuverville garden and arranged "rooms" for themselves among the branches, with André victoriously calling out from the top "I see the sea! I see the sea!" she stayed at the foot of the tree. He was to say of her later on:

She was afraid of everything, even before being afraid of me; and certainly a sense of her own fragility did much to increase her fear. I suggested she take as a motto: *leo est in via* or *latet anguis in herba*. And as the merest trifle satisfied her and she was happy with very little, she considered everything that went beyond the ordinary as excess. The slightest wind became a squall in her eyes. She was meant for continuous calm weather, just as she was for an uneventful, smoothly flowing life.[4]

Of delicate health and constitution, Madeleine was often sick, whereas her two sisters were strong and vigorous. She liked to take walks with her father, whom she held in veneration and for whom she was the favorite. She would listen to him tell about his reminiscences, his journeys, especially his beautiful trip on the Nile with Gustave Rocquigny and Devéria, or read aloud a long novel by Walter Scott. She was as passionately fond of reading as she was indifferent to exercise. When she sat down with a book it seemed as if "the outer world stopped existing for her." Gentle, meditative, somewhat melancholy, she was deeply pious and careful never to do evil. She willingly kept in the background when others were around and seemed to take pleasure in her self-effacement, yet without any affectation whatever. "She constantly withdrew to the background and tried not to attract attention. Never was she heard to say: 'I personally. . . .' Her modesty was as natural to her as the need for pushing themselves forward and shining is to other women," Gide wrote in *Et nunc manet in te;* and in *Si le grain ne meurt:*

She never quarreled; it was so natural for her to give up her turn on her place or her share to others and always with such smiling grace, that one wondered if she did not act that way more from inclination than out of virtue.

[3] *Et nunc manet in te,* p. 22.

[4] *Ibid.,* pp. 43–44.

Even then André saw Madeleine as the embodiment of a kind of moral perfection and his mother often gave her as an example. Sometimes she would make fun of her cousin, whom she considered as a younger brother:

I was growing up too; but it was not the same thing; hard as I tried to seem serious when I was with her, I felt that I was still a child; I felt that she no longer was. The tender look in her eyes was now tinged with sadness, and it fascinated me more especially as I could not fathom it.[5]

More than Mme. Gide's scoldings, a mocking smile from Madeleine helped him to break himself of certain whims and affectations. She hated not only lies but any overstatement, extravagance, and most particularly "acting."

For she had extraordinary perspicacity with regard to anything that was not perfectly genuine. By a sort of subtle intuition, she was warned by an inflection of the voice, a vague gesture, a mere nothing; and that was how, although still very young, she was the first in her family to notice her mother's misconduct.[6]

That precociously serious little girl of fifteen had an unconquerable aversion to anything that was not moral or decent. André Gide was extremely sensitive to Madeleine's judgment:

Even then I lived with my cousin in a conscious community of tastes and thoughts, which with all my heart I worked at making closer and more perfect. I think it amused her; for example, when we dined together at the rue de Crosne, she would make a game of depriving me of my favorite dessert by first refusing it herself, knowing quite well that I would never serve myself anything until she had done so first.[7]

She thus tempted her cousin, and not without malice, to show a spirit of self-sacrifice which was not his strong point.

And so André Gide was marked by Madeleine's influence even in his very early years:

As far back as I can go, I see her; or otherwise, in my earliest childhood, there is merely darkness through which I grope my way. Yet she did not begin to play her benevolent role in my life until the tragic event I recounted in my *Porte étroite* and in *Si le grain ne meurt*. How old were we then? She was fourteen and I twelve, probably. I can't remember more precisely.[8]

At the time of the event, the end of December, 1882, André Gide was thirteen and Madeleine Rondeaux fifteen.

[5] *Si le grain ne meurt*, I, 125.

[6] *Et nunc manet in te*, p. 22.

[7] *Si le grain ne meurt*, I, 125–26.

[8] *Et nunc manet in te*, p. 17.

André Gide did not understand the secret reason for Madeleine's sadness until around New Year's Day, 1883. But he was too sensitive and too curious not to have somewhat suspected that Emile Rondeaux and his wife were not like the other couples in his family, his father and mother, the Démarests, or the Henri Rondeaux. When the three sister-in-laws, Juliette Gide, Lucile Rondeaux, and Claire Démarest got together in the rue de Crosne drawing room, began to speak in low tones, and asked him to play somewhere else, he surmised that the subject of their confidential talks was his frivolous aunt who lived in the rue de Lecat. When he had heard his mother tell Lucile Rondeaux that "Poor Emile has really changed!" he immediately realized that his uncle had in fact changed a great deal and seemed weary and weighed down with grief. André Gide smelled trouble in the rue de Lecat, without knowing exactly what it was.

It is difficult to specify exactly when he began to feel the family's reprobation with regard to Mathilde Rondeaux and to see her as the embodiment of sin. One circumstance seems to have played an important part. When on Paul Gide's death all the women in the family went into mourning and prolonged it for the time prescribed by custom, Mathilde Rondeaux, to whom black was not becoming, refrained from wearing it. And the situation gave rise to a little scene recounted in *La Porte étroite:*

Yes, it was surely the year my father's death; my recollection was confirmed by a conversation that took place between my mother and Miss Ashburton[9] immediately after our arrival. I had unexpectedly come into the room where my mother was talking to her friend; they were discussing my aunt; my mother was indignant at the fact that she had not gone into mourning or that she had already gone out. (To tell the truth it is just as impossible for me to imagine my Aunt Bucolin in black as my mother in a bright dress.) The day of our arrival, as far as I can remember, Lucile Bucolin was wearing a muslin dress. Miss Ashburton, conciliatory as ever, was trying to calm my mother. "After all," she timidly argued, "white is mourning too." "And do you also call that red scarf she's wearing round her shoulders mourning? Flora, you shock me!" my mother exclaimed. I used only to see my aunt during the holiday months and no doubt the heat of summer was her reason for wearing the light and very low-necked bodices I have always seen her in; but what shocked my mother even more than the vibrant scarves my aunt would throw over her bare shoulders was the décolleté.[10]

André Gide, whose descriptions of women are generally remarkably chaste, gave his young and too beautiful aunt an *odor di femina* which seemed to have really disturbed him. "I experienced a strange uneasiness when I was with my aunt; it was a feeling of agitation, combined with a

[9] Miss Shackleton.

[10] *La Porte étroite,* p. 13.

kind of admiration and terror." One day she really gave her young nephew reason to blush:

"Why are you going away so fast? . . . Do I frighten you?" With a beating heart, I drew nearer; I forced myself to smile and hold out my hand to her. She held my hand in one of hers and stroked my cheek with the other. "How badly your mother dresses you, my poor boy!" I was then wearing a kind of sailor shirt with a large collar, which my aunt began to rumple. "Sailor collars are worn much more open!" she said, bursting one of the buttons. "There! see if you don't look better that way!" and taking out her little mirror, she drew my face against hers, put her bare arm around my neck, thrust her hand into my open shirt, laughingly asked if I was ticklish, and pushed further down. . . . I started so violently that my shirt tore; my face was flaming red, and as she cried out: "Oh! Silly boy!" I fled; I ran all the way to the back of the garden; there, in a little cistern in the vegetable patch, I wet my handkerchief, pressed it to my forehead, washed, scrubbed my cheeks, my neck, everything that that woman had touched.[11]

Whether true or imaginary, the scene is no less suggestive. It reveals the young Puritan's modesty, a start too violent to be quite innocent, and a most frantic need for purification after what seemed like contamination.

In *La Porte étroite* Gide also described his aunt's nervous attacks, which revolutionized the household and on which he perhaps unconsciously patterned the attacks he was to have in Montpellier. However, "Lucile Bucolin" was then preparing to leave her home, just as in the rue de Lecat the Emile Rondeaux' marriage seemed to be in jeopardy. Uncle Emile, increasingly gloomy and worried, would shut himself up in his "dismal little office smelling of cigars" for hours at a time and "would come out of it looking much older." One afternoon at the end of December, 1882, when he knew his uncle was not in Rouen, André Gide went to the rue de Lecat with the idea of "discovering" something, convinced that he was going "to see Heaven knows what." He was not mistaken. "That evening my taste for the clandestine was satisfied."

As soon as he was in the door, he sensed something "unusual." The *porte-cochère* was partly open and the evening visitor, although not "the one who was expected," furtively slipped in, when Alice, "a female pest whom my aunt had as a servant," appeared, but she was too late. On the second floor his Aunt Mathilde's room was wide open and brightly lighted: "I caught a glimpse of my aunt, languidly stretched out on a sofa; Suzanne and Louise[12] were with her, bending over, fanning her, and I think giving her smelling salts." He continued up to Madeleine's room on the third floor. There he found his cousin kneeling in the shadows: " 'What have

11 *Ibid.,* pp. 18–19.

12 Jeanne and Valentine Rondeaux.

you come for? You should not have come back. . . .'" She remained on her knees: "I did not realize at once that she was sad. But when I felt her tears on my cheek, my eyes were opened."

It was at that moment and for the first time that André Gide understood the secret of Madeleine's sadness and became aware of her despair:

Today I think that nothing can be more cruel for a child who is all purity, love, and tenderness than to have to judge her mother and disapprove of her conduct; and what intensified her torment was that she had to keep the secret for herself alone and hide it from her father whom she revered, a secret she had somehow discovered and which had devastated her, a secret the whole town was talking about, which the maids were laughing over, and which trifled with the carefree innocence of her two sisters. No, I was not to understand all that until later; but I felt that this little creature, to whom I was already so deeply attached, was prey to a great, an intolerable grief, a grief I would need all my love and all my life to cure.[13]

After having described the scene somewhat differently in *La Porte étroite,* Gide added:

That moment determined my whole life; even today I cannot recall it without anguish. I probably understood very imperfectly the reason for Alissa's grief, but I felt intensely that it was far too strong for her little quivering soul, for her frail body, shaken with sobs. I stood beside her, while she continued to kneel; I was unable to express anything of the new transport in my heart; but I pressed her head against my heart and pressed my lips to her forehead, while my soul flowed out of them. Drunk with love, with pity, and with an obscure mixture of enthusiasm, self-sacrifice, and virtue, I called on God with all my strength and offered myself up to Him, unable to conceive that my life could have any object other than that of sheltering this child from fear, from evil, from life. At last I knelt down, full of prayer; I held her against me; and I indistinctly heard her say: "Jérôme! They didn't see you, did they? Oh! Go quickly! They mustn't see you." Then lower still: "Jérôme, don't tell anyone . . . poor papa knows nothing."[14]

Just as Madeleine appeared to him in a childish aura, wearing the halo of the innocent victims of evil, so André Gide always imagined his heroines—at least those he could not describe without his pen trembling, the Emmanuèles, the Alissas, the Marcelines—as Angels of Suffering, with the same constancy and the same fatality as Edgar Allan Poe imagined his Ligeias, Morellas, and Berenices as Angels of Strangeness. The word *aura* does not seem out of place here, especially if we go back to what André Gide himself wrote when he described the first two *Schaudern* of his childhood as "attacks of this strange aura." Indeed, after having recalled

[13] *Si le grain ne meurt,* I, 134.

[14] *La Porte étroite,* pp. 27–28.

those "two strange shocks," he added: "Had I told about them before, in what would have been their proper places chronologically, it would doubtless have been easier to understand my complete inner upheaval on that autumn evening in the rue de Lecat, when I came into contact with the invisible reality."[15] From then on Madeleine belonged to that invisible reality, to that universe of mystery which leads to the mystical universe. "Until that day, I had been wandering about aimlessly; then suddenly I discovered the mystic orient of my life."

When Jérôme describes his state as being "drunk with love, with pity, and with an obscure mixture of enthusiasm, self-sacrifice, and virtue" and calls "on God with all [his] strength," his enthusiasm, in the etymological sense of the word, is experienced and expressed as a mystical transport. Here, for the first time, appear the name of God and the word prayer, both of which are so strangely missing from Gide's Christian childhood as described in *Si le grain ne meurt*. It would seem that for the first time Gide deeply experienced the religious nature of the opposition between the world of pleasure and sin as embodied by Mathilde Rondeaux, and the world of suffering and virtue as embodied by Madeleine, the religious nature of the choice between the easy way and the strait way. What André Gide as a Protestant child already knew, he then felt with a violence he had never before experienced.

The words with which Gide recalled that "angelic intervention" in *Si le grain ne meurt* are astonishingly serious: "The event seemed most insignificant but was as important in my life as revolutions are for empires —the first scene of a drama which is not yet played out." It would be difficult to affirm more solemnly the symbolic significance of the great event of his thirteenth year. Gide seemed to see it as the passing of an angel, establishing a dividing line between the "darkness" of his childhood and the radiance of a mystical presence, between the world of sin and the world of grace.

Everything of course was not darkness before, and everything after was far from being light, but from then on his life was to oscillate between two poles, two directions. "On the surface nothing had changed." But he was no longer entirely absorbed in "the small events" that made up his life. "In the depths of my heart I was hiding the secret of my destiny." Clearly his memory made the rue de Lecat event a privileged landmark around which he distributed all the recollections of his childhood: this was before, that was after.

Yet given Gide's age at the time he discovered the "mystic orient" of his life, it is very probable that he did not realize just how important the event was until much later. It is probable, for he was still very young, that he

---

[15] *Si le grain ne meurt,* I, 134.

was not immediately aware of the depth of his feeling and did not call it love until a few years had passed. He continued to see his cousin on New Year's Day in Rouen and during the summer holidays at La Roque or Cuverville. When they were separated, they wrote to each other, but never regularly until around 1885–86. Imperceptibly, they came to realize that they were no longer children.

Although Gide began to write to Madeleine more often than to his other cousins, Jeanne and Valentine, each of his letters was read by all three, for the family discipline, to which Madeleine scrupulously conformed, was opposed to any confidential correspondence. This fact probably takes away much of the interest of André Gide's letters—unfortunately destroyed—to his cousin during their early years. When he fell sick in Biskra in 1893, he wrote to Jeanne Rondeaux, asking that Madeleine send back his first letters:

If I get worse, I would appreciate it if you'd send me those old letters Madeleine talks about; I no longer remember them and should like to reread them; then I'll send them back to you as soon as I've finished—it's that past "gentillesse" I should like you to remember me by—it's perhaps the truest—it was at a time when you knew me better.[16]

The tone of "gentillesse," a bit childish, can be felt in a letter addressed to Jeanne, written when he was fifteen and in which he complained about the rarity of Madeleine's letters, his own often going without answer:

Will you please congratulate your most respected sister for me on the alacrity with which she answers the letters that one is kind enough to send her. Remind her that she has only written me one letter since New Year's Day and overwhelm her with well-deserved reproaches. For you it is quite the contrary and I send you only thanks for the letters you write me, which are always most welcome. Out of gratitude for your worthy epistles, I'm doing my best to run your errands and I do hope you will compliment me on them.

Then follow details on the albums of music he had just bought for her, especially on "the three pretty volumes of Beeth. sonatas of which I am jealous," or those he had just received:

Mamma gave me 20 francs worth of Tschaicowski [*sic*], the Russian composer whose music we heard, and I'm delighted with it. I received my Scarlatti.

[16] Letter from André Gide to Jeanne Rondeaux, unpublished. A constraint in André Gide's and Madeleine Rondeaux's relationship, starting with *Les Cahiers d'André Walter,* no doubt explains why he asked Jeanne for the letters instead of asking Madeleine directly.

It's enormous, 25 big albums with 8 toccatas in each. I'm almost dead with joy. The progress I'm making with my piano delights me. I practiced 2 ½ hours today, Sunday, and I already remember the pieces far more easily.

The letter ends with the rather waspish postscript: "Enclosed is a stamp to wound Madeleine's pride."[17]

What is particularly clear is that André's pride was wounded by the rarity of Madeleine's letters and that he felt somewhat disappointed in love (although the word love is perhaps premature). In any case, there is no need to add that the tender relationship he had with his cousin was as chaste then as it continued to be till the end. On the other hand, it seemed to take on its mystical nature, obvious when Gide was about sixteen, not all at once but gradually.

[17] Letter from André Gide to Jeanne Rondeaux, unpublished.

16: Studies with Monsieur Richard

> *"M. Richard had a taste for letters, but
> he was not learned enough for his taste
> to be really good."*
>
> Si le grain ne meurt, *I, 132*

T OWARD the end of 1882, André Gide's health had become so delicate that his mother decided to take him away to the Riviera for
the rest of the winter. Once the New Year's Day ritual in the
rue de Crosne was over, they left, accompanied by Anna Shackleton and
Marie Leuenberger, so that the sickly young boy was anxiously watched
over by his mother, his governess, and his maid.

For the entire time, André Gide "lay fallow." He never opened a book,
he did no homework, he learned no lessons. His mind and body were on
holiday and his mother's only concern was that he avoid any exertion. In
his unpublished notes for *Si le grain ne meurt* Gide summarized his stay
on the Riviera as follows:

Cannes—first Hyères—frightful stomach aches—vomiting etc.—doctor made
me wear an absurd girdle to avoid flatulence—*the first palm trees*—mamma
takes us to Cannes—we cross the Esterel—mad joy—Cannes—ecstasy. The De
Pourtalès—excursions—picking flowers—groves of olive trees (I do nothing but
live, exactly, read nothing, study nothing—I feel)—the islands (ah! if I had
worked at my piano—mamma says I was incapable of it)—The guinea pigs—
The coast road—we can see Corsica—La Turbie—all the way to the border.[1]

The only words André Gide underlined were "the first palm trees," and
it is probable that the discovery contributed to his "mad joy." It is also
clear that he deeply regretted the fact that his mother did not take advan-

---

[1] Unpublished notes for *Si le grain ne meurt*.

tage of his free time on the Riviera to make him work at his piano. In the hotel sitting room in Cannes, there was "a piano, very second-rate, but on which I might have practiced a little every day; alas! my mother had been advised to avoid carefully anything that might cost me any effort. . . . I am furious, like M. Jourdain, when I dream of the virtuoso I might be today, if only I had been somewhat encouraged at that time."[2] André Gide's taste for music, especially for the piano, was gradually awakening. However, obeying the doctor's orders, Mme. Gide even forbade him trying to speak "a little German" with Marie Leuenberger or Anna Shackleton, for she "considered it prudent not to trouble me further."

It was during the month of May, 1883, that Mme. Gide decided to return to Paris and the rue de Tournon apartment, where they had in fact spent almost no time since Paul Gide's death. She then took it into her head that the apartment had become far too big for her and her son and set about finding another. Her search gave rise to the pathetic discussions previously mentioned with her sister Claire Démarest concerning the rent, the neighborhood, the floor, and the *porte-cochère*. As for André, the idea of moving was "immensely" exciting. His mother, duly advised by Aunt Claire, chose a beautiful apartment at 6 rue de Commaille, with windows that had "the costly privilege" of giving onto a marvelous garden.

During the last months in the rue de Tournon, Anton Rubinstein came to Paris to give, in 1883, a series of concerts at the Salle Erard. Mme. Gide found the price of seats "prohibitive"; nevertheless, she allowed her son to go to three of the concerts. André was enraptured by Rubinstein, and of all the early "musical moments" of his childhood, the recollection of that one made all the others "seem pale." He would have really liked to attend the recital devoted to Chopin, but his mother considered Chopin's music "unhealthy" and refused to take him. He was exceedingly vexed. Yet although the decision may appear harsh, it was no doubt justified. Mme. Gide knew her son's extreme nervousness and dreaded anything that might overexcite him, more especially as he seemed to be regaining his balance since his hibernation at Cannes.

Despite the fact that she very much wanted her son to return to the Ecole Alsacienne, she dared not force him to go. Having learned by experience, she did not insist, and while she managed the move from the rue de Tournon to the rue de Commaille, she had him board in Passy with an accommodating professor, "M. Richard," who seemed to suit him. Had she at last found the peace she so much hoped for? After all the tribulations that had led them from Paris to Rouen, from Rouen to La Roque, from La Roque to Montpellier, from Montpellier to Lamelou-les-Bains, from Lamalou-les-Bains to Gérardmer, from Gérardmer to Paris, from

[2] *Si le grain ne meurt,* I, 132.

Paris to Rouen, from Rouen to La Roque, from La Roque to Paris, from Paris to Rouen, from Rouen to Hyères, from Hyères to Cannes, from Cannes to Paris, Mme. Gide aspired to a little stability.

André Gide was happy at M. Richard's.[3] Richard lived in Passy at 12 rue Raynouard in a sunny house with a "little orangery" and a garden that formed a terrace "from which one overlooked half of Paris." His new pupil boarded with him at first, along with two young English girls who "were primarily paying for the fresh air and the beautiful view." Altogether it was congenial, and the professor was not at all a *magister*. The summer holidays soon arrived, and M. Richard spent part of them at La Roque where he continued André's schooling, while a young friend of almost the same age, Armand Bavretel, a pastor's son,[4] was there to accompany him on his walks, for Mme. Gide dreaded her son's increasingly pronounced taste for reverie and solitude.

When school began again in October, 1883, Mme. Gide boldly took action. She tried to make André return to the Ecole Alsacienne, but her attempt was not crowned with success. Indeed headaches—"of the most annoying kind"—reappeared, as well as the unconquerable fatigue and the insomnia. He once again became so nervous that he was sick, and his mother was forced to change back to the old regime, "that desultory, indulgent education which lay no particular stress on the harness." M. Richard, who was hardly inclined to exertion himself, was just the right man to see to it. They came to an understanding, and for two and a half years André Gide lived under the weak rule of the indulgent pedagogue who feared nothing more than overworking.

M. Richard was not a pastor, but he had wanted to be one. That good intention accounted for much of Mme. Gide's confidence in him. His ecclesiastical training had left him with no trace of severity but with a kind of unction. Nonchalant and an idler, the charming man was not a hard worker but had a real taste for conversation, walking, birds, and poets. He had a weakness for lyricism and took his revenge on the too-classical program and *Cinna*'s relatively frigid style by declaiming Hugo's *Le Roi s'amuse* for his young pupil.

André Gide's greatest literary and poetic emotion at the age of thirteen came, alas (Hugo's revenge),[5] from the Marquis de Saint-Vallier's long and redundant speech, beginning "Dans votre lit, tombeau de la vertu des

[3] Actually M. Henry Bauer (unpublished notes for *Si le grain ne meurt*).

[4] Actually Emile Ambresin (*ibid.*).

[5] When Gide was asked whom he considered the greatest French poet, he laconically replied: "Hugo, alas!"

femmes." Gide was rapt in "lyrical amazement." He conceived a boundless admiration for the titan who was able to express such daring things in verse. In June, 1885, a few days after Victor Hugo's funeral, he was indignant because of a certain lack of respect toward the demigod. As he wrote to his cousin Jeanne Rondeaux:

Last Thursday we passed in front of the Pantheon with mamma and believe it or not Victor Hugo's wreaths were still outside on the steps, getting fresh air; those made of pearls are still in good condition, but those made of everlasting flowers are lying all over the steps like stewed fruit. We went in and everyone kept his hat on; the altar and the apse were gone, there was nothing but walls, therefore it seemed so big!! no one stands on ceremony at all anymore, everyone talks and laughs as if he were at home. Children play hide-and-seek behind the columns outside and amuse themselves by jumping over Victor Hugo's wreaths.[6]

The reprobation that can be sensed in the letter for such disrespect shows that André Gide was already filled with veneration for literary glory and for the man who to him was the first to embody it.

Having established the fact that his young pupil was particularly sensitive to lyricism and vibrated "like a violin," M. Richard decided to subject him to even more trying emotions by reading him Richepin's *Blasphèmes* and Rollinat's *Névroses*. Under the bow of his almost pastoral voice, the neophyte's nerves quivered. A very strange education indeed, and it would be interesting to know what Mme. Gide thought of it, for it was at just about that time that she forbade her son to go to the Chopin recital at the Salle Erard.

While Gide was being initiated into literature, at least into the most romantic kind, he was also making progress with his music. And the poetic and musical emotions, genrously meted out by M. Richard and "old Schifmacker,"[7] his piano teacher, made their way so rapidly in André Gide's very precocious soul that on the morning of January 1, 1884, he had the "revelation" that he would be a poet. The anecdote is charming. He had been to Anna Shackleton's to wish her a happy New Year. As he was leaving, at about noon, beaming with joy, he saw a bird alight on his cap "like the Holy Ghost." He immediately felt "the thrilling assurance of having been marked out by a bird sent from Heaven," and delighted and uplifted, ran home to his mother with the "Heavenly creature" in hand:

I was already inclined to believe that I had a vocation; I mean a vocation of a mystical nature; it seemed to me that from then on, I was bound by a kind of

----

[6] Letter from André Gide to Jeanne Rondeaux, unpublished. The letter is not dated but was most probably written a few days after Hugo's funeral on May 31, 1885.

[7] Actually Adolphe W. (unpublished notes for *Si le grain ne meurt*).

secret pact, and when I heard by mother say that she hoped I would have a career in such and such, in the Forest Service for example, which she thought particularly suited to my tastes,[8] I halfheartedly went along with her plans, to be polite, as one would take part in a game, knowing perfectly well that the vital interest lies elsewhere.[9]

The moment of "mad pride," brought about by the canary dropping from Heaven onto his head like a tongue of fire announcing his alliance with the beyond, was strengthened by a feeling of being predestined:

It would not have taken much for me to say to my mother: "How could I dispose of myself? Don't you know that I haven't the right to? Haven't you understood that I am one of the elect?" In fact I think that one day, when she was urging me to choose a profession, I did say something of the kind.

A few days after the annunciation, he saw "another canary" swoop down in front of him and managed to cover it with his cap. This time it was a female. "Wild with delight, delirious," he brought it back to the house and put it in the cage with the male.

In a letter addressed, most likely during the same month of January, 1884, to his cousin Jeanne Rondeaux,[10] André Gide alluded to "two nice little finches, M. Soldat and Pipette," but alas they were merely finches and cannot be identified as the canary messengers. All the same, the letter is significant in that it alludes to a whole little menagerie and reveals Gide's tastes as a young naturalist:

MY DEAR JEANNE,

I don't think I've yet spoken to you about my menagerie. It consists of: 1. a hairy little man with no tail, who is called Fanchon, in short, a delightful little white, brown, and black guinea pig, and his brother Blanchet who, if he doesn't hide in the coal bags as is his habit, is snow white, as his name indicates. Then comes M. Soldat and Pipette, two nice little finches. Then an aquarium of sea water containing for the time being a few shells of various species, one sea urchin, and two very curious beasts such as you have certainly never seen; they resemble two centipedes which instead of legs have appendages that resemble the leaves of a book and are always in motion.

My sea urchins [*sic*] are also very curious; when they are left alone for a time, all their spines become soft and are transformed into so many tentacles that begin to dance about. As soon as they encounter an object, they attach them-

---

[8] In addition, several members of his father's family were inspectors in the Forest Service. Mme. Gide no doubt considered it a peaceful profession, into which her son might be easily admitted.

[9] *Si le grain ne meurt*, I, 187.

[10] The letter is not dated, nor are most of André Gide's early letters to Jeanne Rondeaux.

selves to it and the sea urchin drags after it. You must admit that all that is very curious. But I think I'm spouting a bit and getting away from the point.

Yes my dear Jeanne, this year like the others, and more than the others, I wish you everything I can possibly wish you, can it come true?

Adieu dear Jeanne.

Happy New Year.

Happy return.

Happy Christmas.

Happy return.

ANDRÉ GIDE

Ever since puberty, Gide had fallen back into the solitary habit of his childhood. When he finally succumbed, it was after an obsessing struggle, made even more painful by his real desire for purity. His ideal of resisting sin was strengthened by his growing piety and his admiration for his pure cousin Madeleine. "When I gave in, it was to my vice, I paid no attention whatever to outside provocations." He portrayed himself "at fifteen, unbelievably ignorant of the surroundings of debauchery . . . in spite of my explorations through the apartments of cocottes." His explorations were in fact limited to a few furtive glances. When the rise in the cost of rent and the departure of his English boarders forced M. Richard to leave Passy and look for another apartment, he took his young pupil with him. And the search led to many questionable neighborhoods. However, once M. Richard chose a place in the Batignolles district, the "scabrous" but apparently edifying adventures came to an end.

During the time he was a day boarder with the Richards in Batignolles, one of Gide's fellow boarders was a boy named Bernard Tissaudier. Bernard was "a jovial boy, outspoken, with a ruddy complexion and a black crew cut; he had a lot of good sense, liked to talk, and I felt extremely drawn to him." He too was a Protestant, of puritanical upbringing, and Mme. Gide found him very well-mannered. After she had met him, she saw no reason why the two day boarders should not travel home together after they had left M. Richard's in the evening. But one evening, as she was reading an article in the *Temps* with her usual earnestness, André saw her expression suddenly change. She frowned dramatically and in an appropriately grave voice said: "I do hope your friend Tissaudier does not go through the Passage du Havre when he leaves the *lycée?* . . . I see in the papers that the Passage du Havre is extremely disreputable." And then she was silent.

Badly upset by those mysterious words, young Gide immediately began to imagine the Passage du Havre as "a place of debauchery, a gehenna, the Roncevaux of decency." He pictured the streetwalkers with "a pathetic mixture of the hideous and the poetic." For days to come, he dreamed about the lost creatures, at once attractive and repellent, with all the resources of a fifteen-year-old imagination. And he embellished his dreams with "the indecent, the charming, and the horrible—especially the horrible." He had visions of monstrous seductions and aggressions, more enticing ones no doubt than those of his childhood nightmares, but equally terrifying. "For example, I could see my poor Tissaudier being orgiastically torn to pieces by hetaerae." Clearly the vampires and vamps of the Passage du Havre had different means from the *Crique,* but they used them to the same ends. It was not humanly possible to let good old Bernard run such risks. Overcoming his shyness and gathering all his courage together, André decided to warn him.

As they sat side by side at M. Richard's doing their lessons, André made a great effort and "in a voice choked with anguish," asked his friend:

"Bernard, when you leave the *lycée,* you don't take the Passage du Havre, do you?" "Why do you ask me that?" said he, opening his eyes wide in amazement. Suddenly I felt overwhelmed and panic-stricken by something enormous, religious, like at the time of little Raoul's death or like the day I felt cut off, excluded; completely shaken by sobs, I threw myself down at my friend's knees: "Bernard! Oh! I beg of you: don't go there." My tone of voice, my vehemence, my tears were those of a madman.[11]

Bernard Tissaudier made no mistake about the reason for his friend's anguish, and in the calmest way possible, said: "Do you really think that I don't know about the profession? . . . Go on, you don't have to worry about me!" André Gide's wave of emotion fell and broke on the word "profession," which restored the regimented and financial nature of the streetwalkers' trade. He was dumbfounded at the fact that "the dragon I had made *that* into" could be considered cold-bloodedly and without trembling. Actually, he was not so quick in ceasing to make *that* into a dragon.

Relating this third *Schauder* to the two others, Gide write: "I have done my best to describe the kind of overwhelming suffocation, accompanied by tears and sobs, to which I was subject, and which, in those first three manifestations I have repeatedly talked about, surprised me so very much."[12] The three *Schaudern,* in which the feeling of painful insecurity was carried to its culminating point, were most certainly attacks of anguish. Each one appeared to be released by the intuition of a separation, whether it was little Raoul's death, the feeling of not being like the others, or the mortal danger Bernard was exposed to and with which Gide obviously identified through a kind of *Einfühlung.*

[11] *Si le grain ne meurt,* I, 194.
[12] *Ibid.,* p. 195.

The life of M. Richard's pupil went on as usual, with the days spent at his professor's and the evenings at home with his mother. A real hunger for reading took hold of him; he would devour at least one book a day and from then on forsook his menagerie. The love of literature triumphed over the love of nature. Then an event, which in my opinion is of considerable importance, took place: Gide read Amiel's *Journal.*

In his notes concerning the time he spent at M. Richard's, he wrote: "A little greenhouse where instead of reading Racine and Corneille which he finds terribly boring, we read 'les Névroses' and 'les Blasphèmes' and 'le Roi s'amuse' which makes me sob.—And only later on (in Batignolles), *Amiel.*"[13] The last word is the only one underlined. The precise detail "in Batignolles" makes it possible to situate his reading of Amiel at about the age of fifteen. The *Journal* of Henri-Frédéric Amiel had just been published and "was all the rage." Those *Fragments d'un Journal intime,* which began to come out two years after Amiel's death (1881), were but a very small part of an enormous work, a 16,900-page manuscript, the original of which is in the Geneva Library. The morbid shyness and perpetual anxiety of the Genevan Narcissus are expressed in the *Fragments* with such psychological finesse that the book is a masterpiece of introspective literature.

M. Richard, smitten with Amiel's *Journal,* lent it to his young pupil, who "most sincerely" admired it. The book was a revelation to him and, even more, a revelation about himself. But afterward his initial attraction turned to hostility. Indeed, later on one of the lines of force in André Gide's evolution as a writer was not to be or not to remain an Amiel. Therefore, he was not able to speak of his great juvenile admiration in retrospect with any ease, and more or less hid his own feelings behind those he attributed to Professor Richard:

He found in it a complacent reflection of his own indecisions, relapses, doubts, as if it were an excuse or even an authorization; as for me, I never failed to be sensitive to the ambiguous charm of that moral preciosity, although Amiel's scruples, his groping about, and his nonsensical obscurities so exasperate me today.[14]

Gide succumbed all the more easily to Amiel's ambiguous charm in that he was already spellbound by the magic of ambivalence. He recognized his own difficulties and peculiarities in it as if it were a mirror, for he then was "deplorably shy, stiff with reserve, paralyzed by scruples," torn between contradictory tendencies, a prey to doubt, indecision, and hesitation, incapable of acting and of "simply being."

Amiel's influence on him was all the greater in that he found not only a reflection of certain of his own difficulties but also a "sickness of the

---

[13] Unpublished notes for *Si le grain ne meurt.*

[14] *Si le grain ne meurt,* I, 191.

ideal," to use one of the Genevan's expressions, and reading Amiel helped to make him aware of it. A few months after reading the *Journal,* he began to keep his own personal diary "out of a need to give shape to a chaotic inner agitation." And so M. Richard, although not much of a pedagogue, earned literary recognition by having the future author of an admirable journal read Amiel at a very early age.

Mme. Gide closely supervised her son's choice of books, and it is quite extraordinary how he accepted her restrictions. "I felt honor bound not to deceive her." His mother preferred books of history and criticism, and the walls of the large hall in the rue de Commaille apartment and those of André's room were covered with them. He personally hated history but took great pleasure in the critical works and through them he discovered the writers they were concerned with.

Yet André Gide was then dreaming of poetry. He vainly implored his mother to open Paul Gide's bookcase, "the bookcase of poets," hidden away in a carefully locked room. It was not until he was almost sixteen that Mme. Gide finally allowed him in, having been strongly urged to by Albert Démarest who had some influence on her. And helped by Albert, the little bookcase with its glass doors was opened up, at first parsimoniously, then altogether, allowing a flight of enchanted words to escape toward the dazzled boy, who had been given a sign by the auspicious birds.

17: Three Friendships

> *"Passionate as our relationship was,
> there was not the slightest trace of sensuality in it."*
>
> Si le grain ne meurt, *I, 173*

IRECTLY after André Gide's early childhood, friendships—none of which was at all questionable—played a great part in his life. Albert Démarest, "Armand Bavretel," and "Lionel" were very different in age, social class, and character, and each one opened up a different world to him. None of the three friendships was at all alike, except for the demanding passion Gide brought to each one. Even then he could have said what he was to say later about each of the friends of his youth: "I could not bear to think that any of them might possibly have a more intimate confidant than myself, and I offered myself to all of them just as totally as I demanded that each one give himself to me."[1]

Albert Démarest, born in Rouen on March 7, 1848, was twenty years older than his first cousin. In spite of such a great difference in age, he was the only male cousin with whom André Gide had a really close friendship. There were many reasons for it, some due to the family relationship, others personal. The Démarests, like the Gides, lived in Paris, where Guillaume Démarest, Albert's father, had been a lawyer. The two sisters, Claire Démarest and Juliette Gide, saw each other very often and their friendship became even greater after their husbands' deaths: Guillaume Démarest died in 1879, Paul Gide in 1880. During the holidays the Démarests and the Gides would meet—either in Rouen on New Year's

[1] *Si le grain ne meurt*, I, 259.

Day or in their neighboring country houses in Normandy during the summer. As I have already mentioned, it was in about 1878, after the summer holidays, that Albert Démarest began to pay attention to his young cousin.

Albert, whose father's family was Catholic, had been brought up by his mother as a Protestant. He had a liberal mind, and his "indignation" at the reactionary opinions and the *ne plus ultra* Catholicism that reigned at the Henri Rondeaux' was not without influence upon his young cousin during their visits to the rue de Crosne. He also taught Gide, who at that time was horrified by anything military, what it meant to be patriotic.[2]

The older he grew, the more André admired Albert and wanted his affection:

Even at that time, I had a kind of adoration for Albert; I have already said how ardently I drank in his words, especially when they went against my natural inclination; of course he very rarely countered what I said and I ordinarily found him extraordinarily anxious to understand the part of me that was apt to be the least understood by my mother and the rest of the family.

Although Albert was very attached to his mother and her only companion since Guillaume Démarest's death, he was most independent with regard to the prejudices of his milieu. "His slightest remarks amused me inexpressibly, because he said exactly the things I never dared say, and even the things I never dared think; the mere sound of his voice delighted me." His presence gave André Gide the impression of protection:

Albert was tall; he was very strong and at the same time very gentle . . . I knew he was the winner in all sports, especially in swimming and rowing; and after having experienced the intoxication of the outdoors and of splendid physical development, he was now almost entirely taken up with painting, music, and poetry.

That last characteristic is important. "To me he personified art, courage, and freedom." In André Gide's extremely bourgeois milieu, Albert Démarest was to him "the artist" of the family.

As a young boy, Albert had wanted to be a painter but had been convinced by his parents to study architecture instead. When his father died in 1879, Albert, then thirty-one years old, decided to go back to his former dream and gradually forsook his career as an architect to devote himself exclusively to painting. Since he was just as passionately fond of music and poetry, he was happy to find the same tastes in his young cousin, for they were hardly prevalent in the family. They would meet every Sunday evening, when either Aunt Claire and Albert would come to dine in the rue de Commaille or Mme. Gide and André would in turn go to the boulevard Saint-Germain.[3] After dinner, while the two sisters chatted or

[2] *Ibid.,* p. 140.
[3] The Démarests were then living at 78 boulevard Saint-Germain.

played a game of cards, the two cousins would sit down at the piano. M. Schifmacker's pupil had made progress, and together they tasted "some of the keenest and most profound musical pleasures I have ever known." During Mme. Gide's stay at La Roque at the time of a typhoid fever epidemic, Albert came alone to dine in the rue de Commaille, and for André it was a "treat" to have him all to himself. "We prolonged the evening well into the night, and we played so sweetly the angels must have heard."

Mme. Gide had great esteem for Albert Démarest, and he was one of the members of the family who had the most influence on her. It was therefore to him that André turned when, at sixteen, he wanted to get his mother's permission to open "the little bookcase with the glass doors." At first she energetically refused: "He'll ransack the library"; then she temporized: "He has quite enough to do with the books in the hall and those in his room. Why don't we wait until he has read all those"; she then protested against the accusation of thus giving the books in the library the attraction of forbidden fruit—"In that case, one should never forbid anything"— continued to struggle for a time, and finally, having run out of arguments, came to terms. It was understood that every book André might choose would be read with her, not only in her presence but aloud. She gave up that demand following a reading which embarrassed one of them as much as the other. Then she waived all restrictive clauses and put the library of poets completely at her son's disposal. The victory of the two conspirators was total.

André Gide would have liked to rivet all of Albert's attention, but Albert continued to express his feelings with moderation: "I vaguely suffered from his reserve, and I cannot help thinking today that he would have done me a greater service by throwing it off." I shall come back to that laconic remark.

During the summers of 1882 and 1883 Mme. Gide had a young boy, just slightly older than André, come to La Roque to keep him company. She was worried about her son's lack of exercise, his habit of dreaming or reading on his "small island," or going in exclusively for the "too-contemplative delights of fishing."

Armand Bavretel was a pastor's son and came from a rather poor family. It would seem that through contact with him, André Gide discovered for the first time just how privileged he himself was. "I was privileged without knowing it, just as I was French and Protestant without knowing it; once outside, everything seemed foreign to me." Armand, who was painfully sensitive and already bitter, suffered from his family's poverty. The first time he entered the large drawing room at La Roque, he burst into tears: "As I too was doing all I could to be affectionate, I was more than surprised and almost shocked by his tears. . . . I did not yet understand how offensive the appearance of wealth can be to someone who is poor." André Gide understood far better when on Twelfth Night he was invited to the Bavretels to come and "draw kings," an invitation that was repeated for several years. The six Bavretels—father, mother, two sons, and two daughters—lived in the district of the Halles, the central market of Paris, in cramped lodgings:

Here poverty stopped being merely privative, as the rich are too apt to believe; one felt it as something real, aggressive, attentive; it exercised its frightful sway over minds and hearts, crept in everywhere, touched the most secret and most tender spots, and warped the delicate springs of life.

Armand, mocking and bitterly ironic, his embarrassed mother, his solemn father, his sister whom he teased and humiliated until she dissolved into tears, the uncomfortable guests, all the characters of that scene and the "murky atmosphere I had inhaled at the Bavretels" made a painful impression on André Gide. While Armand "made his mother miserable by exhibiting and pointing out everything she would have liked to conceal— the stains, the torn or unmatched objects"—his friend, in such different surroundings from his own, found the poverty so "foreign" that he completely lost "the notion of reality." He then experienced one of those states of "estrangement" in contact with reality that were to play a great role in the evolution of his vocation as a novelist to whom life appeared as an illusion to be described.

When Gide created Armand Vedel and the Vedel family in *Les Faux-Monnayeurs,* he was describing Armand Bavretel and the Bavretel milieu, basing his description on the recollection of the distressing feasts of the Epiphany:

I especially thought about it again when, a few years later (I had lost touch with him in the interval), I received an announcement of Armand's death. I was traveling and unable to go to his funeral. When I saw his unfortunate mother again somewhat later, I did not dare question her. I then learned indirectly that Armand had thrown himself into the Seine.[4]

François de Witt, the "Lionel" of *Si le grain ne meurt,* was the seventh child of Pauline Guizot and Cornelis de Witt. Born on May 22, 1870, he was a few months younger than André Gide. They would meet during the holidays in Calvados, for the Cornelis de Witts were then living at Val-

---

[4] "That same evening, I learned of Emile A.'s death. He committed suicide, I'm certain of it" (*Journal,* 1891, p. 23).

Richer and the Gides at La Roque–Baignard. Later on, they also saw each other in Paris, where their families lived for the rest of the year. During his early childhood, André Gide was not especially drawn to his neighbor, whom he found too boisterous. Then he got into the habit of playing with him.

Starting with the summer of 1884, when André Gide was alone at La Roque with his mother (neither his cousins nor Armand came that year, and Anna Shackleton had died in May), he saw "Lionel" more frequently. And it was the start of a great friendship that lasted for about three years:

Passionate as our relationship was, there was not the slightest trace of sensuality in it. First of all, Lionel was thoroughly ugly; and no doubt I already felt that fundamental incapacity for mixing the spirit and the senses, which I think is rather special to me and which was soon to become one of the cardinal aversions of my life.[5]

The details he gives about the friendship in *Si le grain ne meurt* are supplemented by an entire notebook "written inside the Alençon Café in Nov. '97." It is interesting to compare the two versions.

In the notebook, after having recalled some of his childhood games with François, Gide added:

One Sunday I went to V.-R. earlier. It was the time for prayer. With the family and the servants, I went into the large drawing room where we all bowed our heads in the same spirit of communion—and François—sitting next to me, took my hand while we were kneeling and held it during the prayer. When I was about to leave him, I wanted to kiss him, and he greatly astonished me by saying: "No! one only kisses women!"[6]

In *Si le grain ne meurt* Gide has recounted the same episode but as two entirely separate anecdotes.

The notebook continues:

He insisted on telling me at that moment that in his brother's library, to which he had the key, there were many pretty queer books he planned to read as soon as he had the time. Among others: *Mémoires d'un chien de chasse!* I remember the title for I turned it over in my mind for a long time trying to figure out what was indecent about it. I think it was the same summer that he was reading the *Encyclopedia,* looking through article after article for information about the sexual organ and what one does with it. He was already advanced with regard to many things (or at any rate I was much less so than he). His cousin de la B. informed him and initiated him into many things and many practices. He told me all about it that summer and talked about what he was reading at that very moment. I was more ignorant than it is possible to be; less depraved than he at

[5] *Si le grain ne meurt,* I, 173.

[6] Alençon notebook, November, 1879, unpublished.

that age and without much curiosity. I naïvely asked what one could do with a woman, and he then used some words that meant nothing to me. He disgusted me sometimes, in fact a great deal. I was already almost incessantly concerned with the idea of training myself, becoming different, better. Actually at that time I had very few weaknesses; my mind was *constantly straining toward something better*.[7] Having admitted our weaknesses, I told him that we ought to use our friendship to break ourselves of them. At first he accepted and seemed to agree with me. We were to confess to each other and by rivaling each other in virtue, find something to cure us from giving in to our vices. For that to work, he would have had to want to improve as much as I; but he did not, I think, consider that which *filled me with horror*[8] as a vice. When on the following Sunday I triumphantly told him that I had not sinned, as I was waiting for the same words from him, I saw him blush a little—he said a bit harshly, "Good for you!"—then we spoke of something else.[9]

That page, which is so important for an understanding of Gide's psychology in that it tells about the "horror" he then felt with regard to his "sin," his desire to improve and to turn his mind energetically "toward something better," has no equivalent in *Si le grain ne meurt*. There he no more than alludes to the "terrific books" in the Val-Richer library which excited Lionel's curiosity.[10]

The sentimental relationship between the two children included studies and games together, as well as the reading of books on religion:

I think it was at that time that we had a great passion for natural history; we wanted to limit our research to cryptogams, so that the research would be more fruitful, not as vast but more thorough.

I took an extraordinary collection of excrescences to Paris in a box. I wanted to examine them under a mounted magnifying glass and under a microscope; so as not to get lost in hypotheses, all the work had to be restricted to describing. The description had simply to be precise. I attached to it a drawing that I colored with a crayon. The diligence I put into the work was worthy of the greatest discoveries. . . .

At the same time, we were beginning to read Pascal, Bossuet, Fénélon, and Saint Augustine: Fénélon's *Le Traité de l'existence de Dieu,* Bossuet's *De la Connaissance de Dieu,* and Saint Augustine's *Confessions,* of course.[11] We made a real study of those three writers; it astonishes me even now. We were so excited about it that we planned to continue in Paris. So during an entire winter, we met together every Wednesday and read Bossuet, Pascal, and Fénélon and managed to write moral commentaries about them. I have kept

[7] The italics are mine.

[8] *Idem.*

[9] Alençon notebook.

[10] *Si le grain ne meurt,* I, 176.

[11] The phrase "Saint Augustine's *Confessions,* of course" was crossed out by Gide.

several of them; they are stupid, but I'm careful not to laugh at them: those little voluntary studies that we passionately made were extraordinarily profitable to us. We were tremendously serious then: we despised everything that was not serious, thinking we were above it.

We also read Massillon's sermon for the third Sunday of Lent and Bossuet's sermons on death, on the passion of Jesus, the panegyric of Saint Bernard—and many others. At that age I would have done better to have read poetry. No, not really: *everything contributed to making me as I am today*.[12]

We also played for the first time those fragments of Bach that were so well-arranged by Saint-Saëns, particularly the great fugue. I was extremely serious.

I was also very disappointed when he told me one day that he did not think he would become a writer when he was older.[13]

In *Si le grain ne meurt* Gide wrote that their friendship finally came to nothing. In the Alençon notebook he also recalled the end of the friendship:

What put an end to such charming relations was his association with O. J.-L.,[14] to whom François became attached and whom I could not bear. I was hurt at the fact that François found good qualities in him and claimed he could not tell me what they were, implying that I possessed those qualities to such a small degree that I was incapable of even understanding them. From that moment on, our relations became more virile, more open, even more seriously cordial—but they completely lacked intimacy. He did not associate with my kind of people, nor I with his—and he made me feel it a great deal.

Here we seen the beginning of that exclusivity Gide brought to his friendships; he could not bear anyone he had chosen as a friend to prefer someone else.

The great friendship began in the summer of 1884, blazed during the summer of '85, fervently continued during the summer of '86, strongly declined in the summer of '87, as a most sarcastic letter to his cousin Jeanne Rondeaux concerning François testifies, and died almost completely in the summer of '88. The young man, who had received his *baccalauréat* and who during his year of preparation at the Ecole Alsacienne had discovered that Pierre Louis[15] was a friend whose tastes in literature were far more similar to his own, could no longer bear Lionel's air of superiority:

[12] The italics are mine.

[13] François de Witt became an army officer not a writer, but he did publish various articles in the *Revue des Deux Mondes* (R.-G. Nobécourt, *Les Nourritures d'André Gide,* p. 86).

[14] Octave Join-Lambert.

[15] The future Pierre Louÿs.

When I saw François again sometime after, he spoke to me a great deal about Napoleon, whose letters, in the great edition published by the Imprimerie Nationale, they had at Val-R. He was then completely involved in politics, dreamt of Pitt and his youth—recited the long speeches of Mr. de Mun.[16]

François had given the place of honor in his room to a photograph of the Duc d'Orléans whom he worshipped as a legitimist. The interests of the two friends were no longer the same. The divorce was consummated.

Each of Gide's first three friendships had decided influence on him. Albert Démarest, who at over thirty had decided to forsake his profession and devote himself exclusively to his vocation as an artist, seemed to him to embody "art, courage, and freedom." Sorrowful "Armand Bavretel" gave him a glimpse of the tragedy of social inequality, which, because of his upbringing, he had hardly suspected; and from that moment on, he was ever mindful of it, even during his years as an aesthete, as evidenced by his personal letters. The mystical turn taken by his friendship for "Lionel" encouraged his religious leanings, which became increasingly marked during the years that preceded and followed his confirmation.

[16] Alençon notebook.

18: At the Pension Keller

> *"I carried a New Testament in my pocket. . . . I took it out continually . . . in the trolley car, for instance, just like a priest, and during the recreation periods at the Pension Keller."*
>
> Si le grain ne meurt, *I, 215*

I N JANUARY, 1886, at the age of sixteen, the erratic pupil of nonchalant M. Richard became the zealous disciple of pious M. Keller. The Pension Keller, on the rue de Chevreuse, was close to the Ecole Alsacienne, on the rue d'Assas, where Mme. Gide still had hopes of sending her son. André was a special student at the Pension. He was the only boy who did not attend the *lycée,* and therefore arrived in the morning and afternoon just when the others were leaving. The absence of schoolmates eliminated the main reasons for his difficulties in adapting to school life, and the affection he felt for his professor did the rest: he became an excellent pupil.

M. Jacob Keller asked to be called M. Jacob, out of respect for his father, the founder of the pension, for whom he had "an almost religious and paralyzing" veneration. The old Keller continued to reign supreme from the third-floor room to which he was confined, appearing before the students only on great occasions. From his "little Huguenot room," sitting between an "enormous Bible" and mountains of school records, he kept watch over the playground from his window. Sometimes André would see the son rush to the sacred room, where his father would transmit orders which he seemed to receive straight from God, and slowly come down again like Moses carrying the holy Tables. In the unpublished notes for *Si le grain ne meurt* there is a floor plan of the Pension Keller, drawn by André Gide and on which the "staircase going up to M. Keller's office" is carefully indicated.

M. Jacob was not only a model son, he was a model professor, one of those born teachers who knows how to put himself on the student's level, "who wore himself out," and who put into practice the words of the Precursor: "He must increase, but I must decrease." As a result, Gide's intellectual growth was rapid, and in eighteen months he made up so well for all the years he "lay fallow" that in October, 1887, he was able to gratify his mother's wishes and enter the top class of the Ecole Alsacienne.

On Sunday mornings André would accompany M. Jacob to church and listen to him play and improvise on the harmonium. During the week he would attend spiritual concerts, in which his teacher took part as a member of the chorus. According to a letter he wrote to Jeanne Rondeaux:

I don't know whether or not I've told you that I have an opportunity to play the harmonium at M. Keller's. You can imagine how I make the most of it . . . —Last Tuesday we went to a splended concert given by the Concordia. I don't know whether or not you've heard of the Society. It's the greatest, most beautiful choral society in France, under the direction of Gounod. The chorus is made up solely of society people like you or me. The concerts are more especially appreciated in that all the seats are given away and cannot be bought for money. The tickets were given to us by M. Keller, who sings in the chorus. I came back enchanted. I still practice my piano 1½ to 2 hours a day, but I'm making very little progress. . . . Do excuse me for not having answered you sooner but I had so much to do these last days I almost got sick to death of work.[1]

Here we are far from the relative idleness of M. Richard's time. Gide was filled with a new fervor.

André Gide had become very pious. Yet his mystical adolescence could hardly have been foreseen from his childhood. The change in direction did date from the rue de Lecat event and his discovery of the "mystic orient" of his life, but the deep emotion he had experienced at that time had not brought about an immediate transformation of his young soul. The mystic turn taken by his friendship for François de Witt has already been mentioned. But many other influences had contributed to his religious evolution: the despair caused by Anna Shackleton's death, the presence of Pastor Allegret at La Roque, starting with the summer of 1885,[2] the correspondence he had begun to carry on regularly with his pious cousin Madeleine, and finally the preparation for his confirmation under the supervision of Pastor Couve.

[1] Letter from André Gide to Jeanne Rondeaux, Jan. 25, 1886, unpublished.

[2] This date is specified in André Gide's unpublished notes for *Si le grain ne meurt*.

On May 14, 1884, Anna Shackleton died. Mme. Gide and her son had taken her to the rue de Chalgrin nursing home, where she was to be operated on for a tumor. "I left her in a little ordinary, clean, cold room, and I never saw her again." André Gide was shattered by the final solitude of the woman who had watched over his childhood with such kindness:

For weeks and months I was filled with the anguish of her solitude. I imagined, in fact I heard her loving soul call out in despair, then sink back, forsaken by all but God; and it is the echo of that call that resounds in the last pages of my *Porte étroite*.

It would be impossible to doubt the almost religious emotion André Gide experienced at Anna Shackleton's death. For him, she was always "an admirable Christian figure," who embodied not only the most rigorous virtue, like his mother, but grace as well. The profound distress he felt then was to inspire, in the following years, his first literary project, which was to be called "Mort de Mlle. Adèle," then "Essai de bien mourir," and finally *La Porte étroite*.

Mme. Gide had been deeply affected by the death of her best friend. She also realized with great regret that her absence would deprive André of a Christian influence she knew to be of irreplaceable quality. She was well aware of the fact that she could not make up for it herself, for André continued to rebel strongly against her. She therefore tried to find someone who could attend to his religious education. During the summer of 1885 she invited Pastor Allegret, a man of great piety and exemplary morality, to come to La Roque, and he came again the following summers. His name is not mentioned in *Si le grain ne meurt* and it is a serious omission, for Pastor Allegret's influence on André Gide became evident at the end of his childhood and particularly during his adolescence. But in his letters of that time, he gave much space to "M. Allegret" and his apostolic zeal as a missionary who took part in the evangelization of the Congo. And it is interesting to note that Pastor Allegret's presence at La Roque during the summer of 1885 coincides with the time André Gide and François de Witt began to "methodically explore" works of mysticism and other reading "of the most serious kind."

With regard to his sixteenth year, Gide wrote: "I was preparing my religious instruction and the correspondence I had begun to carry on with my cousin also pedisposed my mind to it." That remark confirms the fact that his regular correspondence with Madeleine did not begin immediately after the rue de Lecat event but clearly later on, and it took an increasingly large part in his religious fervor. During the time he was at the Pension Keller, his pious cousin's influence on him had become considerable, and from then on she was really "the mystic orient" of his thoughts.

The extreme interest I took in everything from then on came primarily from the fact that Emmanuèle was with me everywhere. I never made a discovery without wanting to inform her of it immediately, and my joy was never perfect unless she shared it.

In every book he read he would write her initial next to the passages he hoped to reread with her during the coming holidays. In the summer they would arrange to meet in the Cuverville garden, near the "little secret gate" described in *La Porte étroite*. At La Roque they would meet in the woods early in the morning while the others were still asleep. Everything was pure and radiant in that tender and mystic relationship. Their love was a prayer, an elevation toward God, and they never felt closer to one another than when they discovered the Gospels together:

But the Gospels . . . Ah! At last I found the reason, the occupation, the infinite exhaustion of love. The feeling I then had explained and strengthened the feeling I had for Emmanuèle; *it was no different from it;*[3] it seemed only to deepen it and grant it its true place in my heart.[4]

When he had left Madeleine to go back to his life as a schoolboy in Paris, he felt that he had found her again through reading the sacred books and in that way could draw near to her. In the evening he read the Bible, during the day the Gospels:

I drank deep of the Bible only in the evening, but in the morning I went back to the Gospels with greater intimacy; and I went back to them again in the course of the day. I carried a New Testament in my pocket; it never left me; I took it out continually, and not only when I was alone but also in the presence of the very people who were apt to make fun of me and whose mockery I most dreaded: in the trolley car, for instance, just like a priest, and during the recreation periods at the Pension Keller . . . and exposed to my schoolmates' jeers, I offered my embarrassment and my blushes up to God.[5]

Few youthful images are as enlightening about the future author of *L'Immoraliste* as this one of the pious young boy, forcing himself to conquer his fear of what people might say in order to pursue his devotional reading. Knowing how painfully the fear of blushing in public obsessed André Gide as an adolescent, the test he voluntarily put himself through seems all the more praiseworthy.

In that state of exceptional piety, André Gide began to prepare for his confirmation with Pastor Couve. The periods preceding and following it were filled with such ardent fervor that they seemed to point to a religious

[3] The italics are mine.

[4] *Si le grain ne meurt*, I, 214.

[5] *Ibid.*, pp. 214–15.

vocation. "For months at a time I lived in a kind of seraphic state, the same state, I suppose, that is recaptured in saintliness." That seraphic state and the desire to act like an angel are indeed what an entire part of *Les Cahiers d'André Walter* is concerned with; the self-mortification it describes in an exaggerated way does somewhat correspond to Gide's adolescence:

Up at dawn, I plunged into a tub of icy water which I had made certain to fill the night before; then, before starting work, I would read a few verses of the Scriptures, or more precisely, I would reread those I had marked the evening before as suitable food for my next day's meditation; then I would pray. My prayer was like a perceptible movement of the soul toward more deeply penetrating into God; and I repeated the movement from hour to hour; I thus broke up my studies, and never changed the object of them without again bringing it as an offering to God. Out of self-mortification, I would sleep on a board; in the middle of the night I would get up again and kneel again, but not so much out of self-mortification as out of impatience for joy. I then felt I had reached the very acme of happiness.[6]

Parallel to the mystic way, the way of art was opening up before André Gide. "But now I am being born into life." It was in those terms that he recalled the happy time at which he discovered the poets. That particular discovery might therefore be considered one of those "second births" or rebirths that were in fact very numerous throughout his life. The reading of Heinrich Heine's poems and the translation of the *Buch der Lieder* was a "most moving discovery" for him. He had, at that time, "a passionate predilection" for verse. He learned Victor Hugo's poems by heart from "a charming little edition" that Anna Shackleton had given his mother. He took it with him on his walks. It contained *Les Voix intérieures, Les Chants du crépuscule,* and *Les Feuilles d'automne,* and he looked forward to reciting them to Madeleine during the holidays, for he never excluded her from anything he admired.

"It was at this time that I began to discover the Greeks, who have had such a decisive influence on my mind." He read them in Leconte de Lisle's beautiful translations which had just been published and given to him as a New Year's present by his Aunt Lucile. "Through them, I beheld Olympus, and the suffering of man, and the smiling severity of the gods; I learned mythology; I embraced Beauty and pressed it to my eager heart." Madeleine shared his enthusiasm:

My friend, for her part, read the *Iliad* and the tragic poets; her admiration excited mine even more and became one with it; I doubt whether we were ever in closer communion, even when we mystically feasted on the Gospels.

[6] *Ibid.,* pp. 215–16.

Strange! That beautiful pagan fervor blazed at the very time I was preparing for my Christian confirmation. Today I admire how little one interfered with the other. . . . The truth is that the temple of our hearts was like those mosques which are always open toward the East, so that light, music, and perfumes may divinely flood in. Exclusion seemed to us irreverent; whatever was beautiful found in us a welcome.[7]

Simultaneous enthusiasm for the miracle of the Gospels and the miracle of Greece did not seem contradictory to the boy who was one day to declare that the Christian and Apollonian ideals were incompatible. The "seraphic state" that was recaptured in grace and the "religious veneration" he felt while reading the *Iliad* and the *Oresteia* seemed to him equally sublime quests for saintliness and beauty. "With me, art and religion became devoutly one, and I tasted my most perfect ecstasy where they fused most harmoniously." Multiple feelings were involved in the first crystallization of his love, feelings that he was later patiently to try and decrystallize.

In 1887, still a pupil at the Pension Keller, André Gide began to take piano lessons with Marc de la Nux. He had studied the piano since his childhood, but his successive teachers, from one Mlle. de Goecklin to M. Schifmacker, had not given him the vocation. However, the teaching of M. de la Nux was a revelation to him. Marc de la Nux's personality charmed André Gide, for it gave him the image of an entire life devoted to art, with no regard whatever to personal advantage, and he found in him the same form of "saintliness" he found four years later in Mallarmé. Marc de la Nux was Leconte de Lisle's cousin and born as he was on the island of Réunion. He had been in contact with many Romantic performers and remembered having seen and heard Frédéric Chopin during his last years, a fact which added to his halo in his pupil's eyes, for Chopin and Schumann were then Gide's favorite composers.

From the very first piano lesson he gave André Gide, Marc de la Nux "undertook to reform completely" his musical education:

I thought I had no musical memory, or very little; the only way I could learn a piece by heart was by going back over it time and again, constantly referring to the music, lost as soon as I took my eyes off it. De la Nux went about it so well that in a few weeks I was able to play several Bach fugues without ever having to open the music; and I remember my surprise when I discovered that the one I thought I was playing in D flat was written in C sharp. Learning with him, everything became alive and clear, everything corresponded to the demand of harmonic necessities and became subtly decomposed and recomposed; I understood! I imagine it must have been with the same rapture that the Apostles felt the Holy Ghost descend upon them. It seemed to me that up until then, I had done no more than repeat, with-

[7] *Ibid.*, p. 212.

out understanding, the sounds of a divine language, which suddenly I had become capable of speaking. Every note took on its own special significance, became a word. With what enthusiasm I sat down to practice![8]

While André Gide was going from enthusiasm to enthusiasm, discovering the emotions of religion, poetry, and music, he could not help yielding to "sinister temptations." Since puberty, and after a time of relative latency, he had fallen back, like many shy and excitable adolescents, into his childhood vice. "The state of chastity, as I was forced to realize, was insidious and precarious; as every other outlet was denied me, I fell back into the vice of my early childhood, and each time I fell back, I despaired anew." He struggled against the sin of solitude, for he considered it shameful and never imagined giving in to more normal temptations:

My puritanical upbringing encouraged to excess a natural reserve, and I saw no harm in it. My lack of curiosity about the opposite sex was total; had I been able to discover the whole mystery of womankind with a single gesture, I should not have made it; I indulged myself by flatteringly calling my repugnance reprobation and taking my aversion for virtue; I lived withdrawn and constrained, and made an ideal of resistance; when I gave in, it was to my vice; I paid no attention whatever to outside provocations. Besides, at that age and with regard to those questions, how generously one fools oneself! On the days when I happen to believe in the devil, when I think of my saintly revulsions, my noble bristling, I seem to hear the *other* laughing and rubbing his hands together in the shadows. But how could I have foreseen what traps . . . ?[9]

And so the separation between love, something angelic, and sexual pleasure, something shameful, grew within him and became the main subject of *Les Cahiers d'André Walter.*

However, the "lack of curiosity," the "repugnance," the "aversion" for the "mystery of womankind" that the resolute pederast attributed to the sixteen-year-old-boy he had been, leave one skeptical. After his pathetic conversation with Bernard Tissaudier, André Gide had become very interested in the workings of certain "bareheaded women." When on Sunday evenings he would go to his Aunt Claire's for dinner, that is, "almost directly across from the Théâtre Cluny," he could not but notice the solitary streetwalkers in the neighborhood. One evening, naturally in the spring, either the "bounteous spring" of his sixteenth year or the following one, he left for Aunt Claire's "earlier than usual" in order to enjoy "the first warm weather," and found himself, as if by chance, among the women who intrigued him so much:

[8] *Si le grain ne meurt,* I, 237–38.

[9] *Ibid.,* pp. 197–98.

I hesitated for half a second as to whether I should not step off the sidewalk so as to avoid going near them; but something within me almost always triumphs *over fear:* namely, the fear of being cowardly;[10] I therefore kept walking. Suddenly, right next to me, another of those women whom I had not noticed at first or who had *sprung*[11] out of a doorway, looked me straight in the face, barring my way. I had to make a quick detour, and how my legs quaked under me as I ran! She had been singing, but she then stopped and shouted at me in a voice at once scolding, mocking, coaxing, and playful: "There's no reason to be so frightened, my pretty boy!" A wave of blood rushed to my face. I was as upset as if I had escaped with my life.[12]

It would indeed appear that the "seeking creatures" terrified him "as much as vitriol throwers," but there is an indication as well of the ambiguous agitation that Tissaudier's young friend had experienced before at the mere idea of those charming and horrible "monsters." In the diary he copied into *Les Cahiers d'André Walter,* dated 1887, we find the following vivid impressions of the girls:

I hate them so much I can't stand them near me, and those words they whisper in one's ear, the vulgar or subtle intonations, the voices of ghouls or of sirens; I hate them! I hate every bit of them. . . . In the street I step off the sidewalk, I race down the road; far off I see them turn around, come and go . . . and their gestures, the remarks I suspect they make intrigue me in spite of it all;—I should like to know . . .

Clearly his lack of curiosity was only relative, and hate is occasionally a very ambiguous form of aversion which does not imply a latent "repugnance" and is, in practice, apt to become quite the reverse.

As I came near her, she turned around, gestured, continuing to sing . . . I ran away. She gave a shrill laugh; another one, prowling around nearby, cried out: "No reason to be so frightened, my pretty boy! . . .

All that would be extremely banal were it not for the "pretty boy's" reaction:

I was so overcome with emotion that I thought I'd faint; the blood rushed to my face; a blush of shame, shame for them; the impression of being contaminated from merely having heard what they said. My temples throbbed, my eyes misted over with tears: I fled. But I shall remember, on that terrifying and very warm spring night, the shadow singing in the shimmering

---

[10] The italics are mine. That fear of being cowardly was given by Gide as the reason for having forced himself, at about the same time, to go into "a revolting little herbalist's shop in the rue Saint-Placide" to buy a smutty song, "simply as a challenge to myself; for, actually, I had not the slightest desire for it" (*ibid.,* p. 202).

[11] The italics are mine. The "spring" of a wild beast should be noted.

[12] *Si le grain ne meurt,* I, 197–98.

gaslight, under the flowering chestnut trees; then, the burst of laughter, as shrill as something that shatters;—and the tears I shed. Yes, I shall always remember; it was extraordinary poetry![13]

The panic, the unforgettable memory, the "extraordinary poetry" imply that the adolescent was not exactly indifferent to "the opposite sex."

While the good M. Jacob Keller was initiating his young pupil into the peace of study and the harmonium, manifold and dissonant emotions were accumulating in the soul of the future André Walter. Some months after having read Amiel's *Journal,* he himself had begun to keep a diary out of a need to untangle the chaos of the contrary tendencies he felt growing within him, "out of a need to give shape to a chaotic inner agitation." He wrote his first notebooks on a little Louis XVI writing desk, with a mirror attached, which Anna Shackleton had left him in her will.[14] Mme. Gide had put it in her son's room in the rue de Commaille.

At that time I felt I could not write, I almost said: think, except in front of that little mirror; in order to become aware of my emotions, of my thoughts, I felt I had first to read them in my eyes. Like Narcissus, I bent over my own image; therefore all the sentences I wrote at the time were also somewhat bent.

And so, in the mirror and in the *Cahier blanc,* André Gide began his practice of reflection at the age of sixteen, the age of Narcissus in the fable.

[13] *Les Cahiers d'André Walter, O.C.,* I, 46–47.

[14] The desk now belongs to M. and Mme. Lambert-Gide.

19: The Transitional Years

"Haven't you understood that I am one of the elect?"

Si le grain ne meurt, *I, 187*

ETWEEN the ages of thirteen and seventeen, a profound evolution, if not an actual "revolution," took place in André Gide's entire being. The anxiety-ridden child, painfully convinced that he was inferior to others, became an adolescent intoxicated with the "thrilling assurance" of being marked out by heaven. What happened between the anguished cry "I'm not like the others!" and the cry of pride "Haven't you understood that I am one of the elect?" How was his feeling of strangeness transformed into one of predestination, and how did his distressing feeling of inferiority become a hope of superiority? If we analyze those transitional years, we come upon two new factors: the awakening of a mystical love and the awakening of a literary vocation. Both certainly contributed to helping a weak and painful ego escape from its prison to reach an ideal. The solitary and sullen child of *Si le grain ne meurt* was no longer either solitary or sullen: he loved and he admired. Yet those rays of light were not enough to dispel the "darkness," and the young adolescent's equilibrium continued to be dangerously precarious. The childish subterfuges were replaced by sublimation, with all the somewhat excessive ascendancy the word implies.

When his cousin Madeleine's pain and despair caused André Gide suddenly to discover the "mystic orient" of his life, the upheaval of his whole being had the flashing intensity of passionate love, but it was actually compassionate love. His affection subsequently crystallized, not around a wave of desire, but around a wave of charity, in the Christian sense of the word: *caritas*. It was a thing of the soul from the very beginning. The impulse of sympathy (in all the etymological force of the term), the intoxication he then experienced through the sublime, "drunk with love, with pity, and with an obscure mixture of enthusiasm, self-sacrifice, and virtue," was a lyrical movement following the *Schaudern* of his childhood, when he was "in contact with the invisible reality," as he himself lucidly specified. But for the first time, his rapture was accompanied by a mystical oblation: "I called on God with all my strength and offered myself up to Him." In the life of an egoist the moment of enthusiasm or divine possession, when the soul "accepts being conquered by God," is a solemn moment which can be the beginning of a true inner revolution. This time it was love, and love meant salvation for the child of *Si le grain ne meurt*. It has been said that "neurotic children would be cured if they were loved"; it would be more correct to say: they would be cured if they loved.

The fact that there was nothing physical about their love at the beginning was quite natural, considering their ages and also the circumstances. But what constitutes a problem is that their love remained ideal to the end and was never consummated, even when both children had become adolescents and then, twelve years later, husband and wife. This problem, one of André Gide's main problems, will be considered in relation to André Walter's malady, for the entire explanation can be found in the *Cahiers*, written when Gide was only twenty. But in the "crystallization," which took place between the ages of thirteen and seventen, following the initial "coup de foudre," to use Stendhal's terms for a love so little Stendhalian, the sublime and incomplete nature of their love was clearly apparent:

Only the best part of me communed with her; however great the impulse of my love, it only served, or so it seems to me today, to divide my nature even more deeply, and I was soon forced to realize that while aspiring to give myself to her completely (however much I remained a child), my worship of her did not succeed in suppressing all the rest.[1]

In that division or, more precisely, in that dissociation between love— a thing of the soul—and desire—a thing of the senses—a dissociation that Gide was to consider a basic peculiarity of his nature, an important factor was an inferiority complex, characterized by both a neutralization of the guilt feeling and an overcompensation for the feeling of a weak ego through the creation of an ideal image of the other, which is in fact an ideal image of oneself.

In André Gide's eyes Madeleine Rondeaux was a kind of model or personification of the puritan ideal that he had built up under the influence

[1] *Et nunc manet in te,* p. 19.

of those "admirable Christian figures," particularly his mother.[2] He could not desire his cousin without reviving his guilt feeling to the point of anguish. What made it possible for him to love her with "seraphic" joy was the very fact of its being disembodied meant that his love was freed of guilt. He loved her, or more accurately, adored her as the angel whose radiant passage drew him out from the "darkness" of his childhood and led him toward God, no longer the God of severity and terror who judges and condemns, but toward the God of love and charity:

My childish love became one with my first religious fervor; or at any rate, because of her, a kind of emulation entered into it. It also seemed to me that by drawing nearer to God, I drew nearer to her, and in that slow ascent, I liked to feel the ground around her and me grow narrower.[3]

The ascent was indeed a mystical sublimation. André Gide's religious feeling awakened at the same time as his love for Madeleine, and throughout his life, their fluctuations remained parallel. He really thought of her as the guardian angel who watched over his safety and salvation, and tried to be worthy of her protection. "Work, effort, charitable acts, I offered everything to Alissa."[4] Then came his extraordinary change of attitude: "The extreme interest I took in everything from then on came primarily from the fact that Emmanuèle was with me everywhere."

Encouraged by that secret presence, he discovered the excitement of beauty imbued with mysticism, and communed with her through the sacred texts and the books of the poets. He wanted his soul to fly ever higher, so that his love was literally a prayer, an elevation toward God. The feeling he had on reading the Gospels was the same that he had for his cousin: "It was no different from it; it seemed only to deepen it and grant it its true place in my heart."[5] But he also noted down a formula so incisive that it verges on cruelty: "Perhaps, as in the case of the divine, my love was too easily satisfied with absence."

Without realizing it, he created an "imaginary figure" of his generally absent cousin, an "ideal figure I invented."[6] And that ideal figure, as different from Madeleine's real personality as Alissa's was to be, was in fact his own ideal. He projected onto her the idealized image of what he would have wished to be had he been able to comply with the pure exigencies of his moral "super-ego" and free himself of all darkness. But whereas he saw only clarity in her, "I was forced to recognize much darkness in

---

[2] The unconscious identification André Gide made between the ideal image he had of his cousin and the idealized image he had of his mother will be analyzed along with André Walter's angelism.

[3] *Et nunc manet in te*, p. 18.

[4] *La Porte étroite*, p. 35.

[5] *Si le grain ne meurt*, I, 214.

[6] *Et nunc manet in te*, p. 12.

myself."[7] A whole part of himself continued to give in to "sinister temptations," so that he was already feeling that separation between the angel and the demon from which the very Manichaean Walter was to suffer. Although the mystical ascent freed him from his feeling of inferiority and gave him a new and unexpectedly high value in his own eyes, the fall was but more hopeless. In other words, his failure in attempting to sublimate his instincts resulted in a new anguish, due not to repression but to the failure of repression. In the abasement he experienced because of it, he dreamed of new elevations.

And so developed the adolescent's fallacious certainty of an incompatibility between the pure, sentimental crystallization of his love for Madeleine and the terrifying realm of sexuality, which he thought of as the "monster," the "dragon," the "sin." He had come to abhor his solitary vice, as can be clearly seen from his words in the Alençon notebook concerning Lionel: "What filled me with horror was that I don't think he considered it a vice." But what really mattered was that the most normal sexual impulse seemed equally sinful to him, due to his mother's puritanical influence. Ever since her son's puberty, Mme. Gide, with increasing severity and "constant worry," kept a sharp eye on his friends, his walks, his piano lessons, his studies, his reading, his thoughts, "constantly" on the lookout for the shadow of evil. One scene, among many, is significant. We know that André Gide finally managed to get his mother's permission to read several books of poetry from his father's library, on condition that he read them with her and aloud. One evening while she was embroidering, he began to read Théophile Gautier's *Albertus,* fortunately subtitled "a theological poem." "I had begun very cheerfully, but as I progressed and the text became spicier, my voice became colder and more impersonal." When he came to a rather lively verse:[8]

"Give me the book for a minute," said my mother, suddenly interrupting me to my immense relief. Then, I looked at her: she held the book under the lamp and glanced through the verses that followed, with tightened lips and the frown of a judge *in camera,* listening to scabrous testimony.[9]

The judge's frown and the accused's voice which became colder and more impersonal are good examples of the psychological attitudes of mother and son.

Mme. Paul Gide's horror of "loose creatures" was not unrelated to her son's "terror" of them. His fright, very strange indeed for a fifteen-year-old

[7] *Ibid.,* p. 19.

[8] ". . . la Dame était si belle
qu'un saint du paradis se fût damné pour elle.
Oh! le tableau charmant! Toute honteuse et rouge . . ."

[9] *Si le grain ne meurt,* I, 202–3.

Parisian, is less so in view of his upbringing and "the dragon" he made "that" into. Yet those monsters of impurity, to the extent that their image became incommensurable with the mother image, seemed to him repulsive but attractive as well. In the future André Walter's Manichaean concept of the world, those damned creatures, excluded from the paradise of virtue, were by that very fact included in the hell of pleasure. To sin with the sinners was no longer unimaginable. Moreover, the anguish such women caused him implied an ambiguous mixture of desire and fear. If there was any trace of a guilt feeling, it was not the feeling of having committed a sin but rather the foreboding of possibly committing a sin. Besides, the sin implied the punishment of being orgiastically torn to pieces, similar to the phantasm of the mutilation through orgasm which has been so frequently discovered in the primitive unconscious and in myth.[10]

The character André Walter doubtless symbolizes a period somewhat later than that of the transitional years, but in his childish double, Boris Lapérouse, Gide portrays the awakening of a mystical love, freed from sexuality, which drew him away from his solitary temptations and redeemed his anguish. Yet the child of *Si le grain ne meurt* was made of stronger stuff than the child of *Les Faux-Monnayeurs,* and his moral upbringing had given him an infinitely tougher backbone. Above all, André Gide had a high card in his deck which the unfortunate Boris did not possess. He knew instinctively that some mysterious promise lay not in the heavens but within himself; along with the poison, he possessed the antidote. The sickly child was a poet who would know how to replace the obscure power of "magic formulas" with his own power of creating a magic universe of forms and words. If Boris had had that gift, he would probably not have committed suicide, and perhaps would have become a young poet: André Walter.

The vocation of an artist often begins as the expression of a drama that was constituted in childhood. A person who will one day accept solitude as his destiny, first has the feeling of being separate from others, incommunicable, "excluded." An artist's intuition of being unique—and his works are the final expression of it—is initially felt with anguish before being felt with pride. The terror of not being "the same as the others" precedes the marvelous calling.

"My works sprang from the anguish of my childhood," wrote François Mauriac, and André Gide himself re-established an invisible link between

---

[10] Either in the myth of the Atridae or in that of Osiris, in the physical form of a chopped-up or castrated body, or in the archetype of Orpheus as victim of the bacchantes. Each one successively played a part in Gide's personal mythology.

the attacks of anguish of his childhood and his first inspirations. Yet such states of poetic grace, no doubt less "gracious" than that of being marked out by a heavenly messenger, are frequent in children or adolescents gifted with intense emotivity and fertile imagination. It is one thing to be divinely moved, and another to be capable of expressing the emotion and channeling the dream. Between the poetic emotion and the *poietic* condition, between the imagination of the awakened dreamer and creation, there is a generally impassable gap which Gide precociously felt capable of crossing. Many are called to that road and few are chosen. It would be impossible to doubt that Gide had been called very early. One is born a poet, and he no doubt already was one when, as an enchanted but hidden spectator, participating in "the holiday mood,"[11] he discovered that between reality and dreams there is a second reality. He discovered the auras of his childhood through the auras of his vocation. But the latter did not take shape until he began to write. The romantic fervor he put into his adolescent years, especially after his mystical love for Madeleine had been awakened, was favorable to his need for freeing himself, through writing, from an overtaxing emotion. But the vocation of a writer can only be put to the test by writing. Before the actual experience of it, one could not speak of a vocation but only of a calling. Yet his comment at fifteen, "haven't you understood that I am one of the elect?" which might seem so presumptuous as to be ridiculous, ceases to be when we think that the timid and proud child was to become André Gide.

The origins of André Gide's literary vocation will be considered with relation to his first book, *Les Cahiers d'André Walter,* but here I should merely like to consider how it was prepared by "a solitary and sullen childhood." "Sullen" implies a disposition to be alone, hence withdrawal or repression. The obstacles and constraints that kept the child of *Si le grain ne meurt* from freely blossoming, forced him to withdraw into himself and flee into the imaginary. The aptitude for dreaming is no doubt a natural bent, differing according to each temperament, and certain constitutions are predisposed to it; but the narcissistic withdrawal in face of life is determined by affective complexes which add to the richness of reveries and lead to preferring "the possession of imaginary goods" to any adjustment to reality.

In André Gide's late childhood, as in that of many future artists, reverie was the great way of escape. He had precociously felt "a clumsy need to give life more density"[12] and to imagine a mysterious and clandestine world. The dual tendency of his nature—the curiosity that led him to be

---

[11] "Poetry," said Baudelaire, "is the state of being in a holiday mood." And he also said that poetic genius was "no more than childhood clearly formulated."

[12] *Si le grain ne meurt,* I, 28.

on the watch for "the play of living matter" and the taste for withdrawing into a country of phantasms—has already been emphasized with reference to his solitary games. As he grew older, games increasingly gave way to dreams. And it was because he was a sick child that Gide was able to protect his solitude and escape from the obligations of a conventional education and upbringing. When speaking of the "disorder" of his studies, he was surprised at the fact that "that desultory an education was able, in spite of everything, to make something of me." But it would seem, on the contrary, that the "unsystematic" regime was excellent for keeping him in the state of an awakened dreamer, which was to lead him to poetic vigilance. The winters on the Riviera, the sudden departures for La Roque, the "idleness," under the vague guardianship of private tutors, were certainly more in tune with his idiosyncrasy than the brilliant scholastic record of a bookworm would have been. The role played by the "idler," M. Richard, seems to have been particularly favorable. The circumstances of André Gide's youth, his family and academic conditions, his position as an only son, in a well-to-do milieu, exempt because of his nervous disorders from the obligations of school and collective distractions, encouraged his aptitude for living in the imaginary, for he was able to live apart. More specifically, his tendency to dream was not thwarted, as it would have been in other circumstances; but it goes without saying that outer circumstances are nothing without an inner predisposition.

Given to dreaming both because of his constitution and because of his complexity, he, like all children with the same temperament, had trouble adjusting to society and to the present, a difficulty often interpreted by naturally active people as "laziness," yet it is not, except in the sense that an accommodation, not visual here but psychological, might seem "lazy." Indeed, reverie relieves one of that effort of accommodation. The more young dreamers are gifted with emotivity and imagination, the more they have the tendency to turn away from reality and take refuge in a more or less magical phantasmagoria. As Sophroniska said with regard to that "lazy" child Boris: "I made him ashamed of having preferred the possession of imaginary goods to that of real goods, which are, I told him, the reward of effort."

We have known ever since Freud—and it was one of his least debatable discoveries—that dream and reverie have a "meaning," an unconscious intentionality. Tendencies that are not satisfied in reality and are repressed because of moral censure or social exigencies, are satisfied in the imaginary, but indirectly, in more or less disguised, masked, and symbolic forms which more or less conceal their origins. The greater the disproportion between the tendencies and the possibility of realizing them, the more young dreamers take refuge in the fallacious but voluptuous efficacy of a fictional world. They acquire or, rather, maintain the primitive belief in the all-powerful magic of thought: "Things BECOME true," said André Walter," one has only to think them.—Reality is within us."

Escape into the imaginary proves an effective subterfuge for protecting the ego from anguish by freeing it from feelings of guilt and inferiority. The guilty, weak, divided, fragmented ego finds magical compensations in reverie. As Denis de Rougemont wrote in his study of the roots of the Romantic malady:[13]

How could total life be recovered in its blessed unity? It was no longer possible here below, in the prison of the guilty and painful ego. It had therefore to be sought in the beyond. And we have seen that the Romantics considered dream, or the descent into the depths of the unconscious, as ways of returning to the lost world, to the "real life" which is "elsewhere," as Rimbaud expressed it. A life of indefinite expansion in the Universe or the divinity. A life of recaptured innocence: for the ego, which loses itself, also loses the feeling of its guilt.[14]

And, it must be added, the ego loses the feeling of its inferiority as well. In that fictional world where everything is possible, the dreamer "bovaryzes," sees himself with undefined, therefore infinite, possibilities, imagines a thousand existences, discovers unsuspected riches within himself. Such escape has its dangers. But while it may be disastrous insofar as it thwarts any adjustment to reality and creates a painful disproportion between life and dream, it may be just as profitable to anyone whose life will one day be devoted to the "possession of imaginary goods" and to the expression of the "second reality."

In the formation of André Gide's literary vocation, his discovery of the poets was of capital importance: "But now I am being born into life."[15] He knew, ever since the time his father read aloud to him in the rue de Tournon study, that the world of books can open up a world of enchantment; he had vibrated "like a violin" listening to M. Richard read Hugo, Richepin, and Rollinat; he had been "gripped" by his reading of the Christian mystics with François de Witt, "rapt" on discovering the Bible and the Gospels with Madeleine Rondeaux. But when he was finally allowed to read Paul Gide's favorite poets, he lived in a kind of lyric fervor. It was then that his passion for poetic literature began, a passion that stayed with him for many years: "At that time I had a passionate predilection for verse; I considered poetry the flower and fulfilment of life."[16]

It was then also that his interest in becoming a naturalist, a possibility

---

[13] The same Romantic malady as that of André Gide's adolescence.

[14] Denis de Rougemont, *Les Personnes du drame,* p. 219.

[15] *Si le grain ne meurt,* I, 205.

[16] *Ibid.,* p. 204.

indicated throughout an entire part of his childhood, seems to have flagged. From that time on, his mind was so taken up with reading—within himself and in those who awakened so many echoes in him—that he could not forget himself long enough to decipher patiently the great book of nature in any other way than through poetic divination, closer to impulses of the heart than to cool observation.[17] At the beginning of his adolescence, he was too mobile, too subjective, too lyrical, and also too anguished to become a scientist. The study of natural sciences made him forget his anguish but did not cure it, and Gide was too enamored of his personal malady not to return to it constantly and try to probe deeply into it through introspection, searching for an inner deliverance, whose secret he was to find only through the poets.

Another early calling, to which Gide more credibly reproached himself with being unfaithful, was that of a musician. Remembering the delight he had taken in the piano and especially in the study of Chopin, he sometimes wondered, in his old age, whether he had not been wrong to have chosen literature as his vocation. Had he taken lessons from "old De la Nux" any earlier, would André Gide's vocation have been changed? "What a pianist M. de la Nux would have made me, if only I had started with him sooner!"[18] Gide's sensitivity to music was indeed remarkable, but it was to find its expression in the balance and movement of his prose, the prose of a writer-musician. André Walter longed to write music, which he in fact finally did and perhaps a bit too much, but literature was to give André Gide the opportunity to express the dual tendency, lyrical and critical, of his nature as poet and analyst, musician and psychologist. He began to write as much out of a need to free himself of his emotions as out of a "need to give shape to a chaotic inner agitation."

A journal and poetry were therefore André Gide's first literary activities, both coming to relatively the same thing, for his first journal is poetic and his poetry is intimate and personal:

The state of preoccupation in which I lived had the serious drawback of introspectively absorbing all my faculties of attention; I wrote and wished to write nothing that was not intimate; I disdained history, and events seemed to me impertinent intruders.[19]

The earliest of those pages that has been kept is dated March, 1886, and show that he was already in the habit of writing. *Les Cahiers d'André Walter,* completed in October, 1890, therefore contain a number of pages

[17] He developed a kind of "naturistic mysticism" (Seillière) similar to Rousseau's.

[18] *Si le grain ne meurt,* I, 237.

[19] *Ibid.,* p. 224.

dating from the four preceding years. In fact they represent the fictional "summa" of Gide's adolescence, between the ages of fifteen and twenty.

At fifteen, the age at which Gide began to write, he was primarily influenced by Amiel's *Journal,* and experienced a kind of deliverance in keeping his own. From then on, far from suffering from not being "like the others," he had specious delight in confiding it to his journal. Had Boris done the same with his troubles and despair, he too would have discovered that the "Strong Men's" gibes are no longer humiliating when transcribed in a schoolboy's notebook. For the notebook serves as practical experience in the use of blessed irony. Reality, transcribed by anyone who is capable of detaching himself from it enough so as to see it from an inner distance—a gift necessary to any arbitrator or artist—becomes, as it were, inoffensive: it is neutralized. Anyone who is successful in that difficult exercise finds that his feeling of inferiority is sooner or later replaced by a certain feeling of superiority. One might say, to use La Rochefoucauld's comment on laziness, that introspective analysis is "a beatitude of the soul which consoles it for all its losses and takes the place of all possessions." In my study of André Walter's malady I shall try to specify the link between the narcissistic condition and that of the confidential writer.

In the top form of the Ecole Alsacienne (1887–88), André Gide, then eighteen, discovered Goethe, a discovery far more important than that of Amiel and which he made thanks to Pierre Louis. Then, and only then, did his real years of apprenticeship begin.

20: At School with Pierre Louis

"A kind of genius dwelt in him."
Si le grain ne meurt, *I, 217*

1

N OCTOBER, 1887, a month before his eighteenth birthday, André
Gide went back to the Ecole Alsacienne after a break of almost
six years. However, the eighteen months he spent at the Pension
Keller helped him catch up on the time he had lost during the "years of
laying fallow," and he was prepared to enter the top form. Yet he somewhat dreaded his return. Toward the end of September, 1887, still on holiday at La Roque, he wrote to his cousin Jeanne Rondeaux:

. . . Two days ago we received a letter from good old M. Rieder, director of
the Ecole Als—a most affable letter which begins by stating the pleasure he
will have, thanks to my return, in renewing our relations. That school will begin on Tuesday at two o'clock with a translation from Latin (oh dear!) and
that I will have nothing to bring but a dictionary. Oh! do please burn three
candles for me on that day.[1]

The letter goes on to tell about a visit from François de Witt, implying
that the relations between the two friends had already grown considerably
cooler, and ends with these words:

Yesterday, Saturday, Alcofribas left. Tomorrow we leave. I haven't written you
as long a letter as I should have liked, but I'm in a great hurry to finish my
classics before going to class. Au revoir. Your affectionate cousin

HIPPOLITE DURILLON

[1] Letter from André Gide to Jeanne Rondeaux, September, 1887, unpublished.

As far as I know, Gide never used that schoolboy's pseudonym except in this one letter; although in the years to come, he was to take many other more literary pen names. In any case the first Tuesday of October, at two in the afternoon, "Hippolite Durillon," full of anxiety but no doubt protected by the candles lit for him by his three cousins, translated from Latin on the benches of the Ecole Alsacienne, not far from Pierre Louis, the future Pierre Louÿs.

Gide found none of his former schoolmates when he got to class. All the faces were new to him. But from the time he arrived, he had eyes for no one but Pierre Louis. Louis, then seventeen,[2] seemed to have everything: he was handsome, he was top in his class, above all he was a poet, and his love of literature was equal to his own:

He was more than a brilliant pupil; a kind of genius dwelt in him and what he did best he did most gracefully. He always unquestionably took first place in French composition; all the others were far behind.

André Gide had such admiration for his fellow student that he did not dare speak to him for several months, that is, until a small incident that took place toward the end of February or beginning of March, 1888. The feeling of inferiority he had with regard to him was one he had already experienced in many other circumstances. And their friendship came relatively late. In Pierre Louÿs' *Journal,* which he kept day by day,[3] there is not even a mention of that obscure André Gide, who nonetheless constantly had him in his thoughts.

In January the perpetual prizewinner noted down in his *Journal:* "Ever since the beginning of the year *all* my homework in French, without exception, has received the highest grades in the class. None of my work has ever been surpassed by any pupil." Yet a few weeks later he was to be surpassed, and by the shy little Huguenot he had hardly noticed. One fine day the professor, M. Dietz, giving the results of the grades in French composition, announced: "First, Gide; second, Louis . . ." "I made such a tremendous effort not to blush that I blushed all the more; my head was swimming." During the recreation period that followed, instead of joining the other boys on the playground, Gide as usual went into a glazed corridor to read. Suddenly he heard steps behind him: it was Louis.

"What are you reading?" he asked. Unable to speak, I held out my book. He skimmed through the pages of the *Buch der Lieder* for a moment. "So you

[2] Pierre Louis was born on December 10, 1870. He was therefore a year younger than André Gide.

[3] Pierre Louÿs, unpublished journal, kept from "Friday, June 24, 1887, nine in the evening" until "Wednesday, May 16, 1888."

like poetry?" he went on, in a tone of voice and with a smile that I had not yet noticed. Well then! he had not come as an enemy. My heart melted. "Yes, I know these," he continued, giving me back the little book. "But in German I prefer Goethe's."

Then the bell rang and it was the end of the recreation period. But it was not long before André Gide saw Pierre Louis almost every day after school, either at Louis' house in the rue Vavin, quite near the Ecole Alsacienne, or at Gide's on the rue de Commaille.

When in his old age Gide said that he had been marked for life by the second part of *Faust* which Pierre Louis had read to him that year, he was not wrong. Although he never mentioned it in *Si le grain ne meurt,* and it was a serious "omission," he made up for it in the years to come.[4] Later on he recalled how shattered he was when Louis, his voice "moist with tears, admiration, and tenderness," read Goethe to him:[5]

Both of us went directly to the densest part of the works, to the heart of the burning bush: to *Faust,* and not even to the first part *of Faust* . . . We recklessly threw ourselves, heart and soul, into the second part. Oh, of course we did not read it all; but what we discovered was enough to revolutionize our aesthetic consciousness, or more precisely, make us aware of aesthetics, dominate our poetic universes, I almost said determine our vocations, and in our common admiration, seal our precarious friendship.

What most shattered the young Huguenot was Faust's monologue, on awakening in the world of nature:

The lines in which the participation of the outer world seems so active that I understood and was ashamed of the fact that up until then (*I was eighteen*)[6] I had opened only my soul to God; I understood that He could also speak to me through my senses, if the screen of books did not come between nature and myself, if I could only make a direct and permanent contact, achieve a physical communion, between my being and the surroundings.[7]

Knowing André Gide's mystical mood at the time, one can understand the strange expression: "was ashamed." Faust's monologue brought him

[4] In his "Goethe," published in the *N.R.F.,* in *Projet,* in *Le Retour du Tchad,* in his *Journal,* in his preface to Marcel Drouin's *La Sagesse de Goethe,* in his preface to the Pléiade edition of Goethe's works.

[5] The second part of *Faust* and *Iphigenia.* Gide did not read *Werther* until March 10, 1890, *Prometheus* until Easter Sunday, 1892, or the *Latin Elegies* until 1892–93. These dates are specified in Gide's *Cahiers de lecture,* unpublished.

[6] Not underlined in the text. This exact date further confirms the fact that Gide read *Faust* during his last year at the Ecole Alsacienne.

[7] "Goethe," *N.R.F.,* p. 370.

a pantheistic message that was completely new to the future author of *Les Nourritures terrestres.*

One cannot overemphasize the importance of Gide's discovery of Goethe at the age of eighteen; it was of course soon to be overlaid by other influences, but never obliterated:

I had the good fortune to come upon Goethe at the beginning of my life. I immediately felt the bonds of a deep fraternity being woven, as though in spite of myself; and however far I may have been carried away from him in my mystical wanderings, I have always let myself return to him with a deep satisfaction of my entire being.[8]

We shall specify further on the different stages of Goethe's influence on André Gide's youth, from 1888 to 1895, the year Mme. Paul Gide, in a letter to her brother-in-law Charles Gide, spoke of her alarm at the deplorable influence on her son of "that Goethe, whom he talks about constantly";[9] but here we are concerned only with Gide's first reading of him with Pierre Louis. For the great and precarious friendship began under the Olympian auspices of Goethe.

Pierre Louis' god was Hugo, whom he worshiped almost religiously. "I would willingly say about him what Mohammed said about Jesus: 'That man is God.' Thus my trinity would be: the Father, the Son, and Victor Hugo." Yet there were a few demigods in the two young poets' literary Olympus, although at some distance from Hugo and Goethe. Both of them, for example, adored Flaubert. Louis preferred *Salammbô* and Gide *L'Education sentimentale,*[10] whose hero, Frédéric Moreau, he thought somewhat resembled the future hero of the novel he was planning, who in turn was as much like him as a brother. They were both also full of admiration for Leconte de Lisle, whose translations of "the Greeks" had a lasting but different influence on each of them, "the Dorian" and "the Ionian."

One day when Pierre was sick, André paid him a visit:

Gide just came . . . I read him my Journal, a few passages, primarily about the books I've been reading. He found it very well written, anyway it showed on his face. He was beaming. I also read him a part of what I wrote a week ago yesterday about my aspirations. My ideas enchanted him, and astounded him! "What, you think that! It can't be! Grace! Poetry! Well, and Hugo, and Aeschylus?" Another one who doesn't know me. But then, who does know

[8] *Ibid.,* p. 368.

[9] Letter from Mme. Paul Gide to Charles Gide, April, 1895, unpublished.

[10] We might also note that of Hugo's works, Pierre Louÿs preferred *La Légende des siècles,* whereas André Gide preferred *Les Voix intérieures.*

me? He wanted something with more emotion. I read him my *Soir à la campagne*.[11] That delighted him.[12]

That little bedside scene, with Gide beaming as he listened to his friend's poetry, is significant in that it shows Gide's real interest in someone else's writings, a rather remarkable trait for a man of letters and one that remained with him: he was one of the most receptive listeners anyone could meet.

Almost as much as literature, music enthralled André Gide and Pierre Louis, and they often went to concerts on Sunday. Gide's preferences went to Chopin and Schumann, Louis' to Wagner and Massenet: "I should like to be in literature what Massenet became in music."[13] Gide hated Wagner even then, and his antipathy grew: "I abhor Wagner's person and his works my passionate aversion has but grown since my childhood. That extraordinary genius is more crushing than exalting . . ."

The two friends' tastes often differed. As Louis noted:

I often talk with Gide, although his opinions about almost everything are the opposite of mine; but he's the only one in the class who has literary tastes, the only one who is enthusiastic as I am, the only one with whom one can talk about anything other than girls, with whom one can talk seriously without him answering: "You bore me!"[14]

When it came to their life at the Ecole Alsacienne, preparing for the first part of the *baccalauréat,* the impetuous Pierre Louis could hardly bear it, whereas André Gide had become very studious, a fact that could never have been predicted from his childhood. The generally disagreeable period of cramming is recalled in a most unusual way in his published notes for *Si le grain ne meurt:*

It was one of the happiest times—yes, I can't remember ever having been happier than when I was preparing for my examinations. My mother was excellent, perfect for me; at such times our intimacy even became very great. She helped me as best she could, listened to me recite my lessons, helped me to set up large chronological tables so as to clarify the history I knew so badly.

I got up very early, about five in the morning—no later.—A tub was prepared in the bathroom next to my room, a tub full of cold water, into which I would plunge for a moment. I would say some sincere prayers, and then set

[11] The poem, written in Dizy on "April 6, 1888, 9–11 P.M.," is in a collection of Gide's and Louis' first poems entitled *Nous Deux.* The handwritten manuscript belongs to M. Henri Mondor, who was kind enough to let me see it.

[12] Pierre Louÿs, unpublished journal, May 14, 1888.

[13] Next to that sentence in his journal, Pierre Louis added in 1897: "It's just about what I have become—alas!"

[14] Pierre Louÿs, unpublished journal, May 14, 1888.

to work. When I finally compared my memory to that of others, I realized that it was extremely mediocre; (I now blame my vice for having made it so) —but then I considered it excellent because I made excellent use of it. I would go over the lessons I had studied before going to sleep and admired the unconscious work the brain does during the night.

Breakfast with my mother was delightful. Summer was radiant outside.

I would go back to sleep for an hour during the day so as to profit again from the unconscious work of sleep.[15] I slept on a board—I even got into the habit of it and still do it every time the habits of the house make it possible.

My brain voluptuously felt every new bit of knowledge enter into it. It was an admirable time—the time of all times I should like to begin again. I was certain that life was coming up from behind me—afterward—and that it was only about to begin.[16]

In July, 1888, the two friends passed the first part of the *baccalauréat* with no trouble whatever and, immediately after, went on holiday. Pierre was determined to make the most of his: "I shan't be able to able to recapture my fervor of today at the age of seventy." André went to La Roque–Baignard, as he did every year.

The arrival of his three cousins, Madeleine, Jeanne, and Valentine Rondeaux, was, as always, the great event of the holidays, and perhaps more especially that year. Madeleine, who was just twenty, had witnessed the legal separation of her mother and father that same year. She was deeply distressed by the despondency of her father, who was not to outlive his misfortune by very long;[17] and she was therefore more sensitive than ever to the tenderness shown her by André. Yet it would seem that she did not want that feeling to become love in the human sense. At least, that is the impression given by André Gide's diary dated the summer of 1888:

It was already late; as the others were tired, they sat down to wait for us. . . . "Oh Lord," I cried out, "it is right that we should stay here! if you wanted to? —let us make our tent here!" Then you smiled, but your smile had such sadness in it that I could feel your forsaken soul; mine quivered for a moment . . . ; you understood all too well, and fearful, quickly turning aside, you painfully tore yourself away from the charm. Your hand, which I had been holding, pushed mine away. "Let us go!" you said, "they're waiting for us. We must leave all that . . ."[18]

---

[15] Gide was faithful to the habit of "napping" almost all of his life. (*Translator's note:* Gide used the English word.)

[16] Uupublished notes for *Si le grain ne meurt*.

[17] Emile Rondeaux died on March 1, 1890.

[18] *Les Cahiers d'André Walter*, O.C., pp. 75–76.

One day as V.[19] was singing a Schumann melody at the piano:

Your emotion was too strong; the tears welled from your eyes; then, ashamed of being touched, troubled about feeling your soul so stirred in spite of yourself, you suddenly fled. I followed you; you ran to your room. "Ah!" you said, "please leave me!" I went away; I wandered in the country until evening, my spirit poised on infinite exaltations undulating to remembered harmonies.

The "Ah! please leave me" and the "O André! you acted in a cowardly way tonight," following a similar scene, give the feeling of simple things that have been said and are in sharp contrast to André Walter's very literary (not always in the best sense of the word) text. We shall come back to it in the analysis of *Les Cahiers d'André Walter*. But it is important now to emphasize the fact that whole passages of Gide's journal, written between 1886 and 1890, were transcribed into *Les Cahiers*. When in January, 1891, Madeleine Rondeaux read the novel for the first time, she was shocked at finding that the story her cousin told was their own and that many of the words were hers. "I shall wait," added André Walter at the end of summer 1888:

I spent all of today with her, but our eyes never tried to meet; I have not drawn nearer to you. . . . We shall go on our ways PARALLEL to one another: It used to make me despair . . . I have begun to read my Bible again. I must climb back up the slope, which I had come down unawares. Oh! how difficult it is![20]

The summer ended and his cousin left. On September 27 André Gide wrote to Jeanne Rondeaux. He was alone at La Roque with his mother and Pastor Allegret, who had joined them there. In the evenings during that end of September, while his mother and Pastor Allegret played a game of bezique, the sentimental pilgrim reread Sully Prudhomme, the melancholy poet of *Les Vaines tendresses*.[21] Gravely, with the deep seriousness that marked his adolescence, he was preparing to become initiated into philosophy, which, as we know, is the love of wisdom.

[19] Valentine Rondeaux, no doubt.

[20] *Les Cahiers d'André Walter, O.C.,* p. 80.

[21] The copy of *Les Cahiers d'André Walter* dedicated to Sully Prudhomme is inscribed: "To monsieur Sully Prudhomme, to the dear poet of solitude and intimate emotions, this tale of a 'vain tenderness,' André Gide."

21: Preparing for the Second *Baccalauréat*

> *"As I wanted my year of philosophy to be an initiation to wisdom, it was necessary, in my opinion, to go into seclusion."*
>
> Si le grain ne meurt, *I, 225*

EITHER André Gide nor Pierre Louis went back to the Ecole Alsacienne for their year of philosophy, the year that prepares for the second part of the *baccalauréat* examination. As Pierre Louis' elder brother, Georges,[1] left the rue Vavin to live in Passy, he put Pierre in the *lycée* Janson de Sailly. And as Mme. Gide allowed herself to be convinced that her dear Ecole Alsacienne was not equal to preparing for the second part of the *baccalauréat,* she sent her son to the *lycée* Henri IV. The two friends were thus separated, one on the right bank, the other on the left, although they often crossed the bridges.

As soon as the first term at Henri IV was over, André Gide left the *lycée.* That new break in his schooling was not motivated by nervous disorders and providential headaches as were the preceding ones, but rather by the need to withdraw to a "heated room" so as to more satisfactorily philosophize, following many illustrious examples: "The study of philosophy seemed to me then to require the kind of meditation that was hardly compatible with the atmosphere of classrooms and the promiscuity of schoolmates." He therefore decided to work alone, under the direction of the professor whose courses he had just taken at Henri IV, "M.L.", that is, M. Lyon.[2]

"My initiation into philosophy was due to Schopenhauer, and to him alone." He read *The World as Will and Idea,* probably in the fine translation Burdeau had made the year before (1888). The work sent him into

---

[1] Georges Louis, a diplomat, was twenty-three years older than Pierre.

[2] Unpublished notes for *Si le grain ne meurt:* "Henri IV 2½ months of philosophy, then M. Lyon and M. Simonnet—and M. Rigaut. Brittany with my dear mamma."

"indescribable raptures." He read it "from end to end" and "with such application of mind that for many months no outside appeal could distract me." He reread it often during the following years, as evidenced by his *cahier de lectures,* and even took it with him into the solitude of his chalet in Menthon, where he wrote *André Walter.* It was an important discovery, less no doubt than that of Goethe had been the year before, but one that probably had a real influence on his mind. He wrote later on: "Schopenhauer and Fichte nourished me, molded me, determined my thinking at an age when the mind finds itself faced with the great problems and becomes avidly questioning."[3] He read Fichte somewhat later,[4] but his reading of Schopenhauer does date from his year of philosophy, and it was doubtless the first time he had read a philosopher in the actual text.

Nothing could be less surprising than André Gide's "rapture" on discovering *The World as Will and Idea.* The great writer's art of composition and style could not have left him indifferent. The esoteric language found in many professional philosophers, and maliciously parodied in *Paludes,* put him off. Although he subsequently took some pleasure in such arduous reading, it was "as an imposition" to discipline his mind. But his real admiration always went to philosophers who were also artists, and curiously enough, after Schopenhauer, his master, to Nietzsche. The same year that Gide was studying philosophy, Henri Bergson's first work was published, his *Essai sur les données immédiates de la conscience.* It seems rather a pity that Gide did not discover Bergson until very late in life, at the time of *Le Retour du Tchad,* when he admitted that he was "Bergsonian without realizing it." Few philosophers were so obviously made to captivate him during his youth as that extraordinary artist. Had André Gide come upon him at an age when the chips were not yet down, it is possible that he would have been as influenced as Marcel Proust was in his youth.

Besides the actual literary attraction of Schopenhauer, the formula "the world is an idea" was perfectly suited to the young poet, and the mortification of "the will to live" perfectly suited to his ascetic ideal. The pessimistic analysis of life into which the philosopher put so much bitter enthusiasm; the glorification of art as a process which reveals the essence of the world and, having shown it to be will, the source of all suffering, makes it inoffensive; the antagonism between dream and reality; and the justification of chastity as a negation of mankind and asceticism as a means to nirvana— all are themes that deeply touched André Gide as he then was. He found that the book interpreted his *Schaudern,* his anguish and his ecstasy, that feeling of a "second reality" he had had since childhood, his passion for music and poetry, and even, he thought, his dislike for history.

[3] *Feuillets, O.C.,* XV, 513.

[4] He noted in his *Journal* of 1894: "During two autumns I also read Fichte."

From Schopenhauer he went on to German Romanticism, which was to have a definite influence on *Les Cahiers d'André Walter*. He later recalled the time he had been "strongly solicited" by Schopenhauer, Fichte, and the German Romantics in the following terms:

I am not certain that they did me nothing but good . . . I demanded that my mind consider appearances as so unreal that the variegated pattern and diversity of the outer world and the veil of Maya lost all importance for me, and that is extremely awkward for an artist. I had some trouble coming back to it.[5]

During that year he also read and reread Flaubert, "the friend always to be hoped for."[6] Beneath the apparent realism of the solitary writer from Croisset, he discovered the basic Romanticism, the Romantic irony, the pessimism, the feeling of universal illusion. He combined Flaubert's aesthetic influence with Schopenhauer's philosophical influence, and began dreaming of a "Nouvelle Education sentimentale," with a Huguenot, Germanic, and philosophizing Frédéric Moreau as its hero. Even Frédéric's platonic love for Mme. Arnoux, and that strange impossibility of desiring the woman one loves, awakened secret correspondences in him. As for Flaubert's style, it was indeed the style he would have then wanted to imitate, and the *Fragment de la Nouvelle Education sentimentale* that has been kept[7] shows clear signs of the cadence, the balance, the harmony, and the imperfect tenses so dear to Flaubert. But that first project came to nothing, and the influence of Flaubert's style was much less evident in *Les Cahiers d'André Walter*. Besides, Gide quickly stopped saying "he" and began to say "I."

Much as the young philosopher-poet of the rue de Commaille wished for solitude, he did not give up seeing Pierre Louis. The two friends met often, and Louis introduced Gide to several of his classmates at Janson de Sailly, in particular Drouin, Quillot, and Legrand, who were also "specializing in literature."

Marcel Drouin was perhaps the most gifted of them all. In his old age Gide, speaking of Drouin who had subsequently become his brother-in-law,[8] told me: "Neither Pierre Louis nor even, a bit later, Paul Valéry[9] gave me the overwhelming impression of intellectual superiority that Marcel Drouin gave me when I knew him." He added: "If he had not gone through the professorial mill, he would have become Leibnitz. I will not say Goethe, but Leibnitz." Maurice Quillot, to whom Gide was to dedi-

---

[5] *Feuillets, O.C.,* XV, 513.

[6] *Les Cahiers d'André Walter,* p. 33.

[7] *Fragments, O.C.,* I, 3.

[8] Marcel Drouin married Jeanne Rondeaux.

[9] André Gide and Paul Valéry first met in December, 1890, in Montpellier.

cate *Les Nourritures terrestres,* and Legrand, the future Franc-Nohain, were both from Nevers. At sixteen

they filled the Nevers newspapers with extraordinary novels, news articles, and art criticism. "Potache-Revue" was founded by Quillot alone, to help pass the time after his friend's departure; during that time at Janson, Legrand struck up a friendship with Drouin and then Louis-Quillot joined them the following year.[10]

Potache-Revue was a bimonthly paper, printed in Nevers, and founded, we discover, by Quillot. Drouin, Louis, Legrand, and Gide began to collaborate on it during that year of philosophy, and Gide above all the following year, using the pseudonyms Zan-dal-Bar and Bernard Durval.

Pierre Louis continued to be his best friend. When Louis lost his father in April, 1889, he wrote to Gide: "I no longer have anyone who knew me as a child: I can feel how much you pity me. Love me even more: I now have only my brother and you. Yours more than ever." However, André Gide's friendship with his cousin Albert Démarest was becoming much closer than it had been in the years before. Until then they had been seeing each other every Sunday; from then on they saw each other every day. As soon as André had passed the first part of his *baccalauréat,* Albert suggested that he paint his portrait, and every evening during the year of philosophy André went to Albert's studio on the rue de la Grande-Chaumière to pose. The artist wanted him to sit for a painting he intended to present at the Salon and in which his cousin would portray a violinist. "Look like you're suffering," he told him, as the young philosopher, armed with a bow, clutched the strings with his fingers. But to spare the rather delicate model too much fatigue, the painting sessions were frequently interrupted by long conversations.

André Gide was an admirable listener, and he always excelled in the art of being a confidant. Albert told him all about his life, his thwarted vocation, his long bitterness concealed beneath a gay manner, a liaison that he hid from his mother so as not to grieve her, his passion for art, his hopes. His example encouraged the young poet to affirm his vocation straight away, without compromising with the exigencies and reprobation of a bourgeois milieu; and the ideals they had in common did much to increase their intimacy. Of all the letters of Gide's youth that I have consulted, there are none, to my mind, in which Gide showed more confidence and affectionate abandon than in his letters to Démarest. Several of them make it possible to clarify certain obscure points and, as evidence, they ring true.

Albert Démarest introduced his cousin into the studio and to the family of his "master," Jean-Paul Laurens. In that cultured and refined circle,

[10] Letter from André Gide to his mother, Oct. 17, 1894, unpublished.

Gide's own taste became formed. Until then he had been so taken up with his inner life that he had paid little attention to his surroundings:

Suddenly my eyes were opened, and I immediately realized that my mother's furnishings were ugly; it seemed to me that something of them stayed with me, and my feeling of unworthiness was so intense that I think I should have fainted with shame and shyness had not my former classmate, Jean-Paul Laurens's son, been present.[11]

Paul Laurens, whom Gide had known in the lower classes of the Ecole Alsacienne and whom he had remembered as being a "disobedient and charming dunce," had become a young man passionately fond of painting, music, and literature. It did not take long for them to become friends. But whenever Gide went to see the Laurens on the rue de Notre-Dame-des-Champs, he was tormented by the fear of being taken for a "bourgeois," a word he hated as much as his dear Flaubert.

Albert Démarest's portrait of André Gide, painted that year and retouched the next, has been kept.[12] Although the treatment is rather clumsy, it does give some idea of the young Romantic that the future André Walter was at that time. His fear of being taken for a bourgeois prompted him to try to look like an "artist." He wore a black flowing bow tie and his hair long, in accordance with the most venerable tradition of "manes." As he wrote to his cousin Jeanne, and not without satisfaction:

With my impossible hair, which horrifies the masses, I should be a great success. My hair has become legendary. Stories are being spread about it. The other day at the Exhibition, a little ruffian walking past me shouted: "Oh, let me have one!!" People from the provinces take me for a *picpoquet* [*sic*], it's most amusing . . . One more word about my hair, I very often now wear it in front of my ears, hanging down from both sides of the brow: you must tell me what I look like that way. Yesterday, at Aunt C.'s dinner, I had pushed it behind my ears. I waited for Maurice[13] to make tremendous fun of me, but not at all! he found that I greatly resembled a fantastic character from the Tales of Hoffmann!!![14]

Gide became very concerned with his physical appearance and intended to look like what he wanted to be: an artist. To the flowing tie and long hair he added a kind of dandyism and mannerism that is clearly evident in certain touching photographs taken in Albert Démarest's studio. Mme. Gide, bound to a strict conformity, was terribly upset by his extravagance and youthful eccentricities, but in vain. Just as she could not overcome his obstinacy as a child, so she could not get him to go to a barber until he had

---

11 *Si le grain ne meurt,* I, 234.

12 It now belongs to M. Dominique Drouin.

13 Maurice Démarest, Albert's older brother.

14 Letter from André Gide to Jeanne Rondeaux, unpublished.

forced people to recognize him as an artist. He considered the excessive growth of his locks a sign of independence. As Gide was very susceptible and changed his soul every time he changed his suit or his attitude, it is probable that his sittings for Albert as a "suffering violinist" helped make him into somewhat of a "poseur," as he was later to describe himself, and encouraged his sentimental melancholia. Moreover, he already knew that he was a born actor. He would study his face in the little mirror attached to the desk he had inherited from Anna Shackleton: "I would gaze upon my features untiringly, study them, train them like an actor, and I searched my lips and my eyes for the expression of all the passions I hoped to feel." André Walter was to remember that training. But the young Huguenot was not long in noticing that "the concern with trying to show emotion supplants the sincere emotion"[15] and reproached himself with such complacency.

Between his studies with M. Lyon and his reading of Schopenhauer, his visits with Pierre Louis and his collaboration on the *Potache-Revue,* his sittings for Albert Démarest and his piano lessons with Marc de la Nux, his correspondence with his cousins and the writing of his journal, the year of philosophy quickly passed. In fact, it passed so quickly that in July of that year, André Gide failed the second part of his *baccalauréat.* Before going back into harness, he wanted, early in the summer, to go on a trip to Brittany.

The hero of the book Gide never stopped thinking about, which was to be called either "Allain" or "La Nouvelle Education sentimentale," had, like Chateaubriand's René, to be Breton: "Had I been able to, I would have had myself born in Brittany in Locmariaquer la Dévote. . . ." And it was partly in order to describe the background he considered suitable a priori to his hero—he would never have imagined him a Gascon or a spicy Burgundian—that he wanted to go to Brittany alone, a pack on his back, with no companion. But his mother would hear nothing of it: she advised Switzerland:

She agreed to let me travel without her; but not exactly alone. When she spoke of enrolling me in a group of Alpine Club tourists, I flatly declared that the atmosphere of the association would drive me quite mad, and that besides, I had come to detest Switzerland.[16]

But Albert Démarest, who had suggested that his cousin read Flaubert's *Par les champs et par les grèves* and therefore felt responsible for his wanderlust, once again intervened, and once again, after much resistance, Mme. Gide compromised. She accepted Brittany, but on the condition that

[15] *Les Cahiers d'André Walter, O.C.,* I, 66.   [16] *Si le grain ne meurt,* I, 243.

she follow her son, from a distance, and meet him every two days at a stopping point decided upon in advance.[17] For all that, the concession was of great importance. It meant that, for the first time, her only son was to travel not quite alone but at some distance from her. Thus nothing could happen to him without her immediately knowing about it.

During his trip Gide met Gauguin, Sérusier, and Filiger at an inn at Le Pouldu. *Si le grain ne meurt* gives a detailed account of the meeting,[18] but there is no mention of an incident that nevertheless had some importance. He was riding in a carriage in the vicinity of Douarnenez and was reading, when suddenly he noticed that the coachman had just slipped off his seat:

When I raised my eyes from my book, there was no more coachman. I leaned forward, he was just about to go under the wheels. I seized the reins, which was not an easy thing to do . . . But if I tell you about this, it is because I remember the strange state I found myself in. It was a kind of sudden revelation about myself. I did not feel the slightest emotion; I was merely extraordinarily interested (*amused* would be more exact), perfectly equal to averting an accident, capable of the proper reactions, etc. But taking part in all that as if at a show *outside* of reality. And if the accident had happened to me, it would have been exactly the same, for you must not see this as a sign of insensitivity . . . I could not manage to take it "seriously"; I acted as I did, with perfect presence of mind and in a state of extreme nervous tension and hypersensitivity . . . but I was amused, simply amused, as if I were at a show. For naturally fear, real fear, then becomes impossible.[19]

When he told me the story in very similar terms, Gide added: "That was the day I discovered irony." He obviously gave that word its transcendent meaning, the meaning intended by German Romanticism and the philosophy of illusion. The experience, not nearly as new an experience as he would have us believe, was no less intense.

When he returned from Brittany, André Gide set to work again preparing for the *baccalauréat,* passed it in October, and then decided to start seriously on a literary career. He wanted to have finished his first book before he was twenty-one.

On July 24, 1889, Pierre Louis wrote him a long letter in verse, somewhat naïve perhaps, but indicative of the desires and hopes they had in common. One line of it reads: "I will go on toward happiness, toward thrills and toward glory . . ." Glory did in fact come very quickly to Pierre Louÿs, whose *Aphrodite* made him famous at twenty-five; it came very slowly to André Gide.

[17] For that reason we have no record of the trip to Brittany in André Gide's letters to his mother.

[18] Gide later saw Gauguin again at Mallarmé's.   [19] *Journal,* p. 800.

22: Great Expectations

"I decided to launch out at once on my own career."

Si le grain ne meurt, *I, 242*

ONE afternoon in the fall of 1889, André Gide and Pierre Louis climbed to the seventh floor of a house in the rue Monsieur-le-Prince, which they thought the perfect place for setting up a literary group. Looking over the roofs of the medical school, the Latin Quarter, the Seine and Notre-Dame in the setting sun, and in the distance the hazy shapes of Montmartre, Gide repeated Rastignac's words to the City: "And now . . . you and I will have it out!"

There was nothing particularly original in that adolescent remark, assuming that Gide had been shaken by the Balzacian fever, and according to his *cahier de lectures,* begun on October 28, 1889, he was then assiduously reading Balzac. But the context is far less banal:

And we both imagined the life of a poor student in such a room, with just enough money to be able to work in freedom. And at his feet, in front of his writing table, Paris. And shut in there with the dream of his masterwork, not to come out until it is finished.[1]

That particular ambition is not a common one; it was not Rastignac's but rather that of the race of young men who are most different from him, that of the Louis Lamberts. Lambert was not eager for outer conquest but for inner victory, and through writing, to make his dream live. His vocation was like that of a scholarly monk who is determined not to be false to him-

[1] *Journal,* 1889, p. 13.

self. That last sentence of André Gide at twenty is more like something André Walter would have said than Rastignac. For Walter "life is a means, not an end"; it is merely a means to the end, and the end is the work to be written. He felt that everything was within him, and the closed-in room—in the rue Monsieur-le-Prince or elsewhere—seemed necessary and quite sufficient for the kind of conquest he dreamed of. He was hardly concerned with the outside world in which—as a reader of Schopenhauer—he saw nothing but illusion and appearances: "Things BECOME true; we have only to think them. Reality is within us; our mind creates its own Truths." The remark shows little more than a naïve idealism, and yet those words of André Walter were part of André Gide's deeper self.

Mme. Gide was not opposed to her son's devoting himself entirely to literature directly after passing his second *baccalauréat*. Considering her character and her background, her tolerance seems extraordinary. André's stubborn will doubtless had had its effect ("I want to be a poet! I am a poet!"), and perhaps her "esteem" for "poetry and generally everything that was above her" was also a factor; but most important was Albert Démarest's influence, which once again was brought to bear on behalf of his young cousin. All that Mme. Gide insisted upon was that he agree to take, regularly, two lessons a week in French from his former professor at the Ecole Alsacienne, M. Dietz.

Gide therefore, at twenty, felt "strangely free, with no responsibilities, no material worries . . . Free? Actually, no, for I was bound by my love and by my plans for the book I have spoken about, which I could not help but consider the most imperious of duties." In fact he was convinced that his book and his love for Madeleine were but one, for the book seemed to him "a long declaration, a profession of love." André Gide's twentieth year was that in which he wrote *Les Cahiers d'André Walter*. Of course he had been planning it throughout his adolescence, but the work had not yet taken shape.

At the same time that he hoped for glory, André Gide was also hoping to marry his cousin "as soon as possible." He imagined his book as a declaration "so noble, so touching, so conclusive, that once it was published, our parents would *no longer* oppose our marriage and Emmanuèle would *no longer*[2] refuse me her hand."[3] These words are highly suggestive. If their parents would no longer oppose the marriage and Madeleine no longer refuse her hand, they obviously had opposed it and she obviously had refused him, which never—up to that point—was even implied in *Si le*

---

[2] "No longer" is not italicized in the text.

[3] *Si le grain ne meurt*, I, 243.

grain ne meurt. Emmanuèle's "Ah! please leave me" in *Les Cahiers d'André Walter,* interpreted by Walter as a Corneillian battle between his cousin's mind, which could neither be conquered nor convinced, and her soul, which wanted nothing more than to give in, must have had some basis in reality.

At the end of February, 1890, Emile Rondeaux—then only fifty-six—had a stroke. He died on March 1 in Rouen, surrounded by his five children and his nephew André Gide. Just as, ten years before, Madeleine had been with André on the day of Paul Gide's funeral, so André was with Madeleine on the day of Emile Rondeaux's death: "She and I had both sat at his bedside, bent over him and brought very close together during his last moments; it seemed to me that in our sorrow for his loss our engagement had been consecrated." This last sentence is significant not only because of the word "consecrated," emphasizing the almost mystical way in which Gide considered his "engagement," but because of the "it seemed to me," which reduced that consecration to an illusion. Gide's reticence here, and his reticence alone, prepared the way in *Si le grain ne meurt* for what was to follow: Madeleine's tender but categorical refusal to marry him when, directly after *Les Cahiers* were published, he proposed to her. Actually, nothing in Madeleine's attitude had given him reason to believe that her tenderness for him was any more than that of a sister for a brother, or that the very deep and sincere feeling she had for him as "an older sister" could be called love, in the usual sense of the word. There had been a misunderstanding.

On the other hand, there is no doubt that during that year and those that followed, all the members of the family who knew about André's matrimonial plans considered them "madness," as much on the Rondeaux side as on the Gide side (certain of Charles Gide's subsequent letters testify to it), with perhaps the exception of Albert Démarest. But the main opposition came from Mme. Gide who, since the Emile Rondeaux had separated, had had great influence on her niece Madeleine, a girl generally "amenable to interdictions" and particularly heedful of her Aunt Juliette's opinion. In the eyes of his mother, André had remained a capricious and disconcerting child; she did not feel that at twenty the "eccentric" adolescent, with his long hair and romantic ideas, was of an age, as they say, to set up a home. She knew that he was temperamental and flighty, and felt that he offered not the slightest security. He had no "practical common sense," which she always deplored but was wrong about. He had no profession, for she could hardly consider literature a profession, and it was the only occupation her son would agree to settle down to. Just the fact of allowing him to become engaged that soon after having finished school seemed to her improper, even incongruous, but that he wanted to become engaged to Madeleine

worried her even more. First of all, Madeleine was his first cousin, a hardly negligible obstacle from the point of view of inbreeding. She was older
than he and appeared even more so, being as serious and steady as he was
excitable and unstable. No doubt she must have foreseen that those very
qualities of her niece would have a good influence on André, and she well
understood it four years later, four years too late, but she then felt perfectly
capable of personally carrying out the mother's role of guidance and had
no intention of delegating her powers. She refused to see the affection she
had watched grow, and not without complications, during those last years
as anything more than brotherly love. She had always had a deep aversion
to her sister-in-law Mathilde Rondeaux. Of course, Madeleine bore absolutely no resemblance, morally, to her mother; she had her father's upright
character. But the very scrupulousness of a child who had already been
painfully ravaged by the tragedy of her parents made Mme. Gide fear that
she would continue to suffer were she to marry André. Mme. Gide, a deeply conscientious woman, and one who examined her conscience every
evening, certainly considered these questions,[4] and although four years
later, overcoming her scruples—for her "good sense always won out"—
she, on the contrary, urged him into the marriage, it was because, feeling
that the game was almost lost, she saw Madeleine as the only haven in the
storm, the only person who seemed liable to lead André back into the ways
of "salvation."

On March 10, leaving his mother and cousin together in Rouen, André
left for Paris. Back in the rue de Commaille, he wrote the following words
in his *cahier de lectures:*

E. Zola's *La Bête humaine.* Bought at the Rouen station—as I went there to
accompany Pierre.[5] Read it immediately after Uncle Emile's funeral. In the
evening, in Fernand's[6] room, back from the rue de Lecat, near the fire,
stretched out in an armchair, two candles on the fireplace—and oblivious of
time—then, traveling, next to Aunt Claire, on the way back to Paris. It is a
physiological, animal study, etc.[7]

What is of most interest to us here is not the long analysis of *La Bête humaine* but the fact that the young Puritan chose that book on the very day

---

[4] Nor, being very bourgeois and very attentive to questions of money, did the considerable difference between André's and Madeleine's financial positions escape her.
In any case it is certain that the upright and delicate Madeleine Rondeaux did allude
in her letters to the "disproportion" in age and fortune between her and André
(October, 1892).

[5] Pierre Louÿs.

[6] Fernand Rondeaux, Henri Rondeaux's son and André Gide's first cousin.

[7] *Cahier de lectures,* March 10, 1890, unpublished.

of his Uncle Emile's funeral and the imaginary "consecration" of his mystical engagement. It shows the need to "leap to the other extreme," which was to become one of the constants of his psychology.

In the letters André Gide wrote to his mother in March, 1890,[8] he reproached himself with not having worked enough and having gone off in too many directions at once. But one can hardly say that he led an idle life. Not only was he writing *Allain* and keeping up his *Journal,* but he read enormously and analyzed what he read in a carefully kept notebook.

From October 28, 1889, to April 11, 1890, there are a great number of commentaries and judgments, sometimes rapidly written, on critical works and especially on novels. He read a great deal of Balzac and commented: "I have the impression that what Balzac had most of was an amorous temperament, oh! a devilish lot of amorous temperament—but not a very artistic one. His unbearable jokes are those of a traveling salesman after a meal." As for Balzac's critics:

Sainte-Beuve: an excellent page on the "efflorescence" of Balzac's style—Paul Albert: a good piece of homework from a stupid freshman—Lamartine: a confused panegyric about a man he cannot very well understand—Gozlan: several well-told anecdotes but too rhetorical.

He read Sarcey: "almost the whole thing is deplorable." He read, pellmell, Gautier, Goncourt, Zola, Anatole France, Loti, Tolstoi, Barrès, George Eliot, Villiers de l'Isle-Adam, Mme. de La Fayette, and others, and every one of his appraisals, often very significant of his own psychology, deserves a long commentary. On March 10 there is a brief note on Goethe's *Werther,* which should be most interesting to literary historians, for several of them, especially Renée Lang in her study of the Germanic sources of André Gide, wondered whether Gide had read *Werther* before *Les Cahiers d'André Walter:*

Goethe's *Werther.* Read a rather large part of it in German—but did not really enjoy the style until the last pages of narrative psychology. Ossian's translation is admirable, to reread before speaking about it—too much to say—not very interested—remains outside like a student's exercise.[9]

The *cahier de lectures* thus makes it possible to affirm that Gide had read *Werther* before finishing his first book, which does not mean that the

[8] One sentence in a letter of March 23, 1890 (unpublished), is highly significant: "I think you must have really excused me for not having written to you, for not having written to both of you (for it comes to the same thing)." Those words in parentheses show, better than any commentary, the curious identification André Gide made between his mother and his cousin.

[9] *Cahier de lecures,* March 10, 1890, unpublished.

influence of *Werther* had any great importance at that point, whatever the alleged resemblances between the two subjects. Yet it was only after having read it that Gide gave Allain the name of Walter. He felt that a Germanic consonance or resonance was implied in the character of his hero, who had been fed—much before Gide's reading of *Werther*—on German poetic and philosophic Romanticism.

Two other books had perhaps some influence on *Les Cahiers:* Gérard de Nerval's *Le Rêve et la Vie,* and most particularly, Turgenev's *Virgin Soil,* whose tone and personal resonance deeply moved André Gide:

Began this book I don't know when, a very long time ago, began it again during the New Year's holiday while going to Rouen and stopped once again at the confessions of Mariane and Nejdanoff. Then, brought it back to the same conditions and the same places, so that the impression would be more lasting, these past days spent in Rouen. Finished it today in the study—by the fireside, in the large armchair—stretched out—then near the window, in the red armchair—with the annoyance (which I commented on) of not being able to lose the feeling of my uncomfortable body.[10]

Often in the notebook one comes across Gide's taste for situating a book with relation to the places in which it was read and even the position in which it was read. But to come back to *Virgin Soil:*

Infinite charm—one of the most beautiful books read—mysterious psychology, very personal although without analysis—grey poetry—strange feeling of life, personal vision of things, even sometimes a bit bewildering precisely because of its great personality. One leaves it somewhat bewildered—with a languishing soul, almost from pessimism . . . no, something more gentle—that word shocks—it would need after it, to correct that little something a bit too harsh, the adjective "sympathetic"—controlled emotion, ready to overflow, always—cello, viola; some flutes in the visions of white birch trees. Sentences one would like to drink.

He liked the book so much ("it moves me extremely") that he wanted to make it his own:

The feeling I like better than any other comes over me—of taking it, of making it mine—whence this suffering. . . . How I should have liked to have said all that; I would have made it shorter, with, had I been able to, less mystery in the outside life and more (but I would have been wrong) in the inner life.

On April 11 Gide wrote that he gave up Mérimée's *Lettres à une Inconnue:* "None of that helps me with *Allain*—my only reading now must be Schopenhauer, Hegel, the Bible, and the ancient classics,"[11] to which he

---

[10] *Ibid.,* April 11, 1890, unpublished.

[11] *Ibid.*

added Saint-Saëns' *Harmonie et Mélodie*—for his book must be written in music—Rémusat's *Abélard,* which is indeed made for the occasion, but also Maupassant's *Bel Ami,* which must have been rather out of place in such company. Then his reading stopped altogether for some months, and the *Journal* of May 8 gives an explanation for it:

May 8. I must do *Allain. Examen d'André Walter.* (Begin at once to collect notes.) *Traité du Narcisse* . . . It is essential to work relentlessly, at one go, and without letting anything distract you; that is the real way to achieve the unity of a work. Then, once it is finished, and while the written pages are at rest, you must read relentlessly, voraciously, as is fitting after such a fast. . . . At the time of production, deliberately stop all reading. For me it is the cause of excessive agitation and stirs up all the ideas in my head at the same time. . . . When you are working, the idea that you stumble on must be the only one you have. You must believe that you are working in the absolute.

At that very moment he decided to go off and live in seclusion and to spend his time exclusively creating, a thing he had been dreaming of for several months. In his *Journal* of March 18 he noted his "rage" at not being able to close himself up 'in a tower," in a cell. "But where? The ideal cell; in the Causses, in the Dauphiné?" In Paris he could not work as he wished. One attempt at seclusion near the lake of Pierrefonds was interrupted on the following day by an unwelcome visit from Pierre Louÿs, and was given up directly. During that month of May in which Gide was grappling with a desire for heroic concentration, his Uncle Charles had invited him to take part in the festivities for the sixth centenary of the University of Montpellier. André Gide was greatly tempted by the invitation, but decided to refuse it and go off alone to write his book in the Dauphiné.

It was Pierre Louÿs who went to Montpellier in his place. Louÿs' letters to Gide were overflowing with enthusiasm. They mentioned the discovery of young literary men from Geneva and especially that of "a young man from Montpellier who spoke to me of *La Tentation* and of Huysmans, of Verlaine and of Mallarmé in such terms . . . you know, I really commend this one to you."[12] The young man from Montpellier, aged nineteen, was indeed commendable: his name was Paul Valéry.

[12] Letter from Pierre Louÿs to André Gide, May, 1890, quoted by Henri Mondor in *Les Premiers Temps d'une amitié, André Gide et Paul Valéry,* p. 4.

23: The First Book

"It was not only my first book, it was my Summa."

Si le grain ne meurt, *I, 247*

SOMETIME during the last half of May, 1890, André Gide left for the Dauphiné in search of "the ideal cell," where he planned to write *Les Cahiers d'André Walter* in the extreme solitude he then judged necessary for creative work. After much difficulty in choosing between Menthon and Talloires—two equally tempting possibilities—he decided on Menthon, rented two rooms in a comfortable chalet, and began work on his book at once. By the end of June he announced to Pierre Louÿs that the book had made great progress: "I believe that the first part will be well-launched in less than two weeks."

Gide returned to Paris at the beginning of July, and spent a few days there before leaving for La Roque, where he planned to complete *Les Cahiers* during the summer. He felt that it was absolutely necessary to finish the book by November at the latest, in other words, before he was twenty-one. The mysterious need of having "to hurry," which Gide experienced throughout his life, as if he were afraid of dying before having said all he had to say, spurred him on then even more than it did later on. Added to it was the feeling that the book he was writing was "one of the most important in the world" and that it would fulfil the anguished expectations of a whole generation:

Yes, my book, I thought, answered such a great need of the times, such a specific demand of the public's, that I even wondered whether someone else would not go about writing it and bring it out quickly, before me. I was afraid of arriving too late.[1]

He had therefore to finish it as soon as possible.

During his short stay in Paris, however, between his withdrawal to the Dauphiné and his withdrawal to Normandy, he allowed himself a certain amount of reading, as can be seen from his *cahier de lectures* of July 6–7, 1890. He read the most varied works, from Shakespeare's *Macbeth* to Alphonse Daudet's *Sapho:* "A bad book—immoral style—smells of musk." He again immersed himself in Flaubert: *La Tentation de Saint Antoine,* several passages of which are quoted in *Les Cahiers d'André Walter; Madame Bovary; La Correspondance,* particularly his correspondence with George Sand: "O Flaubert!" He unexpectedly also read Rabelais, and less unexpectedly, *Paul et Virginie:* "Amusing! J.-J. Rousseau's inclinations amidst apparent benevolence." The notebook also cites: "Episode of *Thérèse* from 'L'Enfance de Michelet.'" It was at Menthon that Gide, with "considerable excitement," had first read Michelet, more precisely, the last chapter of the second volume of his *Histoire de France.* A quite new passion—for a book of history—then awoke in him, as we can see from *Les Cahiers d'André Walter:*

The second volume of Michelet's *Histoire de France.* Ah! how I would have liked that man. His admirable cry of pain: *My own passion began the day my soul fell into this miserable body, which I am finally wearing out through the writing of this.*[2]

His ardent admiration for the historian-poet was doubtless directed more to the poet than to the historian.

We know very little about the months of July and August that Gide spent at La Roque. He was alone at first, then with his mother, and on about August 15 his three cousins joined them. It would appear that almost all his time was spent working, since it was during those two months that he finished *Les Cahiers d'André Walter,* much before the time he had predicted in his letters to his mother and to Pierre Louÿs.

The *cahier de lectures* gives some indication of the books he read during that period of work: in particular, Berlioz' *Mémoires,* which is mentioned by André Walter, Balzac's *Louis Lambert* ("reread"), Edgar Allan Poe's *Ligeia* and *Morella,* and, as always, Schopenhauer. He wrote a long analysis of George Sand's *Elle et Lui* and Paul de Musset's *Lui et Elle,* and reread Tolstoi's *Kreutzer Sonata,* which had left such a deep impression on him: "Read it in one day—at first on top of the Eiffel Tower where I was very uncomfortable.—Frenzied excitement when I saw the subject matter and the boldness of the ideas—I had to run far into the woods to read the book in solitude." Marie Bashkirtsev's *Journal* disappointed him greatly,

[1] *Si le grain ne meurt,* I, 249.   [2] *Les Cahiers d'André Walter, O.C.,* I, 104.

but from that bad example, he learned a "great lesson in rhetoric" which he later put into practice:

Never say: "You can't imagine how beautiful it is. I could never manage to describe it to you." It is so obvious that one can never manage to make others feel one's own emotion in its intensity that it is far better to resign oneself to it from the very beginning and, using one's talent, insinuate the emotion—make it felt symbolically—suggestively.[3]

And we know that Gide was to become a virtuoso of insinuating style.

Starting on August 17, the notebook alludes to reading aloud in the company of his cousins, especially Madeleine: *La Tentation de Saint Antoine,* Renan's *L'Avenir de la science,* the second chapter of Mirbeau's "expurgated" *Calvaire,* and most particularly, *Anna Karenina:* ". . . read at first to myself, then almost immediately after to the others." An analysis of the characters in Tolstoi's novel is followed by these words: "numerous discussions." On the other hand, the letters and personal notes of Madeleine Rondeaux, who was then keeping a diary, allude to the deep impression made by that reading of *Anna Karenina.* At the end of August the reading stopped: André Gide left for Paris in order to read his own book (which he did not want Madeleine to see before it was entirely finished and published) to faithful Albert Démarest. He thus reserved the first reading of it for his cousin and not for Pierre Louÿs, who was most disappointed and deservedly so; for during Gide's stay in Menthon, and even after, Louÿs had sent him some highly discouraging and perfidious letters.

Toward the middle of September, Gide had written to Louÿs that his book was finished. Louÿs showed "real joy" at the news, but his enthusiasm had a false ring:

You produce food for the soul, ha! ha! And art? You don't care a damn? Well, we'll see what it's like. Yet could it be possible that it's passable? eh? old boy?[4]

Although the first reading, to which Gide attached great sentimental importance, was reserved for Albert Démarest, still the second was for Pierre Louÿs. At the time their friendship was especially thriving, they had promised each other that in his first book each of them would leave one page blank for the other to fill in. But their talents were already too different, and Gide's romantic mysticism was not in tune with Louÿs' Parnassian ideal; indeed, it was in opposition to it: "I felt as little capable of writing a sonnet as he of writing a page of my *Cahiers.*" Yet so as to respect somewhat their former vow, Louÿs suggested that he write a preface, presenting *Les Cahiers d'André Walter* as the confessions of a

[3] *Cahier de lectures,* July–August, 1890, unpublished.

[4] Letter from Pierre Louÿs to André Gide, Sept. 19, 1890, quoted by Paul Iseler in *Les Débuts d'André Gide vus par Pierre Louÿs,* pp. 96–97.

young poet who died at twenty. Gide went along with the idea, and when
his book came out, it had no author's name other than Walter's and was
subtitled "posthumous work." Pierre Louÿs, under the pseudonym of
Pierre Chrysis, attended to the obituary notice.

On October 20 Gide offered *Les Cahiers* to Perrin, the publisher of
Barrès' *Un Homme libre,* a rather significant choice in that it showed the
prestige Barrès then had in his eyes. A few days later, Perrin gave his
answer. He agreed to publish *Les Cahiers d'André Walter* but at the
writer's expense. Mme. Gide, who was the obvious backer, gave her consent.

After the fulness of the summer months, Gide felt a great emptiness
within him, which he filled, after a fashion, by working on the piano and
reading. During those months of October and November, 1890, he read
Maeterlinck, Zola, Becque (*Les Corbeaux,* lent to him by Léon Blum),
Mirbeau, Villiers de L'Isle-Adam, and Huysmans. But the most important
reading he did during that period was Baudelaire's posthumous work *Mon
coeur mis à nu:* "When I read between the lines, it really grips me. The
last pages—with the heading Hygiene, Conduct, Ethics—are agonizing—
it would seem to me that everything has still to be said about Baudelaire."
It is interesting to compare these notes from his *cahier de lecture* of November 8, 1890, with the entry in his *Journal,* end of November, 1890, page
18:

Ethics:
First point: Necessity for an ethics.
2. An ethics consists in establishing a hierarchy of things and in using the
lesser to obtain the greater. It is an ideal strategy.
3. Never lose sight of the End. Never prefer the means.
4. Consider oneself as a means; therefore never prefer oneself to the chosen
end, to the work.
Think of one's salvation: egotism.
The hero must not even think of his salvation. He has *voluntarily* and *fatally*
devoted himself, unto damnation, to others; in order to reveal.

Some of these ideas Gide was to develop in a famous note in his second
book, *Le Traité du Narcisse:* "note written in 1890." Moreover, in that
month of November, 1890, during the first days of his twenty-first year,
André Gide was apparently already concerned with but one objective: not
of finding salvation but of writing his works—the sign of an inner evolution, due in great part to the writing of *André Walter,* for the very writing
of it changed him: "My soul, finally freed of that moribund weight it had
been dragging behind it for far too long, caught a glimpse of dizzying possi-

bilities." With his first book hardly finished, André Gide was planning his second.

But at the same time he was hesitating between two very different ways. One was the mystical way:

I imagined a series of "Lay Sermons" on the model of Father Gratry's *Sources,* in which—by means of an immense detour all round the entire earth—I would lead the most recalcitrant souls back to the God of the Gospels (who was not quite what he is ordinarily imagined to be,[5] as I would show in a second and more purely religious series). I also planned a tale, inspired by Anna's death, which was to be called *L'Essai de bien mourir* and which later became *La Porte étroite.*[6]

The other was the aesthetic way, that of *Le Traité du Narcisse,* whose title is already mentioned in his *Journal* on May 8, 1890. André Gide, the Huguenot Narcissus, was still hesitating between whether to let the Huguenot or Narcissus take the lead, the Christian or the aesthete.

Ever since Pierre Louÿs had met Paul Valéry in May, 1890, he had kept up a regular correspondence with him. He had spoken a great deal about Gide to Valéry and about Valéry to Gide. When Gide went to Montpellier to spend the last two weeks in December with his Uncle Charles, the young poet was most anxious to meet him. On December 9 Valéry wrote to Pierre Louÿs: "It is time that Gide came to speak to us of hope and rebirth, the winter hours are slow and bleak."[7]

Gide left for Montpellier on about December 10. His *cahier de lectures,* kept regularly until December 7, says nothing about the Montpellier trip but the following: "Gap. Trip to the south—embarked on *Sous l'oeil des Barbares*[8] and Renan's *Souvenirs . . .* Journey to Montpellier—finished during the evenings in hotels: Loti's *Le Roman d'un enfant.*" As soon as he arrived he saw Paul Valéry, who had received beforehand a curious letter of warning from Pierre Louÿs: "As a favor to me, don't show him your Henri de Régnier, nor any of my letters. I like separate friendships. But I'm very happy that you should see him and I hope he will be as dear to you as he is to me."

[5] This theme was to have great importance subsequently, Gide seeking to oppose the God of the Gospels to the God of the Churches which, to his mind, had deformed the divine teaching.

[6] *Si le grain ne meurt,* I, 247.

[7] Letter from Paul Valéry to Pierre Louÿs, Dec. 9, 1890, quoted by Henri Mondor in *Les Premiers Temps d'une amitié,* p. 8.

[8] He had therefore read *Un Homme libre* (March, 1891) before reading the first volume of Barrès' trilogy *Le Culte du Moi* (December, 1890).

André Gide and Paul Valéry met often during that stay: in the room of "the peaceful rue Urbain V, provincial and musty," where amidst great disorder and cigarette smoke Valéry wrote his first poems; on the high sunny terraces of Le Peyrou, between the sea and the mountains; and in the botanical gardens. "My dear fellow, I am in ecstasy and in raptures over your friend Gide," wrote Valéry to Louÿs. "What an exquisite and rare mind, what enthusiasm for beautiful rhythms and pure ideas!"[9] And Gide's admiration for Valéry was no less.

They talked about their gods, their dreams, their plans. Paul Valéry's masters were then Edgar Allan Poe, the Huysmans of *A Rebours,* and even at that time, Mallarmé; Gide's were Flaubert, Baudelaire, and as always, Schopenhauer. Gide read him pages from the proofs of *Les Cahiers d'André Walter,* as well as a few poems he could not fit in since they were of quite another tone. With the result that Valéry presented Gide with a rather Walterian sonnet, dedicated to him: "Le Bois amical," published the following year in *La Conque* with some variants.

One of their many walks together took them to an arbor in the botanical gardens, near a tombstone bearing the inscription: *Placandis Narcissae manibus.* There lay—according to a disputed tradition—the remains of Edward Young's daughter Eliza, the Narcissa of one of the poems in *Night Thoughts.* Paul Valéry considered using the Latin inscription as an epigraph for the sonnet he had finished on September 28, 1890, and called, by a happy coincidence, *Narcisse parle.*

The Narcissus theme, which since Ovid had inspired so many poets, was no doubt often the subject of their conversations. The following year Gide published his *Traité du Narcisse* and dedicated it to Paul Valéry, probably in remembrance of that first meeting under the auspices of the symbolic myth.

Toward the end of December, André Gide left Montpellier for Arcachon, where he joined his mother and a somewhat ailing Madeleine Rondeaux. It was on January 1 that he received the first copies of *Les Cahiers d'André Walter.* In the daybook that he kept regularly during 1891 he wrote the following words:

> January 1, 1891, Arcachon
> Awake, O north wind; and come, thou tempests; blow upon my garden, that the spices thereof may flow out. *The Song of Solomon.*

[9] The letter from Pierre Louÿs to Paul Valéry and that of Paul Valéry to Pierre Louÿs are quoted by Henri Mondor in *Les Premiers Temps d'une amitié,* pp. 8–9.

Gave Madeleine the copy on rice paper.[10]

Received 4 paper-bound copies from Perrin.

Was most clumsy this evening in insisting too much that Madeleine read my book tonight—as a result, she's balking at it, foreseeing the questions she can no longer put off—and refuses to read it before I leave. Ah well— I shall act differently.[11]

The question Madeleine could no longer put off and which she once again tried to elude was obviously the proposal that, according to Gide's plan, was to have been preceded by her reading of *Les Cahiers*. On January 2 he wrote the following line in his diary: "Why are you not the exile! Alas, or the Stranger!" and on January 3: "We will not have been real lovers, my dear!"[12]

Madeleine's name, which so hopefully opened the 1891 daybook, reappeared on January 8: "I will praise thee; for I am fearfully and wonderfully made (Ps. cxxix, 14).[13] Talked with Madeleine—talked with mamma. Prayers at the G's. Read my Bible." The distressing quotations he inscribed the next day were perhaps related to that conversation: " 'Hope has fled, vanquished, toward the black sky' (Verlaine). 'If thou hadst known, even thou, at least in this thy day, the things which belong unto thy peace! but now they are hid from thine eyes' (Luke, xix, 42). Read my Bible." Then Madeleine's name disappeared from the daybook for long months. What had happened?

Madeleine Rondeaux did not read *Les Cahiers d'André Walter* until after her cousin left. Her diary, which has been kept, shows that she was very moved by it and cried, but she also found that the story was so much their own that he had not the "right" to have written it. She recognized many of the words he had said to her. Moreover, the name of the heroine

---

[10] This copy now belongs to M. Roland Saucier, who has kindly allowed me to reproduce the dedication:

TO MY BELOVED MADELEINE
And now: all things will be made new.

January 1, 1891

"Awake, O north wind; and come, thou south; blow upon
my garden, that the spices thereof may flow out."

The Song of Solomon, IV, 16

"and at our gates are all manner of pleasant fruits, new
and old, which I have laid up for thee, O my beloved."

The Song of Solomon, VII, 14

[11] Daybook, Jan. 1, 1891, unpublished.

[12] Cf. the following lines from *Paludes:*

"We are not,
My dear, among those
Who give birth to the sons of men."

[13] This was to be the epigraph for *l'Immoraliste.*

in a very small number of de luxe copies, including hers, was Madeleine and not, as in the regular edition, Emmanuèle.

Si le grain ne meurt gives the following indications as to what happened, although the first does not seem quite exact:

I had not been able to find out what Emmanuèle thought of my book; all she let me know was that she rejected the proposal that followed it. I declared that I would not consider her refusal as final, that I was prepared to wait, and that nothing would make me give her up. Nevertheless, for a while I stopped writing her letters she no longer answered. I was left terribly distressed by the silence and the vacancy in my heart; but in the meanwhile friendship filled up the time and the place left empty by love.[14]

During his period of great hopes, André Gide had looked upon his book as a declaration of love "so conclusive" that his cousin could not refuse her hand. But Madeleine's answer was a formal refusal. Of course, as we shall see, *Les Cahiers d'André Walter* were hardly apt to put an end to her hesitations. Yet the cruel disillusion he then felt and the despair that followed her refusal were partly obscured by the normal excitement of a young writer who expects nothing less than glory from his first book and by the many people he met in 1890, while he was discovering "Paris and literary life."[15]

As he was writing *André Walter,* André Gide was convinced that the emotional crisis he was portraying would be of the most general interest. In an unpublished letter to his mother dated January 20, 1891, just a few days after *Les Cahiers* came out, he spoke about André Walter—with an absolutely medical objectivity—as a "case." We can therefore imagine how anxiously he awaited not only the critics' appraisals but their diagnoses.

There was no lack of praise on the delicate quality of *Les Cahiers'* style. Stéphane Mallarmé himself commended Gide for having been able to throw "The softest veil over a phase of dead youth, which your book almost leaves to be guessed."[16] Henri de Régnier found *André Walter* "infinitely and delicately shaded," and as cantankerous a judge as Joris-Karl Huysmans wrote that "in the hurly-burly of modern volumes," he was "singularly taken by certain pages of this pale book—pale and tremolant—of convalescence and the beginnings of a sickness of the soul."[17] As for the nature of that sickness of the soul, many shrewd minds were at work analyzing it.

[14] *Si le grain ne meurt,* I, 257–58.

[15] Letter from André Gide to Albert Démarest, January, 1892, unpublished.

[16] Letter from Stéphane Mallarmé to André Gide, Feb. 8, 1891 (Bibliothèque Doucet).

[17] Letter from J.-K. Huysmans to André Gide, 1891 (Bibliothèque Doucet).

As soon as Walter's sad fate was revealed to the literary world, the doctors grouped around his tomb, which they later discovered to be no more than a cenotaph. Gide, who thought that his book answered "a need of the times," was gratified by the publication of a study entitled *L'Ame moderne d'après "Le Canard sauvage" d'Ibsen et "Les Cahiers d'André Walter."*[18] Several consultants diagnosed André Walter's malady as a new *mal du siècle:* "You have most perceptively described," wrote Marcel Schwob, "that terrible sickness of the will experienced by young people in the second half of the century. . . . I have had André Walters—alas—under my eyes—and near me—and as I read your book, their sad plight wrung my heart."[19] Rémy de Gourmont saw *Les Cahiers* as "the condensation of the studies, dreams, and feelings of an entire youth, a withdrawn and timorous youth," and regarding the writer as one of "a romantic and philosophical turn of mind in the tradition of Goethe," he made this singularly lucid diagnosis:

One of these years, after he will have recognized how little power the mind has on the course of things, its social uselessness, the contempt it arouses in that accumulation of corpuscles called Society, he will become indignant, and as action—even illusory action—is forever closed to him, he will wake up armed with irony.[20]

Diverse critics vied with each other in emphasizing the contrast between André Walter's intelligence and his weakness of will, between his taste for analysis and his aversion to action. But actually it was not the *mal du siècle* of one particular century or of "the second half of the century"; it was a malady that can be attributed, at all times and in all places, to a certain type of character. By the same token, when Firmin Roz declared that "André Walter died from the despair of youth, from the conflict of the variously directed forces of his own being, subjected to opposing influences," he ascribed to the malady of youth in general what was merely the malady of one youth.

Other commentators were particularly sensitive to the mystical, moral, and puritanical aspects of the young Huguenot's struggle. If Walter went mad, concluded one pre-Freudian critic of *La Revue encyclopédique,* it was because "he did not want to have a body." More poetically, Maurice Maeterlinck saw *Les Cahiers* as a "sad and marvelous breviary for Virgins" and congratulated the author on his "noble and great book, in which every soul that did not want to fall immediately will rediscover its struggles immortalized."[21] In that perspective André Walter ceased being the victim

18 Letter from André Gide to Albert Démarest, January, 1892, unpublished.

19 Letter from Marcel Schwob to André Gide (Bibliothèque Doucet).

20 Rémy de Gourmont, *Mercure de France,* June, 1891.

21 Letter from Maurice Maeterlinck to André Gide, May 9, 1891.

of *mal du siècle* or of the malady of youth, and became the victim of an imperious religious need for chastity. Thus the critics were agreed on considering the hero as representative, but they were not agreed as to what he represented.

André Gide awaited the diagnosis of Paul Bourget, who had written *Essais de psychologie contemporaine,* with justifiable impatience. On March 6, 1891, he wrote in his diary that the letter he had so hoped for had arrived from Palermo. It was long, serious, kindly, but reserved, and never touched on the really essential question, in other words, the "case." At a much later date Gide told about having gone to see Paul Bourget in November, 1915, at Costebelle. It would seem that the psychologist flatly asked him the following question: "Now that we are alone, tell me, Monsieur Gide, whether your immoralist is or is not a pederast." It would not have taken a great mind to ask that question with regard to Michel in *l'Immoraliste,* but asked with regard to André Walter, it gave evidence of astonishing foreknowledge. Actually, no one appeared to have noticed the short page in which Gide, before any homosexual experience, had expressed—with its precise and unchanging characteristics—the pedophilic phantasm that haunted him throughout his life. Can we then conclude that a more or less unconscious homosexuality was the key to André Walter? It was indeed one of his problems, and not the least of them, but one among many others.

The "spells of anguish" about which André Walter was in such despair are both very particular and very general. The struggles between body and soul, instinct and will, desire and love, morality and nature, dream and reality, the ego and the world, intelligence and action, spontaneity and reflection, sincerity and lucidity, religion and art—all those great human dilemmas were posed at the same time in that adolescent soul which was tortured by antagonism and died of its difficulties. It was not only disturbed and divided; it was itself disturbance and division. Walter was not capable of living; he was doomed to failure. And yet it was from Walter's very substance that Gide created his works, and it was that very romantic chaos that Gide managed to control with a classical style throughout half a century. André Walter's malady is similar to those complicated sicknesses which cannot be diagnosed until there is a crisis; and in the realm of sicknesses of the soul the crisis often lasts a lifetime. Now that Gide's destiny has been fulfilled, it is possible to understand more completely Walter's psychology, retrospectively of course, but not uselessly. "One of the worst kinds of anguish," said the hero of *Les Cahiers,* "is not to know . . . an ignorance about everything, the malady and the remedies." But one must first come to an understanding as to the nature of the malady and as to the value of the remedies.

24: Angelism and Its Other Side

> *"To love only with your soul a soul*
> *who loves you in the same way...."*
> Les Cahiers d'André Walter,
> O.C., *I, 124*

> *"He asks for the superhuman but the*
> *flesh will have its revenge."*
> Ibid., *p. 125*

1 N HIS preface to *Les Cahiers d'André Walter* Pierre Louÿs wrote: "The passion he dared not call love, and which dominated all the others, filled his existence, and he kept it so well hidden that his most intimate friend never knew a thing about it." The hidden passion was that of André Walter for his cousin Emmanuèle.[1]

From the very beginning of *Les Cahiers,* we are warned that his is a hopeless love. André Walter's dying mother says to him:

It would be wise for you to leave Emmanuèle . . . Your affection for each other is fraternal—make no mistake about it . . . Emmanuèle has already suffered a great deal: I should so much like her to be happy. Do you love her enough to prefer her happiness to your own?

As André does not answer, she adds: "Have I counted on you too much, my child—or will I be able to die in peace?" "Yes, mother," answers the obedient son. He leaves, and when he is called back, he sees at her bedside Emmanuèle, hand in hand with the undesirable T., who has just rushed over. Having betrothed them, the mother dies and all three fall to their knees. André feels at once that Emannuèle is lost to him forever, as his mother had wished, and thinks: "Since I must lose her, may I at least find

---

[1] Emmanuèle is a Hebrew name meaning "God with us" and the name with which Isaiah referred to the Messiah. Gide was then too imbued with the Bible for the choice to have been fortuitous.

you again, my God—and may you grant me your blessings for having followed the strait way."[2] His fate is decided, and the sacrifice consummated.

That somewhat naïve scene is, to my mind, extremely important. I think it is significant that from his very first literary venture, from the very first pages of the "Cahier blanc," Gide disclosed—probably unknowingly—one of the deepest secrets of his own psychology: it was the mother who forbade André and Emmanuèle to marry, and she who was responsible for their separation. That opening revelation of the "Cahier blanc" is confirmed—and unambiguously—on the last page:

Mother darling, may God bless you! Our souls met again over your death bed. You were able to separate our bodies only; then *all three of us*[3] rested in the serenity of our virtue; but through a higher and hidden will, the at first harsh virtue that seemed to *separate*[4] us became absolutely glorious and consummated the chaste desire of our souls.[5]

Then there is no further question of the mother throughout the book, only of the inaccessible Emmanuèle.

Now that she is *separated* from him by her marriage to T., whose portrait is limited to that initial, André Walter sorrowfully mulls over his memories of Emmanuèle, one after the other. What he loved in her was her sister-soul. They had been brought up together since childhood, less as cousins than as brother and sister. There was nothing but purity between the two ingenuous children. The dream of a pure love, unmixed with anything carnal, charmed André Walter from the time of his childhood. In his dreams he saw the future and remote princess "as a hazy Beatrice, *fior gittando sopra e d'interno,* as a chosen Lady, immaterially pure." Indeed, the young poet imagined Emmanuèle as a mystical Beatrice out of Dante's universe, the chosen Lady of the troubadours, who were careful that their desire never be satisfied.

But the reader finally finds the absence of any outer manifestation between the two young lovers troubling. Was it Emmanuèle's extreme fragility and her will to resist that caused André to show so little initiative? Probably, but there would appear to be more: "So as not to mar her purity, I shall forego any caress—so as not to trouble her soul—even the most chaste, even holding hands . . . for fear that she may then desire more *of what I am unable to give her.*"[6] Moreover: "I do not desire you. Your body makes me uncomfortable and *carnal possession terrifies me.*"[7]

[2] *Les Cahiers d'André Walter, O.C.,* I, 30.

[3] The italics are mine.

[4] The italics are mine.

[5] *Les Cahiers d'André Walter, O.C.,* I, 89.

[6] The italics are mine.

[7] *Les Cahiers d'André Walter, O.C.,* I, 68; not italicized in the text.

But although he did not desire Emmanuèle, André Walter had other desires. While the soul increasingly idealized the beloved, the body gave in to solitary pleasures:

I separated them to such a degree that now I am no longer in control; each one goes its own way, the body and the soul; one dreams of ever more chaste caresses; the other lets itself go adrift. Wisdom would have them go together, converge in the same pursuits, would have the soul not seek too distant loves in which the body has no part.[8]

That wise old secret of love was already foreign to André Walter; he had already dissociated pleasure and love. And divided between the love-memory of the angelic Emmanuèle and the temptations of the demon of solitude, he was overpowered by the conflict. He finally went mad and died, as the snow fell, reminding him one last time of the Immaculate: "The snow is pure."

André Gide was still not a novelist, and his heroine Emmanuèle remains as vague in the reader's imagination as an extremely "hazy" Beatrice. Nevertheless, there is no doubt that the pure and mystical cousin is Madeleine Rondeaux as Gide then imagined her, if not as she actually was. His adolescent love had remained as "pure and dazzling" as it was when it led him to discover "the mystic orient" of his life. He was marked by the same angelism and a misapprehension that consisted in not loving the other as a real person but through an "ideal figure" that has no common measure with reality. Dostoevsky said that the work of a novelist[9] is done in a "dark room"; when his eyes—accustomed to the semidarkness of his innermost being, the depths in which he creates—return to the light of day, they often behave like the eyes of a hemeralope. Being blind with regard to one's closest relations and friends is a well-known failing. And André Gide projected his "ideal figure," created in his imagination, on to his cousin, attributing to her a psychology that was not her own and a "drama" that was not her own, while remaining "blind to that of reality."[10] He never understood until much later just how wrong he was, but in his youth, despite the cruelest warning, he denied the evidence and doggedly continued his work of the idealization and disembodiment of the beloved object until he had made a perfect angel: the future Alissa.

On the other hand, Madeleine, with her innate modesty and good sense, was afraid that the image he had made of her was different from what she

---

[8] *Ibid.,* p. 50.

[9] At least the introverted novelist who draws his creations from himself.

[10] *Et nunc manet in te,* p. 12.

really was: "You're falling in love with a ghost . . . with an imaginary figure," Alissa was to say to Jérôme. Basically intuitive, she surely had an inkling that her companion would not give her the protection she needed after a childhood so overcharged with emotion. She must have guessed that it would have been up to her, the elder by two years, to play the role of a guardian and replace a mother whose protection he bore with impatience, to say the least. She did, of course, assume that difficult role five years later upon the death of André Gide's mother;[11] but her first answer, after having read *Les Cahiers d'André Walter,* was negative. As I have said, Gide's strange declaration of love was hardly of a nature to put an end to the doubts she had with regard to her disconcerting cousin. She probably did not understand all that was hidden behind "the softest veil," but she was sensitive enough to guess that even then there was something of a mystery in André Gide, and it terrified her to the point of leaving his letters unanswered, thus showing her intention to break off.

At that moment, however, Gide was too closed-in on himself to attribute her categorical refusal to its real reasons. As his angelism was then at its height, he gave an "angelic" interpretation of Madeleine's attitude, an interpretation that culminated in *La Porte étroite,* which was as revealing of his own psychology as it was debatable from the point of view of his cousin's. When I asked Gide if his cousin had been the model for Alissa, he answered: "No, I thought for a long time that she was Alissa, but she was not." Then, after a pause: "She became Alissa"—enigmatic words, the meaning of which I did not understand until later.[12]

When, with regard to its republication, Gide spoke to me bitterly about the "deplorable" *André Walter,* he said that he attached very special importance to Denis de Rougemont's book *L'Amour et l'Occident,* with its remarkably original interpretation of the Tristram myth. "It was in that book," he added, "and not in the works of psychoanalysts, that I found an explanation for a few of my mistakes, a few of my earliest ones."

The medieval myth of Tristram and Isolde symbolizes one type of relationship between man and woman in a given historical group— twelfth- and thirteenth-century chivalry—but the archaic situation continues to live in the dreams of Western man; it belongs, as it were, to his collective unconscious and would represent—in the Jungian sense—an archetype expressing the permanence of certain psychological traits. "He does not love me, nor I him," delared Isolde, but they loved their love until death. The Tristram myth became a symbol for the preference of unsatis-

[11] May 31, 1895.

[12] Our conversation took place in August, 1947, before I read *Et nunc manet in te.*

fied passion to satisfied love, a passion which found fulfilment not in carnal possession but in frustration, in suffering, and at its highest degree, in death. The ring exchanged is the sign of a fidelity that is not of the flesh, and the unconscious objective of the lovers is to create an obstacle which will keep them from so uniting. As soon as Isolde becomes Tristram's wife, he should no longer and does no longer desire her "because he does not love what he has." Through the symbol of this great Western myth, from the time of chivalry to the modern tragedy in which Wagner portrayed "the fundamental catastrophe" of sadomasochistic genius, Denis de Rougemont showed that the secret desire of Tristram and Isolde, as of all couples who unknowingly imitate them, is not to experience love but to experience death.

Like the troubadour who feared nothing more than being satisfied, André Walter might have repeated Fauriel's words: "It is no longer love when it becomes real"; and when on Emmanuèle's death he said: "She dies; *therefore* he possesses her," he was expressing the magic charm of Tristram's love potion, the active passion of the Night. *La Porte étroite,* with its feminine replica of André Walter, is itself an anachronistic book, a novel of chivalry, and its heroine a thirteenth-century virgin, a figure from a stained-glass window. What André Walter and Alissa want is not the happiness of the couple but the obstacle that will prevent it, and of such obstacles death is obviously the most conclusive. Both are victims of the angelic intoxication caused by the love potion, the exaltation of a passion that flees the liberation of the senses and exalts the painful intensity of the feeling.

As that particular concept of love evolved through the centuries, it took both the direction of mysticism and that of romanticism. André Gide's mind was open to one and the other, for at the time of André Walter, Gide was undeniably a Manichaean, although perhaps without knowing it, and a romantic, knowing it perfectly well.

Manichaeanism is based on the divine or angelic nature of the soul or Day, prisoner of matter or Night; the fight between carnal desire and love expresses the anguish of the angels fallen into too human bodies, and the exaltation of infinite passion has as its corollary the condemnation of the flesh. The neophyte in the "cult of Amor" had, if he was married, to swear to abstain from any contact with his wife, for physical possession is a profanation. The condemnation of the flesh is not Christian in essence; it is a dogma of the "cult of Amor," not the church of Rome. This unrealistic mystique tends, then, to oppose within man—like two irreconcilable adversaries—the soul, the principle of good, and the flesh, the principle of evil, an angelic nature and a demoniac nature. It leads to a malign disparagement of the demands of the body and, considering them vile, debases them even further. The noble opponent is the angel, the base opponent the beast, and they never meet or unite in any really human way. André Walter, a reader of Pascal, must have profitably meditated on the famous words: "Man is neither angel nor beast and . . . he who tries to act like an angel, acts like a beast." For Gide, Emmanuèle was the symbol of a hopeless love, for she was the personification of the angel.

However, it is very likely that the influence of the Tristram myth reached Gide primarily through its romantic or profane aspects. If we go back to his reading at that time, we find that he considered Dante's Beatrice as the ideal model for his heroines. On the other hand, German Romanticism, by which Gide was then "very taken," pushed the interiorization of the Tristram myth to its highest point. There is a striking resemblance between the psychology of André Walter and that of Novalis.[13] Both were faithful to the cult of the sister-soul. There is also a certain similarity between Werther and Walter,[14] but perhaps simply on the surface. In French romantic literature a whole courtly tradition, from *Le Roman de la rose* to innumerable modern novels (i.e., *La Nouvelle Héloïse* and *Dominique*), corresponds to the Tristram myth and is in opposition to the Gallic tradition, which ridicules chaste passion as a sickness of the soul and exalts physical love. There is no doubt as to which of these traditions Gide preferred or from which stemmed his worship of *cortegia* and his horror of that Gallic spirit he tended to see only as *gauloiserie*.

And so, through various cultural influences, the magic charms of the Tristram myth cast their spell; but in order for the tradition of Platonism in which it had its origins to obtrude on an adolescent mind as it did on André Walter's, the mind must be predisposed toward it. In other words, and without wanting at all to diminish the importance of Denis de Rougemont's attractive thesis, I believe that only he who is by nature an angelist can be really attacked by the myth of angelism; it would have no effect on a Gallic spirit and would trouble only a courtly spirit, one that is prepared for the potion by temperament, as well as by an early and decisive fixation on the image of a venerated woman. She can be the mother or the sister or another, but for him she represents the "ideal figure," and one he will seek forever more. Generally, if not always, most angelists have spent their childhoods in the presence of an angelic figure or, more precisely, a figure so idealized. The real person has less influence on the child than the image he has made of her, and his image may have no relation to reality. The distortion of reality is all the greater as the imagination is more romantic.

[13] No doubt simply due to a similarity of mentalities, rather than a result of Novalis' direct influence on Gide, for Gide would not appear to have discovered Novalis until a year later, through Maurice Maeterlinck, whom he visited in Belgium.

[14] André Gide's *cahier de lectures* (unpublished) testifies to the fact that he read *Werther* in 1890, before having completed *Les Cahiers d'André Walter*.

André Gide ridiculed the now popularized Freudian interpretation in terms of the Oedipus complex as much as he valued Denis de Rougemont's explanations based on the Tristram myth. As we have shown, there was no Oedipian situation—in the Freudian sense—in Gide's childhood; yet he was the victim of an affective complex determined by the image of a severe and austere mother, who was the embodiment of the puritanical moral conscience which forbade any satisfaction of the flesh. That attitude, revived by all women who resembled the mother image, led to "inhibition," as Gide himself put it.

It is significant that it was the mother who kept André Walter and Emmanuèle from uniting and forced upon them the "harsh virtue" that consummated the "chaste desire" of their souls. His words "You were able to separate our bodies only" might very well be understood as "You were able to separate our bodies only, but it was you who separated them." Now, although in *Les Cahiers* Emmanuèle shows no resemblance to André Walter's mother, the likeness between the mother and the first cousin is indicated with the help of a curious subterfuge: the purely fictional creation of an elder sister, Lucie, who had died, and of whom Emmanuèle is an exact reproduction. "The memory of *her* around you everywhere . . . in the evening I again saw *her* profile in the shadow of your head as it bent over . . . when you spoke, your voice reminded me of *hers*. And soon the memory of you both became fused and indistinct." Might not the blurred image have been caused by the superimposition of two images?

In *La Porte étroite* the resemblance between Alissa and Jérôme's mother becomes apparent. I am not speaking of a physical resemblance, for—as we know—Gide's heroines have almost no bodies and no faces. But the similarity of their characters is striking. Yet Alissa was hardly a portrait of Madeleine Rondeaux, as Gide was later to affirm in *Et nunc manet in te:* "How much simpler she was than Alissa, more normal and more *ordinary* (I mean less Corneillian and less tense) . . ." To what, then, can that distortion of character correspond if not to an unconscious need for a more "Corneillian" and more "tense" model, one whose "constant effort" André Gide claimed to admire? The adjective "Corneillian" was not written by chance. We know how he always associated the theatre of Corneille with the image of his mother and with the ethic of duty she unceasingly advocated. The "ideal figure" was clearly a projection of the mother image: "Miss Ashburton turned toward me and said, almost under her breath: 'Alissa is like your mother.' "

Those words that in *La Porte étroite* Flora Ashburton whispered as a secret to Jérôme have, I believe, real psychological importance. Everything happened as if André Gide, in his imagination, had identified—or at least unconsciously assimilated—the image of his mother with that of his cousin, and combined them to form an ideal image which corresponded to the puritanical ethics of his childhood. The identification explains and, to my mind, alone explains various combinations of circumstance in Gide's life which, without it, remain absolutely enigmatic.[15] This is perhaps not the place to mention it, but I should like to recall the page in *Ainsi soit-il* that contains the most important of Gide's many confessions:

Only in dreams does the figure of my wife often subtly and almost mystically take the place of my mother's and without really surprising me . . . The role played by each one in my dreams is always about the same—that is, *an inhibitory role*.[16]

The fact that the substitution took place "only in dreams" is especially significant of the unconscious or spontaneous nature of that revealing identification.

It does not mean, however, that the "ideal figure" is simply Juliette Rondeaux projected onto Madeleine Rondeaux. It is a composite figure, made up primarily of the "admirable" women who dominated André Gide's childhood: his mother, Miss Shackleton, and his Aunt Claire and Aunt Lucile. The importance of one of those virtuous women must not be underestimated. Anna Shackleton was the model not only for Flora Ashburton, but for a large part of Alissa. In other words, during his childhood Gide's moral conscience, or what psychoanalysts would call his superego, was essentially formed by women, his mother having the greatest but not the only influence. And in his mind he made the extraordinary identification of the feminine sex and virtue: "Desire, I thought, was characteristic of man; I found it reassuring not to admit that women could experience the same thing—or only 'loose women.' "

The role of the inhibition of sexuality played by that ideal figure explains the nature—corresponding to the Tristram myth—of André Walter's love for Emmanuèle and André Gide's love for Madeleine. The surprising lines "I shall forego any caress . . . for fear that she may then desire more of what I am unable to give her" were prophetic of André Gide's unconsummated marriage and express his foreboding of the failure of his virility faced with the woman he considered "the only love" of his life. The fact that Madeleine was not only of the same family but of the same social group, the same religion, the same province, the same traditions, and the same customs as André Gide's mother meant that she revived all the maternal prohibitions with regard to the flesh. Moreover, they were considerably heightened by the fact that she was older than he, appeared even more so, and had been brought up with him as a sister. Thus Madeleine

[15] For example, two weeks after his mother's death, his engagement to Madeleine Rondeaux.

[16] *Ainsi soit-il,* p. 128; the italics are mine.

was doubly sacred—that is, unprofanable—as an image of the mother and as an image of the older sister, both images of Virtue. What Gide took for a long time to be physiological impotence was merely a psychological impossibility, an inhibition that might have been cured, for it had a mental and not a physical basis. He himself wrote in *Et nunc* with regard to his wife:

What I fear she could not understand was that the spiritual force of my love inhibited all carnal desire. For I managed to prove in another connection that I was not incapable of drive—I am speaking of the procreating drive— but only on condition that nothing intellectual or sentimental be mixed with it.[17]

There is no clearer way of saying that the necessary condition for Gide's desire, as for that of all victims of angelism, was that he not be in love. The sexual act was only possible with women who were incommensurable with the ideal figure and who drove out or exorcized the glance of the guardian angel.

If we now go back to André Walter's love, we are more equipped to understand its nature and the fundamental reasons for Walter's physical renunciation of the woman he loved and his attachment to the image he made of her. He was in fact in love with a fictional being and could no more embrace her than Narcissus could his own reflection. Moreover, the ideal figure, although created because of influences outside himself, existed in Narcissus' imagination. It was his soul, or at least the noble and ennobled part of his soul,[18] that he projected into what he called his sister-soul. We notice the obsessive concern in *Les Cahiers* with the resemblance between the hero and his cousin. André Walter becomes irritated whenever he feels that Emmanuèle is not exactly like himself, or more precisely, like the vision he has created of himself—freed from all the demands of the flesh, pure spirit, a veritable angel! Emmanuèle, like Alissa later on, is in fact André Gide not as he was, but as he had at first wanted to be, in accordance with his moral superego that had been formed by a puritanical upbringing, and as he would have become had he allowed the "mystical bud" within him to flower at the cost of all the others. André Walter's love recalls Narcissus' love for an ideal reflection of his soul. Denis de Rougemont was perfectly aware of the fact that the Tristram myth is ultimately an expression of narcissism: "I love myself in the Other." Narcissus did not love the other as he was, but as a supreme identity, and what he

[17] *Et nunc manet in te,* p. 24.

[18] In psychoanalytical language, the superego.

sought in that "twin mirror" was his ideal and, as it were, "bovaryzed"[19] double. With as much psychological truth as Flaubert, when he said: "Mme. Bovary, c'est moi," Gide might have said "Emmanuèle, c'est moi" or "Alissa, c'est moi." Narcissus—in Pausanias' version, if not in Ovid's— is in love with his sister. Would, then, the angelic worship of a sister-soul be ultimately no more than narcissism?

This comparison between André Walter's love for Emmanuèle and Narcissus' for Narcissa, in other words for Echo, his ideal voice,[20] might well seem very hypothetical were it not for certain unequivocal phrases in *Les Cahiers*. Not only does André Walter love Emmanuèle because she is his dream and his creation,[21] but his beloved's death becomes the victory of his love:

Your existence now? Only within me: you live because I dream you, when I dream you, and only then; that is your immortality. *You live only in my thoughts.* Dear soul, how I relish the fact that you live merely by virtue of my undying love! It is through me that you live, through me!

Echo no longer exists except in and through Ego: there can be no further question as to the narcissistic nature of such a love. Echo is no more than Ego's mirage, his idealized and disembodied voice. Moreover, in the last pages of *Les Cahiers* which recount the struggle with the Angel, the Angel shows its true face: "Ah! There you are dear soul! I had long awaited you. . . ." And the face is Emmanuèle's. The soul and the Angel become one, just as in the Tristram myth love and death become one.

I should also like to point out the hecatomb that this immature work entails. The hero's sister is dead, his mother dies, his beloved dies, and he himself dies—but for reasons quite other than an inexperienced novelist's facile desire for pathos. It is an extreme consequence of angelism which, inclined to disembodiment, finds the supreme end of love in the end of those who are loved. The idea "She dies; *therefore* he possesses her" is characteristic, and of many angelists before André Walter, but it was per- haps never put quite so laconically. The angelist has no taste for a "living woman," to use Amiel's expression; rather, he worships the incorruptible fiancée.

---

[19] In the sense that Jules de Gaultier gave to bovaryism (*translator's note:* see In- troduction, p. 11).

[20] In the fable the enamored Echo, scorned by Narcissus, loses her body and is turned into a rock. She is reduced to a voice, a thing of the soul, which finally does disturb Narcissus, for he recognizes it as his own. Echo is the pure symbol of disem- bodied love.

[21] "Things BECOME true; we have only to think them . . . our mind creates its own Truths. . . . The soul must protest against the constraint of things." (*Les Cahiers d'André Walter, O.C.*, I, 54.)

The results of angelism, insofar as the physical fulfilment of love is concerned, are unfortunate. For even if the angelist happens to change his mind, the body he had disdained continues to be unwilling and his disembodied love is in danger of remaining disembodied. In other words, sexual inhibition here is a punishment for men who try to act like angels, a punishment that was not foreseen in Pascal's admirable formula. Yet the instinct that could not be satisfied in an idealized love seeks its satisfaction elsewhere and finds it in indirect, perverse, or neurotic ways. The dissociation between love and pleasure is characteristic of the angelist and often leads to what André Walter called "depraved continence."

André Walter's struggle against his sin was quite the same as André Gide's. And when he fell back into it, his humiliation was in proportion to his mystical exaltation. Of course, Gide did not inflict upon himself the hair shirt and discipline of his hero. Yet his own ascetic rites were meant not only to keep him in a state of fervor that was favorable to literary creation, but to help conquer the demon of solitude and drive out the nocturnal phantasms that provoked his solitary temptations and troubled his nights.

Using almost the same words as Jean-Jacques Rousseau, Gide wrote in his 1893 *Journal*: "Completely . . . virgin and totally depraved."[22] André Walter, in speaking of his "depraved continence," added with a touch of irony: "As a perversity, it is rather delicate!" Was it onanism alone that justified his words or was it the accompanying phantasms? The visions of women that Walter had in his nightmares were all of a disappointing and anguishing nature. He saw the feminine body as "a black hole," a "bag" filled with sand, a balloon that miserably deflates as soon as an extended hand pierces it. But one night, when he was unable to sleep because his "thoughts were too overpowering," André Walter was enchanted by a far less depressing reverie:

I could again see the children . . . bathing in the river, their frail torsos and suntanned limbs immersed in the enveloping coolness. I was overcome by a mad frenzy at not being one of them, one of those little vagabonds who pilfer all day long in the sun and at night stretch out in a ditch with no concern for the cold or rain, who, when they are feverish, dive completely naked into the coolness of rivers. . . . And who do not think.

That vision of naked, suntanned children cheered Walter to such a degree that at five in the morning he went out and walked along the edge of the river, but alas there was no one there. Intoxicated by the air and the colors, he began to run under the low branches and arrived at a forest: "I was

[22] "Until the age of twenty-three I lived completely as a virgin and totally depraved; so crazed that I sought everywhere for some bit of flesh on which to press my lips" (*Journal,* p. 33).

shaken by infinite raptures, lines of poetry rushed to my lips, and I sang them aloud. I painfully enjoyed my solitude; I peopled it with the ones I loved." But who then were the ones he loved? We had been given to believe that he loved only his cousin Emmanuèle, the object of all his thoughts, his "darling mother," and his dead sister Lucie. Yet this time:

Before my eyes, at first rather blurred, hovered the lithe shapes of children who were playing on the beach and whose beauty haunted me; I should have liked to swim around near them and, with my hands, feel the softness of their brown skin. But I was all alone; then I suddenly began to shudder, and I wept for the elusive passing of the dream. . . .

Quid tunc si fuscus Amyntas! So in André Walter's reveries appeared the phantasm that was to haunt all of André Gide's homosexual life until his death. It was there, established, once and for all, *ne varietur,* with its own special nature.

It is difficult to say whether the sexual problem that goes along with angelism is the cause of it or the result of it, for it now appears as a cause, now as a result, now as both at the same time. Apart from exceptional cases in which the sublimation of the sexual instinct succeeds in volatilizing it (as may happen in certain poetic or mystical vocations), the sexual instinct generally somewhat hinders the flight of the soul. Disassociated from love, its demands can be satisfied in different ways, depending on circumstances and temperament: sometimes through onanism; more often through relations with vulgar women, before whom the inhibitions created by the ideal women disappear; and for those who are more or less predisposed to it, through homosexuality or pederasty, at least in certain forms which are occasionally accompanied by an inhibition with regard not only to ideal women but to the entire feminine sex. It goes without saying that there is every possible variation in the habits of the different kinds of angelists, who resemble each other more than they think. The impossibility of desiring the beloved object is their common bond.

When puberty intensified the demands of the sexual instinct, Gide's state of chastity—the state he so valued as an adolescent—became more and more "precarious." Walter wondered whether his "perpetual overexcitement" might not be due to the "ardor" of his "intractable flesh, which perhaps controls everything." But was he a victim of the ardors of the flesh or of their intractability? Actually, the problem here has nothing to do with the dangers of continence, for Walter was anything but chaste; it has to do with the dangers of onanism. The fear of the disastrous consequences of onanism, dramatically exaggerated by certain family admonitions or pamphlets, can create such panic in emotional young people that echoes of it often reach the doctor's office. One of the most common fears is that of a permanent loss of the life force. Sometimes there is the additional fear that the exhaustion will lead to insanity. When in *Si le grain ne meurt* Gide recalled the sad summer of 1892 at La Roque, the summer he wrote *Le Voyage d'Urien,* he noted:

At La Roque, the summer before last, I had thought I was going mad; I spent almost the whole time I was there shut up in my room, where I should have done nothing but work, where I tried to work in vain (I was writing *Le Voyage d'Urien*), obsessed, haunted, hoping to perhaps find some escape in excess itself, to again reach purity [*l'azur*] on the other side, to wear out my demon (I realize that it was his suggestion), and wearing out only myself, I crazily wasted all my energy to the point of exhaustion, to the point of imbecility, of madness.[23]

The experience of nothingness, symbolized in *Le Voyage d'Urien* (or *du rien*), can be felt in this biographical context.

The anguish of guilt linked to onanism, common to the adolescent in *Si le grain ne meurt* and his fictional double, young Boris Lapérouse, reappeared even more strongly in the adolescent André Walter, who experienced the same conflict. But since puberty, both the body and the soul had matured, and with them, their contrary demands. André Gide's moral conscience, formed by his mother's puritanical upbringing, was further elevated by the pure love and mysticism which in this case were inseparable. The adolescent felt all the more guilty for his "monstrous pleasures" in that they led not only to condemnation by a severe judge, as before, but to the shame of not being worthy of an angelic love. Now from this guilt feeling to a feeling, indeed to ideas, of damnation, there is no great distance, and Walter—a Manichaean—constantly dreaded taking the step: "*Rather than burn....*" But since he remained as ambivalent as he was in his childhood, he wanted what he dreaded and he dreaded what he wanted. Moreover, he was in doubt as to the value of his struggle and, doubting, at certain times considered it a dubious battle: he was still in the swamps of ambiguity. Sometimes he exalted chastity and sometimes he considered it no more than trickery and vanity, in every sense of the word.

Apart from anxious feelings of fear or guilt, onanism can encourage—in some sensitive and imaginative adolescents—the tendency to withdraw into themselves and to live in a more or less phantasmagoric world of reverie. "Not, I think, unrelated to solitary practices," wrote Gide in his *Journal.*[24] Psychiatrists have long noticed the relation of one to the other, and Jean-Paul Sartre eloquently expressed it in his *Saint Genêt, comédien et martyr:*

[23] *Si le grain ne meurt,* II, 346.
[24] 1928, p. 891.

We finally discover the secret of that imaginary life: the image is the unsubstantial mediation which reunites Narcissus with himself. The fabulous Opera ends in masturbation. . . . Deciding to prefer appearances to everything else is putting onanism, on principle, above any kind of copulation. . . . A purely demonic act, onanism maintains in the flow of consciousness an appearance of appearances: masturbation results in the world, as well as the person who masturbates, becoming unreal. . . . In one motion the onanist captures the world so as to dissolve it and puts into the universe the order of the unreal: the images must *exist* in order to act. . . . But the worship of appearances leads to impotence, to complete solitude, to the bounds of nothingness.[25]

When onanism corresponds to a whole narcissistic organization of the personality, it is obviously the indication of a neurosis, but desire used on oneself is not a really narcissistic unless it is desire *of* oneself. And such is generally not the case. Desire is provoked not by the image of oneself but by the image of another, of, for instance, a woman one desires but who is not there. Its significance is therefore quite different and almost physiological. The harmless or serious nature of masturbation is not determined by the gesture itself but by the phantasms that caused it. And it is the phantasms that show whether the sexuality is normal or perverse. When André Walter feels overexcited by "visions of women called to mind," it worries no one; but we become more troubled when he says, "Now, I would not really know what to do with them."

At the ambiguous age of adolescence, at André Walter's age, homosexual and heterosexual tendencies can exist at the same time, but it would be impossible to come to any conclusion. The chips are not yet down. For Gide they were not down until several years later, not necessarily during his first trip to Africa when he "made a terrible mistake in taking the wrong road,"[26] but two years after that, when he convinced himself that homosexuality was "the secret" of his nature and decided to build his entire immoralist protest on that original but debatable cornerstone.

[25] Pp. 341–42.

[26] Conversation quoted by Denis de Rougemont, *N.R.F., Hommage à André Gide,* p. 283.

25: Narcissus' Mistake

> *"Like Narcissus, I bent over my image."*
> Si le grain ne meurt, *I, 235*

*T*HE malady that André Walter interpreted as a struggle between the soul and the flesh, or more precisely, between an ideal love and sexual desire, can also be considered from another angle, that of psychological narcissism and the struggle between dream and life. To prefer one's dream to the world and to contemplate oneself rather than to live is characteristic of Narcissus. An ancient metaphor, which no one has ever revived as successfully as Paul Valéry, compares self-consciousness to a mirror. Narcissus is self-conscious. He is an analyzer who can no more escape from the obsessing reflection in the mirror of his consciousness than from his reflection in the water. He lives bent over himself, and his leaning over is the symbol of the division of the ego into actor and spectator, the position characteristic of introversion and introspection, a more or less natural bent but one that can become a vicious plicature.

André Walter is turned toward himself in that way and watches his inner world. It is his inclination and no doubt his "mistake,"[1] but it is not his sin. Dangerous as it may be, it is not morally reprehensible, and although it may cause regret, it does not cause remorse.

There are types of introspection which are not narcissistic. A psychologist or, for example, M. Teste, can take all the dimensions of "The Hon. Myself's" mind, with the impassive glance of a geometrician or, less irrev-

[1] Louis Lavelle, *L'Erreur de Narcisse.*

erently, with the cold blue eye of a Da Vinci, free of concupiscence if not of curiosity.[2] André Walter did not watch himself with such sovereign indifference: he was full of feeling and could not see himself without being moved. And it is indeed the feeling, "love perhaps or, of oneself, hate," that describes the narcissistic behavior. Walter delights himself or detests himself: "I horrify myself! For *if the salt have lost his savour . . .*" But in order to fret because he feels he has become tasteless, he must first have tasted of himself and acquired a taste for his "inimitable savor."

Narcissism may be physical or psychic, depending upon whether it involves the eye or the consciousness. The two aspects, which do not necessarily go together, do in André Walter. André Gide, like Walter, was very concerned with his physical appearance. From the time he was sixteen, Narcissus' age in the fable, he had begun to assiduously study his face in the little mirror he inherited from Anna Shackleton. It was the time of the romantic cape, the artistically knotted and flowing tie, the long hair, the very studied seriousness, the languidly stooped postures, common to the flower *narcissus poeticus,* which, according to the scholar Loiseleur-Deslongchamps, "was perhaps enough to have inspired the creative imagination of the Greeks with the ingenious story told by Ovid." Gide, in his old age, was irritated by the drooping appearance he saw in a photograph of himself as a romantic adolescent: "Ah! It really gives itself away." He added, in German, the words used as a title for one of Schumann's lieder: "a little too serious." Nothing of the languidness in the old picture remained in his taut, sharply defined face, just as nothing of the "uncertain, infinite, inexpressible" style of André Walter's diaries remained in the concise and lively prose of old Theseus. He detested the "complacency" of the body and soul which he saw naïvely revealed in his first portrait and in his first book.[3]

A diary is as necessary to psychological narcissism as a mirror is to physical narcissism. And André Gide, like André Walter, used his diary to satisfy the need for analyzing his moods and giving permanence to his memories of a fleeting youth. He lived in the fear of not keeping an accurate enough catalogue of his emotions. He, in fact, meant to be no more than the memorialist of himself: "Not an event: always the inner life . . . Everything happened in the soul; nothing was visible."[4] Amiel is

[2] M. Teste was not always that detached or objective with regard to "The Hon. Myself": "I adored myself, I detested myself; then we grew old together." His wisdom was acquired.

[3] Preface to the 1930 edition of *Les Cahiers d'André Walter.*

[4] This sentence, like many others in *Les Cahiers,* was transcribed directly from Gide's early *Journal* and was written in verse.

the public hero of that private literary genre and the most glorious victim of what Paul Bourget called "the malady of the personal diary."[5] At eighteen he began to carry on his relationship with himself, never tired of it, and found his vocation in being the vestal of his own flame. At first his *Journal* was "a mystic and hybrid being, kept weekly, a daybook, an official report, an inquisitor, a confidant, a portfolio; but its two main functions are that of the clerk who records and that of the Nestor who preaches." Yet it was to become something quite different:

It is my conversation, my social life, my confidant, my companion. It is also my consolation, my memory, my scapegoat, my echo, the reservoir of my inner experiences, my psychological journal, my protection against a rusty mind, my pretext for living.

Now in a diary the fascinating play of the "I" can be considered either as romantic or neurotic. Both aspects exist in André Walter, as in the adolescent André Gide, then so similar to Amiel.

André Walter, like many of his older brothers in literature—the Hamlets, the Renés, the Werthers—is a romantic Narcissus. He delights in his inner world, in the busily moving succession of vague reveries, painful emotions, fervors, ecstasies, and he has the same contempt for outer reality that he has for action.

Walter was not interested in his mind but in his soul.[6] For him the distinction was not specious, and had he known the terms animus and anima, he would surely have used them. He set small value on cold reason, which is objective, common to all, and therefore common, and kept all his tenderness for the soul, which is complete subjectivity and unique resonance. Walter's psychology is that of an intuitive introvert who means to grasp directly his unique essence without wasting time on the "contingent pluralities" of phenomena. It corresponds to the eternal dream of Narcissus. When he bends over the image reflected in the water, no intermediary would seem able to separate him from it, but the nearer he draws to it, the more blurred it becomes, and when he wants to catch hold of it, it eludes him. A "vain, vain expectation . . ." unless he becomes one with the water, with the current of universal becoming.

There are states of grace in which Narcissus feels he is in direct communion with his soul and experiences "paradisiac fruition." Rather than tension and vigilance, such a state requires relaxation and the deadening of all resistance. *Narcissus* comes from a Greek verb meaning "to cause numbness or stupor," because, according to Littré, "the scent of its flower

[5] Paul Bourget, "La Maladie du Journal intime," *Illustration,* Sept. 27, 1921. Of course, it is not the fact of keeping a diary that is unhealthy, but a certain way of keeping it which corresponds to a way of being.

[6] The word "soul" is used about 175 times in *Les Cahiers.*

goes to the head." And Narcissus' reflection is less a lucid and voluntary analysis of the ego than a vague but willingly enraptured intuition of the self, less a meditation than a reverie, with the same charm, languor, haziness, mobility, undulation, shimmer, and fluidity, the same caprices and vapors, the same trances. Relaxing the mental syntheses which assure an adjustment to reality or, as Bergson put it, an attention to life, results in privileged moments during which Narcissus reaches himself and believes he can possess himself. That supreme reward requires a mental process not unknown to André Walter: "The will must kill itself, voluntarily destroy itself." In other words reason must be numbed and sensibility awakened. Only at that price will the entire being be plunged "in infinite happiness, without that painful resistance of the ego which alone can make us feel it." And then, ecstasy, "an extraordinary nirvana, into which the entire ego would melt, would sink in ecstasy, and yet would voluntarily remain conscious of its vanishing; it would be like a voluptuously visible nothingness." Thus in *Les Cahiers d'André Walter* there is already the Schopenhauerian[7] theme that was to play a great part in Gide's psychology: the search for a "surrender in ecstasy," in which the ego senses itself, while fusing and taking pleasure in the poetic confusion. "Reason falls asleep, the heart is awake—and the soul? The entire soul shudders." And it is the shudder, or rather the quiver, that the lyrical Walter seeks above all.

Like anguish, ecstasy is a purely affective state, hence an ineffable state. One is fear without any apparent object, the other joy without any apparent object. Both are states of panic—that is, total—but one is panic fear and the other panic joy; they resemble one another and are in opposition to one another. Both are spontaneous states of intoxication, "intoxication without wine." To describe their physical effect, Gide used the same words: "deep suffocation." But in anguish the suffocation is painful and accompanied by a constriction; whereas in ecstasy the constriction is replaced by voluptuous anhelation, an expansion of the whole being, an elation. Both, although felt *hic et nunc,* seem outside of space and time, which are abolished, and give the person possessed the impression of being transported outside himself (*ek-stasis*) or of being lifted up, carried away, overcome by an "inner sea" which submerges the consciousness. The consciousness more or less sinks, thus creating in the person the feeling of direct communication with the soul he had been unaware of and which, depending on his personal tendencies, he calls nature or the unconscious, inspiration or mystery, all or nothingness, god or demon, genius or muse. The person who experiences these strange states is apt to seek its origins

[7] Throughout *Les Cahiers* Schopenhauer's influence, the influence of *The World as Will and Idea,* is evident.

outside himself. Gide often spoke of such "miraculous moments" or "eternities of the moment," during which he felt in communion with all of nature, possessing "in his totality" a god who most particularly resembles the great Pan.

Just as at nineteen Gide thought he had spotted his childhood *Schaudern* in Schopenhauer, so later on he thought that he noticed similarities between the auras of Dostoevsky's Myshkin and Kirilov and certain of his own privileged states. Indeed many passages in Dostoevsky recall the basic characteristics of such states: the suddenness, the brevity, the total joy, the suppression of time, the pantheistic contact with nature, the religious vertigo of the soul. "Something enormous, religious, panicky," wrote Gide with regard to his third *Schauder*. There is, of course, nothing in common between the sickness of Dostoevsky's heroes[8] and Gide's emotional intoxication. A trance may have various causes: it merely implies a disturbance of the ego consciousness or, as Bergson said, "a deadening of the active or, rather, resistant powers of the personality, which makes it possible to sympathize with the feeling." This psychological lipothymia is helped along by acute emotivity, favorable to the momentary disintegration of the mental syntheses which insure an adjustment to reality, and by nervous instability, favorable to a dizziness of the ego and a failure of the will, common in both Gide and Amiel. Such quivering or emotional ebriety in Gide sometimes went as far as total confusion and a bewildering duality of the ego. This state, which psychologists somewhat laboriously call "the disintegration of mental syntheses through emotion" was soberly expressed in Racine's well-known line, "Par quel trouble me vois-je emporté loin de moi?" a line Gide was fond of quoting. To be moved means to be transported or carried away, carried out of oneself, and is a state of momentary depersonalization whose high point is anguish or ecstasy.

Certain of André Walter's ecstasies point to the states of intoxication in *Les Nourritures terrestres,* a somewhat breathless succession of swoons. In that little hedonic treatise Gide was to extract a philosophy from his "miraculous moments" and set it up as worship of the moment: "Oh! Oh! Oh! Oh! That little passing pleasure!" Tempered and controlled by art, such "raptures" and transports were to be expressed throughout Gide's works by a well-placed "ah!" There are obviously many "ahs!" and emotional interjections in *Les Cahiers d'André Walter,* whose "ejaculatory" tone later exasperated André Gide. But romantic language suited André Walter's romantic temperament. His ego was all emotion, and it was emotion that he demanded from his profusely poetic and naturalistic, musical, or mystical reveries.

[8] The affective auras, sometimes "marvelous," and the dreamy states of temporal epilepsy.

Walter quivered night and day, out on his solitary walks or closed in his room, in contact with nature and in contact with books. He read so much that it is difficult to distinguish between his personal feelings and those he borrowed from the literature he quite obviously had in his blood. Mentioned at random throughout *Les Cahiers* are: the Bible, Homer, Goethe, Flaubert, Jeremiah, Baudelaire, Shakespeare, Lamennais, John Stuart Mill, Spinoza, Cuvier, Michelet, Taine, Pascal, Stendhal, Bossuet, Massillon, Goncourt, Vigny, Dante, Heinrich Heine, Hugo, Apuleius, Luther, Verlaine, Ribot, Schopenhauer, Berlioz, Kant, Saint Paul, and many others. But one name, although constantly called to mind, is missing: that of Amiel.

André Walter's life, the life of a solitary dreamer, recalls Amiel's. The perpetual introspection, the throbbing and secret emotivity, the shyness, the pietism, the mystic and poetic flights that culminate in fervor and ecstasy, the great ideal and platonic love, the rejection of the outer world and action are comparable in both. "The dream is gigantic, but action is vain," proclaimed Amiel. "Is action necessary?" asked André Walter, and his immediate answer was: "I prefer my dream, O Lord! I prefer my dream." No one ever spoke as lovingly of the delights of reverie and the failure of the ego as the Genevese Narcissus: "It is my opium, my hashish. Disgust for my individual life and the submersion of my private will into the pure consciousness of universal activity is my inclinaton, my weakness, my instinct." What Narcissus implies by the "disgust" for his individual life and what he tries to escape from in the opium of dream is anguish:

I am afraid of objective life and shrink from any surprise, demand, or promise that makes me a part of reality. I am terrified of action and feel comfortable only in the impersonal, detached, subjective life of thought.

Behind the romanticism and trascendental idealism, we see the neurosis.

The romantic Narcissus is often a neurotic Narcissus. His glorification of the imaginary hides a fear of living; his psychology as a dreamer, the psychology of a doubter; his pursuit of the ego, a sickness of the ego. If he constantly looks at himself in a mirror or in a diary, he does it more to understand his malady than to admire himself. He bends over himself more out of anxious concern than out of love. He worries about feeling strange and being a stranger not only to others but to himself; an indefinable mystery troubles him, envelops him, and throws a veil over reality; he is limited, as Góngora said—and not without Gongorism—to "craving the echoes and scorning the fountains." Narcissus and his image are a symbol of the psychological split into actor and spectator, which can become a symbol of the neurotic duality of the personality. Narcissus' duality pushes him into seeking his shadow and makes him wonder whether he himself is not the shadow of a shadow and has not lost his ego. The Prince of Doubt's question, "To be or not to be," expresses his most deep-seated problem: depersonalization. At one extreme the romantic malady is one of the divine postulations of man; at the other it is a sickness of the human personality.

With adolescence, the underlying feelings of insecurity, guilt, and ambivalence of Gide's childhood took on an added intensity, if not really new characteristics. He had become aware of the division and weakness of his ego. An impression of duplicity and duality made him doubt the sincerity of his perceptions, his feelings, his beliefs, and his judgments of reality and values. An impression of complicity, a kind of ambiguous sympathy for the Adversary, kept Gide from fighting him wholeheartedly and thus compromised his will. A prey to doubt, ambivalence, and indecision, he complained about a painful feeling of depersonalization which, in André Walter and in him alone, was to become the sign of a real disintegration of the personality.

André Walter had the impression of being divided into actor and spectator. He suffered at "never losing sight of himself." During his exercises before the mirror or the diary, he found that "the concern with trying to show emotion supplants the sincere emotion," and reproached himself for not feeling the emotion in reality and when he should feel it: "How many times when near you, Emmanuèle, have I felt the real and spontaneous emotion vanish with the too-great effort I made to spurt it out." In like manner André Gide then felt subject to paralyzing thoughts: "At that time I felt I could not write, I almost said: think, except in front of that little mirror; in order to become aware of my emotions, of my thoughts, I felt I had first to read them in my eyes." André Walter sometimes tried to balk at such self-analysis: "I must no longer look backward," but he was quite incapable of putting that into practice. Like his ironic brother, the hero of *Paludes,* he was afflicted with "the sickness of retrospection"; like his Luciferian brother, the future Armand Vedel, he understood— though less forcefully and lucidly—that when one is divided in that way, one can no longer be sincere: "One part of me always steps back and looks at the other." André Walter had the impression of being an actor who doubts his own sincerity.

There is not one belief, not one armature, that is not corroded by those termites of the soul, the doubts as to the authenticity of feelings. The Huguenot Walter's religious faith itself was attacked by the inner enemy and apt to give way at the slightest shock or even at the simple surge of emotion which makes the heart susceptible to God: "Doubt in the middle of ecstasy." The following passage shows a curious ambiguity of feelings and resentment, as well as a doubt as to the existence of the God to whom André Walter was willing to make "so many sacrifices":

A God is not enough, he must see you; that is still not enough, he must love; after that, nothing else matters. You sacrifice every thing, one by one; out of the love of duty, you are perfectly able to destroy your happiness; you become virtuous, sublime; you consent to few knowing about it—only yourself, although yourself has died—and you can even do without that; it is the absolute sacrifice of yourself . . . but may God at least be the last refuge, after everything else has foundered—and may God see us and bless the effort we have made; if not, it is the nothingness of our whole life— and when we have understood that, it is the wild cry of terror in the dark. *Lord! O Lord! How many times have I cried out to you as a child cries out to its father, and you have not answered me!*

It is the prayer of an Alissa who doubts the value of her sacrifice. The sacrifice Walter believed that his God required was that of the flesh, and were the divine guarantee to collapse, he was not determined to "act like an angel." Sometimes he glorified chastity and sometimes saw it as mere vanity, as if he experienced the Gidian feeling par excellence: the fear of being right.[9] In the ambivalent soul of André Walter, there was not only duplicity but complicity with regard to the Adversary, what Kierkegaard called "sympathetic antipathy and antipathetic sympathy," the very source of anguish.

André Walter says that his one objective is to act like an angel, but he immediately wonders whether his objective is "humanly possible" and whether his decision is wise. We feel that he is on the point of wondering whether the values he was taught are not counterfeit. In that perspective his struggle between sexuality and Christian morality is but one of the situations that continued to torment Gide himself for a long time after he had become demoralized, de-Christianized, and free of the guilt he had attached to sexuality: "I cannot decide with assurance that good is here on this side and evil over there on the other."[10] This is not the intellectual doubt of a skeptic who is accustomed to revising methodically his value judgments; it is rather a "natural tendency—far more rare and question-able—which compromises him to the very roots of his will."[11] It signifies a deep affective ambivalence, an equivalence of contraries, a morbid equa-nimity which makes him give equal weight to opposing sides and, no matter which side he takes, makes him an accomplice of the Adversary. In his ambiguous struggle between the angel and the beast, André Walter is already a victim of that "dual and simultaneous postulation, one toward God, the other toward Satan" which Gide found in Baudelaire. The angel attracts him and the demon fascinates him.

[9] "It remained one of the constants of my nature" (*Journal*, 1946, p. 254).

[10] *Ibid.*, 1941, p. 103.

[11] *Ibid.*, p. 109.

But the moral struggle between what he called good and evil is only one aspect of the psychological struggle Gide was to carry on, right to the end, against the coexistence or, more precisely, the attraction of contradictory feelings. When André Gide gave up his belief in both God and the devil, André Walter's malady—"the vertiginous play between heaven and hell" —became a vertigo of the ego. He no longer interpreted it on the moral and metaphysical level but on the psychological level.[12] The supreme ambivalence is an equal attraction to concentration and dispersion, organization and disorganization, integration and disintegration, and finally, being and non-being: to be or not to be. Added to that equal fascination is the fundamental theme of the romantic malady—the attraction of the day and passion for the night, and the theme of the neurotic malady—the rivalry between the life instinct and the death instinct, Narcissus' greatest torment. When he bends over his elusive image in the water, he is tempted to plunge in with it vertiginously. The "submersion" Amiel spoke about as his inclination, his weakness, and his instinct, is the same surrender of the ego that André Walter sought in ecstasy, in voluptuous disintegration, and finally, in alienation.

Narcissus' condition is full of dangers, and when he leans too far over the pure water, he reads in his blurred eyes his fatal desire disguised in symbols. The darkness, the nothingness, the abyss, the chasm seem to fascinate the romantic Walter. The theme of the disintegration or dissolution of the personality, its fluidity, its vaporization, its want of consistency, comes back like a leitmotif in all narcissists. We can imagine how Gide felt when he first read in Amiel's *Journal*:

My own ego evaporates like a drop of water. . . . I am fluid, and must resign myself to it. . . . My want of consistency is like that of a fluid, a vapor, a cloud. . . . You lose the unity of life, strength, action, the unity of the ego. . . . My soul is the possibility of all forms. . . . Everything tempts me, attracts me, polarizes me, transforms me, and temporarily estranges me from my volatile and expansive personality, which is as centrifugal as ether. . . . My being is indifferent, fluctuating, dispersed; I have infinite difficulty in gathering my molecules together; I continually elude myself in spite of my daily meditations and my diary. What gives form to the cohesion of individuality is the will and especially the continuity of willing; as I never continue myself, it is clear that I am several and not one. My name is Legion, Proteus, Anarchy. What I lack is a determining and constant force, a character.

Narcissus' malady has perhaps never been that well expressed; and it is almost needless to emphasize the fact that each sentence, indeed each word, has innumerable counterparts throughout André Gide's *Journal*. The lack of confidence in oneself which leads to such a way of being, or such diffi-

[12] Preface to *Les Fleurs du mal*.

culty in being, explains far more satisfactorily than metaphysical idealism the escape into imaginary life and play, the flight from reality and action.

André Walter's weak ago, assailed by obsessing doubts, was also beset by very special obsessions—musical and numerical—which were very similar to those of André Gide, particularly in periods of fatigue or depression. But all their common feelings of duality, ambivalence, and depersonalization, their doubts, and even their obsessions were to lead André Walter to a still more deadly experience; he stepped over a boundary which, obviously, André Gide never crossed.

An important part of *Les Cahiers* describes a real race to madness between André Walter, the novelist, and Allain, his fictional double:

The race to madness—which one of us will arrive first, Allain or I? I bet on Allain; I hold myself back, apply the brake; him, I push, I accelerate the work, I hasten the denouement: I must make him go mad before I become so myself. Which of the two will climb over the other?

André Walter thus runs after Allain and follows him closely. André Gide also ran after his double and his double's double, but at a great enough distance to allow him to avoid the fatal issue: he "applied his brake" in time and, if we are to believe him, at the very last minute.

He himself wrote apropos of Walter:

I soon could not say which of us was leading the other; for although there was nothing in him which I had not first felt myself, nothing, so to speak, I had not tried on myself, I often pushed my double ahead of me, ventured out after him, and it was in *his* madness that I was preparing to founder.[13]

The pronoun is italicized, which is exceptional in a text of Gide's, but he thus meant to emphasize the fact that whatever the writer's sympathy for his hero's madness, the madness was not his own. André Walter is a double of André Gide's adolescent ego, but in the same restrictive sense that Boris Lapérouse is a double of his childish ego. Boris commits suicide and Walter goes mad, whereas Gide escapes. The conflicts both have to face are essentially the same, as are their defense mechanisms, but André Walter's got out of hand and André Gide's successfully resisted and assured him victory. The differences between the natures of the character and the novelist are more important than the similarities, for what finally determines a character are his limits.

---

[13] *Si le grain ne meurt*, I, 223–24.

26: The Creation of a Double

> *"Leaping right out of my hero, leaving him to sink into madness, my soul, finally freed from him . . ."*
>
> Si le grain ne meurt, *I, 247*

𝒯 HE psychology of *Les Cahiers d'André Walter* leads us into a hall of mirrors. André Walter is in love with his own image, just as he is in love with the image of Emmanuèle, his ideal double, and with the image of Allain, his fictional double. We know that there is a "striking similarity" between Emmanuèle and her first cousin; yet the same resemblance exists between him and Allain, who is not only the mirror of André Walter's soul but the mirror of André Walter's love for Emmanuèle, of which she herself is also the mirror. We can well understand how André Walter finally lost himself, once and for all, in that profusion of dualities: yet André Gide found himself in it. It was not the future Theseus' least important exploit and was assuredly useful training in the "trompe l'oeil" of his inner labyrinth.

In a work of art I rather like to find transposed in that way, on the scale of the characters, the very subject of the work. Nothing can shed a clearer light on it or more surely establish the proportions of the whole. Thus, in certain paintings of Memling or Quentin Metzys, a small convex and dark mirror reflects, in turn, the inside of the room in which the scene of the painting takes place.[1]

---

[1] *Journal*, 1893, p. 41. Gide discovered Quentin Metzys after the publication of *Les Cahiers d'André Walter*, on his 1891 trip to Belgium to see Maeterlinck (1891 daybook, unpublished).

Here the inside of the room in which the scene takes place is André Walter's soul, and the little mirror is Allain's soul, which reflects André's:

A perhaps better explanation of what I meant to do in *Les Cahiers* . . . is a comparison with the device of heraldry[2] that consists in putting a second coat of arms "en abyme" within the first. That retroaction of the subject on itself has always tempted me. It is the model of the psychological novel.

Les Cahiers d'André Walter corresponds to that definition of the psychological novel, at least to an introverted novelist's conception of it. It is an essay about oneself and, as it were, of oneself, an experimental novel, not in the sense meant by Zola, patterned on Claude Bernard, but in the sense of inner experience. André Walter tries to project his own problems on to a double, Allain, and he fails, but André Gide—who attempted the same thing with André Walter—succeeded. The fact that *Les Cahiers* is not a success from the viewpoint of fictional technique is of little matter here. What is important from the psychological viewpoint is that it was effective retroactively. We know that André Gide was very hard on that work of his youth and even declared in a preface that he wrote for the 1930 edition: "I call a book unsuccessful when it leaves the reader intact." But was that all he thought, and would it not have been closer to his own truth to have said: a book seems unsuccessful when it leaves the reader intact, but it *is* unsuccessful only when it leaves its author intact? In his *Journal* of 1893[3] Gide also noted, apropos of *La Tentative amoureuse:*

I wanted to point out . . . the influence of a book on the one who is writing it, and during the very writing of it. For as it issues from us, it changes us, it modifies the course of our life. . . . It is thus a method of acting on oneself.

This problem, which is posed in *Les Cahiers d'André Walter,* is similar to that of literary catharsis. Gide's first book shows how a certain "lack of balance," taken in the very general sense Gide gave the words in his essay on Dostoevsky, could be favorable to literary creation, and how the creation of a double could modify the lack of balance. Actually André Gide, after André Walter, was no longer the same as he was before André Walter, nor, of course, was he exactly someone else.

In his essay on Dostoevsky, André Gide maintained that at the origins of every great moral reform, of every transmutation of values, there is always an anxiety, a dissatisfaction of the flesh, an anomaly. He would also seem to imply that the anomaly was at the origins of all literary creation. Needless to say, his thesis calls for many reservations, but there is

---

[2] The *cahier de lectures* of 1891 mentions Gide's having read a *Traité du blason.*

[3] Pp. 40–41.

some truth in it. A certain lack of balance can—to the extent that it impedes an adjustment to reality—promote creation in artists who use their difficulty in adjusting to create their dreams. Although Gide claimed not to have gone back to the conceptions of Lombroso and Nordau, he did give a new form to the problem of the relationship between neurosis and creation.

André Walter's malady is favorable to literature, at least to a certain form of literature, because of both the temperament and complexes from which it originated. For that matter, literature for André Walter was not a game or a luxurious diversion: it was a vital necessity. It has been said that André Gide, in recalling his youth, had declared: "If I had been kept from writing, I would have committed suicide." When I asked him if he had really made that remark, he waited a moment and then replied: "I don't remember having said it, but I remember having thought it."

Paul Bourget pointed out that the problem of "the animal sensibility of intelligent men" had not been "studied closely enough." Yet it would seem to be at the base of the *genus irritabile vatum,* in which emotional irritability is widespread. "For us," said Rousseau, "to exist means to feel; our sensibility is unquestionably anterior to our intelligence." That is true of everyone, but especially of those whose emotivity is their way of being and whose intelligence appears to have won over the emotion, resulting in a subtle mind, essentially intuitive, and in what Rousseau called the "sensibility of tact" in all the workings of the mind. An intense, susceptible, unstable, and anxious emotivity would seem a part of Gide's temperament itself; and there is a literary virtue that corresponds to every one of those characterisitcs. An inclination to emotional frenzies is inseparable from lyricism, from the gift of enthusiasm. Intense emotivity implies nervous acuity, a hyperesthesia which is precious to a poet. The extreme instability of mood, the oscillation between states of enthusiasm and abjection, between pathetic states and apathetic states, makes that type of nervous person run through the entire range of human emotions with disconcerting speed, while at the same time helps to confirm his feeling of inconstancy, which can be a valuable point of departure for romantic irony. Finally, the anxiety augments the tragic feeling for life and gives thought an aura which is not without poetic charm, nor without philosophical value.[4] Many pessimistic philosophies derive from that type of temperament, just as many aesthetics derive from that esthesia.

Somewhat rarer is the mixture of emotional irritability and a certain form of nervous weakness, which paralyzes action, reinforces the tendency to introspection, and can turn out such virtuosos of the diary as Maine de

---

[4] "It is anxiety," remarked Anatole France, "that gives value to men's thoughts. A mind that is not anxious either irritates me or bores me."

Biran or Amiel, such great poets as Leopardi and Baudelaire, and novelists in the class of Flaubert or Gide. There are many similarities, for example, between Frédéric Moreau in *L'Education sentimentale* and André Walter. In Frédéric Moreau, that "son of Mme. Bovary,"[5] Flaubert described many of the characteristics of his own malady, which was not—as some have thought—epilepsy, but a neurosis, the same neurosis which, if the grain does not germinate, produces a dry fruit (the first title of *L'Education sentimentale* was *Les Fruits secs*) and if the grain does not die, an artist or an arbiter. The same extreme emotivity, anxiety, shyness, doubts, duality of the self, hesitations, obsessions, and above all, the same boredom with reality can be found in Frédéric Moreau, but without the Huguenot Walter's anguish of sexual guilt.[6] A suggestive parallel can be established between Gide's youth and that of Flaubert, who at sixteen saw the world "as a spectacle," was "totally disgusted with the reality that lies so heavily upon us," "constantly dissected" himself, complained about "strange moments of lassitude," rejoiced when he discovered "corruption in something pure," and talked of committing suicide, and all that much before his first nervous spells which did not begin until he was twenty-two. At the same age, that of Frédéric Moreau or of André Walter, both had the same difficulty in adjusting to the world of outer reality, the world of the present, of action, and the same tendency to withdraw, indulge in self-analysis, and take refuge in the imaginary. That substitution of a created life—in which they felt not only normal but superior—for real life, in which they felt deficient, is an eminently favorable condition for a certain type of literature.

Most analysts hold introspection responsible for such disorders, but they take the effect for the cause, for it is the disorder itself that leads a Gide or a Flaubert to self-analysis and introspection. Literature and philosophy only attack those who were already sick and who became writers and philosophers because of their sickness. And although an excess of introspection probably increases certain disorders, it does not create them; rather, it maintains them advantageously and sometimes cures them. The neurotic condition and the literary condition are mutually beneficial.

The very special form of nervous weakness common to Gide and Flaubert, André Walter and Frédéric Moreau, creates a feeling of the inadequacy of reality; a duality—that is, a division of the self into actor and spectator; doubts; and obsessive tendencies which, if they stay within certain limits, may be favorable to the art of literature. Anyone who suffers from a feeling of the inadequacy of reality, and from the impossibility of completely grasping its impact, is impelled to compensate for it

[5] Emile Faguet.

[6] Yet there is the same tendency to dissociate love, which remains platonic (Mme. Arnoux), and desire (Rosanette).

through writing. A moment that is completely and totally experienced is no longer material for art; it must be incompletely experienced and must call for an imaginary end, which is the work of art. The duality, the division of the self into actor and spectator, is one requisite of aesthetic irony. A nervously weak person often complains about watching life—and his own life—as if it were a "spectacle outside of reality"; but for a littérateur it is a privilege. The veil of illusion that comes between him and reality, creating a painful impression of remoteness, becomes the distance necessary to aesthetic perception; the feeling of hypocrisy or of bad conscience, brought about by what little sincerity remains, becomes the play of doubles favorable to aesthetic consciousness. Perception becomes more aesthetic to the extent that it is less "esthesic"; a feeling is easier to act out to the extent that it is less sincere. The nervously weak person, who has always the impression of playing a part, lives in an essentially illusory world which calls for the activities of play. Only by dreaming, in anticipation or in retrospection, does he actualize; only by representing does he grasp the present. Here the secret of a temperament coincides with the artist's need for transposition. For him real life is dreamed life, and what he recopies is never reality but its transposition. He lives at a distance from reality. Life for André Walter was no more than "an echo of his thoughts," just as the voice of the devil was for Flaubert's Saint Anthony.

That type of disposition inevitably leads to preferring portrayed emotion to experienced emotion. When Gide was involved in a carriage accident at the age of eighteen, he had the same feeling of unreality and duality that Frédéric Moreau had during the revolution of 1848: "The wounded and the dead did not seem real." I have already mentioned that in speaking of his carriage accident, Gide told me: "That was the day I discovered irony." And his discovery was no less important for him than it was for Flaubert, "for naturally fear, real fear, then becomes impossible."[7] An innate fear and hatred of reality goes along with the love of a portrayed reality, in other words a reality that is exorcised, canceled out, reduced to nothingness, dead, and—at the extreme—immortalized. "She is dead, *therefore* he possesses her." André Walter's cry of love is of the same nature as a "realistic" novelist such as Flaubert's "love" of reality.[8] André Walter is an essentially Bovaresque hero. To dream life is characteristic of the weak, but to make one's dream live through writing is the secret of literary art.

Doubts, hesitations, and obsessing scruples are a curse for a man of action but a blessing for works of the mind. The "indecision" that Leo-

[7] *Journal*, 1924, p. 800.

[8] "I hate life," said Flaubert. "The word came out; let it stay." André Walter experienced the same "boredom with reality." Flaubert's realism is a revenge on reality.

pardi considered a curse upon the chosen and "one of the greatest afflictions of the human soul" is not without value. Literature owes a great deal to all of its devoted Sisyphi—as much to their mania for questioning and constantly verifying everything, as to their scrupulous slavery to the exact word, accurately placed. Their doubts as to the correct term, the perfectionism of endless retouching, an almost obsessive rigor in their recourse to a unity of tone, necessary because of the variability of their own, are so many obstacles for the mind. An admirable example of that are the men who—weak-willed, undecided, torn between their contradictions, divided, doubting themselves and the world, in short, unhealthy—have created works in which language is at its healthiest. "The work of art is an equilibrium outside of time, an artificial health."[9] Those words from André Gide's early *Journal* would be equally suitable for Flaubert or Baudelaire. There is a striking contrast between the indecision such great writers complained about and the enormous energy it took for them to produce their masterpieces, but the paradox is only on the surface. It was because they mistrusted themselves and felt their weakness that they became slaves to an exclusive worship of literature, to the detriment of all other values. "O Lord," wrote Gide in his *Journal* of 1892, "grant that I may want only one thing and want it constantly."[10]

We can remember Max Nordau's pamphlets against the "degenerate egotist" for whom literature is everything, the "writer who does not hesitate to agree with Mallarmé that the world is made to result in a beautiful book," in contrast to the cobbler who admits that there are more interesting and more important things in life than mending shoes. Yet the conviction that literature is the only important thing in life has less to do with the literary profession itself than with an obsessing concern that can be the same in the art of mending shoes as in the art of writing, the same for the artisan as for the artist. Limited interests are favorable to complete concentration of all the energies on one objective. Writers attacked by diary sickness end by replacing their atrophy of the will by a compensatory hypertrophy—that is, they replace the abulia by an *idée fixe*. Accordingly, Amiel, Flaubert, or Gide can be considered weak-willed or heroes of the will, undecided or the most decided of men, if only in that they aesthetically cultivated their indecision and firmly meant to resolve it only in and through a work of art.

A nervous temperament like Gide's is thus favorable to literature. It encourages both lyricism and introspection, poetic emotion and aesthetic duality. Also, it results in a fundamental conflict between two opposing currents: the coexistence of the spontaneity necessary to lyricism and the

[9] *Journal*, "Littérature et morale," p. 94.

[10] *Ibid.*, 1892, p. 29.

reflection necessary to aestheticism is difficult. The famous words from Flaubert's *Correspondance:* "The less we feel a thing, the more we are apt to express it as it is, as it always is in itself, free of all its ephemeral contingents," were to be brilliantly echoed in Gide's second book, his *Traité du Narcisse.*

To a certain extent, narcissism itself is favorable to aestheticism. Narcissus' apprehensive quest is sterile and can lead only to defeat. He dreams of an impossible adventure: he wants to catch hold of an image that changes as he approaches it and vanishes as soon as he leans over it. The ego is just as fluid and fleeting as a reflection in the water; it refuses to be possessed. "The kiss is impossible. One must not desire an image; any gesture made to possess it destroys it."[11] And Narcissus dies the minute he is "finally disconsolately delivered" from the love of his soul. But if the Narcissus is an artist, he has one recourse: he can give permanence to the elusive image of himself by making it an object outside himself. The work of art is magic, although the work of the artist is as far as possible from the trance of the sorcerer or the languor of reveries.

Freud held that aesthetic activity arises from narcissism, for narcissism implies a fixation at the animistic stage of belief in the omnipotence of thought, which is at the origins of magic or of art. "There is one domain," he wrote, "in which the omnipotence of thought has been maintained right up through our culture: the domain of art. . . . There is good reason to compare the artist to a magician." In studying Gide's childhood and adolescence, we have analyzed the subterfuges that made it possible for him to find a refuge from anguish in solitary reverie—that is, in magical thought and in the imaginary satisfaction of desires, which are both turned away from reality. However, as Freud remarked, "there is one road back from fantasy to reality: art." Schlegel had already written that every poet is a Narcissus. But he is more than that. Narcissus dreams; the poet creates. Reverie, total surrender to subjectivity, is the natural inclination of every introvert, but the artist must constantly climb up out of himself if he wants to express himself. The dream, pure impression, is escape and turns one away from reality, but art—insofar as it is expression—brings one back, for it is objectivization. In order to capture an image, it is necessary to go back to the rules of the game, which require training, knowledge, and technique. Narcissus plays; the poet works. He has the problems of an artisan; he is as earnest as a workman; he applies himself; he accepts difficulties.

If narcissism can explain the withdrawal into oneself and the need for creation, does it also explain the need for communicating to others the products of such creation? The title of one of the most beautiful poems in

[11] *Le Traité du Narcisse, O.C.,* I, 218.

the French language, Paul Valéry's *Narcisse parle,* is splendidly paradoxical; for if Narcissus speaks aloud, he means to be heard by "the others." To be heard only by oneself and to create a language that is understood only by oneself is the expression of complete narcissism, almost never found outside alienation. But the poet, whatever his innate narcissism, means to share his ego and his emotion with others. "Ah! To see oneself," cried André Gide's Narcissus, but he also wanted to be seen. "A God is not enough," said André Walter, "he must see you." In any case he had already understood that an audience is of the greatest importance. A poet retreats into himself, where he prepares to be found, if only by posterity: "I believe that what dominated my life, *what impelled me to write,* was an extraordinary, an insatiable need to love and be loved; an almost mystical need, moreover, for I consented to its not being satisfied during my lifetime."[12] There is no better way of emphasizing the really infinite nature of that love of love; but loving to love is actually loving no one and being enchanted by one's own fervor, which refuses to settle on a definite object:

Some people accused me of egoism; I accused them of stupidity. My claim was to love no one in particular, man or woman, but rather friendship, affection, or love. By giving to one, I would have had to deprive another, and so I only lent myself . . . as I wished to belong to everyone, I gave myself to no one in particular.[13]

As such love is not intended for the creature, it could only be intended for the Creator, for God; but God is within man, and the objective of a narcissistic artist is to express the ideal image of himself. There is at the roots of aesthetic narcissism a more or less acknowledged attempt at self-deification, which finally becomes the will to immortality. "I passionately desired glory," said André Gide in recalling the time of *André Walter,* and as a youth he indeed "burned" with that passion; but he added that he soon consented to its being a posthumous glory.[14] Here we can see the ideal nature and grandeur of aesthetic narcissism and how it contrasts with vulgar narcissism. The transference of the person to the future work somewhat recalls the mystical belief in the immortality of the soul. It encourages the same spirit of renunciation, for the entire life from then on is subordinated to creating the "ideal" statue. Gide came to make that his objective, just as Goethe did before him: "the desire to build the pyramid as high as possible."[15] Aesthetic narcissism is paradoxical because it finally requires a surrender of the self in order to make an ideal image of oneself, a surrender anticipated by Gide in a note added to *Le Traité du Narcisse,* and written in 1890, hence at the same time as *Les Cahiers d'André Wal-*

[12] *Journal,* 1948, p. 302.

[13] *Nourritures terrestres,* p. 75.

[14] *Si le grain ne meurt,* I, 250.

[15] Letter from Goethe to Lavater.

ter: "The artist and the man who is really a man, the man who lives for something, must first have sacrificed himself. His entire life is but a step toward that."[16]

Narcissus' mistake can be aesthetically fruitful in that it leads to a sublimation of narcissism in favor of an ideal image. What the artist adores is never what he is but what he will be *in* and *through* his future work, which will transform him into himself. At that point he is less a Narcissus than a Pygmalion who is completely engrossed in creating a statue that will live when he is no more.

Thus André Gide's entire psychological constitution at the time he was writing *Les Cahiers d'André Walter* predisposed him to literary creation and more especially to the creation of a fictional double. His temperament gave him the vibrant emotivity necessary to lyricism and a duality favorable to aesthetic irony. His complexes were responsible for a narcissism which, after having led him to take refuge in the magic of his imagination, forced Narcissus out of his retreat so as at least to show himself.

As a long confession, *Les Cahiers* gave Gide the possibility of becoming aware of his conflicts and their transference to a double, mechanisms which to a certain extent recall those of psychological catharsis. It is significant that Freud used Aristotle's term catharsis—meaning purgation and mental purification through art—to designate the effects of psychoanalytical treatment. But *Les Cahiers* also required a creative effort as regards composition and style, representing the aesthetic element of catharsis. I should now like to analyze in turn the role of those three processes of the mind: the act of becoming aware, the transference, and the actual "fabrication," all three of which contributed to the psychological liberation produced by the creation of a double.

The tremendous effort Gide made at introspection, from the time he was fifteen until he was twenty, culminating in *Les Cahiers,* was not at all futile. The state of "preoccupation" in which he lived doubtless had the "serious inconvenience of introspectively absorbing" all his faculties of attention, but it also had the enormous advantage of teaching him to know himself. That training in analysis was of prime importance for a future psychologist and a future artist: it made him more lucid and more intelligent, in the sense that intelligence is the art of reading inside (*intus legere*).

At one time the idea that in art it was preferable not to be a fool seemed paradoxical. A certain romantic conception of genius systematically underrated intelligence and scorned common sense as a bourgeois virtue. Now

[16] *Le Traité du Narcisse, O.C.,* I, 215–16, note.

Gide was not only a highly intelligent artist, he was blessed with common sense. That aspect of his personality was no doubt particularly evident in his old age, but even when he was young, André Walter's large romantic felt hat covered a sound, indeed a hard, head. As a descendant of the circumspect peasant Nicolas Rondeaux, he was full of mistrust, reserve, and caution. He did not like to be taken in, even by himself, nor did he like to have counterfeit coins palmed off on him. The malady that conquered André Walter's reason had far to go before it could break down that of the innately crafty author. The sly, even cunning, aspect of Gide's nature was not apparent during his anguished childhood and adolescence, but it was evident in all the more or less skilful subterfuges he used to control his anguish. At first partly unconscious, the subterfuges became more and more conscious as time went on. Inclined to introspection by temperament and upbringing, Gide very soon grew accustomed to analyzing himself, and he considered himself hypocritical enough to become hypercritical and make sincerity to himself his problem.

At the very time he thought he was a poet, André Gide was constantly the happy victim of his Nemesis: his critical turn of mind and sense of proportion. He could never lose his head, much as he may have wanted to, and could never stop being lucid. In his most extravagant wanderings he kept an eye on himself. Even when he felt "lost" in literary creation, as was the case with *André Walter*,[17] he continued—for himself alone—to comment upon his perdition as if it were that of someone else. Split into actor and spectator, he watched himself create, the spectator always ready to learn from the actor and vice versa. Throughout his life Gide suffered from his lack of spontaneity and went so far as to defend the gratuitous act—that is, the impulse, the audacity of the shy, the volition of the undecided, the temptation of the self-analyzers. But his art greatly benefited from an obsessing self-consciousness, which he turned to account in commentaries contemporary with the formulation of each book. The result is a journal in which he is concerned not only with psychology and aesthetics but with the psychology of his own aesthetic: as a writer, he examines his own conscience.

On occasion, the novelist's self-analysis turns out to be far more important than the novel he writes at the same time. Such is the case with André Walter's journal, which he keeps while writing his novel, *Allain*. Indeed, it is in those pages that he most lucidly and concisely puts his malady into words: "To love only with your soul a soul who loves you in the same way. . . . He asks for the superhuman, but the flesh will have its revenge. . . .

---

[17] "I am not even an egoist any longer. Indeed, I am no longer. Lost from the very day I began my book . . ." (*Journal*, 1890, p. 18).

With all that,[18] every doubt. The boredom of reality keeps him a prisoner in his own dream: he will not come out of it. At the end lies madness." Those few sentences indicate an awareness of the main sources of André Walter's malady, and the conjunction "with" shows that there is a conjecture. The writer was conscious of where his "depraved continence" would lead him and of the danger of taking refuge in his imagination and in his journal.

Was Gide's feeling of liberation after having written *Les Cahiers* due to that self-analysis? Was it the awareness of his conflicts "projected into writing" that acted as a cathartic? At the beginnings of psychoanalysis, the effectiveness of the treatment was attributed to an action of that kind: "Our therapy," wrote Breuer and Freud, "acts by bringing the unconscious to consciousness." Repressed tendencies in the unconscious would cease to be detrimental if the subject became aware of them and expressed them. Thus through his self-knowledge and verbal exteriorization he would cure himself. Yet the intellectual awareness alone is not enough; an affective transference from the person analyzed to the analyst is also necessary. The transference makes it possible to overcome the inner resistance which opposes all solitary exploration of the unconscious and generally limits any self-analysis. But there is a way out of that difficulty in literature through the creation of a double. A transference, either positive or negative, takes place between the novelist and his double, and helps him to become aware of his own depths. Fictional as it is, the interpsychological relationship is effective and in certain respects can replace that of patient and doctor.

André Gide transferred all his own conflicts to André Walter, exaggerating them and carrying them to the extreme. He projected all his deepest affective complexes on to him; he inoculated him with his poisons, and the fate of his literary guinea pig instructed him and helped him to become immune. André Walter was André Gide's first experience with a double. Gide could see that Walter was incapable of living, because he was a chaotic mass of contradictory tendencies: he had to die of his contradictions so that his creator could resolve them, slowly and patiently, through his entire works. André Walter was both a mystic and an artist, a Huguenot and an aesthete, an angelist and a demoniac, a Puritan and a sensualist, a musician and a littérateur, an actor smitten by sincerity, a hero and a weakling, at once shy and bold, a lucid analyzer and a dreamer, a romantic enamored of classical beauty. A choice had to be made. Actually, almost everything came out in *Les Cahiers,* but it remained to be expressed with order and clarity. The task took sixty years, but it was finally accomplished. In his old age Gide was able to pronounce the memorable words:

[18] *Les Cahiers d'André Walter, O.C.,* I, 125. The italics are mine.

"Now I have said everything I had to say."[19] But to arrive at that catharsis through expression was hard labor. He had to replace his total double by partial and successive doubles, each of whom represented one of André Walter's tendencies. He had—as long as the French Cartesian lived behind the German Romantic—to divide his difficulties into as many particles as possible, and manage to use each one as a plan for a specific novel.

When André Gide wrote *Les Cahiers,* he had not yet learned the discipline needed to handle a language that tends toward precision. He did not yet possess his instrument. Disapproving of the "ejaculatory tone" of *Les Cahiers,* he later wrote: "My excuse is that at the time of André Walter I was not yet twenty. At that age I did not know how to write."[20] More precisely, he had not yet understood that the most accomplished literary art consists more in hiding the man than in showing him, and thrives on skilful occultations. Walter uses romantic language because he has a romantic soul. But that lyrical "ejaculation" itself is not without interest. It is the spontaneous and—however overliterary it seems—natural expression of a juvenile Narcissus who lets himself go. What is lost by art is gained by psychology. *Les Cahiers* lays bare the basic romanticism of Gide's soul, a romanticism that he later cleverly concealed, using his intelligence and his talent. Moreover, it was not until the end of his life, until his very last book, *Ainsi soit-il ou Les Jeux sont faits,* that he again gave in to really personal statements. The two works of André Gide's that are the least successful aesthetically, *Les Cahiers d'André Walter* and *Ainsi soit-il,* are the most interesting psychologically—the first because the twenty-year-old poet was not yet an artist, the second because the eighty-year-old man, feeling death draw near, did not deign to be one and let his pen run on. The *novissima et ultima verba* touch a psychologist far more than mature masterpieces, and for reasons as foreign to literature as is possible.

Directly after *André Walter,* Gide reduced the problem of form to the following dilemma: to be an artist or to be a poet—a dilemma that contrasts the *artifex* and the *vates,* the artist who "fabricates," in the etymological and higher sense given the word by Paul Valéry, and the poet who follows the dictates of his inspiration. We know how Gide resolved it: "The artist must supplant the poet. From the struggle between the two issues the work of art."[21] The artist in him took the place of the poet, or in other terms, the classic prevailed over the romantic:

The classical work is strong and beautiful only by reason of its subdued romanticism. . . . The romantic writer always remains on this side of his words; the classical writer must be sought beyond them. A certain talent for

19 Preface to the 1930 edition.
20 *Ibid.*
21 *Journal,* 1892, p. 30.

going too rapidly, too easily, from the emotion to the word is characteristic of all the French Romantics—whence the small effort they made to possess the emotion in any way other than by means of the word, the small effort they made to get it under control.

We can see here how that aesthetic of constraint, that morality or propriety of style, may become an effective agent of catharsis. And the catharsis will be all the more durable in that, after the escape from reality into dream or inspiration, it will have necessitated a return to reality, a patient objectivization through the collective conventions of language and its chains, according to the common laws of discourse. Indeed, the finest examples of it can be found in classical art, to the extent that it is a "subdued romanticism" which has succeeded in expressing emotional experience in a form that controls it without limiting it. Because of the discipline it imposes in order to conform to the well-ordered constraints of composition and style, classical writing is in itself a spiritual exercise, an *ascesis,* a purification. André Gide's second book, *Le Traité du Narcisse,* shows that he had already chosen that way. And he may have secretly thought what his renowned master, Goethe, dared to say: "I have found my true self, which is being an artist."

BOOK TWO

From André Walter to André Gide
(1890–95)

PART I

A Period of Transition

27: The Young Symbolist and His Friends

> *"Poetry became a refuge for them; the only escape from hideous realities; they rushed into it with desperate fervor."*
>
> Journal des Faux-Monnayeurs,
> O.C., *XIII*, 37

IDE's first book, *Les Cahiers d'André Walter,* was a "noble" and "touching" declaration of love, but it was hardly "conclusive" and, given Madeleine Rondeaux's character, more likely to increase her uneasiness than bring her to a decision. The recent publication[1] of her letters to André Gide and, more especially, her diary make her position clear. On January 12, 1891, she wrote: "And I've lost my father. And I *must* lose my friend, by childhood brother."[2] She loves her cousin and she is loved by him, but she *must* not marry him and she *must* stop seeing him. In the eyes of a stranger, looking at the situation from the outside, it seems no more than a very Corneillian conflict between duty and love. No religious, moral, or natural law stood in the way of their marriage in any obvious way, not even any social convention. They were majors and free of obligations, even those of a religious nature; of course, they were first cousins, but aside from special cases or hereditary taints, the fact could not be considered a dire impediment. However, the situation seems very different indeed as soon as we understand Madeleine Rondeaux's psychological state: certain obstacles did separate her from her cousin, and to her scrupulous soul they seemed insurmountable.

Apart from the family opposition—and Mme. Gide's influence is not to

[1] Jean Schlumberger, *Madeleine et André Gide.*

[2] *Journal de Madeleine Rondeaux.*

be underestimated—a natural shyness, a Protestant and Victorian upbringing, a puritanical distrust of sex, increased by her mother's infidelity,
helped put a distance between Madeleine and physical life, and sustained
her fear of loving, if not of living. "She was afraid of everything," wrote
André Gide, "even before being afraid of me." That she was afraid of
everything is not very probable, but she was most certainly afraid of him.
She herself admitted, four years later, that the prospect of marrying him
always caused her "moral terror."[3] And although they were kindred spirits
insofar as their common background, sensitivity and intelligence, and all
manner of elective affinities are concerned, their differences prevailed over
their similarities, and Madeleine saw André's failings—his instability, his
inconstancy, his egoism—with a lucidity that was not obscured by the
legendary blindness of love.

Moreover, there is hardly a young girl, however pure, who would be
pleased to hear: "For that matter, I do not desire you. Your body makes
me uncomfortable and carnal possession terrifies me." Admitting that she
shared his apprehension and terror, the promise of an angelism for two
was singularly in contrast with the constant impression of sensual anguish
given by *Les Cahiers*. After the "Cahier blanc" came the "Cahier noir," in
which there was continual question of the flesh, evil, sin, the devil, even
scandal, all of which seemed to be written by a monk who was sorely
tempted. Madeleine had been brought up in complete ignorance of sex,
but it is difficult not to suspect that she noticed an obscure, mysterious side
to André which eluded her. In any case, as moving as she found *Les
Cahiers,* it was not of a nature to make her go back on her decision:

O André, we must separate before the implacable logic of this alternative:
either we consider a folly that would guarantee the unhappiness of both of
us, or we change nothing in our present situation and have the reprobation
of our family and disapproval of the world against us—and even your own
disapproval—the difficulties of the future and the uneasiness of my conscience.
We must separate. . . . My whole heart weeps. . . . O Lord, deliver me from
myself—deliver us one from the other. We must separate.

That passage from Madeleine Rondeaux's diary[4] shows the position she
was in: she did not want to agree to a marriage which she felt would be
unhappy, and she could not continue an intimate relationship that would
incur disapproval. "We must separate." But separation from her "childhood brother" was infinitely painful to her, and as a Christian she be-
seeched God to help her bear it.

André Gide's moral and even religious attitudes were profoundly
changed by Emmanuèle's refusal. As he wrote to his mother in May, 1892,

[3] Letter from Madeleine Rondeaux to André Gide, September, 1894.
[4] June 12, 1891.

he wanted to forget his "old personality" or, as he so often repeated to Marcel Drouin, "to kill Walter." Without Emmanuèle, Walter had no further reason for being, for he existed only in relation to her. Through her, he had discovered the "mystic orient" of his life, and out of a desire to identify with her, the once sullen child had become a religious adolescent, aspiring to reach a perfection consistent with the Protestant and puritanical ideal she embodied. Once the basis for it had disappeared, Walter's moral armature had either to fall apart or to change. As soon as Walter was refused, Gide redirected his mystical tendencies and turned to the quasi-religious worship of literature in the secularized chapel of symbolism.

Until the age of twenty-one, André Gide had remained almost completely within the family circle. After *Les Cahiers* was published, he began to lead a very different life from that of the solitary Walter. The daybook he kept regularly shows that during 1891 he met many people, certain of whom were to have great influence on him: "What did I do in Paris? I underwent a profound change."[5] His transition from the family milieu to a literary milieu was his first real transplantation. From then on, he was surrounded not by Gides, Rondeaux, and Démarests but by men of letters.

Ars non stagnat, art is not immobile. Those words began the important letter from André Gide to Paul Valéry, dated January 26, 1891. He had just discovered that Walter was a "symbolist" without knowing it. He had read, really read, Mallarmé for the first time. "Loving him, I get the impression that I have not yet either loved or admired." At the same time, an issue of *La Plume,*[6] giving "the story of a new school and an account of its dreams," was a revelation to him:

I learn that Maeterlinck is a symbolist (I mean one of their school)—and all their theories, their whole profession of faith, seem to me a straight justification of my book, when my own sentences are not actually transferred from it directly. Well then, I am a symbolist, there is no doubt of it. They say that Moréas is the leader. Oh! no—but surely it's Mallarmé. . . . Mallarmé, then, for poetry, Maeterlinck for drama—and although next to them I feel somewhat of a weakling, I add Myself for the novel.

In his answer Paul Valéry congratulated his "dear caloyer of the symbolic mount" for having come "to adore the very holy Icons of art, in the ultimate and delicious chapel of Symbolism."

A few days later, on February 2, Gide was introduced to Stéphane Mallarmé, master of the symbolist chapel, by Maurice Barrès, for whom—

[5] Letter from André Gide to his mother, May 17, 1892, unpublished.

[6] A review founded in 1889 by Léon Deschamps. The issue of January 1, 1891, devoted to Jean Moréas, gives an account of the symbolist movement.

as his *cahier de lectures* of 1890 testifies—he had such keen admiration. Barrès invited him to the "symbolists' banquet" given in honor of Jean Moréas on the publication of his *Pèlerin passionné*. Gide, who at one time had so envied Pierre Louÿs because he knew men of letters, had the privilege of contemplating, at one go, ninety-four of them: "Mallarmé, etc." The nonchalant "etc." covered many illustrious or well-known names, but in the eyes of André Walter one name eclipsed all the others.

On February 4, two days later, Gide left a copy of *Les Cahiers d'André Walter* at Mallarmé's, 89 rue de Rome, with a letter assuring him that "I have since read your poems (less than two months ago) and you taught me shame for my book and the boredom of poetry, for you have sung all the lines I should have dreamt of writing."[7] Mallarmé's answer, dated— *sub specie aeternitatis*—"Paris, Sunday," was written on Sunday, February 8. Although rarely profuse in his praise, he began the letter with "My dear poet" and ended it with an invitation to the rue de Rome:

PARIS, Sunday

MY DEAR POET

The softest veil over a phase of dead youth, which your book almost leaves to be guessed; and enveloping in silence a face that is still recognizable as that of a rare Intellectual. Thank you: and, if you should like to add a word to *Les Cahiers d'André Walter,* come before anyone else on Tuesday evening, a little before eight; I too will speak to you better. Your hand,

STÉPHANE MALLARMÉ

Sixty years later, Gide still remembered the joy he felt on reading that note. On Tuesday night, "before anyone else" and "a little before eight," he went to the rue de Rome, in the mood of a Levite entering the temple for the first time. It was Mallarmé himself who opened the door.

We would enter Mallarmé's; it was evening; at first one was aware of a great silence; at the door, all the street noises died; Mallarmé would begin to speak in a gentle, musical, unforgettable voice—alas! now stilled forever. Oddly enough: HE THOUGHT BEFORE SPEAKING! And for the first time, close to him, we felt, we touched, the reality of thought: what we were seeking, what we wanted, what we adored in life existed; a man, here, had sacrificed everything to *that*. For Mallarmé literature was the aim, yes, the very end of life.[8]

Those few lines, written by Gide on Mallarmé's death, bring to life the charm of the evenings in the rue de Rome. He admired the some saintliness of the artist in Mallarmé that he had already caught a glimpse of in

[7] Letter from André Gide to Stéphane Mallarmé (Henri Mondor Collection). The letter is dated February 5, but Gide's daybook records his visit ("missed Mallarmé") on February 4.

[8] *Prétextes*, p. 258.

his piano teacher, Marc de la Nux. Mallarmé gave him one of the purest and rarest joys a young writer can know, that of admiring—without reservation—the man whose works he admires. For Gide was just as attracted to the man as he was to his art of poetry.

Of Gide's first meeting with Mallarmé we know only what he confided to Valéry: " 'Your book,' he said, 'is a book of silences. You managed to do the most difficult of all things: to be silent; so that all the thoughts are in the spaces between the lines.' That praise from Mallarmé touched me more than any other."[9] Gide was not mistaken when he retrospectively saw Walter as a symbolist hero whose tastes were those of the school. His assiduous reading of Schopenhauer, the main philosophical influence of his adolescence, had prepared him for Mallarmé's teachings. "Is action necessary?" asked Walter, "I prefer my dream." The divorce of thought from action, the refusal of life and the glorification of dream—Walterian themes par excellence—were carried by the literary group to the heights of a system. An art of escape and evasion, symbolism presented Walter with an ideal refuge. It taught him to see only contingencies in "the prismatic diversity of life," only anecdotes in history, only news stories in the novel, only appearances in reality, from which the artist had to remain separated by the infrangible window, "whether the window be art or mysticism."[10] The almost monastic separation suited the mystique of Walter, who then claimed to "work in the absolute" and disdain everything that did not have more than temporal interest.

If, as Claudel expressed it, the symbolists were "mystics gone astray," no one could have been more influential than Mallarmé in turning André Walter's religious mysticism in the direction of aesthetic mysticism, replacing the poetry of religion by a religion of poetry. Mallarmé's very devout childhood left him with a lofty spirituality which he devoted exclusively to the work of art. He sang the "magnificent vespers of dream" and "the hymn of spiritual hearts" in poems of unequaled perfection, but he considered the belief in an eternal country of souls as pure illusion. He was at once an idealistic Platonist and a convinced nihilist, but he had, as it were, deified literature to the point of thinking that the world was made to result in a beautiful book. His poetics proposed to "take back their own from music." Walter listened to that precept with all the more fervor in that he had hoped to write "not in French but in music," for music alone "sustains the soaring of dreams and reveals the essence of souls." No disciple paid more heed to his lessons, if the word can be used to refer to personal conversations, in which Mallarmé expressed—with supreme clarity—the themes that his writings made hermetic. While listening to the

[9] Letter from André Gide to Paul Valéry, Feb. 21, 1891 (*Correspondance,* p. 52).

[10] Mallarmé, *Les Fenêtres.*

unforgettable talker of those Tuesday evenings, he conceived the plan of a "lesson in artistic rhetoric" which would set forth the theory of the symbol. It was *Le Traité du Narcisse.*

In 1891 the Tuesdays took on "their permanent physiognomy and, one might say, their most rapt atmosphere."[11] That year a whole generation of twenty-year-old poets came to the rue de Rome: Gide, Louÿs, Valéry, Claudel, Mauclair, Fargue. There the newcomers met their elders, the habitués of the literary group: Régnier, Viélé-Griffin, Fontainas, Mockel, Dujardin, Wyzewa, Hérold, Lazare, Quillard. All, or almost all, were symbolist writers. Occasionally a painter would come, and there Gide met Gauguin—whom he had caught a glimpse of during his 1889 trip to Brittany—Whistler, Odilon Redon, and Vuillard. At times there were so many people that more chairs had to be brought into the drawing room which, as we know, was a dining room; at times the group was limited to a few faithful members and pets: the cat Lilith, with its very literary pedigree,[12] and the green parrots Geneviève Mallarmé called the academicians. And it was those intimate soirées that André Walter preferred.

As he had written in his letter to Paul Valéry, André Gide considered as leaders of the symbolist group: Mallarmé for poetry and Maeterlinck for drama. After a volume of poems, *Serres chaudes,* whose damp and monastic atmosphere of imprisoned youth had so pleased Walter, Maurice Maeterlinck devoted himself to the difficult task of transposing the symbolist aesthetic to the theater. He had just published three plays; *La Princesse Maleine, L'Intruse,* and *Les Aveugles.* Reading *La Princesse Maleine* was an event for Gide: "I shan't say anything about it because I shall remember it without having to say anything."[13] In June, 1891, Jules Huret interviewed Maeterlinck and asked him his literary preferences. Among French writers, Maeterlinck mentioned, next to Baudelaire, Villiers, Verlaine, Mallarmé, and Laforgue, the author of *Les Cahiers d'André Walter.* As soon as he had read the declaration in *L'Echo de Paris,* Paul Valéry wrote to his friend: "I was so proud when I read in Maeterlinck's interview that very exact and very glorious line which linked your *Cahiers* to what the tragic Fleming considers great works."[14] The very next month, Gide took himself off to Ghent to meet Maeterlinck. He feared that the twenty-nine-year-old poet—who sang of pale flowers, wilted loves, sickly princesses, and constantly of death—was doomed to consumption and the premature death of a Jules Laforgue: "As I'm terribly afraid that Maeterlinck

[11] Henri Mondor, *Vie de Mallarmé,* p. 624.

[12] Daughter of Banville's cat and granddaughter of Gautier's Eponine, which had inspired Charles Baudelaire.

[13] *Cahier de lectures,* Nov. 4, 1890, unpublished.

[14] Letter from Paul Valéry to André Gide, June 15, 1891 (*Correspondance,* p. 93).

has the same lack of *savoir-vivre,* I want to get to know him as soon as possible."[15] But he found himself in the presence of a robust Fleming, bursting with health and radiating energy; the creator of a world of fragile and erratic characters was a force of nature. How could that vigorous man, who seemed made more for life than for dreams, more for fresh air than for *serres chaudes,* or hothouses, be faithful to the group? "He's not a true esoteric," Gide wrote to Paul Valéry.[16] But he was nonetheless enchanted by *Les Sept Princesses,* which Maeterlinck read to him, and after having made plans to translate Novalis' *Hymns to the Night* together—a plan that, after some work, finally came to nothing—Gide admitted that "Maeterlinck has admirable strength."[17]

Nothing but that meeting interested the young symbolist during his trip to Maeterlinck's country. He visited Ghent, Brugge, Ostend, and then, with his mother who joined him, Antwerp, Amsterdam, the Hague, and Brussels. But in accordance with the principles of the school, which disdained sightseeing, he saw nothing or almost nothing, and kept his eyes closed to outer things, the better to contemplate his inner world. He traveled like a symbolist who will not be distracted from his moods, and projected them on to Brugge, just as the following year, Georges Rodenbach—whose *Règne du silence* he had already read—projected his own. On the way back, he took his bearings:

My mind has just now been quibbling as to whether one must first be and then appear, or first appear and then be what one appears. . . . Perhaps, said my mind, one *is* only insofar as one *appears.* Moreover, both propositions are false when separated: 1. We *are* in order to appear. 2. We *appear* because we are. The two must be joined in mutual dependency; then we get the desired imperative: *One must be so as to appear.* Appearing must not be distinguished from being. . . .[18]

And so ended the reckoning of the young symbolist's trip to Belgium and Holland, and indeed no one could reproach him for behaving like a tourist.

Within the literary geography of Paris in 1891, the rue de Rome literary group corresponded to the Symbolic mount, and a rue Balzac drawing room to the mount Parnassus. Two years before, Gide had read the "exotic and sonorous" name of José-Maria de Heredia in a well-known article by Jules Lemaitre. He had even memorized several sonnets from what was

[15] Letter from André Gide to Paul Valéry, June 29, 1891 (*ibid.,* p. 106).

[16] August, 1891 (*ibid.,* p. 118).

[17] *Journal,* 1891, p. 23.

[18] *Ibid.,* p. 25.

later to be *Les Trophées*. Heredia received on Saturday afternoons. "I spoke to him about you, he is waiting for you," Louÿs had told André Gide, but Gide hesitated and could not make up his mind to go until he received a letter from Henri de Régnier, inviting him to go along with him to the rue Balzac on Saturday, March 7, 1891. Régnier had given the Parnassian a copy of *Les Cahiers d'André Walter*, and Heredia approved of it, with reservations as to the style, which he found "impoverished."

Gide felt as out of his element at Heredia's as he had been enchanted by the almost religious atmosphere at Mallarmé's. On the evening of his first Saturday at the rue Balzac, he wrote to Paul Valéry:

And this afternoon at Heredia's! I was really terrified by that ferocious scramble known as "literary circles." They furiously eat each other up. Ah! What hate one feels in their souls. . . . Everything becomes a matter of journalism and the making of reputations—Heredia's salon is like an advertising agency—and that's why Louis and de Régnier took me there—but today I had quite enough—I'll bet you could not stand it either.

And on Monday he went to the gentle Sully Prudhomme's to console himself for "all the histrionics and such viciousness."[19] Yet on following Saturdays he returned to the rue Balzac, and although the Parnassian salon no longer seemed to him a bloody battlefield or a free-for-all, he was never really at ease there.

The symbolist movement, which had developed as a reaction against realism, also "rose against the Parnassian School." Of course, Mallarmé and Heredia held each other in high esteem, but as often happens, the masters were less antagonistic than their disciples, who felt that by choosing one side, they were necessarily against the other. Gide himself was not influenced by Heredia other than by reaction:

"The style is a bit impoverished," said that excellent Heredia to whom I presented my first book and who was astonished not to find more images in it. I wanted the style to be even more impoverished, more rigorous, more purified, deeming that ornamentation's only reason for being is to hide some defect and that only insufficiently beautiful thought need fear utter nudity.[20]

Yet he considered Heredia one of the "two directors" of his group, all the members of which went both to the rue de Rome on Tuesday evenings and to the rue Balzac on Saturday afternoons. And it was under the combined auspices of Mallarmé and Heredia that *La Conque* was founded in March, 1891, its contributors being exclusively symbolist or Parnassian poets.

[19] Letters from André Gide to Paul Valéry, March 8 and 9, 1891 (*Correspondance*, pp. 63–67).

[20] *Journal*, p. 347.

André Gide and Pierre Louÿs wanted to found a literary review in which their friends could join. In addition to the former team of the *Potache-Revue,* reduced to Drouin and Quillot, there was Henri de Régnier, Paul Valéry, Léon Blum, Fazy, Camille Mauclair, and others. But, above all, it was necessary to insure the collaboration of the great poets in order to combine an "auroral youth" with some of their "ancestors." Thanks to Pierre Louÿs' skill as a mediator, Mallarmé had promised an *Eventail,* Heredia some *Sonnets,* Leconte de Lisle a long poem—*Soleils, poussière d'or,* Maeterlinck a *Lied,* and Paul Verlaine—between two absinthes—a *Mois de Marie.* The brilliant tables of contents of the first twelve issues[21] of *La Conque* testify to the beginners' illustrious collaborators.

The real force behind *La Conque* was Pierre Louÿs, its only editor. Charming, clever, adventuresome, widely known in Paris, he had numerous contacts and knew how to make use of them for himself and for his friends. In fact he was instrumental in drawing the awkward Gide out of his solitude. Yet in spite of their former companionship and their common love of literature, their relationship was no longer what it had been during the year they studied together for the first part of the *baccalauréat.* Their friendship, which had already been somewhat compromised during Gide's writing of *André Walter,* had turned into a stormy series of scenes, estrangements, and short-lived reconciliations. A curious letter that Gide wrote to Paul Valéry,[22] in which he spoke of Louÿs as a "lover" and an "unfaithful mistress," is explained in a way by another of his remarks: "Up until then I wanted to *make friendship* as one 'makes love.' It is ridiculous. And it is all because I do not want to make love. . . . Pure spirit! . . . One must be sufficient unto oneself—with God."[23]

Gide reproached Louÿs for his dissolute ways, but he was just as exasperated by his practical-joke type of humor. Louÿs would write him notes signed by anonymous female admirers, and after Gide had been completely taken in, admit that he was the author. He also sent a series of facetious letters and telegrams, one of which read: "Amo te, ie te ayme, I love you, Ich liebe dich, Ij leebe dij, Ieù te amo . . . ," addressed, with questionable taste, to "Mademoiselle André Gide."

It was partly in reaction to Louÿs that Gide became increasingly friendly with his living antithesis: the serious Marcel Drouin. He called him "the man of integrity," using the same nickname—*vir probus*—that his father had been given by his fellow students at the law school. At the same time that he was losing his esteem for Pierre Louÿs, he wrote in his *Journal:*

[21] The first came out on March 1, 1891.

[22] June 17, 1891 (*Correspondance,* pp. 96–98).

[23] Letter to Paul Valéry, Nov. 3, 1891 (*ibid.,* p. 134).

Marcel Drouin is the person in the world I esteem, and perhaps like, the most. We get absolutely carried away as soon as we are together; we are good for each other. He was tired after his examinations. We both slept on the grass. I read him my notes from Brittany. I am becoming Walter again; and so much the better. Yes, nothing is so beautiful as nobility of soul.[24]

Drouin was also a collaborator on *La Conque*. He wrote his poems under the pseudonym of Michel Arnault. But he was more a philosopher than a poet,[25] and in the little group of *La Conque*, was nicknamed "the Philosopher," whereas Louÿs was "the Parnassian," Gide "the Symbolist," and Paul Valéry . . . "the Decadent." Valéry probably owed his unexpected nickname to his taste for *A Rebours'* Des Esseintes, and not to his first poems, which were hardly in the tradition of decadent aestheticism and showed him to be, even then, a disciple of Mallarmé's. It seems a pity that of all the poets who met every Tuesday evening on the rue de Rome, the one who—more than any other—was destined to receive and perpetuate the symbolist message could not be there. Valéry was unable to leave Montpellier, and did not get to Mallarmé's until October, 1891.[26] Gide, then still at La Roque, came to Paris as soon as possible to join his friend: "Tomorrow, Saturday, wander about under the Odéon from four-thirty to five. I shall be there."[27] On October 16 they took the first of their many walks through the Luxembourg Gardens. Before Valéry's trip to Paris, the two friends had been together in Montpellier in May of that year, but since they were generally far apart, they exchanged an enormous number of letters. Those written in 1891, when they hardly knew one another, are perhaps the most intimate of all and are admirable proof of two pure artistic vocations.

Maurice Quillot, at barely twenty, was one of the most fervent collaborators on *La Conque*. He had known Gide since he was sixteen, at the time of the *Potache-Revue,* but it was not until 1891, after having read *Les Cahiers d'André Walter,* that his friendship for him became really enthusiastic: "Reading you, I admire the serenity of your soul, its great ingenuousness as well, and your heart, which is inept at lying, too sincere, too tender."[28] Quillot practiced occultism: "The occult is my business." He sometimes signed his letters to Gide, written especially on green paper and stamped with seals, "Hermentaire Maurice, bishop of Babylon," and sent

---

[24] *Journal,* 1891, p. 22.

[25] Marcel Drouin became a professor of philosophy. Gide spoke to me of him as the most intellectually gifted "of all the young horses at the post," more than Louÿs, more than Valéry, and, of course, more than himself.

[26] Henri Mondor, "Le Premier Entretien Mallarmé-Valéry," *Cahiers du Sud,* 1946.

[27] Postcard from André Gide to Paul Valéry, October, 1891 (*Correspondance,* p. 132).

[28] Letter from Maurice Quillot to André Gide, June 18, 1891, unpublished.

him messages to commemorate the Eleusinian Mysteries, many poems, and even a "sentimental mass" to celebrate Walter, with *Credo, Introïbo, Confiteor, Kyrie, Gloria,* and so on. Gide went along with the game and wrote to Quillot: "Louÿs is my legitimate husband, you are my gracious adulterer,"[29] a letter which created many complications between the three friends. Quillot had already "given birth" to one novel, *L'Entrainé,* was working on others, and in fact had numerous projects, but two years later, the "prodigal son," whom his friends considered a rival of Rimbaud's, had to give up literature and take himself off to Montigny to run a dairy.

Besides his friends of *La Conque,* Gide saw a great deal of other groups of writers, particularly the group of *Entretiens politiques et littéraires,* the small review in which *Le Traité du Narcisse* was published. He used to see there, among others, Bernard Lazare, Ferdinand Hérold, Pierre Quillard, Paul Adam, and Francis Viélé-Griffin. All were littérateurs, but beyond their mutual interest in aesthetics, several were, socially and politically, violent nonconformists. André Gide was thus abruptly transplanted into a milieu in which the religious, moral, patriotic, and bourgeois traditions he had been taught to hold sacred were completely disparaged: "The ethics according to which I had lived up to then gave way, before long, to an impression—still vague—of a more colorful and shimmering vision of life. It began to dawn on me that duty was perhaps not the same for everyone. . . ."[30]

Among the important names not mentioned in *Si le grain ne meurt* was that of Marcel Schwob. Schwob, who came from a family of rabbis, was only two years older than Gide and was a fount of linguistic and literary learning. It was under his influence that Gide began to read works of philology, a science he found "marvelous," and to develop his taste for foreign literature. Schwob was one of the first in France, perhaps even "the first" (according to his biographer, Pierre Champion), to read Nietzsche, and it is possible that Gide heard him talk about it, for—contrary to what Gide said—he knew at least the philosopher's name[31] in 1891. In any case, Schwob introduced Gide to the writings of Walt Whitman, whom he had just translated, Stevenson, George Meredith, and, above all, Ibsen, whom Gide began to read regularly in 1893.

During his last year at the Ecole Alsacienne, Gide had met André Walckenaër, a student at the *Ecole des chartes,* at a dinner at the home of Claire Démarest. In 1891 Walckenaër would come every Wednesday to the

[29] Letter from André Gide to Maurice Quillot, July, 1891, unpublished (Bibliothèque Doucet).

[30] *Si le grain ne meurt,* I, 275.

[31] "At least Nietzsche is not a philosopher. Aside from that, he can be rather curious seen from a distance." (Letter to Jeanne Rondeaux, November, 1891, unpublished.)

rue de Commaille to spend the afternoon with him. Walckenaër was not a writer—"he does not feel the need to write; the works of others are enough for him"[32]—but he was not interested in much besides literature. He too, as Henri de Régnier phrased it, "worshiped pen and ink," and indeed that was the one common bond between André Gide and his very diversified friends.

In October, 1891, Gide wrote in his *Journal:* "I now have about ten friendships which are constantly on my mind." Ten friends are a lot, and to have them "constantly" on one's mind would seem very harassing indeed; but after *André Walter,* friendship did play a great part in his life, especially as his disappointment in love left his heart and his mind far freer. One thing is certain: he had a keen desire to please his friends: "It is perhaps very dangerous for me to see other people; I always have a too-keen desire to please them."[33] It was in fact dangerous in the sense that he had such a need for being liked, he could not be himself in the presence of others:

And when I chat with a friend, I almost always spend my time telling him what he thinks, and I myself think the same, being concerned only with establishing and measuring the relations between him and things. But when I am with two friends who are of different opinions, I remain on edge between them, no longer knowing what to say, not daring to take sides with one or the other; accepting every affirmative, rejecting every negation.[34]

So excessive a tendency to be friendly necessarily goes along with a feeling of being spurious and even depersonalized: "What deceitful metamorphoses my little prostitute of a soul has undergone, and only out of a desire for love; as it is so often merely a loving reflection of other souls, I hardly know it any more."[35] Such an engrossing desire also implies a need to be preferred, and he would have been flattered to have become any one of his friends' "best friend."[36] What is worse: he was jealous: "I am jealous, Paul Ambroise! I am frightfully jealous. . . . I have despotic affections, which cannot stand to share."[37] Yet such feelings belong more in the category of

[32] *Journal,* 1890, p. 15.

[33] *Ibid.,* 1891, p. 21.

[34] *Ibid.,* 1892, pp. 31–32.

[35] Letter from André Gide to Paul Valéry, September, 1891 (*Correspondance,* p. 124).

[36] *Si le grain ne meurt,* I, 259.

[37] Letter from André Gide to Paul Valéry, September, 1891 (*Correspondance,* p. 124).

"coquetry" than of "prostitution," a much too degrading term. And coquetry, far from implying real love or friendship, implies narcissism—the main obstacle to friendship and love. Along with the desire to please everyone, there is the desire to please oneself through everyone else and, almost always, to compensate for a deep-rooted deficiency, to hide a feeling of inferiority—in other words, to reassure oneself as to oneself. Gide understood that perfectly well, for directly after having recalled the ten friendships that were "constantly on his mind," he added: "A person would have to be quite sure of himself not to feel the need of constantly proving himself."[38]

The following lines from *Si le grain ne meurt* confirm the fact that, despite all his lyrical protests, Gide's relations with his friends and companions were marked by a fundamental narcissism:

They made me feel the truth of Nietzsche's saying that every artist has not only his own intelligence at his disposal but that of his friends as well . . . and while I understood less than what any one of them taken separately understood best, I felt that I understood them all together, and from my perspective at the crossroads, I could look right around and through them, out toward the various prospects which I perceived from their remarks.[39]

Like the young Wilhelm Meister, he wanted everyone and everything to be an education for him, and he expected to get that education not only from his books but also from his friends.

[38] *Journal,* 1891, p. 26.

[39] *Si le grain ne meurt,* I, 258–59.

28: A Year of Reading

> *"Bought a great load of books: I shall*
> *end up with an intellectual disease*
> *from always exciting insatiable desires."*
> Cahier de lectures, *1891, unpublished*

N *Si le grain ne meurt* Gide gave the impression that the year following the publication of *Les Cahiers d'André Walter* was a "period of dissipation." Yet he not only wrote two new books, *Les Poésies d'André Walter* and *Le Traité du Narcisse,* but his *Journal,* his various correspondences, and his reading notebook show that he never lost sight of his "future works." When he found that his production was slowed down, he went back to his *Journal*—"I'm beginning to write again. I stopped for a while because I lacked will power. It would be good for me to force myself to write a few lines here every day"[1]—or else he brought his *cahier de lectures* up to date.

Gide once said that the personal reminiscences of what he read were "among the most important events"[2] in his life. Yet that kind of reminiscence and event is almost completely ignored in *Si le grain ne meurt.* Here psychology loses what art gains, for his literary sustenance had considerable, indeed major, importance in his development. In *L'Influence en littérature* he himself most convincingly expressed what a reader's encounter with an author can be:

I read a certain book; and after having read it, I closed it; I put it back on the shelf in my library—but in that book there was a remark I cannot forget.

[1] *Journal,* 1891, p. 22.

[2] "Goethe," *N.R.F.,* March 1, 1932.

It went so deep within me that I can no longer distinguish it from myself. Henceforth, I am not at all the same as I would have been had I never known it. If I forget in which book I read it, or even forget that I read it, or if I only recall it imperfectly . . . is of no matter! I can never again become the person I was before having read it.[3]

That gap in *Si le grain ne meurt* can be filled in, thanks to his *Journal,* his *Correspondances,* and most particularly, the *cahier de lectures* Gide kept very regularly from October, 1889, to October, 1893—that is, until he left for Algeria with Paul Laurens. During 1891 there is no mention of as decisive an event as his assiduous reading of Goethe the following year, but the notebook of 1891 as a whole is a valuable document on the influences brought to bear on a young literary man between the ages of twenty and twenty-one: "Bought a great load of books: I shall end up with an intellectual disease from always exciting insatiable desires." Through an overindulgence in books, he wilfully brought about the violent "encephalitis" Renan spoke about when he recalled his youth.

When in December, 1890, in Montpellier, André Gide and Paul Valéry had compared their gods, Gide had named Schopenhauer and Flaubert. During 1891 he continued to read *The World as Will and Idea*—"it is that, I think, which will have had the greatest influence on me"[4]—and the *Correspondance* of Flaubert, whose fictional works he had already read.

Although by November Gide seemed somewhat tired of Schopenhauer,[5] he felt that the symbolist aesthetic was a continuation of his philosophy: "Supported by Schopenhauer . . . I considered everything that was not *absolute* as *contingent* (a word then in use)."[6] The formula: the world is an idea, suited the young poet, and the neutralization of the will to live by the means of art corresponded to his ideal. He thought that the object of art was the Idea in its pure state, the Essence as revealed by the genius of music, and not phenomena any more than concepts subject to the laws of reason. A fervent Schopenhauerian, he never mentioned the name of Hegel (of which there is no trace in his *Cahier de lectures* either then or later) except in passing, without realizing, it would seem, that the discovery of Hegel's philosophy had been a considerable event in Mallarmé's inner life.[7]

---

[3] *O.C.,* III, 256.

[4] *Cahier de lectures,* September, 1891, unpublished.

[5] Letter from André Gide to Paul Valéry, Nov. 3, 1891 (*Correspondance,* p. 134).

[6] *Si le grain ne meurt,* I, 264.

[7] Mallarmé started to read Hegel in 1866, having been introduced to his works by Eugène Lefebure, a fervent Hegelian.

Upon his discovery of Flaubert's *Correspondance*,[8] he understood what he had already felt in reading *L'Education sentimentale:* the deep affinity of their temperaments. But what he was most excited about in the *Correspondance* was Flaubert's love for literature, the fact that he worshiped art exclusively: "Life is such a hideous thing that the only way to bear it is by avoiding it. And one avoids it by living in art." Such a systematic disparagement of life, which he found again in *Bouvard et Pécuchet,* later seemed blasphemous to him,[9] but at that point he took it up as his own, along with the recourse to aesthetic escape as the only way out. He was enthusiastic about everything Flaubert said concerning the passion for "great reading," the "frenzies of regular and exhausting" work, the tremendous effort necessary to construct the vain "pyramids" he considered books, an effort which "is perfectly useless, and remains in the desert, yet dominates it extraordinarily." To him the great Flaubertian themes of reality as an "illusion to describe," art for art's sake, the artist's "invisible" presence in his works, were a combination of both Schopenhauer's and Mallarmé's teachings. "The artist must somehow manage to give posterity the impression that he has not lived; the less I imagine him, the greater he seems to me." Of course, we know that Gide was to think quite differently later on.

Another influence, evident during the preceding years but which then took on new importance, was that of Hippolyte Taine. In his *Etude sur Carlyle* Gide witnessed the birth of a hero—that is, "a messenger sent from the mysterious depths of the infinite with news for us." He avidly followed his evolution and learned how the Scottish Puritan had been impregnated by Germanic idealism. He decided to read Carlyle at once, and bought *Heroes and Hero Worship* in Izoulet's translation: "It gives me the desire and already almost the habit of a certain moral defiance, somewhat cantankerous but, on the whole, beautiful, and certainly the only kind of defiance capable of great things."[10]

Besides Taine's work on *Les Philosophes français au XIXe siècle,* he read and reread, with "rare delight,"[11] *L'Histoire de la littérature anglaise,* in which Taine depicts artists as products of their time, and explains their evolution in terms of race, milieu, and the historical moment. Although he

---

[8] Flaubert's *Correspondance* was published in four volumes, from 1887 to 1893. The many passages that Gide copied out into his 1891 *cahier de lectures* are extracts from the third.

[9] *Journal,* 1921, p. 715.

[10] *Ibid.,* 1891, p. 19.

[11] Letter from André Gide to Paul Valéry, June 11, 1891 (*Correspondance,* p. 93).

was one day to contest it,[12] Gide was charmed by the theory. But of all the passages he copied out that had an obvious influence on his *Traité du Narcisse,* the following is especially important:

There is a mysterious self hidden under that clothing of flesh. Deep is its burial under that strange clothing, among the sounds, colors, and forms which are its swaddling clothes and its shroud. . . . For matter is spirit, a manifestation of spirit. All visible things are emblems: what you see is not there for itself. Actually, there is nothing there. Matter only exists spiritually, so as to present some idea and embody it externally. . . . Man is guided and commanded, happy or miserable, by and through symbols; he is surrounded on all sides by symbols, whether they are recognized as such or not. Is not everything he does symbolic? Is his life not a perceptible revelation of God's blessing, of the mystical force within him?[13]

The young Huguenot was captivated by Taine's well-known pages on the contrast between the spirit of the Reformation and the spirit of the Renaissance. Apropos of a violently imaginative and sensual passage on the feasts and customs of the Renaissance, Gide made this unexpected remark:

Perhaps that was true beauty; completely physical. Some time ago, all that display of riches would have left me cold. I am reading about it at the right time, a time when it can intoxicate me the most. My thinking is becoming voluptuously impious and pagan. I must push it even further. I can see the reading I must do: Stendhal, the *Encyclopédie,* Swift, Condillac . . . so as to dry out my heart (drain out is more appropriate; everything in my heart is moldy). Then, the most vigorous writers, especially the virile ones: Aristophanes, Shakespeare, Rabelais. . . . Those are the ones I must read. . . . And not bother with all the rest. There is enough weeping in my soul to irrigate thirty books.[14]

And meaning to undertake the drainage at once, he began to read Stendhal.

Gide was often to go back to Stendhal more because he was "good for him" than out of passion, being more interested in finding "a cuttlebone"[15] than sustenance. Beyle helped him to thwart his Walterian lyricism, for to him he was an anti-Walter. Gide's first Stendhalian breviary was *La Vie de Henri Brulard,* which he read with "extreme interest."[16] He then went on to Stendhal's fictional work, starting with his last novel, *Lamiel:*

[12] *Journal,* 1925, p. 812.

[13] *Cahier de lectures,* May 16, 1891, unpublished.

[14] *Journal,* 1891, p. 21.

[15] *Ibid.,* 1907, p. 255.

[16] *Cahier de lectures,* June 4, 1891, unpublished.

. . . *amusement* was foreign to Lamiel's character; she was too passionate
for that; to spend time calmly and agreeably was almost impossible for her
kind of nature; she could only *amuse herself,* in the vulgar sense of the word,
when she was sick.[17]

The pre-Nietzschean glorification of "living dangerously," the "courage"
in immorality, the contempt not for pleasure but for diversion, such were
the traits of character that struck him in *Lamiel.* Somewhat later, he
judged Beyle's influence as "unfortunate and dangerous," because it encouraged the cultivation of emotion and discouraged "the habit of lofty
thought."[18] Actually, Stendhal was the first genuine immoralist he ever
came upon, before Wilde and before Nietzsche. And it was the Stendhalian egotism[19] that Gide admired in the young Barrès' *Culte de moi.*

Barrès, whose *Un Homme libre* he had read and reread and considered
a major work, was then known as a professor of anarchy. Gide was twenty
in 1889, the very year Paul Bourget, in his preface to *Le Disciple,* urged "the
young people of 1889" to be on their guard against the "delicate nihilist,"
the "intellectual and subtle epicurean," in fact the very picture of *Un
Homme libre:*

For him nothing is true, nothing is false, nothing is moral, nothing is immoral. He is a subtle and delicate egotist whose only ambition, as the remarkable analyzer Maurice Barrès said in his fine novel *Un Homme libre*
. . . consists in "adoring his self" and adorning that self with new sensations.[20]

The nonchalant individualist who in turn praises fervor and lucidity,
spontaneity and constraint, nomadism and withdrawal, sincerity and duplicity, the gratuitousness of emotions and the littérateur's calculated profit
from them ("I take advantage of my emotions"), the virtuoso of alternation who perpetually jumps from one foot to the other without losing his
breath, the acrobat of the inner life who succeeds in contorting himself
into "a great number of souls," some of whom go to "church" and the
others to "low haunts," the egotist who refuses any discipline other than
that he has temporarily chosen and will be bound by no duty except toward himself, who then is this Narcissus if not *Un Homme libre?* We
can see how the early Barrès—the Barrès of *Le Culte de moi,* not the
later one whom he reacted against—was one of the masters of Gide's
youth, in the period when Walter's religious ideal gave way to a worship
of egotism.

[17] *Ibid.,* Oct. 16, 1891.

[18] *Journal,* 1893, p. 38.

[19] In his unpublished notes of March, 1891 (Bibliothèque Doucet), he wrote: "I
noticed that the word *égotiste,* an English import, is already used in *Indiana* (1829?)."

[20] Paul Bourget, preface to *Le Disciple.*

During his adolescence, André Gide had been a great reader of novels. At the end of January, 1891, he bought Balzac's works in thirty volumes, but that year he merely read *Louis Lambert,* one of André Walter's favorites, and it was not until the beginning of the following year that he had his indispensable bout of Balzacian fever.[21] Why such a length of time between the buying and the reading? Perhaps because he wanted a long period of free time in order to plunge into *La Comédie humaine,* or perhaps because he was afraid of Balzac's influence at just the time he was entering the symbolist group. Yet he did continue to read some novels, seeking—by proxy—an experience of life but also lessons in technique and psychology. In his *cahier de lectures* he analyzed the characters, the situations, the construction, and the style, comparing the mentality of the author or the heroes with his own.

The symbolist school considered the naturalistic novel out of date. Gide, who the year before had read a great number of Zola's works, stopped almost completely. Forty-five years later, at the time of his sympathy with communism, he wrote: "My admiration for Zola does not date from yesterday and is in no way provoked by my present 'opinions.' "[22] Gide's *cahier de lectures* of 1890 confirms his admiration for the author of *La Conquête de Plassans*[23]—"extraordinary effect"—and *Germinal.* On the other hand, he found *La Bête humaine* "really too simple," and *L'Oeuvre* made "a rather unfavorable impression." *Une page d'amour* had bored him— "stopped at page 100 by an intolerable impression of boredom"—as did *La Terre:* "never finished." As for *Pot-Bouille:*

The foulest book I ever read—it's enough to make you sick; it's unspeakable. It is also the most pessimistic work I know, after *L'Education sentimentale.* . . . And, after having wanted to get away from the book, I cannot help telling myself that it's really very good—one of Zola's most powerful—I find even that extraordinary—he lives in it as if it were his element—he's not asphyxiated![24]

Among the older members of the Médan group, the only one he still read was in fact its great renegade J. K. Huysmans, author of *A Rebours* and *Là-bas,* but without the enthusiasm—at least with regard to *Là-bas*— of Quillot and Valéry. He set great store by another renegade fram naturalism, J.-H. Rosny, who wrote a satire of it in *Le Termite.* Gide recommended it to Valéry: "It's *very good;* it must be known. I want to know Rosny. . . . I assure you that he and Huysmans are the best in prose."[25] And

[21] He then read Balzac for a month, at the rate of about a novel a day (*Cahier de lectures,* 1892, unpublished).

[22] *Journal,* 1934, p. 1220.

[23] Read in November, 1890, and reread in September, 1891.

[24] Forty years later, he noted: "It is the very excess of *Pot-Bouille* that pleases me, and its perseverance in all that is loathsome" (*Journal,* 1932, p. 1137).

[25] June 11, 1891 (*Correspondance,* p. 92).

in his *cahier de lectures:* "Yes, Rosny and Hervieu are certainly two of the most interesting today."

Like many of his contemporaries, Gide had discovered the Russian novelists through Melchoir de Vogüé's study, *Le Roman russe*—"very remarkable: notes throughout."[26] He had read *War and Peace* during his trip to Belgium and Holland, read *The Kreutzer Sonata* "with frenetic excitement," and *Anna Karenina* had been the object of "numerous discussions" between him and his cousin Madeleine Rondeaux during the summer of 1890. He also read *The Death of Ivan Ilyich:* "An intense, powerful work—not composed enough for me—if the construction were better, it would be a masterwork." But we know that Gide was to prefer Dostoevsky to Tolstoi. Certain critics, emphasizing the fact that he never spoke admiringly of Dostoevsky in his *Journal* until 1903, concluded that Dostoevsky's influence came relatively late. Yet the *cahier de lectures* shows that as early as March, 1890, he had read *The Meek One, The Little Hero,* and then *Crime and Punishment,* which he reread in September, 1891: "Deeper impressions than on the first reading." He claimed that, contrary to Tolstoi, Dostoevsky cannot be understood immediately and at first seems "more complicated than complex, more dense than rich, more curious than interesting"; but the more one rereads Dostoevsky, the more astonishing and admirable each page becomes, and the influence of that underground spirit acts in depth, sometimes long after the first reading. At the time of André Walter, Gide had preferred Turgenev and his *Virgin Soil* to all the Russian novelists: "I have the feeling that I like him better than any other," but he did not find the same "infinite charm" when he read *Torrents of the Spring, Smoke,* and *King Lear of the Steppes.*

He gave up the English novelists that year, especially the puritanical George Eliot, perhaps because she was formerly one of his and his cousin's favorite writers.[27] During the holidays he read Elizabeth Browning's *Aurora Leigh* ("begun with my cousins"), which he found had "a very pure, very lofty, and very tiresome beauty."[28] An article by Théodore de Wyzewa introduced him to the name of the Brontë sisters, but he distrusted the prospector, who decreed that "Emily Brontë got the better of Eliot and all the others,"[29] and waited two years to read *Wuthering Heights,* which was to be one of his greatest discoveries in fiction.[30]

[26] *Cahier de lectures,* September, 1890, unpublished.

[27] Madeleine Rondeaux thought that her character somewhat resembled George Eliot's such as it is described by Browning. Cf. Jean Schlumberger, *Madeleine et André Gide,* p. 51.

[28] *Cahier de lectures,* October, 1891, unpublished.

[29] Letter from André Gide to Jeanne Rondeaux, 1891, unpublished.

[30] "The novel I should have most liked *to have lived* is still, I think, *Wuthering Heights*" (*Cahier de lectures,* September, 1893, unpublished).

André Gide then preferred poetry to all things: "At that time I had eyes only for the soul, and taste only for poetry."[31] With the help of Salomon Reinach's *Grammaire latine* and Havet's *Cours de métrique,* he began to study and memorize Vergil. So began, during his twenty-first year, an intimacy with the Latin poet that was to last until Gide's death; and I think that he never felt a comparable tenderness for any living being:

Finished Vergil's *Eclogues*. Read in Latin, one every morning. Ecstatic surprises at first; a little boredom some time after, because of the monotony of the themes and the fact that they are almost all a bit flaccid. I think the first is the best—and the IVth. I don't like Silenus. The VIIIth is boring. I know by heart the IInd and Xth, which Delacroix brought to my attention.[32]

This brief comment perhaps does not convey the magic spell that Vergil's lines then cast over Gide. In his unpublished La Brévine Journal, dated November, 1894, we read:

I have gone back to Vergil's *Eclogues*. I thought I knew them by heart; I feel as if I had never read them; the poet's marvelous gift of being always new. All the rest, thoughts and numbers, can be grasped, learned, retained. But the actual harmony of the verses, colors, shapes, music remains something *incomprehensible*. Memory can do nothing with it; it remains outside, and stands before us, and every time we behold it, we experience new stupefaction.

The ten eclogues written by Vergil during his youth and known as *The Bucolics* all have an idyllic and pastoral nature. In them we find the source of the names of many Gidian characters: Tityrus, Menaleas, Mopsus, Corydon. For his very next work, *Le Traité du Narcisse,* Gide chose one of Vergil's lines as the epigraph: *Nuper me in littore vidi,*[33] and he did the same for *Le Voyage d'Urien: Dic quibus in terris* . . . But what were the two eclogues that Gide learned by heart? The second tells about the shepherd Corydon's love for Alexis, the tenth, the comfort brought to an unhappy love by the Arcadian landscape.

Apart from Vergil, Gide read almost no French or foreign classics except Shakespeare: "I am reading all of Shakespeare and am infinitely gripped," he wrote to Valéry[34]—and almost none of the Romantics. His sympathies were with the symbolists and all those admired by Mallarmé. Among them was Edgar Allan Poe. He read not only his *Poems* but his

---

[31] *Si le grain ne meurt,* I, 261.

[32] *Cahier de lectures,* June 13, 1891, unpublished.

[33] In a letter to Madeleine Rondeaux on the style of *Le Traité du Narcisse,* Gide spoke about the influence of "Vergil and the *Eclogues*" (June 17, 1892).

[34] July, 1891 (*Correspondance,* p. 109). The *Cahier de lectures* mentions *Romeo and Juliette, Antony and Cleopatra,* and *A Winter's Tale.* He subsequently translated *Antony and Cleopatra* and *Hamlet.*

Extraordinary Tales, Arthur Gordon Pym, and *The Tales of the Grotesque and Arabesque* in the French translations of Baudelaire, Mallarmé, and Hennequin: "Poe has conquered me. I read him every day, and every day he grew. Today I find him colossal—if not he himself, at least his type. But I think he is one of the rare people who fully realized his type."[35] Poe was clearly one of the main aesthetic influences on Gide during his symbolist period and one which became evident in *Le Voyage d'Urien.* Yet in Gide's fascination for Edgar Allan Poe there was something of a deep partiality for his heroines: "While thinking of you," he wrote to Paul Valéry, "I reread for the ?th time, as if out of some morose need, *Ligeia, Morella*—I realize that I never loved anyone but them."[36] I shall come back to the strange identification he made between Emmanuèle and the angelic Morella.

Another poet that Mallarmé ranked very high was Villiers de l'Isle-Adam, of whom he drew an unforgettable portrait. Gide was barely twenty when he read *Axel:*

State of extraordinary excitement—a book which from now on is a friend—I shall reread it—I shall know it—yet the first act alone is admirable—the end is unfortunately very rhetorical and Axelle's [*sic*] struggle, instead of being against true science and higher philosophy, is against a wordy scholasticism—the long speeches are studied with dazzling and almost revealing phrases. The poem's dominant thought is not clear.[37]

Then he went on to *Les Contes cruels* and *Tribulat Bonhonnet:*

Two tales fill up the volume: *Le Tueur de signes* [*sic*] and *Claire Lenoir.* Both are masterpieces, but *Claire Lenoir* much transcends the cruel tales. It is really very good. The whole body of the tale is made up of philosophical dialogues, in which the characters evolve according to the device of Allain.[38] I want to reread them and I want to copy out long passages from them.[39]

He was most disappointed, in *Akédysseril,* not to find the Villiers he was so fond of. "I don't like it—I who like Villiers so much. No, I don't like it. The effects lack subtlety and are brought about by too-brutal means. . . . Then the story itself—which I admit is admirable—is, however, built around a vicious sophistical circle."[40] Actually, his enthusiasm for Villiers was short-lived, and although, during Gide's symbolist period, Villiers as

[35] Letter from André Gide to Paul Valéry, Nov. 3, 1891 (*Correspondance,* p. 134).

[36] August, 1891 (*ibid.,* p. 118).

[37] *Cahier de lectures,* Oct. 29, 1890, unpublished.

[38] He is referring to the device used in *Les Cahiers d'André Walter* for Allain.

[39] *Cahier de lectures,* Nov. 9, 1890, unpublished.

[40] *Ibid.,* October, 1891.

a person was one of his "heroes" insofar as he was possessed by "the literary demon," his works hardly influenced him.

He read a little Rimbaud, whom, until his revolt, he considered no more than "provisional" reading, and a little Verlaine, but on the other hand, he—and his *Poésies d'André Walter*—were influenced by two symbolists: the Maeterlinck of *Serres chaudes* and the early dramas, and Jules Laforgue. Apropos of the "little fragile, shivering, passively pensive people" of his first plays, Maeterlinck wrote:

By painting that enormous and useless debility, you get as close as possible to the final and radical truth of our being, and if you manage to extract a few gestures of grace and tenderness, a few words of sweetness, fragile hope, pity, and love from the characters you thus give up to hostile nothingness, you have done all you can humanly do, having moved existence to the bounds of that great immobile truth which chills the energy and the desire to live. That is what I tried to do in these little dramas.[41]

Walter's *Poésies* originated from that kind of symbolist aesthetic, but with the addition of an ironic tone and a decadent style which came directly from Jules Laforgue.

It was in June, 1891, that Gide discovered Jules Laforgue. He first read his *Hamlet ou les suites de la piété filiale,* which he found "admirable,"[42] then, most of the pieces of his *Moralités légendaires* and *L'Invitation de Notre-Dame la lune.* On June 23 he wrote to Paul Valéry: "Laforgue is my friend."[43] And on June 29:

How much I like Laforgue! I read him every day: but not *Les Complaintes.* You must read *Les Moralités* and especially in *Notre-Dame la lune,* the selenic fauna and flora. . . . It is one of those books of silence, for two legendary writers like us who eat rose leaves together on old tombs. . . . Yet I don't think you would like the jests under which he hides the shyness of his soul. . . . Do you know that Laforgue lived at number 2 of our street, and that I should have liked him, and that I can't help being a bit angry with him for not having waited for me. Twenty-five years old! That is not an age to die![44]

Gide's friendship for the humorist came at the right time, for it corresponded to his temporary mood at the writing of *Les Poésies d'André Walter,* a mood that was no longer the same as when he wrote *Les Cahiers.*

[41] Maurice Maeterlinck, preface to the first volume of his *Théâtre: La Princesse Maleine* (1890), *L'Intrus* (1891), *Les Aveugles* (1891).

[42] *Cahier de lectures,* June 17, 1891, unpublished.

[43] *Correspondance,* pp. 100–101.

[44] *Ibid.,* p. 106. Laforgue died in 1887 at the age of twenty-seven.

29: Narcissus, or the Symbol of an Aesthete (1891)

> *"My* Narcisse *is finished . . . it has clar-*
> *ified my whole aesthetic, my ethics, and*
> *my philosophy."*
> *Letter to Paul Valéry, November 3,*
> *1891* (Correspondance, *p. 133*)

I

N JANUARY, 1892, *Les Poésies d'André Walter,* intended for publication in the last issue of *La Conque,* were completed,[1] but they
had almost all been written during the summer of 1891, from
June to September. One mistake that Gide seems to have made—and he
realized it later—was to have attributed the poems to the deceased Walter.
Walter I was pale, but Walter II was anemic. How could the great soul
of *Les Cahiers* be recognized in that little soul? How could that *animula*
be taken for Walter's *anima?* And yet Walter II is not only the reflection
of other souls—a little of Maeterlinck, a great deal of Laforgue, a shade
of Adoré Floupette; he corresponded to a small side of the great Walter.
He is the same hero ridiculed by a downcast spirit who saw his angelism
as no more than impotence, his struggles as indecision, his surrender as
weakness, his madness as neurasthenia. In fact, by exaggerating that weakly aspect, Gide was to write *Paludes.* Walter II's malady is not André
Walter's; it is a satire of it; it is the malady of Tityrus, who could well
have written *Les Poésies,* for all the poems are in his register.

As for Emmanuèle, Walter's twin mirror, how could she—the proud and
mystical heroine of *Les Cahiers*—be recognized in the poor little creature
who was as miserable as her companion? Madeleine Rondeaux was exasperated by *Les Poésies:*

[1] "I had again begun to work a bit on my mediocre verses of September. It bores me"
(*Journal,* January, 1892, p. 30).

Read *Les Poésies d'A. W.* Very boring and very bad. I assure you that you have not been long in coming down from the pedestal—oh, a very small pedestal—that you have been perched on thanks to *Les Cahiers* and *Narcisse.* Seriously, I was very disappointed. Why did you have that printed?[2]

She must surely have felt the very new tone as a sign that André's soul was not quite the same as it had been. And there lies the psychological interest of the second Walter's poetry. Six months after Emmanuèle's refusal, the author would seem to have unconsciously worked at minimizing and ridiculing the couple that are to reappear in *Le Voyage d'Urien,* in *La Tentative amoureuse,* and most importantly, in *Paludes,* in which Walter's Angel is reduced to Tityrus' Angèle.

Some time after the summer of 1891, during which he had worked on *Les Poésies,* Gide wrote to Valéry with regard to a love story he had read: "It made me disgusted with love (I already had been a little) and with all sentimentality. And with myself as an individual."[3] He may have been disgusted with himself as an individual but not as an artist, and the sicker he was of Walter's sentimentality, the more excited he became about Narcissus' solitary fate. In the same letter he added: "My *Narcisse* is finished."

The Narcissus myth has inspired countless poets, but each one has interpreted it in his own way, and Gide's way was completely personal. He deformed it for his own use, and the fable thus helped make him aware of his own personality. *Les Cahiers d'André Walter* (1890) was an expression of the Walterism of his adolescence; *Le Traité du Narcisse* (1891) is the first real expression of Gidism. Less than a "theory of the symbol" in general, his theory symbolizes the ideal he formulated at the end of his twenty-first year.

In mythology, Narcissus' story is inseparable from Echo's. The suppression of Echo, the total eviction of the nymph, is one of the most curious features of the way in which Gide deformed the legendary myth. There is not a feminine image, not a feminine shadow, not a feminine voice in his whole paradise. It is obvious that Gide's Narcissus does not belong to the "sad race" of Adam, and he seems not to feel the slightest nostalgia because of it. Adam's sin was indeed the original sin, the origin of all evils. For Eve was born and Adam's solitude was disturbed forever. All the unhappiness of man comes from the fact that he was unable to remain seated in the shadow of the large tree.

[2] Letter from Madeleine Rondeaux to André Gide, Aug. 7, 1892 (quoted by Jean Schlumberger, *loc. cit.,* p. 75).

[3] Letter from André Gide to Paul Valéry, Nov. 3, 1891 (*Correspondance,* p. 133).

Narcissus, who was born of spontaneous generation, refuses to be disturbed by the couples lost in their embraces. He wants to ignore them, for he knows that their deadly embraces will only result in the reproduction of another human being, "still incomplete and who will not be sufficient unto himself." Narcissus wants to be sufficient unto himself; he does not want to divide himself, give himself, abandon himself, or reproduce himself, because he in himself is a complete Form, the religious and unsexed being that God made in his own image. He is made for creation and not for reproduction. He must bring forth flowers and not fruit. He must remain the first man, "Elohim's hypostasis, the Divinity's henchman! For him and by him the forms appear."[4] Even spiritually, he does not mean to become "the Androgyne who divides himself in two." He wants to keep not only all his ribs but also the two halves of his psyche, the *animus* and *anima,* for the ambiguous flower—the narcissus—is born from their lack of differentiation. He is a complete being, completely alone, a symbol as representative of solipsism as Mallarmé's virgin, Hérediode: "Oui, c'est pour moi, pour moi, que je flueris, dèserte."

In analyzing Walter's angelic love for Emmanuèle, I concluded that it was basically a form of moral narcissism, Ego's love for Echo, his ideal voice. But Narcissus carries his ostracism to the point of not even wanting to remember Echo's love. Such is the first article of *Le Traité*: Narcissus must be absolutely virginal and absolutely alone. He is by definition intact and separate.

"Everything virtually contains the intimate harmony of its own being, just as every grain of salt has within itself the archetype of its crystal." In order to rediscover the secret of the lost Paradise, Narcissus must seek that original form, that archetype, that golden number, "the intimate, harmonious Number of his Being." The scientist, also, is in search of original forms, the archetype of things, but his way is "through slow and timorous induction," for he stops at appearances and "refuses to guess." Narcissus guesses. Behind Form, he seeks a Number, behind appearances, a Truth, behind phenomena, an Essence. He does not intend to admire merely an image; he wants to penetrate to its deepest meaning, its ultimate design, its message. Narcissus' method is the opposite of the scientist's, for he proceeds by poetic intuition rather than reasonable induction, and claims to attain the absolute, not the relative. His is the same method as that of the romantic Narcissus, André Walter, but enriched by the symbolist theory of "correspondences." It is not a lucid and wilful analysis but, on the contrary, a surrender of reason and the will.

However much Narcissus is Walterian in his way of "contemplating," he differs from Walter in his way of "revealing." The first is romantic, the

---

[4] *Traité du Narcisse, O.C.,* I, 211.

second, classical, and as Gide's style originated in the contrast or conflict between the two, the aesthetics formulated by *Le Traité* is of considerable interest. When the poet wants to express the fleeting vision he has had of his self, he must become "solemn and religious," recover his calm attitude, and allow his contemplation to crystallize slowly in silence, before "revealing" it. But when the time for revealing it comes, he must then do it without complacency. "To prefer oneself—that is the sin." He must not prefer the word to the phrase, nor the phrase to the truth it must convey, for that would be treachery. He must subordinate himself and arrange

all the forms in a reciprocal and symmetrical dependency, in which the pride of words does not supplant the thought—in which the words and the steady rhythmical phrases, symbols still, but pure symbols, are made transparent and revealing.

Or again:

When, as a visionary, he has perceived the Idea, the intimate, harmonious Number of his Being, which supports the imperfect form, he grasps it; then, heedless of the transitory form which clothed it in time, he is able to restore it to its eternal form, its *own* true and fatal Form at last—paradisiac and crystalline. For the work of art is a crystal—a partial paradise in which the Idea flourishes anew in its higher purity.

The crystal is Narcissus' true home. It reveals his essence and reconstitutes the Platonic Eden of eternal Forms. By means of the work of art, in which all the Forms are order and harmony, he can reconquer the lost Paradise. As Gide said in his early *Journal,* the work of art is "an equilibrium outside of time."

When Marcel Drouin, one of Gide's most lucid friends, received *Le Traité du Narcisse,* he at once saw the evolution it represented with relation to *André Walter* and considered it "a massive and precious ingot that will give weight to your works."[5] He was not mistaken. In Gide's complete works the few pages of *Le Traité du Narcisse* are worth their weight in gold. From the viewpoint of form, they signify the birth of a classical writer—that is, one who undertakes to subdue his romanticism. *Le Traité du Narcisse* is truly "a fresh-blown crystal flower in Plato's cavern."[6] Walter's "ejaculatory tone" is replaced by an aesthetic constraint, by submission to an impersonal order of *beauty*. Such is the second article of *Le Traité*: Narcissus must contemplate with lyricism and reveal with propriety, express his romantic frenzies with the moderation of a classic and restrain his pathetic search in the chains of a well-ordered style.

[5] Letter from Marcel Drouin to André Gide, Dec. 9, 1891, unpublished.

[6] Letter from Marcel Schwob to André Gide, June, 1892, unpublished.

If *Le Traité du Narcisse* represents a stage in Gide's aesthetic development—that most important moment at which the artist finds his ultimate
"form"—it also testifies to an important change in his moral attitude.
André Walter was a Narcissus, but a Huguenot Narcissus, religiously
concerned with the problems of good and evil. Here, the ethical mysticism
of *Les Cahiers* is replaced by an aesthetic religion which subordinates all
values to art:

For the artist, what matters morally is not that the Idea he reveals be more
or less moral and useful to the greatest number, but rather that he reveal it
satisfactorily. For everything must be revealed, even the most deadly things:
"Woe unto him through whom offenses come," yet "offenses must come."
The artist and the man who lives for something must first have sacrificed
himself. His entire life is but a step toward that.[7]

And so, faced with the great dilemma of whether to be an artist or a man,
Narcissus chose to be an artist. Moral law is made for Adam, but Narcissus knows only the law of his own truth, and his only ethics will be concerned with revealing it satisfactorily.

His existence as a man will be subordinated to the search for his ideal
essence through his works: for them to grow, he must diminish.[8] The
phrase misquoted from the Holy Scriptures, "offenses must come," shows
that the artist must sacrifice his human reputation to achieve his purpose
and not allow himself to stop because of disrepute or reprobation. From
that time on, Gide wanted to take his place in the host of those then
called the "poètes maudits" or accursed poets. But was it really the demon
of literature alone which demanded such a provocative destiny?

At the end of *Le Traité,* Gide forsakes the myth and speaks in his own
name:

Of course, neither the tiresome laws of men, nor fears, nor modesty, nor
remorse, nor the respect for myself or for my dreams, nor thou, sad death,
nor the terror of anything beyond the grave will keep me from reaching what
I desire; nor anything—anything but the pride, knowing how strong it is, of
feeling that I am even stronger, and conquering it. But the joy of such a
noble victory is not yet as sweet, not as good, as giving in to you, desires,
and being conquered without a battle.[9]

What a curious digression in a theory of the symbol! And the meaning
of that passage is peculiarly clarified when it is compared to the preface
Gide wrote forty years later for *Les Cahiers d'André Walter.* "The struggle
itself seemed vain to me, and how pernicious the pride which resulted in

---

[7] Note added to *Le Traité du Narcisse, O.C.,* I, 215–16.

[8] It was also to become Gide's ultimate ethics—that is, "subordinate to aesthetics"
(*Nouveaux Prétextes,* p. 58).

[9] *Traité du Narcisse, O.C.,* I, 219.

victory, a victory I henceforth ceased to hope for."[10] Had he already ceased to hope for that victory?

Surely, I thought, there are lands other than those disenchanted moors where I led my soul to graze. When will I be able to walk in the sun, filled with joy, far from my gloomy thoughts, and—in the oblivion of yesterday and so many futile religions—embrace the happiness that will come, without scruples and without fear?

In his desire to walk in the sun, Gide would seem to have forgotten that Narcissus must remain immobile, alone in the Tower, and that the drooping flower blooms in the shadow, far from the busy roads. And how strange is the sudden need to embrace happiness without scruples and without fear, like the deplorable Adam and other amateurs of the fruits of the earth. The conclusion of *Le Traité* seems to contradict the premises. And the final digression makes the purity of Narcissus' intentions, as well as his vocation as guardian of the Tower, highly questionable. The Levite is clearly not without "gluttony," even lust, and the habitué of the symbolist group not without a desire to "sight-see."

When Madeleine Rondeaux read *Le Traité du Narcisse* in June, 1892, she was surprised and terrified at the change it represented. She admired its quality as a "lesson in artistic rhetoric" and felt that it showed the nascent maturity of a writer in love with classicism:

If a month ago you had told me, as you did this morning: "I am fundamentally so classical!" I would have laughed and spoken of your vast imagination. But no, I now say: "Perhaps." The feeling came to me as I progressed with *Narcisse*—being sensitive to the accuracy of the proportions, the perfect eurythmy of the whole.

But beyond that illustration of the symbolist theory, she was particularly struck by the strange moral evolution she saw in *Le Traité*:

You haven't told me what you mean by revealing the Truth hidden behind the symbol. What symbol? What Truth? The epitome, according to you, of all morals. You haven't told me how you can claim that the artist—or, in general, anyone who reveals—can ignore the consequences of his proclamations, whether they be good or bad.

She was disturbed by the contempt for action, the proud solitude, the fact of diverting "the contemplation that produces an ethics" to purely aesthetic ends, the estrangement from the God of the Bible, and perhaps other attitudes:

[10] Preface to the republication of *Les Cahiers d'André Walter*, 1930.

And besides, if you were still a little boy, if you were really my brother, I would tell you that your pride frightens me—unless it is purely intellectual—but if it is a pride of the soul, then I am frightened, I am cold—and I feel that it implies some mysterious punishment, like those who attain vainglory in the old legends. And I repeat the prayer I used to say for you when I was a little girl: "O God, give André faith, or increase his faith, and grant that he may learn from you how to be gentle and humble of heart"—and I used to add: "Grant that we may love each other always." Only that I don't ask for any more.[11]

Madeleine Rondeaux was not mistaken as to the significance of that new work in relation to its author. Neither the psychology, nor the aesthetic, nor the ethics of the *Narcisse* are the same as *Walter's*. The voice of the angelic Echo has been silenced, and with it the desire to have the angel triumph. The Romantic is on his way to becoming a classical writer who intends to subordinate himself. The Huguenot has become an aesthete who still quotes the Bible, but as an orator skilled in applying the sacred text to profane ends. Barely one year after *André Walter,* we begin to see the real image of André Gide.

[11] Letter from Madeleine Rondeaux to André Gide, June 17, 1892 (quoted by Jean Schlumberger, pp. 73–74).

30: Meeting with Oscar Wilde

"Wilde is religiously contriving to kill what is left of my soul."

Letter to Paul Valéry,
December 4, 1891

THROUGHOUT 1891, Gide had moved not only in literary circles but also in fashionable ones. He later spoke with some bitterness about the time he "wasted." And yet, although we know he reproached Marcel Proust with doing much the same thing and went so far as to be responsible for the *N.R.F.*'s refusal of Proust's manuscript,[1] he answered his mother's similar reproaches with impatience:

Wasted time! How can you tell—what can you see from *the outside*. How can even *I* tell? Do you think that my mind ever stops working for a minute, often without realizing it myself? Do you think that one can go about in society with as persistent and constant a vision as I have of what I want to do, without everything one sees, everything one hears, everything one does settling and crystallizing *in its place* and bringing something to one's future works?[2]

If we are to believe Gide, he gave the impression in Parisian salons of being a "night bird" or at least cut a somewhat sad figure. His seriousness and shyness made him as uncomfortable as his mother was at the same age, when she had to go out in Rouen society. He therefore always took along either André Walckenaër or Georges Manuel, a "curious person"

[1] Cf. letter from André Gide to Marcel Proust, January, 1914 (Marcel Proust, *Lettres à André Gide,* pp. 9–10). Gide met Proust for the first time on May 1, 1891, at Gabriel Trarieux's.

[2] Letter from André Gide to his mother, May 27, 1892, unpublished.

but one who was accustomed to the afternoon teas of Angèle or her sisters. Actually, he was rather flattered to be invited by "a few women in high society,"[3] and his letters of that time indicate a touch of snobbery, even dandyism. Since his adolescence, he had been very concerned about his physical appearance, but since he had read Barbey d'Aurevilly's study on *G. Brummell et le Dandysme*—"every word should be memorized"[4]—he was even more convinced that to hold sway as a personality, certain manners, attitudes, and clothes were absolutely necessary. "At about twenty, my youth, my long hair, my sentimental manner, and a frock coat that my tailor did a beautiful job on made me rather well thought of in the salons of Mme. Beulé and the Comtesse de Janzé." In addition to them, he paid visits to Mme. Henri Baignères, Mme. Hayen, Mme. Dolfus-Mieg, the Baronne Double, and the Comtesse Robert de Bonnières. Above all, he liked to visit the Princesse Ouroussof, a whimsical, agreeably mad person and an excellent musician. In her drawing room on the Boulevard Haussmann, eccentricity was *de rigueur,* the conversation desultory, the food delicate, and the guests choice. There he got to know Jacques-Emile Blanche and met Oscar Wilde.

Jacques-Emile Blanche was a very literary and fashionable young painter, for whom Gide subsequently posed. In *Mes Modèles* Blanche's description of André Gide is one of the best documents on his appearance during the symbolist period:

That young, very pale Huguenot, with his flat, dark hair, who claims to be shy but asserts such authority . . . I can see him posing in the green dressing room I then had in my Auteuil studio. . . . My model, thin but of sturdy build, sensitive to the cold,[5] and seemingly doubled up, lay his full Inverness cape on a straw armchair so as to sit down . . . A large beauty spot marked the somewhat Chinese face of the young evangelist.

That somewhat Chinese aspect of the face, due to his almost slits of eyes, struck most painters of Gide's portrait.[6] "His sparkling hematite eyes, like slits, stare at you with the expression of a preacher." The word hematite is particularly accurate, for Gide's eyes were not black (as in certain portraits) but gray-green. "The head is supported by a hand with thick,

[3] *Ibid.,* March 18, 1890, unpublished.

[4] *Cahier de lectures,* February, 1891, unpublished.

[5] That sensitivity to the cold was indeed one of Gide's traits, and even at that time he often wore woolen vests and shawls.

[6] "Eyes between two folds," noted Jules Renard that very year, and later, André Rouveyre in *Le Reclus et le Retors:* "The slanting eyes of an old Chinese woman. His Chinese-Latin cryptonymous mask is a trap in which the eyes are not noticed."

spatulate fingers." The strength and thickness of his hands were the most striking feature of Gide's structure,[7] and it was all the more noticeable in that his general morphology was that of a narrow, slender man.

The other hand holds a book placed on one knee; the legs are crossed and float in cheviot trousers of the same grey as the jacket. Extremely romantic, although he denies it, my new friend spoke through clenched teeth and with charming unctuousness; his language was precise, pure, and contrasted strongly with the redundant logomachy of that time.

There is the same contrast here between a fundamental romanticism and a very controlled attitude that Camille Mauclair had noticed when he observed Gide at Mallarmé's.

The name of Oscar Wilde appears in Gide's handwriting for the first time on November 27, 1891, in a letter to Valéry:

A few lines from someone who is completely dazed, who no longer reads, writes, sleeps, eats, or thinks—but who runs around with or without Louÿs to cafés or salons, shaking hands and smiling. Heredia, Régnier, Merrill, the aesthete Oscar Wilde, Oh! an admirable man, admirable.[8]

His name appears again on November 3 in Gide's daybook: "5 P.M.: Oscar Wilde"; then on December 2: "Dinner with Merrill[9] and Wilde"; and on December 3: "Schwob and Oscar Wilde at Bruant's."[10] His letter of Friday, December 4, to Paul Valéry begins with the gloomy words *De profundis* and continues: "Wilde is religiously contriving to kill what is left of my soul, because he says that in order to know an essence, one must eliminate it: he wants me to miss my soul. The effort to destroy is the measure of the thing. All things are made up only of their emptiness . . . , etc." On December 6 he lunched with Wilde at the Princesse Ouroussof's, saw him again next day at Marcel Schwob's, and the day after went back with him to Bruant's. On December 11 and 12, one name covers the entire page of his daybook: *Wilde,* written in enormous letters compared to his usual handwriting. On December 13, dinner again at the Princesse Ouroussof's with Wilde and Henri de Régnier, and on the fifteenth he saw him one last time: "Schwob, Wilde." On "Thursday, Christmas Eve" he wrote to Paul Valéry: "Please excuse my silence: since Wilde, I hardly exist any more." In fact, his meetings with Oscar Wilde during the first two weeks

---

[7] "He did not have the hands of a man of letters, but the hands of a gardener," remarked Mme. Théo Van Rysselberghe.

[8] *Correspondance,* p. 139.

[9] Stuart Merrill, a symbolist poet of American extraction.

[10] Aristide Bruant, the poet-*chansonnier.*

of December, 1891, were one of the most important events in Gide's life since Madeleine Rondeaux's refusal.

And yet in *Si le grain ne meurt* there is as little mention of the second event as of the first. Why the silence? Perhaps because Gide did not want to go back to an episode he had already written about elsewhere,[11] perhaps because, for reasons of structure, he wanted to keep the entire portrait of Wilde for their 1895 meeting in Biskra, or perhaps there were other considerations. Whatever the case may be, no reader of *Si le grain ne meurt* who tries to follow the author's psychological evolution would understand how it had been influenced by the appearance of Wilde or how certain thoughts, Wildeian in spirit and from then on expressed in the *Journal*, came into being. I should like to add that in the manuscript of Gide's *Journal* the pages corresponding to the months of November and December, 1891—the period during which he saw Wilde—have been torn out.

Oscar Wilde was then thirty-seven. He had just published *The Picture of Dorian Gray*, a collection of criticism entitled *Intentions*, and his first play, *Lady Windermere's Fan*, was then in rehearsal. But it was not Wilde's books that impressed Gide, for he had not yet read them and knew them only from hearsay; it was the myth of the man and the charm of his personality and conversation. The Irish aesthete arrived in Paris preceded by an extraordinary reputation:

His expression and his gestures were triumphant. His success was so assured, it seemed that it preceded Wilde and that he himself had only to move forward. His books surprised and charmed. . . . He was rich; he was tall; he was handsome; he was gorged with happiness and honors. Some compared him to an Asiatic Bacchus; others to a Roman emperor; still others to Apollo himself.[12]

Gide had heard about his brilliant gifts as a storyteller who used a thousand paradoxes to justify luxury and vice. And indeed his popularity in England was unquestionable, but his personality gave rise to hatred as well, and that hatred was soon to become evident.

Gide was literally fascinated by Wilde and sensitive to the magnetic spell he cast around him: "The fact is that he was radiant." When he spoke in French, his words lost none of their magic, for he knew the language so well that he was able to write his *Salome* directly in French. He did have a strong accent, but "it gave his words an occasionally new and strange aspect"; and in any case, his voice was "marvelous." More than just talk, he narrated:

[11] The article *In memoriam,* written in 1901, after Wilde's death, was published in *L'Ermitage* in August, 1905, and reprinted in the brochure, *Oscar Wilde.*

[12] *In memoriam,* p. 14.

The astonishing thing was that he never stopped. Did he prepare his conversation in the same way as Mallarmé? Yes, of course; but still, nothing quickened his spirit more than the unexpected; he knew how to extract its most whimsical side; then, almost at the end of his ammunition, he would still extract a kind of wit from the very tone with which he seriously said futile things and futilely said serious things.[13]

In Gide's unpublished notes there is the following passage, which is highly significant of the attitudes of both orator and listener:

I was clearly a past master in the art of listening. "You listen with your eyes," Wilde told me, probably never suspecting the amount of diligence that went into the deliberate expression on my face; not that I forced it much; but I constantly kept watch on it as Wilde made his remarks; and I don't know which of us was more of an actor; but a sincere actor, after all, for each one was acting out his own character. Ah! How well we flattered each other; and with never a compliment. All the same, I now and then gave him to understand that he sometimes really irritated me, for I demanded the best of him; and when the best ran out (he surely prepared his conversations in advance), I found that anything less good was bad.

How curious it must have been to see one Narcissus face to face with the other, one doing his number to the point of exhaustion, the other paralyzed but demanding.

The young Huguenot was enough of an artist to appreciate the form and brilliance of Wilde's stories, but he was particularly sensitive to their deliberate immorality. Had Wilde been merely a brilliant talker, a dealer in frivolities similar to Passavant in *Les Faux-Monnayeurs,* he would never have held Gide; but beyond the witticisms Gide could discern the spirit of evil, and that is what attracted him to the genuine counterfeiter. In his unpublished notes he describes Wilde as "always trying to instil into you *a sanction for evil.*" Although he had of course known areligious or irreligious, amoral or immoral people before, for the first time he found himself confronted with a man who was able to bring about, within him, a transmutation of all values—in other words, a revolution. He himself wrote that he was subsequently less astonished by Nietzsche because he had first known Wilde.

Wilde's influence on Gide was above all that of an immoralist. Their meetings in December, 1891, represent an important stage in Gide's de-Christianization and demoralization. What Wilde denounced in Christianity was the will to mortify the flesh and the condemnation of instincts—in short, everything André Walter had struggled to preserve. The new hedonism rejected all theories and all systems that implied "the sacrifice of any mode of self-expression whatever." It taught men to enjoy the moment

[13] Notes on Oscar Wilde, unpublished.

—*monochronos hedone!*—and "to concentrate on the moments in a life which is itself but a moment." We can imagine Gide's expression as he listened to such ideas, little realizing that he would one day write the breviary of that hedonism, *Les Nourritures terrestres.*

Wilde attacked Christianity not only for its spirit of renunciation but for its spirit of charity, its pity for the weak, the sorrowful, the poor, and its sacred hope of relieving their misery. In terms less vigorous than Nietzsche's, but in a spirit just as basically anti-Christian, he preached the morals of the "strong" as against those of the "weak." And his sophisms devaluated all the virtues, one by one. But of all Wilde's arrows, none struck the Huguenot more forcibly than his justification of the lie and his disparagement of sincerity, the Protestant virtue par excellence: "I don't like your lips; they are straight like those of someone who has never lied. I want to teach you to lie, so that your lips may become beautiful and twisted like those of an ancient mask."[14] A brilliant mythomaniac, the Irish poet proclaimed the virtues of fabrication as a means of multiplying the personality. For him, as for Lord Henry, the lie was not only a fine art but art itself. The artist was first of all a liar.

Wilde also had an aesthetic influence on Gide, for he taught him a completely new way of considering the relations between art and life. In the monastic atmosphere of Mallarmé's group, the young writer had been encouraged to scorn life so as to devote himself to his works, and that mystical disparagement went in the direction of Walter's idealism. But Wilde maintained that the artist's life should imitate art and itself become a work of art. On that point he could not have been more opposed to Mallarmé's principles. Intending to be an artist of existence, he almost preferred to live poetry than to express it.[15] In a notation of Gide's *Journal* on January 3, Wilde's perverting influence can be clearly felt:

One can therefore say the following, which I see as a kind of inverted sincerity (on the part of the artist): Rather than recount his life as he lived it, he must live it as he will recount it. In other words: his portrait, which his life will be, must be identical with the ideal portrait he desires; and, in simpler terms, he must be as he wants to be.[16]

From that moment on, he gave up Mallarmé's and Flaubert's belief that the artist seems all the greater in that he would appear not to have lived,

[14] Wilde, a man of imagination, never bothered to observe. Gide's lips were not straight but sinuous; yet one could hardly conclude that they were that way because of lying.

[15] In 1895, at Biskra, during a conversation with Gide, Wilde conclusively formulated that thought: "I put my genius into my life; I put only my talent into my works." (Letter from André Gide to his mother, Jan. 30, 1895, unpublished.)

[16] *Journal,* p. 29.

and thought of making his masterpiece the story of his life. Now for the story of a life to be captivating, it must include all events, all adventures, and even more importantly, according to Wilde, an "extraordinary, marvelous enumeration of sins."[17] These new precepts or pretexts corresponded most opportunely with the conclusion so curiously expressed on the last page of *Le Traité du Narcisse:* "offenses must come!" If God does not will it, Art does. . . .

Another of Wilde's remarks would seem to have deeply impressed Gide:

"There are," he used to say, "two kinds of artists: some bring answers and the others bring questions. You must know whether you are one of those who answers or one of those who questions; for the one who questions is never the one who answers. There are works that wait and are not understood for a long time, because they brought answers to questions that had not yet been asked; for the question often comes a frightfully long time after the answer."[18]

As a devoted reader of Taine, Gide was then convinced that an artist is the product of his time and must reflect the Form of its spirit. But primarily concerned with his own originality, he soon wondered whether he was among those who must go in the direction of his time or, on the contrary, go against it and impose a new form upon it, anticipating the questions that have not yet been asked. Curiously enough, after his meetings with Wilde, Gide completely stopped reading Taine, as if he were afraid that Taine was a bad guide. Twenty years later, he wrote in his *Journal:*

The most annoying aspect of that theory of Taine's is that it managed to mislead some artists by teaching them to follow their time and to learn from it, whereas all their energy should have gone into *distinguishing* themselves from it. . . . There are, among the greatest, those who—far from following their time—oppose it; who, as Wilde said, bring answers to questions that have not yet been asked.[19]

The germ of that idea, which was soon to dominate his life, had already been put into his mind by Wilde in 1891.

If Wilde's moral and aesthetic influence on Gide was so apparent, can we also assume that their first meetings had turned him toward homosexuality as well? Gide formally denied it. In *In memoriam* he claimed that he had never heard of the Irish aesthete's "strange habits" until the following years. Of course, Wilde came to Paris in 1891 without Lord Alfred Douglas; and he was still careful not to flaunt his liaison with "Bosie,"

[17] *In memoriam,* p. 24.

[18] *Ibid.,* pp. 26–27.

[19] *Journal,* 1925, pp. 812–13.

who was then barely twenty-one. Yet for some time rumors about him had been spreading in England, and it seems very strange that Gide had heard nothing and suspected nothing.

"I think that Wilde did me nothing but harm. In his company I had forgotten how to think. I had more varied emotions, but could no longer get them in order."[20] Those lines, written in Uzès a few days after Gide had left Wilde, are significant of the state of confusion he was in as a result of the sophist's paradoxes and his way of bringing answers to questions that had not yet been asked.

Gide had left Paris for Uzès on December 28, for a month's visit to his ailing grandmother. After the days of dissipation and dispersion, he felt the need to pull himself together and thoroughly examine his conscience, as in the old days. A long letter to Albert Démarest, whom he would seem to have somewhat forsaken during that very social year, gives a better picture of his mood than his *Journal*:

I want to ignore Paris and literary life. I realize that one must be far stronger than I was to be able to take part in that life without being imbued with it and unstrung. . . . These few days here have already completely changed me. I'm back to the difficulty of expressing myself in gestures and words which I had in my childhood: I am once again strangely shy and ill at ease. And since, in addition, my spirits are high again, based on the solid ideas of the past, since I'm disciplining and controlling myself again, thinking more deeply and again beginning to suffer from myself, I conclude that the difficulties in elocution were indicative of a preferable state.

The facility of words and versatility of mind came from the trivial thoughts that were easier and more amusing to manipulate; the "savoir-plaire" came from a greater skill in acting; the charming nonchalance and amiability with others, from a gradual loss of moral maxims. I've really come down since my book, and now I cling to everything I can still find in me to pull myself back up to the state I was in as an unsociable and awkward hard-worker. Everything you do to please others is morally degrading; and it is certainly far better to please yourself than others . . . yourself or God, it comes to the same thing.

The letter is just as interesting for what it reveals about André Gide's feelings for Albert Démarest and Madeleine Rondeaux:

When writing to you, just as when I play the piano for you, I become paralyzed with shyness: I can feel that you judge every line and that you read more into them than what I say: the words don't delude you and I feel completely naked before you, behind the sentences. Add to that the fear of striking you as insincere, bookish, and cold—a fear that chills my words and

[20] *Ibid.,* Jan. 1, 1892, p. 28.

makes everything I write stilted. . . . It all comes from the fact that after Madeleine, you are the person whose judgment means most to me. I don't care a damn for the others . . . but I feel that you and she understand such matters in the same way as I do and I suffer, before you both, at all the points at which I am open to attack; I torture myself and painfully worry myself over it. As you know, in the case of Madeleine, something else—intellectual and heartfelt—is mixed in with it; but what I need from you both is to feel your constant and perceptive sympathy.[21]

As always, Madeleine Rondeaux was the person whose moral judgment meant most to him, because she understood "such matters" in the same way as he. And he never needed her more: "I struggle in this dilemma: to be moral or to be sincere." He, who during that whole year had wanted "to kill Walter," had finally met the person who was quite capable of doing it for him. *"De profundis* . . . Wilde is religiously contriving to kill what is left of my soul." But as it happened, he reacted like a Protestant and now wanted to go back "to nobility of soul": he wanted to "become Walter again." And at night, when all were at rest in the family house, the child of the Uzès Huguenots was unable to sleep, terrified at feeling within him the opposition of two seemingly irreconcilable adversaries, the old man—André Walter, and a new being yet unnamed—the Other.

[21] Letter from André Gide to Albert Démarest, January, 1892, unpublished.

31: Letters from Munich

> *"How I love to hear you reverently speak about Goethe. . . ."*
>
> *Letter from Munich, May 27, 1892*

*I*N 1892 the Germanic influence in French literature was at its height. Taine, who began to learn German in order to read Hegel, had paid noteworthy homage to Goethe. Renan, discovering the historians, philosophers, and philologists across the Rhine, felt as if he were "going into a temple." Wagner was one of the gods of the Mallarmé group, and many young artists were making yearly pilgrimages to Bayreuth. As alert an arbiter as Rémy de Gourmont acknowledged the victory of German idealism and considered symbolism as merely a substitute for it. The reviews were filled with articles about German writers, and translations of Nietzsche began to be published.

During his month of withdrawal in Uzès, André Gide planned a trip to Germany. After an entire year of dispersion, he wanted above all to flee from "Paris and the literary life." He felt that a long and studious stay in the country of science, music, and philosophy would help him once again to become Walter. His uncle, Charles Gide, an earnest partisan of Franco-German exchange, greatly encouraged the plan, and Mme. Paul Gide agreed at once, only too happy to see her son escape from the demoralizing influence of the literary groups and salons. Besides, there was no language difficulty, for André Gide had learned German at home as a child, from Anna Shackleton and Marie Leuenberger, then at the Ecole Alsacienne and at the Pension Keller.

On March 8, 1892, Gide left for Munich. He stayed there for three months, March, April, and May, with a short trip back to Paris to see his mother during the Easter holidays. The many letters he wrote to her and to others while there give up the information lacking in his *Journal* and in *Si le grain ne meurt,* in which there is no mention of his trip whatever.

Having found a room with "three charming old ladies" and supplied with countless letters of introduction, Gide set out to visit the city. But after a very short time, he wrote to his mother:

Before long, I plan to lead the same life in Munich that I led in Paris. And I should like to work. Indeed, I'm going back to being a cenobite. All the hours in a day are not enough as soon as you want to do something; and if you don't protect yourself, your time is completely taken up with mutual obligations.[1]

Although he often went to the theater and rapidly visited the museums, the great events of his trip to Munich were in fact the books he read. It was then that he began his four years of almost uninterrupted reading of Goethe's works. Almost no factor was as important to his development, for Gide was then at the crucial moment when a young intellectual chooses his master, the man he wants to imitate, the man he wants to resemble: his model. "I owe more to that genius," he wrote of Goethe, "than to anyone else, than to perhaps all the others combined."[2] On May 25 he wrote to a friend in Munich:

Oh! Tell me how you came upon Goethe; what he meant to you; when you went to him to find inner consolation? Talk to me of Goethe in relation to yourself, or of yourself in relation to Goethe. For intellectuals an avowal of one's admiration is a page of confessions. When you really know those I love, you will have understood who I am. . . .[3]

As soon as he arrived in Munich he began to read *Torquato Tasso,* and meditated on it from March to May:

O Tasso, you who appeared before me during a troubled period, when active life was beguiling me with its most noble aspect: devotion and religious heroism . . . Who could imagine all the peace I have derived from these pages, all the tranquillity![4]

An inner consolation and a feeling of repose were what first struck Gide in *Tasso,* in which—among other problems—was posed that of the antagonism between the poet and the man of action, between dream and reality, then his main concern as an artist. In addition, Tasso's Eleonora—so wise,

---

[1] Letter from André Gide to his mother, March 22, 1892, unpublished.

[2] "Goethe," *N.R.F.,* March 1, 1932.

[3] Letter to X, Munich, May 25, 1892. The letter is published in Vol. I of Gide's *Oeuvres Complètes,* pp. 543–45, and dated "Munich, May 25, 1893," which is obviously a mistake, for Gide was not then in Munich. Moreover, he speaks of Goethe's *Torquato Tasso, Prometheus,* and *Iphigenie,* which he was reading in 1892.

[4] *Ibid.*

pure, and proper—perhaps called to mind the ideal feminine figure that forever haunted him:

O Tasso! Go no further. There are many things we must seize with ardor; but there are others we can appropriate only with moderation and renunciation. So it is, we are told, with virtue; and so with love, its brother. . . . Think it over carefully.[5]

We know that Goethe, influenced by his passion for Charlotte de Stein, had wanted to show in *Torquato Tasso* the drama of thwarted love. Still another aspect of the tragedy reminded Gide of his own reflections on "the use of illness." He wrote in his *Journal:*

Concerning the illusions we have as to the health of great men . . . The man who has the best things to say about the question is precisely the one generally cited as the model of a healthy man of letters: Goethe . . . . He was unquestionably conscious of the advantage in, etc. See *Torquato Tasso.*[6]

Between his first reading of *Torquato Tasso* in March and his second in May, Gide went to Paris for a few days in April. There he read Goethe's *Prometheus.* On Easter Sunday he noted in his *Journal:* "Read Goethe's poetry; his *Prometheus* . . . I feel that before long I shall again throw myself into a frantic mysticism."[7] The great and perhaps most important battle in Gide's life had in fact already begun on that Easter Sunday of 1892: the battle between the influence of Christianity and the influence of Goethe. What he saw in Goethe's *Prometheus*[8] was essentially the protest of the man who no longer feared Zeus's thunderbolts and affirmed the pre-eminence of fate. Prometheus symbolizes the spirit of revolt against the gods, just as his brother Epimetheus symbolizes the spirit of conciliation. But Gide did not seem to be aware of the fact that Goethe—in his final conception, where Zeus is portrayed as the image of wisdom and harmony —appears far more Epimethean than Promethean.

When he returned to Munich, Gide reread *Torquato Tasso* and then began Goethe's *Iphigenie auf Tauris:*

I'm now reading his *Iphigenie* and find it perhaps even more beautiful. These works have an infinite, almost celestial, radiance. . . . He is absolutely a genius of intelligence; his lines brim over with an ineffable tranquillity; you stroll through his works as you would in a garden of flowers, rays of light, and divinities.[9]

[5] *Interviews imaginaires,* pp. 145–48.

[6] *Journal,* pp. 98–99.

[7] *Ibid.,* 1929, p. 30.

[8] Aeschylus' *Prometheus Bound* had been all the rage in the anarchistic literary groups with which Gide associated in 1891, and the Prometheus myth gradually became a symbol of the human spirit aspiring to total freedom.

[9] Letter to X, May 25, 1892, *O.C.,* I, 543–44.

It was not the Christian Paradise that Gide found in *Iphigenie auf Tauris,* but the Greek miracle, the world of Hellas. For a human being to succeed in transforming destructive passions into an Olympian grandeur, he needs the intercession of a "saving soul," in this case the harmonious Iphigenia, mediator between man and the gods. Such for Gide was the Hellenic ideal of harmony, which he had already caught a glimpse of in Helen of *Faust,* Part II, and then again in *Iphigenie.* And it was just as far from the Christian "holy lack of balance" as it was from Prometheus' revolt. But Gide did not stop at Goethe's works; he read everything he could find about Goethe himself. He devoured Sainte-Beuve's articles on Goethe and Eckermann, and Blaze de Bury's essay on Goethe and Beethoven. He plunged into the great biographies of Goethe: Grimm's and, more especially, Lewes's, in which he studied the interpenetration of the man and his works, and the way his master—for from then on he considered him as such—had resolved the problem of the relations between art and life.

André Gide's correspondence with his mother during his stay in Munich shows the evolution of his feelings toward her. His growing impatience often verges on insolence and points to his approaching revolt. Gide became irritated as much about small things as about far more serious questions. For example, there were his mother's comments concerning his letters:

You mention Maurice's letters and Uncle Emile's, and make me a little ashamed of mine in comparison—go right ahead—what can I do if it amuses them to write letters—but don't ask that of me—I really cannot . . . Writing letters bores me beyond words.[10]

When she asked whether he had paid calls to all the people to whom he had letters of introduction, he answered: "No, I have 'certainly' not 'paid calls to everyone' I should. You don't seem to be much aware of the annoyance that can result from such pleasant letters."[11] And on March 25:

I shall therefore begin by answering you: "Am I nervous, annoyed?" Indeed! After reading your letter, furiously! I had to go out and walk for an hour and a half in order to soothe my irritation. Now it is starting all over again, I think, just writing to you.

He was exasperated: his mother had reproached him with being an egoist, and the reproach hurt him to the quick: "Six long pages of NOTHING but reprimands, and about what! Mercy upon us! . . . You take six pages to prove what?—that I'm a frightful egoist. Please understand that I neither

[10] Letter from André Gide to his mother, March 22, 1892, unpublished.

[11] *Ibid.,* March 24, 1892, unpublished.

can nor wish to answer you." However, he did add a few words with regard to letter-writing:

"I wasn't always like that"—there was a time when I liked nothing better than writing letters; it was also the period when I was constantly writing my journal. That very long period began shortly after my confirmation; the continual self-examination, my inner life and my solitude, all got me into the habit of constantly watching myself; I liked to write about myself in my journal and in my letters—I was vastly interested in myself. Then, when I began to see others to a slight extent, I was passionately interested in them at first. . . . Now, I have completely stopped writing my journal (or only a few moral aphorisms)—and I generally find it disagreeable when people don't leave me alone.[12]

The reproach of egoism certainly affected him the most. When in 1890 Pierre Louÿs wrote in his *Journal:* "Gide is changing a lot. Is he really changing? Or was I mistaken in the past? . . . And gradually the dominant strain of his character came to me: Egoism," Gide was so hurt that his friend immediately suggested tearing out the page, but he had refused. This time, however, Gide defended himself with great subtlety, mentioning his Uncle Charles, who was sacred in Mme. Gide's eyes:

I pay very little attention to myself, I assure you, although you seem really to doubt it. Moreover, I find others hardly more interesting; I'm more and more interested in ideas only. You complain that I pay more and more attention to myself and less to others—oh, less to myself as well, I assure you, but more to my work, which is another matter. What can I do: I'm becoming like Uncle Charles: the *individual* doesn't interest me any more, in himself or in any selfish way. I really find that we still pay too much attention to him. . . . You then prove to me, in the same letter, that I have a nasty disposition; indeed, I'm only too convinced of it, and I even think that I was the first to notice it, although according to you, it would seem that a bad disposition is the art of giving oneself pleasure by being disagreeable to others.—This long-winded letter will answer your question.[13]

Gide was clearly in a state of nervous tension. He felt it and apologized for it, saying that he was "terribly nervous" and unable to work because of his "obligations toward others," the letters he had to write, the calls he had to pay:

Please understand that in this state my sensitivity becomes exacerbated and *to think of Madeleine is as inevitable as it is unbearable.*[14] Or perhaps I'm wrong and that is part of the reason for all the rest. But why make me write all these things when all I ask is not to think of them any more. . . . I'm not at all sure that you're right to send my letters to Rouen: it gives her

---

[12] *Ibid.,* March 25, 1892, unpublished.

[13] *Ibid.*   [14] The italics are mine.

a hold over me, it gives her precise information about me, and I think that she will not fail to judge.[15]

And so, his nerves on edge, he went back to his wound, for Madeleine's refusal was a wound that never healed. And although he denied giving in to despondency, he felt that his great hope was growing more and more precarious. He seemed to be afraid of his cousin's judgment, as if he could sense that it would be without indulgence, as if he could tell that she was ready to look for new grievances against him.

At the end of May, Gide decided to return to Paris on the pretext of having to finish posing for Jacques-Emile Blanche. But Mme. Gide would not hear of it, and another dispute between them began. For several days he beat about the bush, then finally: "Well, no—I'm coming back—this uncertainty is driving me mad." But since he wanted to work freely, he made up his mind not to stay with his mother in the rue de Commaille, a decision that dismayed Mme. Gide. He wanted no one to know about his return, not even his cousins: "I shall therefore try to find a place in Auteuil or in lower-Meudon, thus shortening my trip to Blanche's studio and keeping everyone from noticing my presence in Paris, as well as finally allowing me to work without being disturbed." He also expressly mentioned that he would not promise "to work from morning till night in Paris. I'm too afraid of your violent remonstrances and your 'I told you so's' if ever I have the misfortune of going to see someone."[16]

We can imagine how upset Mme. Gide was on learning that her son was coming back to Paris but would not live at the house. It was an unequivocal manifestation of emancipation, even rebellion. And although she must have had great satisfaction in noting in the margin of his letter dated May 29: "Impossible to get you out of the house once you arrived in Paris. It was with difficulty that I kept you from coming here to live," her triumph was short. During the trip to Munich, there was a distinct deterioration in the relations between mother and son. André Gide liked to reread the thirteenth chapter of Tacitus, "in which Nero slowly loses his meekness and his inborn fears."[17] We know that the young prince, still virtuous and obedient, began to rebel when he suspected his mother's maneuvers to keep him under her wing and make him renounce the object of his love. Relatively speaking, the stormy correspondence of March–May, 1892, indicates, also, an impending crisis, if indeed we can compare the future immoralist to the "incipient monster," and his virtuous mother to the formidable Empress.

[15] Letter from André Gide to his mother, March 25, 1892, unpublished.

[16] *Ibid.,* May 27, 1892, unpublished.

[17] *Journal,* 1893, p. 38.

32: Urien, or *Le Voyage d'Urien* (1892)

"Urien! Urien, sad brother!"
Le Voyage d'Urien, O.C., *I, 356*

As soon as he returned to Paris, at the beginning of June, André Gide set to work on *Le Voyage d'Urien*. He had gone to a hotel, but the fact that Madeleine Rondeau was staying at his mother's on the rue de Commaille doubtless explains why he so often went back "to the house" despite his decision to flee. After she left for Rouen, Gide spent a month of his time between work, reading, and posing at the Auteuil studio. On July 12, Blanche having finally finished his portrait, Gide left Paris, feeling like a schoolboy on holiday, and spent a few days in Montigny in the Côte-d'Or at his friend Maurice Quillot's. But the day after his arrival, he awoke at dawn and worked on *Le Voyage:* "My work enchants me and irritates me; I now think of nothing else and reading is impossible."[1] Then "in a great rush" he left for La Roque.

Gide explained his sudden departure in a letter to Valéry:

I fled from his house in a great rush; for since both of us were absolutely alone in the country house, we were becoming lascivious and my friend provoking. The evening of my departure, I arrived at Pierre Louÿs' and found him even worse. Finally, I got to La Roque; at least I'm alone here.[2]

The episode is recalled in letters from Gide to Louÿs, which show that despite the constant quarrels and attempted ruptures, he continued to feel passionately about him. From Montigny he wrote:

[1] Letter from André Gide to Paul Valéry, July 12, 1892 (*Correspondance,* p. 166).
[2] July 25, 1892 (*Correspondance,* p. 167).

The more I see Maurice, the more I love you. Since I couldn't be with you, I came to Montigny to talk about you. I detested you when I arrived here, but Maurice loves you so much that I realized I had to love you even more. . . . The memory of you puts me in a fever. . . . Here, Maurice makes me steam and I'm becoming dreadful and passionate.[3]

And back at La Roque: "The more we're lovers, the less we're friends. . . . I've gone back to the work I'm always sorry to have left—and although I thought I was pressing you close to me, in spite of myself I let your arms close around a vacuum."[4] All that is highly ambiguous, at least psychologically.[5]

I have already mentioned the state of sexual obsession Gide was in during the summer of 1892 at La Roque.[6] He again felt like the Walter of the "Black Notebook," "haunted" and "obsessed" by his "demon," inclosed in his neurosis, with nothing on the horizon but "a frightful desert, full of unanswered appeals, pointless impulses, anxiety, struggles, exhausting dreams, imaginary raptures, abominable relapses."[7] Such biographical comments have great importance in the interpretation of the symbolic *Voyage d'Urien* and its sexual phantasms.

Later that summer, Gide went back to the biographies of his master Goethe, and read as well a study of Goethe by Arvède Barine and *Iphigenie auf Tauris,* which brought him to the Greek tragedies. He then discovered *Philoctetes, Ajax,* and *Electra.*[8] "I'm reading Goethe, Leibnitz, and Sophocles," he wrote to Valéry.[9] The mention of Leibnitz and Fichte in his unpublished reading notebook, summer, 1892, is important, for the two German philosophers were new to him, and their influence was soon to replace Schopenhauer's. He was once again feeling full of intellectual energy, and *Le Voyage d'Urien* was progressing:

Unbearable and horribly difficult at the beginning, it soon began to amuse me, and these past ten days I've lived in a state of delightful excitement, joyful—as you can imagine one might be—at feeling my head busy and lucid, after all these long months of fog.[10]

[3] July 16, 1892, unpublished.

[4] July 19, 1892, unpublished.

[5] "None of my friendships up to now has been mixed with any attraction or sensual excitement. All have been so free of ambiguity that Quillot, Pierre Louÿs, and myself have been able to play on it and sometimes amusingly simulate it without fear" (Letter to a friend, September, 1894, unpublished).

[6] See above, bk. i, pt. ii, chap. 24.

[7] *Si le grain ne meurt,* II, 345–46.

[8] *Cahier de lectures,* August, 1892.

[9] August, 1892 (*Correspondance,* p. 170).

[10] *Ibid.*

On August 15 he had completed the entire first part of his book, "Le Voyage sur l'océan pathétique," and decided to "flee to Brittany" to write the second part "in the moors and rocks of Belle-Isle." He left with a whole library, including the symbolic combination of *Wilhelm Meister* and the Bible, and there joined Henri de Régnier. But as Mme. Gide refused him the extra money he needed to prolong his trip, he was forced to return to La Roque early in September.

At the end of the month his three cousins, Madeleine, Jeanne, and Valentine, arrived. During their stay he read aloud to them not only Goethe but Stendhal, Poe, Hugo, Balzac, Novalis, Maeterlinck, and Dickens. Yet that amazing amount of reading did not bring Madeleine any closer to him. In fact, during those three weeks at La Roque she not only repeated her decision not to marry him, but also expressed the desire that their lives be completely separated so that both might be free to marry. Never, at least on her part, were they nearer the breaking point. One letter, which he wrote to her in October, 1892, testifies most touchingly to his love for Madeleine, whose disconcerting attitude left him in despair:

I'm sadder than I ever was: I must have a little sympathy to give me the courage to live. Mamma is gone, as one day she will be altogether, and I feel completely alone. Please write me a few lines; if I answer you, I promise to be *sensible.* Please tell me if that's what you really want. Then, we'll consider ourselves brothers, while waiting,[11] and I shan't torment you any more, Madeleine; and you shall no longer be afraid of me, and I'll call you my sister, as before, my poor dear Madeleine.

Despite his discouragement, Gide continued to work and completed the entire second part of *Le Voyage d'Urien:* "La Mer des Sargasses," symbol of stagnation. He then began the third and last part, "Voyage vers une mer glaciale," the theological stage of the journey. And to reach those latitudes, he reread Leibnitz: "I'm reading Leibnitz' *La Théodicée,* which, by proving it reasonable, makes me bored with Christianity."[12]

Mme. Gide was worried about her son's state of depression. Twenty months had passed since the refusal from Arcachon and he was still stubbornly faithful to his love. Obstinate as she was, her "good sense always won out." During the Munich trip, she had felt that a revolt was brewing in André and that it had subsided considerably as soon as he had seen Madeleine in Paris and had begun to hope again. After all, was marriage between them really that unreasonable? From a moral point of view, Madeleine alone had influence on André, the influence she herself was losing from day to day. Compared to that, what was "propriety" and

[11] In the first draft of the letter, the words "while waiting" were crossed out by Gide.

[12] Letter from André Gide to Paul Valéry, Oct. 18, 1892 (*Correspondance,* p. 175).

"disproportion"? And although André was unstable, he did show such constancy in his feelings for his cousin that she might one day succeed in keeping him forever on the right track. Morever, on November 15 he was to begin his military service. What sort of people would he take up with then? Open to influence as he was, with no solid religious faith and no confident hope in Madeleine, she feared—given his state of discouragement —the worst. . . . It was at that point, when André went to her for help, that she gave in and wrote to Madeleine Rondeaux at the end of October. But Madeleine's answer was ambiguous:

> You tell me that I don't know what happiness is—that I'm afraid of it: perhaps your guess is right. With regard to the things of life, I've perhaps really experienced only two moods: anxiety for the future—the sadness of missing papa—and then a state of calm, a passive and tranquil state, like "a maiden's sky," with neither rain nor sun. What is called happiness does perhaps terrify me by its implications of action, living, and the unknown—and then also because—it cannot last.
>
> Adieu, my dear aunt. I must pray God to make me choose the true way. My affection for André fills all my soul; I know now that there is nothing I can do about it—not even diminish its strength—after two years of trying. But I think that if ever it changed in its nature, it could cause us both as much sorrow in the future as it gave me joy—the only joy of my childhood. Tell him that I thank him for his letter with all my heart and that I shall answer him.

Besides Gide's mother, whose resistance was obviously breaking down, Claire Démarest herself, under the influence of Albert, was on the way to becoming an ally. "You know that Aunt Claire is the best of aunts," Gide wrote to Jeanne Rondeaux,[13] "and one who understands the situation awfully well." And so two of the three Fates were giving up their idea of cutting the "magic thread" between André and Madeleine, but in the Rouen stronghold of the rue de Crosne, Aunt Lucile would hear nothing of it and used all her authority, which was great, to remind her niece, were she tempted to forget, of her duties as an "elder sister."

On November 15, 1892, Gide arrived at the barracks in Nancy, leaving his *Voyage d'Urien* and "Sea of Ice" to Eric, the swan slayer, the Eskimos, and Ellis-the-brunette. His first day as a soldier was hardly glorious: looking rather puny and having caught a heavy cold, he was sent at once to the infirmary. He was not unhappy there, but realized that in a relatively military milieu "the faculties of my soul were not employed in relation to their hierarchy. The noblest of them were idle."[14] He spent a week rereading *Werther* and a few of Balzac's novels, especially *L'Illustre Gaudissart*. Then he was sent before the recruiting board and was discharged

---

[13] November, 1892, unpublished.   [14] *Journal*, 1892, p. 32.

from the service on November 22, 1892, the day of his twenty-third birthday.

Gide's permanent exemption was not, as he wrote next day to Jeanne Rondeaux, due "perhaps more to the lack of beds and to the great lack of sanitation in the barracks, than to my own fragility." The doctors of the recruiting board had noticed his thinness, his narrow chest, and the deficiency in his respiratory capacity; the words "weak constitution" and "tuberculosis," or at least a predisposition to tuberculosis, were then pronounced. He was to remember them a year later in Biskra, when he was first attacked by the illness that had killed his father. "*Tuberculosis,* said the form, and I don't know whether I was more delighted by my exemption from service or terrified by the statement."[15] Actually, he had had regular checkups in Paris by a Doctor Miard, who rejected the terrible diagnosis but did find that his patient's lungs had to be closely watched, for he had the "habitus" and the bronchial weakness that were known to indicate a predisposition to consumption.

As soon as Gide got back to Paris, he closed himself up in his tower to write the last part of his book. He went out only twice a week to his friends the Laurens', to take lessons in fencing, which—except for swimming—was the only sport he went in for during his entire youth. Of course, the "priceless evenings of fencing" were mostly a pretext for prolonged conversations and reading aloud. At the end of December he read "My journey to the Pole," as he called his book in his *cahier de lectures* of December, 1892, to Paul and Pierre Laurens. *Le Voyage d'Urien* was finished.

Le Voyage d'Urien is an armchair journey in the symbolist manner. A few young men, tired of "the bitter night of thought, study, and theological ecstasy," weigh anchor with the Orion. The various stages of their imaginary journey take them across the "Pathetic Ocean," the "Sargasso Sea," and the "Sea of Ice." Each of these symbols in its own way expresses the perils that lie in wait for Narcissus, who here is called Urien: "Every climate has its anguish, and every land its disease."[16]

The first stage of *Le Voyage d'Urien* is a cruise in the Pathetic Ocean, which symbolizes the sea of passion and sensual pleasure. Here, every poetic disguise hides a complex. Woman is considered a temptress, as can be seen in the episode of the sirens and that of Queen Haïatalnefus. As soon as the sailors approach the sirens, their bewitching voices become lower and subside, the town falls apart and totters, the minarets and palm trees crumble, the staircases collapse, and the entire city and its captivating

---

[15] *Si le grain ne meurt,* II, 290.   [16] *Le Voyage d'Urien, O.C.,* I, 350.

mirage disappear like a dream of impossible possession. Urien and his companions are afraid of the sirens ("We did not swim that day for fear of them") and they refuse to swim in Queen Haïatalnefus' pool for fear of "crabs" and "cruel crayfish." A psychoanalyst could not fail to think of the wound involved in the sexual act. I have mentioned how André Gide, at the age of fifteen, on learning that his friend Bernard Tissaudier regularly walked down a street where there were prostitutes, imagined him "being orgiastically torn to pieces by hetarae," and was amazed that "the dragon" he had made *that* into could be considered "cold-bloodedly and without trembling in terror." Apropos of the incident, he noted in *Si le grain ne meurt* that "several years later, those seeking creatures terrified me as much as vitriol throwers."[17] Now the fear of having "vitriol" thrown at him, the fear of venereal diseases, does not seem unrelated to the description of the plague that contaminates the sailors as soon as they follow the women. From the beginning of the episode to the end, there is an obsession with so-called shameful diseases. In the eyes of the sad Urien, Aphrodite may perhaps be desirable, but she is dangerous: she wounds, she castrates, or she instils deadly poison. But aside from these punishments, there is a feeling of defilement, a defilement of body and soul brought about by the sexual act. As soon as the men and women "passionately" embrace, the waters become polluted and the whole earth gives off pestilential odors. The theme of water has a symbolic value in *Le Voyage d'Urien*. The cold water of the springs and fountains purify and cause an "angelic gladness," but the water of "tepid pools" leads to sensual pleasure. The "we swam" or "we did not swim," which comes back like a leitmotif throughout the entire first part, is not without significance.

The theme of children bathing in the "over-tepid pools" is also suggestive. Urien and his companions remain "immobile, floating, in a state of abandon, vainly swooning in the marvelous green and blue water, into which filtered only a dim light, turning the arms of the slender children azure." This phantasm is similar to the one I pointed out in *André Walter* and which haunted Gide even in his old age.[18] Urien's pedophilic tastes are as clear as André Walter's. We also notice, in the first part, the perpetual opposition in Gide between the free child, who excited his desire, and the pure, grave, mysterious child, who intimidated him. "We did not swim that day," says Urien, after having met at the edge of the sea a child with eyes as blue "as a sea of ice," skin "like lilies," hair "like a cloud colored by the sun at dawn," and who was sadly sketching his dreams in the sand. That particular child, found in Novalis, is nothing like *fuscus*

[17] *Ibid.,* p. 197.

[18] "Acquasanta," *Feuillets d'automne,* p. 48.

Amyntas. Angelic and pensive, he impedes desire as much as the little sun-tanned vagabonds "who never think" excite it.

The abundance of sexual symbols in the first part of *Le Voyage d'Urien* is significant of the state of obsession in which André Gide lived during the summer of 1892 at La Roque. We can see his desire for boys and especially his fear of women slowly take shape, even before he had any experience. He portrays women as sirens, sphinxes, vampires, demons, homicidal monsters, and carriers of the plague. One gets the impression that he tried to accumulate around them all the deadly forces that would make them into scarecrows.[19]

The second stage of *Le Voyage d'Urien* is the Sargasso Sea, the sea of boredom, into which "raindrops of boredom" fall "on the great surges of desire. Psychology! Psychology! science of all the soul's vanity, may the soul renounce you forever."[20] Narcissus has already had enough of the delights of introspection and inner analysis. He wanted his "desires to disappear," and now that they are gone and he is no longer taken up with anything but the study of himself, he is bored: "Boredom! So it is you, dismal studies of our soul, when around us the splendors and forbidden rays withdraw. The rays are gone, temptation has forsaken us; we are left with nothing to do outside ourselves, in the disenchanted dawn."

Suddenly, in the regions of that sea of boredom, Urien meets his dear Ellis, "sitting under an apple tree," like Eve herself.

She had been there for fourteen days, having taken the more rapid land route; she was wearing a polka dot dress and carried a cherry-red umbrella; next to her was a little suitcase with toilet articles and a few books; a plaid shawl was over her arm; she was eating an endive salad while reading *The Prolegomena to Any Future Metaphysics.*

They help the Kantian traveler into the boat: "Our meeting again was rather dismal, and as we were in the habit of talking only about what we had known together, because of the different roads we had taken, we found nothing to say to each other."[21] Gide himself admitted that Ellis was was somewhat patterned after Madeleine:

And I portrayed her even in my first books, much before we were married: Emmanuèle in *Les Cahiers d'André Walter,* Ellis in *Le Voyage d'Urien* . . . and she constantly appeared in my dreams as an unembraceable, elusive figure; and the dream turned into a nightmare.[22]

---

[19] Adler, who considered pedophilia as "a tendency and practice provoked by the subject's fear of his sexual partner," emphasized the frequency, in the dreams of pedophiles, of the old myth of the *Giftmädchen* or "young girls who are poisoners" (Adler, *The Neurotic Condition*).

[20] *Le Voyage d'Urien, O.C.,* I, 326.

[21] *Ibid.,* p. 327.   [22] *Et nunc manet in te,* p. 35.

After his deep disappointment at her refusal, he had begun to lead a life very different from hers, and when he saw her again during the summer of 1891, and especially 1892, their meetings were "dismal." Urien's symbols suggest that a considerable evolution had taken place in André Gide's feelings for Madeleine since the time of *André Walter*. She begins to bore him and to irritate him. Rereading the Ellis episode with that in mind, the details become rich with intent and, indeed, irony.

"On the peaceful river, between the solid banks" the nights were dreamless, the awakenings without gladness, and the days without happiness. In the boat Ellis reads *Le Traité de la Contingence*. She clearly likes serious books: "Exasperated, I tore the book out of her hands and, having thrown it in the river, shouted: 'Don't you know, unhappy Ellis, that books are temptation?'" The next day, as they are all reading the "moral pamphlets Ellis had distributed," Urien makes an inventory of his companion's small suitcase. Finding it filled with edifying books, he throws it into the Sargasso Sea: "Two large tears ran down Ellis' cheeks. Although I was not particularly moved, the feeling of our common misery calmed my irritation." He then speaks to Ellis of the past, the "majestic and deep night" they had left "for something else." And his allusions to the virtue of resisting, the pride of victory, the quivering thrill of reading books of Truth, the passion for study, and the devout piety are obviously meant for Madeleine. For the very words recall the youth of André Walter and Emmanuèle, or that of André Gide and Madeleine Rondeaux, at the time of their mystical and studious adolescence. But now Urien is tired of books and contemplation; and having wanted to act and to live, he found only disappointment. As for the symbolic Ellis, she understands nothing at all: "The fact that I was suddenly annoyed with her made me notice it; but I kept it to myself. She opens her large questioning eyes...." And their tedious walk continues.

In a grotto full of "lethargic bats" Ellis catches malaria, and it was then, says Urien, "that I had my first doubts as to identity.... I noticed that day—for the first time, I think—that her hair was completely blonde; blonde—and in fact there was nothing more to be said about it." But that blonde Ellis, that pale, insipid, ailing Ellis, seems to be someone else and not the girl he had loved: "At first I told myself, 'Ah! How she has changed!' But I can see now that she's someone else.'" Since he does not feel the same about her, he quite naturally thinks that she has either become different or is actually a different person. As she becomes paler and paler, and the first drift ice floats by, Urien decides that she must "fuse with God" and goes off without her, leaving her on the beach—for "she had almost no reality any longer"—with a few companions who had become "sick with boredom" and seemed to "die of drowsiness." The others go along with him toward the Pole.

It seems unquestionable that the Sargasso Sea episode shows a transformation in André Gide's feeling for Madeleine. At the time he was working on *Le Voyage D'Urien,* he wrote to Jeanne Rondeaux: "Why did your sister write me that gloomy letter—so dull, so weary? How disenchanted I am! And since it takes so little to bring my thoughts back to mind, I could think of nothing at first but how she had hurt me." Just as Urien could no longer recognize his love in the blonde Ellis, so André Gide was occasionally convinced that Madeleine's soul had changed, if not her hair.

The third stage of Urien's journey is toward a Sea of Ice. The travelers begin to feel the same "angelic gladness" they had experienced drinking the crystalline spring water. They have left the "beaches of forbidden joys" and the "gloomy banks of boredom," and are pushing on to "the divine city." Before they arrive, there is a curious episode in which Eric, the swan slayer, joyously slaughters a certain number of birds and destroys their brood. Moreover, to save his companions from scurvy, the disease that is prevalent on the Sea of Ice, he steals an "exquisite" hemostatic solution from the Eskimos. He is thus not only a slayer of birds but a thief, not only ruthless but without scruples.

The psychological interest of the episode lies in the contrast between the sadness of the austere Eskimos and the joyful vigor of the brutal Eric. The Eskimos symbolize the Puritans, and Gide finds their doctrine intolerable, for it leads to a mutilation of the being through refusing the demands of the body. Opposed to that idea is the healthy vitality of Eric, who satisfies his instincts spontaneously and cynically, a remedy later recommended by *Les Nourritures terrestres.* The assertion that puritanical ethics make souls sick and that the secret of healing them is in the recourse to the elementary forces of the being, up to and including cruelty, is a foretaste of Gide's immoralist crisis.

Meanwhile the seven survivors—for one of them, not having taken the solution stolen by Eric, died from scurvy—burn their ship and begin walking toward the North Pole, where in the bitter cold of winter they meet Ellis, sobbing; but this time she is wearing a dress the color of snow, and her hair is darker than the night. She is the real Ellis, not her pale ghost: "One day, on a river bank, I thought I had found you again; but it was only a woman; ah! forgive me! I had yearned for you for so long. And in this darkness, close to the Pole, where will you lead me now, Ellis! my sister?"[23]

Then Ellis speaks: she has her own voice back and, as before, points the way to God:

"Urien! Urien, sad brother! If only you had continued to imagine me! Remember our games of old. . . . I'm waiting for you beyond time, where the

[23] *Le Voyage d'Urien, O.C.,* I, 355.

snows are eternal. . . . Your journey will end, my brother. Stop looking back to the days of old. There are still other lands, lands you will not have known, lands you will never know. What good would it have done you to know them? Everyone has his own road and every road leads to God. But it is not in this life that your eyes will be able to see his glory."

Bent over the snow, she writes: THEY HAVE NOT YET RECEIVED WHAT GOD HAD PROMISED THEM—THAT THEY WITHOUT US SHOULD NOT BE MADE PERFECT. Then after that biblical phrase,[24] she stands up "like an angel laden with prayers," sets out again on the seraphic road, and begins to climb toward the sky, where she disappears into the cloud with the dawn: "She no longer looked in my direction; I saw her climb ever higher . . . and as the cloud opened up, I saw angels. Ellis was in the middle of them; but I was not able to recognize her." And so Ellis disappears among the angels, like the angelic Emmanuèle at the end of *André Walter,* in a veritable Assumption. Once again, the symbol of the incorruptible fiancée fuses with the angel.

Urien and what is left of his companions then take refuge in a block of ice so as not to sink into the snow. As they are carving out corridors and stairways, they make a singular discovery: a corpse lying in the transparent ice, preserved as if in a sepulcher. On the crystal coffin is the inscription: HIC DESPERATUS. The corpse is holding a paper in its hand, but the paper is completely blank: "Had we known beforehand that this was what we had come to see, we should perhaps never have set out; therefore, we thanked God for having hidden the goal from us. . . ." And so, on a rather surrealistic allegory, ends the macabre *Voyage d'Urien,* an experience of decomposition and reduction to nothingness worthy of Poe.[25]

Le Voyage d'Urien is Narcissus' journey not to the ends of the world but to the ends of himself, a disillusioned Narcissus who crosses the Pathetic Ocean with its sensual pleasures of which he is terrified, for they carry the infectious plague; the Sargasso Sea and its boredom, which he dreads because it leads to languishment; the Sea of Ice with its coldness, which he fears even more because it causes scurvy of the soul. "Every climate has its anguish, and every land its disease." Finally, Urien admits that his journey led him to nothing, if not to nothingness.

[24] Hebrews 11:39, 40.

[25] Its similarity to Poe's *Arthur Gordon Pym* is obvious.

33: Luc, or *La Tentative amoureuse* (1893)

> *"We'll call that the temptation to live.*
> *I'm going to write my essay on love to*
> *cure myself of such thoughts."*
>
> Letter to Marcel Drouin,
> March 18, 1893

O F THE painter Jean-Paul Laurens' two sons, Paul and Pierre, André Gide preferred the elder: "We were exactly the same age;[1] we were the same height, and had the same looks, the same walk, the same tastes." With Paul Laurens, Gide did not have to fear Louÿs' wounding jests or Régnier's more subtle irony about his puritanism:

Paul, who was no doubt brought up morally but according to Catholic and not puritanical morals, and who lived in artistic circles, constantly open to the provocation of art students and models, had managed to remain a virgin until he was over twenty-three. . . . Shyness, a sense of shame, disgust, pride, a misunderstood sentimentality, nervous fright due to a rather blundering experience (I think that was Paul's case)—all that holds a young man back.[2]

In short, André and Paul were equally shy, and an emotional inhibition held them back from adventure, just as it had formerly handicapped them at the beginning of school. Furthermore, although Paul was to become an artist, he was as excited about literature as about painting. And Gide, who until then had been rather unresponsive to painting, began reading books

---

[1] Gide was born in 1869, Paul Laurens in 1870, Pierre Laurens in 1875.

[2] *Si le grain ne meurt,* I, 289.

about art, went to the Louvre, studied the history of painting with the guidance of his friend, and even talked about going to Italy with him were Laurens to receive a Beaux-Arts scholarship.

The idea of a trip to Italy fascinated Gide. When Valéry was in Genoa, he had written to him: "Italy! How I dream of being there. Do you know that I want to live there, for several months perhaps, as soon as I am finished with the army—to recover a bit of refinement."[3] He had always been attracted by the Mediterranean shores. But actually, since the young symbolist poet had read Goethe's *Roman Elegies,* he gave the Italy of his dreams of symbolic significance. At the end of 1892 he had noted in his *cahier de lectures:* "Goethe's *Latin Elegies* will have had a greater influence on me than anything else this year. I was perfectly prepared by *Wilhelm Meister* and the rest."[4] One might wonder how reading *Wilhelm Meister* had prepared him for the *Elegies,* and the *Elegies* for a trip to Italy. The sequence corresponds to a psychological moment in the inner evolution of Gide, who from then on was dominated by a will to imitate Goethe.

According to his *cahier de lectures* of March, 1893, Gide was then still reading the *Roman Elegies,* and it was at that time, in Montpellier, that he wrote a letter to Marcel Drouin, which is most relevant to his evolution:

It seems to me that I have never lived. Have I spoken to you of Goethe's elegies? The Latin elegies—there are twenty of them. I don't say that you should read them: perhaps, if you're not predisposed to them, you'll find them just literature. I read them during these holidays, and they have slowly seeped into me; they have awakened all the wishes that were still dormant in me, and all those lines that affirm happiness and the joy of making everything live so that nothing of oneself wilts, every one of those lines is a desire for which I sigh each new day. And I'm completely open to all the temptations. How we shall have waited! This noonday sky torments me like a setting of impossible happiness.

Until the age of twenty-three, I will have lived completely as a virgin and totally depraved, so crazed that I sought everywhere for some bit of flesh on which to press my lips.[5] Laws, propriety, an unrelenting education of the self, the love of mystical tenderness—all that is what made up my first joys— the greatest, most solitary, and most anxious joys—and gave any pleasure in living the bitterness of sin. . . .

And after having quoted in German a few lines of the seventh Roman elegy, which begins with the words: "Oh! What happiness for me to be

[3] Letter from André Gide to Paul Valéry, September, 1892 (*Correspondance,* p. 172).

[4] December, 1892, unpublished.

[5] This sentence can be found almost word for word in Gide's *Journal* of March, 1893, p. 33.

in Rome!" he added: "We'll call that the temptation to live. I'm going to write my essay on love to cure myself of such thoughts."[6]

The essay was *La Tentative amoureuse ou le Traité du vain désir*. Gide got the idea for it at the beginning of January, 1893, from Calderón's *Life Is a Dream*. He had noticed a sentence in Segismundo's monologue which proclaimed the vanity of temporal desire and urged contemplation of the eternal. For one who was both a devotee of Schopenhauer and a symbolist poet, it was certainly a familiar theme, but actually Gide was tired of Schopenhauer and was beginning to feel unfaithful to the aesthetic of the Tower. He was no longer sure that, like Walter, he preferred dream to life. And he was so distracted by thoughts which he had absolutely no desire to "cure" and by new books to read that he worked at his *Traité*, conceived according to the principles of the school, as if it were an imposed task.

It was Marcel Schwob who advised him to read Ibsen, and during January and February, 1893, he read successively *The Lady from the Sea, Ghosts, A Doll's House, The Wild Duck, Rosmersholm*, and *Hedda Gabler*. Although Gide never spoke about Ibsen's influence on him, it was important in the evolution of his moral crisis. Almost all of Ibsen's dramas were based on the themes of revolt and emancipation. In them Gide found a demand for individualism, a protest against social conventions and laws, and the pagan concept of the joy of living as opposed to the Christian concept of renunciation. But he also found in them the prophecy of a natural Christianity, what Ibsen called the "third human state" which, based "on knowledge and on the Cross," tried to reconcile ancient naturalism and the Gospels. And he was particularly sensitive to the nostalgia of the southern sun that could be felt in the tragic works of the northern Protestant.

Of all the Ibsen plays he then read, he was most particularly captivated by *Ghosts*. The ghosts against which the virtuous Mrs. Alving rebels are the teachings of her Christian upbringing and the prejudices of her puritanical ethics. The play is the story of a revolution of the soul, a violent and sometimes frenzied protest, opposing *joie de vivre* to religious melancholy, nature to the law, and the individual to society. At the end of the play, Mrs. Alving, in a kind of wild despair, pushes her son toward everything that she had forever denied herself, toward the pagan ideal, toward the joy of living, toward the sun. "The Sun!" is the last exclamation in *Ghosts*.

What a strange coincidence that at the same moment in Gide's life, the works of Ibsen and Goethe combined to lead him toward the lands of the sun, the symbolic country of *joie de vivre*. The pagan happiness of Goethe's

[6] Letter from André Gide to Marcel Drouin, March 18, 1893 (quoted by Y. Davet in Autour des *"Nourritures terrestres,"* pp. 44–45).

Roman Elegies was complementary to the gloomy despair of Ibsen's heroine, who had wanted to renounce it forever. In his state of agitation at that point, Gide had neither the taste nor the patience for concentrating on his homework in symbolist literature. In fact, he moped about his plan for writing *La Tentative amoureuse* and had the unbearable impression of wasting his time.

During February, 1893, André Gide succeeded in convincing his mother to go along with him on a trip to Spain for the Easter holidays to attend the festival in Seville, a trip he wrote very little about in his *Journal* of the time, as he was too busy with the outside world. On his return to Paris at the end of April, he again started to keep his *Journal,* and wrote the following words, which are "still a prayer" but a prayer with a very new tone:

O God, let this hidebound ethics burst and let me live, ah! fully; and give me the strength to do it, ah! fearlessly, and without always thinking that I'm about to sin. I now have to make as great an effort to let myself go as I once did to resist. That morality of privation had become my natural morality to such a degree that now the other is very painful and difficult for me. I have to strive for pleasure. It is painful for me to be happy. . . . An easy ethics? Oh indeed not! The ethics that up to now has guided me, sustained me, and then depraved me was not easy. But I know very well that when I begin to taste of those things I had denied myself as too beautiful, it will not be secretly, as a sinner, anticipating the bitterness of repentance; no, but rather without remorse, vigorously and joyously. May I finally come out of the dream and live an energetic and full life.[7]

But for a young man who is in the habit of dreaming, it is no easier to "come out of the dream" than it is for a Puritan to taste of the things he had denied himself. "Really, there would be some joy in feeling vigorous and *normal.* I'm waiting."[8] While waiting, the symbolic tower presented him with a refuge and he went back to work on *La Tentative amoureuse.*

One day at the Laurens', one of their friends in common, Eugène Rouart,[9] gave Gide a pamphlet of verses by a poet who was a native of Béarn and still quite unknown in Paris: Francis Jammes. For the first time he heard the pipe of the "good faun from Orthez." He was immediately enchanted by the naïve and tender bucolic poetry, and found that it awakened "harmonics" in him. Gide was extraordinarily open to influence. He had only to discover Jules Laforgue in June, 1891, to feel in the right mood for writing *Les Poésies d'André Walter;* he had only to read a few

[7] *Journal,* 1893, pp. 34–35.

[8] *Ibid.,* p. 35.

[9] Son of the famous art collector, Henri Rouart.

of Jammes's poems in May, 1893, to feel in the right mood for writing *La Tentative amoureuse.* He felt that he had to leave Paris in order fully to enjoy spring in the country, and left for the Laurens' house in Yport, where he spent an entire month. The letters he wrote to his mother during that stay show that he was suddenly relaxed. There was no further mention of a moral crisis, Goethe, or Ibsen, but only of the gentle and peaceful life he was leading in the warmth of a happy home in the country with his friends. There was no trace of the fevers and revolts that constantly came up in his letters from Munich. He clearly seemed appeased.

Yet even in Yport, anxiety—his familiar demon—was not far away. In his unpublished journal, Gide then noted:

In a short while I want to be able to experience very different forms of life, and find in each one this crazed anxiety which becomes intense out of regret for the others. . . . And then other lives! other lives—everything we can manage to live of them, ourselves, and knowing that it's a mistake, savor the emotions so as to tell about them. . . . For Paul Laurens: what good is feeling an emotion, if others know nothing about it? or else it is selfish.[10]

For the moment he was finding happiness in the simple satisfactions he, as an obdurate littérateur, insisted on complicating:

All day I read, I take walks, *I'm going to snatch all the pleasure one can taste without women*[11]: at night I go out again, I'm thirsty and I quench my thirst, and that's very new for me. . . . Every day I go to have a sherbet, as others would go to attend classes—and I often go very far to get it and make myself very thirsy first, and then I get a kind of burning sensation and I patiently study my thirst . . . (my greatest sensual joys have been my slaked thirsts). . . . Besides, I know that this way of living is bad and that the writer must resist things, but today I find pleasure in maintaining the opposite and in creating suffering for myself for the time when I shall no longer gratify myself.

Is it true that a writer must resist things? It was what the author of *La Tentative amoureuse,* as a faithful symbolist, was trying to prove, but the reader of the *Roman Elegies* was not convinced of it any more.

His last letter from Yport, in June, alluded to an "award" that Paul had just received, an award that had serious consequences in Gide's life. As he explained in *Si le grain ne meurt:* "Paul Laurens received, as a prize for some competitive examination, a travel scholarship which obliged him to go into exile for a year; his choice of me as a companion decided my fate."[12] Since the beginning of the year, he and Paul had often dreamed

---

[10] Yport journal, June, 1893, unpublished.

[11] The italics are mine.

[12] *Si le grain ne meurt,* II, 287–88.

of taking a long trip together, preferably to Italy. And suddenly, thanks to a Beaux-Arts scholarship, the plan became feasible. Gide, for his part, was working hard to get his mother's consent, knowing that she had confidence in Paul Laurens, whose family she knew and whom she found well-brought up; and he was not long in convincing her. From that moment on, the painter and the poet spoke of nothing but their departure in October. Before arriving in Italy, Paul—a great admirer of Delacroix and Fromentin—wanted to paint in North Africa, where he expected to be inspired. Gide's imagination took fire. Africa! The Arab world! Ever since childhood he had been in raptures over *The Arabian Nights,* and after, through his reading and his trip *tras los montes,* he was charmed by the ghosts of the Arab world, as were so many Romantic poets and artists. Had not Goethe himself found a promised land in Hafiz' Orient?

In his *cahier de lectures* Gide wrote at the beginning of July, 1893: "From now to my departure, I want to read only what can give me still more of a feeling for life." The moment for trying to live had come, but first he had to finish his imposed task, *La Tentative amoureuse,* which he finally completed during the summer of 1893 at La Roque.

Although *La Tentative amoureuse ou le Traité du vain désir* was written in 1893, the edition of André Gide's complete works places it before *Le Voyage d'Urien.* It seems rather a pity, for its real chronological position is not without interest with regard to Gide's psychological evolution. In *Urien* he had shown the malady that took hold of Narcissus because of the refusal of desire or the absence of desire; he had still to show, so as to remain faithful to aesthetic solipsism, the disappointment that came from its fulfilment.

The preface warns us that the book is not a "very truthful tale" but rather the expression of a dream which "troubled my thought too much and demanded to be brought into existence."[13] The dream is that of carnal possession, which terrified André Walter and which Luc, his brother as far as shyness and squeamishness are concerned, is commissioned to try out. The adventure begins like a fairy tale, but the end is not a happy one.

Parallel to the sequence of seasons, Luc and Rachel's love is born in the spring, blooms in the summer, begins to die in the fall, and is dead by winter. When at the beginning Rachel declares: "My bed invites you," Luc politely remains there every night, but at the end he is no longer even polite: " 'Why do you leave then, Luc? ... Aren't you all my life?' 'But you, Rachel,' said Luc, 'are not all mine.' " The reason Luc is so disagreeable is that he is bored. He is tremendously bored, to the point that, in order to

[13] *La Tentative amoureuse, O.C.,* I, 223.

enhance their walks in spring, summer, fall, and winter, he feels the need to tell stories about the seasons. He tells them mostly for himself, as Rachel listens very little: " 'Talk,' she said, 'I'm listening now; don't stop if I doze off. . . .' " Luc is vexed, especially as his effort to construct his stories is all the more praiseworthy in that he is very tired: "Because of love, they slept very late; they awoke as if from drunkenness—very late, still tired from the night." But then summer came: "There was a moment at which their lives really merged. It was at the summer solstice; in the very blue air, the high branches above us were supremely slender." We never find out any more: "How brief joy is in a book and how quickly told."[14] In the autumn melancholy, Luc dreams of boundless life and coveted storms (horizons, the sea, the ocean, glorious shipwrecks, lost sailors, islands, winds). And the book ends without our having learned very much about Luc and even less about Rachel, except that she danced and she pleased, but less and less.

The affected style of *La Tentative* is delicate and sometimes exquisite; it has a studied awkwardness that recalls the Pre-Raphaelite attitudes which were then very highly thought of and brought back into fashion by Burne-Jones and Ruskin. But aside from that rather antiquated literary interest, the book is often considered a "sparkling trifle." On the other hand, it is not without importance with regard to Gide's personal life. More interesting than the listless intrigues of Luc and Rachel is the Author himself, who fortunately speaks from time to time to indulge in instructive reflections on himself. What is more, the Author is not alone. The couple Luc-Rachel gives rise to comparisons with the couple the Author-Madame, for that is how his companion is designated. And so there is a fourth person, discrete as she may be.

"Madame—I shall tell this story to you . . . this story is for you: in it I looked for what love brings: if I found only boredom, it is my own fault: you made me forget how to be happy."[15] If we allow that the imaginary Madame is a fictional transposition of Madeleine Rondeaux, at the time that her refusal made André Gide despondent, then the sentence is less enigmatic. In fact, *La Tentative amoureuse,* often considered "a silly piece of nonsense," is a bitter book and a cruel one, considering for whom it was destined. Behind a delicate choice of seasonal flowers and rhetoric hides the disappointment of a man who is getting his revenge by ridiculing the satisfaction of love; this explains the vindictive and sharp style of the literary apostrophe to Madame, much as it is couched in flowery forms. After accusing her of having made him "forget how to be happy," which in itself is a lot, the Author continues, but in words so similar to the ones André

14 *Ibid.,* p. 231.

15 *Ibid.*

Walter used to speak to Emmanuèle that there can be no mistake about
whom he is addressing. Luc and Rachel "were unaware of the gesture that
thrusts aside the very thing one would like to embrace—as we did, ah!
Madame—out of fear of possessing and love of pathos." We can see that
the author has no more illusions as to the inner motivations for angelism.
The refusal of the gesture of love is the love of pathos, which identifies
passion with suffering, but it is also, and more deeply, the fear of possession.

The ambitious intention behind *La Tentative amoureuse* is more adequately expressed by its subtitle: *Traité du vain désir,* or "Treatise of Vain
Desire." For not only carnal possession is vain, but any real possession. The
objects of our desires are no more than ashes, and the epigraph of the
work is taken from Calderón's *Life Is a Dream:* "Desire is like a brilliant
flame, and everything it touched is reduced to ashes—a light dust that can
be scattered by a small wind; let us therefore think only of what is eternal." The example Gide chose is that of possession in love. Because Luc
wanted to embody his desire and triumph over his terror of carnal possession, he found boredom and, as Urien would say, fell into the Sargasso
Sea because of his fear of crabs and crayfish. His joy is no more than ashes.
But when the Author ends on the words: "Rise, winds of my thought—
and scatter the ashes," he means rather to collect them and, by means of
inspiration, magically breathe life back into them. No matter by how little,
Luc belongs to the "sad race" of Adam and will be haunted by the regret
of a lost paradise, but the Author is Narcissus, the poet, who will gather up
"the torn leaves of the immemorial Book, which contains the Truth that
we must know."[16] The example of Luc reminds Narcissus that desire must
not be satisfied and that it must remain desire in order to become material
for art. And the example can be generalized. The fact that desire is not
satisfied leads to symbolic satisfaction. For *La Tentative amoureuse* to
remain "amoureuse," it must remain an attempt that can succeed only
through art. "And each book is merely a postponed temptation."[17] Of
course, the poet must try to live, but he must not succeed and must transform every unsuccessful attempt into a work of art. Such is the aesthetic of
failure.

In his *Journal* of 1893, Gide made the following comment:

I wanted to point out, in *La Tentative amoureuse,* the influence of a book
on the one who is writing it, and during the very writing of it. For as it
issues from us, it changes us. . . . For example, I was sad because a dream
of unattainable joy was tormenting me. I relate it, and by detaching the joy
from the dream, I make it my own; my dream is disenchanted and I am

---

[16] *Le Traité du Narcisse, O.C.,* I, 213.

[17] Preface to *La Tentative amoureuse, ibid.,* p. 223.

full of joy. . . . Luc and Rachel want, also, to fulfil their desire; but whereas I fulfil mine in an ideal way by writing about it, they . . . want to plunge into it materially; and it gives them no joy.[18]

As Gide mentioned in a letter to Marcel Drouin, he wanted to write *La Tentative amoureuse* to "cure" himself of the temptation to live: it was meant to act as a catharsis for his desire, a purge for his passions. But did he actually succeed? For the catharsis to have been effective, he would have had to be freed from his "temptation to live." Yet we have only to turn the page of his *Journal* to realize that Gide was by no means "cured" of his "temptation to live" by *La Tentative amoureuse*. He no longer wanted his joy to come from more or less substitutive or sublimated symbolical attempts; he wanted to fulfil his desire. In fact, he could think of nothing but the sea, his "glorious crossing," his North Africas and his Italys. He was meditating on his long journey or, more precisely, premeditating.

[18] Pp. 40–41.

34: Premeditations

*"My impulse drove me not so much
toward a new land as toward* that, *that
Golden Fleece."*

Si le grain ne meurt, *II, 287*

S INCE childhood, André Gide was in the habit of self-examination. After his year of "dissipation" in Paris, he had felt the need to withdraw to Uzès, where he had decided to go back to his former state of being "the old man." After the eighteen-month period between his stay in Munich and his prospective trip with Paul Laurens, he made the contrary decision—to give full scope to "the new being." It was at La Roque, in the summer of 1893, that he became clearly aware of the deep changes that had taken place in him during those transitional years.

Obscure workings of the being—latent travail, births of the unknown, arduous deliveries—drowsiness, waiting; like chrysalises and pupae, I slept; I let form within me the new and already different being I was to become.[1]

It was in those terms that Gide, in *Les Nourritures terrestres,* evoked the chaotic period preceding his journey. He had greatly changed from *André Walter* to *Narcisse:* the Huguenot had become an aesthete. But the transition or, rather, the transformation that took place between the completion of *Le Traité du Narcisse,* in October, 1891, and his departure for Africa, in October, 1893, was just as important. His inner revolution came about not from the effects of his trip and hedonistic experiences but *before,* as he briefly and reluctantly indicated in *Si le grain ne meurt:* "But surely I am anticipating and will spoil my whole story if I give the impression that I

[1] *Les Nourritures terrestres,* I, 22.

had already attained a state of joy which I hardly imagined possible and, above all, hardly dare imagine permissible."[2] We can well understand the scruples of a writer whose story will obviously be improved if he presents his psychological and moral transformations as a consequence of his discovery of "enchanting novelties," and attributes much that came from the fruits of literature to the fruits of the earth. That was no doubt his reason for not mentioning in *Si le grain ne meurt* either the books he had read or the names of those instrumental in bringing about his "liberation," particularly Goethe's. When in 1926 Paul Claudel wrote that in Gide "the Goethean spirit finally prevailed over the Christian spirit," he put his finger on the outcome of a struggle that had begun thirty years before. Thanks to his *Journal,* that striking omission of Goethe's influence was rectified. And when Gide wrote, "But surely I am anticipating," the *Journal* clearly shows that he was not.

Nothing was more considered and more premeditated than Gide's departure toward the "fruits of the earth." It corresponded to a complete change in his moral and aesthetic attitudes, opposing a pagan ethics to Christian ethics and an art close to life to an art far from life. The *Journal* of summer 1893, in which Gide formulated his new ideal before acting on it proves that he had already renounced the Huguenot tower and the symbolist tower.

At the beginning of September, 1893, Gide wrote in his *Journal:*

All my efforts this year have been directed toward the difficult task of finally ridding myself of everything useless and confining with which an inherited religion had surrounded me and which limited my nature far too much; without, however, repudiating anything that could still train me and strengthen me.[3]

For Gide the Christian religion and Protestant ethics he had "inherited" were no longer an end in themselves, and, as such, he repudiated them; but he could still see them as a way of training himself, and, as such, he meant to use them: "You are dependent on everything that formed you. Do not balk at this apparent slavery, and understand that the more numerous the intersecting and mingling laws that hang over you, the more exquisite they are."[4] In addition, for our "free man" all the contrary influences had to stop fighting one another; they had to come to terms and he had to come to terms with them:

[2] *Si le grain ne meurt,* II, 286.

[3] *Journal,* September, 1893, p. 41.

[4] *Ibid.,* p. 46.

The nature of a Christian soul is to imagine battles within itself; after a short time, it is difficult to understand just why. . . . I spent my whole youth opposing two parts of myself which perhaps wanted nothing more than to get along.[5]

The de-Christianization expressed in those lines, which is evident when we realize what the stakes of the battle are for a Christian soul, can be explained by the name that immediately follows:

Goethe. Do we now say, then, that happiness is achieved by suppressing scruples? No. Suppressing scruples is not enough to make one happy; it takes more. But scruples are enough to keep us from being happy; scruples are moral constraints which some prejudices prepare for us. It is all a misunderstood harmony; we think that we can separate ourselves and go on alone, and immediately we oppose ourselves. A soloist must play along with the orchestra. . . . Scrupulous souls, timorous souls, they oppress themselves; they are as afraid of joy as they are of being blinded by a too blazing light.

Instead of struggles, Gide now speaks of harmony; instead of sin, he speaks of scruples; instead of virtue, he speaks of happiness or joy. That is how he interpreted the teachings of Goethe through the *Roman Elegies,* for which he had been prepared by *"Wilhelm Meister* and the rest."

What Gide particularly wanted to learn from Goethe at that time was the art of finding joy and profit in giving in to temptation:

Self-abandon seemed to me a higher wisdom; I had the feeling that I would find in it greater profit for my whole being. I know perfectly well that this was still a form of egoism, but a newer and curious form which satisfied more of my powers. I adhere to that expression: satisfy powers; it had now become my ethics. And then I wanted no more of ethics; I wanted to live powerfully.[6]

Gide's renunciation of the ethics he considered a "higher wisdom" is very similar to the "higher immorality" he found, or thought he had found, in Goethe:

Whence the two states: first the state of struggle; the world is temptation; we must not give in to things. Then the higher state, the state never attained by Proserpina, who always remembered having taken the pomegranate seeds, and into which Goethe soon entered and, no longer refusing himself anything, could write: I felt myself god enough to descend toward the daughters of men.[7]

Yet although the Olympian of the *Roman Elegies* cheerfully descended toward the daughters of men, from Faustina to the young Christiane Vulpius, the author of *Amyntas* was, as we know, to apply himself to other conquests for which Goethe's patronage might seem out of place. Here, a

[5] *Ibid.,* p. 42.   [6] *Ibid.,* Oct. 10, 1893, pp. 44–45.   [7] *Ibid.,* p. 43.

question comes up which is difficult to answer: when Gide took off with Paul Laurens, had he decided to give free rein to his homosexual tendencies? "Yes, Paul and I were resolved when we took off," he wrote in *Si le grain ne meurt*. But Paul Laurens was not at all a homosexual, and the sentence simply means that the two shy boys, both of whom were still virgins at twenty-three, did not intend to remain so.[8] And there is no doubt that his initial intention was to "normalize" himself:

From then on I put all my obstinacy into clinging to the decision that Paul and I had made to "renormalize" ourselves. . . . My natural inclination—which I was finally forced to recognize, but to which I still believed I could not consent—became stronger through my resistance; by struggling against it, I strengthened it, and in despair of ever conquering it, I thought I could change its direction. Out of sympathy for Paul, I went so far as to imagine desire; that is, I adopted his; we each encouraged the other.[9]

The passage, however, is questionable. For although Gide, when he wrote *Si le grain ne meurt*, considered his homosexual inclination as "natural," the young man of 1893 seemed still to consider it abnormal. And that is why he dared not give his consent; it was not out of fear of sinning, for he no longer believed in sin, but out of faithfulness to his new idea of a return to nature and the norm: "what influenced us the most was our horror of anything unusual, strange, morbid, or abnormal. And . . . I remember that we encouraged each other in the ideal of equilibrium, plenitude, and health."[10]

Yet the sophism that made it possible for Corydon to consent to his inclination had already begun taking shape during the crisis of 1893: "In the name of what God or of what ideal do you forbid me to live according to my nature? And where would that nature lead me if I simply followed it?"[11] He at once wondered whether by following his nature he would not be led very far from the general conception of nature, and thus had to reconsider, from his special point of view, the notions of anomaly and the norm. The problem troubled him so that he conceived the plan for a great work in which he would show that "the history of mankind could have been different, that our ways, our habits, our customs, our tastes, our codes, and our standards of beauty could have been different—and remain human all the same."[12] He was already asking the question that was to be at the roots of his future defense in *Corydon,* that of knowing whether what we call nature is not in fact custom. But if the so-called natural laws were

---

[8] *Si le grain ne meurt*, II, 289. It is astonishing that in order to carry through their simple scheme, the two young Parisians had to change continents.

[9] *Ibid.*, pp. 305–6.

[10] *Ibid.*, p. 289.

[11] *Ibid.*, p. 287.

[12] *Ibid.*, p. 291.

merely laws of convention, every individual would have the right to respect "his" nature and to follow his instincts and go anywhere he could find his *joie de vivre*. Even more important, every individual would be duty-bound to respect his original instinct, whose very originality would contribute to the harmony of the whole, a harmony that would not exclude its dissonance:

I began to realize that duty was perhaps not the same for everyone and that even God himself might be horrified at the uniformity against which all nature protested, but toward which, it seemed to me, the Christian ideal tended by claiming to subdue nature. I came to accept only individual moralities, which occasionally proposed contrary imperatives.[13]

All the problems of ethics and habits then troubling his mind could not be resolved immediately. He therefore decided only to "strive for joy . . . In that way was I not following perfectly natural laws?" In his *Journal* of October 10, eight days before his departure, he wrote a few lines that were very significant of his mood:

I was like a sailor who drops his oars and relies on the tide. . . . My will, so constantly strained and taut, relaxed for lack of use; at first I was somewhat uncomfortable; and then even that disappeared and merged with the infinite charm of living—living any way at all. It was the great rest after the long fever; my former anxieties became incomprehensible to me. I was surprised at how beautiful nature was, and called everything: nature.[14]

And for the first time, he addressed an imaginary disciple whom he called Nathaniël and who was to become important in *Les Nourritures terrestres*:

Let us beware, Nathanaël, of all the instruments of happiness. And most important, let us not choose them. We cannot choose, to begin with, but it is even dangerous to think that we do choose; for in order to choose, we must judge; and judging implies . . .[15]

Could the missing word, replaced by ellipsis dots, be "conscience"? It would seem probable, judging from the corresponding passage in *Si le grain ne meurt:* "I was like Prometheus, who was amazed that man could live without an eagle and without being devoured by it. Actually, I unknowingly liked my eagle; but I was beginning to compromise with it."[16] In Gide's mythology the eagle is the conscience. Its most formidable characteristic is its pentrating glance, sharpened by a puritanical upbringing.[17] Our Promotheus, determined to compromise with his eagle, in other words, come to terms with his conscience, and even with heaven, had first to

---

[13] *Ibid.,* p. 275.

[14] *Journal,* 1893, p. 45.

[15] *Ibid.,* p. 47.

[16] *Si le grain ne meurt,* II, 286.

[17] The conscience compared to an eye is an ancient metaphor, brilliantly used by Victor Hugo in his poem *La Conscience.*

attack the aquiline eye. He tried to blind the devouring bird, much before ravenously devouring *it* during a succulent meal at Coclès'.[18] The theme of putting out the eagle's eye, a symbol of the moral blindness to which André Gide was already aspiring, coresponds exactly to the theme of a blind girl's happiness in *La Symphonie pastorale.* And we know from *Si le grain ne meurt* that Gide told Paul Laurens *before* their departure about the subject of his future work:[19] as the heroine was born blind, she could in all innocence give in to her instincts and the impulse of her heart, for according to the Gospels, "If ye were blind, ye should have no sin."

The 1893 *Journal* constantly encourages a surrender of consciousness, as well as of the conscience. Gide seemed to want to renounce not only morality but judgment, reflection, psychological lucidity, and everything that was opposed to his spontaneous impulses, to the "infinite charm of living— living any way at all." After having put all his confidence in the vigilant eye of his conscience, he intended to adopt the policy of the blinded eye.[20] In order to live blindly, he had to put out the eye of his eagle.

Can this moral revolution and glorification of "life for life's sake"[21] be imputed to Nietzsche as well as to the influences previously cited? What did Gide know of Nietzsche before his departure? This historical point is of real importance, since the moral crisis so clearly evidenced in the 1893 *Journal* has often been attributed to the influence of *Zarathustra.* Although there is not one mention of Nietzsche in either his *Journal* or his reading notebook of 1893 or before, Gide did write to Jeanne Rondeaux at the end of November, 1891: "Nietzsche is a . . . Wyzewa is a . . . No, really—the article cannot be taken seriously. . . . In any case, Nietzsche is not a philosopher."[22] He had no doubt read Théodore de Wyzewa's article on Nietzsche in *La Revue Bleue* of November 7, 1891, and perhaps Jean de Néthy's in the April 25, 1892, issue of *La Revue Blanche,* of which he was an assiduous reader. Of course, translations of Nietzsche by Henri Albert and Marcel Schwob, whom Gide had known since 1891, were published in *Le Mercure de France.* And it is easy and logical to conclude from

[18] "I ate it without bitterness: had I not suffered so much from it, it would not have been as plump; had it not been as plump, it would have not been as delectable" (*Le Promethée mal enchaîné, O.C.,* II, 158–59).

[19] *Si le grain ne meurt,* II, 291.

[20] Roger Bastide, in his remarkable article "Les Thèmes gidiens" (*Cahiers du Sud,* 1955), noticed the great symbolical importance of the theme of the blinded eye in Gide's works. Of course, it does not always have the same significance (cf. *Œdipe*), but it often indicates a surrender of moral and psychological lucidity in favor of spontaneity.

[21] *Journal,* 1893, p. 46.

[22] Unpublished.

that, as did Mme. Renée Lang, that Nietzsche had a direct influence on
Gide. However, as the complete absence of Nietzsche's name in the *cahier
de lectures* of that year, from which no page was either pulled out or
crossed out, is certain, it is probable that Gide's only knowledge of the
great philosopher came from magazine articles and the conversation of
friends. Nietzsche's hour was still to come.

Gide's meditations during the summer of 1893 reveal, also, a new way
of considering the artist's personality and the relations between art and
life. Up until then, Gide had seen the artist as a separate being who, like
the Narcissus of his *Traité,* must not mix with other men if he is not to lose
his originality. But, again under Goethe's influence, he proceeded to re-eval-
uate the notions of originality and banality:

Originality: first degree. I am omitting the lower degree, which is no more
than banality, in which man is no more than a group (he constitutes the
crowd). Therefore: originality consists in denying oneself certain things. But
above that, there is a higher state, which Goethe attains: the Olympian. He
understands that originality is limiting, that by being personal, he is just
anyone. And by letting himself live in things, like Pan, everywhere, he
finally rids himself of all limits except those of the world itself. He becomes
banal, in a superior way.[23]

An attitude such as that implies confidence in a kind of pre-established
harmony between the universe and a universal spirit capable of understanding it, a "wild optimism"[24] in the relations between the ego and the
world. It was then that Gide used the following Latin phrase as an epigraph to his *Journal:* "Proprium opus humani generis totaliter accepti est
actuare semper totam potentiam intelectus possibilis"—the motto of a certain humanism or, as he was later to say, of "classicism," which he defined
as the aspiration to a superior banality.[25]

He did see, however, that refusal of limits is a possible danger to the
very existence of the personality:

There is a danger in trying to experience that superior banality too early.
If we do not absorb everything, we lose ourselves in it completely. The mind
must be greater than the world and must contain it; otherwise it pitifully
disintegrates and is no longer even original.[26]

[23] *Journal,* 1893, p. 42.

[24] Preface for a second edition of *Paludes, Mercure de France,* XVI, November,
1895.

[25] "The great classical artist . . . strives for banality. If he attains that banality effort-
lessly, he is surely not a great artist!" (*Incidences,* p. 38).

[26] *Journal,* 1893, pp. 42–43.

But is not the risk of disintegrating, which can be fatal for a man, profitable for a real artist? "The words of Christ, 'whosoever will save his life (his personality) shall lose it,' are just as true in art."[27] The meaning Gide gave to those words in 1893 he put in parentheses: "his personality," signifying the artist's personality. And from that time on, he though only in those terms. This later text gives new scope to his previous remark: "Self-abandon seemed to me a higher wisdom; I had the feeling that I would find in it greater profit for my whole being," in other words, greater profit for his works.

His works! The works still to be written were Gide's main concern, and his entire moral and intellectual transformation was taking place in relation to them. For he not only transformed himself with them in mind, but was equally transformed by them. For example, the creation of his symbolist doubles—Walter II, Narcissus, Urien, Luc, and Tityrus—did much to contribute to the change in his attitude toward symbolism. Walter thought he had found a cure for his malady and his anguish by taking refuge in the symbolist coterie, but in experimenting with the doctrine through fictional heroes who live by proxy, the doctor wondered whether the cure was not worse than the malady. It would thus seem that Gide's symbolist experiences were instrumental in pushing him in exactly the opposite direction, "just as in physics one sees those free-hanging vessels, full of liquid, pushed—as they empty out—in the opposite direction from that of the liquid's flow."[28] Psychoanalysis has sought to define symbol as the representation of a complex; actually, it is not only the projection of a complex but its transformation. In his *Psychanalyse de l'art*, Charles Baudoin rightly emphasized this point of view: "A symbol represents a complex in travail, a complex in the process of transforming and evolving, a complex which tries to assimilate new elements."[29] That heuristic function, coresponding to the workings of a symbol, is similar to what one might call the function of a double. In the "obscure workings," the "latent travail," and the "arduous deliveries" which made for the transition from the old man to the new being, Gide's literary creations played as important a part as that of the literature he was influenced by.

The active influence of symbolism was then followed by a reactive influence. As a reaction to its contempt for reality, nature, and life, Gide wanted to bring about a return to reality, nature, and life. We know that the symbolist movement itself developed in protest to realism and naturalism. For all that, Gide was not to become a naturalist writer, a role for which he was eminently unsuited, but like Goethe, he was to seek a kind of alliance between "truth and poetry." While still far from the classical

[27] *Ibid.,* p. 49.

[28] *Ibid.,* p. 40.   [29] P. 226.

mastery of his model, he was first to train himself in lyric realism, sometimes called naturism, the style of his first "deviation," *Les Nourritures
terrestres.* After his Schopenhauerian pessimism came a "wild optimism";
after Narcissus' solipsism, a form of pantheism; after abstract art, that ab-
stracter of ideas, a return to concrete things, sung with a dogged enthusiasm. "As I drew nearer to the things I once scorned, they appeared to me
more attractive and more beautiful. And it is for them that, completely
beguiled, I set out on my travels."[30] Those lines, as well as many others in
the 1893 *Journal,* show that Gide was in his *Nourritures terrestres* mood
before his departure.

But with what name shall we refer to that mood? Is it possible to symbolize the new metamorphosis of his personality by a myth? Gide is no
longer Walter, and he is no longer Narcissus; he is someone else. To my
mind, the myth of Lynceus, the faithless keeper of the tower, as represented by the Gidian mythology, corresponds perfectly to this new phase
of his inner evolution. Gide did not write a *Lynceus,* but he had been
immediately struck by the character in Goethe's *Faust,* Part II. "To be
Lynceus," he was to write in his 1894 *Journal,*[31] and he used the Goethean
song of the keeper of the tower as an epigraph for the sixth book of *Les
Nourritures terrestres,* entitled "Lynceus."

In Greek mythology Lynceus is one of the Argonauts known for his
penetrating sight which allows him to see what happens in the heavens
and in the hells; his lynx-eye sees through the walls. In *Faust,* Part II,
Lynceus is the watchman who scans the horizon and, lucidly vigilant, gives
notice of everything that approaches the fortified castle. He is the lookout
man, the sentinel, the soldier on guard, always on the alert, always on the
qui-vive to give notice of any danger and to recognize the friend or the
enemy: he is responsible for the security of the others who are able to sleep
because he is on the lookout. "Born to see, he must look."[32] In the third
act Goethe shows the impeccable watchman at fault for the first time: he
neglected to announce Helena's arrival. He admits that he is guilty; he
betrayed his mission and does not try to defend himself: "I completely
forgot my duties as a watchman." But he explains his sin: his eyes were
dazzled by the appearance of Helena, the embodiment of beauty. The
goddess intercedes in his favor and manages to get him reprieved, but he
is still at a loss. Before, he had been proud to watch over the inner treasures
of the castle, but now he doubted their value and his mission. What was

[30] *Journal,* 1893, p. 44.

[31] P. 56.

[32] "Zum sehen geboren. Zum schauen bestellt" (Goethe, *Faust,* Part II).

all that and the satisfaction of fulfilled duty compared to the dazzle of beauty and the intoxication of desire? "I carefully guarded those treasures and considered them my own. ... Now I think they were vain." Compared to the dazzling moment, "all is empty, all is nothingness."

From the Goethean myth of Lynceus, Gide would seem to have drawn a lesson in the surrender of the will: because he had a revelation of beauty and desire, Lynceus understood the vanity of his inner treasures. And deforming the myth for his own use, Gide saw it as an invitation to forsake the "deceitful tower," the Huguenot tower of moral resistance to sin, as much as the symbolist tower of the dream as opposed to life. From an ethical point of view, Lynceus is the antithesis of André Walter; from an aesthetic point of view, he is the antithesis of Narcissus.

"But Nathanaël, here I want to speak to you only of *things*—not of the INVISIBLE REALITY."[33] All the things he speaks of, whether they be springs or thirst, shadows or light, he speaks of for themselves, or more precisely, for the physical, visible, tangible joy they give to his senses. Narcissus lived in the past, seeking in appearances a reflection of the lost paradise. Lynceus lives in the present, in the sole eternity of the moment. He lives in a hazy admiration of everything and repeats, in the manner of Goethe's Lynceus: "O my blessed eyes—Whatever may come to pass—Everything that you saw was so beautiful!" He is no longer like Narcissus, bent over his reflection in the water; he has become a hunter of sensations, emotions, and images.

No doubt the Gidian Lynceus' sensations, emotions, and images belong to a later period than the one we are studying, for they were gathered during his journey; but what is important to bring out here is that the "Panic" frame of mind of the fruits of the earth's poet was but a development of the "inclination to pantheism" emphasized in the 1893 *Journal. Les Nourritures terrestres* was to be the realization and illustration of Gide's summer–1893 program, his "constant preoccupation" with joy, his "emotions which opened out like a religion," his renunciation of judgment and choice, that receptive frame of mind which was soon to be called "availability," and above all, the "self-abandon" he represented as a voluptuous surrender of the personality. "For have you noticed that there was *no one* in this book? And that even I myself am nothing but Vision? Nathanaël, I am the keeper of the tower, Lynceus."[34]

The encounter that changed Gide's inner destiny, like Lynceus' encounter with Helena, was above all that of the pagan ideal of joy and beauty found in Goethe, "the ideal of equilibrium, plenitude, and health," which he, like Goethe, embodied in the Greek goddess, the symbolic

[33] *Les Nourritures terrestres,* VI, 134.

[34] *Ibid.,* p. 145.

Helena of *Faust,* Part II. For him, as for many other poets of his time, Helena was the Hellenic ideal of the harmonious development of all man's forces, as opposed to the "sacred lack of balance" he henceforth considered Christianity: "I do think it was my first aspiration toward what is today called 'classicism'; I could never convey just how contrary it was to my early Christian ideal."[35] To Gide, as to Edgar Allan Poe[36] and Goethe, Helena was a psyche, a symbol for the achievement in a human personality of the return to the soul of ancient Greece, at least as he imagined ancient Greece. She represented the psyche in which all Olympia was in equilibrium. And that is why he described himself as setting out to conquer a harmony which "must be my supreme objective and my tangible reason for living."[37] The young traveler became so haunted by that Mother of the classical ideal that he went so far as to find the image of his new psyche in the form of a city, and walked around in it as if in search of a shadow. Thus in evoking his first vision of the "white, serious, classical Tunis in autumn," he confessed that "in the evening, wandering through its regular streets," it made him think of "Helena of *Faust,* Part II, or of Psyche, 'the agate lamp in her hand.' "[38]

In point of fact, when he set out on his long journey, his frame of mind was that of his Lynceus, after he had resigned his post as keeper of the tower:

The night had lasted long enough. From the top of the tower I called out to you, dawns! Dawns that are never too radiant! Until the night ended, I clung to the hope of a new light; I don't see it yet, but I'm hoping; I know on which side daylight will break. Indeed, a whole people is getting ready; from the top of the tower I hear a clamor in the streets. The day will break! The people feel festive and are already walking to meet the sun. What have you to say of the night? What of the night, watchman? I see one generation climbing up and I see one generation going down. I see a vast generation climbing up, climbing up all armed, all armed with joy, toward life. What do you see from the top of your tower? What do you see, Lynceus, my brother? Alas! Alas! Let the other prophet weep; night is coming and so is day. Their night is coming and so is our day. And let those who will sleep, sleep. Lynceus! Come down from your tower now. The day breaks. Come down into the plain. Look at each thing more closely. Come, Lynceus! Draw near. Here is the day and we believe in it.[39]

[35] *Si le grain ne meurt,* II, 289–90. The meaning Gide gave to the word "classicism" is open to discussion; "paganism" would probably be more exact.

[36] Cf. André Gide's letters to Paul Valéry, June 21 and July 25, 1892 (*Correspondance,* pp. 153–67) and *Feuillets de route* (1896), p. 69.

[37] *Si le grain ne meurt,* II, 287.

[38] *Journal,* 1896, p. 69.

[39] *Les Nourritures terrestres,* VI, 145–46.

35: Departure

"I decided not to take my Bible with me."

Si le grain ne meurt, *II, 290*

AVING considered André Gide's new amoralistic, or at least hedonistic, frame of mind, one might surely wonder how it could have been compatible with his steadfast love for Madeleine Rondeaux. Gide himself explains in *Si le grain ne meurt*. After declaring that his heart was "completely taken up" by his love, he went on to say:

But I had decided not to let it stand in my way. After my *Cahiers* was published, my cousin's refusal had perhaps not discouraged me, but it had forced me to suspend my hopes; besides, as I have already said, my love was still almost mystical; and I could not then have realized that the devil was deceiving me by making me consider as offensive the idea of mixing it with anything carnal. *In any case, I had made up my mind to dissociate pleasure and love;* and I even felt that the separation was desirable, that if the heart and the flesh were kept apart, pleasure would be purer and love more perfect.[1]

What André Gide says about the constancy of his love for Madeleine certainly corresponds to reality, but in *Si le grain ne meurt* he never mentions the one fact that would exonerate him: his cousin's utterly discouraging attitude. Ever since October, 1892, when she had expressed the desire that each one feel free to marry if he saw fit, they had been seeing each other very infrequently and their correspondence had become irregular and without any real intimacy. Nothing in his cousin's attitude gave Gide the

[1] *Si le grain ne meurt*, II, 288–89. The italics are mine.

right to consider her as his future fiancée. Yet although he felt free to do as he pleased, he continued to love "Emmanuèle" as much as ever. That emotional tie with the past kept him from completely repudiating the religion and the Christian ethics to which he was more attached than his *Journal* would give us to believe. An analysis of the days before his departure gives ample proof of it.

From September 15 to September 22, Gide again stayed with the Laurens in Yport. He then went to Paris to join his mother, and left her on October 6, stopping in the vicinity of Nîmes to say goodbye to his Uncle, Charles Gide. On October 8 he wrote his first letter to his mother:[2]

As I don't want you to be too sad, I am writing to you immediately; then you will feel that I have not quite left yet. . . . I shall arrive in Marseilles on the 12th; you must send me (and quickly) to the Hotel Terminus: 1. my visiting cards, which are in the middle drawer of Anna's[3] little desk—2. a book bound in black cloth and leather—*La Logique de Port-Royal*—which is on the edge of papa's bookcase, on the left—in a pile—3. *The Elective affinities*—in German—Goethe—which I think you can find rather cheaply at Fichbacher's or some other foreign bookstore—4. a thin Bible (Segond) cloth-bound.

Nathanaël had thus not yet decided to burn all the books, and in fact he took a cargo of them in his trunks. But the choice of those he intended to add at the last minute is most interesting, especially the Bible, the last but not the least. Speaking about his new ideal in *Si le grain ne meurt,* he did write:

I could never convey just how contrary it was to my early Christian ideal; and I once understood it so well that I decided not to take my Bible with me. Although this perhaps seems insignificant, it was of the highest importance: up until then, not a day had passed without my going to the Holy Book for moral sustenance and advice. But it was for precisely that reason, because the sustenance had become indispensable, that I felt the need to cut myself off from it. I did not bid Christ farewell without a deep struggle, so that now I wonder if I ever really left him.[4]

There is no doubt he wanted to detach himself from the Bible to begin with, but he finally broke down and asked his mother to send it to him, which she did with alacrity. Hardly had he returned to his Protestant family's surroundings than he went back on his decision. And the same thing can be said for his choice of *La Logique de Port-Royal*, a masterpiece of Jansenist rigor by "the great" Arnauld and Pierre Nicole. The third book he asked his mother to send him, Goethe's *Elective Affinities,*

[2] Unpublished.   [3] Anna Shackleton.   [4] *Si le grain ne meurt*, II, 290.

would appear to be just as significant a choice in quite another way. Gide, who had brought along many other books by Goethe, had already read *Elective Affinities* and knew what it represented with relation to his illustrious model's life and works. At the core of the novel there is the mystical figure of Ottilia, whose resemblance to the "ideal image" of Emmanuèle as André Walter had imagined her seems particularly striking. Nothing could be more different from Ottilia's "mysticism" than Helena's "classicism." Between the heroine of *Faust,* Part II, and the heroine of *Elective Affinities* lies all of Christian civilization.

Gide's change of heart on October 8, 1893, is an interesting development in his general evolution. He wants to bid Christ farewell, but he takes along the Bible. He wants to renounce logic and morality, but he takes along the most moral of logical treatises, that of Port-Royal. He wants to give up chastity and freely enjoy his body, but he takes along the *Elective Affinities.* Prometheus still loves his eagle; or at any rate, the young Theseus, just as he is about to confront the "dragon" of sexuality, tries to find Ariadne's clew, which ties him to his pure love.

After a visit with his paternal grandmother in Uzès, Gide met Paul Laurens in Toulon and proceeded to Marseilles. On October 18 he wrote to his mother:

Our boat leaves in an hour; we have our tickets and we've checked our baggage. I have but a moment to let you know that all is well. . . . Although the weather is still very fine, thin clouds are beginning to appear—not enough to spoil this admirable view of Marseilles—from the room in which I'm writing to you, at Paul's family's where I have just lunched, I can see the entire harbor, the islands, the mountains, the city in a splendid light. We are up on a hill, just a bit lower than Notre-Dame de la Garde. At the Hotel Terminus I received your two excellent letters which touched me deeply. I like everything you tell me. I shall "answer" you—as soon as I have more time—received another letter from Georges Pouchet—very pleasant, with regard to my book—from Rouart a letter of introduction to General Leclerc—Paul has one too, so it's really excellent. Adieu. I must leave now—you shan't receive any more letters until Tunis—that is, in almost a week I think. Much love to Aunt Claire.—Your André.[5]

And so on October 18, 1893, André Gide took a boat from Marseilles and set off across the Mediterranean on the journey he imagined as his odyssey: "The elite of Greece, setting sail on the *Argo,* did not tremble with more solemn enthusiasm."[6] The escaped prisoner from the Tower no longer compared himself to the sad passengers of Urien's boat but to the adventurous Argonauts, among whom was the young Theseus.

[5] Unpublished.   [6] *Si le grain ne meurt,* II, 288.

PART II

Transformation

36: Illness in New Surroundings

> *"Africa! I kept repeating the mysterious word, filling it with terrors, alluring horrors, expectation. . . ."*
>
> Si le grain ne meurt, *II, 292*

s soon as he arrived in Tunis, André Gide had the feeling of being out of his element, especially as the city then had all of its oriental character:

The rue Marr and the Place des Moutons were still such that one had no idea where one had been taken to, and I don't think that the farthest point of the Far East or the most central part of Central Africa would have had a more stupefying taste of exoticism. A different form of life, in which everything is accomplished on the outside—very full, ancient, classical, established; still no compromise between Eastern civilizations and ours.[1]

His first letters to his mother conveyed his enchantment with the exoticism of a people out of *The Arabian Nights:* "Tunis is marvelous: every time we go out, we are inexpressibly dumfounded; Tunis is more different and bewildering than is possible to believe; you never meet a Frenchman."[2]

Delighted as he was, he from time to time complained of overwhelming fatigue, which he attributed to the climate—"we live in the midst of the Sirocco"—and he could not get rid of a cold he had caught before he left. At night, unable to sleep and perspiring continually, he wrote verses he

[1] *Journal,* 1896, p. 69.

[2] Letter from André Gide to his mother, Oct. 22, 1893, unpublished.

thought wonderful until dawn, at which point he found them execrable. They were the first fragments of *Les Nourritures terrestres.*

The two travelers set out for Biskra, stopping en route at Zaghouan, Kairouan, and Sousse. But at Sousse Gide was so weary and short of breath that Laurens had to go out and look for a doctor. In order not to worry his mother, Gide concealed the seriousness of his condition from her, but he did write to Albert Démarest that the "medical officer" had diagnosed his case as pulmonary tuberculosis:

My very good and dear Albert,

I'm so sorry that my first news to you is bad news. But there it is: we have promised you and Pierre the sad truths whenever there were any. And there are. We are stuck in Sousse. Ever since I arrived in Tunisia, my bronchial tubes or my lungs have worried me daily; now it's come: one lung is almost broken down and the other is in almost the same condition. Both are terribly congested. Suffocation, chills, sweats, some pain when breathing, a slight fever, great despondency—my voice has become a memory, nothing is missing. I had the medical officer come. He told us expressly that we should not go to see Souf and Djerid but rather Algiers, Biskra, or any city in which I should be able to recover—and as quickly as possible—for in two days' time. I could become consumptive and spit blood. These things are not madly gay, when one thinks that Sousse is a nasty city, where cholera is still almost rampant, and in fact all Tunisian cities are, more apt to weaken you than cure you, etc.—in other words, a city that is easier to enter than to leave. . . .

I'm going to write to mamma that as I was somewhat weakened by a cold, I consulted a medical officer who strongly advised me against crossing the desert—so that we must reach Biskra by sea and by rail, etc. I'll arrange that. . . . If by chance I get worse, I shall try to take advantage of her desire to travel, without worrying her, so as to try to get her to come to Algeria. . . . Adieu—I am your sickly—André.[3]

While in Sousse, despite his illness, Gide did not stay in bed. He would often join Paul Laurens, who was out painting in picturesque sites. Since he shivered even out in the bright sun, he would take blankets with him, carried by Arab children who were habitually on the lookout for foreigners at the hotel exit. "The one who went with me that day was a very young, brown-skinned Arab, whom I had noticed on the previous days among the group of little rascals who were loafing around near the hotel." Ali was his name. He offered to carry Gide's shawl and coat to the dune, and when they arrived, "laughingly" offered himself. Gide made no mistake about the invitation: "On the threshold of what is called sin, was I still hesitating? No; I should have been too disappointed had the adventure ended with the triumph of my virtue—which I had already come to despise and ab-

[3] Letters from André Gide to Albert Démarest, Nov. 12 and 14, 1893, unpublished.

hor." After a short feigned delay, he gave in: "His body was perhaps burning, but my hands found it as refreshing as the shade. How beautiful the sand was! In the divine splendor of the evening, what radiance clothed my joy!"[4] And so it was in Sousse, a few days before his twenty-fourth birthday, that André Gide had his first homosexual experience or, in the case that he had previously had ambiguous relations with one or another of his friends, which he formally denied—his first experience as a pederast, a man who loves young boys.

In Biskra, André Gide lived in "complete ignorance of day and date,"[5] a fact that would have stood in the way of any chronological classification of his letters had his very systematic mother not dated them herself. He and Paul Laurens settled down in the mission house of the Pères Blancs, a former convent that had been transformed into a hotel, in an apartment recently occupied by Cardinal Lavigerie. Upon arrival in Biskra, Gide found telegrams and letters from Mme. Gide, to whom Albert Démarest, despite his cousin's instructions, felt obliged to show the alarming letter he had received from Sousse. She asked for a medical report so that she might show it as soon as possible to Dr. Miard, André's doctor in Paris. He went to be examined by a Dr. Dicquemare who reassured him and found that his lung condition was improving.

He was also in a better state of mind. Gide found Biskra marvelous and his apartment, with its terrace that looked out on the palm trees, ideal. He and Paul got themselves a servant, a fifteen-year-old Arab boy, a veritable "black pearl": Athman.

He is the color of *racahout* and has very frizzy hair. I shan't give you any more information about him, knowing perfectly well that this much is all you need to start explaining to us, in your usual way, that he is no more than a rascal, that he'll surely take advantage of us—in other words, try to disgust us with him as much as you can.[6]

He then had a piano sent to him from Algiers, and asked his mother to send over certain scores of Schumann, Brahms, and Chopin, as well as some books he wanted to reread: Barbey d'Aurevilly's *Une vielle maîtresse,* Sainte-Beuve's *Volupté,* and Heinrich Heine's *Book of Songs,* which he had first read at the age of sixteen. He had again begun to write verses: "The beauty of the race here fills us with a vaguely erotic but rather more lyrical exaltation: I write verses the whole day."[7]

---

[4] *Si le grain ne meurt,* II, 300–302.

[5] Letter from André Gide to his mother, Nov. 24, 1893, unpublished.

[6] *Ibid.,* Nov. 30, 1893, unpublished.

[7] Letter to a friend, November, 1893, unpublished.

The general improvement did not last long. A nervous condition soon complicated his lung condition:

I suddenly had a serious nervous breakdown and as a result, everything about my condition is confused. . . . Really these past days there were times when I actually felt far from life. . . . Although I've been very solemn, I've not stopped being joyous. I notice that I love life with a strange passion. . . . I feel better when I sense the presence around me of some beautiful child who breathes.[8]

In the same letter Gide added: "During this period of debility I've been going through (will I ever get through it?), any emotion of sympathy has become exaggerated; I live mostly through affection." He then effusively thanked his cousin for his letter:

What you tell me about Rouen touches me—Rouen—it was there that we began to talk together. . . . I remember everything—the cemetery—and your visit with my three friends. One of them I love more than ever—without hope—*without any desire*[9]—and anyway why speak of such things . . . but they are impossible to forget.

He could not forget and, at grips with his illness in the solitude of Biskra, his thoughts went to Madeleine far more than to his mother, whose constant concern occasionally moved him, but was more often a source of irritation. Although he wrote to her regularly and not to his cousin, his letters were also meant for Madeleine, and he reproached his mother for not showing them to her as she had promised: "Yet you know that when one is far away, it is very painful to feel that one's confidence has been misplaced." He did not dare write to Madeleine, however—"I have not yet dared write to her"—and his silence shows how anxious he was about her feelings toward him, but he did not forget to congratulate her governess, Fraülein Siller, on her birthday, no doubt well aware of the duenna's influence.

Gide could not bring himself to stay in bed in Biskra any more than he could in Sousse. There was no question of his accompanying Paul on his painting expeditions, but he did walk about on the terrace of his apartment or in the public gardens. There, he liked to watch the Arab children at play. Their health, familiarity, and intimacy delighted him: "I was not in love with any one of them in particular but rather, indiscriminately, with their youth in general."[10] He tried to find models for Paul among the young boys, many of whom were related to Athman.

Athman himself was taking an increasingly important place in the

---

[8] Letter from André Gide to Albert Démarest, November, 1893, unpublished.

[9] The italics are mine.

[10] *Si le grain ne meurt*, II, 305.

household. His *joie de vivre,* his indolence, his general dawdling about, his beautiful stories, his colorful and naïve way of speaking (he called the lungs "the fan of the heart") enchanted Gide and Laurens:

He is indeed a charming little boy, who has unbounded esteem and affection for us; he is puffed up with vanity, so that he is very easy to manage; all of his monthly wage that he does not give to his mother he uses to buy vests of all colors, astounding *chiachias,* etc., so that he does us great honor.[11]

An enormous package of toys, which Gide had asked his mother to send for his little friends, arrived on January 8, and there is no doubt that it increased his popularity. When he went out, he was escorted by at least three of them, one carrying his jacket, another his raincoat, and a third the hood to his ulster. Yet during his first stay in Biskra, there was no reoccurrence of his Sousse adventure. Nothing sexual was mixed in with the childish games, which recall Michel's in *L'Immoraliste,* with the one difference that Michel was an unconscious pederast, whereas Gide was already aware of his inclination and still determined to struggle against it. After all, he had set out on his travels with the idea of "renormalizing" himself.

The plan of the two Parisians was helped along by the presence in Biskra of numerous Oulad Naïls. The girls of that Algerian tribe are known to prepare themselves for marriage by prostitution, and through selling their bodies, earn enough to buy themselves husbands. Gide was not insensitive to their exotic beauty: "Strangeness attracts me as much as the ordinary puts me off." One evening he and Paul went to a café and watched Meriem ben Sala and her "beautiful" cousin En Barka dance:

Meriem had amber-colored skin and firm flesh; her figure was full but *still almost childlike,*[12] for she was just a little over sixteen. I can only compare her to some bacchante, like the one on the Gaeta vase—also because of her bracelets which jingled like castanets and which she was continually shaking.

Even more than by Meriem's beauty and dark golden skin, the future author of *Amyntas* was attracted by her still childish youth, her turbulent liveliness, and her air of "savageness" and "vulgarity." While the girls danced, their brother, little Mohammed, thumped on his tambourine: "How beautiful he was! Half-naked under his rags, black and slim as a demon, his mouth open, a wild look in his eyes . . ."[13]

A few days after the family spectacle, Paul Laurens met Meriem and arranged for her to come to their flat that very night. She arrived in a whirlwind, jingling like castanets, dropped her double haik, then her dress,

---

[11] Letter from André Gide to Jeanne Rondeaux, Biskra, 1893, unpublished.

[12] The italics are mine. Given Gide's pedophilic tastes, the fact that Meriem was a woman-child or, better still, a child-woman, is not without interest.

[13] *Si le grain ne meurt,* II, 310.

kept on only her bracelets, and at once followed Paul into his room, before joining André in his. When on the following morning Athman, "his eyes lowered," entered his master's room, he saw Meriem ben Sala and André Gide in the bed that shortly before had been occupied by a cardinal.

Gide found the need to apologize for his prompt victory by invoking attenuating circumstances: "If I was valiant that night with Meriem, it was because when I closed my eyes, I imagined I was holding Mohammed in my arms."[14] Whether or not his phantasm of the young tambourine player contributed to his success, the desired result came about in the most natural way. Gide suddenly felt in a state of "extraordinary well-being" and optimism:

Meriem had done me more good, straight away, than all the doctor's counter-irritants. . . . My condition was so much a matter of hidden nervousness that it was not astonishing to find the congestion of my lungs relieved by that extreme diversion, and a certain equilibrium re-established.[15]

Whatever we may think of Meriem's role as a counterirritant, there is no doubt that the sickly young man had the keenest desire to continue a cure that was both agreeable and useful. It was decided that the Oulad Naïl would divide her nights between the painter's room and the poet's room. They really organized a life together, undisturbed by any jealousy, and André Gide found pleasure in sharing the "bacchante's" charms with Paul Laurens: "The fact was that we both then considered the carnal act rather cynically, and no feeling, at least in this case, was mixed in with it." As Pierre Louÿs had just sent him his last book, *Chrysis,* a poem about a courtesan, Gide answered, congratulating him on his work "of exquisite delicacy," and added: "I certainly admit that Chrysis is charming; in Biskra she is called Meriem: a delicate name and one I'm not yet sure how to spell . . ."[16] And so thanks to Meriem, the two friends lived happily until a telegram arrived, like the *deus ex machina* of Fate: Mme. Gide was arriving in Biskra.

"I was of course happy to see her again and show her the country," he wrote in *Si le grain ne meurt* with obvious kindness, "yet we were dismayed: our life together was beginning to shape up so well; would it be necessary to interrupt the re-education of our instincts that had only just begun?"[17] Gide blamed his mother's untimely arrival on Paul Laurens, who had sent an alarming letter to his parents concerning his friend's health, but in fact he himself was fully responsible. On January 26, 1894, he wrote to his mother:

[14] *Ibid.*

[15] *Ibid.,* pp. 310–11.

[16] Feb. 1, 1894, unpublished.

[17] *Si le grain ne meurt,* II, 311.

Why wouldn't you want to come? Just think: all the little boys are waiting for you and hope to see you; they have already told me several times that they had taken some other woman for you, made me walk over to look at her, thinking that she looked pleasant enough to be my mother.[18]

Of course on February 3 he tried to delay her: "If I understand correctly, this expedition will take place toward the end of March, for we plan to stay here another two months."[19] He did not know that Mme. Gide had already left to join him: she left Paris on February 2, arrived in Marseilles on the third, in Algiers on the fourth, and was in Biskra on the seventh. But meanwhile Meriem had turned up, and André Gide, who had imprudently provoked his mother's arrival, would have then liked to postpone it.

Nevertheless, on February 7, 1894, Mme. Paul Gide, followed by her faithful maid, Anna Leuenberger, and a considerable number of suitcases, arrived at the Biskra station. The best room in the mission house of the Pères Blancs had been prepared for her. But out of some mad imprudence or daring, André Gide and Paul Laurens had decided not to "cancel" Meriem, who came that night as usual to join the painter and then, in the early hours of the morning, knock at the poet's window. What happened was this: the shutters of Mme. Gide's room opened, and she bent out of the window just in time to see Meriem fleeing "like a ghost about to dissolve at the cock's crow."[20] But alas, the realistic Mme. Gide did not take the Oulad Naïl for a ghost, and she went to her son's room, indignant at the behavior of young Laurens. Then, "making a great effort," he dared say to her: "Besides, you know, she doesn't come only for him. She should be coming back." He expected an explosion of outrage, and what he got was a deluge of tears. It must have been a strange scene between the twenty-four-year-old man and his mother, a scene which perhaps partly determined Gide's sexual future. He did not have the heart or, as he put it, "the courage" to grieve his mother further, and he gave up Meriem.

However, the desires awakened by the Oulad Naïl were so harassing that André Gide and Paul Laurens went, clandestinely, "far from the hotel" where his mother was on the lookout and, for lack of Meriem, visited her cousin En Barka in her room. Unfortunately, "Caresses, provocations, nothing worked; I remained silent, and left her without having been able to give her anything but money."[21] In other words, this new attempt at "renormalization" ended "miserably" in failure.

The fiasco, to again use Stendhal's expression, was, in itself, probably not in the least alarming. The clandestine and forbidden nature of the nocturnal

---

[18] Unpublished.

[19] Unpublished.

[20] *Si le grain ne meurt,* II, 313.

[21] *Ibid.,* p. 314.

visit was enough to upset the emotional young man, so easily inhibited by any apprehension. But Gide did not attribute his fiasco of imagination, of which there are many examples in literature, to mere stage fright, and he was afraid; he thought it was something "irreparable." Like any man who suffers from an inferiority complex with regard to his virility, he saw his sexual failure as a catastrophe. Actually, from that point on, the fear of failure becomes the reason for failure, and if ever such unfortunate attempts are repeated, an anxiety-ridden man takes his inhibition for impotence. In a letter to Albert Démarest, Gide alluded to that consequence of his mother's presence:

I was really afraid that the harm done, most unintentionally, by her presence was irreparable, and I shan't begin to feel reassured for a few weeks yet. Put in this way, such things sound brutal; it would take too long to explain them to you . . . besides, we have never stopped showing (in fact, feeling) the deepest cordiality toward one another, and it has never entered mamma's mind that things might have been different before her arrival. But as I was just beginning to live—I mean, to be open to joy—I felt that having painfully come out of a cave, I suddenly fell back into it from the sixth floor.[22]

Gide made no new attempts and there was no further question of Meriem. He walked about in the country with the Arab children, and Mme. Gide indulgently watched her big son take pleasure in such safe companionship. His health was much improved and he could make rather long excursions. Spring was on its way, and Gide was as enchanted by his new surroundings as he was by a rejuvenation characteristic of of the convalescent: "With the combined help of climate and illness, I felt my austerity melt away and my brows unknit."[23] It was from that combination of new surroundings and illness that *Les Nourritures terrestres* was born:

I was lucky to be taken ill over there—very seriously ill, it's true—but my illness did not kill me—on the contrary—it only weakened me for a while, and had the distinct effect of giving me a taste for the rarity of life. It would seem that a weakened organism is more porous, more transparent, tendérer, more perfectly receptive to sensations. In spite of my illness, if not because of it, I was all receptivity and joy.[24]

Gide's senses were awakening and, in his dealings with his small companions, sensual pleasure was already "insidiously creeping into the idyll."[25] In his unpublished notes for *Se le grain ne meurt* he evoked his little friends in great detail. Although the notes never got beyond the draft stage, they show the extraordinary interest Gide took in each child:

---

[22] March, 1894, unpublished.

[23] *Si le grain ne meurt*, II, 305.

[24] *Le Renoncement au voyage, O.C.,* IV, 301.

[25] *Ibid.*

At the French school I knew even more little boys: there was Teli, who never came into my apartment; Madani, whom mamma called Magali; and Nöouï, whom mamma called Noé . . . they had masses of little brothers—but the only one of them I knew was little Mohammed, who was always making faces at me. Hamma (still Mohammed) . . . seemed to be a great friend of Ashour, the eldest of the class, a Negro, blacker than any of them, slender, handsome, with the eyes of a girl, very shy, and supposedly very studious. . . .

Another Hamma, older than the little one but younger than Ashour, had the reputation among all the children of being a thief—he always looked as if he were on the prowl, and was often found around the bend of a wall, crafty, defiant, laughing—he attracted me quite a bit; I should have liked to know him better, but the other little ones would have held it against me. . . .

What can I say about Ali? Haven't I already spoken about him a bit elsewhere?—that little face, more delicate than the others, that bulging forehead, that cruel mouth, that pinched nose . . . he was always playful or angry—his emotions followed one another too quickly. He never slept; he had headaches; he played frantically; he probably loved no one—but when he wanted something from you, he would become affectionate, charming, as coaxing as a girl. . . .

Lachmi and Achani were the two sons of the gardeners at Ouardi. . . . There were Mhamharr and Larbi, both of whom worked for Charles B. Mhamharr was black—completely black—and one day, turning a somersault, his *gandoura,* his only piece of clothing, stayed behind; Larbi, who was with us, shouted laughingly: "O! Monsieur Gide! Monsieur Gide! How black he is!!" But what can this story mean to anyone who did not hear that laughter as I did?

Larbi had several brothers; he was the youngest; and the next youngest, Bachir, I did not get to know until much later, for fear of attracting him at first, for I was afraid that so many others, hanging about the streets, would follow him to our apartment. Bachir was as elegant as a faun; and his snub-nosed face made you think of one. He soon came along with me on all my errands, whereas Athman followed Paul—each one of them chose his master that way, rather than our having chosen our valets. Bachir never asked for anything, perhaps because he thought he could manage better that way. He had an older brother, Lachmi, whom I saw only rarely. . . .

Sadeck, Athman's brother, although older than Lachmi, was, on the contrary, most affable to us. Sadeck was handsome, gigantic . . . The last evening that I saw him, I had gone to find him in a café near the Oulads; he was waiting for me; he knew that I was leaving at dawn the next day and kept repeating: "Ah! Monsieur Gide! Monsieur Gide!!"—knowing no other words in our language but saying that at least in a tone that touches me every time I think back on it. We went into a café . . . but I forgot to say this—the most exquisite of all—after having taken my hand, he kept it in his—my left hand in his left hand, so that it seemed very intimate—and we walked that way down the street.

Of all those young characters, the one who intrigued Gide the most was the disturbing Mohammed, Meriem's brother. He described him in the following terms:

Mohammed—Fantasio—Heinrich Heine—The tassel of his *chechia* was attached to his hair—a sneering head—or a serious death-head—vice or madness in his eyes—his burnoose constantly hiding the side of his face one could have seen in profile—a torn burnoose, an enormous flap of it always thrown over his arm—constant gestures with his hands. A highway prowler, he shot birds with stones which he threw admirably. You meet him at night in the Oulad quarter, always prowling, always in the shadows. He goes into the long and narrow café and chats—sitting in a circle with other children. Brushing against women, training for vice. . . . I had been out looking for him every day; so as to vary the opportunities, I would go down the road at different hours . . . and I dared not talk about him to anyone.[26]

No doubt the forsaken Meriem did not yet suspect that her former lover was that interested in her young brother. Otherwise the strange situation described at the end of *L'Immoraliste* would have already taken place: "She was not angry, but every time I met her, she laughed and joked about the fact that I preferred the child to her. She claims that I remain here principally on his account. Perhaps she is somewhat right. . . ."

After a month and a half in Biskra, Mme. Paul Gide, reassured as to her son's health and satisfied with his behavior, agreed to return to France alone, leaving André and Paul to make their way to Italy. As before, the two friends first spent a few days in Tunis. But there Gide's enthusiasm turned to boredom: "I am irritated with this boredom and I am becoming horribly depraved. Only *La Vie de Goethe* distracts me a little, even though it's in German."[27] During his stay in North Africa he had often gone back to the biographies of Goethe and to his *Roman Elegies* and *Elective Affinities,* in which his attention was drawn to the famous quotation from Lessing: "Es wandelt niemand unbestraft unter Palmen." He was already regretting the oasis of Biskra and the shepherds playing their flutes. "The palm trees bore me, but the shadow of the palms delights me."

[26] Unpublished notes for *Si le grain ne meurt.*

[27] Letter to a friend, March 30, 1894, unpublished.

37: Convalescence in Italy

> *"Europe bores me. . . ."*
> Letter to his mother, June 17,
> 1894, unpublished

AT THE time of his first reading of Goethe's *Roman Elegies,* Gide had anticipated the greatest joy on discovering Italy. But in April, 1894, he approached it in a precarious state of health. In Malta, as during the worst period in Biskra, he suddenly felt feverish, short of breath, and prey to overwhelming fatigue. He no more than crossed Syracuse, too weary and feverish to look at anything, and barely stopped at Messina and Naples, "sweating in the sun, shivering in the shade, and able to walk only on absolutely flat ground." As Paul Laurens wanted to see Pompeii, Gide left him in Naples and took off as soon as possible for Rome to consult a doctor.

When he arrived on April 13, he went to M. Guillaume, then director of the Villa Medici and to whom he had been recommended by Jean-Paul Laurens, to ask for the address of a lung specialist: "I must surely have asthma. The doctor found that I had no fever." Gide himself wondered whether he was not "more nervous than sick," and all the symptoms he described in letters to his mother are repeated almost verbatim in *L'Immoraliste* apropos of Michel's illness: "I think that in addition to my illness, I had some nervous disorder."[1] His diagnosis would appear to be correct. Meanwhile, back in Paris, Mme. Gide went to a great deal of trouble to deny the alarming news that was circulating about her son's health. Some people were already burying the pale Walter. But Gide did

---

[1] *L'Immoraliste*, p. 53.

not want to be thought cured, for if he returned to Paris, he had every intention of "returning as a self-avowed invalid and not seeing anyone— or at any rate, not going to see anyone."[2] His idea was to take advantage of his illness in order to secure the peace he would need in order to write.

Gide and Laurens settled down "very near both the doctor and the Villa Medici," in two ground-floor rooms facing one another on the via Georgiana. Gide rented a piano, as he had done in Menthon Saint-Bernard and Biskra, began to write again, and only left his lodgings to go to the gardens, to which he was driven, as walking winded him so: "I lead a fairly pleasant and monotonous life either in a public garden near my door, or at my piano, or before blank sheets of paper. I had to give up *seeing*—and nothing is more pleasant," he wrote to Albert Démarest.[3] And to his mother: "As walking quickly makes me short of breath and the streets exhaust me, I have decreed that Rome bores me and I propose to prove it. On the other hand, I one day propose to prove the contrary, if ever I come back in good health."[4] Letting Paul visit the Eternal City without him, he spent his days working.

He was then writing the poetry or poetic prose that was soon to become *Les Nourritures terrestres*. He sometimes worked closed in his room and sometimes walking alone in the public gardens, those of the Villa Medici— "as beautiful as Vergil's poetry"—the Villa Borghese, and the Pincio: "I spent the whole day in the hanging gardens of the Pincio, sitting down, or walking, writing verses, or thinking of Vergil, or just giving in to joy."[5] Those walks in the Pincio were evoked in *Les Nourritures terrestres,* and such moments of lyricism alternated with depression and nostalgia for Africa: "It is becoming a fixed idea with us, a morbid obsession. . . . I couldn't possibly express how bored we are here and how much we miss Kairouan and Biskra."[6] The covered tray on which their meals were sent in they named "Athman," in memory of the little servant at the Pères Blancs hotel:

Would you believe that our only joy at present is when we get together for meals—and talk about "over there"—oh, not Paris!—Africa—we would each give twenty Romes for twenty days of beginning again. Last night I awoke in tears: I was dreaming about it.[7]

[2] Letter from André Gide to his mother, April 19, 1894, unpublished.

[3] April, 1894, unpublished.

[4] April 13, 1894, unpublished.

[5] Letter to his mother, May 12, 1894, unpublished. In his letters there are frequent allusions to Vergil, whose influence was to be considerable in *Les Nourritures terrestres,* as Justin O'Brien has pointed out.

[6] *Ibid.,* April 22, 1894, unpublished.

[7] *Ibid.,* April 25, 1894, unpublished.

The letters from Athman and Dr. Dicquemare, giving news of Biskra and proof of how they were missed, only increased their nostalgia.

At the same time as he was writing *Les Nourritures terrestres,* Gide had started on another book which was to be the "negative" of it: *Paludes.* When in Biskra he received news of the Parisian literary groups, the contrast between his former existence as a littérateur and his new fervor as a wandering poet had given him the idea of writing a satire on sedentary life. He felt the need of ridiculing the temptations of the Tower he had known after *André Walter,* and in order to help himself "get beyond" them, he was to hold them up to ridicule by means of a comic character. "I'm working at something rather long and which is progressing rather well, but when my relatives read it, they will have me put in the lunatic asylum," he wrote to his mother; and in another letter:

I'm working at something rather difficult and which will give me a lot of trouble, for half of what I thought was completed has to be done over; but if I succeed, it will be pretty terrific. I'm dedicating it to young Rouart. . . . He is a charming boy, deliciously mad, whom I like very much.[8]

As we know, *Paludes* was indeed dedicated to Eugène Rouart.

The most important document on Gide's state of mind during his stay in Rome is the letter he wrote to Marcel Drouin on May 10, 1894:[9]

I have reached the happy state in which one no longer has any personal faith; this state, which for the philosopher would be skepticism, is for a man of letters what one might call a *state of dialogue;* it comes from an insight into the beliefs and morals of others, and from an ever-increasing and, above all, more profound comprehension of them; from the possibility of being touched in turn as much by one as by another—sincerely, passionately touched; and finally, from complete detachment from one's own opinion. Once again, it implies no *skepticism*—I mean, no psychological anxiety, no sadness, and no smile—only a more immediate perception of *life.*

And after having thus defined his new mentality, he set out to give "an historical account of this state" in a page of capital importance which must be quoted in its entirety:

You know that I was tending in that direction with all my might when we parted: literature was perhaps a little the reason, others' as much as my own; I was afraid it would get lost because of exclusively associating with Bacon's "idola," having got into the bad habit of considering nothing but *substitutes* for *things.* As for me, who had squeezed my soul like a sponge so as to draw out *Les Cahiers* which you've read, the habit of keeping a journal had made me know myself so well that introspection became insipid the day it held no further surprises for me. I felt more and more that the best in me was

---

[8] *Ibid.,* May 22 and 28, 1894, unpublished.

[9] Quoted by Y. Davet, pp. 65–68.

that unknown resonance, that possibility for sympathy which would recall that of the chameleon if it became green of its own will because it *thought* of leaves—and not solely through a kind of transparency or, more precisely, an adaptation to its surroundings. From that period on, you probably remember that I could no longer keep up any discussion; in the most pleasant conversations my silences were unbearable; they could be attributed to the absence of thought, to boredom, or to fatigue. It was not—that; it was due to an almost inexplicable disturbance; others' thoughts immediately interested me more than my own; actually, I had no thoughts or, more precisely, mine no longer existed as soon as others began to speak: The psychological truth of such thoughts *with relation to the person* who expresses them interested me more than their *absolute truth* (do you get what I mean?). I was therefore almost uniquely concerned with "understanding" (what joys!); I cared about nothing less than subsequently forming my own opinion; it would have been very difficult for me to give "my opinion" or to explain "my belief"—but even then I think I could have constructed a character without any big psychological mistakes or—if you prefer the metaphor—draw a figure without any big drafting mistakes. I then began to consider that for a littérateur (between us, we can still talk of that without laughing, and for me nothing is more serious) the important thing was to bring light to all points; lucidly, coldly, and passionately, he had to present the various forms of *Life,* and his conclusions had to be direct questions to the reader: I rather like the reader to be backed up against the wall and made to *answer.* But once again, and more strongly than ever, having the conviction that for a *moral act* to be *valid* it must be a free choice, and believing with Fichte that moral life begins with a *personal decision* and that acceptance of others' decisions is a state of death or nonlife—I refrain from trying to make *my thoughts* accepted (from now on, what good does it do me to have any?), seeing it as a Jesuistic encroachment ("And compel them to come in," etc.) on others' thoughts; limiting my role, or rather increasing it to the point of trying to make others think for themselves, finally provoking that important personal decision. Catholicism seems not to permit that, Bossuet no more than the quietists: their convictions were admirable, but I suffer from them. Why have I never suffered from them in Pascal? Isn't it true that he exalts thought?

The inner evolution that had preceded his trip was reinforced by it:

My life all these past months has been marvelously useful to this course; too sick, too overwhelmed, or too uniquely concerned with living to think very much—feeling around me no possibility of understanding, but feeling within myself—on the contrary—the sympathies of an invalid—that is, passionately fond of all those Arabs around me, who at least *were living,* with no thoughts, with all our passions, and with other morals—which is what makes them seem different. And as I no longer had any morals, I could understand theirs more fully—and as I was concerned uniquely (I must always add: "almost") with living, I tasted of more joys in a few days than the pride of many triumphs had given me in the past—and at a time when

I was without hope and had said farewell to life. That very sympathy for those around me made me give up *my thoughts even more since they* would not have understood them. Can you understand that at present Italy (Rome, at least) bores and exasperates me; that I think of Shelley, who did not want to go into churches. . . . I spend my days in the Pincio gardens, watching the light; I write verses; at the house I work; I read very little: Leibnitz' *New Essays,* Stendhal's *Promenades dans Rome,* and *Vanity Fair* are on my table; I patiently work at my piano. All that is enough for me—for the moment. Above all, don't think I've become idiotic through trying to live— never have I found my thoughts healthier and more capable of creating.

André Gide stayed in Rome from April 13 to May 22. Despite his decision to give up *seeing,* he made a few excursions to the Christian city and to the ancient city: "I saw the Pope yesterday . . . blessing the excited crowd in such a serene and beautiful way that I was choked with sobs."[10] A month later, the young Huguenot wrote to his mother:

I often go back to St. Peters, almost in spite of myself . . . that architecture, more papal than Catholic, is awe-inspiring . . . it's enormous and not very mystical; it's exactly as it should be; when there, I thought of those words of Victor Hugo—the title of one of his works: "Stability is assured."[11]

He walked out of the Vatican Museum "indignant": "I saw the Vatican Museum yesterday; . . . is it possible that they sacrificed everything to ostentation! The perfection of the statues is ridiculous: there's not a hair missing. . . . What treachery!"[12] As for painting, he wrote to his mother: "Painting is at present what interests me the least," and summed up his impressions of the Italian School as follows:

Except for two or three great names—(let's say four: Michelangelo, Titian, Da Vinci, and occasionally Raphael, as well as Botticelli and a few others of that time)—the Italian School bores me more than I could have ever imagined.

Subsequently, he was to retract those hasty impressions.

As for the monuments of ancient Rome, Gide generally let Paul Laurens visit them alone: "The beauty of Rome is so severe that one must be strong to begin with in order to bear it. . . . It's a somewhat tiring city for me."[13] Yet during his walks he had some happy surprises—the Forum, and the Colosseum: ". . . it's really more beautiful than the amphitheatre at Nîmes —the proportions are perfect." Actually, his impressions of Rome varied from day to day. He was later to write: "I have found the secret of my boredom in Rome: I don't find myself interesting here."[14] He had already

[10] Letter from André Gide to his mother, April 16, 1894, unpublished.

[11] *Ibid.,* May 4, 1894, unpublished.   [13] *Ibid.,* April 30, 1894, unpublished.

[12] *Ibid.,* May 6, 1894, unpublished.   [14] *Journal,* 1896, p. 65.

explained that "secret" in a letter to his mother, following a visit to the Palazzo Borghese:

I really understand very well the kind of pleasure one might find in this Italian life—palaces, perfect shade, a manorial, courtly, and polite life—but you must realize that we cannot lead that life, nor can we that of the Romans in the Forum, nor that of the Christians in the catacombs—we will never be anything but spectators—or, at any rate, that's all we can be now (I'm thinking of Byron and Shelley in Ravenna); the palaces remain closed to us—and anyway, what would we do there without "costumes?"[15]

As his health improved, he again had a thirst for travel, perhaps more tempted by the desire to retrace his steps than by any new horizons. Yet although he planned to return to Algeria during the coming winter, he had decided to spend the summer in La Roque in order to see Madeleine again:

It would be real heartbreak for me not to see Madeleine again. I fear she has not taken seriously what I have and that she considers the whole thing no more than the whim of a spoiled child, just as the Charles Gides did in the past.[16]

He should have liked his cousin to feel pity for his lot, and he could not get over the fact that she had almost stopped writing to him.

In Rome a student at the Villa Medici had introduced Gide and Laurens to a "high-class prostitute" whom they had nicknamed "the lady." He was exasperated by the "distinction" and "affectation" of the too-stylized Italian girl, and it would seem that he experienced the same fiasco with her as with the "too beautiful" En Barka:

I begin to understand that I had put up with Meriem only because of her cynicism and savageness; with her at least one knew what to expect; nothing in her remarks or her gestures aped love; with the other one, I profaned all that was most sacred in my heart.[17]

And so the former angelist Walter was feeling more and more resolved, or obliged, to dissociate pleasure and love, the latter still pledged to the distant Madeleine.

On May 23 Gide arrived in Florence and at once wrote to his mother:

This morning the weather promised to be mild: never has it been worse. . . . But nothing suits Florence better than this very low and uniformly gray sky, so that despite the drizzle, there is not a cloud to be seen. . . . After

[15] April 25, 1894, unpublished.

[16] Letter from André Gide to his mother, May 12, 1894, unpublished.

[17] *Si le grain ne meurt,* II, 317.

Rome, everything seems marvelous to me; the mere fact of knowing that I'm in the city of the Medicis and Savonarola really moves me; I always found the history of Florence more beautiful than all the others, perhaps because having learned a little of it, I wanted to learn still more. I think I find more beauty here; in Rome I feel nothing but strength and vigor.[18]

He was bored in Rome, but Florence delighted him:

I *once again feel much better in every respect* and briskly go down to the street, *but*—and I think it's nerves—at the end of ten minutes, wham—for no reason at all I start to sweat abundantly, then suffocation, my clothes weigh heavy on me—impossible to go on—I'm ready to sit under the omnibuses. . . . But Florence is so beautiful that it's going to cure me. . . . I travel passionately; and that is how I love Florence—passionately.

A few days after his arrival, Gide unexpectedly met Oscar Wilde, who was stopping in Florence with a young Englishman, Lord Alfred Douglas:

Whom should I meet here? Oscar Wilde! He has aged and is ugly, but always an extraordinary storyteller, a little as I imagine Baudelaire must have been, but perhaps not as sharp and more charming. He was only here for another day, and as he was leaving an apartment he had rented for a month and had lived in for only two weeks, he kindly offered it to me. It consisted of two very large rooms giving onto the river, between the Ponte Vecchio and that marvelous bridge I was just talking about.[19]

Gide made another allusion to their meeting in a letter to Valéry a few weeks later:

It was in Florence that I met one of the rare Englishmen I know: Oscar Wilde; and he seemed hardly delighted by the meeting, for he thought he was in hiding. With him smiled another poet of a younger generation. I had two vermouths and listened to four stories. He was leaving next day; that was four weeks ago. I didn't tell you about it because you were in Paris and would have repeated it! But now that silence is easier, I still ask for your silence.[20]

That last suggestion is quite significant. Gide, who in December, 1891, had not hesitated to be seen everywhere with Wilde, had since learned that the proximity of a reputed homosexual was compromising, and he obviously knew about the relationship between the Irishman and his young traveling companion, "Bosie." Besides, two years before, he had nothing to hide, but since his trip to North Africa, the same did not hold true. Whatever the case may be, their second meeting was so brief that Gide

[18] May 23, 1894, unpublished.

[19] The Ponte Santa Trinitá. Letter from André Gide to his mother, May 28, 1894, unpublished.

[20] June, 1894 (*Correspondance*, p. 206). In the *Correspondance,* the letter is dated as of July, but it was sent from Florence and Gide left there on June 23.

said in *In memoriam*: "That short a meeting in Florence a year before does not count."[21] But the third, a year later in Biskra, was to have a decisive influence on the course of his life.

He continued to work alternately on *Paludes* and *Les Nourritures terrestres,* which extolled the beauty of the Tuscan city. He also continued to keep well-informed on everything that was published in Paris, through the many reviews and books his mother forwarded to him. He was delighted with Maurice Barrès' *Les Deux Femmes du bourgeois de Brugges:*

It's a little marvel, most revolting and particularly so when you know that it's the story of Barrès, Madame Barrès, and some Russian lady with whom he traveled in Spain a short time after his marriage. But that is Barrès' great strength: his life and his writings are one.[22]

In fact, Gide's own ambition then was that his life and writings be one. And he felt that despite the charm of Florence, the most original part of his trip had been the complete change in Africa. As he wrote to Paul Valéry:

I think of nothing but leaving for Cairo; were I healthier, I'd go to Batavia. Houses with windows, men wearing hats, and women who go to confession bore me. I dream of Africa where I had a terrific time. I shall return there as soon as the temperature is favorable.[23]

And to his mother: "Florence bores me; the houses have windows and the men hats—I might as well be in Paris—*Europe bores me.* I find it difficult not to think constantly of Cairo."[24] Or, one beautiful morning in Fiesole, while "the fields were filled with cicadas" and their shrill cries: "How splendid Oumach must be now!!"[25]

However, his health began to worry him again—"I was breathing with great difficulty"—and again he went to see a doctor:

The doctor—scrupulous, intelligent, really very good, I think—listened to my lungs and to *my heart* for a long time; he found the action of the latter very nervous indeed, but no hypertrophy and great muscular vigor. As for the lungs: *nothing at all*—not the shadow of a congestion, he told me. I had explained "my case" to him at length—that alone, he said, could give him information, for otherwise he would have judged me perfectly able-bodied. That's about it.—Nevertheless, I have continued to feel very indisposed for two days—let's say that it's nerves.[26]

---

[21] P. 29.

[22] Letter from André Gide to his mother, June 15, 1894, unpublished.

[23] June, 1894 (*Correspondance,* p. 207.)

[24] June 17, 1894, unpublished.

[25] Letter to his mother, June 23, 1894, unpublished.

[26] *Ibid.,* June 17, 1894, unpublished.

He was only half reassured by the doctor's opinion and decided to go to Geneva to consult Dr. Andreæ, an eminent specialist whom his aunt, Mme. Charles Gide, had been suggesting to him for a long time.

It was in Florence, on June 23, that André Gide and Paul Laurens parted company: "For our last day Paul and I are going to lunch in the country. I think it's really the last day of our companionship. It's ending gloriously —and we have the impression that it was a success—something accomplished."[27] After nine months of Africa and Italy, Paul Laurens, his Beaux-Arts scholarship at an end, had to return to Paris. For his part, André Gide had definitely decided to continue his peregrinations alone and prolong them as much as his mother—who in her letters was beginning to complain about expenses and to urge him to come back—would allow. He himself dreamed of nothing but exoticism and new departures. The once sedentary young man was now convinced that he "passionately" loved traveling, "independently of the things I see."[28] Although he denied that he "resembled Byron," he wanted to belong to the race of romantic travelers who leave for the sake of leaving.

[27] *Ibid.,* June 23, 1894, unpublished.

[28] *Ibid.,* May 28, 1894, unpublished.

38: From Champel to La Roque

> *"Dr. Andreæ, a new Tronchin, con-*
> *vinced me that the only thing wrong*
> *with me was my nerves."*
>
> Si le grain ne meurt, *III, 318*

ANDRÉ GIDE's sole reason for going to Geneva was to seek the advice of Dr. Andreæ: "Did I tell you that I'm now on my way to Switzerland? Not for pleasure, but for medical care," he wrote to Paul Valéry from Florence.[1] He arrived in Geneva on the morning of June 27 and found the weather splendid, "just slightly cooler, a peaceful and pure serenity throughout the city, the feeling that I'm going to be cured."[2] He at once went to see his aunt, Mme. Charles Gide, who had arranged an appointment for him with the doctor that very day: "Dr. Andreæ came to see me at four this afternoon. I think he plans to send me to Champel where I shall go to ruin completely."[3] Yet in *Si le grain ne meurt* Gide praised Dr. Andreæ and claimed that he owed his "salvation" to the wise specialist. He "soon convinced me that the only thing wrong with me was my nerves and that a cure of hydrotherapy at Champel first, and then a winter in the mountains, would do me more good than caution and medicines."[4] Determined to follow the prescription, the convalescent took off for Champel immediately.

On June 29 Gide wrote to his mother:

[1] June, 1894 (*Correspondance*, p. 207).

[2] Letter from André Gide to his mother, June 27, 1894, unpublished.

[3] *Ibid.*

[4] *Si le grain ne meurt*, II, 318.

And so I'm at Champel—almost at the border but still quite enough in horrible Switzerland for my taste . . . the country is too chaste for me. You know what I wrote in defense of chastity; and I'm quite ready to go back to it—but I don't much like learning about it from the country. On the contrary, I like the country to tempt me with sensuality so that I have some merit in often refusing it. . . . No matter; this plateau of Champel is beautifully shaded and the very air I breathe is curing me. The doctors here, the one in Champel and my aunt's, are agreed that everything is due to my nerves.[5]

It was then that telegrams and letters began arriving from Mme. Paul Gide. She was incensed at the fact that the cure had been decided on without her permission. Furthermore, André—on arriving in Geneva and embarrassed in front of the Charles Gides because he was not in mourning for his grandmother who had died a few months before—had dared order some black clothes without consulting his mother. Added to that, he had told her that he meant to return to La Roque in June and that he wanted his three cousins, Paul and Pierre Laurens, Maurice Drouin, and Eugène Rouart to be there. At that point, an epistolary controversy began that was as bitter as the one in Munich during the spring of 1892:

Your two telegrams rather irritated me by their complete futility: since morning I've been wearing the black suit I just ordered, and you tell me to order a gray one. Two excellent doctors of authority advise me to take showers, and you tell me that they've always been bad for me (wonderful for my morale!). I'm sent to Champel, and you seem to regret it. Nothing could be more bewildering than such telegrams; you should refrain from sending them, dear mamma.

And he added, as if to alarm her: "Rest assured that *I am not at all cured* —and that if my condition is not somewhat improved before the approach of winter, I may just never leave here." As for the August reunion at La Roque:

Given the fact that the doctors consider my return to the North[6] very imprudent and are worried about it, and that it would interrupt the cure I've begun here and take me away from the mountains just when they might do me the most good—if the reunion cannot take place at La Roque as we have planned it, I think I shall do without coming back at all. It would be a heartbreaking disappointment and great wisdom.[7]

But his little sentimental blackmail did not have the expected result. Mme. Gide, who was apprehensive about Madeleine and André's seeing one another again during the holidays, jumped at the opportunity so rash-

---

[5] Unpublished.

[6] By "North" he means Normandy.

[7] Letter from André Gide to his mother, July 4, 1894, unpublished.

ly offered and advised her son not to come back to La Roque at all. He at once persisted in considering the family reunion indispensable. A letter written to his cousin Jeanne Rondeaux shows how exasperated he was by his mother's attitude:

What's wrong with mamma? Since I've been here, I have received *daily* letters and a shower of telegrams. . . . I announce that the doctors are sending me to Champel—1st telegram: "Champel strange why not the mountains?" I write that I'm taking showers—answer: "Showers have always been bad for you." Having arrived here in blue, I find my relatives in deep mourning for grand-mamma—disgrace—I'm forced to order something black to wear. I inform mamma of the fact and three days later receive—both the suit and a telegram from La Roque: "Mourning almost over; not black, gray." Finally, and it's the only thing important to me: I arrive here indisposed; I have serious doubts as to whether I can go back to Normandy without being most imprudent—I try to make mamma understand that perhaps the doctors will keep me here; at that point the daily messages read: "You must absolutely come back; return indispensable." Now that I'm allowed to return—having wanted to so much, actually living for it—and the doctors don't think it imprudent, for I'm much better—I write that I'm coming—and that I'm happy. What do I receive: "Dear, dear, dear child, I understand you—no, don't come back—you had better . . ." Gradually the formula becomes: "Above all, don't come back." One last thing: since I have been advised to try winter in the mountains (which mamma wanted so much for me), mamma advises me to go to the Balearic Islands! ! ! And when I have the misfortune to say one word, mamma at once writes me the same as she says about Edouard and Georges:[8] "One can feel the foreign influence!" (In this case it's my Aunt Charles, as you can well imagine.)[9] Or else: "My poor child, how nervous you were when you wrote me your last letter!" Then I decided to send only telegrams for six days, one each morning; each and every one says: "I'm coming back end of the month; beg you to change nothing about the reunion. . . ." Nothing has been inter-fered with, has it, my dear sister, and we shall soon be together again, just as if we had parted only to sleep.[10]

At that point of the conflict, the question of the holidays at La Roque became a test of the mother's strength against the son's. Every day Mme. Gide renewed her attack with interminable letters; every day André an-swered her with a brief telegram saying exactly the same thing. After six telegrams, he decided to write her a long letter:

[8] Edouard and Georges Rondeaux were the brothers of Madeleine and Jeanne.

[9] It would seem that Mme. Paul Gide was very jealous of the influence she thought her sister-in-law, Mme. Charles Gide, had on her son.

[10] July, 1894, unpublished.

Why do you persist so in continuing this either open or hidden opposition, when you can see that I have made my decision . . . ? When you have made up your mind about something . . . ah!—And now here you are beginning a whole new series: "Don't spend the winter in the mountains, go to the Balearic Islands.". . . It's not in the Balearic Islands that I'll end up but in the lunatic asylum. . . . The following was decided—agree that it still is: *Reunion at La Roque* beginning August 1—and don't tell me there's no room for Rouart; *there must be and there will be* . . . Please tell me positively what will completely cure me: that I shall soon see *my cousins, the Laurens, Drouin,* and ROUART down there together. I MUST. If not, next month I take off for Madagascar.

Far from being intimidated by the Madagascan perspective, Mme. Gide countered him with renewed vigor and took advantage of the situation to bewail once again the fact that André had not wanted to tie himself down to a regular career, a reliable and stable profession. His answer was utterly nonchalant:

Nothing is as uncertain as my life; what will become of me—what will I do—where will I go? That's precisely why I find life admirable. This morning the weather is splendid; that's at least one thing to the good. I enjoy life; I enjoy life; I madly enjoy life.—How astonishingly miserable that any occupation might distract one from enjoying the divine beauty of the air; if I *had a career now, I would resign or hang myself.* I'm the happiest of men and I think I would be in spite of everything. . . . Solitude may sometimes make me cry out a little with boredom and I may feel extremely miserable, yet indeed I hope so; I'm in this world to write about those emotions as well as the others; for me the real misfortune would be not to be able to cry them out. But do realize that this manifestation contains its own remedy. How can I make you understand that? I can work well only in boredom; boredom must drive me to the wall so that I'm forced to work, so that work is my *refuge*—so that I throw myself into it madly. . . . Dear mamma, I assure you that I taste of more happiness in one week than others do all their lives. I don't want to be any more pitied than envied, because I lead the life I must lead—and even this long illness will have done me good as a writer.[11]

Never was André Gide's sole vocation as an artist expressed more clearly than in that letter to his mother. He knew where he wanted to go and what existence he had to lead in order to create his works out of all his joy and all his sadness, all his enthusiasm and all his boredom, all his sympathies and all his solitude. He could no longer be turned away from the goal he had set himself. He now put all his will power not only into his works but into the style of life he felt they necessitated, and he meant not to give in to anyone any more.

[11] Letter from André Gide to his mother, July 8, 1894, unpublished.

During the second week in July, when Pierre Louÿs and Ferdinand Hérold—en route to Bayreuth—stopped at Champel to see André Gide, whom they thought was very sickly indeed, given the alarming rumors that had circulated about his health, they found him in superbly good shape. Sun, waters, and inspiration had transformed him. He read them *La Ronde de la Grenade:*

> —Joys of the flesh and joys of the senses
> Let another condemn you if he will.[12]

We can imagine the former Chrysis' astonishment upon hearing the former Walter extol the joys of the senses. But there were more surprises to come. Gide told him and Hérold a very self-complimentary story about his love affair with the beautiful Meriem, no doubt taking an even more revengeful pleasure in it inasmuch as his two friends had once made fun of his chastity. Who then was this Meriem, who had transformed the austere Huguenot into a dionysiac poet? Louÿs, touched to the quick, gave up his plans for going to Bayreuth and decided to get to Biskra as soon as possible. He had immediately to get to know "the bacchante of the Gaeta vase," and Gide urged him on. The two Wagnerians, betraying the Valkyrie, sailed off to Africa, taking with them a silk scarf for Meriem and a barrel organ for Athman.

Gide wrote to Valéry[13] from Champel and told him how he had convinced Louÿs and especially Hérold—who "will never manage to finish *Le Victorieux*[14] because I'm introducing him to women"—to leave for Biskra. His victory gave him "the joy of feeling my will-power laugh," a completely new joy for him. Who would have thought that the shy André Walter would one day speak in that provocative tone and nonchalantly hand the Parnassians over to the bacchantes? In relation to Louÿs and Hérold, it was he who now appeared to be the roué. Added to the man of letters' wicked pleasure in compromising *Le Victorieux* was the joy of an ironic experimenter, a joy Gide was often to seek by meddling in other people's lives and giving rise to adventures whose development he would follow with curiosity.

Meanwhile, at La Roque, Mme. Paul Gide, with the help of her faithful Marie, set about getting the large house ready for her son and all the guests he demanded be present—not one less, but not one more. He refused, in a threatening way, to have the Rondeaux brothers and the

[12] *Les Nourritures terrestres,* IV, 83.

[13] July 16, 1894 (*Correspondance,* p. 210).

[14] Hérold's poem, *Le Victorieux,* was to be published in 1895.

Widmers,[15] whom Mme. Gide vainly insisted upon, for she had already invited them. "That's just too bad," he answered. "Besides, they had better get accustomed to being shocked by me." From that time on, the mother obeyed and the son gave the orders. The roles were reversed.

The main objective of the great reunion in August was for André Gide to see Madeleine again, and that is why he so carefully prepared the meeting, eliminating all those he considered unfavorable to his plans in order to be surrounded only by his "three sisters" and devoted friends. When he wrote to Jeanne Rondeaux from Champel: ". . . we shall soon be together again, just as if we had parted only to sleep," it was doubtless meant for Madeleine. But during the ten-month separation, he had done many other things besides sleep, and he had become singularly strong-willed: he no longer accepted that anyone hold out against him. Therefore, as soon as he arrived, he set out to convince Madeleine to marry him, but he came up against such invincible resistance that, for the first time, he seriously considered giving up the idea altogether.

This is confirmed by a letter he received from his cousin on August 18:

You think that up until now I could not read your letters without apprehension: perhaps—I was not aware of it. But whose fault is it if, in my relations with you, I had to keep myself from any self-abandon and any spontaneity—to the point that I infinitely preferred your absence to your presence?[16]

And above all:

I can't leave you, dear André, without thanking you for the assurance you give me of the constancy of your affection. Really, I never quite doubted it. I must also tell you how relieved I am that you gave up any idea of marriage—which has always caused me mortal terror and to which I have a constantly increasing aversion. You can't know what an oppressive weight of anxiety disappeared forever upon reading your letter. How much more I would have enjoyed La Roque had I known it beforehand. But I regret nothing—not even the very unhappy days I spent because of your deadly obstinacy—my brother . . . In spite of what you say, never have I really wanted you to forget me or love me less; I only wanted our lives, now too united, to be liberated one from the other. I thank God that it has been done, and done simply.[17]

But André Gide's nature was such that as soon as he felt anyone or anything eluding him, he persisted all the more. He, in any case, at once took advantage of the situation by asking his cousin to resume their correspondence, which—although she sensed a "trap"—she agreed to do.

[15] Albert Démarest's sister, Isabelle, had married Edouard Widmer.
[16] Quoted by Jean Schlumberger, p. 99.
[17] September, 1894, *ibid.,* p. 98.

We know almost nothing about those two weeks in August at La Roque, for with the exception of Pierre Louÿs, who was in Biskra, and Paul Valéry, all of André Gide's regular correspondents were with him. But his return was in no way similar to the prodigal son's. He had traveled far from the family house, but regretted it not at all, and he was no sooner back than he began thinking of leaving again: "Now it's Bursa (via Constantinople) that attracts me, but I shan't be able to go there for quite a while."[18] However, he did leave La Roque on August 15, thus shortening the holiday he had looked forward to with such joy.

[18] Letter from André Gide to Paul Valéry, Aug. 6, 1894 (*Correspondance,* p. 212).

39: From La Roque to Neuchâtel

*"As for my hasty getaway, what can I
possibly say except what I always say:
if I did it, it was because I thought I
had to."*

Letter to his mother, September
18, 1894, unpublished

I N MID-AUGUST Gide left La Roque with Eugène Rouart and
stopped off in Paris. None of his friends was there except Henri
de Régnier. They naturally talked about Algeria and about
Pierre Louÿs and Hérold, who had carried Meriem off and set her up near
Constantine, where Louÿs was writing *Les Chansons de Bilitis,* dedicated
to André Gide in remembrance of M.b.S. Gide spoke about Biskra in such
an eloquent way that he convinced Régnier to go there with him in the
spring. He also read him the beginning of *Paludes,* written in Rome and
Florence. According to his *Journal* of August, 1894:

Friday, lunch with Henri de Régnier at the *Soufflet.* In the morning visited
Aunt Claire; bought some books under the Odéon arcades. Henri de Régnier
came along with me to the rue de Commaille; I read him the beginning of
Paludes. Talked about Biskra. Saturday, left for Lausanne in the morning.[1]

He no sooner got to the boarding house in Lausanne where the Charles
Gides were staying than his cousin Valentine Rondeaux arrived. That trip
made by the youngest of the three cousins has never been explained, but
there is a possibility that André was at the bottom of it. He was perhaps
not unhappy about playing a trick on Madeleine or arousing her jealousy
a little. Valentine, the most romantic of the "three sisters," had a very deep
feeling for her cousin.[2] All the same, the family was upset, especially one

---

[1] *Journal,* 1894, p. 50.

[2] Juliette, Alissa's sister in *La Porte étroite,* was no doubt patterned after Valentine
and not after Jeanne Rondeaux.

aunt, Mme. Henri Rondeaux, and they sent the governess, Fraülein Siller, to separate her from her cousin and take her back to the fold. Gide protested and at the same time tried to bring his mother into his game by exploiting the family rivalries in the manner of a court intrigue:

What a stupid squabble this Valentine business is; why call such a natural thing an "escapade"? I think they (Le Houlme)[3] were a little afraid of you; they were afraid you'd agree with us, on the side of Valentine and *the Gides;* they probably didn't let you know about Le Houlme's indignation till the last minute. The real trouble is that Aunt Claire and Isabelle happened to be with Aunt Henri; Aunt Henri forced her way of thinking on them, which Aunt Claire didn't dare refute and which delighted Isabelle, since she doesn't much like Valentine.[4]

André, formerly so worried about the family's opinion, would seem to have decided to pay no further attention to it. But he wrote to his mother very affectionately:

I still remember your last letter—the letter of a poor solitary widow, abandoned by her son . . . and I now wonder how I so meanly had the heart to leave you, to prefer *my* health and *my* career to you. . . . When will this temporary period be over? When will I be able to work peacefully at your side, full of visions, telling about the past and dreaming of a future that includes you?[5]

If he left for Switzerland, it was not, he said, for pleasure: "Yes, Switzerland is indeed frightful; I'm very prejudiced against it—it's better to be sick in Biskra than healthy in Switzerland; everything here displeases and exasperates me." But he felt that there he would have enough of the necessary boredom to write *Paludes,* and of course it was advisable for his health. In Lausanne he was examined by the well-known Dr. Bourget, who confirmed his Genevan colleague's prescription of a winter in the mountains at La Brévine. But as the season had not yet come, Gide decided to travel a bit.

On August 31 he was in Chur. He lyrically wrote to Paul Valéry: "I'm happy tonight, for this afternoon I bathed completely naked in a green mountain torrent; afterward, to dry myself off, I rolled about in the warm grass."[6] He added that for three weeks he had been reading nothing but Rimbaud, whose poetry certainly had an influence on *Les Nourritures terrestres.* As he told Paterne Berrichon in a letter of June 4, 1911: "*Les*

[3] "Le Houlme" was the country estate of the Henri Rondeaux.

[4] Letter from André Gide to his mother, Aug. 31, 1894, unpublished.

[5] *Ibid.*

[6] Aug. 31, 1894 (*Correspondance,* p. 213; letter dated Sept. 3).

Illuminations was my viaticum and about my only sustenance during the most important month of convalescence in my life."[7]

From Chur, Gide went to Samaden, Saint-Moritz, and then to Lecco, where,

Following M. Bourget's advice, I took a shower bath of sun and fresh air—that is, almost completely naked, on a heated plateau where probably no one would come, I let the sun and wind on my skin act like a hot and cold shower—marvelous—exquisite—O nature, Pan, physical permeation, aerial warmth, etc.

In order to corroborate that evocation of the great Pan who, as we know, was none other than Bacchus: "I had stolen some grapes from the vine harvest (I saw them for the first time and ate them straight from the vine). I found them delicious."[8] And in his *Nourritures terrestres* the taste of those grapes stolen in Lecco is described in *La Ballade de toutes le rencontres.*

The next step was Milan, where he walked about in the public gardens, thinking of *Paludes,* and felt the whole book "take shape" within him around a few little insignificant phrases: "Path bordered with aristolochia" and " 'Why, when the weather's always so unsettled, did you take only a parasol?' 'It's an *en-tous-cas,*' she told me. . . ."[9] Such was to be the very tone of *Paludes.* A "certain sense of the ridiculous," less obvious here than in *Le Voyage d'Urien,* and more a certain sense of the innocuous, which sprang from the disproportion between his former squeamish refinement and his present "fervors," plus a sense of "estrangement," gave him the form necessary for humorous platitudes.

From Milan he went to Como, where he stayed from September 12 to 17, and lived there in a constant state of "fervor." A month before in Paris, Henri de Régnier had spoken to him, "in a marvelous way,"[10] about what he had been reading, particularly Jean Paul's *Titan* and Casanova's *Mémoires.* On the banks of Lake Como, Gide was reminded of Jean Paul, but his adventure in a boat on the same lake was hardly reminiscent of Casanova:

After my adventure in Sousse, I had miserably fallen back into vice. Although I had occasionally managed to snatch some sensual pleasure in passing, it always seemed to be furtively; yet deliciously one evening, in a boat on Lake

---

[7] Quoted by Y. Davet, p. 42.

[8] Letter from André Gide to his mother, Sept. 11, 1894, unpublished.

[9] *Si le grain ne meurt,* II, 322. Although in *Si le grain ne meurt* Gide says he was there "before my stay at Champel," it was in fact before his stay in La Brévine and after Champel.

[10] Letter from André Gide to his mother, Aug. 20, 1894, unpublished.

Como with a young boatman (a little before arriving at La Brévine), when my ecstasy was wrapped in moonlight, which fused with the misty enchantment of the lake and the moist perfumes of the banks.[11]

Mme. Gide was not told about those furtive delights, fusions, and effusions, but in his letter of September 15 Gide did allude to them:

. . . last evening, my dinner finished—I rented a little boat, and sometimes rowing myself, sometimes being rowed, I moved ahead in the moon's reflection . . . we dropped the oars and just remained there, immobile in that marvelous serenity. The child who was leading me then came and sat near me; he murmured: "Como è bello." I took his hand and we stayed there a long time without saying a word. The moon had slowly gone down; it soon disappeared behind the dome of the city; and Como, thus gently lighted, seemed even more Italian. Everything was dark when we got back. Such evenings can never be forgotten.[12]

He was feeling happy: "I don't think I could ever leave if my work were not calling me." But his work—in other words, his duty—was indeed calling him, and since happiness was not suitable to the writing of *Paludes*, he took off for virtuous Switzerland, renouncing Como, its banks, and its boats.

In Neuchâtel Gide moved into a "house of temperance," frequented by frugal and abstemious old maids, and found the atmosphere he needed. As the comical aspect of *Paludes* had to be expressed in as flat a style as possible, it implied constant control over his thoughts and his pen. Yet he was also anxious to embark on other works. A letter to Marcel Drouin, written from Neuchâtel, shows the state of overstimulation he was in during that period:

I have no time: I must work—it's a vital necessity (I'm speaking Swiss)— every day four to six hours of piano, three to four hours of walking (I would stop if I didn't think it was so good for me—besides, I got into the habit of doing my best thinking and imagining while walking)—an hour and a half of hygiene (baths, sponge baths, rubdowns, exercises, etc.). Add to that, besides work, the letters to my mother and you'll see what's left for my translation, horribly stiff, of Novalis; for *Paludes,* which is not progressing at all; and for all the rest I'm working on at almost the same time: *Philoctètes,* which I finished preparing in the Engadine, and wrote some passages of *Proserpine;* the novel I was telling you about at La Roque and which is coming along terrifically—the death of my old maid, paralleled by the death of a bachelor!— my book "of pure lyricism" which I'm working on most of all—and many more things. Up till now, I've accomplished (somehow or other) *everything* I at first dreamed of—and everything I'm now dreaming of is dreamed with

---

[11] *Si le grain ne meurt,* II, 345.   [12] Unpublished.

a view to accomplishment in the very near future. I write all the time and everywhere—I do my correspondence during meals. I read Emerson and Goethe while playing my scales on the piano, I correct my translation of the day before while dressing in the morning. Add to that my *longing* to read (you know what that is), one would like to be closed in with *one* book so as to finally be able to finish with it. I haven't finished Darwin; I've read nothing good recently: except *The Pretenders* and Strindberg's horrifying *Miss Julie*.[13]

And so not only *Paludes,* but *Philoctètes, Proserpine, La Mort de Mlle. Claire*—which was to become *La Porte étroite*—*Les Nourritures terrestres,* and "many more things" were all in his mind at the same time. As for his reading, apart from the inseparable Goethe, there is a new name: Strindberg.

Apropos of Strindberg's *Miss Julie* and Ibsen's *Pretenders,* a passage about Protestantism in one of Gide's letters to his mother is, I think, of the greatest importance, for it contains a rough sketch of several ideas he was later to formulate and which played a vital part in his religious and moral crisis:[14]

I'm reading the translations of Strindberg. *Miss Julie* is terrifying—there's no cynicism like it—in anything I've read up till now—but we must be ready for some queer experiences. It's the work of an obstinate man; it's voluntarily divested of beauty and to such a degree that one rebels against it. I've read nothing really strong that displeases me as much. Also read another of Ibsen's plays: *The Pretenders.* . . . It seems to me that nothing that might be said about Ibsen has yet been said—perhaps an article is in order—and people like M. Doumergue[15] irritate me when they claim that "they don't see what Ibsen wanted to say!"—I should think it was clear enough—and I personally see it very distinctly—more especially as every play hits the same nail. Ah! They're in good shape, the Protestant races! Bravo!—and above all, they will be in good shape. We're going into some interesting periods, and I'm strangely excited about it all—what Arvède Barine so nicely calls "the infamy of this *fin de siècle*—the decay of ideas."[16] I'm no more upset about it than I am about the disappearance of the old moons. Since an idea is immaterial, it cannot decay. . . . That northern literature is terrifying; it's as brutal as their ancient gods; the history of Protestantism continues on in it; when Luther proclaimed free inquiry, the powers in the shadow must have laughed. *The history of Protestantism is a chapter in the history of free thinking.*[17] How admirable to have shown (as it did) that free thinking can be religious. Etc., etc. I'm sure you understand how passionately interested I am in these things.

[13] September, 1894 (quoted by Y. Davet, pp. 55–56).

[14] See below, chap. 46.

[15] A good friend of the Gides, whom Gide saw in Lausanne. His family were Protestants from Uzès.

[16] Mme. Arvède Barine had just published an article about the "emancipated women in England."

[17] The italics are mine.

You told me in a letter, after having quoted a very beautiful passage from *Virgin Soil*—that "you're silent, you say nothing, but your mind keeps work-ing all the same"— (or something like that—I don't have the letter with me)— yes, my mind is very active—but from fear of going too far, going too fast, I'm silent—not wanting to have to retract. I'm silent, but I don't think any less, and pretty queer things. How exciting our age is! You need a warm heart and a perfectly cool head to *get involved in it*—I've got the warm heart, but I'm too hot-headed and the blood rushing up makes me dizzy. Yet I'm beginning to have a few clear ideas; but I won't be satisfied with them until I've put them to all the tests, natural and supernatural.[18]

In the Swiss city, where the Protestant church, with its two towers, bears the inscription, "Neuchâtel, city of studies and abode," in the theological city, where "the old Neuchâtelian quarrel about eternal punishment was not yet dead,"[19] André Gide once again examined his conscience. Did he still believe in God? No doubt, but in the immanent and pantheistic god extolled in *Les Nourritures terrestres:*

And I love God because he is within me; I admire him because he is beautiful; for God is everything, and everything is beautiful to him who can understand. . . . Once perceived, we have a greater and greater need to find his adorable presence everywhere. I no longer wish to know God other than through the study of all things. What others call "gratitude" is, I think, my admiration.[20]

God is the name he gives to his own fervor:

A clear understanding of God makes one wish to go in the direction of things, in the direction of oneself. . . . I want to honor God with every part of myself, seek him everywhere, and suppress nothing with a view to partial exaltation; doing that, it seems to me, is praying badly. Prayer is praise of God; our entire life is constant prayer, and I want to know no other; it can be love, distress, or humility. I should like it to be only love.[21]

That same naturalistic quietism can be found in *La Symphonie pastorale,* of which one important scene takes place in Neuchâtel, and doubtless the memory of Rousseau,[22] always present in Gide's mind in Neuchâtel, as in La Brévine, is not unrelated to it. He wants no part of "angelic ardor," which he henceforth considers madness: "I used to wish for such madness; I want no more of it." And since everything in nature can come only from God, he means to honor him by satisfying his "natural desires."[23] Gide expressed, in a picturesque way, the benefit he expected to derive from such

[18] Sept. 22, 1894, unpublished.

[19] Blaise Allan, "André Gide et Neuchâtel. Hommage à André Gide," *N.R.F.*, 1951, p. 50.

[20] *Journal*, 1894, pp. 55–56.

[21] *Ibid.*, pp. 53–54.

[22] *Si le grain ne meurt*, II, 323.

[23] *Journal*, 1894, p. 53.

pantheistic tendencies, in a letter to a friend, which dates from Neuchâtel: "Let's not be strange particularities—let's mix with nature—we're the ones who'll gain from the *association*. From now on, I sign only *Gide and Pan*."[24]

Ever since he had read Goethe, Gide's thoughts always turned to him in the long run:

Laws and morals are for the state of childhood; education is an emancipation. A perfectly wise city or State would live and judge without laws, the norms being in the minds of its Areopagus. The wise man lives without morals, according to his wisdom. We must try to reach a higher immorality.[25]

And his Neuchâtel *Journal* ends with this conclusion: "*Take upon oneself the most humanity possible,* that's the right formula."[26] It was exactly the same formula as Wilhelm Meister's at the end of his years of apprenticeship.

In *Si le grain ne meurt* Gide says that his month in Neuchâtel was "one of the happiest times I can remember."[27] But as winter was approaching, he soon had to leave. After a short visit to his friend Maurice Quillot, who, since he had been helping his brother run a dairy in Montigny, felt that "my heart is sterilized, like my milk,"[28] Gide took off for his studious retreat. In the train he could not help thinking how fortunate he was in relation to Quillot. Several generations of Rondeaux, hard-working and economical industrialists, had resolved the deadly question of money for him. Most of his young friends, who—like him—had dreamed only of literature, had been forced to take up some work or profession: Quillot was in business; Legrand was in government service; Drouin was at the University; Blum was preparing for the Council of State. The feeling of social inequality, which he spoke about in a letter to his mother as the painful issue between them, was one of the reasons he worked so hard, as if to rectify an injustice: "Only frantic work can excuse my wealth in my own eyes. Affluence considered solely as the permission to work freely."[29] Being moral in spite of himself, he meant to pay the price for his freedom by leading an ascetic life in La Brévine, thus justifying his privileges in his own eyes.

24 Oct. 5, 1894, unpublished.

25 *Journal,* 1894, p. 55.

26 *Ibid.,* p. 56.

27 II, 324.

28 Letter to André Gide, Dec. 29, 1893, unpublished.

29 *Journal,* 1893, p. 48.

40: Tityrus, or a Satire on an Aesthete (1894)

> *"Despite my exasperation with Switzerland, I managed to stick to it as long as it took to finish* Paludes.*"*
>
> Si le grain ne meurt, *II, 326*

L A BRÉVINE, a village in the Neuchâtel region of the Jura where Jean Jacques Rousseau had stayed twenty-five years before, was chosen by Dr. Andreæ partly for psychological reasons: he felt it was important to take his patient's mind "off Africa and off himself."[1] It was a difficult task, and from that point of view the cure was, as we shall see, a complete failure; but that winter in the mountains was also meant to strengthen the convalescent and calm his nerves. As for the lung condition, Andreæ had already found it quite satisfactory, and a few months later, in Lausanne, Dr. Bourget had told Gide "that if he had to buy a new lung, he would take mine without hesitation."[2]

On October 2, André Gide left Neuchâtel to take a look at La Brévine and prepare his winter quarters there. For months he had been dreaming of the Jura retreat:

I've already taught lots of little urchins, gone along with the doctor to see some eyes plucked out, skated on the tips of my toes, killed four wolves, saved the lives of a whole squad of travelers, thoroughly studied several philosophical systems, memorized all the Bach fugues, and written the first volume of my complete works.[3]

[1] Edouard Martinet, *André Gide—L'amour et la divinité*, p. 129.

[2] Letter from André Gide to his mother, Sept. 28, 1894, unpublished.

[3] *Ibid.*, Oct. 2, 1894, unpublished.

And so it was with the greatest curiosity that he went off to explore the country. He then rented a piano in Neuchâtel, had it sent off to La Brévine, and on the evening of October 17 he himself moved in.

In *Si le grain ne meurt* Gide gave a very harsh account of his "three-month" stay.[4] He described himself as living in complete solitude; associating with no one, for "the inhabitants of this region are the least affable in the world"; and disappointed in the pastor and the doctor, who never invited him to go along with them on "their rounds among the poor and the sick." He found the village people's attitude not only indifferent but hostile:

One must have lived in this region to understand the passages of Rousseau's *Confessions* and *Rêveries* that refer to his stay in Val-Travers. Ill will, nasty remarks, eyes full of hate, mockery—no, he made up none of it; I experienced all that, even to the pebbles thrown at strangers by the pack of village children.[5]

Although such assertions are not in the least astonishing from Jean Jacques, they are surprising from Gide, who was little given to ideas of persecution.

Actually, when he arrived, he was most obligingly welcomed by the pastor, who could not find him "the Athman of La Brévine" he wanted, but did produce a buxom Swiss woman, Augusta. One day she fell right into his arms: "With great effort, I dragged her over to the couch; then, as she was clinging to me . . . I suddenly shouted: 'I hear voices!' and, pretending to be terrified, I broke loose from her arms like another Joseph, and rushed off to wash my hands."[6] At least one woman from La Brévine could not be accused of having given him a cold reception. As for the doctor, if he never asked him to go along with him on his rounds, it was because his presence would have been superfluous, for Gide was no more "useful in accidents" than *Paludes'* Tityrus. Therefore, neither the pastor, nor the maid, nor the doctor would seem to have deserved the La Brévine misanthrope's bitter reproaches. The hostility he attributed to the natives, although still difficult to explain,[7] can no doubt be put down to the fact that he missed Biskra terribly, and perhaps the "eyes full of hate" and the "nasty remarks" were but a projection of the young Huguenot's remorse, for his uneasy conscience saw reproaches in the eyes of others and could have made nature itself seem hostile.

[4] Actually, it was two months: October 18 to December 14, 1894.

[5] *Si le grain ne meurt,* II, 326.

[6] *Ibid.,* p. 325.

[7] Blaise Allan points out (p. 51) that Gide knew nothing about the political events that were then upsetting that part of the Jura, "the anarchists who had triumphed a short while back . . . and the victorious Marxists."

Gide's letters to his mother show him "macerating," sometimes with satisfaction, sometimes with exasperation, in the ugliness of La Brévine, and haunted by a nostalgia for Africa: "For a hole, it's a hole!—every new day I go into raptures over how ugly it is! No—I can't get over it."[8] The state of exasperation he lived in while writing *Paludes* was accompanied by "Nervous disorders again—how can I explain that? . . . It's extremely peculiar." He complained of partial anesthesia and "nervous thirst," which is "a kind of anxiety, an irritation at the top of the pharynx. . . ." He slept very badly: "My nerves are overstrained and my mind gets overtired—I've had more than enough." But he did feel that his state of nervous exasperation was necessary to the writing of *Paludes,* which was to be a book about an exasperated man. And that is why he was sometimes pleased with "macerating" in La Brévine. He had understood that every book required not only a particular mood but an appropriate way of life. There is no doubt that the winter in La Brévine and the creation of *Paludes* are an example of what Gide considered a *self-willed* state, in which the will power is led exclusively by what the work requires—a technique for living that seems directly drawn from the one advocated by Maurice Barrès in *Un Homme libre,* in the chapter entitled "L'Eglise militante."

From that period on, Gide fully understood that "the strangely special importance of an artist's *life*" is comparable to no other. And he explained it to his mother as follows, in one of his letters from La Brévine:

I can't really understand what you tell me about careers when you compare mine to that of doctors and engineers; I'm afraid that you're seriously mistaken. . . . *Is not every artist necessarily an exception to all the rules?* a unique case and one that will never be found again?—or a nonvalue, if someone like him existed already. For you must understand that the great works remain and are not like doctors' operations, which must be repeated with every patient. The other professions, whatever they may be, present one permanent subject to the worker—this one, not at all; one works on oneself. Hence the strangely special importance of an artist's *life.*

The idea that an artist's life must be like no other because his work is specifically devoted to the expression of a unique being, this key to the Gidian protest is directly expressed here in the simplest way, in October, 1894, before taking a more elaborate form and becoming the exaltation of the "most irreplaceable of beings,"[9] *Les Nourritures terrestres.*

Gide's real difficulty in writing *Paludes* was that he had to renounce temporarily all his possibilities, to limit himself to the singularly restricted character of Tityrus. And there is where he had to concentrate all his will power. Yet the "I really don't care, because I'm writing *Paludes*" was not

---

[8] Oct. 26, 1894, unpublished.

[9] *Les Nourritures terrestres,* "Envoi," p. 184.

Gide's own remark, and the well-known insensitivity of a creator was not his strong point, as can be seen from his reaction to another call for help from Montigny, during that winter in La Brévine. Indeed, he proved to be a generous friend to Maurice Quillot. The businessman-aesthete, to whom *Les Nourritures* was to be dedicated, found he had very heavy bills to pay; in spite of Gide's advice, he had wanted to mix poetry and business, and took some very costly initiatives, such as commissioning Steinlen to do a poster advertising his model dairy. Without any financial backing, relatively important at that time, he was heading for bankruptcy. Gide did not hesitate to help him out, despite his "natural stinginess" and his mother's reproaches:

Not to have had confidence, or more precisely: *not to have had faith* in some-one—if by chance that someone is Someone—is a stain I don't want to have on my life. That's about it—I'm looking after my biography. (Oh, it's not for others' eyes—they won't know anything about it—it's for myself—I detest the *doubt* that is an act of cowardice.) What can I do? Its my way of being moral.—You talk about inexperience—youth, etc.; you've missed the point and I don't see it that way. This is the point: Was I wrong to have made Quillot my friend?[10]

He clearly made the generous gesture only because he believed in Quillot's value as an artist. He was already subordinating everything to literature and, as he admitted, to his own biography as a writer. Of course, Gide's friendships continued to play a large part in his life, as evidenced by his letters to Drouin, Valéry, Louÿs, and Régnier, but they were always friend-ships for men who worshiped the same god. While Eugène Rouart was spending a few days with him at La Brévine, Gide wrote to his mother: "Besides, nothing has been taken away from work, for we furiously talk about literature, and in discussing plans together, they become clearer."[11]

He had a great deal of trouble making headway with *Paludes,* and explained it to Pierre Louÿs:

Since I last saw you, I've certainly worked on it a lot, but the actual results are almost nonexistent. Nor would you see anything new in me . . . and heavens knows! . . . I'm going through a period in which I feel that all my intellectual value will be determined; I have never thought so much or so well. It's a time of both violent activity and great calm; my thinking is becom-ing more certain and more orderly. I'm working at everything at the same time: that explains the delays with *Paludes;* I'm accumulating notes for many other things; *I'm connecting all my ideas.* That requires sustained attention and is very absorbing.[12]

[10] Letter from André Gide to his mother, Oct. 17, 1894, unpublished.

[11] *Ibid.,* Nov. 3, 1894, unpublished.

[12] Letter from André Gide to Pierre Louÿs, Oct. 19, 1894, unpublished.

He had so many more important literary projects that it was painful for him to give them all up, even temporarily, and restrict himself to *Paludes*. Yet he ended by resigning himself to it: "I'm beginning to understand that *Paludes* will never be completed unless I finish it; the poor old book has no one but me to do it; Gawd help us, with such vocations!"[13] When he sent Pierre Louÿs a chapter that was to be published in the *Revue Blanche* in January, 1895, he decided to have the first third of his book printed in order to force himself to write the rest as quickly as possible. And on December 6 he was able to write to his mother:

Paludes is finished. I've had to give all these past days to it. . . . Think how wonderful: the day after the evening I completed the book, I received the first proofs. Hence a lot of extra work. I had to edit the whole manuscript from beginning to end and go over it for certain typographical indications. I'm madly pleased about *Paludes; and about having finished it*. No one will ever again get me to write in December. . . . Imagination is of the same nature as a marmot; it sleeps in the winter. I had to overtax it terribly in order to work out my story; but I'm tired. I've had more than enough of La Brévine.[14]

He immediately sent the whole manuscript, 120 pages written on one side in black ink, to Paul Valéry.

Pierre Louÿs was surprised to learn that *Paludes* was already completed: "Why in the devil is *Paludes* finished? Right away like that? It must be tiny?" And in a postscript:

I'm explaining *Paludes* to the population as follows: am I wrong? Last winter I wrote to Gide: "What are you doing?" Actually, he was doing nothing, yet he answered: "I'm writing *Paludes*." And Régnier asked him: "What are you doing, dear friend?" Actually, he was still doing nothing, but he answered Régnier: "I'm writing *Paludes!*" And his disciples wrote to him: "What are you doing, master? What are you doing?" Actually, he was copulating with my future companion. But he seriously answered, in the voice that you well know and with his hand raised: "I'm writing *Paludes!*" And that's how the idea came to him (*Paludes* was originally a book of verse) of telling about the situation of a gentleman who "is writing *Paludes*."[15]

But a few weeks later, and despite his disappointment at seeing that *Paludes* was not dedicated to him, Louÿs wrote to Gide: "It's terrific."[16] And, indeed, it was a little masterpiece of taste, malice, and style.

Before analyzing *Paludes,* we must go back to André Gide's correspond-

[13] *Ibid.,* Nov. 22, 1894, unpublished.

[14] Dec. 6, 1894, unpublished.

[15] Letter from Pierre Louÿs to André Gide, Nov. 11, 1894 (quoted by Paul Iseler, p. 98).

[16] Dec. 16, 1894 (*ibid.,* p. 101).

ence with his mother and cousin during that winter at La Brévine, for it helps to clarify his relations with them. We know that since the last family reunion at La Roque, Madeleine and André had again begun to write to each other affectionately. On October 18 he wrote to his mother:

MAMMA DARLING,

I beg you with all my soul to leave our relationship—Madeleine's and mine—alone as it is. At least wait until I've spoken to you. You'd never believe how your persistence in coming back to the subject—even without openly approaching it—fills me with dread and takes away my confidence. . . . I believe that each one of us has just enough wisdom to direct the events of his own life and that there comes a point at which others have nothing to do with it and advice no longer penetrates.

Beloved mamma, I beg you to be careful: when times were bad, I expected everything from you; I turned to you for help. Now that all is well, let it remain that way. One rash word from you can do all of us a lot of harm—all of us—I say all of us—for I may warn you that if anyone interferes in what I hold most dear—anything, the worst, is possible.

. . . We're hoping to meet this spring, in a foreign city—this meeting, which I hardly dared hope for, becomes more possible and probable every day. I don't talk about it—I dare not talk about it—but Madeleine writes that she so much hopes to see me again! and hasn't seen me for four years.

I'm perhaps very wrong in telling you these things, because I don't tell you enough for you to understand. Wait until we've been able to talk it over—wait, I beg you—do nothing about anything, or you'll drive me to despair.

Forget everything I just told you—have enough confidence in your two children—and leave them free to play with happiness, and don't always think that they don't know the rules of the game. With one clumsy word you can do us irreparable harm. I can't wait to have a long conversation with you. Meanwhile, don't speak, mamma darling.[17]

On November 22, 1894, the day of his twenty-fifth birthday, he received a long letter from Madeleine Rondeaux:

For how many winters have I been unable—not to have a special thought on November 22, for it has never gone by forgotten—but to send you all the joyous—serious—proud and confident good wishes that come from my tenderness for you? This renewal, or rather resurrection, of the *expression* of our intimacy makes me wonder a lot about you. On this eve of your 25th birthday, and may God bless my brother, I unintentionally stop, as if I were at one of the bends in a road. . . . I suddenly have strange scruples. . . . I'm almost afraid of the place you've given me in your life. . . . Happy, gravely happy, as I would be to have a moral influence, I reject—almost as an ill deed—the idea, the possibility, of having any intellectual influence whatever.

. . . Never do anything—that is, *never write anything to please me*. Most often—and up until now for our happiness and our own good—my mind has been the one to yield—the one to follow yours—without wanting to, without

17 Unpublished.

even knowing it—since so much of the unknown has covered us with darkness. There are so many truths which you already recognized as such, while I was still calling them obscurities, if not just empty—in which I now believe—and it is best that it remain that way in the intellectual realm, between you and me.[18]

We don't know what Gide's reply was, for it was destroyed along with all his letters to Madeleine Rondeaux, but he certainly alluded to the necessity of becoming "an object of scandal," for she wrote to him at once: "O dear André, will we ever be grateful enough for having each other? You miraculously express all my thoughts. But you make me go cold, I shiver with apprehension: to be an object of scandal—what do you mean?"[19]

Meanwhile, a letter had arrived from Mme. Mazué, owner of the Pères Blancs hotel in Biskra, asking whether her client planned to return soon. Gide immediately considered "rushing off to Biskra" in February, before meeting his mother and cousin: "Tell me what you think of the possibility of a meeting—in April—either in Italy—or in Barcelona—or in Cannes— or anywhere—with M., who seems to want to, although in our letters I don't breathe a word about this secret plan?"[20] Mme. Gide answered with a sixteen-page letter:

A terrifying letter from you (16 pages)—I'm not complaining about the length but about the fact that the letter is filled with completely futile arguments—which I shall certainly not answer—for you would re-answer in turn and when would it end? . . . 4 pages to inform me that some people can't travel because of their careers!

On December 6, the day on which he finished *Paludes,* he received a second letter from Mme. Mazué, telling him that an apartment in Biskra would be reserved for him in February:

I'm so angry to see that you're against my return there . . . why? I shall be very upset about going if it's against your will—but if I don't take this trip, it will be so much against my own! I put up with La Brévine only because of that hope. . . . I'd rather go on foot! . . .

And at the end of his letter, he went back to his plans for spring:

Oh! May it be so—mamma darling—I beg you with all my soul . . . if only she agrees to it—for if not—the wills of others must not be forced—and each one must act as freely as possible—in fact, each one must be given, so far as possible, the means of acting according to his own will—It seems to me that Madeleine's will, her desire, is to "see some great, beautiful, and *new* country" with me—you alone can make it possible—and you are enough to make it possible. [21]

[18] Nov. 21, 1894 (quoted by Jean Schlumberger, p. 100).
[19] Dec. 1, 1894 (*ibid.,* p. 101).
[20] Letter from André Gide to his mother, Nov. 22, 1894, unpublished.
[21] *Ibid.,* Dec. 6, 1894, unpublished.

He thus ardently wished to see Madeleine again and, there is no doubt, to marry her; but he also dreaded setting up a home:

Ah! Family! Family! It's like Aesop's meal of tongues—the worst or the best of things. Woe to those who are excluded—they have the right to find it detestable. . . . If ever I have a home, I want it to be wide open—if not, it makes the others too sad. That's what would make me hate a home—the intimacy is strangely delicious; I understand how one can be afraid of feeling too happy there . . . the doors you close to concentrate the delicious warmth of the home and to keep your *family* around you—are doors to keep the others out—and double doors to keep you from hearing them knock.[22]

In that last letter from La Brévine he again spoke about *Paludes:*

Since that's "all everyone talks about" in Paris—you must have known (you and Madeleine) where and when the first chapter of *Paludes* is to be published. *I should like you to wait to read it until the book comes out.* For I'm afraid that because of lack of time, the first chapter has not been printed to my taste—and the arrangement of the text has an importance that only "practitioners understand." Tell that to Madeleine—*really, I should like you please to wait.*

Madeleine was impatiently awaiting that new work: "I love and am delighted about—in joyous and proud expectation—everything you want to write as an extension of *Les Cahiers.*"[23] But *Paludes* was nothing less than an extension of *Les Cahiers;* the most it did was to unearth the second Walter's mood by ridiculing it in the character Tityrus.

Paludes is a satire, but "a satire on what?"[24] Gide himself answered the question in various commentaries. He wanted to hold up to ridicule the life he had led in Paris in literary coteries and salons, from the publication of *Les Cahiers d'André Walter* to his departure for Africa. In his preface to the second edition of *Paludes,* published in the *Mercure de France,*[25] he explained how the book originated from the contrast between his sedentary life among the symbolist aesthetes and his strange and exotic life in North Africa.

Tityrus is a composite figure, whose characteristics are borrowed from several people Gide had actually known:

I've made Tityrus solitary in order to concentrate the monotony; it's an artistic device; surely you wouldn't want me to make all six of them go fishing? . . .

[22] *Ibid.,* Dec. 11, 1894, unpublished.

[23] Nov. 16, 1894 (quoted by Jean Schlumberger, p. 99).

[24] Dedication of *Paludes:* "For my friend Eugène Rouart, I wrote this satire on what?"

[25] XVI, November 1895, p. 199.

But why tell the same story six times? But since the impression they give is the same—yes, exactly, six times . . .[26]

As *Paludes* is an ironic work, Gide kept only the ridiculous aspects of the literary coterie and deliberately rejected everything noble in the great intellectual adventure of symbolism, from Mallarmé to Valéry. It would be futile to try to recognize the characters, thinking that so and so resembles someone "in that clan of almost intimates, in which Hérold played such great parts."[27] Moreover, the protagonist, Tityrus, is of far greater interest than the secondary characters, in that he is a double of the author. Just as Gide himself was a part of André Walter, the second André Walter, Narcissus, Urien, and Luc, so he is a part of Tityrus.

A "satire on what"? The answer is, no doubt, a satire on himself,[28] but on only one of his selves, on only one aspect of his charatcer, which he had come to detest and wanted to hold up to ridicule so as to rid himself of it. "If I were no more than the hero (I don't say the author) of *L'Immoraliste,* I would really feel myself shrink." Those words of Gide's are even more applicable to *Paludes.* The hero of *Paludes,* Tityrus I, who writes the Vergilian Tityrus' journal, is shrunken to the point of atresia, reduced to tiny and ridiculous proportions. In his *Journal* of 1892, Gide wrote: "What makes us laugh is the feeling of atrophy, of something that could be full but is not. And what exalts us is the feeling of fulness."[29] What makes us laugh in *Paludes* is that confrontation of a new "feeling of fulness" with a former "feeling of atrophy."

Tityrus is a weakly sort of man. We don't see him, for Gide hardly ever describes his characters, but we can imagine him as being slight, fragile, slim, wan, fastidious, finical, full of affectations, wearing his shoes out only at the tips, drinking tea with his little finger raised, or murmuring in a thin voice: *"Dic cur hic?"* He has no muscle and very little bone, but his nerves are of bristle. When his feathers are ruffled, he squeaks; when he is thwarted, he sobs and feels on the verge of a little attack. He droops, his posture is sloping, and he would willingly live lying down, like his Vergilian ancestor who, as we know, remained *recubans.* He was born tired, not only depressed but irritable. He is a slight sleeper and a mere nothing disturbs him. The smell of others' coffee makes him nervous and is enough to keep him awake. He has a small appetite, is sensitive to the

[26] *Paludes, O.C.,* I, 393.

[27] Letter from Paul Valéry to André Gide, Dec. 11, 1894 (*Correspondance,* p. 227).

[28] On May 20, 1894, Gide wrote to Eugène Rouart: "I'm working on *Paludes.* My objective is to make the reader laugh and think: you can see that I've put myself into it. Besides, it's a satire on ourselves."

[29] P. 39.

cold, loathes physical exercise, and his morals are disturbingly good. He is a natural bachelor, "for more simplicity," as he says.

Angèle is the only woman in his life, and he visits her regularly to read to her, "with all the desirable atony," Tityrus' journal, to which he adds a running commentary. The evanescent Angèle is more sedentary than her cousin, the traveling Ellis. For lack of exoticism, metaphysics, and ethics, much psychologizing goes on in Angèle's salon. Tityrus and his friends are not dauntless sailors like the passengers on the Orion; they are drawing-room "menofletters" [*sic*]. They have no intention of risking their lives on the Pathetic Ocean or the Arctic Sea; they are satisfied to come together at the same time for what Anglophile Frenchmen call *le five o'clock,* and drown their precious thoughts in Angèle's cups of tea. Tityrus is even more reserved with Angèle than Urien was with the blonde Ellis. Is it out of angelism? Not at all. The Huguenot Walter's angelism came from an emotional struggle between the soul and the flesh, the angel and the demon. In André Walter, a tragic character, there was a conflict; in Tityrus, a comic character, there is merely deficiency. Walter and Emmanuèle's platonic relationship was not laughable; Tityrus and Angèle's is. Was Gide thinking at all of Madeleine Rondeaux when he drew the portrait of Angèle? It might not seem so, but he himself wrote in *Et nunc manet in te:* "Even for Angèle in *Paludes,* I was somewhat inspired by her . . . and she constantly appeared in my dreams as an unembraceable, elusive figure; and the dream turned into a nightmare."[30] As it happens, in *Paludes* Tityrus has a nightmare in which the idea that he has lost Angèle comes back like an obsession, amidst dreamlike visions and plays on words.[31] Gide obviously felt the need to project, even in a satirical farce like *Paludes* and a grotesque character like Tityrus, not only the platonic nature of his relations with his cousin but the anguishing fear of her eluding him.

Another aspect of André Walter's malady—his narcissism, or more precisely, his Hamletism—is caricatured in *Paludes.* Klaus Mann found the work "a satirical treatment of the Hamlet complex." Undoubtedly; however, not with reference to Shakespeare's tragic character but to the comic character ridiculed by Laforgue in his *Moralités légendaires.* Tityrus has extraordinary difficulty with social actions; he finds it impossible to act or decide, a condition that is made worse by his perpetual need for analyzing: he is incapable of wanting anything; he has merely inclinations. The ironic levity of the text artfully conceals the psychological study of a certain type of character, that of the undecided person, whose traits are carried to a

[30] P. 35.

[31] *Paludes, O.C.,* I, 425–27.

morbid extreme, verging on neurosis. In general, it recalls the weakness of the will described by Pierre Janet as psychasthenia,[32] with its very special symptoms: feeling of unreality or little reality, "estrangement" or strangeness, "deconsistency" or inconsistency, inadequacy or deficiency, sterility, emptiness, monotony, forced and repeated beginnings, and above all, boredom. As we saw in the study of Gide's childhood and adolescence, that nervous weakness corresponded to an aspect of his personality which he owed to his complexes and to his temperament.[33] He comes back to it in *Paludes* apropos of Tityrus, and will again in *Les Faux-Monnayeurs,* in a tragic manner, apropos of Armand Vedel, author of *Un Traité de l'Insuffisance.*

Tityrus has Narcissus' posture: he lives bent over himself, but more because of his temperatment than his complexes. A deficiency in vital impetus keeps him from projecting himself into the outer world and acting: he constantly observes himself and spends his time in obsessive ruminations and ratiocinations. At a gathering of littérateurs at Angèle's, he diagnoses himself with the eloquence of exasperation:

Yes, gentlemen, yes! Tityrus has his sickness! ! ! All of us, all of us do, and throughout our lives, just as in these periods of deterioration in which the mania of doubt takes hold of us: did we lock the door tonight? we go back to see; did we put a tie on this morning? we finger our collars; did we button our trousers this evening? we make sure. . . . Note that we knew we'd done the thing perfectly; we do it again because of our sickness—the sickness of retrospection. We do it again because we've already done it; every one of our yesterday's acts seems to call out to us today; it's like a child to whom we've given life and whom we henceforth must keep alive. . . .

To him every act seems enslaving because it makes us depend on it:

Everything we cause to happen, we feel we must keep up; hence the dread of acting too much, for fear of becoming too dependent—for once an act is performed, instead of thrusting us forward, it becomes a hollow bed on which we fall back—*recubans.*[34]

He is afraid of acting, and wants to act as little as possible for fear of subsequently having doubts about his acts or being enslaved by them; as every involvement is likely to condemn him to the torture of retracting, he ends by choosing the psychological life with the lowest buying power.

The sickness of retrospection is one aspect of nervous weakness; another

[32] There are similarities between Gide's Tityrus and Goncharov's Oblomov. Gide did not read Goncharov's book until 1929 and then found it "dreary and mediocre" (*Journal,* 1929, p. 906).

[33] See above, bk. one, pt. i, chap. 11, and bk. one, pt. ii, chap. 22.

[34] *Paludes, O.C.,* I, 417–18.

is the sickness of introspection. Tityrus constantly analyzes himself instead of living; he is perpetually in the dual state of actor and spectator, and the spectator paralyzes the actor. He is constantly aware of himself and of his slightest intentions, and of the awareness he has of his awareness of his intentions, so that his consciousness (raised to various powers) becomes an instrument of his powerlessness to decide: he never extricates himself from his complications and puts all his effort into analyzing, with sincerity, the slightest flutter of his delicate and miserable soul. It is interesting to compare the state of mind we find in *Paludes* to what Gide was to write in 1900, in the *Revue Blanche,* about a "book by a little manofletters"— an article called "Sincérité." He had just learned of the death of "the very young Maurice Léon," who had killed himself after having published his first book. And he wrote a commentary on the news, no doubt questionable but very revealing of his own psychology:

We might as well say that he died of that book; for there are no objective reasons for his suicide, no sickness, no intrigue, no love affair. . . . The reason for his slow and complicated death, finished off by a pistol shot, must be sought solely in his thought, which he has so thoroughly expounded here. A sad autopsy! which will perhaps interest no one but psychologists and psychotherapists, but them it will interest passionately. On every page of the book we reflect, we think: What, then, is there in it that's so deadly?

Gide's analysis here of the "little manofletters" malady is very similar to "the great Valentin Knox's" diagnosis of Tityrus' malady. He begins by saying that the main character of the book is "obsessive retrospection"; and we know that Tityrus, also, described his malady as the sickness of retrospection:

My autobiography, he went on to say, I want to be cold, meticulous . . . that, a biography! Not a fact, not an emotion—I almost said: not a thought, so obviously does the study or criticism of thought take the place of new thought. It's like Orpheus' attempt to catch a glimpse of Eurydice, and his disappointed astonishment at never grasping more than her corpse. . . . Why didn't Orpheus simply move ahead without looking back?

The malady described here is indeed the malady of those who analyze. "And from then on he is inhabited by this attendant concern: *being sincere.* It is essential to note that this concern inhabits, and can only inhabit, those who have *nothing to say. . . .*"

Gide's conclusion is worth considering in its entirety:

Understanding everything and feeling nothing . . . Again the question comes up: what is there in it that's so deadly? Oh, nothing perhaps—for actually, and generations have proved it, we can very well live that way without dying from it, without even suffering too much from it, and above all, without suspecting it. It's the awareness of a malady, more than the malady itself, that leads to suicide, and we resign ourselves, without virtue, to suffering that we share. But as the world turns, it changes a little. . . . For a long time, intelligence was enough; if Léon is dead, it's probably because intelligence is *beginning not to be enough any more.* [35]

These little-known pages of Gide's have a special importance. The deficiency he criticizes in "the little manofletters," as in Tityrus and later in Armand Vedel, is not a deficiency of intelligence; on the contrary, it is a deficiency of instinct, a deficiency of vital impetus, whose flow is either too weak or runs dry too quickly because of obsessive self-awareness, obsessive reflection.

In order to force himself to act, Tityrus keeps an agenda, in which he writes in advance the program of what he must do, or rather, what he should do, and which, naturally, he does not do. The following is an example of one of Tityrus' days: "I began it [the agenda] three days ago. For example, this morning, across from the notation: try to get up at 6 o'clock, I wrote: got up at 7—then in parentheses: a negative unforeseen element." That brilliant formula, "a negative unforeseen element," makes it possible for Tityrus to bring a little of the unexpected into his monotonous life:

Next on the agenda were various notes: Write to Gustave and Léon. Be surprised at not receiving a letter from Jules. Go to see Gontran. Think about Richard's individuality. Worry about the relationship between Hubert and Angèle. Try to find time to go to the Jardins des Plantes; study there the variety called the little potamogeton for *Paludes.* Spend the evening at Angèle's. Next came the thought (I write, in advance, one for every day; they determine my sadness or my joy): "There are things that one repeats every day simply because one has nothing better to do; it's not a question of progress or of keeping things in order—but still, one can't do nothing at all. . . ."

That exemplary page, on which a program of feelings and reactions is decided in advance, is a model of what has been called "the rigidity of a psychasthenic," and contains the irresistible comic force that arises, according to the Bergsonian point of view, from the mechanical superimposed on the living.

In a life which is that regulated, even with regard to the emotional attitudes that should go along with every action, we can understand how expedient the "negative unforeseen element" is to Tityrus. But we can also understand the temptation of a positive unforeseen element—that is, an impulse, an act that springs forth directly, without the control of that exasperating self-awareness. Here we touch upon an important problem in

[35] "Sincérité." In *Morceaux choisis,* pp. 81–85.

Gide's psychology, and one just barely indicated in *Paludes:* that of the gratuitous act.

When Tityrus calls on Angèle who lives on the fifth floor, he stops on the third floor to "catch his breath" and notes down on a slip of paper the following thought: "Be blind in order to believe you're happy." This is hardly an original idea, but the author interprets it in his own way. Weary of perpetual introspection, of that vigilant eye of consciousness that always watches him and keeps him from acting, he advocates the idea not of pursuing himself but of fleeing from himself in blind and happy unconsciousness. Gide personally never managed to do it, but he entrusted his heroes with performing a gratuitous act (not an unmotivated act—there is no such thing—but an unconsciously motivated act. Now doing something on impulse gives weak-willed people the feeling of new-found freedom and unrestrained power. The gratuitous act, which has often been considered a Machiavellian invention of Gide's, is actually very common in people who suffer from a sickness of the will.

In *Paludes* the gratuitous act is still called a free act, but it comes to the same thing. Of course, Tityrus, who has few if any impulses, does not perform a gratuitous act, but his state of stagnation calls for it. We would not be especially surprised should the delicate aesthete, in a moment of exasperation, really strangle Angèle, just as in Baudelaire the bored man does away with the perfect woman in order to accelerate the course of a life that passes "too slowly," and, in a sense, as a nervous joke.

At times the sedentary Tityrus is choked with anguish and has the feeling of being at a dead end. Yet the futility of all action is his favorite theme, and he likes to discourage others from activities that he finds sterile. He is convinced of the futility of all effort outside of writing *Paludes,* which is in fact a treatise on the futility of effort and on the insignificance of any attitude, including the spectator's. But he himself writes, and literature is his reason for being, or at any rate, his pretext. In *Paludes,* Tityrus describes the feeling his own life gives him: "Boredom, monotony, futility." Next, he will write *Polders,* in which he will describe the "futility, monotony, and boredom" of that same life, and so on. He only likes literature in which nothing happens, literature that is disenchanted with vulgar action and reduced to the style which is the man—that is, himself—whom actually he likes very much. Yet behind Tityrus' self-love there is also self-hate. Basically, he is unhappy. "Why do you write?" Angèle asks him. "Me? I don't know—probably because it's a way of acting." Probably, but above all it is because he cannot keep himself from it and because if he did not write, he would no longer exist. Who is Tityrus? The author of *Paludes.* And who will Tityrus be after *Paludes?* The author of *Polders.* The whole thing is a marvelous caricature on deficiency in the form of literature.

The reaction of Gide's family to *Paludes* was far more moderate than he had anticipated. The severe uncle, Charles Gide, wrote to his nephew: "I find it a literary exercise like *Urien,* although in a very different chord, which proves that you have many you can use."[36] As for Madeleine Rondeaux, who had very discriminating taste in literature, she appreciated *Paludes,* but she did ask her cousin: "With such faith in life, such hope, and such love, how did you write *Paludes?* (Note that this is not a *criticism;* I find *Paludes* excellent in itself.)"[37]

On the whole, the literary critics paid little attention to *Paludes.* Some saw it as "a parody of M. Barrès' psychological self-cultivation." Barrès himself found it a "strange little book. You add disrespect and fantasy, when I thought that Heine had left the poets nothing to express on that level."[38] But Mallarmé's letter about *Paludes* is one of the most flattering of all those he ever wrote to Gide:

VALVINS, PAR AVONS, SEINE-ET-MARNE, July 21

The first of all, before anyone in the world, I should have answered you, dear friend, for having presented me with the A copy of *Paludes:* but I preferred to work out my answer at leisure. I make no allusion at first to your tart and precious drop of irony which is maintained for a hundred pages, its essence is unique; but, otherwise, the spiritual arrangement of facts approaches the marvelous and you have found, in the suspense and asides, a form that had to be introduced and will not be recaptured. I think that it's really yours, Gide, or full of genius, this discreet and terrifying banter on the surface of the soul. Thank you for the affectionate honor of having mentioned my name in it.

Yours always,
STÉPHANE MALLARMÉ[39]

The most pertinent of the few reviews devoted to *Paludes* was Camille Mauclair's in the *Mercure de France.* "I like *Paludes,*" he remarked, "because it is the book of a man who has had enough." And he saw that man (whom he knew well) as haunted by "new perfumes, bigger flowers, untried pleasures," just as Flaubert was by the visionary desires of *La Tentation de Saint Antoine. Paludes* was indeed the book of a man who had had enough. By ridiculing the confined existence of an aesthete, Gide showed his desire to escape once and for all from the salons and literary coteries. Had the nosy Angèle asked him: "But why, then, are you writing *Paludes?*" he would have been sincere in answering: "So that I can set out

[36] Unpublished (Bibliothèque Doucet).

[37] July 23, 1895 (quoted by Jean Schlumberger, p. 119).

[38] Unpublished (Bibliothèque Doucet).

[39] Unpublished (Bibliothèque Doucet). The glorious name of Mallarmé is mentioned on p. 439 of *Paludes, O.C.,* I.

again." And where was friend Hubert leaving for, as the chronicler Tityrus, his short treatise finished, continued to be bored to death writing *Polders?* "For Biskra."[40] This satire on sedentary life was merely the preface to a justification of a nomadic life: *Les Nourritures terrestres.* By making fun of the kind of nature that is primarily defined by privatives, Gide was strengthening his will to protest, to assert himself; and by stigmatizing faintheartedness, he was urging himself on toward a dangerous life. *Paludes* was no more than a curtain raiser; but the tragedy—which, according to the classical definition, is a crisis nearing its end—was about to begin.

[40] *Paludes, O.C.,* I, 452.

41: Wilde and Douglas

> *"Met Wilde in Blidah!—terrifying evo-
> lution toward evil—voluntary surrender
> of the will."*
>
>

Unpublished notes for
Si le grain ne meurt

WHEN he left La Brévine sometime during the last two weeks in December, 1894, Gide was not yet decided to take off for North Africa. Ever since he had finished *Paludes,* he felt that he was prey to a "curious disease," in which overexertion no doubt played a part: ". . . a kind of torpor which is perhaps no more than sleep; I feel like sleeping all the time; I think it's a great need for a free and complete-ly physical life, for I'm also always hungry as a wolf."[1] In Montpellier, where he was visiting the Charles Gides, he continued to complain about overwhelming fatigue, and he once again felt shy and self-defiant. Even conversation became difficult for him: "It takes effort to listen to what people say to me and I feel forced to smile in order to prove to myself that I understood." Even so, he was not overly alarmed about his state of de-pression, for he knew by experience that it was only momentary: "These are bad temporary periods during which you'd like to hide yourself in a hole, during which you bore yourself, during which you tell yourself that you've overdone it."[2] Actually, those short-lived periods of depression corresponded to one aspect of his nervous temperament.

When in a state of nervous fatigue, Gide's natural indecision took on even greater proportions. Was he going to leave for Africa? Was he going

[1] Letter from André Gide to his mother, Jan. 1, 1895, unpublished.

[2] *Ibid.,* Jan. 17, 1895, unpublished.

to return to Paris? He could not bring himself to make up his mind about that, or about whether or not to write to Madeleine: "Tell Madeleine that I think of nothing more than of writing to her, but that at present the only things I could tell her would be dull and mediocre. I prefer to wait, for I owe her, I wish her, nothing but joy."[3]

On January 17 Gide left Montpellier for Marseilles, where he was to take his boat. But he no sooner arrived than he was overcome by anguish and wrote to his mother, begging her and Madeleine to come along with him on his trip. That very important letter, dated January 18, has a tone of pathetic entreaty. It shows a sincere attempt to clutch at his love as though it were his one chance for salvation:

May I confess it? . . . I'm waiting . . . I'm waiting for you both!—Yes! I'm so obsessed with wanting you to come that I don't dare take off and leave Marseilles without knowing whether you'll come. . . . Answer quickly, for this waiting wears me down: Why wouldn't you come—immediately. . . . The idea now is to be able to carry it off with enthusiasm, make it something joyous, glorious, and keep the heart and mind so busy that no time is left to know whether it's really reasonable or not. You *yourself* have had, and still have, time to think it over[4]—Madeleine musn't be allowed to think it over too much —she would be afraid and would wear herself out in futile reflection. . . . The more I think about it, the more I see it as the only way out, the only loophole in that cornered a situation. Otherwise, nothing will be done—and nothing will be undone either. So I won't leave if I have no answer—but since I get panicky from waiting too long—wire me, I beg of you, and may it be "we're on our way." I can't tell you how grieved I'd be by any other answer. Imagine what the crossing would be like, together, all three of us, in the splendid weather that's on its way back—If not, imagine what my wretched solitary crossing would be.[5]

The tone of that letter is the tone of a man who feels himself in danger and who is afraid. A sentence like "The more I think about it, the more I see it as the only way out," probably remained obscure for Mme. Gide, but surely it was not for the man who wrote it. He perhaps wrote it thoughtlessly, but certainly not unconsciously. He knew that leaving alone for North Africa inevitably meant giving in to his sexual inclinations. And although the "new being" was intellectually convinced of the "profit" in "satisfying desires," the Walter in him was not dead and "the old man" was calling for help. But on the next day, January 19, he seems to have pulled himself together:

[3] *Ibid.*

[4] Gide had already written to his mother about his plan for all three of them to travel together, and in his letter of January 1 (unpublished), asked her to speak to Madeleine about it.

[5] Unpublished.

Let Madeleine do what she wants; she must be the one who desires and wants this trip. If she's against it, she must know that nothing will be changed between us, that I'll take off at once alone as if nothing had been said, and that I shan't even be sad about it, convinced that if she refuses to come, some higher reason is leading her, to which I want to submit fully, acknowledging her authority and determined never to go against it. Besides, I don't want to allow the happiness of us both to depend on circumstances. It is within us, deeply, and no one could do anything about it.

Yesterday I wrote to Madeleine; this morning I'm sorry that I sent the letter; it seems full of confusion and anxiety;—*it deforms me;*—I'm neither confused nor anxious; I'm only tired—and I think my fatigue comes from the fact that I can't work. When work is, as it has become for me, a need, it is work itself that is restful.—This morning I'm in better spirits, after finally having had a better night; I'm again beginning to see things and beings as one must, that is, from their angle of beauty. . . .

He added the following *special* postscript:

I'm coming back to it again, mamma darling, it means so much to me, I attach such capital importance to it: Madeleine must read this four-page letter herself —give it to her without saying anything.—Perhaps she'll understand it in a special way, which you can only imperfectly imagine. I think it's *indispensable.* You'll realize it afterwards.[6]

We notice to what point Gide, although proud to get on alone, would appear subject, if not to his mother's authority, at least to that of Madeleine, who seems to have already taken Mme. Gide's place. The transfer of authority shown in that letter is of the greatest significance. But by leaving the decision to his cousin, he avoids having to decide for himself, and is free, as it were, from responsibility. If Madeleine comes, he will give the old man every chance; if she refuses to come, he will give the new being every chance. So much the worse or so much the better. . . . Therefore, when on the afternoon of that same day he received a letter from his mother refusing to take that "costly" trip to Algeria, and putting André and Madeleine's meeting off till later, probably during the following summer at La Roque, he resigned himself to it at once:

Don't think that there is any spirit of rebellion in me. I'll accept everything very simply. . . . I accept the idea of La Roque with pleasure—gratitude—I shall enjoy it with no reservations, I won't even consider it a last resort—but you must understand that it is not *suitable* at present—and know how to take a small hint.—Besides, I'm not bent on any one place more than any other, but I had hoped that it would be in a *new and distant* land . . . for me it's a condition *sine qua non.* . . . I'm afraid La Roque will be charming but insignificant —we're all in danger of suffering from it. You talk about expenses—let me

[6] Letter from André Gide to his mother, Jan. 19, 1895, unpublished.

tell you that I find that the height of absurdity! and even completely unjusti-
fiable in this situation.[7]

It is certain that Mme. Gide did not take the small hint and considered
the whole thing no more than a caprice. Moreover, the next day she received a letter that could not have been more optimistic:

Ah! dear, dear mamma! What has happened to me? Just that I've started to be
madly joyous again. Seeing, feeling, understanding; loving God through all
things . . . One might say it was like a cataract operation, or more precisely,
an ear that suddenly opens up—bang! . . . Oh! what special physiologies we
have!

He had seen a doctor who completely reassured him as to the state of his
lungs, and had spent the day with a journalist from Marseilles, Léon Parsons,[8] who introduced him to a woman lost in admiration for *Les Cahiers
d'André Walter*. He was in a real state of exuberance and ended his letter
with these words: "Read this news to my cousins, I want them to know
that I'm happy again."[9]

Gide arrived in Algiers on January 22, after a "terrible crossing," and his
initial enthusiasm had not withstood seasickness. Moreover, he had hoped
to see white Algiers in radiant sunlight, and it was raining.[10] But no
sooner did the clouds disappear and the sky become luminous once again
than he got back his confidence in life: "Yes, I'm certainly at the mercy of
the sky. . . ." On January 23 his barometer registered darkness; on January
24 it was pointing to fair weather. He even went so far as to attribute his
beseeching letter from Marseilles solely to the influence of his aunt, Mme.
Charles Gide. If he begged his mother and Madeleine to go along with
him, it was "simply for the sake of appearances, as I knew the answer beforehand. . . . Don't consider it either as insanity, or as frenzy, or as any
kind of confusion—not even as anxiety."[11] In other words, he would seem
to be denying the fact that he had called for help, and his letters—which
contradict each other—again prove his basic ambivalence. Actually, the
only point on which he never changed was that of making all his joys and
sorrows contribute to his literary works:

[7] *Ibid.*, Saturday, 3 P.M., unpublished.

[8] There is also a question of Léon Parsons in a letter to Paul Valéry, Jan. 20, 1895
(*Correspondance*, p. 232).

[9] Letter from André Gide to his mother, Jan. 20, 1895, unpublished.

[10] *Ibid.*, Jan. 23, 1895, unpublished.

[11] *Ibid.*, Jan. 24, 1895, unpublished.

Please understand, mamma darling, that all that, the fog and the joys, is fertilizer for literature, and that I'm maturing accordingly and growing richer with every exchange of emotion, for like Aladdin, I do no more than turn in a worn-out lamp for a new lamp.[12]

On January 24 he left Algiers for Blidah: "In a few hours I'm leaving Algiers, that frightful bazaar, for Blidah, where I shall try to live." But he found Blidah, "flower of the Sahel! little rose!"[13] under a gray sky and very faded indeed. The mountains that rise above the Sahel were covered with clouds and snow, and the entire plain seemed to him insipid. He vainly sought suitable lodgings in and around Blidah: "I've seen everything that is possible to see: *there is absolutely nothing.*" He shut himself up in his hotel room, wired Mme. Mazué to find out whether he could come to Biskra, and continued reading *Barnaby Rudge,* which he had begun in Montpellier. As the rain fell outside, he was prey to the saddest of thoughts. He tried to work: "The lowering sky weighed on my thoughts; I wanted to work, but I felt uninspired; I was languishing in unspeakable boredom. Mixed in with my revolt against the sky was a revolt against myself; I thought of myself with contempt, with hate."[14] He reproached himself with his idleness and egoism; he was horrified by his hedonistic aspirations. He felt inclined to put himself once again under constraints, and would have liked to give himself up to serious study.

Yet on January 25 he wrote to his mother: "Here I am, with a clear mind, starting *to write* again. I'm saved!" He stayed on in Blidah for two days more, Saturday and Sunday. He had received a telegram from Mme. Mazué informing him that he was expected in Biskra. He planned to isolate himself and work very hard. On Sunday afternoon he closed his trunks and had them put on the hotel bus, keeping Fichte's *Vocation of the Scholar* with him to read in the train. When he went downstairs to pay his bill, he glanced at the slate, where the names of new arrivals were written in chalk: "I wanted to leave at four o'clock: my trunks were ready, I was ready.—When what name should I see in passing the list of travelers? . . . Oscar Wilde!"[15]

As soon as Gide saw the name of Wilde, and that of Lord Douglas a little beneath his, his "first reaction" was to erase his own and head immediately for the station on foot. On the way he changed his mind, had

[12] *Ibid.,* Jan. 28, 1895, unpublished.

[13] *Les Nourritures terrestres,* III, *O.C.,* II, 105.

[14] *Si le grain ne meurt,* II, 239.

[15] Letter from André Gide to his mother, Jan. 28, 1895, unpublished.

his trunks and suitcases taken off the bus, and went back to the Grand Hotel de l'Orient. In his unpublished notes for *Si le grain ne meurt* he wrote:

Met O. W. in Florence in '94, with L. A. D. The following year in Blidah—the evening I was leaving the hotel, I saw his name and his *vade mecum*'s hanging up in the list of Foreigners. I began by erasing mine; an act of cowardice which I was sorry for at once. I had my trunks carried up again and stayed to dinner with them.

He commented on his recantation in *Si le grain ne meurt,* attributing it either to "self-consciousness," as Wilde's proximity had become compromising, or to the "unsociable mood" he was in after a period of depression.

In the letter to his mother, directly after having said that he had seen Oscar Wilde's name, he added: "Perhaps he had seen my name—leaving without shaking his hand, I couldn't have escaped from the suspicion of fleeing from him. He had gone out—I therefore missed my train and stayed to wait for him." He waited in the hotel lobby for Wilde and Douglas to return:

He came back in the evening, that terrifying man, the most dangerous product of modern civilization—still, as in Florence, escorted by young Lord Douglas, both of them on the London and Paris blacklists, and, if one weren't far away, the most compromising people in the world to be with. Besides, just as in Florence, and in spite of abundant smiles, apparently very annoyed at meeting anyone. Fortunately, as a play of his is in rehearsal in London,[16] he will have to leave in a few days; otherwise, I would not be able to avoid him in Biskra. I must add that he's charming—unbelievable, and everything considered, a very great figure. It was a great piece of luck that I saw so much of him and knew him so well a few years ago in Paris, for it was his best period, and never again will he be as good.

Gide remained perplexed about the strange couple. Sometimes he had the impression that Wilde was a gentle, weak, irresolute man, completely dominated by the young and terrifying Bosie, who had made a toy of him; sometimes, on the contrary, he felt that Wilde was a "terrifying man" and incongruously advised his mother of it:

Impossible to understand the worth of that young Lord Douglas, whom Wilde seems to have depraved right down to the marrow—in the manner of a Vautrin, far more terrifying (I find) than the one in *Père Goriot*—because he does everything under the pretext of aestheticism. Lord Douglas plans to come to Biskra, where I hope to see him a little better and understand how much in

[16] *An Ideal Husband* was performed for the first time on January 3, 1895, at the Haymarket. After its enormous success, Wilde took off for North Africa with Douglas, leaving the rehearsals of *The Importance of Being Earnest* in the hands of George Alexander. (Lord Queensberry-Percy Colson, *Oscar Wilde and the Douglas Clan.*)

that madness of deprivation is sincere and how much affected. Otherwise, he doesn't interest me enormously; he would interest me more if I knew something about English society, for he is representative of all that is the most lord, the most Brummel, the most Byronian.

He dined and spent Sunday evening with his two companions. It was raining in torrents. A guide led them to a shady café, where they witnessed a brawl between Spaniards and Arabs. He described it in a letter to his mother, but fortunately kept silent about Lord Douglas' comment as to the "rather ugly guide" who took them around in the rain from café to café: "These guides are stupid: explain to them as you may, they always take you to cafés full of women. I hope that you're like me: I have a horror of women. I only like boys."[17] And Wilde did not conceal his desire to meet young Arabs "as beautiful as bronze statues."

Nothing else happened that evening, which, "everything considered, was rather dreary." The next morning Gide left "almost surreptitiously" for Algiers, where he spent the day. The letter he wrote to his mother begins with the words: "My swith mother," which testifies to the very recent English influence and a rather approximate idea of the language:

Had I told you that I bolted out of Blidah because of that terrifying Wilde who was stopping there.—I found him again here. The first evening, dinner together, evening together—the young Douglas having stayed over in Blidah for an extra day. Marvels! marvels! the two of them . . . and that young lord, whom I'm beginning to see very clearly, that future marquis, that son of kings, that 25-year-old Scotsman, branded, ruined, devoured by a sickly thirst for infamy, who seeks shame and finds it, and despite everything, retains an ambiguous distinction . . . ah! how badly I write all that—but how much I could say about it! You see types like that in Shakespeare's historical tragedies.

And Wilde! Wilde! what life is more tragic than his!—if he paid more attention, were he capable of attention, he would be a genius, a great genius. But he himself said it and knows it: "I've put my genius into my life; I've put only my talent into my works. I know it, and it's the tragedy of my life."

That's exactly why those who will have known him well will have had, when near him, that shudder of terror, which I always have with him—from something very great, and beautiful—but it's not possible that he quite realizes it. I don't know his works and don't believe that his works are up to him; I shall have known the best of him, deeply and very intimately, I'm happy to meet him far away, and even Algiers isn't far enough for me to see him without apprehension; I spoke to him very frankly; I managed to tell him that if I should meet him in London or Paris, I wouldn't recognize him—and I'd do that if only to safeguard our friendship, and to be able to defend him when I'm with people who attack him. He was born to be a Roman emperor—Heliogabalus or some other one. He's going away tomorrow—and I'm glad; if he came to Biskra, I would leave.

[17] *Si le grain ne meurt,* II, 334.

Lord Douglas is staying on; he's coming to Biskra; I shall be able to watch him at leisure. If Wilde wasn't being played in London, with a run of three hundred performances, and if the Prince of Wales did not attend the premières, he would be in jail, and Lord Douglas as well. In France we've only had Verlaine and Rimbaud—in England almost all their great poets are outside the law —marvels! marvels!

It's unfortunate that all that is deformed by detestable literary theories. They are right for Oscar Wilde—but his disciples! his disciples!

André Walckenaër has been here since yesterday; I was unable to see him until this evening. The De Linsecs keep him on a leash. They're at the same hotel as Oscar Wilde, whom M. de Linsec knows well enough by reputation to turn his back on him openly. It was therefore impossible to introduce André Walckenaër.[18]

There is no way of knowing whether Gide met Wilde again by chance or if their meeting had been planned. At any rate, Lord Alfred Douglas arrived from Blidah unexpectedly on Tuesday, January 29. That evening Gide and Wilde were at the hotel bar, and the Irishman was showing his new friend some "love letters" which had been forwarded to him from London: "Oh! this one is from a young . . . how do you say?[19] . . . acrobat? Yes, acrobat; absolutely delightful." Suddenly Douglas, whom they were not expecting, came in:

He brushed past me, as though he didn't recognize me, planted himself in front of Wilde, and in a hissing, contemptuous voice, full of hate, rapped out in one breath a few sentences which I didn't understand at all; then he suddenly turned on his heel and walked out. Wilde had weathered the storm without saying a word; but he had turned very pale. . . .[20]

Seeing to what degree Bosie's companionship obsessed and dissipated Wilde, and "what a lover's pleasure" he seemed to take in "allowing himself to be dominated" by a boy who took every opportunity to involve him in scandals, made a strong impression on Gide. He was also struck by Wilde's "excessive assurance" with regard to his pending trial, and by his most singular conception of "tragic pleasure," which had long since given him a taste for "little perverse messenger boys,"[21] bellboys, and stable boys, and for walking through the streets of Algiers, escorted by "an extraordinary gang of ruffians"[22] to whom he threw handfuls of the money he owed to the triumphal success of his plays:

[18] Monday, Jan. 30, 1895, unpublished.

[19] English in the text.

[20] *Si le grain ne meurt*, II, 336–37.

[21] A newspaper article on the publication of *The Picture of Dorian Gray* (quoted by Robert Merle, *Oscar Wilde*, p. 99).

[22] *Oscar Wilde. In memoriam*, p. 31.

"I hope I've really demoralized this city," he told me. I thought of what Flaubert answered when he was asked the kind of fame he aspired to the most: "That of a demoralizer." I looked upon all that with great astonishment, admiration, and apprehension. I knew about his shaky situation, the hostilities, the attacks, and the somber anxiety he hid beneath his bold joy. . . . "But if you go back there, what will happen?" I asked him. "Do you know the risk you're taking?" "One must never know that. . . . I must go as far as possible. . . . Something must happen . . . something else."[23]

The author-actor was out in quest of a fifth act.

On Wednesday the 30th, Douglas left for Blidah: "He was working on a plan to carry off a young *caouadji,* whom he intended to take along to Biskra. . . ."[24] In the absence of Douglas, who was retained by that singular "work," Gide and Wilde spent not several days, as Gide wrote in *Si le grain ne meurt,* but Wednesday evening, January 30, together. As soon as Douglas had left, Wilde asked Gide whether he wanted to go with him to a Moorish café.

Like most perverts, Wilde was proselytizing. He took André Gide to an Arab café, the one described in *Amyntas.* Some old Arabs, squatting on mats, were smoking kef. As the two men were drinking ginger tea, "a marvelous adolescent," willowy, slender, and of much the same color as the one in *fuscus Amyntas,* appeared in the half-open doorway. Upon a sign from Wilde, he came over, sat down near them, and "exquisitely" played a reed flute, accompanied by a *darbouka* player. A few minutes later, on leaving the café, Wilde said to Gide in a low voice: " 'Dear,[25] do you want the little musician?' Oh! how dark the alley was! I thought my heart would fail me; and how I had to brace myself to get up the courage to answer: 'Yes,' and in what a choked voice!"[26] The word "courage," which André Walter reserved for the struggle against his desires, André Gide used here to designate the act of giving in to them. In the carriage the Irishman burst out into interminable laughter, apologized for it, and then started laughing again even harder. They arrived at a house with a double entrance, which was being watched by the police. Wilde closed himself into a room with one of the little musicians, Gide with the other.

That episode, in which Oscar Wilde played the part of a procurer, had decisive importance in Gide's sexual life: "The attempt with Meriem, that effort I made at 'normalization,' was not repeated, for it did not correspond

---

[23] *Ibid.,* pp. 31–33.

[24] *Si le grain ne meurt,* II, 339.

[25] English in the text.

[26] *Si le grain ne meurt,* II, 343.

to my nature; I now found what was normal for me."[27] That very considerable statement in *Si le grain ne meurt* would appear ill-considered and calls for some reservations completely missing from Gide's text and which we shall come back to. "Since then, each time I have sought pleasure, I have tried to capture the memory of that night. . . . My joy was so great that even were love to be mixed in with it, I cannot imagine anything more complete."[28] Thus love had no part in that fundamental experience, any more than it was to have in subsequent experiences.[29] Be that as it may, after having described his rapture "at clasping in my bare arms that wild, lascivious, mysterious, and perfect little body," Gide added:

After Mohammed had left me, I spent a long time in a state of quivering jubilation, and although I had already achieved pleasure five times *with him*,[30] I revived my ecstasy over and again, and back in my hotel room, prolonged the echoes of it until morning.[31]

The most interesting thing about this record performance, remarkable as it was, is the way in which it was achieved—that is, by means of the same vice, reciprocal or solitary, from which he had so much wanted to free himself.

The overexertion of the Algerian night seems not to have depressed him:

At the first pale rays of dawn I got up; I ran, yes really ran, in sandals, well beyond Mustapha; feeling not the slightest fatigue from my night, but on the contrary, a liveliness, a kind of lightness of body and soul, which stayed with me all through the day.[32]

He immediately informed his mother of his liveliness. . . . And on Thursday, January 31, he wrote to her:

Oscar Wilde left this morning. I'm glad. . . . *I'm counting on a radiant springtime.* I'm writing all sorts of notes for my *Nourritures terrestres*. That frightful title is exactly right—and now I shan't change it any more. It's frightful as long as it's not accepted—*retrospectively* it could become superb—because of its very candor and brutality.[33]

Thus on January 31, 1895, the day of Wilde's departure, Gide conclusively decided on a title for his now-famous book.

He was determined to start work immediately. But that same letter to

27 *Ibid.*, p. 346.

28 *Ibid.*, pp. 345–46.

29 With one exception, which was to be evoked in *Les Faux-Monnayeurs*.

30 The italics are mine.

31 *Si le grain ne meurt,* II, 346–47.

32 *Ibid.*, p. 347.

33 Unpublished.

his mother ended with the announcement that a wire from Lord Douglas had "just arrived." He enclosed the wire in his letter and added the strange postscript: "Ah! Ah! Lord Alfred! What do you want of me?" Gide seemed very interested indeed in getting to know Douglas. . . . And while the author of *Les Nourritures terrestres* was preparing to sing of rejuvenation, Oscar Wilde was sailing off to old England and hard labor.

On Sunday, February 2, Gide was at Sétif, awaiting Alfred Douglas and the young *caouadji* he had "carried off" for the purpose of his debauchery. While waiting for the train, he wrote to his mother:

I'm waiting for Lord Douglas. He begged me not to leave Algiers without him —to delay my departure 24 hours. There was perhaps a measure of cowardice in my refusal—for fear of scandal—for fear of the impression it would make. I reproached myself for it. And I'm waiting for him here; tomorrow we shall travel together and arrive in Biskra together. I told him yesterday, very frankly, that I didn't want to leave Algiers with him, being a serious-minded man and wanting to be respected because I seemed respectable to myself. I now consider all that as ridiculously personal considerations—the important thing is *To Be,* and *to appear* signifies nothing until afterward.—Lord Douglas is traveling with a little Arab boy twelve or thirteen years old, whom he picked up in Blidah—a real kidnapping.

These lines he so curiously addressed to his mother do show that Gide seemed no longer to fear the opinions of others. He went on to say that he heard a mysterious voice call out to him:

"Come—don't tarry—there are still other things and always new things. . . ." And it's madness to regret the lands we have left; it's the vanity of wanting to prolong our youth into our maturity. I now feel that my youth is over. In this book I'm planning to write, I should like to bury it altogether. I feel myself maturing and ready for more serious and stronger works.—You might find it indecent that I talk so much about myself—but it's because I'm unable to write a line or a sentence so long as I'm not in *complete possession* (that is, WITH FULL KNOWLEDGE) of myself. I should like very submissively to follow nature—the unconscious, which is within myself and must be *true*. The strange thing is that those who see me now[34] say that I'm becoming the man I was when I was writing *André Walter*. And I don't think they're wrong. I'm on my way back to that point, but richer because of a huge profit from my travels. . . . I'm still "basically" the same. . . . At Biskra I want to work, work, work. Really, I think of nothing more than of that, and at the present time I would trade the most beautiful countries for a peaceful study to work in.[35]

[34] He probably means André Walckenaër.

[35] Letter from André Gide to his mother, Feb. 2, 1895, unpublished.

Such was his state of mind when he saw Lord Douglas and his *caouad-ji*, a very handsome young Arab nobleman, get off the train. But Ali's beauty had no effect on him: "Nothing put me off more than the effeminate appearance of his whole being, which is no doubt exactly what would have seduced others."[36] Gide did not envy Bosie, and in reaction to the spectacle of his eccentricities and debauchery, he was all the more inclined to remain in "a state of chastity." The state lasted, if we are to believe *Si le grain ne meurt,* during his "entire stay" in Biskra. Thus his return to Biskra was not a return to dissipation but a return to laborious concentration: "I buried myself in my work all the more, with the flattering feeling that I was atoning for something." The Huguenot took over from the hedonist: "Lord Douglas. Ali. I react to Lord Douglas with a horror of evil and debauchery, but not calm enough—no, frantic and almost with the desire to kill."[37] The relationship between André Gide and Alfred Douglas became more and more strained until Douglas' departure on February 18.

On February 16, Gide—now at the Royal Hotel in Biskra—received a letter from Madeleine Rondeaux. She had not written a word since her cousin had asked her to go along with him on his trip, and he had been tormented about it:

Perhaps, without wanting to admit it to myself, my former state of gloominess came from Madeleine's silence: her last letter, so delightful, overcame all the clouds, doubts, confusion, etc. I should like to answer her at once: I think about it constantly, but am too continually disturbed. Events, emotions, and new ideas are piling up, and every hour of the day brings its own beauty. I see quite a bit of Lord Douglas, while keeping my distance from him: I learn more from watching him than I would from reading many books. The spectacle of life is more profitable than . . . I'm talking nonsense.—I've seen extraordinary things, and am again just intoxicated enough to enjoy everything. What dominates everything is Madeleine's letter; please tell her that—don't fail to tell her. Her letter crossed one that I was writing to her. I receive avalanches of pamphlets, books with dedications, letters, etc.—I answer nothing—I live; I enjoy the sky, the wind, the voices of the children who play around my window. Since my apartment is on a level with the ground, they're often there, laughing, chatting, I'm delightfully disturbed. My role is being on a level with life; I like not to prefer my occupations to those of others for a while.

[36] *Si le grain ne meurt,* II, 349.

[37] Unpublished notes for *Si le grain ne meurt.* The word "enough" was crossed out by Gide.

And on February 19 he went back to the subject of Madeleine's letter:

Yesterday I wrote a long letter to Madeleine; I could not leave her exquisite letter any longer without an answer. Her silence tormented me; I was afraid she was misjudging me, after my very mad proposition: she considered it only great love and does not reproach me at all. She continues to wait and to hope that we will see new countries together; she still talks about it and her insistence delights and surprises me:—what can it mean?—How we shall have waited! . . .

And so, even in the most exotic states of mind, a "mysterious thread" continued to bind the adventurous Theseus to his past love. Being uncertain of his own "victory," he did not yet know that even then, he and nothing else was leading him in the labyrinth. In love as he was with his youthful freedom, one single message from Madeleine was enough to make him again dream of making her his companion. In his troubled state he turned yet again toward Ariadne.

42: Open Rebellion

"I was not satisfied to free myself from the rule; I claimed to justify my frenzy and to vindicate my madness."

Si le grain ne meurt, *II, 361*

FTER Douglas' departure, Gide went through a period of over-activity and lyrical exaltation that lasted until his return to France in mid-April. Leaving early in the morning, with pencils and notebooks, he would go off alone on "exhausting excursions" through the desert, "sometimes following the dry bed of the wadi, sometimes going up into the large dunes, where at times I would stay until nightfall, intoxicated with boundless space, strangeness, and solitude, my heart lighter than a bird."[1] It was then that he composed large fragments of *Les Nourritures terrestres*. He wrote to his mother: "Biskra pleases me more than I can say; it's not the oasis that I like, but the desert, the Arabs, and the only reason I prefer Biskra to the other small oases is because a Frenchman can live there more comfortably."[2] He was no longer attracted by the local picturesque quality or "the small particularities of the country": "What charms me here is the light, the monotony, the desert, the *likeness*."[3] And he said that he could now stand the sirocco "like an old desert palm tree."[4]

In the evenings he would meet Athman, who had gone back to his job as a guide, an occupation that consisted primarily in leading foreigners to the Oulads. Athman would tell Gide about the profits he made each day, and when he explained how by increasing the commissions he received both from the foreigners and the Oulads he substantially rounded off his

[1] *Si le grain ne meurt,* II, 352.

[2] Feb. 19, 1895, unpublished.

[3] *Ibid.*

[4] Feb. 25, 1895, unpublished.

baksheesh, Gide became indignant: "I accepted his being a procurer; but
that he be dishonest, no, that I would not tolerate." By appealing to his
"sense of dignity," Gide urged him to give up his illicit profits, explaining
that he wanted him "to be worthy of my friends when you meet them in
Paris."[5] And indeed he had made plans to take Athman to Paris with him.

He informed his mother of it on February 19, presenting his plan in the
most innocuous and even reasonable way:

Expenses being what they are, I'm no longer thinking of looking for other
places but will stay here until April, then come back to Paris at once. I must
finally tell you about my plan for bringing Athman. He'll help in the house
at La Roque and Marie will thus be all the more relaxed. Everything is arranged and worked out with his family (although it's not completely settled
yet)—they're all charming. His good mother, whom you know, tells me that
she would not let her son go that far away with anyone but me, but she also
remembers you and says she's happy that her son will learn "good manners"
with us. Athman himself is extraordinary, far funnier than last year, affectionate (I was going to say devoted—but I prefer to wait), and *brave* [good-
natured] (in the *Midi* sense of the word).[6]

Presented in that way, it was all meant to seem quite natural. Gide went
on to tell his mother about another plan of his, that of buying a plot of
land in Biskra and building a small house on it "with two apartments—
which I can rent every time I don't live there." The letter ended with the
affectionate words: "Adieu. I should like to come back and spend a long
time with you. I've finished with my youth and with this apprenticeship in
life. Traveling tires me and I'm no longer curious. Adieu—Your beloved
son." Was he then ready to settle down, as the saying goes? No, not yet. . . .
For in the same letter: "Tired of seeing, I want to make others see, and all
my passion will again awaken in contact with a beginner's curiosity."

However, Mme. Gide, who at the beginning seemed not to have attached great importance to her son's new caprices, began to worry seriously about them and add objection to objection. "Concerning the plot of
land," he answered, "it would take too long to explain to you that your
arguments are excellent only from far away; besides, the matter is now in
the hands of the notary public."[7] As for carrying off Athman, André Gide
was absolutely determined, and in his replies to his mother, his tone was
becoming sharper and sharper:

Carrying off Athman presents lots of difficulties—you almost never mention
the real ones;—it was not until after I had turned the plan over and over in
my mind for about ten days *without mentioning it to him,* until after I had
seriously considered the pros and the cons—until after I had spoken to him

[5] *Si le grain ne meurt,* II, 354.

[6] Unpublished.   [7] March 6, 1895, unpublished.

about it as an idle and improbable notion—that I now am getting him accustomed to seeing it as a serious probability—at the point when for me it's already a well-established resolution. I therefore really don't know what you're alluding to, going back to that old grievance: you never keep all of your promises—I really don't see anything in me that justifies such an accusation, for I think that, on the contrary, I'm extremely scrupulous in such things and of a faithful nature—and I think that my friends know it well—seeing the way they're all now asking favors of me. And I'm delighted about it. I don't like your trying to get me by my conscience as another would get someone by the hair. Anyway, it's just too bad.—As for the Ramadan, be assured that I have no intention of bringing the delinquent until it's over. Etc., etc.

On March 10 he seemed completely exasperated:

Everything you tell me with regard to Athman is *outrageously* absurd—please let me tell you that—besides, it's useless to talk about it further; I've put the arguments before him . . . , etc., etc. The arguments against it, *which I feared* and which seem to me most serious, you don't even mention. Which means that everything is for the best.[8]

It is quite clear that Mme. Gide did not yet suspect her son's sexual habits and the reasons that made Athman's abduction a scabrous affair.

On March 14 he wrote his mother a perfectly insolent letter:

All that rigmarole about Athman is beside the point and therefore very irritating. I never said that he was to replace Marie—and to do the bedrooms—where did you ever get that idea?—You have the habit of always looking for as many arguments as possible without worrying about whether or not they're worth anything.—I said that he would help Marie (polishing shoes—and almost nothing in Paris—but at La Roque bringing water up to the bedrooms, carrying plates from the kitchen to the dining room—lots of little diverse chores); besides, I never claimed that he could completely replace a servant. Remember that he's just 15 and is being trained, in fact . . . you must find a place to put him up—and not at a hotel—with us—and if you don't find a way to do it, then you'll force me to ask Paul to take him in his studio, for I don't want to leave him free to associate with just anybody. I have perfect confidence in him in that respect, but I don't want to expose him . . . you know perfectly well that there's a room on the 7th floor that's only used to store trunks . . . oh the terrible bad faith of Mme. Gide—or else we could sleep together in the guest room [when all the others are taken], which personally would be completely immaterial to me.

Athman's dirty? You know that he's as vain as a peacock and is easily ashamed—my answer to you is that he'll soon be clean—I take the responsibility for it.

Madeleine will take me less seriously because of Athman—?!—I think it's quite the contrary and besides, such things are absolutely none of your business. . . .

[8] Letter from André Gide to his mother, March 10, 1895, unpublished.

As for the *face* Marie will make, let me tell you that what she does depends entirely on you. . . . Remember your *absurd* behavior on my return from La Brévine and how by your lack of confidence you turned Marie against both of us. . . .

And now I don't know how to go about . . . begging you to get rid of your resentment and your righteous indignation on me alone and to welcome, with a smile and gently and with open arms, a 15-year-old child who is going to be away from his family for the first time. . . . And try to make Marie understand the same thing.[9]

The next day he repeated the whole thing, but this time he extended the debate, using the affair about the plot of land and the abduction of Athman as an opportunity for a violent and open protest against his mother and the ethics she represented. He meant to live the way he wanted, without ever again worrying about prohibitions:

I find your advice unbearable, in that it is not meant to light my way as much as to change my behavior, and that sometimes makes me think that you understand *Life* so differently than I do that it's almost useless for me to listen to your advice, other than out of respect, I know so well in advance that, before formulating it, you will not have taken into consideration the most important thing: the reasons or the passions that determine our acts.

A life is not necessarily more or less beautiful because it is more or less reasonable. If I spent my time leading the life you "advise" me to, it would be in constant contradiction with my thoughts. Nothing irritates me more than your need to interfere in the actions of others, which perhaps makes them a bit more sensible, but makes them lose all their value since they come from you more than from the other person—makes them lose all their "originality" (and please don't take the word in any way other than in its etymological meaning). All these seem to me the most important questions of religion, ethics, and philosophy—they seem to be leading us away from Athman and my plot of land —but understand, decide beforehand, and resign yourself to not suppressing all the peculiarities in my existence that might grow there like natural grass (and I call them "peculiarities" to satisfy you, for they don't appear to me as such, but rather as natural things), and I have a horror of the perpetual feeling that you do your best to give me—that I don't act as everyone else acts. . . .

I'm buying my plot of land—and I'm bringing Athman—and . . . *If you don't give me a good welcome in the rue de Commaille*—and with Athman, and *if you don't manage to have Marie look at him cheerfully—I shall settle down with him either in Grignon or in the Passy apartment that Pierre Louÿs has kept*—but once again, it is difficult for me to write you these words which seem like threats—it's very contrary to my nature—and I wish for nothing more than to spend my life very calmly near you; I beg you not to make me believe that it's impossible. . . .

Letters like your last four, which unfortunately—coming from you—no

9 March 14, 1895, unpublished.

longer surprise me, give me a good idea of the real conjugal hell it would be were I ever to marry, because you could never give up playing the role of the experienced person and adviser. Oh! terror!—And do you think that I don't feel, at the very thought of the future, made of bronze and steel so as to resist you, even when I might have had some real joy in giving up, at your request, some wild, whimsical decision!—No, no, no; nothing doing. Many of the best things in my life come solely from my stubborn resistance to the invasion of your will. I'm afraid that if I ever had children they would be badly and insufficiently brought up, because of the horror the extremes of your system have given me for any upbringing "whose objective is not to abolish itself"— as the sages and admirable old De Lanux so excellently put it.—Can you really not understand that? Didn't papa think exactly that? . . . how is it possible not to think that?[10]

He reproached his mother with turning his friends—especially the Laurens, Albert Démarest, and Marcel Drouin—against Athman, thus making his return to Paris "as tiresome as possible." He had tried to get Madeleine into his little game, but on March 10 she answered him with a perfectly clear letter, in which nothing would indicate that she, any more than her aunt, understood the real obstacles in the way of that abduction:

You gave us some good laughs with your whole passage about Athman. But, dear friend, how could you have been mistaken for a moment as to my opinion about this plan? I condemn it absolutely. I know that your mother does too. I know all the arguments that she's given you against it. I condemn this plan of bringing Athman to France, because I think it has nine chances out of ten of turning against the poor boy. After all, just look at it clearly: it's less for him than for you that you're bringing him. I think that all his qualities that are somewhat negative in Biskra will be transformed into very positive faults in our civilized world. You're going to make him into someone who's baffled and rootless. You said of La Brévine: "Those countries have their inhabitants." One could say of Athman and the others: those people have their country; and only in his country is Athman a happy and attractive child. *Punktum damit.*[11]

A long letter to his mother on March 17 shows him just as resolved. Yet there is a short passage in it which does much to clarify the sequence of events: "No interesting news. Don't fail to send me everything you can in the way of clippings about the scandalous proceedings that the Marquis of Queensberry is bringing against Wilde."[12] Now from that day on, Gide stopped writing to his mother. For seventeen days he merely sent her news of himself by telegram, and there was no further question of bringing Athman home with him.

[10] March 15, 1895, unpublished.

[11] Quoted by Jean Schlumberger, p. 105.

[12] March 17, 1895, unpublished.

In *Si le grain ne meurt* Gide recalled his epistolary polemics with his mother and his resistance to the coalition she tried to organize in order to get him to give up Athman, but according to him it was a letter from Marie Leuenberger that made him drop the whole thing: "she swore that she'd leave the house the day 'my Negro'[13] came into it. And what would have become of mamma without Marie? I gave in; I had to."[14] Yet about two weeks after Gide's last letter to his mother, on April 5, 1895, Wilde was arrested. It is probable that the trial and a fear of scandal made André Gide think twice and finally convinced him to give up, at least temporarily, taking Athman back with him. On March 12 he had written to his mother: "Carrying off Athman presents lots of difficulties—you almost never mention the real ones." Oscar Wilde's trial was to point up the "real" difficulties.

Athman, who had been rejoicing about his trip to Paris, was terribly disappointed when he learned that he had to give it up. As for Gide, the more he saw the date of his departure approach, the more miserable he was at having to leave the boy and his little friends. However, after a "paradisiac"[15] two-day trip with Athman, Gide arrived at the station and looked about for him in vain, but as the train pulled out of El Kantara, he caught a glimpse of him at the edge of the wadi, "a little motionless figure, lost in the desert, overwhelmed with grief, the image of my despair." He was often to think of Athman, whom he saw again the following year in Biskra when he returned with Madeleine, then Mme. André Gide, and four years later took him to Paris: "It rarely happens that I give up something; a postponement is the most a setback can get out of me."[16]

In Algiers, Gide spent three days with Pierre Louÿs. But the two friends were not together for fifteen minutes before they began quarreling about the Oscar Wilde trial. Pierre Louÿs was known to be pugnacious, but he found himself faced with an adversary he no longer recognized. He had been stupefied at Champel to see how the mystical André Walter had become a worshiper of bacchantes: he now discovered a hard, sharp, sarcastic antagonist, who was determined not to give in and to defend his point of view without yielding. Proteus had once again changed his face. *"My character is changing; I'm becoming violent and immoderate,"* he had written to his mother,[17] and in *Si le grain ne meurt* he pointed out that he was then "not exactly easy to get along with." He showed his friend that he had become "violent," and he also wanted to prove to him that he had

---

[13] In fact, Gide himself had already used the word "Negro" in a letter to his mother: "My best to Marie—prepare Pauline for the idea of seeing a Negro near her" (March 6, 1895, unpublished).

[14] *Si le grain ne meurt*, II, 355.

[15] *Ibid.*, p. 357.

[16] *Ibid.*, p. 355.

[17] March 17, 1895, unpublished.

become "immoderate" by agreeing to go along with him to an Algerian brothel called "Les Etoiles Andalouses," which would have been absolutely unthinkable at the time of André Walter: "I now prided myself on not resisting a thing."[18]

Gide's disgust with the vulgarity of the brothel was not enough to keep him from closing himself in with one of the girls and trying again. But this time he was "more successful" than he had been with En Barka. The fears that had been created by his former fiascoes might have been removed had Pierre Louÿs not immediately hastened to persuade him that the girl was one of those "vitriol throwers" of whom, as he well knew, Gide had been so terrified. After describing in detail the "illness I should probably soon be suffering from," Louÿs tried hypocritically to console him by explaining that "quantities of great men certainly owed more than three-quarters of their genius to syphilis."[19] From Maupassant to Nietzsche, the list of those who could serve to illustrate that absurd thesis was long. Exasperated, Gide went into a rage: "Decidedly, we could no longer get along, no longer bear each other." And so ended, under the disreputable sky of the "Andalusian Stars," the great friendship that had begun under the Olympian auspices of Goethe.

After Louÿs' departure, Gide remained alone in Algiers, unable to bring himself to return to France. As he wrote to a friend:

It seems to me that I have not yet seen enough, savored enough . . . the desire, no, the *will* to push everything right to the very end and the horrible realization that one is never at the end of anything . . . ; the *will to dare* to do everything, understanding that our whole life is compromised by each one of our acts. I'm staking everything I have in this tragic game.[20]

He alludes to associating with "vagrants" and to ambiguous promiscuities:

You know that one of my great pleasures is to shadow people; here, another pleasure no less rare is to be shadowed by them. Be assured that Blidah is a city of quite biblical corruption—O Corazin, Bethsaida!—and that all those who are not there to buy are there to sell themselves. . . . But as my behavior has remained platonic, can I really speak?

One evening he went into a café that was "a little more disreputable" than the others, and "among the horrible faces," caught a glimpse of an "extraordinarily sweet" one, that of a child: "I didn't exactly desire him, yet I dreamt about him that night, and the next day it was because of him that I went back." He then noticed that the child was a poor cripple with a frightfully deformed body. The others called him "Crapaud," or Toad, and the word, pronounced by the Arabs, became Karappo:

[18] *Si le grain ne meurt,* II, 359.

[19] *Ibid.,* p. 360.   [20] April 3, 1895, unpublished.

When the next day I saw that little creature jump down and crawl, helping himself along with his hands and his crooked feet, he seemed so exactly like a toad that I had to call him by that name, although his lawful name was Mohammed. I held out a cigarette to him. Everyone in the café laughed. . . . I sat down next to him, troubled by indescribable anguish. I was thinking that the poor child had never been fondled, and yet he was living amidst such prostitution—"Karappo, how old are you?"—"Twelve."—"What is your name?"—"Mohammed." "Mohammed, I come here for you, not for the others; the others follow me and I amuse myself by losing them so that I can come back and be near you when they're gone."—And Karappo curled up against me and I very gently stroked his sad little face, and I could have sobbed with unaccountable tenderness. . . .

That episode is related to the strange attraction that crippled, sickly, deformed, and even monstrous children always had for Gide. As Pierre Herbart pointed out:

It seemed that between him and those scrofulous creatures, those village idiots, those cripples, there was some common measure. He then expressed what was perhaps the best of himself (and it was not pity). As though he felt bound up with their deformities; as though he *recognized* himself in them.[21]

I have already emphasized the psychological value of that characteristic.[22]

The same letter to a friend of April 3 is also very revealing as to the change in attitude of both Gide and his mother toward the prospect of his marriage to Madeleine:

I'm eager to see my poor mother, whose unaccountable anxiety increases every day. . . . The basis for her anxiety is my marriage to my cousin . . . she thinks of nothing else and desires it to such a degree that she's becoming sick over it. And I'm terrified at the thought that perhaps what she desires will never take place.

Shattered by the letters she had received from Biskra, Mme. Gide finally understood that the hour had come to give over her powers to her niece, for no doubt Madeleine alone would be capable of "saving" André by having a moral and Christian influence on him. After having struggled against that plan for five years, she adopted it, but now that she wanted it to work out with all her strength, it was her son who considered it "perhaps" unfeasible.

The violence of Gide's letters to his mother and even his peremptory attitude toward Louÿs are obvious signs that he was resolved to translate his rebellion into action and to affirm his protest. Formerly so anxious to

[21] *A la recherche d'André Gide*, p. 58.   [22] Cf. above, pp. 103–5.

please and to win the sympathy of others, he now aggressively assumed his new personality and had no intention of yielding ever again:

The very moment I was beginning to discover myself was hardly the time to wish to turn my back on myself, just as I was on the point of discovering the inner tables of my new law. For I was not satisfied to free myself from the rule; I claimed to justify my frenzy and to vindicate my madness.

The words no doubt apply to the assertion of his homosexual habits, but they have an infinitely broader scope. Not only did Gide mean to justify an anomaly he henceforth considered "normal" for himself; he meant, above all, to follow no ethics other than those that were suited to his purpose and to defend his "originality" against all comers. The subordination of collective rules to an individual destiny, an aesthetic and no longer an ethical concept of the personality; praise for actions which are apparently gratuitous but in no way detached from a secret purpose or from *amour-propre,* in La Rochefoucauld's sense of the word; the acceptance of scandal, indeed, a demand for it; the glorification of a bold existence, resolved to pride itself on contempt and hate for most others—all those great Gidian themes can be found substantially in the letters of March 15 and 17. To a certain extent, the immoralist protest of 1895 is but an illustration and the practical application of the formulas in the 1893 *Journal* about the artist's "higher immorality." But the long premeditated crisis came to a head with new violence, and the moral rebellion took the form of rebellion against the mother.

The long conflict of authority, characteristic of the mother-son relationship during Gide's entire youth, reached its denouement. For the first time he stands before her as an accuser. He marks her out as his Adversary and talks to her as though she were his enemy. He criticizes the way she brought him up and congratulates himself on finally escaping from a law which tended primarily to "suppress" his own personality. He tells her that he will no longer follow her advice, which has become "unbearable," and that he is determined to pay no further mind even to her suggestions. The best things in his life had come from his dogged will to resist her, and he will go right on, without troubling himself about what she thinks. He will not allow himself to be "limited," and will protect his happiness from her. And when he thinks of the future, he feels himself made of "bronze and steel" so as to stand up against her disastrous influence; if he marries, he will not tolerate her ruling over his household, which she would immediately turn into a "conjugal hell," or taking care of his children, over whom she would wield her "tyranny." Written in a fit of temper, his letters express a resentment that touches on hate. Mme. Gide was deeply hurt by his cruel words, and her son, feeling that this time he had gone too far, vainly tried to reassure her:

POOR DEAR MAMMA,

What's wrong? Why such sadness? What can I write to you? What can I do to conquer your persistent anxiety? If I write to you, you see insanity or nervous irritation in my letters. If I don't, you infer the worst things from my silence. I wired you several times that I'm well and that everything is going according to your wishes. . . .[23]

Mme. Gide's anguished questions and "sadness" are hardly surprising. She felt that her son was becoming detached from her and that the moral education she had given him had collapsed. She had also begun to feel that he was detached once and for all from the Christian religion, and nothing could have been more tragic for that ardent Protestant who had devoted her entire life to her own salvation and that of her family. And yet she was wrong in believing that he was henceforth separated from Christ. For it was in fact at the height of his moral crisis, during those feverish days in Biskra and Algiers, that he felt the need to reread the Gospels. He himself wrote in *Si le grain ne meurt*, ". . . how, beyond that desert into which my worship led me, going ever more deeply into it in pursuit of my own thirst, how and with what raptures of love I rediscovered the Gospels. . . ."[24] But actually, the Christ he saw in them did not resemble the Christ worshiped by Mme. Gide. A Protestant in spite of himself, Gide was then meditating on the most heretical of all his enterprises, that of showing that the Church in general and his mother in particular had betrayed the teachings of Christ, and that the real believer was himself.[25] He had had the revelation that the Churches had "distorted" the teachings of Christ, and thus intended writing a book which he would call "Christianity against Christ." If he did not get down to that theological treatise at once, it was not from lack of conviction but because he was afraid of distressing "someone"[26] very dear to him, and he later regretted the fact that sentimental ties, in that instance, had kept him from thinking it through to the end.

"I'm searching through the Gospels, vainly searching, for a commandment, a threat, an interdiction. . . . All that comes uniquely from Saint Paul." Those words from *La Symphonie pastorale*[27] sum up the entire argumentation that had been sketched out in 1895. Saint Paul betrayed the teachings of Christ, who had come only to bring the world a promise of joy *et nunc*—right now—and to teach people to be happy without forbid-

---

[23] April 3, 1895, unpublished.

[24] II, 361.

[25] Cf. Gide's *Journal*, 1895, p. 57, and *Si le grain ne meurt*, II, 362.

[26] He was obviously referring to Madeleine Rondeaux.

[27] P. 105.

ding anyone to live according to his own ideal and his own nature. Gide could not find any trace of interdiction or prohibition in the Gospels, only an incentive to "many kinds of anarchy."[28] Christ appeared to him, above all, as an emancipator:

I think we shall soon come to isolating the words of Christ, in order to let them appear more emancipatory than they have appeared up till now. Less buried, they will appear more dramatically, finally repudiating the family (and that will give us the permission to suppress it), pulling man himself out of his environment so that he may have a personal career, and teaching him by his example and his voice not to have any possessions on this earth or any place on which to lay his head. Oh! all my soul longs for the advent of that "nomadic state," in which man, without a snug home, will not localize his duty or his affection on particular people, any more than he will his happiness.[29]

Those lines insinuate tendentious similarities between the author of *Les Nourritures terrestres,* as he sees himself, and Christ, as he sees him. The former hates families and would like to teach children "not to love their families and gradually to leave them"; the latter would also be an enemy of the family. Gide particularly emphasized the distance that Christ would have put between himself and his mother: " 'Woman!' he says to his mother, who continues to love him with special affection—'Woman, what have I in common with thee?' " The necessity of not attaching oneself to any special affection or special possession is a leitmotiv of *Les Nourritures terrestres,* and the author is not far from seeing the Gospels as a justification of being uprooted. He noticed subtle connections between the Savior's message and the message of Nathanaël, who also preaches individual emancipation and the search for happiness. And he closed his eyes before the drama, the Calvary, the Golgotha, so that the Gidian Christ seems like a Christ without a Cross, a quasihedonistic philosopher who teaches man to break free from his cumbersome possessions so as to have a "personal career" according to his own nature and with a joyous heart—in other words, to live in exactly the opposite way from the one Mme. Gide sanctioned, the one obviously inspired by Saint Paul.

Thanks to that naturistic distortion of the word of Christ to his own ends, Gide no longer saw that antagonism between Christian ethics and pagan ethics which he did in 1893. And he declared himself "ready to entrust Christ with the settlement of the dispute between Dionysus and Apollo."[30] Without contesting the at least momentary sincerity of that intention, would he not have been more sincere in declaring himself ready to entrust Apollo with the settlement of the dispute between Dionysus and

[28] *Journal,* p. 96.

[29] *Ibid.*   [30] *Si le grain ne meurt,* II, 361.

Christ? Actually, during those days of moral and religious anxiety, he did not entrust himself to Christ but to Goethe, the Apollonian arbiter: "Nothing will have soothed me in life so much as the contemplation of that great figure," he then noted in his *Journal*,[31] and he wrote to his mother:

I'm finishing Goethe's memoirs; everything in that great man teaches you something and I'm learning more by reading about how Goethe blew his nose than I would by reading about how a *concierge* received Holy Communion. . . . It's slow absorption. And that's why it's very difficult to understand.—Anyway, I'd like you to read these memoirs; you would perhaps be as surprised as I am, about the extraordinary amount of madness that that most reasonable of men could *absorb, adopt,* and *neutralize*—just as I think Mithridates could get his body accustomed to poison. And that reminds me of the sentence from Taine quoted by Sorel in his speech and which I'm going to quote incorrectly: "The value of a writer is in relation to his nervous capacity (his nervous receptivity)."[32]

As always with Gide, the discussion about the hierarchy of values ends with a reference to the only one that really mattered to him: literary value. And he finally comes back to the guide whom, for four years, he had never really left. Nothing is further from the sublimity of the Cross or the intoxication of Dionysus than the influence of Goethe, the reasonable artist par excellence, devoted exclusively to the harmony of his works, and who, for aesthetic ends, converted all his madness into wisdom, all his poisons into antidotes, all his demons into mediators. One cannot serve both Christ and Apollo; one cannot be both the Walter of *Les Cahiers* and the Narcissus of *Le Traité*. One must choose, and Gide chose.

On April 5 he wrote his mother the last letter dated from Algiers:

Now that we're so close to seeing each other again, I don't want to discuss any further the few points you take so to heart. I'd like to see you accept things a little more, for anxiety will not be able to change them. I'd like to see you, not more resigned, but more confident.—Perhaps by associating with Arabs, some of their calm philosophy has rubbed off on me; in this life I'm getting used to taking God more and more into account, which is a way of taking man less and less into account.—When I write you these words, you see them only as literature, as sophisms, as infatuation, etc.—you don't believe them . . . or far worse: you don't believe in the feeling that makes we write them. Well, that is a pity. Certain thoughts are beginning to dominate my life; it's natural enough for me to want to live and write according to them.

. . . I know that in every being, even in the maddest, lies a bit of wisdom; but the more I know her, the more I seem to see in Madeleine a radiance of celestial and infinite wisdom; I sometimes feel that only in her have I found wisdom, and in thinking of her I'd like to say what Goethe said about Madame

[31] 1895, p. 57.   [32] April 5, 1895, unpublished.

de Stein: "She sees—she reflects things, without passion."—There is more intelligence in her than you seem to think and you should try to listen to her rather than want to advise her. Let things take their course and consider what Madeleine has decided as very wise.—I always find that when anyone speaks to me about her or about us, it's always somewhat beside the point, but the loves of men have the self-complacency of always believing that they're misunderstood.

Although that last paragraph hurt Mme. Gide, it did revive her hopes for an imminent marriage between André and Madeleine:

Au revoir—I'll soon be with you, dear mamma. Your state of anxiety is more to worry about, I assure you, than my state of great calm; my life is completely out at sea and you try to pull me back with the lifeline just when I'm admiring the way I swim. Try to convince yourself that I'm perfectly well, that I'm only just mad enough to be a poet and that what happens pleases God.

And so ends André Gide's correspondence with his mother.

43: His Mother's Death

"I felt my whole being sink into an abyss of love, grief, and freedom."

Si le grain ne meurt, *II, 368*

WHILE André Gide was in Algiers, letting "four or five steamers" go off without him, "on the pretext that the sea was too rough,"[1] the Charles Gides were waiting for him in Montpellier. They even expected him to arrive "with his following," for he had said he was coming with Athman and had never informed them of his change in plans. On March 25 and on April 10 Mme. Charles Gide wrote to her sister-in-law of her surprise at having no news of the traveler.

Those two significant letters[2] show how anxious the family was about André's "madness." "I also know that his nerves are in a bad state and that people's minds are not very stable nowadays." His aunt felt that a quick marriage was the only way of saving him: "You must make haste: marriage and life in the country. If your niece loves him tenderly, she will devote herself to him." Of course, she did not find Madeleine Rondeaux "the ideal wife for someone as unbalanced as André," but since they loved one another, she considered that the opportunity was not to be lost. She was strongly against the possibility of the unconsummated marriage she thought Madeleine had in mind: "When a young girl admits that she loves a young man, there's nothing for her to do but give herself to him; those

[1] *Si le grain ne meurt,* II, 358.

[2] They belong to M. Dominique Drouin, who allowed me to consult them.

are *my* morals. . . . It's hard to imagine that André would accept. . . . I'm really afraid that your niece, too, is unbalanced." And so the plan for their marriage, which both families had opposed, found an active ally in Mme. Charles Gide.

In all probability, the letters made Mme. Paul Gide sit back and think. She was no doubt sorry for not having taken her sister-in-law's advice and failing to listen to André in January, 1895, when she refused to allow him to take a long trip with Madeleine, with her as a chaperone, of course. Since then, a great deal had happened, and she had lived in a state of increasing anxiety. André's meeting with Oscar Wilde and Lord Douglas, whose depravity she was given a clear account of in her son's letters; his plan for bringing Athman to Paris; the plot of land he wanted to buy in Biskra; the state of overexcitement and rebellion that was so obvious from his letters; his immoral ideas, which she found quite mad; an almost threatening tone of arrogance, without the slightest indication of repentance—all of that deeply upset her. It was clear that her son was going through a very serious crisis. When she received the letter written from Algiers on April 5, which contained a lyrical eulogy on Goethe, she thought she had found the person who was responsible for it all. She now knew the name of the evil spirit that had so dangerously transformed her son, and wrote at once to Charles Gide, whom, since her husband's death, she had considered somewhat as her counsel in guiding André.

Her letter about "that Goethe" absolutely exuded anguish. Charles Gide answered it very calmly on April 16: "What André confided to you about Goethe and the passage about the experiments in life he is making seem innocent enough to me—at any rate, I should have to see the letter to be able to judge." As a matter of fact, André had arrived in Montpellier the day before, on April 15, and did not appear to be in an alarming state. Charles Gide advised his sister-in-law to calm down. He once again regretted that André had no profession. And as for the marriage plans, he considered them in the following terms:

If he does not marry, it will be one more reason for a breakdown added to the first[3]—but as far as this particular marriage is concerned, I'm less affirmative than Anna[4] and would hesitate to press either Mlle. R. or himself on that score. It's not at all certain that the marriage will be a happy one, and pushing them into it would mean taking a great responsibility. Yet it's true that if it does not take place, both of them will probably be unhappy, so that there is little more than a choice between that which is certain to cause harm and that which is liable to.

[3] The first being his lack of a profession.

[4] Mme. Charles Gide.

He concluded by warning Mme. Gide against inopportune letters and "calls for help." "I learned indirectly that you have written to Valéry. You would do better not to write to André's friends; it can do no good." And his letter ends with a very dry "Yours . . ."[5]

Gide soon left Montpellier to join his mother, who was awaiting him with immeasurable anguish. She found him less "harmed" than she had feared, and was at first overjoyed at having her prodigal son back. But the very fact that he was prodigal, in the economic sense of the word, was to be the cause of some painful disputes. She had always thought that André, despite his intelligence, was absolutely lacking in practical sense and that he was like a child when it came to material questions. Now she found herself face to face with a man who demanded an accounting of his money and pointed out to her that she had never informed him of the inheritance he had come into from his father upon his majority. She had not wanted him to be free to dispose of his wealth, in order that she might keep him under her thumb, and he would put up with it no longer. Bitterly, they argued about figures; but he refused to be persuaded and finally suggested that he pay his mother board "whenever I should live with her."[6] In that way the disagreement that had poisoned their first days together was brought to an end.

During the two weeks that followed, they were far more "relaxed and had made a truce." The word "truce" shows that he considered it a kind of armistice between two adversaries. And his polite attitude was no doubt more effective than the former quarrels in making Mme. Gide realize that she had lost the game and that her son had escaped from her once and for all. Thanks to their mutual concessions, they spent two full weeks with no scenes, no clashes, not even any "clouds." André was surprised that their life together, which had been so stormy just a short while back, was again becoming possible; his mother was so conciliatory and for the first time seemed to him so defenseless that he again began to love her:

I felt nothing in her but a mother and enjoyed feeling that I was her son. . . . As if to insure a more perfect harmony between us, mamma finally confessed to me that she wished for nothing so much as to see me marry the girl she had long looked upon as her daughter-in-law. Perhaps, too, she felt that her strength was failing and was afraid of leaving me alone.[7]

Mme. Gide was then sixty. Her health, which had once been robust, had declined during the past years. She who had never complained could no longer hide the overwhelming fatigue she sometimes suffered from in the

[5] Unpublished.

[6] *Si le grain ne meurt,* II, 364.

[7] *Ibid.,* p. 365.

evenings. She had aged a great deal, and her son loved her all the more for it.[8]

When André and Madeleine saw each other again, it was thus with Mme. Paul Gide's blessings. The former interdiction, pronounced by Walter's mother, was officially lifted, and Emmanuèle's attitude changed at once. As Madeleine wrote to André on May 24:

I must tell you how many beautiful and good moments, during this stay which I somewhat dreaded, I owe to you. I'm not thanking you but I thank God. . . . The hours with you were the best that I've spent in a long time—and one thing I no longer believed possible, I'm delighted at the thought of seeing you again.[9]

Gide, for his part, wrote to Paul Valéry:

Even during the hours I spent far from M., I thought of her with fatiguing steadiness. It now makes almost seven years that I've been waiting for such hours; and the anxiety, although leading to happiness at last, was still a great strain; but this kind of torment is only momentary.[10]

It was decided that both fiancés-to-be would meet at La Roque at the beginning of July, and Mme. Gide left at once with Marie to prepare the house, while André went to Grignon to see his friend Eugène Rouart.

During that month of May, 1894, the newspapers gave an account of the Oscar Wilde trial, and we can imagine how fascinated Gide was in attentively following its course. On May 25, 1895, the jurors handed in their verdict: Wilde was sentenced to two years of prison and hard labor. Justice Wills made the verdict even worse by solemnly adding that it was the most repulsive case he had ever had to judge, and that he regretted the maximum punishment provided by law was not more severe. Madeleine wrote to André at once:

Did you read about the sentence given the two English defendants? Inclosed is a newspaper clipping on the subject. If the details are accurate, the penalty of hard labor would be worthy of being added, as an extra chapter, to those of the sinister *House of the Dead*—or else Dante should have thought of it. It's frightful, isn't it?[11]

---

[8] It is interesting to compare that attitude to a passage in *Et nunc manet in te,* p. 62, concerning Madeleine Gide in her old age: "I never loved Madeleine more than when she was old, bent, suffering from varicose sores on her legs which she allowed me to dress, almost crippled, and giving in at last to my attentions with sweet and tender gratitude."

[9] Quoted by Jean Schlumberger, p. 108.

[10] May, 1895 (*Correspondance,* p. 237).

[11] May 30, 1895 (quoted by Jean Schlumberger, p. 106).

Meanwhile, as Gide was beginning to worry about not having received any news from his mother, a telegram from Marie arrived, telling him to come to La Roque immediately: his mother had just had an attack.

In the big bedroom at La Roque, alone with his mother who was unconscious but still alive, Gide could not manage to control his sobs:

And suddenly, watching those poor hands which I had just seen laboring so desperately, I imagined them on the piano, and the thought that just a short time ago they too had awkwardly tried to express a little poetry, music, and beauty . . . that very thought filled me with tremendous veneration, and falling to my knees at the foot of the bed, I buried my face in the sheets to stifle my sobs.[12]

That emotional outburst *in extremis,* suddenly made possible by his mother's slight talent as a pianist, is one of the most singular of André Gide's revelations about himself. The feeling that shook him was not aroused by any remorse for having made his mother suffer, or by any guilt at not having been with her before her death throes, but by the thought that she had somewhat served, however clumsily, the only god he was to worship from then on.

Yet Gide would seem to have watched "the solemn invasion of death" like a man of letters: "And I listened to the troubled beats of that unyielding heart echo within me. How it still struggled! I had already been present at other death agonies, but I had not found them as pathetic."[13] The mixture of sincere emotion and the dual state of being divided into actor and spectator which once again made him watch a pathetic reality "as if it were a spectacle outside reality" was characteristic of his psychological ambivalence.[14] But he meant to experience that most serious of all moments properly. He wanted no one to distract him, and insisted that no member of the family, either Rondeaux or Démarest, be notified, so that he could remain alone with his mother during that last tête-à-tête: "I was anxious to watch over her alone. Marie and I helped her in her last moments, and when her heart finally stopped beating, I felt my whole being sink into an abyss of love, guilt, and freedom."

[12] *Si le grain ne meurt,* II, 366–67.

[13] *Ibid.,* p. 368.

[14] Very late in life he wrote in *Ainsi soit-il:* "Strictly speaking, there is not even the duality that makes someone within me a spectator of the one who acts. No: it is the very one who acts, or who suffers, who doesn't take himself seriously. I even think that at the point of death I shall say to myself: 'Well, well! He's dying.' "

There is no doubt that the basic conflict in André Gide's youth was the conflict of authority and submission; and the emotional confusion he experienced on the death of his mother, just when he had thought he was morally out from under her wing, the evocation of the "abyss of love, grief, and freedom" into which he felt his heart sink, is a sign of the deep ambivalence of his filial feelings. Of course, one whole part of his personality had been built up in reaction and in protest, so to speak, to the way his mother had brought him up, but he remained no less attached to the woman who in his eyes embodied the virtue and moral duty he had been taught by his childhood religion. As soon as his mother disappeared, and with her the last obstacle to his complete freedom, he took fright; he temporarily forgot the hostile resentment that had become strengthened in the struggle and, as is usual in such pathetic circumstances, nothing remained but his veneration. Gide had not become so hardened as not to be a prey to remorse, as anyone would have been in his place. It is true that during his 1895 crisis he had decided to become hard; but in January he was still writing to his mother, begging her to go along with him on his trip. It is true that many of his letters show an exasperation that touched on hate; but what extraordinary emotional dependency is also shown by that almost daily correspondence! The need for keeping his mother informed about his every action, including the most preposterous ones, testifies to the importance he attached to her judgment, even were it only to defy her.

André Gide's extraordinary emotional reaction after his mother's death is similar to the ambiguous states described as the intoxication of mourning. This expression designates the exaltation that follows the death of someone beloved but whose love had held the person captive.[15] In that state of exhilaration "due to the sublime," he began by distributing to all his relatives, even to those who had hardly known his mother, the jewels and objects that had belonged to her.[16] It is psychologically interesting to see how Gide's liberation was accompanied by acts of liberality that were not in his nature, for he was just as stingy as his mother. But he felt that he had to give everything away and that he had to give up all self-control: "The very thought of reserve would have seemed shameful to me. . . ."[17] Dizziness and choking, fear and trembling, anguish and lyrical exaltation were all mixed together in this new *Schauder,* just as it had been during his childhood. But now his mother was not there as before to shelter in her arms the pathetic child who did not feel "the same as the others." Lacking that maternal protection at an intense moment of crisis, he did not know

[15] It has been compared to the frenzy of a slave on the death of his respected master (the mourning mania).

[16] *Si le grain ne meurt,* II, 368.

[17] *Ibid.*

whether to grieve about her absence or to rejoice about it. He was on the verge of both laughter and tears. He was afraid and he was intoxicated. He did not know where to turn.

"The only thing left for me to cling to was my love for my cousin; the will to marry her was all I still had to guide my life."[18] In the emotional tempest that shook him to his very depths, he again went toward her as toward hope. In the stormy sky above, he saw the light of the morning star of his adolescence, the "mystic Orient" of his life. Barely free of a mother's ties, he was thinking of again binding himself by conjugal ties. And by the same token, he was going back to the values he had wanted to free himself from but from which, basically, he was not at all sure that he was right to free himself: "Was it not virtue itself that I loved in Emmanuèle?"[19]

Mme. Paul Gide died on May 31, 1895. Seventeen days later, on June 17, André Gide and Madeleine Rondeaux became engaged. Coming so soon after Mme. Gide's death, neither the Gides nor the Rondeaux particularly welcomed the news. Only Albert Démarest gave his approval and, as always, wholeheartedly took his side. In a letter Gide wrote to him shortly after, he spoke with obvious sincerity about his love for his fiancée but also about his anxiety for the future:

At the present moment, my patience is gone; I should like to see her again and stay with her from tomorrow on; the thought that she continues to see, love, and listen to my aunt[20] who, in spite of everything, is doing her best [to undermine all our plans]—it's driving me crazy and making me worry dreadfully about the future. . . . Later on, if anything at all should happen to us, what a thing to remember, those dissolving conversations—I mean dissolving in the sense that they might break up our marriage. . . . Will I ever manage to make her forget? . . . Of course, you can understand that I never speak to her of my fears and that they will vanish at the first moment of happiness like night birds at the sight of day.

He hoped with all his heart to make her happy. "Out on the balcony, one of our last evenings together, Madeleine said to me: 'I'm like someone who puts his hands in front of his eyes so as not to see the sun; and in spite of myself, I can tell that its rays are shining through my fingers.'" And he recalled a conversation that might seem surprising between two young fiancés but which is very much in the same tone as the conversations between André Walter and Emmanuèle:

[18] *Ibid.,* p. 369.

[19] *Ibid.*

[20] Mme. Henri Rondeaux.

"Will we really learn English together? For I'll have to learn it again, I know it so badly."

"—And Italian!" I said.

"—And Italian!" she repeated.

Albert! Albert! How extraordinary it was those last evenings together gradually to revive each desire to live! in that poor devastated soul—each joy! first, so as not to frighten her, by arousing the most serious and solemn ones, those of study, of *knowledge,* those that have up till now given us, both of us, our most intense, our most fervent, our most austere moments of happiness.[21]

The same brotherly words were also used by Madeleine: "Dear André, am I not your friend, your sister, your fiancée? *Sister* might perhaps seem ridiculous to others—to me it also corresponds very well to what I am, to what I feel."[22] It would appear that she still wanted no more than a brother-sister relationship: *"I'm not afraid of death. but I'm afraid of marriage."*[23]

André Gide spent the month of July at La Roque, in the big house of his childhood summers, where everything reminded him of his mother. He was alone there with Marie. Mme. Gide's old servant could not get over the death of her "dear unforgettable mistress," and thought that André's marriage was coming much too soon after the bereavement: "Everything is happening so fast, I was not prepared for it." During the twenty-two years she had been in the family, she had become very domineering, and she was so touchy that even her mistress had never dared reprimand her. Madeleine Rondeaux dreaded being under her supervision, and for that reason the two fiancés had decided that the next fall they would give Marie a pension, making it possible for her to retire to her native country. Marie accepted: "I have enough intelligence and experience not to want to force myself on a young couple," but the prospect of being separated from them seemed to her "night and day like a black, black ghost." She had watched André from the time of his difficult childhood to the day he took off on his travels, and she did not think that the future mistress of La Roque would have an easy time of it: "André has often been the subject of my prayers . . . how he suffered as a child! and his long trip? and his sickness in Tunis, and his last stay in Algeria? . . . Oh yes I'm also one of those who pray for you," she wrote to Madeleine Rondeaux. "Even his literature made me sigh to heaven, for I couldn't understand his views and had heard someone say that what he wrote wasn't good. It really made me

[21] June or July, 1895, unpublished.

[22] Letter from Madeleine Rondeaux to André Gide, June 22, 1895 (quoted by Jean Schlumberger, p. 117).

[23] *Ibid.,* June 27, 1895, p. 117. The italics are mine.

suffer." As Marie was writing, André had "gone off to pick up his friend Valéry."[24]

Paul Valéry came to La Roque in July. Gide had written to him, informing him of his coming engagement: "Don't think that because I am a lover, *I am any less your friend.*" And Valéry had answered: "May I ask you not to worry about me and not to lose a spark of your feelings: 1. because such moments are rarer than the troubles of your friend, and 2. because there is nothing anyone can do about the latter." Since December, 1890, when Gide had confided to him that he hoped to marry "Emmanuèle," Valéry had often heard about Gide's disappointments, and the moments of happiness his friend was now experiencing, after having waited so long, seemed to him "rarer" than the "great mental game" he humorously referred to when he wrote: "I realize that I've become like an alcoholic."[25] When he arrived at La Roque, he brought with him an "article" which was nothing less than *L'Introduction à la méthode de Léonard de Vinci.* The two friends talked about literature at leisure, just as they had years ago in Montpellier. Then Gide left for Cuverville to join his fiancée, and remained there until August 17.

During those weeks in August he would appear to have put an end to the anxieties he had about Madeleine, and the days he spent with her were the happiest of their "difficult engagement."[26] Back at La Roque, the letters he received from Madeleine showed her confident in their future for the first time:

Through a sort of providential instinctive perception, I've always felt *the real you.* How? I don't know. I feel it for you only. But I never doubt that secret vision. It's an inner voice, which at once gives me a precise idea of your *intention,* behind everything that hides it from the eyes of others: embellishments, exaggerations, or mistakes. It's as natural for me to understand you— near or far away—as it is to open my eyes to see. And for that I thank God, for *generally* what I felt and the others did not feel was to your advantage.[27]

Never had she written to him so tenderly: "My tenderness for you is so clearly associated with my own existence that often I don't *think* it any more; it exists because I exist, it existed because it did us so much good, it will exist because *we will walk toward God.*"[28] Or: "I am yours with all my soul; I know neither how, nor why, nor since when." She did not suffer from their temporary separation, for André's letters filled in the time:

[24] Letters from Marie Leuenberger to Madeleine Rondeaux, July 10 and 28, 1895, unpublished.

[25] Letter from Paul Valéry to André Gide, May, 1895 (*Correspondance,* p. 238).

[26] Letter from André Gide to Francis Jammes, Oct. 23, 1895 (*Correspondance,* p. 57).

[27] Sept. 8, 1895 (quoted by Jean Schlumberger, p. 119).

[28] Sept. 17, 1895 (*ibid.,* p. 120). The italics are mine.

"We shall always have to be able to separate from time to time, so as to have our letters—they are irreplaceable and they are even more so because we don't dare speak to each other. . . . Ah! What queer people we are!"[29]

It was not long, however, before Gide got bored at La Roque. He could not bear solitude when it was not creative. As his approaching marriage made him incapable of becoming engrossed in his work, he was as far as he could possibly be from the mood in which he had begun *Les Nourritures terrestres* two years before. The letters from his pure and mystical fiancée sometimes reduced him to tears. He read them and reread them, walking alone through the woods of La Roque, where they had spent so much of their childhood together. Autumn was drawing near and always made him feel somewhat like the old Walter. What had he accomplished? Where exactly was he going? He dared not start keeping his journal again, for fear that any state of duality would change the sincerity of his feelings. Perhaps he was also afraid of self-analysis because it would have forced him to examine his conscience. He had kept so many things hidden from Madeleine! He had so many secrets from her! In July she had written to him: "With such an unsullied and pure life, how could you have written certain pages of *Le Voyage d'Urien,* pages that made me close the book the other day? . . . Why are you afraid of telling me your thoughts as they come to you? Am I not your friend?"[30] *Urien* had been written three years before, during a terrible summer at La Roque. And since then, he had had many adventures which he obviously could not confide to Madeleine just as she was at last beginning to be reassured about him. Gide had a bad conscience, and when he thought about it with his usual lucidity, he could not help but ask himself many questions and recall many shadows! In the old family house, haunted by his mother's soul, his recent adventures appeared to him in quite a different light than they had in Biskra or Algiers. A letter from Maurice Quillot informed him that *Madame l'Esthète* would be dedicated to "Oscar Wilde, martyr." The friend of Madeleine Rondeaux's fiancé was henceforth convict C. 33 in Reading Gaol.

Gide had planned to go to Noirmoutier in September to visit the Charles Gides, who were spending the summer there. He left La Roque on that pretext, but actually he meant to take a short trip with his friend Eugène Rouart. Old Marie, who had been well trained by her mistress to be on the alert, was not taken in and felt obliged to reprimand him by letter:

I'll bet, judging from a telegram I've seen lying around, that you've made another *mad trip* through France. I should have thought that a fiancé doesn't

[29] *Ibid.,* p. 115.

[30] *Ibid.,* p. 119.

go running around with his friends like that. So you've pushed your relatives aside for your friends? . . . When I saw that telegram from M. Rouart, I was furious with him, and I should have thought that you were more responsible too. Think about it again; once you're married, you can't wildly run around with friends. . . . How you do change your mind all the time. You leave for Noirmoutier, and no, you can't just peacefully go your way without being led astray.[31]

Marie did not find that his engagement had made the perpetual traveler any more reasonable, and she became alarmed: "That made me very annoyed because I hoped that you'd really give your nerves a rest at Noirmoutier. I don't care if you're angry at me, I had to tell you that." She scolded him just as she had heard her "dear unforgettable mistress" do so often; but it was for the last time.

[31] Sept. 3, 1895, unpublished.

44: Medical Advice

> *"Yet I could not help but worry about my own nature, I mean that of my desires . . . I had therefore decided to talk freely about it to a doctor."*
>
> Et nunc manet in te, *p. 1130*

A T THE very end of *Si le grain ne meurt* Gide wrote of his engagement to Emmanuèle: "I believed I could give myself to her *completely*,[1] and did so without any reservations." Apparently, at the time of his engagement he had decided to put an end to that dissociation of pleasure and love which had governed his sexual life until then. When he married Madeleine "without any reservations," did he really mean to give up his homosexual habits?

It was a marriage between heaven and my insatiable hell; but at the actual moment, that hell was temporarily suppressed: the tears of my mourning had put out all its fires; it was as if I were dazzled by the glare of azure, and everything I refused to see had stopped existing for me.[2]

Barely two weeks after his mother's death, that celestial glare, that blinding exaltation, favored an immediate engagement; but as the emotional intoxication wore off, his usual temptations probably returned, and with them, some hesitations and doubts as to his physiological aptitude for marriage. It would be difficult to affirm that "at the time he married, Gide's illusion about his normalcy was complete."[3] In October, 1893, he had set out on his travels with the intention of "normalizing" himself; his first

---

[1] The italics are mine.

[2] *Si le grain ne meurt,* II, 369.

[3] Jean Schlumberger, *Madeleine et André Gide,* p. 121.

attempts with Meriem had been successful, but all the others had "pitifully failed," whereas his homosexual experiences had been so easy and conclusive that he had believed he had found what was "normal" for him. Gide was thus faced with a serious problem and was well aware of it, for he decided to tell a doctor all about his fears.

In *Et nunc manet in te* he wrote about that prenuptial consultation, unmentioned in *Si le grain ne meurt*. He went to see "a rather well-known specialist," and made a confession that was "as cynical as possible." The "neurologist" listened to him "smilingly," examined him, and then drew comforting conclusions:

And yet you say that you're in love with a young girl; and that you hesitate to marry her because, on the other hand, you're aware of your tastes. . . . Get married. Get married without fear. And you'll quickly realize that all the rest exists only in your imagination. You give me the impression of someone who is starved and who up until now has tried to subsist on pickles. (I'm accurately quoting his words; by heaven, I could hardly forget them!) As soon as you're married, you will quickly understand what natural instinct is and will quite spontaneously go back to it.[4]

The practitioner who displayed such hardy optimism no doubt believed he was dealing with an emotional and shy young man who lacked self-confidence, and that all he had to do was to reassure him good-naturedly. That kind of attitude would have been justified had Gide been simply anxious and tormented by the fear of sexual inhibition, but the situation was far more complicated and should never have been treated lightly. We have now come to the point in this study where an analysis of Gide's sexual problem, as it stood in 1895, seems in order. In a plan for a preface to *Si le grain ne meurt,* Gide wrote:

Rousseau says that he wrote his *Confessions* because he believed he was unique. I am writing mine for exactly the opposite reasons, and because I know that a great many will recognize themselves in them.—But to what purpose?— I believe that everything that is true can be instructive.[5]

It is precisely because of his intention to tell the truth for representative purposes that it is necessary to reconsider that important question from an angle which has nothing to do with literature.

Given Gide's way of understanding confessions, it is probable that he omitted no detail that might have enlightened the doctor, save that he could not have pointed out a whole group of family circumstances which at that time were considered to have no connection with the sexual question. Moreover, many doctors, even the most learned in the field of nervous

---

[4] *Et nunc manet in te,* p. 1130.   [5] *O.C.,* X, 454.

illnesses, then knew very little about sexual neuroses. Once they had ascertained that their patient's constitution was normally virile (and Gide's was) and that he had already been capable of heterosexual relations (which was indeed his case), they were of the idea that he had no actual medical problem, as if the doctor could ignore the implications of the mind and the body, or, as they say, the psyche and the soma. The neurologist cannot be personally blamed for his mistake, for it is ascribable to a certain purely somatic conception of medicine, which was far more widespread then than it is today.

Before trying to explain Gide's sexual habits, they must be defined. With regard to his experience in January, 1895, he said: "I now found what was normal for me." What did he mean by "normal" for him? The one word "homosexual" designates "types" that are very different from one another, with one trait in common: the subject and object of desire are of the same sex. "If only, instead of becoming indignant, people would just try to find out what is being talked about. Before discussing, one should always define. Most quarrels further a misunderstanding."[6] In regard to himself, Gide wanted to avoid any possibility of a misunderstanding: he was bent on saying what he was and what he was not. "I call a *pederast* the man who, as the word indicates, falls in love with young boys . . . pederasts, of whom I am one. . . ."[7] He was a pederast or a pedophile—that is, a man whose object of desire is neither man nor woman but the male child or adolescent, at least as long as the adolescent remains the *molliter juvenis* spoken of by Pliny. For Gide, childishness or youthfulness was the condition *sine qua non* of desirability; mature virility was as horrifying to him as effeminacy. On that point he hardly ever varied, and the homosexual phantasms we remarked in *Les Cahiers d'André Walter* and *Le Voyage d'Urien,* conceived before he had had any experience, were indeed those of a pedophile. Giving a quite different meaning to certain terms in medical language, he called a *sodomite* "the man whose desire is directed to mature men," and an *invert* "the man who, in the comedy of love, assumes the role of a woman."[8] The author of *Amyntas* never hid the fact that he was repelled by one and the other, and said about the different types of homosexuals: "The difference between them is so great that they feel profound disgust for one another." As early as October, 1894, after having read Moll's book on homosexuality, he wrote:

He does not differentiate enough between two classes: the effeminate men and the others—he constantly mixes them together, and nothing is more different, more *contrary*—because one is opposed to the other—because for that kind of psychophysiology, that which does not attract repels—and each horrifies the other.[9]

[6] *Journal,* p. 671.   [8] *Ibid.*
[7] *Ibid.*   [9] Letter to a friend, unpublished.

Gide was specific about the forms of his homosexual relations.

We always have great difficulty in understanding the loves of others, their way of practicing love. . . . But nothing is more disconcerting than the gesture, so different from species to species, by means of which each one of them achieves sexual pleasure. . . . It is perhaps, on the contrary, in what M. de Gourmont calls "the physics of love" that we find the most marked differences not only between man and animals but often even from one man to another—to the point that were we allowed to watch our neighbor's practices, they would often seem as strange, as preposterous, and indeed as monstrous as the coupling of batrachians or insects—but why go that far afield? as that of dogs and cats. And that is no doubt why the incomprehension on this point is so great and the intransigence so ferocious.[10]

He himself was always to remain the André Walter who was "terrified by carnal possession" and as unresponsive to virile aggressivity as to feminine passivity. As Baudelaire wrote:

There is something in the act of love that is similar to torture or to a surgical operation. . . . Love wants to come out of itself, fuse with its victim like the conqueror with the conquered, and yet keep the conqueror's privileges.[11]

Copulation, whether natural or against nature, provoked a kind of terror in Gide, in that it called to mind a semblance of combat or, to use Baudelaire's expression, the conqueror and the conquered, whatever the assent or the agreement between the partners as to the respective roles they play in the pantomime. In *Si le grain ne meurt* he told about how during one of his trips in Algeria, he was the horrified witness to an act of homosexual fornication between a sodomite and an invert:

He seemed like a huge vampire feeding on a corpse. I could have screamed out with horror. . . . As for me, whose only way of taking pleasure is face to face, reciprocally and without violence, and who, like Whitman, am often satisfied by the most furtive contact, I was horrified both by Daniel's way of going about it and by Mohammed's very complacent submission to it.[12]

His homosexual habits were limited to the voluptuous play of his childhood, and differed from it only in that the solitary onanism had become reciprocal onanism with childish partners. Certain of the great writer's self-disparaging remarks, such as: "I shall never be a man, but only a child who has grown old," or: "I'm only a little boy having a good time . . . ," do make sense with regard to his sexual behavior, which was to remain infantile.

It seems surprising that Gide, always so careful when it came to distinguishing between pleasure and love, would have picked up the expression

[10] *Si le grain ne meurt*, pp. 595–96.

[11] Charles Baudelaire, *Fusées*.

[12] *Si le grain ne meurt*, pp. 595–96. The allusion is obviously to Walt Whitman.

cited above, "the physics of love," when he was clearly referring to the physics of pleasure. When he specified that love had played no part in his experience of January, 1895, he was speaking of pleasure for what it was, without mixing in any sentimental or moral considerations, and could not honestly assimilate it to Greek love. But later on, he had Corydon, that Victor Cousin of pedophiles, do just that when he claimed to justify pederasty in the name of the true, the beautiful, and the good. What happened was that in the meanwhile Gide had rationalized his tastes and proceeded to defend them with a whole dialectic, in which so many sophisms were mixed with valid arguments that a passage from *Le Journal des Faux-Monnayeurs* could well have been used as an epigraph for *Corydon:*

Someone with a so-called false turn of mind? Well! I'll explain it to you: it's someone who feels the need of convincing himself that he's *right;* someone who uses his reason to serve his instincts, his interests, which is worse, or his temperament. . . . He is the first victim of his own false reasoning; he ends by convincing himself that he is being led by those false reasons.[13]

In any case, Gide's homosexual problem in 1895 was far simpler and much less involved in sophistries than it was to become later on, for he had not yet constructed the theory that was meant to justify his inclinations. The very fact that he went to consult a doctor and accepted the assurance that he was sexually normal proves that he was not yet sure that pederasty was "normal" for him.

When he recalled the prenuptial consultation that had put an end to his hesitations and doubts as to his aptitude for marriage, Gide added:

I should have realized at once how very wrong the theorist was. He was wrong in the same way as all those who persist in thinking that as soon as someone is physiologically normal, his homosexual tastes are merely acquired tendencies and can therefore be changed with the help of education, promiscuity, and love.[14]

If the first theorist was wrong out of overoptimism, was not the second wrong out of overfatalism? The passage clearly hints at the thesis that was to be upheld by the doctrinary Corydon. If one believes homosexuality to be innate, it seems fatal and represents a destiny; if one believes it to be acquired, it seems modifiable and represents a choice. The homosexual who claims that his inclinations are "natural" considers them inevitable, thus discouraging beforehand any attempt at a struggle and allowing for only one reasonable solution: acceptance, if, of course, he is determined to

[13] Pp. 58–59.

[14] *Et nunc manet in te,* p. 1130.

follow his "nature" despite all moral or social interdictions. That, we know, is the viewpoint of Corydon, who invokes Goethe's words:

Pederasty is as old as humanity itself and we can therefore say that it is natural, that it is based upon nature although it goes against nature. What culture has gained, what it has won over nature, should never be allowed to escape; at no price should it be let go.

In other words, Goethe believed that the approbation of heterosexuality and the reprobation of homosexuality represent a cultural victory, but that nature proposes one as well as the other. Corydon, who thinks his habits are "against custom," not "against nature," is convinced of it, but he is completely opposed to Goethe in the sense that he considers "culture's" gain in that realm unfortunate. Indeed, basing his point of view on a whole documentation borrowed from the history of aesthetics and ethics, sociology and biology, he believes that pederasty, far from being any kind of human inferiority, is a superiority in the scale of values. There is little point in discussing so specious an argument here, for it would lead us far from the problem at hand: was it possible, at the time of the 1895 consultation, to know whether Gide's homosexuality was innate, and therefore fatal, or acquired, and therefore modifiable? Was it, as he proclaimed, inscribed in his nature, or was it, on the contrary, produced by outer influences which turned his instinct from its habitual finality and kept him from reaching maturity? In his *Discours sur l'origine de l'inégalité,* Jean Jacques Rousseau remarked: "It is no small undertaking to distinguish the native from the artificial in man's present nature." Difficult as it may be, it is still necessary, in tracing the evolution of habits, to distinguish how much is native and how much artificial—that is, how much is constitutional and how much institutional, how much organic and how much environmental.

Gide's physical constitution was normally virile, and we know in another connection that he was not at all incapable of "the impulse that procreates." He apparently had none of the anomalies of the sex characteristics, primary or secondary, which make it possible to consider a hormonal factor at the roots of some homosexuality. Besides, *Corydon* deals only with the pederasty of men who are completely virile biologically, as Gide himself was. Yet modern research in the determination of the "genetic sex" shows that the biological problem is infinitely more complicated than one might have believed. It is possible that any profound and lasting perversion of the sexual instinct implies a constitutional predisposition. Freud himself, who upheld the psychogenesis of the homosexual neurosis, admitted that "without a constitutional predisposition, no neurosis could exist." Be that as it may, the only notable anomaly in Gide's constitution was not of a sexual but of a nervous nature. His temperament was that of someone nervously weak, predisposed to emotional inhibitions and self-doubt, *naturally* shy, exposed to difficulties in social relations and, most particularly, in sexual relations. Many anxious people of that irritable and suggestible temperament might say with Amiel: "Sexuality will have been my Nemesis, my torment since childhood," and invoke "my extraordinary shyness, my embarrassment with women, my violent desires, the fervor of imagination . . . the eternal disproportion between a life of dream and real life, my deadly propensity for detaching myself from the tastes, passions, and habits of those of my own age and my own sex . . ." to explain an inhibition, if not a perversion, of which that idiosyncrasy can be a predisposing, but not a determining, factor.

When endocrinology discovers nothing abnormal in the distribution of male and female hormones, whose relative preponderance determines the secondary sex characteristics, when the possibility of a biologically characterized inversion or intersexual state is eliminated, the explanation for pederasty must be sought in the psychological history of the development of the instinct. This field of research has largely benefited from psychoanalytical studies. Freud, in his far-reaching analysis of infantile sexuality, has shown that the libido, which is present from the beginnings of life, goes through different stages. At first autoerotic—that is, turned toward itself—it then becomes alloerotic—that is, turned toward an object outside itself. But, at the beginning of the alloerotic stage, it is not unusual for it to direct its energies toward an object of the same sex before directing them toward an object of the opposite sex. Many adolescents who go through a homosexual stage reach the heterosexual stage all the same. But maturity is not complete until both desire and love are concentrated on an object of the opposite sex: the capacity to desire and love an individual outside oneself and of a different sex characterizes adult sexuality. Now most perversions are the expression of fixations or regressions at one or another of the stages of the instinct's development, perpetuating, so to speak, a period of apprenticeship. It is what Freud expressed in the laconic formula: "One does not become perverse; one remains perverse." Any lasting sexual anomaly would be a fixation on some former hedonism, either a stopping point or a return to infantile or juvenile stages.

Corydon is indignant at the fact that a pederast could be considered "backward."[15] And, of course, he is not at all backward in the physical and intellectual sense, but from the particular viewpoint of the maturation of instinct, he has indeed "remained" at a stage of immaturity. With relation to solitary onanism, as an expression of integral narcissism and the total introversion of desire, and from the viewpoint of the philosophy of instinct, some progress has been made, since the libido directs its energies toward an object outside itself; but that progress is incomplete and does

[15] *Corydon,* p. 137.

not reach the last stage, that at which the libido directs its energies toward an object sexually different from itself. It is, as it were, an intermediary stage between the desire of the onanist and the desire of the heterosexual, between narcissism and heterosexuality. This concept finds confirmation in the basic narcissism of the huge majority of pederasts: "Proceeding as from narcissism, they seek their own image in young people."[16]

In that perspective, the problem is to determine the influences that hindered the maturation of the instinct and arrested its normal development. But on this particular point, different schools have different doctrines. Gide reproached psycshoanalysts for their sense of system. As he told me: "They want to apply their theory to everyone, instead of reconsidering the dogma, or what they take to be such, with relation to each individual case."[17] With no fixed prejudice, I shall try to bring out everything in the first twenty-five years of his life that can clarify his "individual case." Various complex-creating situations, various psychic factors, moral and social, encouraged a neurotic condition that was highly compromising for the future of his virility.

"My puritanical upbringing made a monster of the demands of the flesh."[18] A puritanical upbringing has often been blamed for the sexual neuroses of a Rousseau, an Amiel, a Nietzsche, a Loti, a Gide, to give only a few literary examples, and many psychological novelists have treated the theme of the young Protestant who has become sexually neurotic because of the severity of his confessional mold. There is no doubt that the Calvinist regulation of habits is particularly stern. As a Protestant philosopher, M. Arbousse-Bastide, has emphasized: "In bourgeois society, the greatest sin is stealing; for a Puritan society, it is any sexual infringement." Yet the repressions and sexual deviations provoked by a too severely moral upbringing are less dependent on any one particular religion than on the personality of the educator and on that of the child he educates. The benefits or dangers of a rigorous upbringing depend, above all, on the one who gives it and the one who receives it. Both Gide, a Protestant child, and Rimbaud, a Catholic child, were brought up by narrow-minded mothers who saw religion as a constant constraint, and proved to be more concerned with having them live under the law than in the loftiness of grace. Even more rigid, intolerant, and domineering in that each had to react against a secret weakness, they increased the prohibitions and cast such a categorical interdict over sex that their anxious children imagined all the

---

[16] Freud, *Three Essays on the Theory of Sexuality.*

[17] "Dernières années. Hommage à André Gide," *N.R.F.,* 1951, p. 363.

[18] *Si le grain ne meurt,* I, 247.

temptations of the flesh as coming from the devil.[19] Now by condemning sex as a "monster," a "dragon," a "demon," the Puritan ends by considering normal sexual satisfaction just as mortal a sin as any other kind of sexual satisfaction.[20] When in 1893 Gide made every effort to give his consent to the "demands" of his flesh, he added: "Even had those demands been more commonplace, I doubt whether I should have been any less perturbed."[21] That was characteristic of his puritanical turn of mind. The attitude of André Gide's family toward sex can be seen in all its rigor in a letter written to him by his uncle, Charles Gide, reproaching him for his relations with a "prostitute from Biskra," and going so far as to evoke the ghost of Lady Macbeth: "What's done cannot be undone."[22] Such intransigence, so foreign to Gallic humor, was not apt to encourage the young traveler in his attempt at "normalization."

What Freud said about Leonardo da Vinci's mother, namely that she had "stripped him of part of his virility," might be repeated, with more likelihood, about André Gide's mother.[23] Although her intentions were of the best, she seems to be that type of virile mother, so threatening to a son's virility, whom psychoanalysts do not hesitate to call "castrating." We know the role Freud gave to "that maternal divinity with the head of a vulture," and in most representations "endowed by the Egyptians with a phallus," in the evolution of certain homosexual cases. In the fable, Osiris—the child cut up into bits—managed to put all his pieces together with the exception of the male organ, and that legendary version has been used to represent symbolically the so-called castration complex. To go from there and claim that the threatening "crique" of Gide's childhood nightmares was merely a mother symbol is a big step and one an orthodox Freudian would not hesitate to take. But without turning to the elements of the psychology of the unconscious, particularly hypothetical in this case, we can find in Gide's history many proofs of his mother's inhibiting influence on his sexual development.

When at the time Gide was sent away from the Ecole Alsacienne and Mme. Gide learned that her nine-year-old son had "bad habits," she took him to a doctor who threatened to castrate him, but the prospect of such bodily punishment seemed not to have terrified the boy nearly as much as his

[19] See above, bk. one, pt. i, chap. 12.

[20] I must also add that certain puritanical educators, Protestant or Catholic, would seem to have more indulgence for the onanism of adolescents than for any first normal sexual relations, as though in their eyes woman represented the sinner par excellence, as though Adam's sin, which lost him Paradise, had far more deadly consequences.

[21] *Si le grain ne meurt,* II, p. 287.

[22] January 20, 1895, unpublished.

[23] See above, bk. one, pt. i, chap. 3.

mother's reproaches and the pain it caused her. He was fifteen when his mother warned him against streetwalkers in such a dramatic way that a few days later he had a fit of anguish, imagining one of his friends, a habitué of certain disreputable districts, as being "orgiastically torn to pieces by hetaerae." When he would read aloud to Mme. Gide, he was terrified by the idea of coming upon a "daring" passage, at which point his voice would "freeze," while his mother glared at him with an expression he described as either that of the captain of a ship, responsible for the fate of his fragile skiff during a tempest, or as that of an examining magistrate. When at the end of his adolescence he informed his mother of his plan to marry Madeleine Rondeaux, she categorically opposed it. He was so dependent upon her that his friends Louÿs and Régnier teased him about behaving like a "little boy." And he was already a twenty-two-year-old man when, in Biskra, Mme. Gide was so upset about his affair with Meriem that he agreed to break with the Oulad-Naïl and kept his word. Those are but a few of the more significant episodes.

"Each one," said Nietzsche, "forms his image of women from his mother; and according to the impression he keeps of his mother, he will esteem women or despise them, or be generally indifferent to them." That fairly questionable assertion would seem valid insofar as Gide is concerned: he formed a very special image of women from his mother, imagining them as paragons of virtue, respectable but not desirable, devoted to austere duties but unrelated to sensual pleasures. Yet ever since childhood he had embodied the opposite of such virtuous women in the image of his aunt, Mathilde Rondeaux, near whom he had felt "singularly uneasy," troubled both by "admiration and terror"; but the misconduct of Madeleine's mother caused her to be excluded from the family circle, and, anguished by the reprobation that weighed on the sinner, he had felt contaminated at the slightest contact with her.[24] Mme. Paul Gide's horror of sensual and frivolous women, and even more of "loose women," contributed to her son's "terror" of them.

In the evolution of homosexuality, psychoanalysts attribute major importance to the reactions of identification or rejection with regard to the parental images. Now among the very diverse family situations that have been invoked to explain disturbances in the normal development of the sexual instinct, that of Gide during his childhood is considered one of the most characteristic: the only child of an ill-sorted couple, with the father playing a very small part and the tyrannical and dreaded mother in authority. A homosexual is rarely the son of a happy couple, the image of complete conjugal understanding. And Gide was very young when his intuition told him that his parents were hiding a secret misunderstanding;

[24] See above, pp. 142–46.

furthermore, he persisted in trying to discover the flaw. On the other hand, the obliteration of the father image, whether due to the father's absence, estrangement, or general discretion, is one of the traits psychoanalysts have often noticed in homosexuals. It was certainly part of Gide's condition, not only because he was only eleven when his father died, but because his intellectual, gentle, meditative, somewhat distant father, who dreaded domestic disputes, had given over to his domineering wife the task of bringing up their only son. "If my father had seen to my upbringing himself, my life would have been very different," André Gide told me when he was old, implying that he had lacked a father's presence; and indeed it would seem that the masculine influence in his development was insufficient in relation to the preponderant feminine influence. If it is true that in the case of many homosexuals one finds an abnormally close and prolonged dependency on the mother or on a maternal substitute, the dependency can exist in very different emotional types, going from enraptured love to more or less unconscious hate, and including all the ambivalent forms of love-hate. The love identification can be so intense that it leads to the desire for "dreaming, feeling, and loving like a woman," and even to the point of wanting to actualize "a woman's soul in a man's body"; but the mothers who inspire such abnormal, passionate feelings are usually very feminine, thus very different from Mme. Paul Gide. None of that applies to André Gide, whose dependency on his mother was doubtless close and prolonged but apprehensive and ambivalent, a mixture of the feelings of veneration and aggressive resentment, which contributed a great deal to making him a divided child.[25] Marcel Proust's love dependency on Mme. Adrien Proust, and André Gide's hostile dependency on Mme. Paul Gide, no doubt contributed to making them both homosexuals, but different kinds, for one became effeminate and not the other.

"Our most serious vices are acquired in our most tender childhoods," remarked Montaigne. Now as Gide himself specified in his *Journal* and even in *Ainsi soit-il,* his main vice was onanism, and actually his homosexual practices were merely substitutes for it. Although episodic masturbation is relatively commonplace, the same is not true when the habit becomes so inveterate that it defines the entire sexual behavior of a man as that of an onanist. This autoerotic fixation can provoke other perversions, assuming that they are also the expression of narcissism, and it is in that way that the variously interpreted link between onanism and homosexuality has often been emphasized. "I didn't give up one of the two *vices* for the other. I mixed them together. Or rather, as each one took it upon itself to break all the obstacles of thought and feeling which might have stopped the other, it also seemed to provoke it," wrote Marcel Proust in *La Confession d'une jeune fille.*

[25] See above, pp. 124–25.

When the organism is accustomed exclusively to solitary vice, as though it were a kind of "toxicomania," the sexual instincts become centered exclusively on the organ that gives the habitual pleasure, and desire cannot be transferred except to a human object endowed with the same advantage. Thus the very finality of the instinct—the complete union of the two opposite sexes—is thwarted; the homosexual is not attracted by the difference but by the homology that recalls his own sexual organ, the object of all his complacency. According to Freud:

The high esteem in which homosexuals hold the male organ is what decides their fate. In their childhood they choose woman as the sexual object so long as they credit her with possessing that part of the body which to them is indispensable. Once they have acquired the firm belief that woman has disappointed them on that score, woman becomes unacceptable to them as a sexual object.

Very early in life, Gide imagined the female body as a mutilated body which nature had considerably diminished by depriving it of a captivating organ. Moreover, when in his hallucinated daydreams Walter evoked the vision of "women's flesh," he at first found those visions tempting but in the end disappointing: "And I was afraid of seeing; I wanted to turn my eyes away, but in spite of myself, I looked. Under the dress there was nothing; it was dark, dark as a hole; I sobbed in despair."[26] He found the image not only distressing but terrifying; for the phantasm of sexual possession was linked in his youthful imagination to the fear of being "orgiastically torn to pieces." He dreaded the ailments suffered by those of Urien's companions who gave in to women, and dreaded even more the truly mutilating torture endured by Osiris or Orpheus. His was the same childish fear of mutilation through orgasm that psychoanalysis has discovered in the unconscious of certain homosexuals terrified by carnal possession.

In Gide's childhood and adolescence there is no trace of those ambiguous "friendships" which are often considered the starting point of homosexual habits. Yet apropos of his cousin Albert, twenty years his elder, he declared: "I vaguely suffered from his reserve, and I cannot help thinking today that he would have done me a better service by throwing it off." It is interesting to compare that laconic sentence from *Si le grain ne meurt* and a comment Gide made later in life: "If my cousin had initiated me, instead of letting me wear myself out all alone, I should have been an excellent family man." Here we have one of the strangest and most questionable ideas the writer of *Corydon* ever expressed. He deemed solitary habits so dangerous for any future virility that the sexual education of a young boy by an older man appeared to him advantageous and more normal. He actually believed that it would have made him "more virile" with women.

[26] *Les Cahiers d'André Walter, O.C.,* I, 170.

All that is highly questionable, but there is no doubt that Gide's extraordinary and prolonged ignorance of sexual realities and his lack of any education in that realm did contribute to his deviation. He himself emphasized in *Si le grain ne meurt* the strangeness of his "themes of physical enjoyment," in order to bring out "to what point a child's instinct can go astray."[27]

Adler considered pederasty, in men of neurotic temperament, as the expression of an inferiority complex with regard to their virility; this interpretation is valid only in certain cases, but it is not unlikely in Gide's and seems to contain a measure of truth. According to Adler, the nervously weak man, who has doubts about himself and about his own virility, dreads, above all, the deep humiliation implied in sexual failure, and seeks a way to assert, beyond question, his own superiority.[28]

Gide, still a virgin at the age of twenty-four, made, like Walter or Corydon, the sexual act into something terrifying, and feared that his "ridiculous ignorance" would make *him* ridiculous. Again and again, Corydon dwells on the difficulties an inexperienced young man has in approaching "the other sex" for the first time, and the ease offered by homosexual intercourse:

Do you remember Daphnis' mistake and how he groped . . . And that is why, in Vergil, we see Damoetas still crying over Galatea's flight under the willows, while Menalcas was already taking his pleasure with Amyntas, and without reserve. . . . *At mihi sese offert ultro, meus ignis, Amyntas.*

His interpretation is specious, for desire is generally stimulated by difficulty, not thwarted by it; and the flight under the willows is merely flirtatiousness and should have provoked a chase, not, as with shy people, intimidation. Gide, whose Galatea obstinately fled from him for five years, and hardly out of flirtatiousness, was not obliged to make the slightest effort to get young Arabs, who offered themselves "without reserve," and the pleasure he took with them demanded no training whatever, for they merely revived his old habits. No inhibition intervened in his North African experiences with childish partners, especially as the differences in race and social class tended to neutralize the feeling of inferiority. Everything happened as if circumstances had helped him to follow his inclinations. His initiations took place in a country where pederasty is not particularly disapproved of.[29] The young boys he knew during his first two trips were accustomed to such practices and had no feeling of guilt about them. In the eyes of the little vagabonds who hung around the hotel, in Sousse

[27] *Si le grain ne meurt*, p. 62. See also, above, pp. 115–17.

[28] Adler, *The Neurotic Constitution* and *Inferiority Complex and Sexuality*.

[29] " 'Love is very difficult in our country,' Athman said, 'because the women are guarded by dogs and by the whole family' " (*Journal*, p. 87, n. 1).

as in Biskra, he was a rich and powerful lord, and all the more attractive in that he took part in their games with real amusement. He met just exactly the little sunburned boys Walter had dreamed of, and with them the puritanical convalescent, out of his element under that oriental sky, felt his austerity "melt away." Quite obviously, he tried to identify with the little foreigners, seeking an estrangement from himself which was also a return to the natural self he might have been before the puritanical and maternal ethics had intervened and at a time when sin did not exist. In fact, it seemed like a return to health. The blond, pure, wise, and dreaming child, contemplating some northern sea, whom he described in *Le Voyage d'Urien,* would doubtless have intimidated Gide by his whiteness, his purity, his wisdom, and his dreams, for he would have awakened the guilt feeling in him; but Gide had no guilt when a little Arab "smilingly" offered himself in a strange country which left him no place for reflection. Of course, his desire was especially awakened by the bad little boys, but his tenderness went out to the others; and when he attached himself to one of them, Athman, for example, he at once began to moralize, wanting to bring him up—in the literal sense of the word. As he emphasized so many times, that tendency thwarted his sexual inclinations, as though the pedagogue inhibited the pederast. The "dissociation of pleasure and love" also regulated his homosexual habits; in him sensuality and sentimentality were opposed, but they are not opposed in *Corydon,* which is a theory of André Gide's habits not as they were but as he would have wished them to be.

There is no doubt that Gide's pedophilic experiences during his two trips in Algeria had considerable influence on the direction and determination of his sexual habits, and he himself confided to Denis de Rougemont that at that point he had made "a terrible mistake in taking the wrong road."[30] But was his attempt at "normalization" really compromised from that time on? His relations with Meriem had been satisfying. The fact that they were combined with a homosexual phantasm changes nothing essentially: if Gide had had a real "aversion"[31] to the female sex, as he subsequently declared, his first attempt would not have been brought to so successful and natural a conclusion.

Yet if that first experience was fully satisfying, why was it not followed up? Here, a series of adverse circumstances came into play and revived all the interdictions that had been cast over the female sex. First of all, Mme.

[30] Denis de Rougemont, "Un Complot de Protestants. Hommage à André Gide," *N.R.F.,* 1951, p. 283.

[31] *Si le grain ne meurt,* I, 197.

Gide's despair, tears, and "inconsolable, infinite sadness" immediately transformed her recently emancipated son into the guilty child of old, and although he had the "cheek" to abide by his decision of seeing Meriem again, he did not, he said, have "the courage" to keep his word. As we know, his guilt feeling and anguish were such that his next attempt with the "much too beautiful" En Barka "failed miserably," and as he wrote to Albert Démarest, he felt that the harm done was "irreparable." Many months later he did get back some assurance in an Algiers brothel, perhaps because of the very "vulgarity" of the place and the girl, but the psychological benefit of his accomplishment was at once reduced to nothing by Pierre Louÿs' disastrous remarks on the girls' general state of hygiene. And so his heterosexual experiences were thwarted by anguishing feelings of guilt, inferiority, and insecurity, whereas none of those inhibitions intervened in his pedophilic relations.

If it is true that an unbroken chain linked the neurotic difficulties of a childhood and adolescence to Gide's choice of homosexuality, his fate as a homosexual was not definitely established until he had made the choice itself. The actual moment he became aware of being, or thinking he was, a pederast, and chose to assert himself as such, was at the end of January, 1895, in Algiers. "I now found what was normal for me." That categorical an awareness of his state, whether genuine or fallacious (there are homosexuals by conviction), had a decisive influence on the determination of his sexual habits, for self-awareness is a powerful agent of transformation, and man becomes, to a great extent, what he thinks he is. Was it the homosexual revelation in Algiers that led him to the highly assertive attitude so unusual in a doubter for whom every affirmation was a demand for asserting the contrary? The experience itself was probably less determinant than the circumstances under which it took place, the most important of which was the presence of Oscar Wilde. "There are people who would never have loved if they had not heard about love," wrote La Rochefoucauld, and that is even truer about sexual habits which go against nature. There is, of course, no reason to say that Gide would not have become a homosexual if he had not met Wilde, but it is likely that he would not have so soon adopted, within himself, the attitude of the arrogant pederast, determined to assert his anomaly as his norm. It was directly after his meeting with Wilde in Algeria that he began to think that what he had, until then, considered an inferiority could represent, or be represented as, a superiority. His letters of January and February, 1895, show the naïve, if not ingenuous, fascination Wilde and Douglas held for him. The luxury with which the aesthete and his Bosie surrounded themselves, their insolence, their extravagance, their provocations, and their pretensions of being patricians above the laws and morals of the plebs seemed, for a time, to the son of the conventional and economical Mme. Gide, to be the "higher immorality" toward which he had been aiming but to which he had not yet dared aspire. There would be little point in dwelling on such details were the pomp with which certain pederasts surround themselves not part of the prestige they have with the very young. Oscar Wilde's vice, stripped of all the glamor—the fame, the wit, the money—is no more than M. Melmoth's sad habit. It has been said that a vice cannot live without mystery; actually, to certain people it is not viable without prestige. Of course, a homosexual cannot have influence on anyone who has not the same latent tendencies, but if it is true that such tendencies are more or less latent in many adolescents whose tastes are not conclusively established, an illustrious example can be partly responsible for numerous deviations. Gide was fascinated by the "courage," or at any rate, the audacity, with which Wilde had dared "be himself" and defy public opinion. The authority with which the writer-actor had played the part of a homosexual character seemed to give Gide a kind of authorization to imitate him.

The minute a young man whose instinct has been repressed by moral and social constraints decides to free sexuality from guilt, he also generally rebels against the constraints themselves. Would Gide's change in attitude have been very different if, instead of deciding to free his "anomaly" from guilt, he had continued his attempt at "normalization" despite his mother's prohibitions? It would seem doubtful, given his essential puritanism, but the exceptional and censurable nature of the "originality" he asserted from then on helped to intoxicate him with pride and strengthen his protest. Determined to struggle for his sexual nonconformity, he was led to extend his struggle to every other kind of conformity. As he later wrote to Ramon Fernandez:

I think it's quite right to say (as you have done so well) that sexual nonconformity is the first key to my works; but I'm particularly grateful to you for already having indicated, after that monster of the flesh, the first sphinx on my way, and the most devouring of them, through what evolution and because of what invitation my mind, its appetite whetted, went even further and attacked all the other sphinxes of conformity, which henceforth it suspected of being the brothers and cousins of the first.

This passage would seem to show that those—and they are numerous—who consider Gide's attitude toward morality a consequence of his sexual anomaly are right. They base their theory on Charles Du Bos's diagnosis, namely that he was suffering from "generalized inversion,"[32] and playing on those words, they see his sexual inversion as the point of departure for a general inversion of values. This thesis, which satisfies a widespread tend-

[32] Charles Du Bos, *Le Dialogue avec André Gide.*

ency to see a link of cause and effect between immorality and "immoralism," is simplifying to an extreme. Sexually abnormal people, outside of their anomaly, may go along either with the conformist's code of moral and social values or with the nonconformists': each one's reaction to his particular problem depends essentially on his only nature. The psychological motivations for Gide's immoralist protest were infinitely more complicated than the preceding thesis would give us to understand. What interests us at present is the fact that Gide considered his homosexual problem an integral part of his personality, for it thus took on major importance in his eyes. Just as Walter's psychology was constructed around Emmanuèle's love, so the "new being's" psychology was to be constructed around the justification of a vice. Needless to say, Gide was to find it all the more difficult to give up homosexuality in that he came to consider it the cornerstone of his personality, fallacious as that opinion may have been. His "virile protest," in the Adlerian sense of the words, was to be all the more uncompromising in that he came to consider his homosexuality as closely linked to his virility itself. Through a strange paradox, which was in fact not peculiar to him, giving up pederasty would have meant symbolic castration, because his assertion of homosexuality was so integral a part of his will to power.

It was one of Wilde's sophisms that largely contributed, if not to Gide's choice of homosexuality, at least to his rationalization of it: the idea, so often put forward, of the aesthetic superiority of the homosexual. Corydon not only claims that for a man to prefer the body of an adolescent to that of a woman is a proof of taste, but he asserts that "all periods of artistic efflorescence are accompanied by an outburst of uranism," and he enlists a long procession of artists behind Amyntas' crook, from Plato[33] to the present. There is no doubt much of homosexual inspiration to be found in the works of creative geniuses, as, for example, Freud remarked in Da Vinci, Carpenter in Shakespeare, and Proust in Baudelaire, but it is impossible to conclude from that fact that they themselves were homosexuals. In the same way, the psychological makeup of many artists shows an astonishing mixture of feminine and masculine traits, or so-called from a Jungian perspective, yet there is no way of judging their sexual behavior from that. It is true that uranism is far more widespread in aesthetically inclined groups than in others, but the fact is open to various interpretations. "I accept only one thing in the world as not being natural: the work of art," said Corydon. But once that axiom is stated, he refuses to use it as an argument for his thesis, as Wilde did, for example,[34] for the good

[33] For a refutation of this point see Etienne Gilson, *L'Ecole des muses,* pp. 22–23, 228.

[34] Gide's axiom, "vice is the father of all the arts," was directly inspired by Wilde's remarks.

reason that he means to prove that pederasty is "natural." We might wonder with more probability whether the frequency of the link between the homosexual condition and the aesthetic condition does not come from the fact that both may be dependent, at least to a certain extent, on the narcissistic condition, without claiming, of course, as Schlegel did, that "every poet is a Narcissus." Some artists, completely devoted to the creation of their works, dread passionate love and procreation as though they were rivals: *aut liberi aut libri.* Since neither Gide's heart nor his mind was involved in his homosexual relations, they had no lasting consequences and therefore did not compromise his freedom. Moreover, the fact that homosexuality was then considered so reprehensible, especially by his own Protestant and Victorian bourgeoisie, seemed to him part of that necessary scandal—" 'Woe unto him through whom offenses come,' yet 'offenses must come' "—which, according to the author of *Le Traité du Narcisse,* had to be part of an artist's life. In his unpublished journal of December 31, 1891, two weeks after his first meeting with Wilde, Gide wrote, and then crossed out, the revealing words: "The artist must know how to be something of a martyr." But such strategic intentions were to be brutally put to the test by the Wilde affair.

During the months of January, February, and March, 1895, the period that conclusively determined Gide's choice of homosexuality, he tried to justify his inclinations and worked out some of the arguments Corydon was later to develop with a far greater fund of information. But the first bit of rationalization or "crystallization" was suddenly compromised by the dramatic effect of the Oscar Wilde trial. A pervert cannot be intimidated, but candidates for perversion can very well be. Justice Wills's speech about Wilde's monstrous attempt at corrupting young people was addressed, beyond Oscar Wilde, to André Walter. Had the implacable verdict been pronounced in December, 1891, instead of four years later, Gide's fate as a homosexual might have been changed, for he was then still easily intimidated. He was far less so in 1895, but although he had foreseen the possibility of scandal and had consented to being "something of a martyr," he had never imagined that his attempt at sexual emancipation could lead to jail and hard labor. The last thing a free man wants is to be a convict. Noble as it may have seemed to defy the norms and judgment of society as Wilde did, "so certain of impunity," as soon as society avenged itself, he took fright at the atrocious punishment. And while the poet was on his way to Reading Gaol, Gide was shattered by another dramatic situation: his mother's death. In *Si le grain ne meurt* he affirmed that his mother had not even suspected his homosexual habits and had attributed his impassioned letters from Biskra and Algiers to an "affair," which she had begged him to break up. "The truth, had she known it, would have terrified her even more."[35] But was she really unaware of the truth? As she read about the details of the trial in the newspapers, had she not suddenly understood what was behind her son's strange attitude? She had read, reread, dated, annotated, and kept all the letters he wrote to her during the time he was seeing Wilde and Douglas, without quite understanding what they implied. Yet did she not suddenly understand, with deadly grief, the meaning of certain enigmatic phrases? Between Wilde's conviction on May 25 and the attack that paralyzed André Gide's mother at the end of May, the chronological coincidence is indeed disturbing. Did he himself never think of it? As a child, and like many other religious and scrupulous children, he was inclined to make his "sin" responsible for any unfortunate events that may have occurred in his immediate surroundings; in *Les Faux-Monnayeurs* he described his alter ego, little Boris, as terrified by the idea that his vice made him responsible for the death of his father, and I have already pointed out the chronological link between Paul Gide's death and his son's fits of anguish.[36] Fifteen years later, upon the death of his mother, at the point when moral suffering causes childish terror in even the most reasonable of adults, did he not feed his guilt feeling on that kind of remorse? This hypothesis would more clearly explain the state of panic brought about by his bereavement, and the immediate and absolute need he had for "clinging" to his love for Madeleine, a pure Beatrice floating over the hells, the ideal image of a *vita nuova*. Such, in my opinion, were the circumstances that made Gide's prenuptial consultation a sincere undertaking.

Ruling out the possibility of a constitutional predisposition, and nothing would seem to indicate that there was one, Gide's homosexuality was not innate, and therefore fatal, but acquired, and therefore modifiable. It was not inscribed in his nature, but produced by diverse factors which had arrested the normal development of his sexual instinct, factors so entangled that to disentangle them would have been a difficult, but not impossible, task. He had a homosexuality neurosis—in other words, a sexual neurosis—which is susceptible of medical treatment, at least today. But in 1895 the methods of psychoanalysis were still in their infancy. Much later, when he was almost fifty, his discovered, and became interested in, the theories of Freud and especially of Stekel; he wondered whether he at one time could have been helped by such methods, and his reflections on the subject led to the episode of little Boris' psychoanalysis in *Les Faux-Monnayeurs*. But his inquiry was merely informative. Gide had long since decided that his

[35] *Si le grain ne meurt*, II, 361.

[36] See above, pp. 118–19.

sexual habits could not be changed; his sexual neurosis had become a perversion to which he gave his full consent and with which he shamelessly came to terms.

As for his physical aptitude for marriage, the doctor saw no problem because of the fact that he formerly had had normal sexual relations. Homosexuality, when not exclusive, is not, in itself, necessarily an obstacle to marriage. But the marriage of André Gide and Madeleine Rondeaux presented almost insurmountable difficulties, due not only to him but to her and to their whole relationship. What might still have been possible with another woman was not with her because of the inhibitions of both partners. Not only had Madeleine steadily refused him for five years, but she had clearly given André to understand that their union caused her "mortal terror," and even during their "difficult engagement" she had written to him: "I'm not afraid of death, but I'm afraid of marriage." And so Mme. Paul Gide's death had not miraculously removed the obstacles which were temporarily concealed by the exaltation of one and the compassion of the other. For reasons relatively independent of the homosexual problem, it was to be expected that André Gide's marriage, given the conditions under which it was contracted in October, 1895, would be unconsummated.

45: The Unconsummated Marriage

> *"It was a marriage between heaven and my insatiable hell."*
>
> Si le grain ne meurt, *I, 369*

IDE spent the days preceding his marriage in a state of great hope, the very same hope that had once moved André Walter. He wrote to Jeanne Rondeaux:

O dear Jeanne, is it true then that the reward has finally come, the crowning of such a long period of waiting; as I see the great expanse of pure and cloudless azure through my constantly open window, my heart overflows with a tenderness and gratitude that rises to heaven every morning like a cry of wild joy.—Perhaps our poor friend, after so many years of suffering, deserves to be loved as we love her, but I feel that I now love her more than ever before, when I had already thought I loved her so very much. Would you believe that I've spent completely sleepless nights, my mind was so taken up with her, and in the mornings I was so full of joy that I didn't even feel tired. . . .[1]

Four months after Mme. Paul Gide's death, André Gide and Madeleine Rondeaux were married. The wedding took place on October 7 at the Cuverville town hall, and on October 8 in the Etretat Protestant church. Because they were still in mourning, only a very few relatives and intimate friends were invited. Madeleine's mother, Mme. Charles Talabart, did not attend. The faithful Albert Démarest was André's best man. The "ceremony" was simple and very similar to that described in *L'Immoraliste*:

[1] October, 1895, unpublished.

In the little country church in which I was married . . . There were very few people and the presence of true friends turned that generally commonplace ceremony into a touching one. I had the impression that everyone was moved, and therefore I myself was moved. After leaving the church, you joined us at my bride's house for a short meal, at which there was no laughter and no shouting; then the carriage we had ordered took us away, according to the custom that associates in our minds the idea of a wedding with the vision of a departure.[2]

The traditional honeymoon began with a stay at the Charles Gides' estate near Nîmes. From there the newlyweds went to Switzerland, stopping off at Neuchâtel, with its peaceful lake which Gide liked so well, and where, a year before, he had spent such a splendid autumn. He wanted to retrace his steps and rediscover, with his wife, the places in which he had been happy. But Madeleine, who had never been terribly robust, fell ill, and her husband spent his days with her in a hotel overlooking the lake.

After Neuchâtel, the young couple set out for Saint-Moritz. In *L'Immoraliste* there is a coldly detailed description of Gide's growing annoyance, at every stage in the trip, as he saw how weak his wife was and how she was unable to eat at the country inns and unable to sleep in the hotels. Like Michel with Marceline, he also became irritated at her timorous nature, for Madeleine wished for nothing so much as a smooth, calm, adventureless life. He, who considered himelf cured of his pusillanimity and weakness, would have liked to take her along with him everywhere, and was exasperated at feeling that neither could she go nor did she wish to, making fun, with gentle irony, of what she called "stormy happiness."

It was then that Gide received a letter from Edouard Ducôté, the new editor of *L'Ermitage,* asking him to write a piece to "open" the first issue, which was to come out in January, 1896:

I don't think that anything in my career ever flattered me more; for Ducôté did not yet know me. I was on my honeymoon in the Engadine; it was at Saint-Moritz that I received his letter. I was working on my *Nourritures terrestres.* And I immediately sent him the tale of *Ménalque.*[3]

Actually, it was at Saint-Moritz, from November to December, that he wrote the tale of "Ménalque":

I remember that I wrote it at Saint-Moritz, at one go, in answer to Ducôté's request. . . . It is there [in *L'Ermitage*] that this tale was published, a tale rather different in ethics from the one in the already written pages of *Les Nourritures,* which I thought too fragmentary for me to agree to release immediately. . . . The figure of *Ménalque* is better drawn in *L'Immoraliste.*[4]

[2] *L'Immoraliste*, pp. 20–21.

[3] *Journal*, 1929, p. 947.

[4] *Ibid.*, 1935, p. 1222.

The psychological interest of this passage lies in the fact that it indicates a kind of transition between the mood of *Les Nourritures terrestres,* already one of the past, and the mood that was to inspire *L'Immoraliste.* It is worth analyzing at length, for it establishes a moment in Gide's development from which we can reconsider his "ethics."

Indeed, in *L'Immoraliste* it was during Michel and Marceline's honeymoon that Michel, weary of working in the field of history, tried for the first time to formulate his immoralist protest, seeking nothing but an answer to a "new question," the very one Gide asked, by implication, in his "Ménalque":

> What more can man do? That's what was important for me to know. Is what man has said till now all that he could say? Has he not overlooked something in himself? Is there nothing left for him to do but repeat himself? . . . And every day there grew stronger within me an obscure feeling of untouched riches, covered over, hidden, and stifled by cultures, proprieties, and ethics. I then felt that I had been born to make discoveries of an unknown kind; and I grew strangely and passionately interested in my darkly mysterious work, for the sake of which I know the investigator most renounce and thrust aside all culture, propriety, and ethics. I got to the point of appreciating only the wildest outbursts in others, and of regretting the fact that they could be curbed by any constraint whatever. I very nearly came to consider honesty as merely restriction, convention, or fear. I should have liked to cherish it as something rare and difficult; but our customs had turned it into a reciprocal and commonplace form of contract. . . . I understood that Marceline needed it; yet I did not hide my new train of thought from her.[5]

Michel did not hide his feelings or thoughts from Marceline, any more than Gide, writing "Ménalque," did from Madeleine, even though it shocked her deeply. Here, the situations are obviously analogous. The more Marceline praised the fundamental "honesty" of the Swiss, the more irritated Michel grew and the more he wanted to leave. Gide's reaction was much the same, though he had no intention of leaving until he had finished his "Ménalque." Once the struggle against his mother's moralism was over, he seemed to feel the need of beginning the same struggle all over again, but this time against his wife, for what he loved in her was "virtue," and it was virtue he was fighting.

The chronological coincidence between the manifesto, "Ménalque," and the young couple's relationship in Saint-Moritz was not fortuitous. "Ménalque," with its cynical protest, its unrestrained appeal to all the delights and sensual pleasures, its lyrical eulogy of Dionysus, and its defense of the fruits of the earth, was the work of an impotent husband, humiliated by his impotence. Such is the brutal fact, and Gide found it so hard to admit that in spite of his deliberate choice of sincerity and his bold-

[5] *L'Immoraliste,* pp. 222–23.

ness in disclosing all his most personal secrets, he never dared own up to it until very late in life. To my mind, there is a link of cause and effect between the humiliating failure of his virility and the frantic nature of his new assertion of strength, as though strength represented the overcompensation for an intolerable feeling of inferiority with regard to his virility.

After over two months of marriage, the couple was still not united by any physical bond, and so it was to be right to the end. That situation of failure was as painful for one as for the other during the early part of their married life. It has been said that they came to an agreement about it, and even that it corresponded to what they both wished. But the hypothesis does not hold.

At the time of *Les Cahiers d'André Walter,* when in the most Manichaean way he rigorously contrasted the soul and the flesh as the angel and the demon, it is likely that André Gide had anticipated a purely spiritual union with Emmanuèle. Yet in spite of the fact that he wanted to "act like an angel," could he really have thought that "it would be only fraternity," he who at once added: "But in spite of you, in spite of us . . ."? His prenuptial consultation proves that he himself considered that type of union impossible, and the inquiry he made to find out whether his children would suffer because of inbreeding confirms it. But after he was married, as the days and nights went by, he had to acknowledge the fact that the doctor's "get married without fear" was an ill-considered remark. The situation of failure that had so humiliated him with En Barka was being repeated in far more serious circumstances—that is, in the presence of the woman he loved, not a "woman of absolutely no consequence," as Stendhal phrased it. Thus the reasons he gave in *L'Immoraliste* as an explanation of why his wife irritated him during their honeymoon are hardly convincing, for Gide was quite aware, and had been for some time, that Madeleine was in weak health and had little taste for physical exercise; such reasons were merely pretexts which concealed the real cause of his irritation: his own inadequacy. "And she no doubt modestly attributed that deficiency of my desires to her lack of charms."[6] He had no confidence in himself, and she had no confidence in herself. Madeleine's anxiety, sadness, and fatigue can probably be explained by that very situation, whose anomaly was all the more flagrant during a wedding trip. Gide declared in *Et nunc manet in te:* "It was not until much later that I began to understand how cruelly I had wounded and devastated the woman for whom I was ready to give my life."[7] But here his alleged "unawareness" is open to question. He himself quoted the extraordinary remark that Gorki ascribed

---

[6] *Et nunc manet in te,* p. 1130.   [7] *Ibid.,* p. 1128.

to Tolstoi: "Man survives earthquakes, epidemics, the horrors of sickness, and all the agonies of the soul, but the tragedy that always has tormented him, does torment him, and will torment him the most is—and will be— the tragedy of the bedroom." And in letters to Paul Claudel and particularly to Francis Jammes[8]—although it is true they were written much later—he spoke of that "thorn in the flesh" as the drama of his life, which stood in the way, not of his love for Madeleine, but of his body's assent to that love.

When "Ménalque" was finished, André and Madeleine Gide left Switzerland for Italy, just as Michel and Marceline were to do during their honeymoon. Madeleine had not yet been to Italy, but as her father had often told her about his marvelous journey there, Emile Rondeaux's memory was constantly with them as they crossed the Apennines in a carriage. However, each time they went through a village, the little boys, the *ragazzi,* would escort the carriage, and their presence strangely excited Gide. Did Madeleine then suspect that the young boys were awakening her husband's sensuality, a sensuality she had had no proof of? Gide himself seemed convinced of it.[9] All those who imagine that an exceptionally intelligent and cultured young woman of twenty-eight is unaware of the existence of homosexuality, as were many of her puritanical and Victorian contemporaries, are deluding themselves. She knew about her cousin's relations with Oscar Wilde and Douglas, and she had read all about the details of the trial in the newspapers, for she had written to André about them.[10] At that time she had probably not yet associated the defendant's homosexual habits with André's curious enthusiasm for young Arab boys. But at Saint-Moritz, Gide had read "Ménalque" to her before sending it to *L'Ermitage,* and its allusions to pederasty might have escaped the notice of an ordinary reader but not that of so subtle and "perceptive" a listener.[11] Were not the "scandal" that Walter dreaded and the strange sexual obsession that permeated *Le Voyage d'Urien*—a book so disturbing that she had to stop reading it—allusions to the same thing? She was on the alert. During the long carriage trip from Saint-Moritz to Florence, the observant young woman, deprived of her husband's attentions, could not have helped but notice how calm he was with her and how upset he became as soon as young boys appeared on the scene. When Gide was possessed by his "demon," when he was a prey to his pedophilic obsessions, he would lose

[8] This particular letter to Francis Jammes has not been published.

[9] Cf. *Et nunc manet in te,* p. 1133.

[10] On May 30, 1895.

[11] *Et nunc manet in te,* p. 1127.

all control and any feeling of decorum, respect for others, or even the most elementary caution. His features and his eyes would change; he would become someone else. It is probable that at such times he gave a terrifying impression of "insecurity,"[12] the same impression he later gave to other lucid witnesses. Dominated by a passion which the ancients compared to a temporary state of insanity, he would start "gasping" and "panting," and became so different from himself that it is not hard to believe how Mme. Gide, a few months later, after beholding a scene that could not have been misinterpreted, came to say to her husband: "You look like either a criminal or a madman."[13] Even before they arrived in Florence, she had understood that the man she loved with all her heart and soul, and whose genius she sensed more than anyone else, was sexually abnormal. And yet, neither of them mentioned it, either then or later.

In Florence they went into the churches and museums Gide had so infrequently visited during his first stay with Paul Laurens in May and June, 1894. In the city of Brunetto Latini, the master whom Dante was to meet in hell amongst those "who have done violence to nature," he found correspondent desires in the works of the Renaissance. *Les Feuillets de route,* which he wrote at the time, shows how singularly attracted he was by Donatello's sculpture and even more by his models. "Looked especially at Donatello, whom I admire most of all. . . . Astonishing preference for the male body and strange understanding of the child's forms."[14] André Walter did not like sculpture; it was too cold an art for him. But André Gide would seem to have learned how to see a statue come to life. He constantly went back to the Bargello, "for the purpose of study":

Donatello's marvelous *David!* A little bronze body! adorned nudity; oriental grace . . . Smile on the lips; softness of the cheeks. His small delicate body with its somewhat frail and unnatural grace;—the hardness of bronze . . . I should like to conjure it up before me at will. I looked at it for a long time—trying to learn and retain those delightful lines, that fold in the belly directly under the ribs and hollowed out by his breathing, and even that leanness of the muscle joining the top of the breast to the right shoulder—and that somewhat broken fold at the top of the thigh—and that extraordinary flatness of the loins directly above the sacrum. . . .[15]

He also admired "the *Zuccone* of the Campanile, of which, alas, we see only the bust here."[16]

It would seem that he was combining the pleasure of study with a less austere pleasure, and the pure aesthetic emotion with a less aesthetic emo-

[12] Roger Martin du Gard, *Notes sur André Gide.*

[13] *Et nunc manet in te,* p. 1134.   [15] *Ibid.,* p. 63.

[14] *Journal,* December, 1895, p. 61.   [16] *Ibid.,* p. 64.

tion that satisfied the demon. Gide had no further thoughts of writing the story of Savonarola in Florence, a literary project he had been considering for some time and one strongly encouraged by his Uncle Charles. Donatello's "David" and its oriental grace awakened his nostalgia for the skies of Africa, and just as before, on the banks of the Arno, he dreamed of Biskra, his paradise:

Obsessions of the Orient, the desert, its ardor and its emptiness, the shadow of palm gardens, full white garments—obsessions in which my senses go mad, my nerves become exasperated, and which, at the beginning of each night, make me think that sleep is impossible.[17]

Madeleine, suffering from migraine headaches or fatigue, spent long hours at the hotel, and sometimes, during his walks in the country or in the streets, he reproached himself with abandoning her:

Some sort of loving anxiety and the fear that she was bored made me hurry back to her; and sometimes I summoned up my will, rebelled against that hold on me, and said to myself: "So that's all you're worth, you bad excuse for a great man!"—and forced myself to prolong my absence.[18]

Was that curious exercise of the will inspired by the very Nietzschean idea that for the really great man to "dare to be himself" he had to repress his pity and consent to be cruel? It was certainly true, in *L'Immoraliste,* for Michel, who never hesitated to develop his new theories in front of his wife, despite her fear of them. Gide, too, was sometimes "brutal" with Madeleine, and in his unpublished journal we can see how he reproached himself with it—for example, one day during their stay in Florence:

This morning, admirable walk in the Cascine . . . Shall I tell my story about the bunch of flowers? No—for whom would I tell it? not for me, who will remember it *usque ad finem*. The poor little roses are there, and I look at them constantly. The little roses of the poor—bought from someone poor. I was clumsy and brutal and did not understand at once just how exquisite the voluntary modesty of the gift was. I thought that Madeleine, too weak, had not been able to resist the persistence of a poor man offering her his merchandise. . . . A strange story, that, and one that made me sick with worry. Should Madeleine one day separate from me, I would become a vagabond.[19]

The passage gives every psychological indication that Gide's state of mind was then much the same as Michel's, and the last sentence shows the motive for each one's irritation: his wife's tenderness and fragility—the wife he loved, and suffered to make suffer—kept him from giving in to the temptations of vagabondage and all those temptations resulting from it. Gide had not gone back to his homosexual practices in Florence, but a few weeks later,

[17] *Ibid.*

[18] *L'Immoraliste,* pp. 229–30.   [19] Jan. 1, 1896.

in Rome, he was unable to resist "Saraginesco's young models,"[20] whom he took home with him on the pretext of photographing them in the "small apartment" he and his wife had rented in the Piazza Barberini:

. . . as neither my heart nor my mind was involved, I did not feel that I was being unfaithful in seeking from someone other than her a satisfaction of the flesh I was unable to ask of her. Besides, I was not reasoning. I was acting irresponsibly. I was inhabited by a demon.[21]

At the same time, André Gide was inhabited by another demon: that of literature. In Florence he had met the young novelist Roberto Gatteschi, whom he and Paul Laurens had seen often the year before. Gatteschi introduced him to Gabriele D'Annunzio, whom he found "a little cruel perhaps, but perhaps it is only the appearance of his delicate sensuality that makes him seem that way to me."[22] There are those who considered D'Annunzio one of the models for Menalcas,[23] but when Gide met him, "Ménalque" had already been written. But he had read *The Intruder* in Algiers in April, 1895: "I just finished D'Annunzio's admirable *Intruder*. It's a beautiful book, many pages of which I should have liked to have written myself."[24] That cruel novel had sharply struck his imagination during his period of revolt, and he had wanted to meet the man who had written it. But what most stood in his way was that Gabriele D'Annunzio was a "terrifying worker" who wrote twelve hours a day and had already produced about twenty volumes. Every time Gide met a writer who was impelled by a creative force, the impulse communicated itself to him and he himself was led to work. Such was the case in Ghent with Maeterlinck, and now in Florence with D'Annunzio. He reproached himself with his idleness. What had he produced since *Les Cahiers d'André Walter?* Five little booklets, which seemed to him of small importance compared with what he still had to write. Of course, *Les Nourritures terrestres* was almost finished, but he had yet to accentuate its "sensational lyricism," its pantheistic naturism, its sensuality: "I want to write the beginning of a poem, in which I shall make this voraciousness, this desire to be penetrated, brutalized, filled by nature, into Pasiphae's love for the bull."[25] More than ever, he felt the need of African inspiration in order to finish that treatise of fever and fervor, far from an overcivilized Europe:

[20] *Et nunc manet in te,* p. 1133.

[21] *Ibid.,* pp. 1133–34.

[22] *Journal,* December, 1895, p. 62.

[23] In particular, Paul Valéry. See his letter to Gide, Sept. 21, 1897 (*Correspondance,* p. 300).

[24] Letter from André Gide to his mother, April 5, 1895, unpublished.

[25] Unpublished journal, Jan. 13, 1896. The seven lines that follow were carefully crossed out by Gide.

More and more, I've understood that only the desert has pleased me; I'm obsessed with soon going back *there,* and some nights it keeps me from sleeping. Piles of books in preparation await an approaching withdrawal; I've given up writing while traveling, but as soon as I get back to France, I think that writing will make me give up all *the rest.*[26]

He was divided between the desire to travel and the duty to withdraw, a duty he considered only in relation to the demands of his work, which required long and arduous concentration.

Meanwhile, the year 1895 was drawing to a close. On the evening of December 31 in Florence, Madeleine, who was ailing, had gone up to her room quite early. Gide had remained in the hotel lounge, where the usual New Year's Eve diversions had been organized. He reproached himself with "not having stayed with her," but could not make up his mind to join her. Three months had gone by since their marriage, and "at the end of the evening, around midnight," as the couples danced past him, he was overcome by sadness:

I should have liked to have been able to leave and never was I so anxious to get back to her. I also thought, amidst the laughter, of that so peaceful and solemn evening Paul and I spent in Biskra two years ago. I wondered how I could have been so determined not to have any personal sadness and if I was really that determined. Instead of all the dancing and shouting at this approach of the Hour, a time we like to be particularly gripping, I longed for communal prayers, a church service, or simply a solemn moment of waiting. Horror of anything that is not serious—I've always had it.—What was Em. thinking about all alone, during that time? . . .[27]

It is on this question that the 1895 *Journal* ends. And we have now reached the chronological end of the period I established as André Gide's youth after André Walter (1891–95). Yet if we turn to the page of Gide's unpublished journal dated January 1, 1896, we read: "How often, with Madeleine in the next room, have I *mistaken her for my mother.*"[28] And that sentence suddenly throws light on the drama of an unconsummated marriage.

At the end of the chapter concerning Gide's prenuptial consultation, I pointed out that the problem of his unconsummated marriage was relatively independent of his homosexual problem. In the great majority of cases, a homosexual is merely one who prefers homosexual relations to

[26] Letter from André Gide to Paul Valéry, Jan. 24, 1896 (*Correspondance,* p. 258).

[27] *Journal,* Dec. 31, 1895, pp. 64–65.

[28] The italics are mine.

others, but he is perfectly capable of marrying and having children. Wilde himself, to take only one significant example, was married and the father of two children. Gide's inhibitions with regard to his wife were indeed independent of his homosexuality, but only relatively so, in that the role of the mother was a determining factor in one and the other. If the interdiction Mme. Paul Gide cast over her son's sexuality contributed to the evolution of his homosexual inclinations, it was even more obviously a factor in his unconsummated marriage, for in his imagination Gide identified the image of his mother with the image of his wife. That unconscious identification between Juliette Rondeaux and Madeleine Rondeaux had begun very early.[29] After *Les Cahiers d'André Walter,* Gide's ambiguous correspondence with his mother shows that when he venerated her, he felt the same love for her as for Madeleine, and that when he was in revolt against her, he opposed one image to the other. But that dissociation, which corresponded to a far more lucid view of the very real differences between his mother and his cousin—"I have met fierce Puritans: she was not like them in any way . . ."[30]—was reduced to nothingness by Mme. Paul Gide's death, for his tears quenched the resentment and blurred his eyes. In the "exhilaration due to the sublime" which he then experienced, he merged their images into one "ideal figure," the symbol of "Virtue," and having temporarily become Walter once again, hastened to tie himself anew to his mother, for without that bond he was at a loss.

The note he wrote three months after his marriage: "How often, with Madeleine in the next room, have I mistaken her for my mother," confirms these hypotheses. It was impossible for Gide to desire a woman he mistook for his mother, not only because the interdictions and prohibitions of incest were involved, but because no image was more apt to inhibit his virility than that of the puritanical Mme. Paul Gide. As a general rule, neurotics—and Gide was sexually a neurotic—tend to repeat throughout their lives the complex-ridden situations of their childhoods in relation to substitutes for the parental images, thus perpetuating the early basic conflict. Gide's struggle against his wife, which began as soon as they were married, was simply the unconscious repetition of his struggle against his mother.

When the couple finally settled down in La Roque, after the nine-month journey through Switzerland, Italy, and North Africa, it became less and less probable that the inhibition could ever be removed. In the family environment, which had been created by Mme. Paul Gide, all the habits and memories helped to accentuate the unconscious identification between the two images of mother and wife. Moreover, Madeleine had taken over at once his mother's role of the impeccable mistress of the house.

[29] See above, pp. 221–23.   [30] *Et nunc manet in te,* p. 1125.

Strachis the gate

Yet Gide's imaginary identification between Juliette and Madeleine Rondeaux, between Juliette and Madeleine Gide, did not correspond to reality. Of course, both of them stood for the same family, the same class, the same ethics, the same religion, the same Protestant ideal, but the differences predominated over the similarities. Physically, Madeleine resembled her aunt in no way except perhaps in her bearing, which was as characteristic of a perfect Victorian upbringing as the type of handwriting learned in the Convent of the Sacred Heart: she was far more like her mother, with a touch of "Creole grace" in her features and particularly in her smile. Those who knew Mme. André Gide when still young noticed the rather exotic charm that went along with her distinction, the solemn tenderness in her eyes, the delicacy of her hands, and the freshness of her smile, for she often laughed, whereas her aunt never did. Nothing about her recalled the hard, virile, austere appearance of Mme. Paul Gide, that strong woman par excellence. The differences in intelligence and character were just as noticeable. Infinitely more intelligent and cultured than her narrow-minded, petty, inartistic aunt, she had a most subtle mind, an unerring intuition when it came to the quality of people, a sense of reality far superior to her husband's, great generosity, tact, and kindness. Like most people who are both very sensitive and very lucid, she had a sense of humor. Certain of her letters—for example, those to Francis Jammes[31]—have an impulsive, spontaneous, witty, and often malicious tone that could hardly be said to grace Mme. Paul Gide's letters. Rather, they recall those of Anna Shackleton, also a fervent and scrupulously moral Protestant, but so different in nature from Juliette Rondeaux.[32] By managing to identify the figure of his wife with that of his mother or even the "Corneillian and tense" figure of the Jansenist Alissa, how strangely André Gide's imagination must have distorted reality! In *Et nunc manet in te* he reproached himself with deforming the personalities of others, a part of his fundamental Bovarysm— that is, his faculty of seeing people differently from what they were. He concluded the passage with: "I don't think that Dante acted any differently with regard to Beatrice."[33]

As Gide so often made that comparison, it is worth analyzing in detail. The construction of the "ideal figure" he invented and superimposed on the real figure of Madeleine cannot be explained solely in terms of its neurotic origins—namely, the complex-ridden situation because of which he identified the image of his wife with that of his mother; it can also be explained in terms of the aesthetic finality that was so deeply a part of his personality as an artist. In a work entitled *L'Ecole des muses,* Etienne Gil-

[31] Mme. Francis Jammes very kindly made them available to me.

[32] See above, pp. 21–23, 222.

[33] P. 1124.

son remarks apropos of certain famous artists and their purely platonic love for an "ideal" woman:

The real danger that threatens the muse is not seeing that if everything is centered around her, everything takes place in the poet's heart as if it were a holy ecstasy, of which she would be less the cause than the occasion . . . Every muse is what Boëthius called an image of the real good which cannot lead to beatitude, or, in Dante's magnificent interpretation, one of those false images which never completely keep their promise.[34]

Some of the greatest poets refused, voluntarily or involuntarily, any carnal bond with the women who divinely inspired them, as though they themselves became holy and unprofanable. Such was the case, for example, with Dante and Beatrice, Petrarch and Laura, Baudelaire and Mme. Sabatier. Was it solely the result of a Catharist influence, as Denis de Rougemont concludes in *L'Amour et l'Occident?* In the platonic loves of such men of genius, far more than courtly love was involved. There was no doubt, in the mystical couple that each one formed with the beloved object, a third and mysterious power neither of the intelligence nor of the senses, which Goethe called *daemonic*. In a conversation with Eckermann apropos of Lili Schönemann, Goethe, having recalled the two elements of the couple, added: "And then, what we must not forget is that there is a third power involved in love—the daemonic, which goes along with every passion and finds its true element in love." The daemonic is not the demoniac; indeed, it is quite the contrary:

What Goethe called daemonic is that power outside the man of genius; the greater he is, the more strongly it acts upon him, and he must always welcome its influence, although less by giving into it than by directing it himself to his own ends.[35]

A true artist cannot turn away from that personal finality without betraying himself, for it is one with the direction of his life.

André and Madeleine Gide's love might be added to the long and renowned list of platonic loves evoked in *L'Ecole des muses,* and it could no more escape history than those that preceded it. There is no question that Madeleine had been Gide's inspiration from *Les Cahiers d'André Walter* to his final confession, *Et nunc manet in te;* the figure of one single woman, always the same, is represented throughout, at least in the masterpieces: Alissa in *La Porte étroite,* Marceline in *L'Immoraliste.* Yet if he had really written his works to "convince" Madeleine, as he claimed in *Et nunc manet in te,*[36] he would not have written them the way he did.

[34] Pp. 20–29.

[35] Etienne Gilson, *L'Ecole des muses,* p. 209.

[36] P. 1157.

From his very first book, *Les Cahiers d'André Walter,* had he thought of her and not of himself, he would never have made certain confessions, those that were the most apt to shock her. He would not have written the cynical "Ménalque" during their honeymoon, nor would he have written *L'Immoraliste* later on, a book in which every feature seemed to have been prompted not by a wish to "convince" her but, on the contrary, by a wish to fight her. How strange a lover is the one who kills what he loves! He would not have ridiculed everything she respected, attacked everything she venerated, destroyed everything she worshiped. His one and only passion was his work, and it was to that alone that he subordinated not only his own destiny but that of Madeleine, who was so closely bound to him. Everything he wrote, that long "plea,"[37] was not meant to justify him in her eyes, for its only justification was that of art. Madeleine was like every other literary genius' muse: she was not the "cause" but the "occasion." "Was it not virtue itself that I loved in Emmanuèle?" We must constantly go back to that key phrase to understand the role played by the "ideal figure" in Gide's works, where she appeared, according to Boëthius' ancient definition, as "the image of the real good." Whether he called her Emmanuèle or Alissa or Marceline, she always represents (except during the period of the ironic distortion of the myth, following Madeleine's refusal) the angel of suffering, symbolizing Christian virtue. Pure and sorrowful, pious and resigned, the touching victim ready for every sacrifice and every self-denial, she is all soul and spirituality: "What I fear she could never understand was that the spiritual force of my love is what inhibited any carnal desire."[38] The daemonic power led to the creation of an image of saintliness that prohibited physical intimacy as surely as Tristram's sword. "You're falling in love with a ghost . . . an imaginary figure," Alissa was to say to Jérôme. But the projecting force of that "imaginary figure" was such that it hid the real figure and made Gide act toward his wife as "toward a being who, for him, very like the divinity, inspires extreme love and extreme respect."[39]

In the myth of Emmanuèle, forged by an angelist's imagination, he loved not only "the virtue" but Walter's religious soul and his struggling but persistent attachment to the God of his childhood. Anyone who overlooks that mystical bond is unaware of the most important aspect of André Gide's unconsummated marriage. His identification of Madeleine's love with divine love branded his passion with the indelible mark: *ego christianus.* Throughout his life the vicissitudes of his love and his religious feeling were parallel. "It seemed to me . . . that by drawing nearer to God, I

---

[37] *Ibid.*

[38] *Ibid.,* p. 1130.

[39] These are the words Stendhal used to designate the "fiasco of imagination."

was drawing nearer to her,"[40] and by the same token, by drawing nearer to her, he felt he was drawing nearer to God. She was the friend of the Christian half of Gide's being, *dimidium animae meae,* and the enemy of his pagan half. He belonged to her to the extent that he remained faithful to the "old man"; he betrayed her to the extent that he became the "new being." Madeleine was never André Gide's wife; she continued to be André Walter's eternal fiancée, linked to him by an engagement that was not of this world and the stakes of which could have been what a Christian calls salvation. As she said to him one day: "I have had the best of your soul, the tenderness of your childhood and youth, and I know that, living or dead, I would have the soul of your old age."

Indeed, it was the Christian significance of Madeleine's presence that made André Gide exclude her from the atheistic universe of *Les Faux-Monnayeurs.* He wrote it at the time when the future of their relationship seemed conclusively compromised by his mad escapade with M. A., the time at which he thought he had "lost" the "game" he could have "won only with her." And yet the mystical image had such force that, even in such a godless world, he embodied it in the figure of the angelic Bronja, whose death took away little Boris' only hope for salvation: "Without her how could be believe in the angels . . . ? Even heaven was now empty. Boris went back to the classroom as one might plunge into hell."[41] More than a fictional episode, it was, at the heart of the book, the representation on a childish level of the drama that the fifty-year-old man was experiencing on an adult level. "And some days I feel evil invade me to such an extent that I already have the impression that the bad prince is instituting the creation of a hell within me."[42]

Madeleine's influence delayed, within the bounds of possibility, the creation of that hell. Thanks to her, the "tension" between the forces of good and evil—an element that went into the making of the best of his works—was maintained for a long time. Were one to remove Emmanuèle and her sisters, Alissa or Marceline, from his works, the feeling of moral tragedy would disappear at once. Without her, he might have written more books like *Les Caves du Vatican* and *Thésée,* but he would not have written either *La Porte étroite, L'Immoraliste,* or *Numquid et tu.* And in the counterpoint of Gide's works, the solemn resonance is given by that struggle between the "old man" and the "new being," the same struggle that will always keep him from being mistaken for a hedonist à la Wilde or a skeptic à la Voltaire. In his *Journal* of 1940 he wrote:

[40] *Et nunc manet in te,* p. 1126.

[41] *Les Faux-Monnayeurs,* III, 480.

[42] *Journal des Faux-Monnayeurs,* last sentence.

If I had listened to myself (I mean: the self of yesterday listening to that of today), I should have gone round the world four times . . . and I should never have married. As I write these words, I tremble as at an act of blasphemy. For in spite of everything, I have remained very much in love with what constrained me the most, and I cannot swear that that very constraint did not get the best out of me.[43]

A strange admission, and one that reduces his marriage to a simple enterprise meant to get the best out of him in accordance with his destiny as an artist, a destiny to which he dedicated himself "even to damnation." He seems grateful to his marriage for having produced "constraints" which furthered not his salvation, in the Christian sense, but his success, in the aesthetic sense. He knew that it was not only art which lives on constraints and dies of freedom, but the artist as well. Indeed, the author of *Le Traité du Narcisse* knew it very early in life. And at the age of twenty-two, did he not subordinate all sentimental, moral, and even religious virtues to the future of his works and to his own future? Was not "Gide's vertiginous game between heaven and hell"[44] the most vertiginous of them all, that of art? The most striking of Mauriac's words is the simplest: *game*. It superlatively marks out the boundary between a Christian, for whom the stakes of the struggle are salvation or the loss of his soul, and an artist, for whom the stakes of the literary portrayal of the struggle are simply the success or failure of his works.

Recalling his marriage to Emmanuèle, Gide wrote in *Si le grain ne meurt:* "Our sincerest acts are also the least premeditated; the explanation one tries to give after the event is always futile. I was led by a fatality." Part of that fatality was the "daemonic power," or the demands of an artist's vocation. Gide translated William Blake's *Marriage of Heaven and Hell*, and often quoted Blake as having said that the work of art is the "marriage ring" of heaven and hell. One cannot help but compare that phrase to the very striking one from *Si le grain ne meurt:* "It was a marriage between heaven and my insatiable hell." Anxious to preserve all the complexity of his nature and to carry his contradictions to the extreme, was his choice not secretly inspired by some obscure foresight? Did he not sense that Emmanuèle would be the irreplaceable muse of that marriage of heaven and hell, its "marriage ring" being his works?

[43] *Journal*, Sept. 9, 1940, p. 84.

[44] François Mauriac.

46: Menalcas, or the New Being (1895)

> *"The Gospels lead to it, said Euclid; we shall call your doctrine Nomadism, from the fine word:* nomos, *pasture."*
> *Epigraph, "Ménalque," L'Ermitage, January, 1896*

1

N HIS preface to the German translation of *Les Nourritures ter- restres,* Gide specified that the book had been "written in 1895."[1] He had begun to think about it in 1893, for the *Journal* and the *Feuillets* of that year are filled with phrases characteristic of his new mood —"I want to speak here of life for life's sake"—and even the first invoca- tions to Nathanaël. His "idea" for a book always preceded the workings of his "imagination,"[2] and although he had had the idea for *Les Nourritures terrestres* before his departure in October, 1893, he was able to imagine it only because of the wealth of sensations collected during his years of travel.

In his *Memoirs,* Goethe spoke of a time in his youth during which he had decided to give himself up to the outer world and let all the influences act on his being indiscriminately. *Les Nourritures terrestres* was inspired by a similar surrender to nature. Most of the impressions described in it were prompted by Gide's personal experience: the book is a lyrical autobiogra- phy. In 1895 he wrote to his mother: "I now feel that my youth is over. In this book I'm planning to write, I should like to bury it altogether. I feel myself maturing and ready for more serious and stronger works." Just as *Les Cahiers d'André Walter* had been the mystical *summa* of the first part of his youth, so *Les Nourritures terrestres* was to be the lyrical *summa* of the second. The work was not published until 1897, but the tale of Menal-

[1] *N.R.F.,* XXIV (1930), 122. [2] *Journal,* 1893, p. 49.

cas—written in November, 1895, and published in the first issue of *L'Ermitage* in January, 1896, before becoming Book IV of *Les Nourritures terrestres*—was something of a preface which announced the main themes of the new book:

> Make no mistake, Nathanaël, about the brutal title I chose to give this book; I could have called it *Menalcas,* but Menalcas, like yourself, never existed. The only man's name that might have been appropriate to the book is my own; but then how could I have dared to sign it?[3]

Menalcas is no more than a myth, but a representative myth, and he was to become the central figure of *Les Nourritures terrestres.*

What interests us in the Menalcas episode is not the fictional story of his life but the philosophy that comes through; for there Gide introduced an "ethic" almost identical to that of *Les Nourritures terrestres* and which points to that of *L'Immoraliste.* "The figure of Menalcas is better drawn in *L'Immoraliste,*"[4] he was to say. True, but there is not one trait of *L'Immoraliste*'s Menalcas that had not already been sketched out or even embodied in the first Menalcas of 1895: they are one and the same character, or, more precisely, the expression of one and the same myth, that of the "new being," who was as contrary as possible to the "old man," represented by André Walter.

Menalcas was brought up very strictly, but as soon as he reached adolescence, "exasperated by constraints," he decided to free himself and seek, quite alone, the ways of his freedom. He set his mind to emancipating himself from all the moral teachings that had been lavished upon him. "That unlearning was slow and difficult; it was more useful to me than all the learning imposed by men, and was really the beginning of an education."[5] He believes that the laws and conventions that govern men are likely to deform the individual, for each one must follow his own nature and develop according to his own law: "The part of us that we feel is different is exactly the part that is rare, the part that gives each one his own value—and it is that part we try to suppress."[6] This determined individualist sees the conformist as one of Panurge's sheep who imitates the others, not daring to be himself.[7] The idea that one must make a clean sweep of all pre-established rules and customs to invent one's destiny all alone is

---

[3] Preface to *Les Nourritures terrestres,* p. 19.

[4] *Journal,* 1935, p. 1222.

[5] *Les Nourritures terrestres,* I, 13.

[6] *L'Immoraliste,* pp. 162–63. One of Menalcas' comments.

[7] *Ibid.*

curiously similar to what today we call the existentialist attitude. In fact, Menalcas is in many ways a premature existentialist hero.

Menalcas hates men of principle.[8] For him good and evil do not exist in themselves; he considers them conventional and somewhat artificial notions, established by religious or social authorities in order to deprive man of his freedom and to keep him from living according to that which is original and unique in his own individual destiny. He reproaches others with suffering from "moral agoraphobia," but he himself is so afraid of being caught in the mechanism of a pre-established system that will deprive him of his freedom, and of being closed in a "labyrinth" with no exit, that he seems to be suffering from moral claustrophobia. He sees any attachment as slavery, and any faithfulness as a prison: "I claimed that every new thing must always find us wholly available."[9]

Yet living means choosing; man is constantly faced with the necessity of making a choice. And that is precisely what torments Menalcas.[10] The systematic rejection of all the usual rules which help men make decisions would, to begin with, not seem to lend itself to eliminating the difficulties in choosing:

All choice is terrifying, when you come to think of it; and *freedom no longer guided by duty is terrifying.*—It is like choosing a path in an entirely unexplored country, where each one makes *his own* discovery and, please note, *makes it for himself alone* . . . so that even the most dubious trail in the most unknown region of Africa is less uncertain. . . .[11]

Here we are right in the middle of existentialist anguish. Having refused any guide other than himself, by what will Menalcas be guided? Actually, in order to put an end to his indecision, this otherwise hesitant individual has to make a series of choices of considerable scope, which, as a whole, constitute what philosophy textbooks call a system. He chooses an attitude to life, a "position," a way of being.[12]

To begin with, Menalcas decides, as an act of faith, to find life excellent in itself, which is a first and clearly optimistic choice. André Walter declared that "Life is a means not an end; I will not seek it for its own sake." Menalcas, on the contrary, believes in life for life's sake; for him life is not a means but an end in itself.[13] All of *Les Nourritures terrestres* is a hymn

[8] *Ibid.,* p. 165.

[9] *Les Nourritures terrestres,* IV, 70.

[10] *Ibid.,* pp. 67–68.

[11] *Ibid.,* I, 14. The italics are mine.

[12] "I choose myself not in my being but in my way of being," wrote Sartre in *L'Etre et le néant.*

[13] *Notices, O.C.,* II, ix.

of gratitude to "the inestimable gift of life," to "the manifold forms of life," which Menalcas claims to taste *indiscriminately*. He loves life; he adores life. Walter's Protestant and Schopenhauerian pessimism is replaced by an enraptured optimism.

André Walter said, with reference to *Les Cahiers:* "Those who seek happiness will not understand this book"; Menalcas chooses to be happy, which is a second and clearly eudaemonistic choice. But there are many ways of understanding happiness:

Of the thousand forms of life, each of us can know but one. It is madness to envy the happiness of others; we would have no idea what to do with it. Happiness refuses to be ready-made; it must be made to measure.—I'm leaving tomorrow; yes, I know: I've tried to cut happiness to my own size . . . keep the untroubled happiness of your home. . . .[14]

He thus does not want just any form of happiness, but happiness made to measure, cut to his own size, which eliminates many possibilities and implies a renunciation of many other and less singular ways of being happy.

For Menalcas happiness means pleasure, which is a third and clearly hedonistic choice. He professes to love and adore pleasure. The "joys" of the flesh and the senses, which Walter found reprehensible because he considered them sinful, are the very ones sought by Menalcas, who no longer believes in sin.[15] Living in the moment, he chooses to have as little to do with feelings of responsibility or guilt as the birds in the sky, to whom he compares himself. Sensation is his guide:

The *sincerity* of my pleasure, Nathanaël, is the most important of my guides. I know how much sensual pleasure my body can desire each day and how much of it my mind can bear. And then my sleep will begin. Heaven and earth have no value beyond that.[16]

Far more than an Epicurean, Menalcas is a Cyrenaic. He could have used the following text of Socrates' dissident disciple, Aristippus of Cyrene, as his program:

Our sensations are our only knowledge; the object of these sensations, like the sensations of other men, elude our grasp. Happiness is not derived from virtue, nor virtue from science, as Socrates affirmed. Happiness consists in pleasure, whatever it may be and wherever it may lead, but one must always remain master of it; virtue lies in the search for pleasure, and freedom in the satisfaction of desires.

[14] *L'Immoraliste,* p. 171. One of Menalcas' comments.

[15] *Ibid.,* p. 174.

[16] *Les Nourritures terrestres,* II, 37.

Menalcas is all the more ardent a follower of the religion of pleasure in that he practices it as a duty.[17] A Sisyphus of sensual pleasure, a wandering Jew of desire, this freeman seems rather more like a convict condemned forever to pleasure. "A harrowing existence, Nathanaël, rather than tranquillity. I wish for no rest other than the sleep of death. I fear that every desire and every force I have not satisfied during my life may survive to torment me."[18] We can see to what exhausting labor this earnest profligate will have to subject himself. He is not an Epicurean, for while Epicurus taught that the pleasure of the body is the principle of all good, he added that the pleasures of the mind, consisting of the memory of past bodily pleasures and the anticipation of future ones, were greater than those of the body limited to the present. He preferred *pleasure at rest,* consisting of the absence of pain, to *pleasure in motion,* such as *Aristippus* conceived it, and his doctrine, tending to suppress and restrain desires other than those that are "natural and necessary," finally resulted in a kind of asceticism. Such moderation is far from the intoxication of Menalcas, who sometimes consents to asceticism, but only to give more spice to his sensations.[19] Walter consented to prolonged fasting to be more capable of conquering nature; Menalcas does the same to enjoy nature more fully. Walter was a Puritan; Menalcas is a hedonist.

There would have been nothing very new in Menalcas' philosophy, which after all is that of the Cynics, had it not illustrated a personal method for attaining a blissful life: nomadism. Its doctrine, or rather its technique of living, comes straight from the Gospels, and no less unduly than the young Barrès used Ignatius of Loyola's *Spiritual Exercises* to create in himself, ad libitum, profane emotions. We know the conclusion of Barrès' free man, who chose, as a rule of life, to be "a stranger even to myself ... a stranger even to my past ... knowing only the swift emotions that I will have chosen: truly a free Man!" and summed up his program with the troubling word: *Alienus!*[20] There are, of course, similarities between Barrès' anarchistic "Stranger" and Gide's "Nomad." But the differences in their ethics and emotions are just as considerable, and no one would contest the fact that Menalcas raised the art of flight to the height of a strategy.

We can well imagine how astonished a careful reader of *Les Cahiers d'André Walter* might have been upon discovering, five years later in *L'Ermitage,* a provocative "Ménalque," which seemed to indicate that its

[17] *Notices, O.C.,* II, ix.

[18] *Les Nourritures terrestres,* I, 16.

[19] *Ibid.,* IV, 73.

[20] M. Barrès, *Un Homme libre,* p. 240.

author had undergone a moral transformation, if not metamorphosis. Gide's small group of intimate friends were scarcely less surprised. Francis Jammes praised the "magnificent prose," but added:

If I thought it was absolutely sincere on your part, it would be painful and disagreeable to me, and you would have done better, in that case, not to have brought it to my attention. . . . That exhibition of moral luxury and egoism is an insult to those who, like me, live in bitter retirement. . . .[21]

Marcel Drouin did not much appreciate the flaunting of immoralism, and somewhat later, upon the publication of *Les Nourritures terrestres,* wrote Gide a severe letter:

And I have read the terrible book. . . . If you were considering only yourself, did the need of speaking, of shouting, outweigh the security necessary to the best of your life? If you were thinking of your works, did you see it as an indispensable means of expression? But no, for if it becomes obscure and false for the others, if at the place you wrote *joy* they *very naturally* read *disgust,* if, in a word, after having heard you, Nathanaël no longer dares to go out. . . .[22]

Paul Valéry considered "Ménalque" "an excellent piece." On the other hand, that first fragment of *Les Nourritures terrestres* made him feel once again just how different his turn of mind was from Gide's: "You know that I am not acquainted with your God, and that I cannot look for one. Alas! I am not a man of God, nor am I a man of the country. Ecstasy and grass overexcite me for no more than half a day."[23]

With the exception of Francis Jammes' "Réponse à Ménalque" in *L'Ermitage,*[24] no critical article referred to Gide's new creation. But when *Les Nourritures terrestres* was published, the controversy broke out around Menalcas. Francis Jammes' "Lettre à Ménalque"[25] was "frightfully painful"[26] to Gide. In the name of "simplicity" and Christian charity, Jammes reproached Gide with his luxurious and lecherous gospel of joy, so indifferent to the suffering of others. On the other hand, Léon Blum congratulated the author on "walking in the fresh air, finally discovering life, and seeking, behind all appearances, joy, beauty, and justice"; Henri Ghéon found that "handbook of pantheism" a poetic masterpiece; and the young

[21] Letter to André Gide, Feb. 7, 1896 (*Correspondance,* pp. 63–64).

[22] Letter to André Gide, May 13, 1897, unpublished. Marcel Drouin had then become André Gide's brother-in-law by his marriage to Jeanne Rondeaux, Madeleine's sister.

[23] Letter to André Gide, Jan. 11, 1896 (*Correspondance,* p. 255).

[24] I, 1896, 325.

[25] "En faveur de la simplicité chrétienne. Lettre à Ménalque sur les 'Nourritures terrestres,' " *Le Spectateur catholique,* July, 1897, p. 51.

[26] Letter from André Gide to Francis Jammes, July, 1897 (*Correspondance,* p. 117).

Edmond Jaloux wrote: "It gives evidence of something absolutely new in the realm of thought, and it may be that the literature of the next century will be influenced by Menalcas, the hero of *Les Nourritures,* just as the literature of this century was influenced by Werther and René."[27] Edmond Jaloux was not wrong in predicting that Menalcas, or at any rate the immoralist protest first expressed by the myth in Gide's work, would have considerable influence on the literature of the coming century.

It would be a great error to mistake Menalcas' ethics for Gide's, and here more than ever, it is necessary to distinguish between the character and the author. In his *Journal,* without quite repudiating Menalcas, Gide wanted to show the distance between them:

Jef Last finds fault with Menalcas' ethics. He is right. I myself disapprove of it and, even at that time, presenting it only with reservations, I made a point of giving the responsibility of it to another. That is true; but my partial disapproval remains almost imperceptible and what little irony I thought I had put into certain sentences . . . is not sufficiently brought out.[28]

And yet, in creating the character Menalcas, Gide freed himself from him and established his traits "as a novelist establishes those of a hero who resembles him, but whom he invents. . . . I did not establish those traits without separating them from myself, so to speak, or, if one prefers, without separating myself from them."[29] Here the writer's (in a sense) professional immunity becomes apparent, for through his powers of mithridatization or catharsis, the writer can neutralize deadly poisons for men who have not the same resources. Gide did not choose to be Menalcas; he chose to be a writer who created Menalcas before choosing to be a writer who created Saul as an antidote for the preceding character. Involved as he may have been in an existential attitude, he never was completely, and he kept a distance from, his double. He was able to indulge in all sorts of moral acrobatics, take stock of an ethical position by pushing it "to the absurd, to exhaustion,"[30] and immediately change and "leap to the other extreme"; yet he was certain to fall back into the net of his works. "Whom would I educate if not myself?" The mistake, then, would be to take for a guide the man who claimed to be "the most irreplaceable of beings"[31] and who was deeply concerned only with his works.

---

[27] Léon Blum's article was published in the *Revue Blanche,* Henri Ghéon's in the *Mercure de France,* and Edmond Jaloux's in *Indépendance Républicaine,* all in 1897. They are quoted in Y. Davet, *Autour des "Nourritures terrestres."*

[28] *Journal,* 1935, I, 1222–23.

[29] 1927 preface to *Les Nourritures terrestres, O.C.,* II, 228.

[30] Letter from André Gide to Henri Drain, July 18, 1932.

[31] *Les Nourritures terrestres,* "Envoi," p. 184.

What most particularly revolted Francis Jammes in the tale "Ménalque" was the "evangelic parallel" Gide had tried to establish between his "false prophet" and Christ, using as an epigraph the words "the Gospels lead to it," an epigraph he did not repeat in *Les Nourritures terrestres*. "A heretic among heretics, I was always drawn to dissimilar opinions, extreme deviations in thinking, divergencies."[32] Indeed, one must have rare heretical tendencies to relate Menalcas' doctrine to Christ's, denounce the treason of the Churches for "deforming" the divine teaching, proclaim that "our Western world is perishing" because of a false interpretation of the Gospels, believe that "the duty to denounce this evil is imperative for me," and plan to write "Christianity against Christ."[33] The mystical inspiration he experienced in the spring of 1895, amidst the delights of Biskra and under the hot African sun, corresponds to one of the important aspects of Gide's psychology: his inclination toward a Christian immoralism, which represents the most singular deviation from his early Protestantism.

It is not enough to say that the Protestant is a Bible reader; he must, in addition, live "face to face" with the book, without any sacerdotal intermediary, and interpret it freely. That principle, which had been instilled in Gide during his childhood, led him to an extremely personal interpretation of the holy texts. But it is probable that some intercessors came between the text and himself, especially Rousseau, whom he was reading assiduously in 1894 and 1895. Gide did not write "Christianity against Christ," but he often developed the theses he planned to uphold in it, for there is no doubt that all the Gidian themes were youthful ideas developed in maturity. The suggestion of experiencing happiness *hic et nunc,* the avoidance of all possessions, the advent of the "nomadic state," the renunciation of any lucid intelligence that might compromise spontaneity, the surrender of the personality in the blind joy of the moment, all those leitmotivs of *Les Nourritures terrestres* were picked up by Gide at various times in his life—for example, in *La Symphonie pastorale* and in his *Dostoevsky.*

Behind Gide's sophisms, ever since *Le Traité du Narcisse,* there is always the same finality, that of stretching the meaning of Christ's words to make his gospel into a perfect gospel of the artist. It is in that perspective that we must reconsider the Gidian metaphors of salvation through "self-abandon," of "leave everything and you will find everything," and of a fervor that cannot be permanently attached to any earthly possession. Menalcas has as a double a man of letters who considers nomadism, availability, the worship of the moment, and even certain sacrifices or renunciations of the "self" as integral parts of the literary condition. "Christ's words are equally true in art. 'Whosoever will save his life (his personality) shall

[32] *Ibid.,* p. 16.   [33] *Si le grain ne meurt,* p. 362.

lose it.' "[34] We must go back to that sentence from the 1893 *Journal* to understand that when Gide quoted the Gospels, he did not think of a Christian's destiny but of an artist's destiny. Whoever will save his life shall lose it, say the Gospels; whoever will lose his life shall save it. The words Gide added in parentheses, "his personality," signify that the poet-Narcissus must lose his personality as a man in order to save his personality as an artist. And the mysterious epigraph of *Si le grain ne meurt,* taken from the word of John, has the same meaning: "Except a corn of wheat fall into the ground and die, it abideth alone: but if it die, it bringeth forth much fruit."

Gide sought to use Christ's teaching for his own ends, opposing the tolerance of the Gospels, which allowed him to "preserve the complexity of his nature," to the rigor of puritanical ethics, which did not allow that kind of compromise. Yet a whole part of himself remained attached to his Protestant upbringing. At the time he had resolved to "rid myself of everything useless and confining with which an inherited religion had surrounded me and which limited my nature far too much," he added: "without, however, repudiating anything that could still train me and strengthen me."[35] He thus saw his childhood religion as no more than a culture, but one he did not reject entirely. "You are dependent on everything that formed you. Do not balk at this apparent slavery. . . . In debt to so much, you merely buy your good qualities through so many dependencies."[36] Menalcas represents someone integrally "uprooted," but the author of "Ménalque" valued his roots. He balked at his dependencies when they interfered with the fulfilment of his vocation; he gave in to them when they promoted it. The result was a perpetual contradiction between the assertion of complete freedom and the no less clearly affirmed necessity of constraint, a perpetual oscillation between nonresistance and resistance, which was evident not only during his difficult youth but throughout his life. Having, at Biskra in 1895, protested against Alfred Douglas' dissipation, Gide tried to discover what motives then caused "my mechanism to rebel, in spite of myself" and made him "bury himself in work" as though he needed to atone: he attributed his behavior to "the remains of a former ethic," of which nothing in him approved any longer, but on which his "moral reflexes"[37] still depended. Those reflexes of self-preservation were to stay with him as an expression of the survival of the "old man," and it was to them that he owed the fact that he did not end up like his Saul. Even when he finally decided no longer to refuse anything and voluntarily give up his will power, the experimental atony was short-lived and did not

[34] *Journal*, 1893, p. 49.   [36] *Ibid.*, p. 46.

[35] *Ibid.*, p. 41.   [37] *Si le grain ne meurt*, II, 350.

result in degradation, because a reaction to it was not long in coming. Much as he wanted to allow himself complete license, he never managed it. "It was a long time before I understood to what extent I was subject to my heredity. In other and simpler words: I was far less free than I had supposed, extraordinarily held, held back, and held in by the feeling of *duty*."[38] The artist in him was much too lucid for him not to have used his mind to justify that strong feeling of duty, which he owed to his Huguenot upbringing, for he knew that unchecked pleasure, disorder, and disintegration would have kept him from creating his works. He thus accepted constraints and sacrifices of which, Menalcas, the hedonist, would seem to know nothing.

Once his youth was over, despite his lasting attachment to the person of Christ and, to a certain degree, to the Huguenot tradition, Gide appeared to have lost his religious faith. André Walter himself had written:

Had I known you, O Lord, I should have loved you with all my soul. And yet I love you in spite of not knowing you; I love you even if you do not exist, for at least you exist in my mind, and my mind projects your image before me, and it is encompassed by my worship.[39]

Five years later Gide no longer seemed even concerned about God's existence, other than in his "lay of fine proofs" in *Les Nourritures terrestres,* but he never stopped talking about God: "We all believe we shall eventually discover God. While waiting to find him, we have, alas, no idea of where to offer our prayers. . . . Then we end by telling ourselves that He, the unfindable, is everywhere, anywhere, and we kneel down at random."[40] That profession of pantheism must not hide the fact that, intellectually, Gide had become a freethinker, but the important thing is that he tended to consider this evolution as a continuation of his Protestantism, and, in that sense, deemed that he was in no way unfaithful to the spirit of the Reformation. In fact, he first expressed the idea in a letter to his mother, dated September 22, 1894: "The history of Protestantism is a chapter in the history of freethinking." Of a naturally dialectic turn of mind, Gide saw Protestantism as a religion which negates itself, thus becoming a factor of uneasiness, which—to his mind—meant progress. On the grounds of having been marked by the same religion, he compared his evolution toward freethinking to Nietzsche's, and after having read *Thus Spake Zarathustra,* he commented: "And so that is where Protestantism is bound to lead?— I think so—and that is why I admire it;—to the greatest liberation."[41]

[38] *Ainsi soit-il ou Les Jeux sont faits*, p. 27.

[39] *Les Cahiers d'André Walter, O.C.,* I, 11.

[40] *Les Nourritures terrestres*, I, 14.

[41] *Lettre à Angèle, O.C.,* III, 233.

Gide claimed that when he wrote *Les Nourritures terrestres,* he did not yet know Nietzsche "even by name," and he added:

Those (and they are many) who recognize the influence of Zarathustra in my *Nourritures terrestres* are somewhat anticipating. . . . There is a kinship of minds, but no descent. The emotion I felt when I later read Nietzsche would not have been as strong if I myself had not already been well on my way, a way on which I thought I was venturing alone, on which suddenly I saw a huge shadow rise up before me.[42]

Renée Lang's study,[43] of which Gide himself approved, and my own findings, clearly proving that he knew at least Nietzsche's name as early as 1891, force us to dispute such claims. He could not have written to Marcel Drouin in November, 1895, that he was drawn to Nietzsche "in such a way as to make me dizzy," had he not had some knowledge of him already. But it was very likely not until the following years that he really devoured his works. Therefore, the Menalcas of 1895, the one in *Les Nourritures terrestres,* is relatively pre-Nietzschean, whereas the Menalcas of 1900, the one in *L'Immoraliste,* is obviously post-Nietzschean. Nevertheless, a comparison of those two aspects of the character shows such similarities in ethics that Gide would seem to have been correct in stating that he himself was well on the same way that Nietzsche had taken. Moreover, he himself emphasized the fact that other literary influences—especially that of Wilde, Goethe, and Rimbaud—had prepared him for Nietzsche. Whether or not he was directly influenced by him before the end of 1895—a disputable point which is still difficult to resolve—one finds, relatively speaking, a certain "kinship" between the mood of *Les Nourritures terrestres* and the inclination to Nietzscheism. When Gide first read Nietzsche, he thought he had spotted a magnified portrayal of the crisis he had gone through in his youth: his attempt to replace the "old man" by a "new being." He admired his Dionysiac vision of the world—"Here Dionysus triumphs"—that is, a vision at once lyrical and immoralist, similar to the one he had meant to establish in *Les Nourritures terrestres.* This book, too, expressed a revolt against intellectualism and moralism.

The cry: "Ah! Who will deliver us from the heavy chains of logic!" corresponds to Nietzsche's sarcastic remarks about "reason at any price, the cold and clear life." André Walter had rebelled against reason. But Gide had continued to consider lucid analysis, "the clearest perception," as his best guide. It was during his crisis of 1893–95 that he wanted to stop subjecting his acts to "that approbation which implied, before acting, a kind of deliberation and counterbalance in the imagination, by means of

[42] Preface to the German translation of *Les Nourritures terrestres,* N.R.F., XXIV (1930), 322.

[43] *André Gide.*

which action was that much delayed and impeded."[44] It was then that he resolved to change his tactics and, renouncing lucidity, decided in favor of spontaneity. Gide claimed to have given up reason, to have voluntarily surrendered his will-power, and to have found the disorder of his mind "holy," in the manner of Rimbaud, but the critical sense, his Nemesis, was always far too alert to allow him to succeed in such a Dionysiac attempt. "I'm throwing myself wholly into this tragic game. . . . 'Dreadful fanfare in which I never stumble.' It's from Rimbaud."[45] No, all of Gide was not involved in the game; he played it with only part of himself, and that is why it was never really tragic but rather very literary: he was always in the dual state of being actor and spectator, and the spectator kept watch on the actor; he was "just mad enough to be a poet,"[46] but not enough to be wholly a poet and justify his reference to Rimbaud. His lyricism was too irregular, his emotional outbursts too quickly interrupted by contrary currents, to allow him to play the part of Dionysus without forcing himself. But, as it happens, he did make the effort, and that is precisely why *Les Nourritures terrestres* is, with respect to his complex personality, an exaggerated, oversimplified, and biased book. At the time he was writing it, he said: "The game was difficult and dangerous: given the premises, such as carrying everything to its conclusion—and experimenting on myself—everything I've written till now had to be written sincerely."[47] The words "game" and "experimenting" show very precisely the limits of such artificial sincerity, the sincerity of an artist. "Let's mix with nature—we're the ones *who'll gain* from the association. From now on, I sign only Gide and Pan."[48] By thus limiting the role of the great Pan to that of a literary collaborator, Gide rather comically put his finger on the controlled nature of his identification with Dionysus. With regard to the *Schaudern* of his adolescence, he said: "I quickly understood that intoxication without wine is nothing other than the state of lyricism, and that during the happy moment at which I was shaken by that ecstasy, I was being visited by Dionysus." In *Les Nourritures terrestres* the will to sustain that "Panic" inclination is far too obvious, and the uninterrupted series of moments experienced as so many intoxicating revelations becomes labored. The intoxication itself often seems contrived. Menalcas' "Dionysia" is much less convincing than the strong alcohols of a Rimbaud or a Nietzsche, and the

[44] *Journal,* 1923, p. 776.

[45] Letter from André Gide to a friend, April 3, 1895, unpublished.

[46] Letter from André Gide to his mother, April 5, 1895, unpublished.

[47] Letter from André Gide to Marcel Drouin, n.d., unpublished.

[48] Letter from André Gide to a friend, Oct. 5, 1894, unpublished. The italics are mine.

invitation to a lyrical life remains far from the lyricism of *Les Illuminations* or *Zarathustra*.

To Gide, Nietzsche symbolized not only a lyrical vision but also an immoralist vision of the world, as contrary as possible to the puritanical ethics according to which they both had been brought up. In that sense, Menalcas' protest sprang from the same reaction of opposition. Nietzsche, the son of a pastor from Röcken, had been brought up by his mother according to rigorous Protestant doctrine, but he rebelled against the Christianity he had been taught, and presented the Christian ethic as a sickness of the soul. He believed he had found the remedy for his own malady in the radical criticism of all the "counterfeit coins" inherited from Christianity, which passed off shadow for substance, evil for good, sickness for health. Because of his hate for "counterfeiters," he opposed the ethic of slaves with an ethic of masters, thus transmuting all values. To counter the debilitating poisons of the spiritual food chosen by Christian idealism, he advocated "the food of the serpent, the earth," a return to the instinctive joys without which man wastes away from starvation. Counterfeiters, immoralists, and the fruits of the earth are three familiar expressions in Nietzsche's vocabulary. Now Gide underwent a similar evolution, from Walter's Christian idealism to Menalcas' pagan naturism. But Menalcas' immoralist protest is not only the freethinker's revenge on the Huguenot; it is also the artist's "challenge" to the bourgeois, as representative of certain moral and social conventions according to the tradition of Flaubert, whose idea was to "demoralize," if not "corrupt," the young. Gide had long been convinced that the artist must cause offense. The phrase from *Le Traité du Narcisse:* "offenses must come," may refer to his homosexuality, but it can also be said to refer to the perpetual offense to society of the way of life of an artist determined to live according to his own destiny, outside norms and conventions, duties and laws. "I know of no form of thought more contrary to the work of art (and to my works in particular) . . . than Calvinism. It was that fact that estranged me from it the day I took up my pen."[49] This laconic but extraordinary admission would seem to indicate that beyond the assertions of his particular nature, it was his aesthetic finality itself which led him to repudiate his early Calvinism. That constant aesthetic finality is one of the traits that most differentiates Gidian immoralism from Nietzschean immoralism. Whatever Nieztsche's literary genius, it was no literary aspiration that made him "set up Dionysus over and against the Crucified." Nietzsche was primarily a philosopher, Gide an artist. The very ways in which the two Protestants rebelled against their early religion were strikingly opposed. The fanatical Nietzsche hated Christianity to such a degree that he actually identified himself with the antichrist; the ambivalent Gide claimed

---

[49] Quoted by E. Martinet, *André Gide—L'Amour et la divinité,* p. 75.

to dissociate the "true Christ" from his Church, and continued to support his claim with the Gospels, as though he were still attached to them.

In a letter to Marcel Drouin,[50] Gide interpreted the violence of Nietzsche's "early crisis" not only in terms of his vocation as an artist and his "Protestant past," but in the light of a third explanatory principle: "His very sickly temperament (because of which, for him, everything he preached was unattainable)." The problem here is to know whether the psychological mechanism Gide spoke about with relation to Nietzsche had not in fact been at work within himself. In his early *Journal*,[51] apropos of the use of illness, Gide spoke of a "system of compensations" and declared that if Sparta had not produced great men it was because it had suppressed all weak children. It is quite extraordinary to find that in 1896 he expressed the idea that was to underlie Adler's *Individualpsychologie*. Far removed from Freudianism, Adler showed that certain personalities are formed out of protest to an inferiority feeling which often originated in an insecure, difficult, and humiliating childhood. The weaker the ego, the higher an ideal of himself the neurotic builds up, for he uses that fictional objective to neutralize his insecurity. A perpetual need for outdoing himself, an obsession with "going beyond," leads him to exploit all his possibilities, all his resources, and to conceive his life as a strategy: he wants to be a superman and forever escape from the fear of failure that had dominated his childhood. He reconstructs the world and the others and himself according to his own perspective. He exhausts himself, says Adler, "for a world which is not our world" or, at any rate, the world of men living in relation to the norms of the group. A frantic individualist, he is always opposed to his environment and tends to reverse its moral values in a way that brings about a re-evaluation of the superior and the inferior to his own egotistical ends. According to Adler,[52] he tries to shift everything that is in a high position to a low position, switch everything that is at the right to the left, and transform the front to the back, because his guiding fiction demands such reversals. Should he fail, he remains neurotic and as incapable of adapting to others as he is of affirming his own personality; should he succeed, he becomes an original personality and, in the broadest sense of the word, an artist who creates his own way of being and intends to make his life a work of art. At the extreme, the neurotic technique of life becomes an aesthetic technique of life. As Stekel said, neurosis is an attempt, and its successful outcome the man of genius. But a personality formed in that way will always remain deeply ambiguous and full of contradictions, because the superman's other side is a weak child, the famous man's other

[50] March 30, 1898 (quoted by Y. Davet, p. 61).

[51] 1896, p. 98.

[52] *The Neurotic Constitution,* p. 355.

side an anguished and guilt-ridden creature, the bold man's other side a coward. On Menalcas' other side there are Boris, Walter, and Tityrus.

Menalcas, the provocative superman who flaunts his debauchery and brags about his vices, was created by Gide at precisely the time he was on a trip with his wife to Saint-Moritz and humiliated by a physical inhibition; that marital failure painfully revived the feeling of being inferior in virility to others, a feeling he described so well apropos of the child in *Si le grain ne meurt* and his fictional double, Boris, apropos of André Walter in a tragic mode, and of Tityrus in a comic mode. On the other hand, from the viewpoint of an inferiority complex, Gide was all the more obliged to mask his inadequacy and give himself new value in his own eyes by glorifying his pedophilic activities as proof of his virility. Important as the sexual aspect of the inferiority complex is, however, it is but one aspect, and the "thorn in the flesh" does not necessarily or sufficiently explain it; in fact, it can be more a consequence than a cause. Indeed, originally, Gide had had an inferiority complex which led to an individual protest according to the mechanisms of psychological "overcompensation."

Even more than the search for pleasure, the passion that guides Menalcas is pride: he wants to be "the most irreplaceable of beings." On March 27, 1895, Gide wrote to his mother: "I am filled with more pride than I can hold."[53] That sentence could have been used as an epigraph to Menalcas' protest and would have been more suitable than the reference to the Gospels. "I would hear nothing but that which allowed me to admire myself,"[54] Gide declared with regard to some extravagant gestures he had made after his mother's death. The magnificently immoderate gestures of Menalcas— who believes himself to be the most disinterested of men and even the most gratuitous when he laid waste to domains just for the spectacle of the thing: *qualis artifex!*—are similarly motivated. And it is always pride, the need to admire oneself or to be admired, that guides the Gidian heroes of the gratuitous act, Menalcas' numerous posterity: Philoctetes, King Candaule, Lafcadio, Boris. For them, not only their virtues but their vices are lost in "self-interest," like rivers in a sea. It may not seem obvious to those who judge "self-interest" according to the moral and religious norms, but it becomes so as soon as we put ourselves in the place of one who wants to astonish or be astonished by "something dangerous, absurd,"[55] and more particularly one who wants to become "the most irreplaceable of beings." We are dealing less with a cult of the "I" than with the cult of "He"— that is, less with a cult of the ego than with a cult of an ideal of oneself; their interests may be contradictory, for in order that the "He" grow, it

[53] Unpublished letter.

[54] *Si le grain ne meurt*, II, 368.

[55] *Les Faux-Monnayeurs*, III, 481.

may be necessary for the "I" to diminish, take risks, get lost, put an end to itself. That sort of pride is very similar to La Rochefoucauld's conception of *amour-propre*.[56] Menalcas may pass himself off as a hedonist, but he is more especially one of "the proud," and most of his crimes can be ascribed to "braggadocio."

The creation of "Ménalque" corresponds to the most intense moment, the acme, as it were, of the crisis in Gide's youth. Recalling the creation of *Les Nourritures terrestres,* he remarked:

I was writing that book at a time when I had just settled down in life by getting married; when I willingly parted with a freedom which my book, a work of art, immediately asserted all the more. And needless to say, I was perfectly sincere in writing it; but just as sincere in my heart's denial of it.[57]

It was thus at a time when he had just become involved, sincerely, in the bonds of marriage that he wrote, sincerely, a eulogy of nomadism. Nothing is more important than those two acts of sincerity, in understanding the differences between Menalcas, the character, and Gide's personality as it was at the end of his twenty-fifth year. Whereas his marriage to Emmanuèle affirmed the survival of the "old man," Gide felt the need to establish, "at one go," the traits of the "new being" in an aggressive form. Over and against the former Huguenot Walter, with his shyness, his anguish, and his ideal of virtue and resistance to sin, he set up that arrogant hedonist, "with no modesty and decked out in glorious guilt,"[58] as though in that way he could more successfully confront the two entelechies. "Ménalque" is an exaggeration of tendencies which existed in Gide but were neutralized to a certain degree by opposite tendencies. And it was that very ambiguity that characterized his own behavior, not only in 1895, when it seemed to be carried to its climax, but throughout his life.

On January 23, 1895, André Gide had written to his mother: "I have the feeling that I'm going through a very important crisis, a decisive crisis perhaps and one from which I should emerge full-grown."[59] During his youth the periods of crisis were numerous, but the year 1895, considered from the beginning to end, was indeed of crucial importance in the story of his life and personality.

[56] We know, of course, how Gide attacked La Rochefoucauld's system (*N.R.F.,* July, 1910) by countering it with the gratuitous hero, but he finally retracted his criticism: "I find that the position I tried to take with regard to La Rochefoucauld could not rightfully be maintained. My first mistake was to attempt to assimilate what he calls *amour-propre* to egoism" (*Journal,* 1921, p. 698).

[57] 1927 preface to *Les Nourritures terrestres, O.C.,* II, 228.

[58] *Notices, O.C.,* II, ix.   [59] Unpublished letter.

A state of crisis generally calls for a denouement, but in human psychology there are crises without denouements and which last a lifetime. So it
was with André Gide. At the end of 1895, a time he had hoped would be
decisive, he seemed to be more torn apart than ever by his contradictory
tendencies. Not only were his heart and his senses pulling in different directions; his whole personality was that of a divided man. He desired young
boys he did not love, and he loved a woman he did not desire; he seemed
to have accepted the situation by convincing himself that "pleasure was
thus purer and love more perfect if the heart and the senses were kept
apart." The organization of his sexual habits was established once and for
all. Can the same be said for his ethics and his personality? It is significant
that the three great tendencies underlying his entire evolution came together and were combined during that telling experience of his twenty-fifth
year: his Dionysiac tendency, first represented by Menalcas and soon
strengthened by the reading of Nietzsche; his so-called Christian tendency,
marked by a very personal heretical interpretation of the Gospels; and his
Apollonian tendency, of which Goethe seemed to him the incomparable
example. Yet the aesthetic finality he laid down for himself in *Le Traité
du Narcisse* was a sign that he would always subordinate his attitudes
toward ethics and religion to the demands of his literary vocation, conceived
as the well-ordered expression of his contradictory possibilities.

"I spent my whole youth opposing two parts of myself which perhaps
wanted nothing more than to get along," Gide declared in his *Journal* of
1893,[60] but he soon understood that this agreement between two irreducible
adversaries would be possible only by bringing in a third factor, the artist,
whose arbitration would be only aesthetic. The moment at which he decided to make his works the representation of the "games of heaven and
hell," giving his life no objective other than that representation itself, marks
the end of the drama and the birth of the *Homo litterarius,* whose writings
became a way of living.

On November 11, 1894, Gide wrote to Paul Valéry:

I like only vicious circles. I think that the important thing for each one is to
know that he has really put on all his skins one after another and not too much
of other people's clothing. . . . There lies my wisdom, I say wisdom since that
is the name we give to a recipe for happiness.[61]

That wisdom was something quite different from a recipe for happiness;
it was an author's strategy. The attitude itself in no way excludes sincerity,
but the sincerity is that of an actor who more easily puts on the skin of a
character when the character is part of his personal repertory. As André
Walter had said long before, practicing in front of his mirror: "An actor

---

[60] P. 42. [61] *Correspondance,* pp. 219–20.

perhaps, but I play myself." Gide often emphasized that need of leaping "to the other extremity" of himself,[62] which forced him, once a book was finished, to write another disconcertingly different from it. He expressed this perfectly in a letter to Francis Jammes:

Each of my works is an immediate reaction *against* the preceding one. No one of them ever completely satisfies me, and I never dance on more than one foot *at a time;* the main thing is to dance well all the same; but with every book I change feet, as one is tired from having danced, and the other from having rested all that time.[63]

And so he was to live on only one foot, but not on the same one for long. For the rest of his life he was to alternate from one half of his being to the other. "Extremes move me" is the epigraph he was to choose for his *Morceaux choisis,* and it was from the struggle between those "extremes" that all his characters were born. The successive opposition between them was to be the expression of his own antagonisms artificially resolved.

At the end of 1895 Gide was torn between contradictory tendencies, but he appeared to have stopped really suffering from it. It is not the fact of being divided that is painful, but the feeling that one should not be divided: André Walter suffered from being divided because he found it contrary to his moral duty; André Gide made the best of it because he found it not only consistent with his nature but profitable for his works. Divided as a man, he intended to become whole as an artist by making his works the experience of his contradictions. He was fifty-four when he wrote:

I have never been able to renounce anything; and protecting both the best and the worst of myself, I have lived in a state of being torn asunder. But how can I explain that this cohabitation of extremes in me led not so much to anxiety and suffering as to a passionate intensification of the feeling of existence, of life? The most opposite tendencies never succeeded in making me a tormented man; but rather perplexed—for torment goes along with a state one wishes to come out of, and I did not wish to escape what carried into effect all the potentialities of my being; that *state of dialogue* which, for so many others, is almost intolerable, became necessary for me. This is also because, for those others, it can only be harmful to action, whereas for me, far from resulting in sterility, it, on the contrary, invited me to the work of art, immediately preceded creation, and resulted in equilibrium and harmony.[64]

That need for preserving his contradictions and living in a dialectic state in the interest of creation explains that Gide did not want to come out of his early crisis so that it would have no other denouement than his complete works.

[62] *Si le grain ne meurt,* I, 251.

[63] Aug. 6, 1902 (*Correspondance,* pp. 199–200).

[64] *Journal,* 1923, pp. 777–78.

Persona

> *"I convinced myself that everyone, or at any rate, everyone of the elect, had a part to play in the world, his very own part, which was unlike any other. . . ."*
>
> Si le grain ne meurt, I, 275

O THE comment he made to his mother at the age of fifteen: "Haven't you understood that I am one of the elect?" Gide added: "I was already inclined to believe that I had a vocation; I mean a vocation of a mystical nature."[1] The aesthetic mysticism that had been so deeply involved with his religious beliefs broke away from them at the time of *Le Traité du Narcisse,* the first formulation of the Gidian ideal. Every time Gide defined the part he intended to play in life, he recalled the words of the Gospels: "Ye are the salt of the earth: but if the salt have lost his savor, wherewith shall it be salted?" but gave it a different interpretation from that of the Uzès Huguenots:

I convinced myself that everyone, or at any rate, everyone of the elect, had a part to play in the world, his very own part, which was unlike any other; so that every effort to submit to a common rule became treachery in my eyes; yes, treachery, and I likened it to that great sin against the Holy Ghost "which shall not be forgiven," and by which the individual loses his precise and irreplaceable significance, his "savor," which cannot be restored to him.[2]

Gide, more than most, identified his personality with a character—that is, according to the ancient and theatrical meaning of the word *persona,* with a part. He conceived his part as that of an artist passionately devoted to

[1] *Si le grain ne meurt,* I, 187.   [2] *Ibid.,* p. 275.

the realization of his very unique works—"Is not every artist necessarily an exception to all the rules? a unique case and one that will never be found again?"[3]—passionately devoted to "what others call a literary career and what I choose to call my life."[4] Faith in his vocation was for him the *quid inconcussum* that religious faith is for others; he doubted everything else. "I've begun to write again; I'm saved," he wrote to his mother in January, 1895; and indeed from youth to old age, writing was his salvation. He himself said that had he been kept from creating his works, he would have committed suicide, which shows to what point he considered them his only hope: they were his true love, his one religion. A few minutes after André Gide's death, Roger Martin du Gard told me of his friend's confidence in the survival of his works, and compared it to "a Christian's belief in the immortality of the soul." When an aesthetic vocation is taken up with such total devotion and constant passion, it does recall a mystical vocation, but its ends are completely different and the conception of immortality remains foreign to Christianity.

"O Lord, grant that I may want only one thing and want it constantly," implored André Walter. The young Huguenot poet may have appeared to be equally attracted by the mystical way and by the aesthetic way, but in 1895 there was no further room for doubt. André Gide chose, and he chose to subordinate everything to his literary vocation and make everything contribute to it—his virtues and his vices, his good qualities and his faults, his sincerity and his hypocrisy, his temperament and his upbringing, his culture and his experiences, his submission and his rebellion, daemons and gods, Dionysus and Christ. From that point on, "the Goethean spirit conclusively prevailed over the Christian spirit," as Paul Claudel was to say in 1926.

During the entire transition from André Walter to André Gide, Goethe was his guide: "To take my mind off my momentary concerns, I am reading Rod's essay on Goethe. Nothing will have soothed me in life so much as the contemplation of that great figure."[5] This was the only mention of Goethe in the 1895 *Journal,* but in Gide's private correspondence his name is ever present. Mme. Gide was not that mistaken when she attributed her son's transformation to "that Goethe, whom he talks about constantly." For four years he not only read Goethe every day and in every clime—in Paris and in Munich, in La Roque and in Uzès, in Tunis and in Sousse, in Biskra and in Algiers, in Rome and in Como, in Neuchâtel and in La Brévine, in Saint-Moritz and in Florence—but he endlessly studied his biography, especially in the translation of Lewes' book, never separating

[3] Letter from André Gide to his mother, November, 1894, unpublished.

[4] Letter from André Gide to Saint-Georges de Bouhélier, January, 1897.

[5] *Journal,* 1895, p. 57.

the man from his works, admiring the way in which he had resolved the problem of the relations between art and life. Gide was, of course, so different from his model that any comparison of their destinies would seem ill-considered, but he did find that Goethe represented exactly what he wanted to become, and drew upon his "strategy" to conceive his own personality as an artist. He was convinced very early in life that an *homo artifex* had to have his own special philosophy, ethics, and aesthetics.[6] In his 1892 *Journal,* apropos of the artist's "inverted sincerity" and his destiny conceived as the realization of an "ideal portrait," he had already written: "He must be as he wants to be!"[7]

"The aesthetic point of view is the only one from which to judge my works in any sound manner," Gide said at the end of his life, thus confirming the conclusion of *Le Traité du Narcisse.* Generally, it is not judged in that way, but rather from a moral viewpoint, which makes it practically indefensible. At the time of *Le Traité du Narcisse* he stopped considering moral obligation as a categorical imperative and an end in itself, and began to see ethics merely as "a dependency of aesthetics." He shaped his varied and contradictory attitudes vis-à-vis the moral problem according to the value they would have for his works. "It seemed to me that the doctrine of art for art's sake owed its failure only to its refusal to embrace moral questions. It was entirely up to the artist, I found, to enlarge his realm so as to include them as well."[8] In other words, moral questions should be annexed to literary ends, which in itself is neither immoralism nor moralism but an amoralism which takes stock, in turn, of different systems of ethics, without becoming attached to any one of them. "Nothing amuses me more than a system of ethics," we read in *Les Nourritures terrestres,*[9] and the playful nature of the remark must not hide the fact that for the artist, ethical systems were actually only games subordinated to art, the game of games. Shocking as that nonchalant attitude may seem to men who are committed, and perilous as it may be for those who are not yet committed, it can be explained (which does not mean justified), in Gide's case, both by the fact that he had the morbid temperament of a doubter and by his exclusive vocation as an artist. An ambivalent moralist and a questionable immoralist, he was in fact an amoralist. In his unpublished journal of 1894, after having written the following passage, entirely reproduced in the *Journal:*

Laws and moral codes are essentially educative, hence provisional. All education that is properly understood aims at being able to dispense with them.

[6] *Ibid.,* p. 94.

[7] *Ibid.,* 1892, p. 29.

[8] Letter to Henri Drain, July 18, 1932.

[9] II, p. 42.

All education aims at negating itself. Laws and moral codes are for the child-hood state: education is an emancipation. . . . The wise man lives without a moral code, according to his own wisdom. We must try to reach a higher immorality.[10]

He had added the sentence: "It is more an amoralism," which he then crossed out. Yet it contained the right word.

In this passage from the 1894 *Journal,* Goethe's influence is obvious, and of course Gide meant to use him as a model for the artist's "higher immoral-ity," which ends by being more of an exigency than an ethic. In the Goethean perspective of the aesthetic development of the personality con-ceived in relation to the work of art, moral laws and values are of only relative importance and are judged solely by the individual. For him, there is no extrinsic duty but rather an intrinsic exigency—that of fulfilling him-self, not as he should be in accordance with the canons of religion and society, but as he is. He must not say: this is good and this is bad in itself, but this is good and this is bad in relation to me; he must not say: this is healthy or this is unhealthy, but this is healthy and this is unhealthy in relation to my nature. He must "carry his originality to the extreme." Any-one who replaces all the obligations he has not chosen himself by a personal exigency, for which only he is answerable, is no more an enemy of the gods than he is an enemy of the laws: he looks upon them with indifference. He acts less in a spirit of rebellion than in a spirit of revolution. Moreover, there is no doubt he is an egoist—and Goethe himself said: "The purest and most rigorous egoism is alone capable of saving us"—but one who claims to find his justification in the fulfilment of an ideal of himself and the aesthetic finality toward which he directs all his energy. Apropos of Goethe's transcendent egoism, Gide quoted the following lines of Renan which, he said, summarized his own thoughts on the matter: "Goethe's duty was to be an egoist for his works. The artist's transcendent immorality is, in its way, the supreme morality."[11]

At the end of 1895, having written to his friend Drouin that Goethe's influence on him had reached its maximum, Gide added:

Goethe's hold on me is, as with Novalis, that of an enemy. You must sense in everything I've written and in everything I want to write that I'm as far from him as you are, as far from him as from the Parnassians; but I've always thought that I learn more in the camp of my adversaries than in the clan of my allies.[12]

He thus repudiates the Goethean wisdom, but he repudiates it half-heartedly, and so it was always to be. He more than once felt that such

[10] *Journal,* 1894, pp. 54–55.

[11] *Attendu que,* p. 111.   [12] Dec. 3, 1895, quoted by Y. Davet, p. 50.

wisdom had been prompted by "a concern for tranquillity and comfort" that was contrary to his need of restlessness, but however far his "wanderings"—Nietzschean or Christian—carried him from the great mediator, he was always to come back to him, as to an Apollonian arbiter.

It was from Goethe that Gide got the idea of freeing himself and surrendering himself to nature, like the author of the *Roman Elegies:* "By letting himself live in things, like Pan, everywhere, he managed to rid himself of all limits except those of the world itself." However, man must be "god enough" to take the risks of such an adventure, for if not, he "pitifully disintegrates."[13] At the time he was experiencing and writing *Les Nourritures terrestres,* Gide was often apprehensive about such pitiful disintegration, and it was from that fear that his *Saül* was born. Although he wrote the play very much after his crisis of 1895, all the tendencies that went into its creation were already evident, and he had already felt the need to "mithridatize" himself, to make himself immune to Menalcas' hedonist adventure by showing how *Les Nourritures terrestres'* doctrine of "receptivity" could lead to one's downfall. This is clearly indicated in the episode in which Hylas, the proudly free man, becomes the slave of his desires.

And every one of my senses had its desires. When I wanted to return to my inner home, I found my manservants and maidservants at my table; there was not even the smallest place for me to sit down. The place of honor was taken by Thirst; other thirsts contested his right to the fine place. The whole table was quarrelsome; but they conspired together against me. When I tried to come closer to the table, all of them—already quite drunk—rose against me; they chased me out of my own house; they dragged me outside, and again I went off to gather them grapes.[14]

Written in 1895, those lines contain the entire subject matter of *Saül:* a man's reduction to slavery by the desires over which he is no longer the master, and his eviction by so many heady abnegations. Even at the height of his Dionysiac intoxications, Gide never danced on more than one foot, and was never blind in more than one eye; the other, with no indulgence whatever, watched him acting like a drunken helot and deemed that his state of drunkenness might well lead to a bad end. He was then, as he was always to be, split into actor and spectator, and just as sincere in one role as in the other, divided between a positive tendency, from which Menalcas, hero of *Les Nourritures terrestres,* was born, and a negative tendency, from which *Saül,* antidote of *Les Nourritures terrestres,* was to be born.

Describing the "difficult and dangerous game" of experimenting on himself with the ethics of *Les Nourritures terrestres,* Gide wrote to Marcel Drouin:

[13] *Journal,* 1893, p. 43.   [14] *Les Nourritures terrestres,* IV, 96–97.

This anguish (sometimes horrible), this confusion of my entire being, this distress, this dispossession—this sickness, perhaps more intellectual than you would believe—I consider on certain days (the good ones) as no more than the state of being pregnant with the new book that is on its way—this *Saül* perhaps, in which—having deliberately chosen to put into my *Nourritures* only the joy of desire—even if the joy was mad—I should like to sing of all the anguish, distress, and confusion caused by *that*. (*That* has still to be defined: it's an unclassified sickness which must be *created*—which will be explained by Valentin Knox, as slightly different—one of the forms of lunacy, let's say—for which we shall try to find a terrifying name.)[15]

That terrifying name, which the psychiatrist Valentin Knox would have surely derived from Greek, was replaced to advantage by the expression "disintegration of the personality," which Gide himself used: "The disintegration of the personality, caused by an overpassive inclination to receptivity, is the very subject matter of my *Saül,* which I wrote directly after my *Nourritures,* as an antidote to it or a counterweight," he was to write to Pastor Ferrari.[16] The naturalist in him saw Saul's destiny in terms of the chrysalis in which, instead of finding a hawk moth, he found a great number of another insect's cocoons. "Thus, I thought, my Saul would say: 'I am totally suppressed.' "[17] The idea that self-abandon, as Menalcas conceived it, leads to self-suppression, is the moral in *Saül,* and in direct opposition to the moral in "Ménalque."

This ethics of ambiguity, which Gide evolved because he found it so well suited to his destiny as an artist, consists in counterbalancing one excess by another and finding an equilibrium in the aesthetic representation of contraries. In as much as it means seeking and finding a way of salvation through the liberation and release of literary creation, it is more a kind of "wisdom," in the Goethean sense, than an ethic. Because of its Apollonian principle of equilibrium, it kept Gide from ever giving in, body and soul, to the Nietzschean temptation of "life for life's sake," to the unconditional glorification of the instincts, or even to a fanatic immoralism.

At the other extreme, the author of *Numquid et tu* was often tempted to go back to Christianity: "O God, grant that I may be happy—not with the tragic and wild happiness of Nietzsche, which I also admire nevertheless, but with that of St. Francis, with that adorable, radiant happiness";[18] or "On certain days, if only I let myself go, I would roll straight under the Communion table."[19] However, faithful to his method of arbitration, he had every intention of protecting himself from the lures of religion by embodying them in Christian characters, whom, like his

---

[15] Undated letter, probably written in 1896, unpublished.

[16] *O.C.,* XV, 532.

[17] *Journal,* 1942–49, pp. 165–66.

[18] *Ibid.,* 1921, p. 713.

[19] *Ibid.,* 1931, p. 1065.

Nietzschean characters, he would lead to ruin. He sought to free himself from the lures of an anarchistic Christ and Christian quietism in *La Symphonie pastorale,* whose denouement is clearly catastrophic: Gertrude commits suicide and the pastor discovers his own fraudulence. He sought to free himself from the lures of an exclusive Christ and Christian Jansenism in *La Porte étroite.* That "essay on dying well" was originally meant to be an ironical book—that is, "a warning": its author wanted to show how the puritanical ideal leads a very noble soul to complete self-resignation, the renunciation of love, and the renunciation of life, in accordance with Nietzsche's comment on "that horrible way of perishing, the most famous example of which is Pascal." But it happened that Gide was so deeply attached to Alissa, who was to embody the ethics of his adolescence, that the book written to nullify Christianity turned out to glorify it.

A writer does not always write the book he wants to.

Suddenly, the spirit of irony was silent and the writer's pen trembled. Alissa's sublimity stirs the reader, who feels gripped by something that resembles the feeling of moral grandeur. Gide may well have affirmed that he was an atheist, but the author of this masterpiece is clearly a man marked by *Christianus sum. La Porte étroite* is Protestantism's most insidious revenge on its renegade child.

The characters most contrary to one another, those descended from Nietzsche and those descended from Christianity, were all potentially contained in that true matrix of Gide's works, his crisis of 1895. But a third type of character was also already in evidence, one as foreign to the madness of Dionysus as to the religion of Christ: Theseus, the Athenian. Of course, the work of which Gide said: "This is my last will and testament,"[20] belongs to his old age, but he had thought about the myth of Theseus ever since his youth, and alluded to it in "Ménalque," written in 1895. Indeed, for him the Argonaut was the most perfect figure of the "new being" he dreamed of becoming when he took off in October, 1893, in search of his new personality as though it were "the golden fleece."[21] Theseus represented the embodiment of pagan amoralism, which to him seemed consistent with the Greek or Goethean ideal, and was clearly opposed to his "first Christian ideal." Gide always said that the Goethean influence and the Hellenic influence had led him in the same direction: "The great influence I have perhaps really *undergone* is that of Goethe, and even then, I'm not certain whether my admiration for Greek literature and Hellenism would not have been enough to counterbalance my early Christian formation."[22] For the Greek hero as for the Olympian sage, the problem was "to keep his

[20] Shortly after, the bitter codicil, *Et nunc manet in te,* was published.

[21] *Si le grain ne meurt,* II, 290.

[22] *Journal,* 1927, p. 895.

private Olympus in equilibrium, and not to subjugate or limit any of the gods,"[23] substituting aesthetic values for moral values, preferring intelligent and beautiful figures to virtuous figures, and going so far as to think that the spectacle of a pleasing harmony "would contribute more to the happiness of others than hard and painful struggles against their misfortunes."[24] The 1893 *Journal* contains a rough sketch of the program the symbolic Theseus was to try to put into effect. From his severe, if not puritanical, upbringing, he kept the precept that "nothing great, nothing of any value, and nothing lasting can be obtained without effort."[25] Theseus first applied that effort to "living with strength, living joyously,"[26] and breaking away from the duties and conventions he had been brought up to believe in. He refused to close himself up in the labyrinth of any doctrine, any religion, any ethic, any love, any human ties, and he explained his position more openly than Menalcas did: "I want above all to remain free. It is to myself that I owe myself." But there was Ariadne and the precious thread that tied Theseus to his past. He was to hesitate a long time before cutting the roots of his own personality by cutting the clew. Yet "the mysterious thread that bound Theseus to his past love did not prevent him from moving on to newer regions":[27] it was thus a very slack and unobtrusive thread, one which allowed him many deviations and perhaps made him somewhat uncomfortable, but never stood in his way. Actually, the main episode in the story of Theseus does not take place in the labyrinth, nor even when, once out of the labyrinth, he cuts the thread, but before, at the point when Daedalus tells him of his fate:

But know this (since my eyes have learned the art of discerning the future through the present), know that you have still to do great things, and in a realm quite different from that of your past exploits; things compared to which those exploits will seem, in the future, like child's play. You have still to found Athens, and there establish the sovereignity of the mind. Therefore, do not linger in the labyrinth or in Ariadne's arms. . . . Move on. Consider indolence as treachery. Know that you must seek no rest until, your destiny fulfilled, you find it in death. Only in that way, and beyond what seems like death, will you live, inexhaustibly recreated by the gratitude of mankind. Move on, go forward, follow your own road, O valiant assembler of cities.[28]

Strengthened by that promise of immortality, Theseus will be courageous enough not to yield to the heady perfumes of the labyrinth, and hard enough to keep from being moved by Ariadne's despair. A ruthless and lucid hero behind his apparent playfulness, he "moves on" and makes his

---

[23] *Ibid.*, p. 777.

[24] *Ibid.*, 1893, p. 44.

[25] *Thésée*, p. 11.

[26] *Journal*, 1893, p. 35.

[27] *Les Nourritures terrestres*, IV, 71.

[28] *Thésée*, pp. 74–75.

way straight to the throne of Athens, where he knows he is called upon to establish the unity of Attica and create a work whose wisdom and order, seemingly inspired by Apollo himself, will astound mankind. There is nothing less wild and less charitable, less "Dionysiac" and less "Christian," than this Greek of the Renaissance—subtle and calculating, crafty and Machiavellian, for whom the end justifies the means—this cheerful incarnation of the Prince.

Gide clearly meant to draw a parallel between the art of politics and the "strategy" of creation, between the symbolic situations of Theseus' youth and of his own. What gave him the courage to fight the "monster" of conformity, the will to escape from the "labyrinth," and the energy to disregard many interdictions and incur public reprobation was the feeling of being one of the "elect," the mysterious promise that his vocation as an artist would be fulfilled in spite of anything and everything—a promise in which he continued to believe from his adolescence on. He believed he was called upon not to assemble cities but to assemble his own virtualities by creating a world of diverse characters integrated into an Attic work, whose "style alone" would give proof of its unity.[29]

Much as Gide wanted to take Goethe as his model and submit to his influence, the anomaly of his sexual habits, his emotional and nervous instability, and his neurotic complexes were great handicaps to reaching a Goethean equilibrium. Although he, also, sought harmony, he was too concerned with trying to include his "dissonance" for his works to have that universal a resonance. On the other hand, he was relatively wanting in a "sense of reality"[30] and in Goethe's remarkable ability to adapt to life. Goethe established an astonishing compromise between the demands of his freedom as an artist and the demands of social constraints; his "obliging" individualism is a human accomplishment of a generality and scope that Gide's purely aesthetic accomplishment could not even approach. Yet the fact that the child of *Si le grain ne meurt,* given his weakness and his morbidity, became the author of masterpieces, certain of which reached classical perfection, is no less admirable.

"I call the classic *healthy,*" said Goethe, "and the romantic *sickly.*" He himself was at first a romantic, and if he became classical, it was by means of a constant struggle to find an equilibrium among his antagonisms and create a harmony out of all his dissonance. As Gide would accept classicism only if it were subdued romanticism, it was that struggle which he particu-

[29] "The style alone will reveal its unity," Gide wrote, defining an artist's work according to his own ideal.

[30] Cf. above, pp. 110–12, 197, 245–47.

larly admired in Goethe: the difficult triumph of order and measure over inner romanticism.

The more rebellious the subdued elements were to begin with, the more beautiful the work. If the substance is subdued in advance, the work is cold and without interest. True classicism is comprised of nothing restrictive or suppressive; it is more creative than conservative.[31]

André Walter was a romantic poet. He saw literature as sincere lyricism, as a song that reveals "the intoxication" of a soul, and he would have preferred to write his book in music, which—far more than words—is the language of emotion. Gide was to return to an even more spellbinding lyricism in *Les Nourritures terrestres,* but that romantic "deviation" in his works was short-lived and cannot be considered representative of the literary art as he conceived it once and for all in *Le Traité du Narcisse.* Faced with the ethical dilemma of "whether to be moral or sincere," he chose the values of sincerity; faced with the aesthetic dilemma of "whether to be an artist or a poet," he chose the values of construction. "The old man is the sincere man. And I find this to be true: the old man is the poet. The new man, whom one prefers, is the artist. The artist must take the place of the poet. From the struggle between the two, the work of art is born."[32] The more or less debatable but constant opposition Gide saw between the poet, or "natural being," and the artist, or "artificial being whom one prefers," corresponded in his mind to the opposition between spontaneity and reflection, lyricism and analysis, inspiration and conscious creation, or more generally, the *vates* and the *artifex.* We note that for him expressions like "the old man" and "the new being" meant one thing on the aesthetic level and exactly the opposite on the ethical level. This obvious contradiction is of the greatest importance, for it corresponds to a specifically Gidian maneuver, a kind of "change partners," which consists in re-establishing in art the very constraints from which he wanted to free himself in ethics. Here he chooses the natural state and freedom, impugning the artificial being; there he chooses composition and subordination, impugning the spontaneous being. The need for aesthetic "subordination" affirmed in *Le Traité du Narcisse* as early as 1891 was again emphasized by Gide thirty years later, in answer to an inquiry about classicism:

Classical perfection implies not at all a suppression of the individual (I very nearly said: on the contrary) but the submission of the individual, his subordination, and that of the word in the sentence, and the sentence on the page, and the page in the whole work. It is the *perfect example of a hierarchy.*[33]

This hierarchy becomes evident in the composition and style.

[31] "Réponse à une enquête de la Renaissance sur le Classicisme, 1921." In *Morceaux choisis,* p. 453.

[32] *Journal,* 1892, p. 30.   [33] *Morceaux choisis,* p. 453.

Nothing is more composed than Gide's books, even the earliest ones, with the exception of *Les Cahiers d'André Walter* and *Les Nourritures terrestres*. In the latter, the absence of composition was intentional: "I'm cutting up my nutriment into small slices and I admire how many little pieces it makes!"[34] During the year 1896 he worked at cutting and chopping up the fragments he had previously composed—indeed, overcomposed—of *Les Nourritures terrestres,* according to an aesthetics more consistent with "sensational lyricism"; but that sort of splendid disorder is an effect of art, and the magical device was "very thought out." Perhaps there he was forcing his talent. In any case, the Dionysian was short-lived. "I cannot help but compose as a classicist, which, at bottom, I have always been," he wrote to Pierre Louÿs apropos of *Le Voyage d'Urien*,[35] and in his La Brévine journal: "Today the novel must prove that it can be something other than a mirror carried down the road—that it can be superior and a priori—that is, deduced; that is, *composed;* that is, a work of art."[36] Directly after *Les Cahiers d'André Walter,* he understood that he had been wrong to want to express, at one go, in one character, all his inner contradictions. He had to bring order to the chaos, and create as many doubles for Walter as would be necessary to express each of his tendencies and difficulties. He was going to have to work with method. Like many other writers for whom order and clarity become governing qualities, Gide originally had not only a very complicated mind but a very mixed-up mind. In several of his early letters, particularly those from Munich, he found his ideas so "confused" that he was miserable about being in such an "inextricable mess"; he complained about not being able to move them without them catching on to one another like Renan's "bundle of twigs." He realized that he had to carry all his ideas "to their conclusion,"[37] but that he had also to separate them, clarify them, and prune them to make a work of art. And here he is concerned with ideas, not images:

Imagination (in my case) rarely precedes the idea; it is the latter, and not at all the former, that excites me; but the latter without the former produces nothing in itself; it is a fever without virtue. *The idea of a work is its composition.* The reason so many artists today create weak and very poorly composed works is that they imagine too quickly.[38]

Gide was not one of those born poets who naturally think in images; an intuitive intellectual, his real difficulty lay in making the transition from schema to image. For that matter, every character he created was the illustration of a pre-existing, a priori *schema,* or in other terms, the concrete form of an idea which, before being embodied in a fictional hero and so given life,

---

[34] Letter from André Gide to Paul Valéry, Jan. 24, 1896 (*Correspondance,* p. 258).

[35] July 30, 1892, unpublished.   [37] *Paludes, O.C.,* I, 458.

[36] End of October, 1894, unpublished.   [38] *Journal,* 1893, p. 49.

had been abstract. There is something Cartesian in the way he divided his inner difficulties into as many parcels as he could break up.

The experimental method, which consists in maintaining the state of mind and heart necessary to the elaboration of an ideally simplified character, required certain sacrifices on the part of an innately complicated and inconstant writer. To begin with, although eager to live the totality of his life in the present moment, he had to rid himself systematically of everything that was unsuitable to the "self" of his current hero, however limited that hero may have been. He who extolled availability had to imprison himself in a character and not move an inch away from him. He was as compressed within Tityrus or Menalcas, Alissa or Michel, as the sage in Phalaris' bull. "As soon as the idea of a work has taken shape—in other words, as soon as the work becomes organized—the elaboration consists in little more than suppressing everything that is useless to its *organism*."[39] But after having been temporarily limited so as to fulfil himself in that "organismic" form, he gives it up and goes on to another character who, in general, will be exactly the opposite of the one he has just described. In his letter to Marcel Drouin of 1893, Gide—barely twenty-four years old—announced that the importance of each of his works would only be explained afterward, "so that one can be a good judge of one part only after having known the whole— that is, after me."[40] Now that his works are complete, it would indeed seem that their pattern corresponds to a general plan. It was because of no whim that Gide leaped from one extreme to another, but, as it were, in obedience to the demands of his inner logic:

Don't you sense, with your good and simple nose, that the only way I can write a simple work of art is first to rid myself, in another work, of all my complexity? . . . Don't you sense that if I had not written *Paludes,* I should not have written *Saül?* That without my *Prométhée,* my *Candaule* would have remained absolutely cluttered, and without my *Immoraliste* . . . I might well have become him? I purge myself. And this is not the last time.[41]

That general plan—formulated in Gide's youth, perhaps not in detail but in its ultimate design—was precisely to express all the complexity of his nature, using the device of alternation. He only once tried to give up the plan, and that was in *Les Faux-Monnayeurs,* a symbolic counterpoint of all his tendencies. Although it has been criticized for its lack of composition, this book was, on the contrary, very skilfully composed with regard to its author's personality. It is the fifty-year-old man's *summa,* just as *Les Cahiers d'André Walter* was the *summa* of the twenty-year-old man.

[39] *Ibid.*

[40] *O.C.,* I, 545.

[41] Letter from André Gide to Francis Jammes, Aug. 6, 1902 (*Correspondance,* p. 199).

We can understand why Gide, bent on very consciously objectivizing his contradictory tendencies in a series of psychological diagrams, made such great use of classical myths, from Narcissus to Proteus, from Prometheus to Philoctetes, from Candaule to Proserpina, from Oedipus to Thesus. He saw how helpful symbolic situations, crystallized in fable, are for psychological analysis:

Every myth is first, and solely, addressed to reason, and we have understood nothing of that myth as long as reason has not accepted it. Greek fable is fundamentally reasonable. . . . The great mistake is refusing to acknowledge the myth as anything other than the expression, in images, of physical laws, and seeing all the rest as merely the play of *Fate*. . . . I should say that the more we limit the part of *Fatum* in the fable, the more we learn. For lack of a physical law, the psychological truth will out, a truth I find far more appealing . . . the fatality here in question in an inner fatality . . . a psychological fatality.[42]

An analysis of that fatality dissolves it, bringing it back to laws; and each of the Gidian myths is the psychological elucidation of one of his personal problems. "Hell, too, has its laws," said Goethe, who was planning to destroy the terrifying *Fatum* through the knowledge of psychological laws, by teaching how to use them "to human ends."[43]

The predominance of intelligence "over feeling and instinct,"[44] by which Gide defined classicism, is evident not only in the composition of a work but in the writing itself, in a style free from so-called romantic failings such as excess, complacency, extravagance, and eccentricity. The exaggerated *pathos* of *Les Nourritures terrestres* is in no way representative of the *ithos* toward which Gide's style was tending:

There is more emotion in each of our classical writers than at first meets the eye. Because of his lavishness of expression, the Romantic always tends to appear more filled with emotion than he is in reality, with the result that in our Romantic writers the word constantly precedes and overlays the emotion and the thought. . . . For lack of the necessary perception and the ability to take a hint, we have up till now found our classical writers cold, and considered their most exquisite quality—their reserve—as a failing.[45]

However, reserve calls for a control which tends to diminish the emotion. Any writer with a nervous temperament as subject to *Schaudern* as Gide's was can acquire a restrained style only at the price of disciplining his lyricism and making a constant effort to master his inclination:

I allow that Paul-Ambroise is right when he considers inspiration as one of the most harmful things to art; and I'm willing to believe that to be an artist

---

[42] "Considérations sur la mythologie grecque." In *Morceaux choisis*, pp. 186–87.

[43] *Interviews imaginaires*, p. 133.

[44] *Morceaux choisis*, p. 95.   [45] *Incidences*, pp. 40–41.

one must master the lyrical state; but in order to master it, it is essential to have first experienced it.[46]

Those words of Edouard's were to recall the compromise between spontaneity and restraint that had already been indicated in the 1892 *Journal* and from which the Gidian style was born. It is understandable that Bernard was puzzled when Edouard told him that it was "good to follow one's inclination, provided one ascends," for where is high and where is low for someone who accepts no moral or psychological hierarchy? Let Bernard not seek a lesson in life in that fine phrase, for it is only a lesson in aesthetics. Edouard accepts a hierarchy of values in art, and in art alone. He thinks he must struggle against his innate romanticism, but the strategy of his continually sustained battle demands infinite tact, for if "the artist must take the place of the poet," he must also know how occasionally to accept defeat, on condition that he consent to it "with difficulty."[47] Edouard will sometimes consent to letting himself be vanquished by lyricism: "Look at it this way: I think I call lyricism the state of a man who consents to letting himself be vanquished by God,"[48] and we know that André Gide identified that God with Dionysus. Goethe, also, thought that "the *Schaudern* is the best part of man," but finally remained "on the side of Apollo."[49]

André Gide reproached André Walter's style with its "complacency" and its overindulgence in adjectives such as "uncertain, infinite, inexpressible," as though "the genius of a language that tends toward precision" was not equal to expressing his ineffable moods: "I tried to adapt the language: I had not yet learned how much more one learns by adapting to it, and how much of a lesson are those laws which at first are troublesome and at which the mind balks, longing sometimes to reject them."[50] The more he freed himself from moral rules, the more he gave in to aesthetic rules, which—and it was characteristic of his conversion of values—he liked to call moral: "It would seem to me that the qualities we like to call classical are above all moral qualities, and I would readily consider classicism as a harmonious cluster of virtues."[51] The more the man preached an essentially romantic individualism, the more the artist became formally classic.

No one was more convinced than Gide that "the work of art flourishes only with the participation and complicity of all the virtuous elements of the mind."[52] Of course, his conception of duty and virtue was different from his mother's, but both he and his mother had the same constant need of making

---

[46] *Les Faux-Monnayeurs,* III, 400–401. "Paul-Ambroise" designates Paul Valéry.

[47] "I don't care about sincerity in art unless one has consented to it with difficulty" (*Morceaux choisis,* p. 86).

[48] *Les Faux-Monnayeurs,* III, 400.   [49] *Journal,* p. 1282.

[50] Preface to the second edition of *Les Cahiers d'André Walter,* 1930, O.C., I, 201.

[51] *Morceaux choisis,* p. 452.   [52] *Journal,* 1910, p. 310.

an effort—one in the realm of ethics, the other in the realm of aesthetics. Indeed, Gide put the same discipline, earnestness, order, care, integrity, punctuality, obstinacy, perseverance, and economy into the organization of his works as Mme. Paul Gide put into the organization of her moral and material resources, converting, as it were, the maternal virtues into aesthetic ends.[53] But there is more to it than that. One might say that the more detached he became from puritanical ethics, the more he felt the need to make his work a "penalty" for his pleasures and to find, once again, in the realm of art, the values of constraint that had almost ceased being of any use in his life. Henri Massis speaks of Gide's "stilted anarchism."[54] The expression, although no doubt meant pejoratively, brings out very precisely the contrast between the freedom of tenor and the rigor of manner. Everything happened as though Gide had wanted to redeem the peccability of the substance by an impeccability of the form, replacing, as it were, the Protestant's puritanism by a writer's purism, the morality of habits by a morality of life. The artist took a singular revenge on the man by developing a style whose qualities compensated for his own failings and offset them, so to speak—in other words, by giving proof of a steadfastness, a constancy, and a virtuous control in which his character was lacking. In certain writers, such as Gide or Baudelaire, the concern with purity and soundness of form seems all the more exacting in that they had to express murky and unhealthy tendencies. "The work of art is an equilibrium outside of time, an artificial health."[55]

Now that we have analyzed, step by step and over a period of five years, the psychological evolution we termed "From André Walter to André Gide," we have come to the point where Gide's literary vocation has acquired its specific character. Gide had found his way, and understood that his originality would consist in remaining faithful to the ambivalence that had been his weakness and would be his strength, if he could manage to bring out all his contradictions in the work of art, with the sole objective of expressing them with order and beauty. Through patience, tact, and revision, he did in fact succeed in completing an extraordinary portrait of the ambivalent man, which perhaps has no equal in all literature.

[53] That little trait has its amusing side: "My mother taught me always to empty my glass of cider before leaving the table, and never to take more bread than I could eat. No doubt some of that idea of economy still exists in the urgent need I feel for measure. I should like the whole of the work of art to be gratuitous, but I cannot tolerate any insignificant profusion in it, and never esteem that perfection has been reached if there is more ink at the tip of my pen than is necessary for the rigorous expression of my thought" ("Conseils au jeune écrivain," *N.R.F.*, Aug. 1, 1956, pp. 224–25).

[54] *Jugements*, p. 9.   [55] *Journal*, 1896, p. 94.

In that sense, it is true that he remained "faithful" to his youth and prolonged it indefinitely, making every effort to attain a serenity within his
ambivalence. Everything happened as though he had wanted to settle into a
state of crisis and sustained it to the end. His essentially divided personality,
whose inconstancy could have passed for inconsistency, was—like Edouard's
in *Les Faux-Monnayeurs*—to take on consistency only through the practice
of literature. The depersonalization of Gide's successive character-doubles
was to be the professional secret of the novelist Edouard, whose *self* the
others were never able to discover: "His being constantly unforms and re-
forms. One thinks one has grasped him ... and he is Proteus."[56] There is no
trait in that integral man of letters that was not already evident in Gide at
the end of his twenty-fifth year, except that Edouard had already acquired
complete mastery in the art of using his basic ambivalence to maintain the
artificial condition he deemed necessary to creation. At that point the chips
were down, for the "role," even though it involved as many masks as
Proteus', was wilfully assumed.

Gide was more than gratified at being reproached with having expressed
only his youth, and with being "unconcerned about expressing anything
else, hoping only to express it more perfectly." He had reached Edouard's
age when he wrote in his *Journal*:

Very few of my contemporaries have remained faithful to their youths. Almost all of them have compromised. It is what they call "learning from life."
They have repudiated the truth that was in them. Borrowed truths are the
ones we cling to most tenaciously, and all the more so in that they remain
foreign to our inner self. It takes far more caution to deliver one's own message, far more audacity and prudence, than it does to give one's adherence
and add one's voice to an already established party. Whence that accusation
of indecision and uncertainty that some throw at me, precisely because I believed
that the main thing was to remain faithful to oneself.[57]

Some have seen that refusal of commitment, so generally characteristic of
his attitudes of hesitation or retraction, as proof of immaturity, proof that
the adolescent continued to persist in making Narcissus' mistake. "Make
haste. Be a man. Choose," Charles-Louis Philippe kept telling Gide. But
Gide did not think that the word "maturity" had the same meaning for the
man as for the artist, especially one who chose to make his works an expression of his youth, with everything that implies of irreducible antagonisms
and profound irresolution. One might say that he meant to remain permanently attached to the age of life in which the future still seems completely open, in which the undefined being feels unbounded and enjoys an availability that is so pure it gives the illusion of freedom.

[56] *Les Faux-Monnayeurs*, p. 258.   [57] *Journal*, 1921, p. 711.

Index